# Correctional Ethics

**The International Library of Essays in Public and Professional Ethics**
*Series Editors: Seumas Miller and Tom Campbell*

**Titles in the Series**

# Correctional Ethics

*Edited by*

# John Kleinig

*John Jay College of Criminal Justice, USA and Charles Sturt University,*
*Australia*

ASHGATE

Published by
Ashgate Publishing Limited
Gower House
Croft Road
Aldershot
Hants GU11 3HR
England

Ashgate Publishing Company
Suite 420
101 Cherry Street
Burlington, VT 05401-4405
USA

Ashgate website: http://www.ashgate.com

**British Library Cataloguing in Publication Data**
Correctional ethics. – (The international library of essays
   in public and professional ethics)
   1. Corrections – Moral and ethical aspects  2. Prison
   administration – Moral and ethical aspects  3. Restorative
   justice  4. Correctional personnel – Professional ethics
   I. Kleinig, John, 1942-
   364.'01

**Library of Congress Cataloging-in-Publication Data**
Correctional ethics / edited by John Kleinig.
       p. cm. — (The International library of essays in public and professional ethics)
   Includes bibliographical references.
   ISBN 0-7546-2413-5 (alk. paper)
       1. Corrections—Moral and ethical aspects. 2. Punishment—Moral and ethical aspects. 3.
   Correctional personnel—Professional ethics. 4. Restorative justice. I. Kleinig, John, 1942-
   II. Series.

   HV8665.C67  2005-11-08
   174'.93646—dc22

                                                                                                2004062750


ISBN 0 7546 2431 5



Printed in Great Britain by The Cromwell Press, Trowbridge, Wiltshire

# Contents

## PART IV    CORRECTIONAL POLICY

## PART V    CORRECTIONAL ETHICS AS PROFESSIONAL ETHICS

# Acknowledgements

The editor and publishers wish to thank the following for permission to use copyright material.

American Society of Criminology for the essay: Lawrence W. Sherman (2003), 'Reason for Emotion: Reinventing Justice With Theories, Innovations, and Research', The American Society of Criminology 2002 Presidential Address, *Criminology*, **41**, pp. 1–36.

Blackwell Publishing for the essays: H.L.A. Hart (1959–60), 'Prolegomenon to the Principles of Punishment', *Proceedings of the Aristotelian Society*, **60**, pp. 1–26; Jeffrie G. Murphy (1973), 'Marxism and Retribution', *Philosophy and Public Affairs*, **2**, pp. 217–43; Jean Hampton (1984), 'The Moral Education Theory of Punishment', *Philosophy and Public Affairs*, **13**, pp. 208–38; Jeffrey H. Reiman (1985), 'Justice, Civilization, and the Death Penalty: Answering van den Haag', *Philosophy and Public Affairs*, **14**, pp. 115–48.

Cambridge University Press for the essay: Anthony O'Hear (1984), 'Imprisonment', in *Philosophy*, Supplementary Volume **18**, A. Phillips Griffiths (ed.), 'Philosophy and Practice', pp. 203–20. Copyright © The Royal Institute of Philosophy. Published by Cambridge University Press and reproduced with permission of the author and publisher.

Copyright Clearance Center for the essay: Richard Delgado (2001), 'Prosecuting Violence: A Colloquy on Race, Community, and Justice', *Stanford Law Review*, **52**, pp. 751–75.

Hart Publishing for the essay: Antony Duff (2003), 'Restoration and Retribution', in Andrew von Hirsch *et al.* (eds), *Restorative Justice and Criminal Justice: Competing or Reconcilable Paradigms?*, Oxford: Hart Publishing, pp. 43–59.

Macmillan Publishers Ltd for the essay: Richard Sparks (1996), 'Penal "Austerity": The Doctrine of Less Eligibility Reborn?', in R. Matthews and P. Francis (eds), *Prisons 2000: An International Perspective on the Current State and Future of Imprisonment*, Basingstoke, UK: Macmillan, pp. 74–93.

The Monist for the essay: Herbert Morris (1968), 'Persons and Punishment', *The Monist*, **52**, pp. 475–501. Copyright © 1968, *The Monist*: An International Quarterly Journal of General Philosophical Inquiry, Peru, Illinois, USA 61354. Reprinted by permission.

Oxford University Press for the essays: John Braithwaite and Stephen Mugford (1994), 'Conditions of Successful Reintegration Ceremonies: Dealing with Juvenile Offenders', *British Journal of Criminology*, **34**, pp. 139–71; John Braithwaite (2002), 'Setting Standards for Restorative Justice', *British Journal of Criminology*, **42**, pp. 563–77. Copyright © 2002 The Centre for Crime and Justice Studies (ISTD); James B. Jacobs (2004), 'Prison Reform Amid the Ruins of Prisoners' Rights', in Michael Tonry (ed.), *The Future of Imprisonment*, New York: Oxford University Press, pp. 179–96. Copyright © 2003 Oxford University Press, Inc. Used by permission of Oxford University Press, Inc.; John Kleinig (1998), 'The Hardness of Hard Treatment', in Andrew Ashworth and Martin Wasik (eds), *Fundamentals of Sentencing Theory*, Oxford: Clarendon, pp. 273–98.

Pearson Education for the essay: Francis T. Cullen, Jody L. Sundt and John F. Wozniak (2001), 'The Virtuous Prison: Toward a Restorative Rehabilitation', in Henry N. Pontell and David Schichor (eds), *Contemporary Issues in Crime and Justice: Essays in Honor of Gilbert Geis*, Upper Saddle River, NJ: Prentice Hall, pp. 265–86. Copyright © 2001. Reprinted by permission of Pearson Education Inc.

Rowman & Littlefield for the essays: Kenneth Kipnis (2001), 'Health Care in the Corrections Setting: An Ethical Analysis', in John Kleinig and Margaret Leland Smith (eds), *Discretion, Community and Correctional Ethics*, Lanham, MD: Rowman & Littlefield, pp. 113–24; John Kleinig (2001), 'Brokering Health Care', in John Kleinig and Margaret Leland Smith (eds), *Discretion, Community and Correctional Ethics*, Lanham, MD: Rowman & Littlefield, pp. 141–48; Kevin N. Wright (2001), 'Management-Staff Relations: Issues in Leadership, Ethics, and Values', in John Kleinig and Margaret Leland Smith (eds), *Discretion, Community and Correctional Ethics*, Lanham, MD: Rowman & Littlefield, pp. 203–18; Michael Jacobson (2001), 'The Ethical Dilemmas of Corrections Managers: Confronting Practical and Political Complexity', in John Kleinig and Margaret Leland Smith (eds), *Discretion, Community and Correctional Ethics*, Lanham, MD: Rowman & Littlefield, pp. 219–33.

Southern Illinois University Press for the essay: Jess Maghan (1998), 'Cell Out: Renting Out the Responsibility for the Criminally Confined', in Jack Kamerman (ed.), *Negotiating Responsibility in the Criminal Justice System*, Carbondale, IL: Southern Illinois University Press, pp. 49–67.

Springer for the essay: Daniel W. Van Ness (1993), 'New Wine and Old Wineskins: Four Challenges of Restorative Justice', *Criminal Law Forum*, **4**, pp. 251–76.

Every effort has been made to trace all the copyright holders, but if any have been inadvertently overlooked the publishers will be pleased to make the necessary arrangement at the first opportunity.

# Series Preface

'Ethics' is now a considerable part of all debates about the conduct of public life, in government, economics, law, business, the professions and indeed every area of social and political affairs. The ethical aspects of public life include questions of moral right and wrong in the performance of public and professional roles, the moral justification and critique of public institutions and the choices that confront citizens and professionals as they come to their own moral views about social, economic and political issues.

While there are no moral experts to whom we can delegate the determination of ethical questions, the traditional skills of moral philosophers have been increasingly applied to practical contexts that call for moral assessment. Moreover this is being done with a degree of specialist knowledge of the areas under scrutiny that previously has been lacking from much of the work undertaken by philosophers.

This series brings together essays that exhibit high quality work in philosophy and the social sciences, that is well informed on the relevant subject matter and provides novel insights into the problems that arise in resolving ethical questions in practical contexts.

The volumes are designed to assist those engaged in scholarly research by providing the core essays that all who are involved in research in that area will want to have to hand. Essays are reproduced in full with the original pagination for ease of reference and citation.

The editors are selected for their eminence in the particular area of public and professional ethics. Each volume represents the editor's selection of the most seminal essays of enduring interest in the field.

SEUMAS MILLER and TOM CAMPBELL
*Centre for Applied Philosophy and Public Ethics (CAPPE)*
*Australian National University*
*Charles Sturt University*
*University of Melbourne*

# Introduction

This volume is intended to be a resource in more ways than one. It reproduces a set of essays that help to frame the development of an ethically informed correctional ethic. Correctional ethics is thus embedded in a set of wider discussions that help to shape it and give it substance. In addition, though, it seeks to alert those who are engaged in the more practical task of articulating such an ethic or are involved in correctional practice to resources on which they can draw in linking the framing debates to those that take place in the day-to-day activities of correctional institutions and practices. Both kinds of resource are important. Correctional institutions reflect – or should reflect – broad social values and commitments. But there is no simple way in which the concrete decisions of those involved in the correctional enterprise can be 'deduced' from those broader values. Various mediating principles must first be established and then applied – via judgement rather than deductive techniques – to the concrete situations in which the participants of correctional practice find themselves. If not in the broader framing discussions then in the notes and references, it is hoped that a path will be traced from broader to more particularized concerns. A more fully articulated project would result in a series of case studies.

I am grateful to various people for assisting in this project. Most of the work was done under the auspices of a fellowship at the Centre for Applied Philosophy and Public Ethics (Charles Sturt University). I received helpful criticism of earlier drafts from David Biles, John Braithwaite, Derek Brookes, Tom Campbell, Todd Clear, Stephen Coleman, John Dawes, James Jacobs, Michael Jacobson, Richard Lippke, Seumas Miller, Larry Sullivan, and Matthew Zommer. Stephen Coleman provided a great deal of additional research support. As is standard, although the final product is much better than it would have been without their assistance, I must take responsibility for what I have done with their advice.

## Developing a Correctional Ethic

Even the term 'correctional ethics' reflects history and begs questions. Were we to trace its roots, we would discover that, had it been labelled, what is now referred to as correctional ethics might have once been spoken of as 'penitentiary ethics' or, somewhat later, as 'prison ethics'. Such shifts of nomenclature would have reflected changes in our ways of conceptualizing a particular institution. What emerged in the eighteenth century as a regularized institutional response to crime – the penitentiary – has been redrafted to reflect – or at least espouse – evolving understandings. Nevertheless, even correctional ethics, the latest evolution, will appear dated to some, because the ideology that spawned it had its heyday in the mid-twentieth century and it now has only token representation in many of the institutions that bear the correctional name.[1] What is more, the institution itself, and not merely its purpose, is under challenge, and some would question the very possibility of an ethic related to it.[2]

Since Robert Martinson's controversial but influential 1974 report,[3] which – somewhat misleadingly – concluded that 'nothing works', there has been, for the most part, a contraction of the rehabilitative and educational/vocational programmes that might have given some credence to the idea that prisons were correctional institutions. During the same period there has been – at least in the United States – a massive increase in incarceration.[4] Apart from the retributive functions traditionally associated with penality, incarcerative institutions have become primarily incapacitative and secondarily deterrent. Rehabilitative programmes have lost out to the economic exigencies and political popularity of austere incarcerative responses to social dislocation.

Putting to one side the vexed question of institutional *tele*, the idea of correctional ethics, if construed along the lines of business, medical and legal ethics, is also striking for its lack of articulation. A search of 'correctional ethics', its cognates and substantive treatments of issues that it could be expected to cover turns up precious little. There are reasons for this. First, institutional and professional ethics are largely nineteenth- and twentieth-century creations, reflecting the increasing division of labour and the depersonalization of social and public services. There are numerous fields in which the development of an occupational or professional ethic is still in its infancy. Second, institutional and occupational ethics have developed in response to the demands of a client public. There has, however, been relatively little public concern for 'troublemakers' beyond the desire that they be dealt with or put away.[5] Third, although 'correctional institutions' have usually been 'outfitted' with various formal social functions – such as rehabilitation, retribution, incapacitation, specific and general deterrence – the interrelations of, and tensions among, these have not been carefully worked out and institutional priorities have tended to reflect external pressures – how the need to 'do something' with those who have fallen foul of the formal constraints of an increasingly urban society can be most efficiently implemented. Fourth, the fact that prison officers and administrators have not usually been expected to undergo the extensive tertiary or professional training required of many other social providers of services has meant that their preparation for the ethical challenges of their work environment has not engaged the attention of the academic scholars who would normally address such issues. The additional and not insignificant fact that what goes on in correctional institutions is mostly hidden from public sight has helped perpetuate this lack of attention and concern. Even the courts – especially in the United States – have been reluctant to intrude,[6] despite the fact that, when they have done so, they have often uncovered what can be generously described as a lack of professionalism.[7]

That said, certain foundational or framing issues in correctional ethics have been given a great deal of attention. The view that wrongdoing or, more narrowly and problematically, crime, in some sense warrants punishment has engaged philosophers and others from ancient times. Although the latter precipitating response – crime – has itself engendered a lively and often polarized debate,[8] there has always been strong support for the view that it warrants punishment. How crime warrants punishment – as a deserved or vindicatory imposition or alternatively or in addition as justified on rehabilitative, incapacitative, deterrent or other consequentialist grounds – has generated a vast and rich literature, influential examples of which are included in this volume. If, as it is sometimes argued, punishment is warranted by wrongdoing on retributive grounds – that is, as a deserved response – one might wonder what connection there could be between punishment and correctional ethics. One answer might be that to the extent that we institutionalize punishment we must look at its social benefits as well as the distribution of deserts. Another, developed by Antony Duff (Chapter 11, this volume), is that correction of an appropriate kind must be mediated by punishment.

In most recent discussions, the inclusion of imprisonment among punishment options has been taken for granted, and it is easily forgotten that imprisonment as punishment is a modern development.[9] Rationales for imprisonment, along with its problems, were articulated by eighteenth- and nineteenth-century theorists, but until the recent turn towards restorative alternatives, the phenomenon of confinement as such has attracted little philosophical attention.[10] Such discussion as there is has focused on the purposes and terms of incarceration. For most, it has seemed reasonable that, as Kenneth Kipnis (Chapter 22) puts it, those who violate the conditions of a democratic society should find their enjoyment of its 'preeminent political good' – liberty – limited for a time (p. 534). Those who accept that position will be likely to consider the conduct of those who work in so-called correctional institutions – primarily prison officers and administrators, but also other professional and ancillary staff – an important focus of correctional ethics.[11] One purpose of this volume is to foster increased scholarly interest in the ethical issues that (ought to) engage correctional staff.

Although there has always been active resistance to imprisonment as punishment, particularly in Europe,[12] it has been only in the past 30 years that disenchantment has developed a momentum that now requires formal administrators of justice to give serious consideration to alternatives. Among the reasons have been the increasing and almost indiscriminate use of imprisonment by some Western democracies (sometimes referred to in the United States as an 'imprisonment binge'), a sense that many of those who come before criminal justice authorities (especially juveniles and drug users) are not appropriately dealt with by means of imprisonment,[13] an acute sense of racial and jurisdictional disparities in sentencing practices,[14] frustration on the part of a society that has sensed rampant recidivism and the ineffectiveness of incarceration, victims who feel let down by the criminal justice process, and the sheer economic and social cost of maintaining 'the prison industrial complex'. Questioning imprisonment has also tapped into deeper doubts concerning the 'crime warrants punishment' formula. Even if 'crime' deserves some significant social response, the idea that this response should take the form of punishment (as usually understood) is claimed to be a matter of convention rather than of moral necessity. Once the nexus of crime and punishment is challenged, the nexus of crime and imprisonment is also called into question. We may have reached the nadir of the incapacitative response to criminality. Although the movement for alternatives is diverse,[15] the frequent appeal to what is referred to as 'restorative justice' now constitutes a formidable challenge to conventional wisdom.

Mirroring its diversity, how the restorative critique and alternative is construed varies considerably. For some, such strategies are viewed simply as supplements to, or opportunities provided by, incarcerative punishment. Other restorative responses belong on a continuum that includes aspects of what has traditionally been known as 'community corrections'.[16] But, for some of its proponents, the restorative approach offers a radical alternative to punishment. It focuses on the healing or mending of breached relations, not simply of those between the offender and the wider community but also and especially between the offender and those who have been more directly victimized by the offender's acts. On this understanding, punishment is not imposed, although shame and apology might be evoked and various forms of restitution agreed to. The emphasis is on reconciliation and reintegration rather than on retribution.

In its less radical forms, restorative justice offers a welcome antidote not only to the preoccupation with harsh incarcerative responses to crime, but also to a damaging depersonalization of criminal justice processes in which a proper concern for impartiality has failed to accommodate the human sensibilities that crime has affected. In its more radical forms, however, restorative approaches must confront problems of equity and the possibility that, without some form of retribution, a morally acceptable restoration cannot be effectuated – issues that are canvassed by Antony Duff and Richard Delgado in Chapters 11 and 12 of this volume. Despite sometimes significant gains in victim satisfaction through restorative approaches, there is still a substantial argument to be made for the view that victims are more likely to consider that they have been taken seriously if the response is taken to include an expectation of punishment.

Whatever our judgement on this important debate, restorative approaches do not dispense with the need for a correctional ethic, even though they transform it. The relationships and techniques of restorative justice generate important ethical challenges for their practitioners as they do for those who administer and work in prisons and other instrumentalities of the traditional criminal justice system.

## About this Volume

The purpose of this collection, in line with the series of which it is a part, is to provide, in a single volume, core essays that those researching the field might want to have at hand. Of necessity, the volume has to recognize the controversial and divided nature of the field and must therefore encompass, on the one hand, the ethical challenges implicit in the administration of prisons and other forms of intensive supervision and, on the other hand, those posed by alternative (restorative) practices that call into question, both ethically and practically, the dominant incarcerative response to crime.

Even so, a formidable logistical problem remains. The ethical issues encountered in corrections are myriad and range from the most general, such as the links between wrongdoing, crime and punishment, and the forms to be taken by punishment or other responses to crime, through detailed policy issues relating to general conditions of confinement or the structuring of restorative encounters, to the minutiae of human relationships – individual cases in which the interests of the various stakeholders have to be confronted and mediated.

Although some scholarly discussions of correctional workplace ethics exist, their numbers are depressingly low and at this point could not constitute the centrepiece for an anthology of this kind. For the most part, the relevant work remains to be done. It has therefore seemed most appropriate, given the absence of an established literature, to conceive of the present anthology as one in which a framework is provided for the more detailed work that is needed. Although some of the essays gesture towards and, in some cases, footnote the more concrete problems that need to be addressed, for the most part they are stage-setting. To give some shape to what a more fully developed correctional ethic might look like, I have therefore included an Appendix (A) that sets out the kind of detailed research agenda that might be pursued. As part of that research agenda I have noted some books or articles that might help to initiate a discussion of the issues they identify. If the developments that have taken place in police ethics over the past 15 years can be taken as a guide to what we might reasonably anticipate in correctional ethics, we also have reason to expect that over the next 10–15 years there will emerge a body of work comparable to that found in other occupations. Of course, just because correctional ethics is, and is likely to remain, problematic at its core, it may have very different instantiations.

Part I of the anthology includes several formative contributions to the contemporary debate over wrongdoing, crime, and punishment. Although the essays by H.L.A. Hart, Herbert Morris, Jeffrie Murphy and Jean Hampton may be viewed as abstract treatments of punishment theory, the conceptions they articulate and discuss still dominate correctional practice. Sentencers and institutional managers must confront, even implicitly, the issue of what morally justifies the practices they prescribe and superintend. Jeffrie Murphy's essay (Chapter 3) has the additional merit of addressing the possibility that there is a radical disconnection between punishment as it is theorized and institutions of punishment as we find them. Two practically important ancillary issues are also dealt with in this section: whether, and if so how, capital punishment might be justified and the moral challenge posed by the 'collateral consequences' of conviction – the various disqualifications that may be imposed on people in addition to a formal sentence.

The essays included in Part II explore certain aspects of the frequently taken-for-granted nexus between punishment and imprisonment. In a sense, it supplements the contributions of Part I, which, in seeking to articulate various justifying desiderata (such as retribution, deterrence and incapacitation) usually intend that these sustain the use of imprisonment as a form of punishment. As the essays included in Part II show, however, imprisonment as punishment raises numerous ethical concerns of its own.

The essays included in Part III serve two purposes. On the one hand, they draw attention to an emerging critique of the ways of thinking that underlie both Parts I and II – the 'restorative' critique that is sometimes said to provide an appropriate role for victims in the social response to crime, but which often constitutes a much more fundamental probing of the moral link between crime, punishment and imprisonment. Although they do not reflect the full range of such accounts, those included (by Lawrence Sherman, John Braithwaite and Daniel Van Ness) bring into sharp focus some of the main ideas involved. Restorative approaches are not concerned merely – if at all – with imposing a burden on those who have breached social norms, but with the restoration of relationships that have been breached by wrongdoing and with a healing of social fractures. That, of course, may require that the offender accept compensatory or restitutive burdens, along with an acceptance of responsibility, but this is seen more as the outcome of a form of negotiation than as an externally administered imposition.

As noted earlier, it cannot be presumed that the contrast drawn between retributive and restorative responses to wrongdoing is a legitimate one, and that restorative approaches represent a legitimate alternative to traditional punitive responses to wrongdoing. This is the thrust of Antony Duff's critique in Chapter 11. And to the extent that they constitute a radical alternative, restorative approaches must confront significant procedural challenges, some of which are developed in Richard Delgado's essay (Chapter 12). Even if restorative strategies are included in our response to crime, their distinctive techniques will raise distinctive ethical questions. Restorative justice mediators, no less than prison officers, need to develop their own correctional ethic. Some of the framing ethical issues are addressed by John Braithwaite in Chapter 14.

Part IV approaches a few of the broad ethical questions of correctional policy that arise in the context of the dominant correctional paradigm. Who should, and how should we frame correctional policy?[17] Should correctional facilities be privatized and, if so, what should be the terms under which the private correctional facilities operate? How hard should we make the experience of prison? Responses to such questions are not absent from some of the essays considered in Parts I to III, yet they also warrant separate treatment since they are questions to be addressed when social policy is being considered – when decisions are being made about the allocation of social resources and the impact of those decisions on institutions has to be taken into account. Despite their frequent geographical isolation, itself an ethical issue,[18] what happens in prisons is not immune to – and, indeed, is often strongly affected by – decisions taken many miles away. A central policy concern is the tacit, and occasionally explicit, commitment to what is sometimes referred to as the doctrine of penal austerity, the notion that conditions 'inside' prison ought not to be better than those an inmate might have encountered 'outside'. The doctrine taps into the sense that punishment is to be seen as an imposition, not a benefit. Yet it cannot ignore the obligation that a state takes upon itself when it chooses to exercise almost total control over the conditions of a person's life.

The essays included in Part V begin to detail some of the broad questions of professional ethics that confront prison personnel. More detailed explorations await the further development of correctional ethics, though some beginnings are noted in the research agenda (Appendix A). Although Parts IV and V are often deeply interconnected, they cannot be collapsed. How prison officers deal with the constraints under which they must work is not wholly determined by broader social policy.

Ideally, this collection ought to have included a further section dealing with institutional and professional issues that are parasitic on imprisonment – probation, parole, diversionary programmes such as drug courts, and community corrections (intermediate sanctions). There is a growing sociological/criminological literature dealing with these supplements/alternatives, but for the most part it is not oriented in a focused and scholarly way to the ethical questions that are implicit in them. Some of the extant literature is indicated in Appendix A.

Finally, despite their significant deficiencies as deliberative articulations of ethical concerns, professional codes of ethics identify many of the recurring ethical issues encountered by those who work in various forms of correctional practice. Judiciously used, however, they can be articulated into a valuable ethical toolkit or handbook for those who work in the correctional field.[19] A listing of some of the main correctional codes of ethics, along with their website addresses, is included as Appendix B.

### Appendix A: A Research Agenda for Correctional Ethics[20]

*Crime*
- Ethical issues in criminalization
    - What sort of acts should be criminalized?[21]
    - The politics of criminalization[22]
    - Criminalizing corporations[23]

*Responses to crime punishment versus alternatives*[24]

*Punishment*
- What justifies punishment?
    - The classic options: retribution (desert, vindication and so on), deterrence (specific and general), rehabilitation, moral education, incapacitation and so on.[25]
    - What justifies state punishment?[26]

- How is severity of punishment to be determined?[27]
- What types of punishments are justifiable?
  - Corporal punishment and torture[28]
  - Capital punishment[29]
    - Ethical issues in the appeals process
    - Methods of capital punishment[30]
    - Ethical issues for executioners[31]
    - The role of medical personnel in capital punishment[32]
- Imprisonment versus non-incarcerative alternatives[33]

*Imprisonment*[34]
- Who should be imprisoned?[35]
  - Ethical issues arising from imprisonment rate disparities, sentencing disparities and racial disproportion[36]
- Plea bargaining[37]
- Ethical issues relating to judicial discretion, sentencing guidelines, mandatory minima, and substantial assistance departures[38]
- Sentencing juveniles[39]
- Ethical issues relating to cross-cultural punishment, international convictions and transfers[40]
- Private and public prisons[41]
- Ethical issues confronting the minimum, medium, and maximum distinction[42]
  - The supermax challenge[43]
- Conditions of confinement[44]
  - Ethical issues relating to basic conditions of confinement (cell size, double celling, overcrowding, smoking policies, noise, temperature control, food)[45]
  - Basic rights (associational rights, provisions for religious observance, free speech, privacy; safety; health care, mental and physical)[46]
  - Amenities[47] – recreational[48] (gym, TV, amount available), educational/vocational (including library and other resources), labour[49] (including chain gangs[50])
  - Visitation and outside contacts (telephone policies, conjugal visits, children of prisoners, voting rights)[51]
  - Security issues (strip searches, drug testing, lockdowns, solitary confinement)[52]

*Prison administrators*[53]
- Responsibilities and responsiveness to wider community and political overseers
- Ethical issues in supervision of officers and the development of prison policies
- Changing prison demographics (racial disparities, aging prisoners; female prisoners)

*Ethical issues for prison officers*[54]
- ethically defensible training policies[55]
- ethical issues in officer/inmate relationships[56]
- exploitation of cliques
- friendships and other intimacies[57]
- the use of force[58]

- deception
- corruption[59]

*Ethical issues for professional staff*
- ethical issues relating to training and competence
- relations between security needs and provision of professional service
- distinctive issues for medical personnel, social workers, mental health workers, chaplains, teachers and so on.

*Release issues*
- extending confinement[60]
- preparation for release
- post-release conditions (for example notification laws and the like)[61]
- civil disqualifications[62]
- Parole[63]
  - conditions for the award of parole[64]
  - imposing special conditions on parolees[65]
  - conditions for revocation

*Non-incarcerative alternatives*
- Fines and forfeitures[66]
- Corporal punishment[67]
- Community corrections[68]
- Probation[69]
  - appropriate conditions for probation
  - role of a probation officer[70]
  - training and caseload issues
  - supervisory issues
  - conditions of probation
  - curfews
  - drug-testing[71]
  - special conditions
- Drug courts[72]
- Community service[73]
- Boot camps, shock incarceration[74]
- House arrest
- Electronic monitoring[75]

*Alternative responses*
- Treatment
  - Ethics of a treatment response[76]
  - Treatment conditions
- Reconciliation programmes[77]
  - A restorative/retributive dichotomy?[78]
  - Do restorative programmes accept too much of a problematic status quo?[79]

- Restorative processes and the problem of expressing social disapproval
- Varieties of, and the ethical issues dealt with or raised by each[80]
- Issues of implementation[81]
- Training issues
- Relations with police and other criminal justice personnel
- The eliminability of processual shortfalls
- Dealing with intransigence
- Recidivism and responsibility to the community
- Fairness and the limits of the victim's role
- Ethical issues in program evaluation

## Appendix B: Correctional Codes

United Nations, Standard Minimum Rules for the Treatment of Prisoners
 <http://www.unhchr.ch/html/menu3/b/h_comp34.htm>

Council of Europe, European Convention for the Prevention of Torture and Inhuman or Degrading Treatment or Punishment
 <http://conventions.coe.int/Treaty/en/Treaties/Html/126.htm>

International Association of Correctional Officers, Correctional Officers Creed

International Association of Correctional Training Personnel (IACTP), Trainers= Code of Ethics
 <http://www.iactp.org/doc_codeofethics.pdf>

American Correctional Health Services Association (ACHSA), Code of Ethics
 <http://www.corrections.com/achsa/ethics.html>

International Council of Nurses, Nurses Role in the Care of Prisoners and Detainees
 <http://www.icn.ch/psdetainees.htm>

American Correctional Chaplains Association, Code of Ethics
 <http://www.correctionalchaplains.org/what_is_the_acca.htm>

American Probation and Parole Association, Code of Ethics
 <http://www.appa-net.org/about%20appa/codeof.htm>

United Nations, Basic Principles on the Use of Restorative Justice Programmes in Criminal Matters (UN), 2000
 <http://www.restorativejustice.org/rj3/UNdocuments/UNDecBasicPrinciplesofRJ.html>

Restorative Justice Consortium, Statement of Restorative Justice Principles
 <http://www.mediate.com/articles/rjprinciples.cfm>

## Notes

1 For a valuable set of essays detailing the development of the prison, see Norval Morris and David J. Rothman (eds), *The Oxford History of the Prison* (New York: Oxford University Press, 1998).

2 See Derek Brookes, 'The Possibility of a Correctional Ethic', in John Kleinig and Margaret Leland Smith (eds), *Discretion, Community and Correctional Ethics* (Lanham, MD: Rowman & Littlefield, 2001), pp. 39–68.

3 Robert Martinson, Judith Wilks and D. Lipton, *Effectiveness of Corrections Treatment: A Survey of Treatment Evaluation Studies* (New York: Praeger, 1975) was an analysis of over 200 rehabilitation programmes from 1945–1967. Its main conclusions – and the slogan 'nothing works' – became widely known through Martinson's essay, 'What Works? Questions and Answers about Prison Reform', *Public Interest*, **35** (Spring 1974), pp. 22–54. Although Martinson later conceded that the situation was not quite as bleak as he had made it appear (see his 'New Findings, New Views: A Note of Caution Regarding Sentencing Reform', *Hofstra Law Review*, **7** (1979), pp. 243–58), and his research was strongly criticized, the position he had popularized was formally accepted by the US Supreme Court in *Mistretta* v. *United States*, 488 US 361 (1989).

4 In 1972 the inmate population of the United States was 330 000. In June 2002 there were over 2 million, an increase in the incarceration rate from approximately 100 per 100 000 to 702. A further 4 million were under intensive court supervision. The former world leader, Russia, had reduced its imprisonment rate to 628. By comparison, the rates in England and Wales were 139, in Australia, 112, and in India, the world's largest democracy, it was about 27! It is interesting to reflect on the significance of these differences. It is at least arguable that whereas the United States figures are evidence of an excessively punitive society, those in India reflect a breakdown of the criminal justice system. Comparative imprisonment rates can be accessed via The Sentencing Project: <http://www.sentencingproject.org>.

5 There are some notable exceptions. Gresham M. Sykes's sociological study, *The Society of Captives: A Study of a Maximum Security Prison* (Princeton, NJ: Princeton University Press, 1958) shows considerable sensitivity to the ethical dimensions of prison life. Kelsey Kauffman, *Prison Officers and Their World* (Cambridge, MA: Harvard University Press, 1988) also displays an awareness of how ethical issues impinge on the experience of prison officers. More recently, Ted Conover, *Newjack: Guarding Sing Sing* (New York: Random House, 2001), a study of the socialization of prison officers, provides a useful insight into prison officer training and the context in which ethical decision-making by officers must take place.

6 Some of the reasons are canvassed in John Kleinig, 'The Hardness of Hard Treatment', included in this volume; but see also Kenneth C. Haas, 'Judicial Politics and Correctional Reform: An Analysis of the Decline of the "Hands-off" Doctrine', *Detroit College of Law Review*, **4** (1977), pp. 796–831.

7 See, for example, Audrey J. Bomse, 'Prison Abuse: Prisoner-Staff Relations', in Kleinig and Smith (eds), *Discretion, Community and Correctional Ethics*, pp. 79–104. As the US Supreme Court has become more conservative, it has become less responsive to 'prisoners' rights'. See *Lewis* v. *Casey*, 518 US 343, 116 S. Ct. 2174 (1996), and James B. Jacobs, 'Prison Reform Amid the Ruins of Prisoners' Rights', Chapter 15 in this volume.

8 Of fundamental concern has been the identification of those kinds of act appropriately criminalized. Not all wrongdoing is appropriately criminalized, and behaviour that is criminalized may protect improperly partisan interests. Some of the issues are powerfully canvassed in Jeffrie Murphy, 'Marxism and Retribution', Chapter 3 in this volume. But see also R. Antony Duff, 'Conceptions of Crime', in P. Apps, C.E. Herlitz and L. Holmqvist (eds), *Flores Juris et Legum: Festskrift till Nils Jareborg* (Uppsala: Iustus Förlag, 2002).

9 See Morris and Rothman (eds), *The Oxford History of the Prison*. We need to distinguish firmly between imprisonment *as* punishment and imprisonment *for* punishment. Even if the latter has often seemed to be the case, only the former has public justification.

10 For classical discussions, see John Howard, *The State of Prisons* (London: J.M. Dent, 1929), first published 1777; Jeremy Bentham, *The Panopticon Writings*, ed. Miran Bozovic (London: Verso, 1995); James Mill, 'Essay on Prisons and Prison Discipline' in *James Mill: Political Writings*, ed. Terence Ball (Cambridge: Cambridge University Press, 1992), first published 1823. More recently,

see Michel Foucault, *Discipline and Punish: The Birth of the Prison,* trans. Alan Sheridan (New York: Pantheon, 1977). Excellent, largely sociological, studies of the contemporary prison are provided in Sykes, *The Society of Captives*; Norval Morris, *The Future of Imprisonment* (Chicago: University of Chicago Press, 1974); James B. Jacobs, *Stateville: The Penitentiary in Mass Society* (University of Chicago Press, 1977); and idem, *New Perspectives on Prisons and Imprisonment* (Ithaca, NY: Cornell University Press, 1983).

11   Not to leave prisoners themselves out of consideration, though their lack of power in the institution makes a consideration of their *duties* less urgent and our concern is more likely to be for their *rights*. (We might compare the relative lack of emphasis on the ethical responsibilities of patients vis-à-vis medical personnel.). See H.A. Bedau, 'Prisoners' Rights', *Criminal Justice Ethics,* **1**(1) (Winter/Spring,1982), pp. 26–41; Donald H. Wallace, 'Prisoners' Rights: Historical Views', in Edward J. Latessa, Alexander Holsinger, James W. Marquart and Jonathan R. Sorensen (eds), *Correctional Contexts: Contemporary and Classical Readings*, 2nd edn (Los Angeles: Roxbury, 2001), pp. 229–38; James B. Jacobs, 'The Prisoners' Rights Movement and Its Impact', in Norval Morris and Michael Tonry (eds), *Crime and Justice: An Annual Review of Research* Vol. II (Chicago: University of Chicago Press, 1980), pp. 429–70. I endeavour to link a professional correctional ethic to prisoner concerns in 'Professionalizing Incarceration', in Kleinig and Smith (eds), *Discretion, Community and Correctional Ethics*, pp. 1–15.

12   See, especially, Thomas Mathiesen, *Prison on Trial: A Critical Assessment* (London: Sage, 1990); Louk Hulsman, 'The Abolitionist Case: Alternative Crime Policies', *Israel Law Review*, **25**(3–4) (Summer/Autumn, 1991), pp. 681–709. In addition, Quakers have been in the forefront not only of prison reform but also of alternatives to incarceration. See Fay Honey Knopp *et al.*, *Instead of Prisons: A Handbook for Abolitionists* (Syracuse, NY: Prison Research Education Action Project, 1976) <http://prisonsucks.com/scans/instead_of_prisons/index.shtml>.

13   Added to this is the large number of people in prisons who suffer from mental disorders. See Human Rights Watch, 'Ill-Equipped: U.S. Prisoners and Offenders with Mental Illness', September 2003 at <http://www.hrw.org/reports/2003/usa1003/>.

14   See Michael Tonry, *Malign Neglect: Race, Crime, and Punishment in America* (New York: Oxford University Press, 1995).

15   See, for example, Howard Zehr and Harry Mika, 'Fundamental Concepts of Restorative Justice', *Contemporary Justice Review*, **1**(1) (1998), pp. 47–55.

16   For a review of the standard 'community corrections' options, see Todd R. Clear and Anthony A. Braga, 'Community Corrections', in James Q. Wilson and Joan Petersilia (eds), *Crime* (San Francisco: ICS Publishers, 1995), pp. 421–44; and a special issue of the *Federal Sentencing Reporter* on Risk Assessment, **16**(3) (2004).

17   For a broad official statement, see Home Office, 'The Correctional Policy Framework: Effective Execution of the Sentences of the Courts so as to Reduce Re-Offending and Protect the Public' at <http://www.homeoffice.gov.uk/docs/framecont.html>. Information on policy development in the United States can be accessed through the US Department of Justice's National Institute of Corrections website at <http://nicic.org/>.

18   Consider National Institute of Corrections, *Issues in Siting Correctional Facilities* [An Information Brief] (US Department of Justice, NIC, n.d.); Ryan S. King, Marc Mauer and Tracy Huling, 'Big Prisons, Small Town: Prison Economies in Rural America' (Washington: The Sentencing Project, February 2003) at <http://www.soros.org/initiatives/justice/articles_publications/publications/bigprisons_20030201/bigprisons.pdf>.

19   For a good example of this, see Andrew Coyle, *A Human Rights Approach to Prison Management: Handbook for Prison Staff* (London: International Centre for Prison Studies, 2002); cf. <http//www.kcl.ac.uk/depsta/rel/icps/restorative_prison.html>.

20   See, generally, Timothy Stroup, 'Correctional Ethics', in *Encyclopedia of Ethics*, ed. Lawrence Becker and Charlotte Becker, 2nd edn (London: Routledge, 2001), Vol. 1, pp. 338–43.

21   See Joel Feinberg, *The Moral Limits of Criminal Law* (New York: Oxford University Press, 1984–88), 4 vols.

22   See Richard Quinney, *Class, State, and Crime* (New York: Longman, 1977); Louk Hulsman, 'Critical Criminology and the Concept of Crime', *Contemporary Crises*, **10** (1986), pp. 63–80.

23    Celia Wells, *Corporations and Criminal Responsibility*, 2nd edn (New York: Oxford University Press, 2001).

24    See John Braithwaite, *Crime, Shame and Reintegration* (Cambridge: Cambridge University Press, 1989); Antony Duff, 'Alternatives to Punishment – or Alternative Punishments?' in Wesley Cragg (ed.), *Retributivism and Its Critics* (Stuttgart: Franz Steiner, 1992), pp. 44–68.

25    See C.L. Ten, *Guilt and Punishment* (Oxford: Clarendon Press, 1987); Finn Hornum, 'Corrections in Two Social Welfare Democracies', *Prison Journal*, **58** (1988), pp. 63-82; Edgardo Rotman, *Beyond Punishment: A New View on the Rehabilitation of Criminal Offenders* (Westport, CT: Greenwood, 1990); Franklin Zimring and Gordon Hawkins, *Incapacitation: Penal Confinement and the Restraint of Crime* (New York: Oxford University Press, 1995); R.A. Duff, 'Penal Communications: Recent Work in the Philosophy of Punishment', in Michael Tonry (ed.), *Crime and Justice: A Review of Research*, (Chicago: University of Chicago Press, 1996), Vol. XX, pp. 1–97; Andrew von Hirsch, Anthony E. Bottoms, Elizabeth Burney and P-O. Wikstrom, *Criminal Deterrence and Sentence Severity: An Analysis of Recent Research* (Oxford: Hart, 1999).

26    See John Kleinig, *Desert and Punishment* (The Hague: Martinus Nijhoff, 1973), ch. 4; Nicola Lacey, *State Punishment, Political Principles and Community Values* (London: Routledge, 1988); Marc Mauer and Meda Chesney-Lind (eds), *Invisible Punishment: The Collateral Consequences of Mass Imprisonment* (NY: The New Press, 2003).

27    See Kleinig, *Desert and Punishment*, ch. 7; Andrew von Hirsch, *Censure and Sanctions* (Oxford: Clarendon, 1993); Jeremy Waldron, 'Lex Talionis', *Arizona Law Review*, **34** (1992), pp. 25–51.

28    See Graeme Neuman, *Just and Painful: A Case for the Corporal Punishment of Criminals*, rev. edn (New York: Harrow & Heston, 2000); Henry Shue, 'Torture', *Philosophy and Public Affairs*, **7** (Winter, 1978), pp. 124-43; Rod Morgan, 'The Utilitarian Justification of Torture', *Punishment and Society*, **2** (2000), pp. 181–96.

29    See Hugo A. Bedau, 'The Case Against the Death Penalty' at <http://archive.aclu.org/library/case_against_death.html>; Louis Pojman and Jeffrey Reiman, *The Death Penalty: For and Against* (Lanham, MD: Rowman & Littlefield, 1998); Evan J. Mandery (ed.), *Capital Punishment: A Balanced Examination* (Sudbury, MA: Jones and Bartlett, 2005); Ethics Updates (L. Hinman): 'Punishment and the Death Penalty' at <http://ethics.acusd.edu/Applied/deathpenalty>.

30    See A. Camus, 'Reflections on the Guillotine', in *Resistance, Rebellion, and Death* (New York: Alfred Knopf, 1961); Paul Leighton, 'Fear and Loathing in an Age of Show Business: Reflections on Televised Executions', in Paul Leighton and Jeffrey Reiman (eds), *Criminal Justice Ethics* (Prentice Hall: Upper Saddle River, 2001), pp. 512–25.

31    See Arthur Applbaum, 'Professional Detachment: The Executioner of Paris', *Harvard Law Review*, **109** (1995), pp. 458–86; Robert J. Connelly, 'Role Morality and the Executioner's Intention', *Professional Ethics*, **6**(1–2) (1997), pp. 77–102.

32    See Human Rights Watch, 'Breach of Trust: Physician Participation in Executions in the United States' at <http://www.hrw.org/reports/1994/usdp/index.htm>; Michael Davis, 'What is Unethical About Physicians Helping at Executions', in *Justice in the Shadow of Death* (Lanham, MD: Rowman & Littlefield, 1996), ch. 4.

33    Richard B. Brandt, 'Conscience, (Rule) Utilitarianism and the Criminal Law', *Law and Philosophy*, **14**(1) (February 1995), pp. 65–89.

34    William Spelman, 'What Recent Studies Do (And Don't) Tell Us about Imprisonment and Crime', in Michael Tonry (ed.), *Crime and Justice*, Vol. XXVII (2000), pp. 419–94. Reflections on imprisonment (and other aspects of traditional criminal justice) by academically-inclined ex-convicts can be found in Jeffrey Ian Ross and Stephen C. Richards (eds), *Convict Criminology* Belmont, CA: Wadsworth, 2002).

35    Bruce Western and Katherine Beckett, 'Governing Social Marginality: Welfare, Incarceration, and the Transformation of State Policy', *Punishment and Society*, **3**(1) (January 2001), pp. 43–59.

36    Michael Tonry, 'Racial Disproportion in U.S. Prisons', *British Journal of Criminology*, **34** (1994), 97–115; Prison Reform Trust, *Sentencing: A Geographical Lottery* (London: Prison Reform Trust, 1997).

37    Albert Alschuler, 'Plea Bargaining and Its History', *Columbia Law Review*, **79** (1979), pp. 1–43; idem, 'The Changing Plea Bargaining Debate', *California Law Review*, **69** (1981) pp. 652–730.

38  Andrew von Hirsch and Judith Greene, 'When Should Reformers Support Creation of Sentencing Guidelines?', *Wake Forest Law Review*, **28** (1993), pp. 329–43; Adina Schwartz, 'A Market in Liberty: Corruption, Cooperation, and the Federal Criminal Justice System', in William C. Heffernan and John Kleinig (eds), *Private and Public Corruption* (Lanham, MD: Rowman & Littlefield, 2004), pp. 173–222.

39  See Franklin Zimring, 'Towards a Jurisprudence of Youth Violence', in Michael Tonry and Mark H. Moore (eds), *Youth Violence: Crime and Justice: A Review of Research* (Chicago: Chicago University Press, 1998), Vol. 24, pp. 477–501; Lucia Zedner, 'Sentencing Young Offenders', in Andrew Ashworth and Martin Wasik (eds), *Fundamentals of Sentencing Theory* (Oxford: Clarendon Press, 1998), ch. 7; Donna Bishop, 'Juvenile Offenders in the Adult Criminal Justice System', in Tonry (ed.), *Crime and Justice*, Vol. 27, pp. 81–168.

40  See Duncan Ivison, 'Justifying Punishment in Intercultural Contexts: Whose Norms, Which Values?' in M. Matravers (ed.), *Punishment and Political Theory* (Oxford: Hart, 1999), pp. 88–107; Prison Reform Trust, *Foreign Nationals in the Prison System* (London: Prison Reform Trust, 1996).

41  See C. Logan, *Private Prisons: Cons and Pros* (New York: Oxford University Press, 1990); D. Schichor, *Punishment for Profit: Private Prisons/Public Concerns* (Thousand Oaks, CA: Sage, 1995); Douglas McDonald, Elizabeth Fournier, Malcolm Russell-Einhourn and Stephen Crawford, *Private Prisons in the United States: An Assessment of Current Practice* (Cambridge, MA: Abt Associates, 1998); Richard Harding, 'Private Prisons', in Tonry (ed.), *Crime and Justice*, Vol. 28 (2001), pp. 265–346; Michael D. Reisig and Travis C. Pratt, 'The Ethics of Correctional Privatization: A Critical Examination of the Delegation of Coercive Authority', *The Prison Journal*, **80**(2) (June, 2000), pp. 210–22.

42  Kelsey Kauffman, *Prison Officers and Their World* (Cambridge, MA: Harvard University Press, 1985).

43  Leena Kurki and Norval Morris, 'The Purposes, Practices, and Problems of Supermax Prisons', in Tonry (ed.), *Crime and Justice*, Vol. 28, pp. 385–424; Richard L. Lippke, 'Against Supermax', *Journal of Applied Philosophy*, **21**(2) (2004), pp. 109–24; Craig Haney and Mona Lynch Haney, 'Regulating Prisons of the Future: A Psychological Analysis of Supermax and Solitary Confinement', *New York University Review of Law and Social Change*, **23** (1997), pp. 477–570; Chase Riveland, *Supermax Prisons: Overview and General Considerations* (Washington, DC: US Department of Justice, National Institute of Corrections, 1999); National Institute of Corrections, *Supermax Prisons: Legal Issues and Considerations* (Washington, DC: US Department of Justice, National Institute of Corrections, 1999); Human Rights Watch, 'Out of Sight: Human Rights Watch Briefing Paper on Supermaximum Prisons' at <http://www.hrw.org/reports/2000/supermax/Sprmx002.htm>.

44  Hugo Bedau, 'Prisoners' Rights', *Criminal Justice Ethics*, **1**(1) (1982), pp. 26–41; Richard L. Lippke, 'Toward a Theory of Prisoners' Rights', *Ratio Juris*, **15** (2002), pp. 122–45; Prison Reform Trust, *The Rising Toll of Prison Suicide* (London: Prison Reform Trust, 1997); Alison Liebling, 'Prisoner Suicide and Prisoner Coping', in Tonry and Petersilia (eds), *Crime and Justice*, Vol. 26 (1999), pp. 205–81; Andrew Ashworth and Elaine Player, 'Sentencing, Equal Treatment, and the Impact of Sanctions', in Andrew Ashworth and Martin Wasik (eds), *Fundamentals of Sentencing Theory* (Oxford: Clarendon, 1998); Richard Sparks and Anthony E. Bottoms, 'Legitimacy and Order in Prisons', *British Journal of Sociology*, **46**(1) (1995), pp. 45–62; Jennifer Wynn, *Inside Rikers: Stories from the World's Largest Penal Colony* (New York: St Martin's Press, 2001).

45  Gerald G. Gaes, 'The Effects of Overcrowding in Prisons', in Tonry and Morris (eds), *Crime and Justice*, Vol. 6 (1985), pp. 265–346; Gerald G. Gaes, 'Prison Crowding Research Re-examined', *Prison Journal*, **73**(3) (September 1994), pp. 329–64; Joe Levenson, *A System Under Pressure: The Effects of Prison Overcrowding* (London: Prison Reform Trust, 1999); *Helling v. McKinney*, 509 US 25 (1993).

46  Douglas C. McDonald, 'Medical Care in Prisons', in Tonry and Petersilia (eds), *Crime and Justice*, Vol. 26, pp. 427–78; Anthony E. Bottoms, 'Interpersonal Violence and Social Order in Prisons', in ibid., pp. 205–82.

47  A. Wunder, 'The Extinction of Inmate Privileges', *Corrections Compendium*, **20**(6) (1995), pp. 5–24; A. Lomax and P. Wright, 'Prison TV: Luxury or Management Tool?', in D. Burton-Rose (ed.), *The Celling of America: An Inside Look at the U.S. Prison Industry* (Monroe, ME: Common Courage, 1998), pp. 48–54.

48    Richard L. Lippke, 'Prisoner Access to Recreation, Entertainment and Diversion', *Punishment and Society*, **5**(1) (2003), pp. 33–52.

49    Rex Martin, 'The Right of Inmates to Work', *A System of Rights* (New York: Oxford University Press, 1993), ch. 11; Richard L. Lippke, 'Prison Labor: Its Control, Facilitation, and Terms', *Law and Philosophy*, **17** (1998), pp. 533–57.

50    Tessa M. Gorman, 'Back on the Chain Gang: Why the Eighth Amendment and the History of Slavery Proscribe the Resurgence of Chain Gangs', *California Law Review*, **85** (March 1997), pp. 441–78.

51    James B. Jacobs and Eric H. Steele, 'Sexual Deprivation and Penal Policy', *Cornell Law Review*, **62** (1977), pp. 289–312; Richard L. Lippke, 'The Disenfranchisement of Felons', *Law and Philosophy*, **20**(6) (November 2001), pp. 553–80; Michael Cholbi, 'A Felon's Right to Vote', *Law and Philosophy*, **21** (2002), pp. 543–65; John Kleinig and Kevin Murtagh, 'Disenfranchising Felons', *Journal of Applied Philosophy*, **22** (2005), pp. 217–39.

52    James Bonta and Paul Gendreau, 'Solitary Confinement Is Not Cruel and Unusual Punishment: People Sometimes Are', *Canadian Journal of Criminology*, **26** (1984), pp. 467–78.

53    See John DiIulio, *Governing Prisons: A Comparative Study of Correctional Management* (New York: Free Press, 1987); Kevin N. Wright and Lynne Goodstein, 'Correctional Environments', in Lynne Goodstein and Doris Layton MacKenzie (eds), *The American Prison: Issues in Research and Policy* (New York: Plenum Press, 1989), pp. 253–70; Linda L. Zupan and Ben A. Menke, 'The New Generation Jail: An Overview', in Joel A. Thompson and G. Larry Mays (eds), *American Jails: Public Policy Issues* (Chicago: Nelson Hall, 1991), pp. 181–94.

54    Lucien X. Lombardo, *Guards Imprisoned: Correctional Officers at Work* (New York: Elsevier, 1981); Alison Liebling and David Price, *The Prison Officer* (Winchester: Waterside Press, 2001); Robert Johnston and S. Price, 'The Complete Correctional Officer: Human Service and the Human Environment of Prison', *Criminal Justice and Behavior*, **8**(3) (September 1981), pp. 343–73; Roslyn Muraskin, 'Corrections/Punishment: Ethical Behavior of Correctional Officers', in Roslyn Muraskin and Matthew Muraskin (eds), *Morality and the Law* (Upper Saddle River, NJ: Prentice Hall, 2001), pp. 140–50; Paul Gendreau, 'Principles of Effective Intervention with Offenders', in A.T. Harland (ed.), *Choosing Correctional Options that Work: Defining the Demand and Evaluating the Supply* (Thousand Oaks, CA: Sage, 1996), pp. 117–30; Mark A. Harris, *Making Ethical Choices: A Guide for Staff* (Lanham, MD: American Correctional Association, 1999).

55    Ted Conover, *Newjack: Guarding Sing Sing* (New York: Vintage Books, 2001).

56    Hans Toch, 'Is a "Correctional Officer," by Any Other Name, a "Screw"?', *Criminal Justice Review*, **3**(2) (1978), pp. 19–35; Jay Farbstein and Associates, and Richard Werner, 'A Comparison of Direct and Indirect Supervision Correctional Facilities', *Forum on Corrections Research*, **3**(2) (1991), pp. 7–11.

57    Amnesty International, *'Not Part of My Sentence': Violations of the Human Rights of Women in Custody* (Washington, DC: Amnesty International, 1999); Amnesty International, *Abuse of Women in Custody: Sexual Misconduct and Shackling of Pregnant Women*, 2001 at <http://www.amnestyusa.org/women/custody/abuseincustody.html>.

58    Patrick Henry, Jeffrey D. Senese and Gwyn Smith Ingley, 'Use of Force in America's Prisons: An Overview of Current Research', *Corrections Today*, **56**(4) (July 1994), pp. 108–12.

59    Bernard J. McCarthy, 'Keeping an Eye on the Keeper: Prison Corruption and its Control', in Michael Braswell, Bernard McCarthy and Belinda McCarthy (eds), *Justice, Crime and Ethics* (Belmont, CA: Wadsworth, 1991), pp. 239–53.

60    Robert Allen Prentky, Eric Janus and Michael Seto (eds), *Sexually Coercive Behavior: Understanding and Management* (New York: Annals of the New York Academy of the Sciences, **989** (2003), pp. 1–514).

61    Megan's Law, 42 USC § 13701 (2001); Virginia B. Baldau, *Summary of State Sex Offender Registries: Automation and Operation*, NCJ 177621 (Washington, DC: US Department of Justice, 1999) at <http://www.ojp.usdoj.gov/bjs/pub/pdf/sssorao.pdf>.

62    Special Project, 'The Collateral Consequences of a Felony Conviction', *Vanderbilt Law Review*, **23**(5) (October 1970), p. 929; Andrew von Hirsch and Martin Wasik, 'Civil Disqualifications Attending Conviction: A Suggested Conceptual Framework', *Cambridge Law Journal*, **56**(3) (1997), pp. 599–626; Hugh LaFollette, 'Collateral Consequences of Punishment', *Journal of Applied Philosophy*, **22** (2005), pp. 241–61.

63  Jonathan Simon, *Poor Discipline: Parole and the Social Control of the Underclass* (Chicago: University of Chicago Press, 1993); Joan Petersilia, *When Prisoners Come Home: Parole and Prisoner Reentry* (New York: Oxford University Press, 2003); Norman Holt, 'The Current State of Parole in America', in Joan Petersilia (ed.), *Community Corrections: Probation, Parole and Intermediate Sanctions* (NY: Oxford University Press, 1997); John T, Whitehead, 'Ethical Issues in Probation and Parole', in Michael Braswell, Bernard McCarthy and Belinda McCarthy (eds), *Justice, Crime and Ethics* (Cincinnati, OH: Anderson, 1996), pp. 243–59; Roslyn Muraskin, 'Probation and Parole Officers: Ethical Behavior', in Muraskin (ed.), *Morality and the Law*, pp. 119–29.

64  James B. Jacobs, 'Sentencing by Prison Personnel: Good Time', *UCLA Law Review*, **30** (December 1982), pp. 217–70.

65  John Kleinig and Charles Lindner, 'AIDS on Parole: Dilemmas in Decision Making', *Criminal Justice Policy Review*, **18**(1) (January 1990), pp. 1–27.

66  See S. Hillsman and J. Greene, 'The Use of Fines as an Intermediate Sanction', in J. Byrne, A. Lurigio and J. Petersilia (eds), *Smart Sentencing: The Emergence of Intermediate Sanctions* (Newbury Park, CA: Sage, 1992), pp. 123–41.

67  See World Corporal Punishment Research at <http://www.corpun.com>.

68  Norval Morris and Michael Tonry, *Between Prison and Probation: Intermediate Punishments in a Rational Sentencing System* (New York: Oxford University Press, 1990); Andrew von Hirsch, 'The Ethics of Community-Based Sanctions', *Crime and Delinquency*, **36**(1) (January 1990), pp. 162–73.

69  Joan Petersilia, *Community Corrections* (New York: Oxford University Press, 1998); John T. Whitehead, 'Ethical Issues in Probation and Parole', in Michael Braswell, Bernard McCarthy and Belinda McCarthy (eds), *Justice, Crime and Ethics* (Cincinnati, OH: Anderson, 1996), pp. 243–59; Roslyn Muraskin, 'Probation and Parole Officers: Ethical Behavior', in Muraskin (ed.), *Morality and the Law*, pp. 119–29.

70  Robert B. Mills, 'Ethical Guidelines in Corrections', in *Offender Assessment: A Casebook in Corrections* (Cincinnati, OH: Anderson, 1980), pp. 51–55.

71  Susan Turner, Joan Petersilia and Elizabeth Piper Deschenes, 'The Implementation and Effectiveness of Drug Testing in Community Supervision: Results of an Experimental Evaluation', in D. MacKenzie and C. Uchida (eds), *Drugs and Crime: Evaluating Public Policy Initiatives* (Thousand Oaks, CA: Sage, 1994), pp. 231–52.

72  See Lana D. Harrison and Frank R. Scarpitti (eds), 'Special Issue: Drug Treatment Courts', *Substance Use & Misuse*, **37**(12–13) (2002), pp. 1441–832; James L. Nolan Jr (ed.), *Drug Courts in Theory and Practice* (New York: Aldine deGruyter, 2002).

73  D. McDonald, 'Punishing Labor: Unpaid Community Service as a Criminal Sentence', in J. Byrne, A. Lurigio and J. Petersilia (eds), *Smart Sentencing: The Emergence of Intermediate Sanctions* (Newbury Park, CA: Sage, 1992), pp. 182–93.

74  Doris Layton MacKenzie and Gaylene Styve Armstrong (eds), *Boot Camps: Studies Examining Military Basic Training as a Model for Corrections* (Thousand Oaks, CA: Sage, 2004).

75  Stephen Mainprize, 'Electronic Monitoring in Corrections: Assessing Cost Effectiveness and the Potential for Widening the Net of Social Control', *Canadian Journal of Criminology*, **34**(2) (April 1992), pp. 161–80; Prison Reform Trust, *Electronic Tagging: Viable Option of Expensive Diversion* (London: Prison Reform Trust, 1999).

76  C.S. Lewis, 'The Humanitarian Theory of Punishment', *Twentieth Century*, **12** (1949), pp. 1–12.

77  John Braithwaite, 'Restorative Justice: Assessing Optimistic and Pessimistic Accounts', in Tonry (ed.), *Crime and Justice*, Vol. 25, pp. 1–127; idem, 'Theories that Might Explain Why Restorative Justice Works', in *Restorative Justice and Responsive Regulation* (Oxford: Oxford University Press, 2002), pp. 73–136; Gerry Johnston (ed.), *A Restorative Justice Reader: Text, Sources, Context* (Cullompton, Devon: Willan Publishing, 2003); Lawrence W. Sherman, 'Two Protestant Ethics and the Spirit of Restoration', in John Braithwaite and Helen Strang (eds), *Restorative Justice and Civil Society* (Cambridge: Cambridge University Press, 2001), pp. 35–55.

78  Kathleen Daly, 'Revisiting the Relationship between Retributive and Restorative Justice', in *Restorative Justice: Philosophy to Practice* (London: Dartmouth/Ashgate, 2000), pp. 33–54.

79  Sharon Levrant, Francis T. Cullen, Betsy Fulton and John F. Wozniak, 'Reconsidering Restorative Justice: The Corruption of Benevolence Revisited', *Crime and Delinquency*, **45** (1999), pp. 3–27.

80   Kathleen Daly, 'Restorative Justice: The Real Story', *Punishment and Society*, **4**(1) (2002), pp. 55–79.
81   Robert E. MacKay, 'Ethics and Good Practice in Restorative Justice', in *Victim-Offender Mediation in Europe: Making Restorative Justice Work*, ed. The European Forum for Victim-Offender Mediation and Restorative Justice, intro. Tony Peters (Leuven: Leuven University Press, 2000), pp. 49–67.

# Part I
# Wrongdoing, Crime and Punishment

# [1]

## PROLEGOMENON TO THE PRINCIPLES OF PUNISHMENT

*By* Professor H. L. A. HART

### INTRODUCTORY

THE main object of this paper is to provide a framework for the discussion of the mounting perplexities which now surround the institution of criminal punishment, and to show that any morally tolerable account of this institution must exhibit it as a compromise between radically distinct and partly conflicting principles.

General interest in the topic of punishment has never been greater than it is at present and I doubt if the public discussion of it has ever been more confused. The interest and the confusion are both in part due to relatively modern scepticism about two elements which have figured as essential parts of the traditionally opposed " theories " of punishment. On the one hand, the old Benthamite confidence in fear of the penalties threatened by the law as a powerful deterrent, has waned with the growing realisation that the part played by calculation of any sort in anti-social behaviour has been exaggerated. On the other hand a cloud of doubt has settled over the keystone of " Retributive " theory. Its advocates can no longer speak with the old confidence that statements of the form " This man who has broken the law could have kept it " had a univocal or agreed meaning; or where scepticism does not attach to the *meaning* of this form of statement, it has shaken the confidence that we are generally able to distinguish the cases where this form of statement is true from those where it is not.[1]

---

[1] See Barbara Wootton *Social Science and Social Pathology* for a clear and most comprehensive modern statement of these doubts.

2                                   H. L. A. HART

Yet quite apart from the uncertainty engendered by these fundamental doubts, which seem to call in question the accounts given of the efficacy, and the morality of punishment by all the old competing theories, the public utterances of those who conceive themselves to be expounding, as plain men for other plain men, orthodox or common-sense principles, untouched by modern psychological doubts are uneasy. Their words often sound as if the authors had not fully grasped their meaning or did not intend the words to be taken quite literally. A glance at the parliamentary debates or the *Report of the Royal Commission on Capital Punishment* shows that many are now troubled by the suspicion that the view that there is just one supreme value or objective (*e.g.*, Deterrence, Retribution or Reform) in terms of which *all* questions about the justification of punishment are to be answered, is somehow wrong: yet, from what is said on such occasions no clear account of what the different values or objectives are, or how they fit together in the justification of punishment, can be extracted.[2]

No one expects judges or statesmen occupied in the business of sending people to the gallows or prison, or in making (or unmaking) laws which enable this to be done, to have much time for philosophical discussion of the principles which make it morally tolerable to do these things. A judicial bench is not and should not be a professorial chair. Yet what is said in public debates about punishment by those specially concerned with it as judges or legislators is important. Few are likely to be more circumspect, and if what they say seems, as it often does, unclear, one-sided and easily refutable by pointing to some aspect of things which they have overlooked, it is likely that in our inherited ways of talking or thinking about punishment there is some persistent drive towards an over-simplification of multiple issues which require separate consideration. To counter this

---

[2] In the Lords' debate in July 1956 the Lord Chancellor agreed with Lord Denning that " the ultimate justification of any punishment is not that it is a deterrent but that it is the emphatic denunciation of the committing of a crime " yet also said that " the real crux of the question at issue is whether capital punishment is a uniquely effective deterrent." See 198 *H. L. Deb* (5th July) 576, 577, 596 (1956). In his article " An Approach to the Problems of Punishment " (*Philosophy*, 1958) Mr. S. L. Benn rightly observes of Lord Denning's view that denunciation does not imply the deliberate imposition of suffering which is the feature needing justification (325 n.1).

drive what is most needed is *not* the simple admission that instead of a single value or aim (Deterrence, Retribution, Reform or any other) a plurality of different values and aims should be given as a conjunctive answer to some *single* question concerning the justification of punishment. What is needed is the realisation that different principles (each of which may in a sense be called a " justification ") are relevant at different points in any morally acceptable account of punishment. What we should look for are answers to a number of different questions such as: What justifies the general practice of punishment? To whom may punishment be applied? How severely may we punish? In dealing with these and other questions concerning punishment we should bear in mind that in this, as in most other social institutions, the pursuit of one aim may be qualified by or provide an opportunity, not to be missed, for the pursuit of others. Till we have developed this sense of the complexity of punishment (and this prolegomenon aims only to do this) we shall be in no fit state to assess the extent to which the whole institution has been eroded by or needs to be adapted to new beliefs about the human mind.

## II

### JUSTIFYING AIMS AND PRINCIPLES OF DISTRIBUTION

There is, I think, an analogy worth considering between the concept of Punishment and that of Property. In both cases we have to do with a social institution of which the centrally important form is a structure of *legal* rules, though it would be dogmatic to deny the names of Punishment or Property to the similar though more rudimentary rule-regulated practices within groups such as a family, or a school, or in customary societies whose customs may lack some of the standard or salient features of law (*e.g.*, legislation, organised sanctions, courts). In both cases we are confronted by a complex institution presenting different inter-related features calling for separate explanation; or, if the morality of the institution is challenged, for separate justification. In both cases failure to distinguish separate questions or attempting to answer them all by reference to a single principle ends in confusion. Thus in the case of Property we should distinguish between the

4                                   H. L. A. HART

question of the *definition* of Property, the question why and in
what circumstance it is a *good* institution to maintain, and the
questions in what ways individuals may become *entitled* to
property and *how much* they should be allowed to acquire.
These we may call questions of *Definition, General Justifying Aim*,
and *Distribution* with the last subdivided into questions of
*Title* and *Amount*. It is salutary to take some classical exposition
of the idea of Property, say Locke's Chapter ' Of Property ' in the
*Second Treatise*,[3] and to observe how much darkness is spread by
the use of a single notion (in this case " the labour of (a man's)
body and the work of his hands ") to answer all these different
questions which press upon us when we reflect on the institution
of Property. In the case of Punishment the beginning of wisdom
(though by no means its end) is to distinguish similar questions
and confront them separately.

### (a) Definition

Here I shall simply draw upon the recent admirable work
scattered through English philosophical[4] journals and add to it
only an admonition of my own against the abuse of definition
in the philosophical discussion of punishment. So with Mr.
Benn and Professor Flew I shall define the standard or central
case of ' punishment ' in terms of five elements:

  (i) It must involve pain or other consequences normally
      considered unpleasant.

 (ii) It must be for an offence against legal rules.

(iii) It must be of an actual or supposed offender for his
      offence.

 (iv) It must be intentionally administered by human beings
      other than the offender.

  (v) It must be imposed and administered by an authority
      constituted by a legal system against which the offence
      is committed.

---

[3] Chapter IV.
[4] K. Baier " Is Punishment Retributive?" *Analysis*, March 16, p. 26
(1955). A. Flew " The Justification of Punishment ", *Philosophy*, 1954,
pp. 291–307. S. I. Benn, *op. cit*, pp. 325–326.

PROLEGOMENON TO THE PRINCIPLES OF PUNISHMENT      5

In calling this the standard or central case of punishment I shall relegate to the position of sub-standard or secondary cases the following among many other possibilities:

(*a*) Punishments for breaches of legal rules imposed or administered otherwise than by officials (decentralised sanctions).

(*b*) Punishments for breaches of non-legal rules or orders (punishments in a family or school).

(*c*) Vicarious or collective punishment of some member of a social group for actions done by others without the former's authorisation, encouragement, control or permission.

(*d*) Punishment of persons (otherwise than under (*c*)) who are neither in fact nor supposed to be offenders.

The chief importance of listing these sub-standard cases is to prevent the use of what I shall call the " definitional stop " in discussions of punishment. This is an abuse of definition especially tempting when use is made of conditions (ii) and (iii) of the standard case against the utilitarian claim that the practice of punishment is justified by the beneficial consequences resulting from the observance of the laws which it secures. Here the stock ' retributive ' argument [5] is: If *this* is the justificaion of punishment, why not apply it when it pays to do so to those innocent of any crime chosen at random, or to the wife and children of the offender? And here the wrong reply is: That, by definition, would not be " punishment " and it is the justification of punishment which is in issue.[6] Not only will this definitional stop fail to satisfy the advocate of ' Retribution '; it would prevent us from investigating the very thing which modern scepticism most calls in question: namely the rational and moral status of our preference for a system of punishment under which

---

[5] Ewing, *The Morality of Punishment*, D. J. B. Hawkins, *Punishment and Moral Responsibility* (The Kings Good Servant, p. 92), J. D. Mabbott, " Punishment." *Mind*, 1939, p. 153.

[6] Mr. Benn seemed to succumb at times to the temptation to give " The short answer to the critics of utilitarian theories of punishment—that they are theories of *punishment* not of any sort of technique involving suffering " (*op. cit*. p. 322). He has since told me that he does not now rely on the definitional stop.

6                         H. L. A. HART

measures painful to individuals are to be taken against them
only when they have committed an offence.   Why do we prefer
this to other forms of social hygiene which we might employ
instead to prevent anti-social behaviour and which we do employ
in special circumstances sometimes with reluctance?   No
account of punishment can afford to dismiss this question with a
definition.

*(b) The nature of an offence*

Before we reach any question of justification we must identify
a preliminary question to which the answer is so simple that the
question may not appear worth asking;  yet it is clear that some
curious " theories " of punishment gain their only plausibility
from ignoring it, and others from confusing it with other
questions.   This question is:  Why are certain kinds of action
forbidden by law and so made crimes or offences?   The answer
is:  To announce to society that these actions are not to be done
and to secure that fewer of them are done.   These are the common
immediate aims of making any conduct a criminal offence and
until we have laws made with these primary aims we shall lack
the notion of a ' crime ' and so of a ' criminal '.   Without
recourse to the simple idea that the criminal law sets up, in its
rules, standards of behaviour to encourage certain types of conduct and discourage others we cannot distinguish a punishment
in the form of a fine from a tax on a course of conduct.[7]   This
indeed is one grave objection to those theories of law which in
the interests of simplicity or uniformity obscure the distinction
between primary laws setting standards for behaviour and
secondary laws specifying what officials must or may do when
they are broken.   Such theories insist that all legal rules are
" really " directions to officials to exact " sanctions " under
certain conditions, *e.g.*, if people kill.[8]   Yet only if we keep alive

---

[7] This generally clear distinction may be blurred.   Taxes may be imposed
to discourage the activities taxed though the law does not announce this as
it does when it makes them criminal.   Conversely fines payable for some
criminal offences because of a depreciation of currency, became so small that
they are cheerfully paid and offences are frequent.   They are then felt to be
mere taxes because the sense is lost that the rule is meant to be taken seriously
as a standard of behaviour.
[8] *cf.* Kelsen, *General Theory of Law and State*, 30–3, 33–34, 143–144 (1946).
" Law is the primary norm which stipulates the sanction. . . ." (*id.* 61)

the distinction (which such theories thus obscure) between the primary objective of the law in encouraging or discouraging certain kinds of behaviour and its merely ancillary sanction or remedial steps, can we give sense to the notion of a crime or offence.

It is important however to stress the fact that in thus identifying the immediate aims of the criminal law we have not reached the stage of justification. There are indeed many forms of undesirable behaviour which it would be foolish because ineffective or too costly to attempt to inhibit by use of the law and some of these may be better left to educators, trades unions, churches, marriage guidance councils or other non-legal agencies. Conversely there are some forms of conduct which we believe cannot be effectively inhibited without use of the law. But it is only too plain that in fact the law may make activities criminal which it is morally important to promote and the suppression of these may be quite unjustifiable. Yet confusion between the simple immediate aim of any criminal legislation and the justification of punishment seems to be the most charitable explanation of the claim that punishment is justified as an " emphatic denunciation by the community of a crime ". Lord Denning's [9] dictum that this is the ultimate justification of punishment can be saved from Mr. Benn's criticism, noted above, only if it is treated as a blurred statement of the truth that the aim not of punishment, but of criminal legislation is indeed to denounce certain types of conduct as something not to be practised. Conversely the immediate aim of criminal legislation cannot be any of the things which are usually mentioned as justifying punishment: for until it is settled what conduct is to be legally denounced and discouraged we have not settled from what we are to *deter* people, or who are to be considered *criminals* from whom we are to exact *retribution*, or on whom we are to wreak *vengeance*, or whom we are to *reform*.

Even those who look upon human law as a mere instrument for enforcing " morality as such " (itself conceived as the law of God or Nature) and who at the stage of justifying punishment wish to appeal not to socially beneficial consequences but simply

---

[9] In evidence to the Royal Commission on Capital Punishment, Cmd. 8932. §53 (1953). *Supra*, p. 3, n.2.

8                    H. L. A. HART

to the intrinsic value of inflicting suffering on wrongdoers who have disturbed by their offence the moral order, would not deny that the aim of criminal legislation is to set up types of behaviour (in this case conformity with a pre-existing moral law) as legal standards of behaviour and to secure conformity with them. No doubt in all communities certain moral offences, *e.g.*, killing, will always be selected for suppresion as crimes and it is conceivable that this may be done not to protect human beings from being killed but to save the potential murderer from sin; but it would be paradoxical to look upon the law as designed not to prevent murder at all (even conceived as sin rather than harm) but simply to extract the penalty from the murderer.

*(c) General Justifying Aim*

I shall not here criticise the intelligibility or consistency or adequacy of these theories that are united in denying that the practice of a system of punishment is justified by its beneficial consequences and claim instead that the main justification of the practice lies in the fact that when breach of the law involves moral guilt the application to the offender of the pain of punishment is itself a thing of value. A great variety of claims of this character designating ' Retribution ' or ' Expiation ' or ' Reprobation ' as the justifying aim, fall in spite of differences under this rough general description. Though in fact I agree with Mr. Benn[10] in thinking that these all either avoid the question of justification altogether or are in spite of their protestations disguised forms of Utilitarianism, I shall assume that Retribution, defined simply as the application of the pains of punishment to an offender who is morally guilty, may figure among the conceivable justifying aims of a system of punishment. Here I shall merely insist that it is one thing to use the word Retribution *at this point* in an account of the principle of punishment in order to designate the General Justifying Aim of the system, and quite another to use it to secure that to the question " To whom may punishment be applied? " (the question of Distribution) the answer given is " Only to an offender for an offence". Failure to distinguish Retribution as a General Justifying Aim from

---

[10] *Op cit.*, pp. 326–335.

retribution as the simple insistence that only those who have broken the law—and voluntarily broken it—may be punished may be traced. in many writers even perhaps in Mr. J. D. Mabbott's[11] otherwise most illuminating essay. We shall distinguish the latter from Retribution in General Aim as " retribution in Distribution ". Much confusing shadow-fighting between Utilitarians and their opponents may be avoided if it is recognized that it is perfectly consistent to assert *both* that the General Justifying Aim of the practice of punishment is its beneficial consequences and that the pursuit of this general aim should be qualified or restricted out of deference to principles of Distribution which require that punishment should be only of an offender for an offence. Conversely it does not in the least follow from the admission of the latter principle of retribution in Distribution that the General Justifying Aim of punishment is Retribution though of course Retribution in General Aim entails retribution in Distribution.

We shall consider later the principles of justice lying at the root of retribution in Distribution. Meanwhile it is worth observing that both the most old fashioned Retributionist (in General Aim) and the most modern sceptic often make the same and, I think, wholly mistaken assumption that sense can only be made of the restrictive principle that punishment be applied only to an offender for an offence if the General Justifying Aim of the practice of punishment is Retribution. The sceptic consequently imputes to all systems of punishment (when they are restricted by the principle of retribution in Distribution) all the irrationality he finds in the idea of Retribution as a General Justifying Aim; conversely the advocates of the latter think the admission of retribution in Distribution is a refutation of the utilitarian claim that the social consequences of punishment are its Justifying Aim.

The most general lesson to be learnt from this extends beyond the topic of punishment. It is, that in relation to any social institution, after stating what general aim or value its maintenance fosters we should enquire whether there are any and if so what principles limiting the unqualified pursuit of that aim or

---

[11] *Op cit.* It is not always quite clear what he considers a " retributive " theory to be.

10            H. L. A. HART

value. Just because the pursuit of any single social aim always
has its restrictive qualifier our main social institutions always
possess a plurality of features which can only be understood as
a compromise between partly discrepant principles. This is true
even of relatively minor legal institutions like that of a contract.
In general this is designed to enable individuals to give effect
to their wishes to create structures of legal rights and duties and
so to change, in certain ways their legal position. Yet at the
same time there is need to protect those who in good faith
understand a verbal offer made to them to mean what it would
ordinarily mean, accept it, and then act on the footing that a
valid contract has been concluded. As against them, it would
be unfair to allow the other party to say that the words he used
in his verbal offer or the interpretation put on them did not
express his real wishes or intention. Hence principles of
" estoppel " or doctrines of the " objective sense" of a contract
are introduced to prevent this and to qualify the principle that
the law enforces contracts in order to give effect to the joint
wishes of the contracting parties.

### (d) Distribution

This as in the case of property has two aspects (i) Liability
(Who may be punished?) and (ii) Amount. In this section I shall
chiefly be concerned with the first of these.[12]

From the foregoing discussions two things emerge. First,
though we may be clear as to what value the practice of punishment is to promote we have still to answer as a question of
Distribution " Who may be punished? " Secondly, if in answer
to this question we say " only an offender for an offence " this
admission of retribution in Distribution is not a principle from
which anything follows as to the severity or amount of punishment; in particular it neither licenses nor requires as Retribution
in General Aim does more severe punishments than deterrence
or other utilitarian criteria would require.

The root question to be considered is however why we attach
the moral importance which we do to retribution in Distribution.
Here I shall consider the efforts made to show that restriction of

---

[12] Amount is considered below in Section III (in connexion with Mitigation) and Section V.

punishment to offenders is a simple consequence of whatever principles (Retributive or Utilitarian) constitute the Justifying Aim of punishment.

The standard example used by philosophers to bring out the importance of retribution in Distribution is that of a wholly innocent person who has not even unintentionally done anything which the law punishes if done intentionally. It is supposed that in order to avert some social catastrophe officials of the system fabricate evidence on which he is charged, tried, convicted and sent to prison or death. Or it is supposed that without resort to any fraud more persons may be deterred from crime if wives and children of offenders were punished vicariously for their crimes. In some forms this kind of thing may be ruled out by a consistent sufficiently comprehensive utilitarianism.[13] Certainly expedients involving fraud or faked charges might be very difficult to justify on utilitarian grounds. We can of course imagine that a negro might be sent to prison or executed on a false charge of rape in order to avoid widespread lynching of many others; but a *system* which openly empowered authorities to do this kind of thing, even if it succeeded in averting specific evils like lynching, would awaken such apprehension and insecurity that any gain from the exercise of these powers would by any utilitarian calculation be offset by the misery caused by their existence. But official resort to this kind of fraud on a particular occasion in breach of the rules and the subsequent indemnification of the officials responsible might save many lives and so be thought to yield a clear surplus of value. Certainly vicarious punishment of an offender's family might do so and legal systems have occasionally though exceptionally resorted to this. An example of it is the Roman *Lex Quisquis* providing for the punishment of the children of those guilty of *majestas*.[14] In extreme cases many might still think it right to resort to these expedients but we should do so with the sense of sacrificing an important principle. We should be conscious of choosing the lesser of two evils, and this would be inexplicable if the principle sacrificed to utility were itself only a requirement of utility.

---

[13] See J. Rawls " Two Concepts of Rules ", *Philosophical Review*, 1955, pp. 4–13.
[14] Constitution of emperors Arcadius and Honorius.

12                          H. L. A. HART

Similarly the moral importance of the restriction of punishment to the offender cannot be explained as merely a consequence
of the principle that the General Justifying Aim is Retribution
for immorality involved in breaking the law.   Retribution in the
Distribution of punishment has a value quite independent of
Retribution as Justifying Aim.   This is shown by the fact that
we attach importance to the restrictive principle that only
offenders may be punished even where breach of this law might
not be thought immoral: indeed even where the laws themselves
are hideously immoral as in Nazi Germany, *e.g.*, forbidding
activities (helping the sick or destitute of some racial group)
which might be thought morally obligatory, the absence of the
principle restricting punishment to the offender would be a
further *special* iniquity;   whereas admission of this principle
would represent some residual respect for justice though in the
administration of morally bad laws.

### III

#### Justification, Excuse and Mitigation

What is morally at stake in the restrictive principle of Distribution cannot, however, be made clear by these external examples of
its violation by faked charges or vicarious punishment.   To make
it clear we must allot to their place the appeals to matters of
Justification, Excuse and Mitigation made in answer to the claim
that someone should be punished.   The first of these depends
on the General Justifying Aim; the last two are different aspects
of the principles of Distribution of punishment.

#### (a) Justification and Excuse

English lawyers once distinguished between ' excusable '
homicide (*e.g.*, accidental non-negligent killing) and ' justifiable '
homicide (*e.g.*, killing in self-defence or the arrest of a felon) and
different legal consequences once attached to these two forms of
homicide.   To the modern lawyer this distinction has no longer
any legal importance: he would simply consider both kinds of
homicide to be cases where some element, negative or positive,
required in the full definition of criminal homicide (murder or
manslaughter) was lacking.   But the distinction between these

two different ways in which actions may fail to constitute a criminal offence is still of great moral importance. Killing in self-defence is an exception to a general rule making killing punishable; it is admitted because the policy or aims which in general justify the punishment of killing (*e.g.*, protection of human life) do not include cases such as this. In the case of ' justification ' what is done is regarded as something which the law does not condemn or even welcomes.[15] But where killing (*e.g.*, accidental) is excused, criminal responsibility is excluded on a different footing. What has been done is something which is deplored, but the psychological state of the agent when he did it exemplified one or more of a variety of conditions which are held to rule out the public condemnation and punishment of individuals. This is a requirement of fairness or of justice to individuals independent of whatever the General Aim of punishment is, and remains a value whether the laws are good, morally indifferent or iniquitous.

The most prominent of these excusing conditions are those forms of lack of knowledge which make action unintentional: lack of muscular control which make it involuntary, subjection to gross forms of coercion by threats, and types of mental abnormality, which are believed to render the agent incapable of choice or of carrying out what he has chosen to do. Not all these excusing conditions are admitted by all legal systems for all offenders. Nearly all penal systems make some compromise at this point as we shall see with other principles; but most of them are admitted to some considerable extent in the case of the most serious crimes. Actions done under these excusing conditions are in the misleading terminology of Anglo-American law done without " mens rea ";[16] and most people would say of them that they were 'not voluntary' or 'not wholly voluntary'.

### (b) Mitigation

Justification and Excuse though different from each other are alike in that if either is made out then conviction and punishment

---

[15] In 1811 Mr. Purcell of Co. Cork, a septuagenarian, was knighted for killing four burglars with a carving knife. Kenny, *Outlines of Criminal Law*, 5th Ed., p. 103, n.3.

[16] Misleading because it suggests moral guilt is a necessary condition of criminal responsibility.

14           H. L. A. HART

are excluded. In this they differ from the idea of Mitigation which presupposes that someone is convicted and liable to be punished and the question of the severity of his punishment is to be decided. It is therefore relevant to that aspect of Distribution which we have termed Amount. Certainly the severity of punishment is in part determined by the General Justifying Aim. A utilitarian will for example exclude in principle punishments the infliction of which is held to cause more suffering than the offence unchecked, and will hold that if one kind of crime causes greater suffering than another then a greater penalty may be used to repress it. He will also exclude degrees of severity which are useless in the sense that they do no more to secure or maintain a higher level of law-observance or any other valued result than less severe penalties. But in addition to restrictions on the severity of punishment which follow from the aim of punishing special limitations are imported by the idea of Mitigation. These, like the principle of Distribution restricting liability to punishment to offenders, have a status which is independent of the general Aim. The special features of Mitigation are that a good reason for administering a less severe penalty is made out if the situation or mental state of the convicted criminal is such that he was exposed to an unusual or specially great temptation, or his ability to control his actions is thought to have been impaired or weakened otherwise than by his own action, so that conformity to the law which he has broken was a matter of special difficulty for him as compared with normal persons normally placed.

The special features of the idea of Mitigation are however often concealed by the various legal techniques which make it necessary to distinguish between what may be termed 'informal' and 'formal' Mitigation. In the first case the law fixes a maximum penalty and leaves it to the judge to give such weight as he thinks proper in selecting the punishment to be applied to a particular offender to (among other considerations) mitigating factors. It is here that the barrister makes his 'plea in mitigation'. Sometimes however legal rules provide that the presence of a mitigating factor shall always remove the offence into a separate category carrying a lower maximum penalty. This is 'formal' mitigation and the most prominent example of it is Provocation which in English law is operative only in relation to homicide.

It is not a matter of Justification or Excuse for it does not exclude conviction or punishment; but " reduces " the charges from murder to manslaughter and the possible maximum penalty from death to life imprisonment. It is worth stressing that not every provision reducing the maximum penalty can be thought of as " Mitigation ": the very peculiar provisions of s. 5 of the Homicide Act 1957 which (*inter alia*) restricted the death penalty to types of murder not including, for example, murder by poisoning, did not in doing this recognise the use of poison as a " mitigating circumstance ". Only a reduction of penalty made in view of the individual criminal's special difficulties in keeping the law which he has broken is so conceived.

Though the central cases are distinct enough the border lines between Justification, Excuse and Mitigation are not. There are many features of conduct which can be and are thought of in more than one of these ways. Thus, though little is heard of it, duress (coercion by threat of serious harm) is in English law in relation to some crimes an Excuse excluding responsibility. Where it is so treated the conception is that since *B* has committed a crime only because *A* has threatened him with gross violence or other harm, *B's* action is not the outcome of a ' free ' or independent choice; *B* is merely an instrument of *A* who has ' made him do it '. Nonetheless *B* is not an instrument in the same sense that he would have been had he been pushed by *A* against a window and broken it: unless he is literally paralysed by fear of the threat, we may believe that *B* could have refused to comply. If he complies we may say ' *coactus voluit* ' and treat the situation not as one making it intolerable to punish at all, but as one calling for mitigation of the penalty as gross provocation does. On the other hand if the crime which *A* requires *B* to commit is a petty one compared with the serious harm threatened (*e.g.*, death) by *A* there would be no absurdity in treating *A's* threat as a Justification for *B's* conduct though few legal systems overtly do this. If this line is taken coercion merges into the idea of " Necessity "[17] which appears on the margin of most systems of criminal law as an exculpating factor.

In view of the character of modern sceptical doubts about

---

[17] *i.e.*, when breaking the law is held justified as the lesser of two evils.

16                                     H. L. A. HART

criminal punishment it is worth observing that even in English law the relevance of mental disease to criminal punishment is not always as a matter of Excuse though exclusive concentration on the M'Naghten rules relating to the criminal responsibility of the mentally diseased encourages the belief that it is. Even before the Homicide Act 1957 a statute[18] provided that if a mother murdered her child under the age of 12 months " while the balance of her mind was disturbed " by the processes of birth or lactation she should be guilty only of the felony of infanticide carrying a maximum penalty of life imprisonment. This is to treat mental abnormality as a matter of (formal) Mitigation. Similarly in other cases of homicide the M'Naghten rules relating to certain types of insanity as an Excuse no longer stand alone; now such abnormality of mind as " substantially impaired the mental responsibility "[19] of the accused is a matter of formal mitigation, which like provocation reduces the homicide to the category of manslaughter which does not carry the death penalty.


                                        IV

                        THE RATIONALE OF EXCUSES

The admission of excusing conditions is a feature of the Distribution of punishment is required by distinct principles of Justice which restrict the extent to which general social aims may be pursued at the cost of individuals. The moral importance attached to these in punishment distinguishes it from other measures which pursue similar aims (*e.g.*, the protection of life, wealth or property) by methods which like punishment are also often unpleasant to the individuals to whom they are applied, *e.g.*, the detention of persons of hostile origin or association in war time, or of the insane, or the compulsory quarantine of persons suffering from infectious disease. To these we resort to avoid damage of a catastrophic character.

Every penal system in the name of some other social value compromises over the admission of excusing conditions and no system goes as far (particularly in cases of mental disease) as many would wish. But it is important (if we are to avoid a

---

[18] Infanticide Act, 1938.
[19] Homicide Act, 1957, sec. 2.

superficial but tempting answer to modern scepticism about the meaning or truth of the statement that a criminal could have kept the law which he has broken) to see that our moral preference for a system which does recognise such excuses cannot, any more than our reluctance to engage in the cruder business of false charges or vicarious punishment, be explained by reference to the General Aim which we take to justify the practice of punishment.   Here, too, even where the laws appear to us morally iniquitous or where we are uncertain as to their moral character so that breach of law does not entail moral guilt, punishment of those who break the law unintentionally would be an added wrong and refusal to do this some sign of grace.

Retributionists (in General Aim) have not paid much attention to the rationale of this aspect of punishment; they have usually (wrongly) assumed that it has no status except as a corollary of Retribution in General Aim.   But Utilitarians have made strenuous, detailed efforts to show that the restriction on the use of punishment to those who have voluntarily broken the law is explicable on purely utilitarian lines.   Bentham's efforts are the most complete, and their failure is an instructive warning to contemporaries.

Bentham's argument was a reply to Blackstone who in expounding the main excusing conditions recognised in the criminal law of his day,[20] claimed that " all the several pleas and excuses which protect the committer of a forbidden act from punishment which is otherwise annexed thereunto reduce to this single consideration: the want or defect of will " . . . . [and to the principle] " that to constitute a crime . . . . there must be first a vitious will ".   In the Principles of Morals and Legislation [21] under the heading " Cases unmeet for punishment " Bentham sets out a list of the main excusing conditions similar to Blackstone's; he then undertakes to show that the infliction of punishment on those who have done what the law forbids while in any of these conditions " must be inefficacious: it cannot act so as to prevent the mischief ".   All Blackstone's talk about want or defect of will or lack of a " vitious " will is he says " nothing to the purpose ", except so far as it implies the reason (inefficacy of

---

[20] *Commentaries*, Book IV, Chap. 11.
[21] Chap. XIII.

**18**                          H. L. A. HART

punishment) which he himself gives for recognising these excuses.

Bentham's argument is in fact a spectacular *non-sequitur*. He sets out to prove that to *punish* the mad, the infant child or those who break the law unintentionally or under duress or even under " necessity " must be inefficacious; but all that he proves (at the most) is the quite different proposition that the *threat* of punishment will be ineffective so far as the class of persons who suffer from these conditions are concerned. Plainly is it possible that the actual *infliction* of punishment on those persons, though (as Bentham says) the *threat* of punishment could not have operated on them, may secure a higher measure of conformity to law on the part of normal persons than is secured by the admission of excusing conditions. If this is so and if Utilitarian principles only were at stake, we should, without any sense that we were sacrificing any principle of value or were choosing the lesser of two evils, drop from the law the restriction on punishment entailed by the admission of excuses; unless, of course, we believed that the terror or insecurity or misery produced by the operation of laws so Draconic was worse than the lower measure of obedience to law secured by the law which admits excuses.

This objection to Bentham's rationale of excuses is not merely a fanciful one. Any increase in the number of conditions required to establish criminal liability increases the opportunity for deceiving courts or juries by the pretence that some condition is not satisfied. When the condition is a psychological factor the chances of such pretence succeeding are considerable. Quite apart from the provision made for mental disease, the cases where an accused person pleads that he killed in his sleep or accidentally or in some temporary abnormal state of unconsciousness show that deception is certainly feasible. From the Utilitarian point of view this may lead to two sorts of ' losses '. The belief that such deception is feasible may embolden persons who would not otherwise risk punishment to take their chance of deceiving a jury in this way. Secondly, a murderer who actually succeeds in this deception will be left at large, though belonging to the class which the law is concerned to incapacitate. Developments in Anglo-American law since Bentham's day have given more concrete form to the objection to this argument. There are now

PROLEGOMENON TO THE PRINCIPLES OF PUNISHMENT    19

offences (known as offences of " strict liability ") where it is not
necessary for conviction to show that the accused either intentionally did what the law forbids or could have avoided doing it
by use of care: selling liquor to an intoxicated person, possessing
an altered passport, selling adulterated milk [22] are examples out of
a range of ' strict liability ' offences where it is no defence that
the accused did not offend intentionally, or through negligence,
*e.g.*, that he was under some mistake against which he had no
opportunity to guard.   Two things should be noted about them.
First, the justification of this form of criminal liability can
only be that if proof of intention or lack of care were required
guilty persons would escape.   Secondly, ' strict liability ' is
generally viewed with great odium and admitted as an exception
to the general rule with the sense that an important principle has
been sacrificed to secure a higher measure of conformity and
conviction of offenders.   Thus Bentham's argument curiously
ignores both the two possibilities which have been realised.   First,
actual punishment of those who act unintentionally or in some
other normally excusing condition may have a utilitarian value
in its effects on others; and secondly, that when because of this
probability, strict liability is admitted and the normal excuses
are excluded, this may be done with the sense that some other
principle has been overriden.

On this issue modern extended forms of Utilitarianism fare no
better than Bentham's whose main criterion here of ' effective '
punishment was deterrence of the offender or of others by example.
Sometimes the principle that punishment should be restricted to
those who have voluntarily broken the law is defended not as a
principle which is rational or morally important in itself but as
something so engrained in popular conceptions of justice [23] in
certain societies, including our own, that not to recognise it would
lead to disturbances, or to the nullification of the criminal law
since officials or juries might refuse to co-operate in such a
system.   Hence to punish in these circumstances would either
be impracticable or would create more harm than could possibly

---

[22] See Glanville Williams *The Criminal Law*, Chap. 7, p. 238, for a discussion
of and protest against strict liability.

[23] Wechsler and Michael " A Rationale of the Law of Homicide " 37,
*Columbia Law Review*, 701, esp. pp. 752–757, and Rawls *op cit.*

20                          H. L. A. HART

be offset by any superior deterrent force gained by such a system. On this footing, a system should admit excuses much as, in order to prevent disorder or lynching, concessions might be made to popular demands for more savage punishment than could be defended on other grounds. Two objections confront this wider pragmatic form of Utilitarianism. The first is the factual observation that even if a system of strict liability for all or very serious crime would be unworkable, a system which admits it on its periphery for relatively minor offences is not only workable but an actuality which we have, though many object to it or admit it with reluctance. The second objection is simply that we do not dissociate ourselves from the principle that it is wrong to punish the hopelessly insane or those who act unintentionally, etc., by treating it as something merely embodied in popular *mores* to which concessions must be made sometimes. We condemn legal systems where they disregard this principle; whereas we try to educate people out of their preference for savage penalties even if we might in extreme cases of threatened disorder concede them.

It is therefore impossible to exhibit the principle by which punishment is excluded for those who act under the excusing conditions merely as a corollary of the general Aim—Retributive or Utilitarian—justifying the practice of punishment. Can anything positive be said about this principle except that it is one to which we attach moral importance as a restriction on the pursuit of any aim we have in punishing?

It is clear that like all principles of Justice it is concerned with the adjustment of claims between a multiplicity of persons. It incorporates the idea that each individual person is to be protected against the claim of the rest for the highest possible measure of security, happiness or welfare which could be got at his expense by condemning him for the breach of the rules and punishing him. For this a moral licence is required in the form of proof that the person punished broke the law by an action which was the outcome of his free choice, and the recognition of excuses is the most we can do to ensure that the terms of the licence are observed. Here perhaps the elucidation of this restrictive principle should stop. Perhaps we (or I) ought simply to say that it is a requirement of Justice, and Justice simply consists of principles to be observed in adjusting the competing claims of human beings which (i) treat all alike as persons by attaching special significance to human voluntary action and (ii) forbid the use of one human being for the benefit of others except in return for his voluntary actions against them. I confess however to an itch to go further; though what I have to say may not add to these principles of Justice. There are, however, three points which even if they are restatements from different points of view of the principles already stated, may help us to identify what we now think of as values in the practice of punishment and what we may have to reconsider in the light of modern scepticism.

(*a*) We may look upon the principle that punishment must be reserved for voluntary offences from two different points of view. The first is that of the rest of society considered as *harmed* by the offence (either because one of its members has been injured or because the authority of the law essential to its existence has been challenged or both). The principle then appears as one securing that the suffering involved in punishment is a return for the harm done to others: this is valued, not as the Aim of punishment, but as the only fair terms on which the General Aim (protection of society, maintenance of respect for law, etc.) may be pursued.

(*b*) The second point of view is that of society concerned not as harmed by the crime but as *offering* individuals including the criminal the protection of the laws on terms which are fair, because they not only consist of a framework of reciprocal rights and duties, but because within their framework each individual is given a *fair* opportunity to choose between keeping the law required for society's protection or paying the penalty. From the first point of view the actual punishment of a criminal appears not merely as something useful to society (General Aim) but as justly extracted from the criminal as a return for harm done; from the second it appears as a price justly extracted because the criminal had a fair opportunity beforehand to avoid liability to pay.

(*c*) Criminal punishment as an attempt to secure desired behaviour differs from the manipulative techniques of the Brave New World (conditioning propaganda, etc.) or the simple incapacitation of those with anti-social tendencies by taking a

22                          H.  L.  A.  HART

risk.  It defers action till harm has been done;  its primary
operation consists simply in announcing certain standards of
behaviour and attaching penalties for deviation, making it less
eligible, and then leaving individuals to choose.  This is a method
of social control which maximises individual freedom within the
coercive framework of law in a number of different ways, or
perhaps, different senses.  First, the individual has an option
between obeying or paying.  The worse the laws are, the more
valuable the possibility of exercising this choice becomes in
enabling an individual to decide how he shall live.  Secondly,
this system not only enables individuals to exercise this choice but
increases the power of individuals to identify beforehand periods
when the law's punishments will not interfere with them and to
plan their lives accordingly.  This very obvious point is often
overshadowed by the other merits of restricting punishment to
offences voluntarily committed, but is worth separate attention.
Where punishment is not so restricted individuals will be liable
to have their plans frustrated by punishments for what they do
unintentionally, in ignorance, by accident or mistake.  Such a
system of strict liability for all offences, it is logically possible,[24]
would not only vastly increase the number of punishments, but
would diminish the individual's power to identify beforehand
particular periods during which he will be free from them.
This is so because we can have very little grounds for confidence
that during a particular period we will not do something
unintentionally, accidentally, etc.;  whereas from their own
knowledge of themselves many can say with justified confidence
that for some period ahead they are not likely to engage intentionally in crime and can plan their lives from point to point in
confidence that they will be left free during that period.  Of course
the confidence justified does not amount to certainty though drawn
from knowledge of ourselves.  My confidence that I will not
during the next 12 months intentionally engage in any crime and
will be free from punishment, may turn out to be misplaced;
but it is both greater and better justified than my belief that I will
not do unintentionally any of the things which our system
punishes if done intentionally.

---

[24] Some crimes, *e.g.*, demanding money by menaces, cannot (logically)
be committed unintentionally.

V

REFORM AND THE INDIVIDUALIZATION OF PUNISHMENT

The idea of Mitigation incorporates the conviction that though the amount or severity of punishment is primarily to be determined by reference to the General Aim, yet Justice requires that those who have special difficulties to face in keeping the law which they have broken should be punished less.  Principles of Justice however are also widely taken to bear on the amount of punishment in at least two further ways.  The first is the somewhat hazy requirement that ' like cases be treated alike '.  This is certainly felt to be infringed at least when the ground for different punishment for those guilty of the same crime is neither some personal characteristic of the offender connected with the commission of the crime nor the effect of punishment on him. If because at a given time a certain offence is specially prevalent a Judge passes a heavier sentence than on previous offenders (" as a warning ") some sacrifice of justice to the safety of society is involved though it is often acceptable to many as the lesser of two evils.

The further principle that different kinds of offence of different gravity (however that is assessed) should not be punished with equal severity is one which like other principles of Distribution may qualify the pursuit of our General Aim and is not deducible from it.  Long sentences of imprisonment might effectually stamp out car parking offences, yet we think it wrong to employ them; *not* because there is for each crime a penalty ' naturally ' fitted to its degree of iniquity (as some Retributionists in General Aim might think); nor because we are convinced that the misery caused by such sentences (which might indeed be slight because they would need to be rarely applied) would be greater than that caused by the offences unchecked (as a Utilitarian might argue).  The guiding principle is that of a proportion within a system of penalties between those imposed for different offences where these have a distinct place in a common-sense scale of gravity.  This scale itself no doubt consists of very broad judgments both of relative moral iniquity and harmfulness of different types of offence: it draws rough distinctions like that between parking offences and homicide, or between ' mercy

24                          H. L. A. HART

killing ' and murder for gain, but cannot cope with any precise
assessment of an individual's wickedness in committing a crime
(Who can ?)   Yet maintenance of proportion of this kind may
be important: for where the legal gradation of crimes expressed
in the relative severity of penalties diverges sharply from this
rough scale, there is a risk of either confusing common morality
or flouting it and bringing the law into contempt.

The ideals of Reform and Individualization of punishment
(*e.g.*, corrective training, preventive detention) which have been
increasingly accepted in English penal practice since 1900 plainly
run counter to the second if not to both of these principles of
Justice or proportion.   Some fear, and others hope, that the
further intrusion of these ideals will end with the substitution of
" treatment " by experts for judicial punishment.   It is, however,
important to see precisely what the relation of Reform to punishment is because its advocates too often mis-state it.   ' Reform ' as
an objective is no doubt very vague; it now embraces any
strengthening of the offender's disposition and capacity to keep
within the law which is intentionally brought about by human
effort otherwise than through fear of punishment.   Reforming
methods include the inducement of states of repentance or
recognition of moral guilt or greater awareness of the character
and demands of society, the provision of education in a broad
sense, vocational training and psychological treatment.   Many
seeing the futility and indeed harmful character of much traditional
punishment speak as if Reform could and should be the General
Aim of the whole practice of punishment or the dominant
objective of the criminal law:

> " The corrective theory based upon a conception of
> multiple causation and curative rehabilitative treatment
> should clearly predominate in legislation and in judicial and
> administrative practices."[25]

Of course this is a possible ideal but is not an ideal for punishment.   Reform can only have a place within a system of punishment as an exploitation of the opportunities presented by the
conviction or compulsory detention of offenders.   It is not an

---

[25] Hall and Gluck *Cases on Criminal Law and is Enforcement*, 8 (1951).

alternative General Justifying Aim of the practice of punishment but something the pursuit of which within a system of punishment qualifies or displaces altogether recourse to principles of justice or proportion in determining the amount of punishment. This is where both Reform and individualized punishment have run counter to the customary morality of punishment.

There is indeed a paradox in asserting that Reform should " predominate " in a system of Criminal Law, as if the main purpose of providing punishment for murder was to reform the murderer not to prevent murder; and the paradox is greater where the legal offence is not a serious moral one: *e.g.*, infringing a state monopoly of transport. The objection to assigning to Reform this place in punishment is not merely that punishment entails suffering and Reform does not; but that Reform is essentially a remedial step for which *ex hypothesi* there is an opportunity only at the point where the criminal law has failed in its primary task of securing society from the evil which breach of the law involves. Society is divisible at any moment into two classes (i) those who have actually broken a given law and (ii) those who have not yet broken it but may. To take Reform as the dominant objective would be to forgo the hope of influencing the second and—in relation to the more serious offences—numerically much greater class. We should thus subordinate the prevention of first offences to the prevention of recidivism.

Consideration of what conditions or beliefs would make this appear a reasonable policy brings us to the topic to which this paper is a mere prolegomenon: modern sceptical doubt about the whole institution of punishment. If we believed that nothing was achieved by announcing penalties or by the example of their infliction either because those who do not commit crimes would not commit them in any event or because the penalties announced or inflicted on others are not among the factors which influence them in keeping the law then some dramatic change concentrating wholly on actual offenders would be necessary. Just because at present we do not entirely believe this we have a dilemma and an uneasy compromise. Penalties which we believe are required as a threat to maintain conformity to law at its maximum may convert the offender to whom they are applied into a hardened enemy of society; while the use of measures of Reform may lower

26                   H. L. A. HART

the efficacy and example of punishment on others. At present
we compromise on this relatively new aspect of punishment as
we do over its main elements. What makes this compromise
seem tolerable is the belief that the influence which the threat
and example of punishment exerts is often independent of the
severity of the punishment and is due more to the disgrace
attached to conviction for crime and to the deprivation of
freedom which many reforming measures at present used, would
in any case involve.

———————————

# [2]

## PERSONS AND PUNISHMENT

### Herbert Morris

They acted and looked . . . at us, and around in our house, in a way
that had about it the feeling—at least for me—that we were not people. In their eyesight we were just things, that was all. [Malcolm X]

We have no right to treat a man like a dog. [Governor Maddox of
Georgia]

Alfredo Traps in Durrenmatt's tale discovers that he has
brought off, all by himself, a murder involving considerable ingenuity. The mock prosecutor in the tale demands the death penalty "as
reward for a crime that merits admiration, astonishment, and
respect." Traps is deeply moved; indeed, he is exhilarated, and the
whole of his life becomes more heroic, and, ironically, more precious. His defense attorney proceeds to argue that Traps was not
only innocent but incapable of guilt, "a victim of the age." This
defense Traps disavows with indignation and anger. He makes
claim to the murder as his and demands the prescribed punishment
—death.

The themes to be found in this macabre tale do not often find
their way into philosophical discussions of punishment. These
discussions deal with large and significant questions of whether or
not we ever have the right to punish, and if we do, under what
conditions, to what degree, and in what manner. There is a
tradition, of course, not notable for its present vitality, that is
closely linked with motifs in Durrenmatt's tale of crime and punishment. Its adherents have urged that justice requires a person be
punished if he is guilty. Sometimes—though rarely—these philosophers have expressed themselves in terms of the criminal's *right to*

* All of the essays in this issue of THE MONIST were presented in their
initial form at the Conference on Human Rights at Tuskegee Institute March 2-
5, 1967, sponsored by the Council for Philosophical Studies and directed by R.
Wasserstrom—the Editor.

*be punished.* **R**eaction to the claim that there is such a right has
been astonishment combined, perhaps, with a touch of contempt for
the perversity of the suggestion. A strange right that no one would
ever wish to claim! With that flourish the subject is buried and the
right disposed of. In this paper the subject is resurrected.

My aim is to argue for four propositions concerning rights that
will certainly strike some as not only false but preposterous: first,
that we have a right to punishment; second, that this right derives
from a fundamental human right to be treated as a person; third,
that this fundamental right is a natural, inalienable, and absolute
right; and, fourth, that the denial of this right implies the denial of
all moral rights and duties. Showing the truth of one, let alone all,
of these large and questionable claims, is a tall order. The attempt
or, more properly speaking, the first steps in an attempt, follow.

1. When someone claims that there is a right to be free, we can
easily imagine situations in which the right is infringed and easily
imagine situations in which there is a point to asserting or claiming
the right. With the right to be punished, matters are otherwise. The
immediate reaction to the claim that there is such a right is
puzzlement. And the reasons for this are apparent. People do not
normally value pain and suffering. Punishment is associated with
pain and suffering. When we think about punishment we naturally
think of the strong desire most persons have to avoid it, to accept,
for example, acquittal of a criminal charge with relief and eagerly,
if convicted, to hope for pardon or probation. Adding, of course, to
the paradoxical character of the claim of such a right is difficulty in
imagining circumstances in which it would be denied one. When
would one rightly demand punishment and meet with any threat of
the claim being denied?

So our first task is to see when the claim of such a right would
have a point. I want to approach this task by setting out two
complex types of institutions both of which are designed to maintain some degree of social control. In the one a central concept is
punishment for wrongdoing and in the other the central concepts
are control of dangerous individuals and treatment of disease.

Let us first turn attention to the institutions in which punishment is involved. The institutions I describe will resemble those we
ordinarily think of as institutions of punishment; they will have,

however, additional features we associate with a system of just punishment.

Let us suppose that men are constituted roughly as they now are, with a rough equivalence in strength and abilities, a capacity to be injured by each other and to make judgments that such injury is undesirable, a limited strength of will, and a capacity to reason and to conform conduct to rules. Applying to the conduct of these men are a group of rules, ones I shall label 'primary', which closely resemble the core rules of our criminal law, rules that prohibit violence and deception and compliance with which provides benefits for all persons. These benefits consist in noninterference by others with what each person values, such matters as continuance of life and bodily security. The rules define a sphere for each person, then, which is immune from interference by others. Making possible this mutual benefit is the assumption by individuals of a burden. The burden consists in the exercise of self-restraint by individuals over inclinations that would, if satisfied, directly interfere or create a substantial risk of interference with others in proscribed ways. If a person fails to exercise self-restraint even though he might have and gives in to such inclinations, he renounces a burden which others have voluntarily assumed and thus gains an advantage which others, who have restrained themselves, do not possess. This system, then, is one in which the rules establish a mutuality of benefit and burden and in which the benefits of noninterference are conditional upon the assumption of burdens.

Connecting punishment with the violation of these primary rules, and making public the provision for punishment, is both reasonable and just. First, it is only reasonable that those who voluntarily comply with the rules be provided some assurance that they will not be assuming burdens which others are unprepared to assume. Their disposition to comply voluntarily will diminish as they learn that others are with impunity renouncing burdens they are assuming. Second, fairness dictates that a system in which benefits and burdens are equally distributed have a mechanism designed to prevent a maldistribution in the benefits and burdens. Thus, sanctions are attached to noncompliance with the primary rules so as to induce compliance with the primary rules among those who may be disinclined to obey. In this way the likelihood of an unfair distribution is diminished.

Third, it is just to punish those who have violated the rules and caused the unfair distribution of benefits and burdens. A person who violates the rules has something others have—the benefits of the system—but by renouncing what others have assumed, the burdens of self-restraint, he has acquired an unfair advantage. Matters are not even until this advantage is in some way erased. Another way of putting it is that he owes something to others, for he has something that does not rightfully belong to him. Justice— that is punishing such individuals—restores the equilibrium of benefits and burdens by taking from the individual what he owes, that is, exacting the debt. It is important to see that the equilib- rium may be restored in another way. Forgiveness—with its legal analogue of a pardon—while not the righting of an unfair distribu- tion by making one pay his debt is, nevertheless, a restoring of the equilibrium by forgiving the debt. Forgiveness may be viewed, at least in some types of cases, as a gift after the fact, erasing a debt, which had the gift been given before the fact, would not have cre- ated a debt. But the practice of pardoning has to proceed sensi- tively, for it may endanger in a way the practice of justice does not, the maintenance of an equilibrium of benefits and burdens. If all are indiscriminately pardoned less incentive is provided individu- als to restrain their inclincations, thus increasing the incidence of persons taking what they do not deserve.

There are also in this system we are considering a variety of operative principles compliance with which provides some guaran- tee that the system of punishment does not itself promote an unfair distribution of benefits and burdens. For one thing, provision is made for a variety of defenses, each one of which can be said to have as its object diminishing the chances of forcibly depriving a person of benefits others have if that person has not derived an unfair advantage. A person has not derived an unfair advantage if he could not have restrained himself or if it is unreasonable to expect him to behave otherwise than he did. Sometimes the rules preclude punishment of classes of persons such as children. Some- times they provide a defense if on a particular occasion a person lacked the capacity to conform his conduct to the rules. Thus, someone who in an epileptic seizure strikes another is excused. Punishment in these cases would be punishment of the innocent, punishment of those who do not voluntarily renounce a burden others have assumed. Punishment in such cases, then, would not equalize but rather cause an unfair distribution in benefits and burdens.

Along with principles providing defenses there are requirements that the rules be prospective and relatively clear so that persons have a fair opportunity to comply with the rules. There are, also, rules governing, among other matters, the burden of proof, who shall bear it and what it shall be, the prohibition on double jeopardy, and the privilege against self-incrimination. Justice requires conviction of the guilty, and requires their punishment, but in setting out to fulfill the demands of justice we may, of course, because we are not omniscient, cause injustice by convicting and punishing the innocent. The resolution arrived at in the system I am describing consists in weighing as the greater evil the punishment of the innocent. The primary function of the system of rules was to provide individuals with a sphere of interest immune from interference. Given this goal, it is determined to be a greater evil for society to interfere unjustifiably with an individual by depriving him of good than for the society to fail to punish those that have unjustifiably interfered.

Finally, because the primary rules are designed to benefit all and because the punishments prescribed for their violation are publicized and the defenses respected, there is some plausibility in the exaggerated claim that in choosing to do an act violative of the rules an individual has chosen to be punished. This way of putting matters brings to our attention the extent to which, when the system is as I have described it, the criminal "has brought the punishment upon himself" in contrast to those cases where it would be misleading to say "he has brought it upon himself," cases, for example, where one does not know the rules or is punished in the absence of fault.

To summarize, then: first, there is a group of rules guiding the behavior of individuals in the community which establish spheres of interest immune from interference by others; second, provision is made for what is generally regarded as a deprivation of some thing of value if the rules are violated; third, the deprivations visited upon any person are justified by that person's having violated the rules; fourth, the deprivation, in this just system of punishment, is linked to rules that fairly distribute benefits and burdens and to procedures that strike some balance between not punishing the guilty and punishing the innocent, a class defined as those who have not voluntarily done acts violative of the law, in which it is evident that the evil of punishing the innocent is regarded as greater than the nonpunishment of the guilty.

At the core of many actual legal systems one finds, of course, rules and procedures of the kind I have sketched. It is obvious, though, that any ongoing legal system differs in significant respects from what I have presented here, containing 'pockets of injustice'.

I want now to sketch an extreme version of a set of institutions of a fundamentally different kind, institutions proceeding on a conception of man which appears to be basically at odds with that operative within a system of punishment.

Rules are promulgated in this system that prohibit certain types of injuries and harms.

In this world we are now to imagine when an individual harms another his conduct is to be regarded as a symptom of some pathological condition in the way a running nose is a symptom of a cold. Actions diverging from some conception of the normal are viewed as manifestations of a disease in the way in which we might today regard the arm and leg movements of an epileptic during a seizure. Actions conforming to what is normal are assimilated to the normal and healthy functioning of bodily organs. What a person does, then, is assimilated, on this conception, to what we believe today, or at least most of us believe today, a person undergoes. We draw a distinction between the operation of the kidney and raising an arm on request. This distinction between mere events or happenings and human actions is erased in our imagined system.[1]

----

[1] "When a man is suffering from an infectious disease, he is a danger to the community, and it is necessary to restrict his liberty of movement. But no one associates any idea of guilt with such a situation. On the contrary, he is an object of commiseration to his friends. Such steps as science recommends are taken to cure him of his disease, and he submits as a rule without reluctance to the

There is, however, bound to be something strange in this erasing of a recognized distinction, for, as with metaphysical suggestions generally, and I take this to be one, the distinction may be reintroduced but given a different description, for example, 'happenings with *X* type of causes' and 'happenings with *Y* type of causes'. Responses of different kinds, today legitimated by our distinction between happenings and actions may be legitimated by this new manner of description. And so there may be isomorphism between a system recognizing the distinction and one erasing it. Still, when this distinction is erased certain tendencies of thought

---

curtailment of liberty involved meanwhile. The same method in spirit ought to be shown in the treatment of what is called 'crime.' "

Bertrand Russell, *Roads to Freedom* (London: George Allen and Unwin Ltd., 1918), p. 135.

"We do not hold people responsible for their reflexes—for example, for coughing in church. We hold them responsible for their operant behavior—for example, for whispering in church or remaining in church while coughing. But there are variables which are responsible for whispering as well as coughing, and these may be just as inexorable. When we recognize this, we are likely to drop the notion of responsibility altogether and with it the doctrine of free will as an inner causal agent."

B. F. Skinner, *Science and Human Behavior* (1953), pp. 115-6.

"Basically, criminality is but a symptom of insanity, using the term in its widest generic sense to express unacceptable social behavior based on unconscious motivation flowing from a disturbed instinctive and emotional life, whether this appears in frank psychoses, or in less obvious form in neuroses and unrecognized psychoses. . . . If criminals are products of early environmental influences in the same sense that psychotics and neurotics are, then it should be possible to reach them psychotherapeutically."

Benjamin Karpman, "Criminal Psychodynamics," *Journal of Criminal Law and Criminology*, 47 (1956), p. 9.

"We, the agents of society, must move to end the game of tit-for-tat and blow-for-blow in which the offender has foolishly and futilely engaged himself and us. We are not driven, as he is, to wild and impulsive actions. With knowledge comes power, and with power there is no need for the frightened vengeance of the old penology. In its place should go a quiet, dignified, therapeutic program for the rehabilitation of the disorganized one, if possible, the protection of society during the treatment period, and his guided return to useful citizenship, as soon as this can be effected."

Karl Menninger, "Therapy, Not Punishment," *Harper's Magazine* (August 1959), pp. 63-64.

and responses might naturally arise that would tend to affect unfavorably values respected by a system of punishment.

Let us elaborate on this assimilation of conduct of a certain kind to symptoms of a disease. First, there is something abnormal in both the case of conduct, such as killing another, and a symptom of a disease such as an irregular heart beat. Second, there are causes for this abnormality in action such that once we know of them we can explain the abnormality as we now can explain the symptoms of many physical diseases. The abnormality is looked upon as a happening with a causal explanation rather than an action for which there were reasons. Third, the causes that account for the abnormality interfere with the normal functioning of the body, or, in the case of killing with what is regarded as a normal functioning of an individual. Fourth, the abnormality is in some way a part of the individual, necessarily involving his body. A well going dry might satisfy our three foregoing conditions of disease symptoms, but it is hardly a disease or the symptom of one. Finally, and most obscure, the abnormality arises in some way from within the individual. If Jones is hit with a mallet by Smith, Jones may reel about and fall on James who may be injured. But this abnormal conduct of Jones is not regarded as a symptom of disease. Smith, not Jones, is suffering from some pathological condition.

With this view of man the institutions of social control respond, not with punishment, but with either preventive detention, in case of 'carriers', or therapy in the case of those manifesting pathological symptoms. The logic of sickness implies the logic of therapy. And therapy and punishment differ widely in their implications. In bringing out some of these differences I want again to draw attention to the important fact that while the distinctions we now draw are erased in the therapy world, they may, in fact, be reintroduced but under different descriptions. To the extent they are, we really have a punishment system combined with a therapy system. I am concerned now, however, with what the implications would be were the world indeed one of therapy and not a disguised world of punishment and therapy, for I want to suggest tendencies of thought that arise when one is immersed in the ideology of disease and therapy.

First, punishment is the imposition upon a person who is

believed to be at fault of something commonly believed to be a deprivation where that deprivation is justified by the person's guilty behavior. It is associated with resentment, for the guilty are those who have done what they had no right to do by failing to exercise restraint when they might have and where others have. Therapy is not a response to a person who is at fault. We respond to an individual, not because of what he has done, but because of some condition from which he is suffering. If he is no longer suffering from the condition, treatment no longer has a point. Punishment, then, focuses on the past; therapy on the present. Therapy is normally associated with compassion for what one undergoes, not resentment for what one has illegitimately done.

Second, with therapy, unlike punishment, we do not seek to deprive the person of something acknowledged as a good, but seek rather to help and to benefit the individual who is suffering by ministering to his illness in the hope that the person can be cured. The good we attempt to do is not a reward for desert. The individual suffering has not merited by his disease the good we seek to bestow upon him but has, because he is a creature that has the capacity to feel pain, a claim upon our sympathies and help.

Third, we saw with punishment that its justification was related to maintaining and restoring a fair distribution of benefits and burdens. Infliction of the prescribed punishment carries the implication, then, that one has 'paid one's debt' to society, for the punishment is the taking from the person of something commonly recognized as valuable. It is this conception of 'a debt owed' that may permit, as I suggested earlier, under certain conditions, the nonpunishment of the guilty, for operative within a system of punishment may be a concept analogous to forgiveness, namely pardoning. Who it is that we may pardon and under what conditions—contrition with its elements of self-punishment no doubt plays a role—I shall not go into though it is clearly a matter of the greatest practical and theoretical interest. What is clear is that the conceptions of 'paying a debt' or 'having a debt forgiven' or pardoning have no place in a system of therapy.

Fourth, with punishment there is an attempt at some equivalence between the advantage gained by the wrongdoer—partly based upon the seriousness of the interest invaded, partly on the state of mind with which the wrongful act was performed—and the punishment meted out. Thus, we can understand a prohibition on 'cruel and unusual punishments' so that disproportionate pain and suffering are avoided. With therapy attempts at proportionality make no sense. It is perfectly plausible giving someone who kills a pill and treating for a lifetime within an institution one who has broken a dish and manifested accident proneness. We have the concept of 'painful treatment'. We do not have the concept of 'cruel treatment'. Because treatment is regarded as a benefit, though it may involve pain, it is natural that less restraint is exercised in bestowing it, than in inflicting punishment. Further, protests wth respect to treatment are likely to be assimilated to the complaints of one whose leg must be amputated in order for him to live, and, thus, largely disregarded. To be sure, there is operative in the therapy world some conception of the "cure being worse than the disease," but if the disease is manifested in conduct harmful to others, and if being a normal operating human being is valued highly, there will naturally be considerable pressure to find the cure acceptable.

Fifth, the rules in our system of punishment governing conduct of individuals were rules violation of which involved either direct interference with others or the creation of a substantial risk of such interference. One could imagine adding to this system of primary rules other rules proscribing preparation to do acts violative of the primary rules and even rules proscribing thoughts. Objection to such suggestions would have many sources but a principal one would consist in its involving the infliction of punishment on too great a number of persons who would not, because of a change of mind, have violated the primary rules. Though we are interested in diminishing violations of the primary rules, we are not prepared to punish too many individuals who would never have violated the rules in order to achieve this aim. In a system motivated solely by a preventive and curative ideology there would be less reason to wait until symptoms manifest themselves in socially harmful conduct. It is understandable that we should wish at the earliest possible stage to arrest the development of the disease. In the punishment system, because we are dealing with deprivations, it is understandable that we should forbear from imposing them until we are quite sure of guilt. In the therapy system, dealing as it does with benefits, there is less reason for forbearance from treatment at an early stage.

Sixth, a variety of procedural safeguards we associate with punishment have less significance in a therapy system. To the degree objections to double jeopardy and self-incrimination are based on a wish to decrease the chances of the innocent being convicted and punished, a therapy system, unconcerned with this problem, would disregard such safeguards. When one is out to help people there is also little sense in urging that the burden of proof be on those providing the help. And there is less point to imposing the burden of proving that the conduct was pathological beyond a reasonable doubt. Further, a jury system which, within a system of justice, serves to make accommodations to the individual situation and to introduce a human element, would play no role or a minor one in a world where expertise is required in making determinations of disease and treatment.

In our system of punishment an attempt was made to maximize each individual's freedom of choice by first of all delimiting by rules certain spheres of conduct immune from interference by others. The punishment associated with these primary rules paid deference to an individual's free choice by connecting punishment to a freely chosen act violative of the rules, thus giving some plausibility to the claim, as we saw, that what a person received by way of punishment he himself had chosen. With the world of disease and therapy all this changes and the individual's free choice ceases to be a determinative factor in how others respond to him. All those principles of our own legal system that minimize the chances of punishment of those who have not chosen to do acts violative of the rules tend to lose their point in the therapy system, for how we respond in a therapy system to a person is not conditioned upon what he has chosen but rather on what symptoms he has manifested or may manifest and what the best therapy for the disease is that is suggested by the symptoms.

Now, it is clear I think, that were we confronted with the alternatives I have sketched, between a system of just punishment and a thoroughgoing system of treatment, a system, that is, that did not reintroduce concepts appropriate to punishment, we could see the point in claiming that a person has a right to be punished,

486                         THE MONIST

meaning by this that a person had a right to all those institutions
and practices linked to punishment. For these would provide him
with, among other things, a far greater ability to predict what
would happen to him on the occurrence of certain events than the
therapy system. There is the inestimable value to each of us of
having the responses of others to us determined over a wide range of
our lives by what we choose rather than what they choose. A person
has a right to institutions that respect his choices. Our punishment
system does; our therapy system does not.

Apart from those aspects of our therapy model which would
relate to serious limitations on personal liberty, there are clearly
objections of a more profound kind to the mode of thinking I have
associated with the therapy model.

First, human beings pride themselves in having capacities that
animals do not. A common way, for example, of arousing shame in
a child is to compare the child's conduct to that of an animal. In a
system where all actions are assimilated to happenings we are
assimilated to creatures—indeed, it is more extreme than this—
whom we have always thought possessed of less than we. Fundamental to our practice of praise and order of attainment is that one who
can do more—one who is capable of more and one who does more is
more worthy of respect and admiration. And we have thought of
ourselves as capable where animals are not of making, of creating,
among other things, ourselves. The conception of man I have
outlined would provide us with a status that today, when our
conduct is assimilated to it in moral criticism, we consider properly
evocative of shame.

Second, if all human conduct is viewed as something men
undergo, thrown into question would be the appropriateness of that
extensive range of peculiarly human satisfactions that derive from a
sense of achievement. For these satisfactions we shall have to
substitute those mild satisfactions attendant upon a healthy well-
functioning body. Contentment is our lot if we are fortunate;
intense satisfaction at achievement is entirely inappropriate.

Third, in the therapy world nothing is earned and what we
receive comes to us through compassion, or through a desire to
control us. Resentment is out of place. We can take credit for
nothing but must always regard ourselves—if there are selves left to

regard once actions disappear—as fortunate recipients of benefits or unfortunate carriers of disease who must be controlled. We know that within our own world human beings who have been so regarded and who come to accept this view of themselves come to look upon themselves as worthless. When what we do is met with resentment, we are indirectly paid something of a compliment.

Fourth, attention should also be drawn to a peculiar evil that may be attendant upon regarding a man's actions as symptoms of disease. The logic of cure will push us toward forms of therapy that inevitably involve changes in the person made against his will. The evil in this would be most apparent in those cases where the agent, whose action is determined to be a manifestation of some disease, does not regard his action in this way. He believes that what he has done is, in fact, 'right' but his conception of 'normality' is not the therapeutically accepted one. When we treat an illness we normally treat a condition that the person is not responsible for. He is 'suffering' from some disease and we treat the condition, relieving the person of something preventing his normal functioning. When we begin treating persons for actions that have been chosen, we do not lift from the person something that is interfering with his normal functioning but we change the person so that he functions in a way regarded as normal by the current therapeutic community. We have to change him and his judgments of value. In doing this we display a lack of respect for the moral status of individuals, that is, a lack of respect for the reasoning and choices of individuals. They are but animals who must be conditioned. I think we can understand and, indeed, sympathize with a man's preferring death to being forcibly turned into what he is not.

Finally, perhaps most frightening of all would be the derogation in status of all protests to treatment. If someone believes that he has done something right, and if he protests being treated and changed, the protest will itself be regarded as a sign of some pathological condition, for who would not wish to be cured of an affliction? What this leads to are questions of an important kind about the effect of this conception of man upon what we now understand by reasoning. Here what a person takes to be a reasoned defense of an act is treated, as the action was, on the model of a happening of a pathological kind. Not just a person's acts are taken from him but also his attempt at a reasoned justification for the acts. In a system of punishment a person who has committed a crime may argue that what he did was right. We make him pay the price and we respect his right to retain the judgment he has made. A conception of pathology precludes this form of respect.

It might be objected to the foregoing that all I have shown—if that—is that if the only alternatives open to us are a *just* system of punishment or the mad world of being treated like sick or healthy animals, we do in fact have a right to a system of punishment of this kind. But this hardly shows that we have a right *simpliciter* to punishment as we do, say, to be free. Indeed, it does not even show a right to a just system of punishment, for surely we can, without too much difficulty, imagine situations in which the alternatives to punishment are not this mad world but a world in which we are still treated as persons and there is, for example, not the pain and suffering attendant upon punishment. One such world is one in which there are rules but responses to their violation is not the deprivation of some good but forgiveness. Still another type of world would be one in which violation of the rules were responded to by merely comparing the conduct of the person to something commonly regarded as low or filthy, and thus, producing by this mode of moral criticism, feelings of shame rather than feelings of guilt.

I am prepared to allow that these objections have a point. While granting force to the above objections I want to offer a few additional comments with respect to each of them. First, any existent legal system permits the punishment of individuals under circumstances where the conditions I have set forth for a just system have not been satisfied. A glaring example of this would be criminal strict liability which is to be found in our own legal system. Nevertheless, I think it would be difficult to present any system we should regard as a system of punishment that would not still have a great advantage over our imagined therapy system. The system of punishment we imagine may more and more approximate a system of sheer terror in which human beings are treated as animals to be intimidated and prodded. To the degree that the system is of this character it is, in my judgment, not simply an unjust system but one that diverges from what we normally understand by a system of punishment. At least some deference to the choice of individuals is built into the idea of punishment. So there would be some truth in saying we have a right to any system of punishment if the only alternative to it was therapy.

Second, people may imagine systems in which there are rules and in which the response to their violation is not punishment but pardoning, the legal analogue of forgiveness. Surely this is a system to which we would claim a right as against one in which we are made to suffer for violating the rules. There are several comments that need to be made about this. It may be, of course, that a high incidence of pardoning would increase the incidence of rule violations. Further, the difficulty with suggesting pardoning as a general response is that pardoning presupposes the very responses that it is suggested it supplant. A system of deprivations, or a practice of deprivations on the happening of certain actions, underlies the practice of pardoning and forgiving, for it is only where we possess the idea of a wrong to be made up or of a debt owed to others, ideas we acquire within a world in which there have been deprivations for wrong acts, that we have the idea of pardoning for the wrong or forgiving the debt.

Finally, if we look at the responses I suggested would give rise to feelings of shame, we may rightly be troubled with the appropriateness of this response in any community in which each person assumes burdens so that each may derive benefits. In such situations might it not be that individuals have a right to a system of punishment so that each person could be assured that inequities in the distribution of benefits and burdens are unlikely to occur and if they do, procedures exist for correcting them? Further, it may well be that, everything considered, we should prefer the pain and suffering of a system of punishment to a world in which we only experience shame on the doing of wrong acts, for with guilt there are relatively simple ways of ridding ourselves of the feeling we have, that is, gaining forgiveness or taking the punishment, but with shame we have to bear it until we no longer are the person who has behaved in the shameful way. Thus, I suggest that we have, wherever there is a distribution of benefits and burdens of the kind I have described, a right to a system of punishment.

I want also to make clear in concluding this section that I have argued, though very indirectly, not just for a right to a system of punishment, but for a right to be punished once there is in existence such a system. Thus, a man has the right to be punished rather than treated if he is guilty of some offense. And, indeed, one can imagine a case in which, even in the face of an offer of a pardon, a man claims and ought to have acknowledged his right to be punished.

2. The primary reason for preferring the system of punishment as against the system of therapy might have been expressed in terms of the one system treating one as a person and the other not. In invoking the right to be punished, one justifies one's claim by reference to a more fundamental right. I want now to turn attention to this fundamental right and attempt to shed light—it will have to be little, for the topic is immense—on what is meant by 'treating an individual as a person'.

When we talk of not treating a human being as a person or 'showing no respect for one as a person' what we imply by our words is a contrast between the manner in which one acceptably responds to human beings and the manner in which one acceptably responds to animals and inanimate objects. When we treat a human being merely as an animal or some inanimate object our responses to the human being are determined, not by his choices, but ours in disregard of or with indifference to his. And when we 'look upon' a person as less than a person or not a person, we consider the person as incapable of rational choice. In cases of not treating a human being as a person we interfere with a person in such a way that what is done, even if the person is involved in the doing, is done not by the person but by the user of the person. In extreme cases there may even be an elision of a causal chain so that we might say that $X$ killed $Z$ even though $Y$'s hand was the hand that held the weapon, for $Y$'s hand may have been entirely in $X$'s control. The one agent is in some way treating the other as a mere link in a causal chain. There is, of course, a wide range of cases in which a person is used to accomplish the aim of another and in which the person used is less than fully free. A person may be grabbed against his will and used as a shield. A person may be drugged or hypnotized and then employed for certain ends. A person may be deceived into doing other than he intends doing. A person may be ordered to do something and threatened with harm if he does not and coerced into doing what he does not want to. There is still another range of cases in which individuals are not used, but in which decisions by others are made that affect them in circumstances where they have the capacity for choice and where they are not being treated as persons.

But it is particularly important to look at coercion, for I have claimed that a just system of punishment treats human beings as persons; and it is not immediately apparent how ordering someone to do something and threatening harm differs essentially from having rules supported by threats of harm in case of noncompliance.

There are affinities between coercion and other cases of not treating someone as a person, for it is not the coerced person's choices but the coercer's that are responsible for what is done. But unlike other indisputable cases of not treating one as a person, for example using someone as a shield, there is some choice involved in coercion. And if this is so, why does the coercer stand in any different relation to the coerced person than the criminal law stands to individuals in society?

Suppose the person who is threatened disregards the order and gets the threatened harm. Now suppose he is told, "Well, you did after all bring it upon yourself." There is clearly something strange in this. It is the person doing the threatening and not the person threatened who is responsible. But our reaction to punishment, at least in a system that resembles the one I have described, is precisely that the person violating the rules brought it upon himself. What lies behind these different reactions?

There exist situations in the law, of course, which resemble coercion situations. There are occasions when in the law a person might justifiably say "I am not being treated as a person but being used" and where he might properly react to the punishment as something "he was hardly responsible for." But it is possible to have a system in which it would be misleading to say, over a wide range of cases of punishment for noncompliance, that we are using persons. The clearest case in which it would be inappropriate to so regard punishment would be one in which there were explicit agreement in advance that punishment should follow on the volun-

tary doing of certain acts. Even if one does not have such conditions
satisfied, and obviously such explicit agreements are not characteristic, one can see significant differences between our system of just
punishment and a coercion situation.

First, unlike the case with one person coercing another 'to do his
will', the rules in our system apply to all, with the benefits and
burdens equally distributed. About such a system it cannot be said
that some are being subordinated to others or are being used by
others or gotten to do things by others. To the extent that the rules
are thought to be to the advantage of only some or to the extent
there is a maldistribution of benefits and burdens, the difference
between coercion and law disappears.

Second, it might be argued that at least any person inclined to
act in a manner violative of the rules stands to all others as the
person coerced stands to his coercer, and that he, at least, is a person
disadvantaged as others are not. It is important here, I think, that
he is part of a system in which it is commonly agreed that forbearance from the acts proscribed by the rules provides advantages for
all. This system is the accepted setting; it is the norm. Thus, in any
coercive situation, it is the coercer who deviates from the norm,
with the responsibility of the person he is attempting to coerce,
defeated. In a just punishment situation, it is the person deviating
from the norm, indeed he might be a coercer, who is responsible, for
it is the norm to restrain oneself from acts of that kind. A voluntary
agent diverging in his conduct from what is expected or what the
norm is, on general causal principles, regarded as the cause of what
results from his conduct.

There is, then, some plausibility in the claim that, in a system of
punishment of the kind I have sketched, a person chooses the
punishment that is meted out to him. If, then, we can say in such a
system that the rules provide none with advantages that others do
not have, and further, that what happens to a person is conditioned
by that person's choice and not that of others, then we can say that
it is a system responding to one as a person.

We treat a human being as a person provided: first, we permit
the person to make the choices that will determine what happens to
him and second, when our responses to the person are responses
respecting the person's choices. When we respond to a person's

PERSONS AND PUNISHMENT 493

illness by treating the illness it is neither a case of treating or not treating the individual as a person. When we give a person a gift we are neither treating or not treating him as a person, unless, of course, he does not wish it, chooses not to have it, but we compel him to accept it.

3. This right to be treated as a person is a fundamental human right belonging to all human beings by virtue of their being human. It is also a natural, inalienable, and absolute right. I want now to defend these claims so reminiscent of an era of philosophical thinking about rights that many consider to have been seriously confused.

If the right is one that we possess by virtue of being human beings, we are immediately confronted with an apparent dilemma. If, to treat another as a person requires that we provide him with reasons for acting and avoid force or deception, how can we justify the force and deception we exercise with respect to children and the mentally ill? If they, too, have a right to be treated as persons are we not constantly infringing their rights? One way out of this is simply to restrict the right to those who satisfy the conditions of being a person. Infants and the insane, it might be argued, do not meet these conditions, and they would not then have the right. Another approach would be to describe the right they possess as a prima facie right to be treated as a person. This right might then be outweighed by other considerations. This approach generally seems to me, as I shall later argue, inadequate.

I prefer this tack. Children possess the right to be treated as persons but they possess this right as an individual might be said in the law of property to possess a future interest. There are advantages in talking of individuals as having a right though complete enjoyment of it is postponed. Brought to our attention, if we ascribe to them the right, is the legitimacy of their complaint if they are not provided with opportunities and conditions assuring their full enjoyment of the right when they acquire the characteristics of persons. More than this, all persons are charged with the sensitive task of not denying them the right to be a person and to be treated as a person by failing to provide the conditions for their becoming individuals who are able freely and in an informed way to choose and who are prepared themselves to assume responsibility for their choices. There is an obligation imposed upon us all, unlike that we have with respect to animals, to respond to children in such a way as to maximize the chances of their becoming persons. This may well impose upon us the obligation to treat them as persons from a very early age, that is, to respect their choices and to place upon them the responsibility for the choices to be made. There is no need to say that there is a close connection between how we respond to them and what they become. It also imposes upon us all the duty to display constantly the qualities of a person, for what they become they will largely become because of what they learn from us is acceptable behavior.

In claiming that the right is a right that human beings have by virtue of being human, there are several other features of the right, that should be noted, perhaps better conveyed by labelling them 'natural'. First, it is a right we have apart from any voluntary agreement into which we have entered. Second, it is not a right that derives from some defined position or status. Third, it is equally apparent that one has the right regardless of the society or community of which one is a member. Finally, it is a right linked to certain features of a class of beings. Were we fundamentally different than we now are, we would not have it. But it is more than that, for the right is linked to a feature of human beings which, were that feature absent—the capacity to reason and to choose on the basis of reasons—, profound conceptual changes would be involved in the thought about human beings. It is a right, then, connected with a feature of men that sets men apart from other natural phenomena.

The right to be treated as a person is inalienable. To say of a right that it is inalienable draws attention not to limitations placed on what others may do with respect to the possessor of the right but rather to limitations placed on the dispositive capacities of the possessor of the right. Something is to be gained in keeping the issues of alienability and absoluteness separate.

There are a variety of locutions qualifying what possessors of rights may and may not do. For example, on this issue of alienability, it would be worthwhile to look at, among other things, what is involved in abandoning, abdicating, conveying, giving up, granting, relinquishing, surrendering, transferring, and waiving one's rights. And with respect to each of these concepts we should also

## PERSONS AND PUNISHMENT 495

have to be sensitive to the variety of uses of the term 'rights'. What it is, for example, to waive a Hohfeldian 'right' in his strict sense will differ from what it is to waive a right in his 'privilege' sense.

Let us look at only two concepts very briefly, those of transferring and waiving rights. The clearest case of transferring rights is that of transferring rights with respect to specific objects. I own a watch and owning it I have a complicated relationship, captured in this area rather well I think by Hohfeld's four basic legal relationships, to all persons in the world with respect to the watch. We crudely capture these complex relationships by talking of my 'property rights' in or with respect to the watch. If I sell the watch, thus exercising a capacity provided by the rules of property, I have transferred rights in or with respect to the watch to someone else, the buyer, and the buyer now stands, as I formerly did, to all persons in the world in a series of complex relationships with respect to the watch.

While still the owner, I may have given to another permission to use it for several days. Had there not been the permission and had the person taken the watch, we should have spoken of interfering with or violating or, possibly, infringing my property rights. Or, to take a situation in which transferring rights is inappropriate, I may say to another "go ahead and slap me—you have my permission." In these types of situations philosophers and others have spoken of 'surrendering' rights or, alternatively and, I believe, less strangely, of 'waiving one's rights'. And recently, of course, the whole topic of 'waiving one's right to remain silent' in the context of police interrogation of suspects has been a subject of extensive litigation and discussion.

I confess to feeling that matters are not entirely perspicuous with respect to what is involved in 'waiving' or 'surrendering' rights. In conveying to another permission to take a watch or slap one, one makes legally permissible what otherwise would not have been. But in saying those words that constitute permission to take one's watch one is, of course, exercising precisely one of those capacities that leads us to say he has, while others have not, property rights with respect to the watch. Has one then waived his right in Hohfeld's strict sense in which the correlative is a duty to forebear on the part of others?

We may wish to distinguish here waiving the right to have others forbear to which there is a corresponding duty on their part to forbear, from placing oneself in a position where one has no legitimate right to complain. If I say the magic words "take the watch for a couple of days" or "go ahead and slap me," have I waived my right not to have my property taken or a right not to be struck or have I, rather, in saying what I have, simply stepped into a relation in which the rights no longer apply with respect to a specified other person? These observations find support in the following considerations. The right is that which gives rise, when infringed, to a legitimate claim against another person. What this suggests is that the right is that sphere interference with which entitles us to complain or gives us a right to complain. From this it seems to follow that a right to bodily security should be more precisely described as 'a right that others not interfere without permission'. And there is the corresponding duty not to interfere unless provided permission. Thus when we talk of waiving our rights or 'giving up our rights' in such cases we are not waiving or giving up our right to property nor our right to bodily security, for we still, of course, possess the right not to have our watch taken without permission. We have rather placed ourselves in a position where we do not possess the capacity, sometimes called a right, to complain if the person takes the watch or slaps us.

There is another type of situation in which we may speak of waiving our rights. If someone without permission slaps me, there is an infringement of my right to bodily security. If I now acquiesce or go further and say "forget it" or "you are forgiven," we might say that I had waived my right to complain. But here, too, I feel uncomfortable about what is involved. For I do have the right to complain (a right without a corresponding duty) in the event I am slapped and I have that right whether I wish it or not. If I say to another after the slap, "you are forgiven" what I do is not waive the right to complain but rather make illegitimate my subsequent exercise of that right.

Now, if we turn to the right to be treated as a person, the claim that I made was that it was inalienable, and what I meant to convey by that word of respectable age is that (a) it is a right that cannot be transferred to another in the way one's right with respect to objects can be transferred and (b) that it cannot be waived in the ways in which people talk of waiving rights to property or waiving, within certain limitations, one's right to bodily security.

While the rules of the law of property are such that persons may, satisfying certain procedures, transfer rights, the right to be treated as a person logically cannot be transferred anymore than one person can transfer to another his right to life or privacy. What, indeed, would it be like for another to have our right to be treated as a person? We can understand transferring a right with respect to certain objects. The new owner stands where the old owner stood. But with a right to be treated as a person what could this mean? My having the right meant that my choices were respected. Now if I transfer it to another this will mean that he will possess the right that my choices be respected? This is nonsense. It is only each person himself that can have his choices respected. It is no more possible to transfer this right than it is to transfer one's right to life.

Nor can the right be waived. It cannot be waived because any agreement to being treated as an animal or an instrument does not provide others with the moral permission to so treat us. One can volunteer to be a shield, but then it is one's choice on a particular occasion to be a shield. If without our permission, without our choosing it, someone used us as a shield, we may, I should suppose, forgive the person for treating us as an object. But we do not thereby waive our right to be treated as a person, for that is a right that has been infringed and what we have at most done is put ourselves in a position where it is inappropriate any longer to exercise the right to complain.

This is the sort of right, then, such that the moral rules defining relationships among persons preclude anyone from morally giving others legitimate permissions or rights with respect to one by doing or saying certain things. One stands, then, with respect to one's person as the nonowner of goods stands to those goods. The nonowner cannot, given the rule-defined relationships, convey to others rights and privileges that only the owner possesses. Just as there are agreements nonenforceable because void is contrary to public policy, so there are permissions our moral outlook regards as without moral force. With respect to being treated as a person, one is 'disabled' from modifying relations of others to one.

498                          THE MONIST

The right is absolute. This claim is bound to raise eyebrows. I
have an innocuous point in mind in making this claim.

In discussing alienability we focused on incapacities with
respect to disposing of rights. Here what I want to bring out is a
sense in which a right exists despite considerations for refusing to
accord the person his rights. As with the topic of alienability there
are a host of concepts that deserve a close look in this area. Among
them are according, acknowledging, annulling, asserting, claiming,
denying, destroying, exercising, infringing, insisting upon, interfering with, possessing, recognizing and violating.

The claim that rights are absolute has been construed to mean
that 'assertions of rights cannot, for any reason under any circumstances be denied'. When there are considerations which warrant
refusing to accord persons their rights, there are two prevalent views
as to how this should be described: there is, first, the view that the
person does not have the right, and second, the view that he has
rights but of a prima facie kind and that these have been outweighed or overcome by the other considerations. "We can conceive
times when such rights must give way, and, therefore, they are only
prima facie and not absolute rights." (Brandt)

Perhaps there are cases in which a person claims a right to do a
certain thing, say with his property, and argues that his property
rights are absolute, meaning by this he has a right to do whatever
he wishes with his property. Here, no doubt, it has to be explained
to the person that the right he claims he has, he does not in fact
possess. In such a case the person does not have and never did have,
given a certain description of the right, a right that was prima facie
or otherwise, to do what he claimed he had the right to do. If the
assertion that a right is absolute implies that we have a right to do
whatever we wish to do, it is an absurd claim and as such should not
really ever have been attributed to political theorists arguing for
absolute rights. But, of course, the claim that we have a prima facie
right to do whatever we wish to do is equally absurd. The right is
not prima facie either, for who would claim, thinking of the right to
be free, that one has a prima facie right to kill others, if one wishes,
unless there are moral considerations weighing against it?

There are, however, other situations in which it is accepted by
all that a person possesses rights of a certain kind, and the difficulty

## PERSONS AND PUNISHMENT 499

we face is that of according the person the right he is claiming when this will promote more evil than good. The just act is to give the man his due and giving a man what it is his right to have is giving him his due. But it is a mistake to suppose that justice is the only dimension of morality. It may be justifiable not to accord to a man his rights. But it is no less a wrong to him, no less an infringement. It is seriously misleading to turn all justifiable infringements into noninfringements by saying that the right is only prima facie, as if we have, in concluding that we should not accord a man his rights, made out a case that he had none. To use the language of 'prima facie rights' misleads, for it suggests that a presumption of the existence of a right has been overcome in these cases where all that can be said is that the presumption in favor of according a man his rights has been overcome. If we begin to think the right itself is prima facie, we shall, in cases in which we are justified in not according it, fail sufficiently to bring out that we have interfered where justice says we should not. Our moral framework is unnecessarily and undesirably impoverished by the theory that there are such rights.

When I claim, then, that the right to be treated as a person is absolute what I claim is that given that one is a person, one always has the right so to be treated, and that while there may possibly be occasions morally requiring not according a person this right, this fact makes it no less true that the right exists and would be infringed if the person were not accorded it.

4. Having said something about the nature of this fundamental right I want now, in conclusion, to suggest that the denial of this right entails the denial of all moral rights and duties. This requires bringing out what is surely intuitively clear that any framework of rights and duties presupposes individuals that have the capacity to choose on the basis of reasons presented to them, and that what makes legitimate actions within such a system are the free choices of individuals. There is, in other words, a distribution of benefits and burdens in accord with a respect for the freedom of choice and freedom of action of all. I think that the best way to make this point may be to sketch some of the features of a world in which rights and duties are possessed.

First, rights exist only when there is some conception of some things valued and others not. Secondly, and implied in the first point, is the fact that there are dispositions to defend the valued commodities. Third, the valued commodities may be interfered with by others in this world. A group of animals might be said to satisfy these first three conditions. Fourth, rights exist when there are recognized rules establishing the legitimacy of some acts and ruling out others. Mistakes in the claim of right are possible. Rights imply the concepts of interference and infringement, concepts the elucidation of which requires the concept of a rule applying to the conduct of persons. Fifth, to possess a right is to possess something that constitutes a legitimate restraint on the freedom of action of others. It is clear, for example, that if individuals were incapable of controlling their actions we would have no notion of a legitimate claim that they do so. If, for example, we were all disposed to object or disposed to complain, as the elephant seal is disposed to object when his territory is invaded, then the objection would operate in a causal way, or approximating a causal way, in getting the behavior of noninterference. In a system of rights, on the other hand, there is a point to appealing to the rules in legitimating one's complaint. Implied, then, in any conception of rights are the existence of individuals capable of choosing and capable of choosing on the basis of considerations with respect to rules. The distribution of freedom throughout such a system is determined by the free choice of individuals. Thus any denial of the right to be treated as a person would be a denial undercutting the whole system, for the system rests on the assumption that spheres of legitimate and illegitimate conduct are to be delimited with regard to the choices made by persons.

This conclusion stimulates one final reflection on the therapy world we imagined.

The denial of this fundamental right will also carry with it, ironically, the denial of the right to treatment to those who are ill. In the world as we now understand it, there are those who do wrong and who have a right to be responded to as persons who have done wrong. And there are those who have not done wrong but who are suffering from illnesses that in a variety of ways interfere with their capacity to live their lives as complete persons. These persons who are ill have a claim upon our compassion. But more than this they have, as animals do not, a right to be treated as persons. When an individual is ill he is entitled to that assistance which will make it possible for him to resume his functioning as a person. If it is an injustice to punish an innocent person, it is no less an injustice, and a far more significant one in our day, to fail to promote as best we can through adequate facilities and medical care the treatment of those who are ill. Those human beings who fill our mental institutions are entitled to more than they do in fact receive; they should be viewed as possessing the right to be treated as a person so that our responses to them may increase the likelihood that they will enjoy fully the right to be so treated. Like the child the mentally ill person has a future interest we cannot rightly deny him. Society is today sensitive to the infringement of justice in punishing the innocent; elaborate rules exist to avoid this evil. Society should be no less sensitive to the injustice of failing to bring back to the community of persons those whom it is possible to bring back.

HERBERT MORRIS

UNIVERSITY OF CALIFORNIA,
LOS ANGELES

# [3]

## Marxism and Retribution

JEFFRIE G. MURPHY

*Punishment in general has been defended as a means either of amel-
iorating or of intimidating. Now what right have you to punish me for
the amelioration or intimidation of others? And besides there is history—there is such a thing as statistics—which prove with the most
complete evidence that since Cain the world has been neither intimidated nor ameliorated by punishment. Quite the contrary. From the
point of view of abstract right, there is only one theory of punishment
which recognizes human dignity in the abstract, and that is the theory
of Kant, especially in the more rigid formula given to it by Hegel.
Hegel says: "Punishment is the right of the criminal. It is an act of his
own will. The violation of right has been proclaimed by the criminal
as his own right. His crime is the negation of right. Punishment is the
negation of this negation, and consequently an affirmation of right,
solicited and forced upon the criminal by himself."*

*There is no doubt something specious in this formula, inasmuch as
Hegel, instead of looking upon the criminal as the mere object, the
slave of justice, elevates him to the position of a free and self-deter-*

An earlier version of this essay was delivered to the Third Annual Colloquium
in Philosophy ("The Philosophy of Punishment") at the University of Dayton
in October, 1972. I am grateful to the Department of Philosophy at the University of Dayton for inviting me to participate and to a number of persons at the
Colloquium for the useful discussion on my paper at the time. I am also grateful
to Anthony D. Woozley of the University of Virginia and to two of my colleagues,
Robert M. Harnish and Francis V. Raab, for helping me to clarify the expression
of my views.

*mined being. Looking, however, more closely into the matter, we dis-*
*cover that German idealism here, as in most other instances, has but*
*given a transcendental sanction to the rules of existing society. Is it*
*not a delusion to substitute for the individual with his real motives,*
*with multifarious social circumstances pressing upon him, the ab-*
*straction of "free will"—one among the many qualities of man for man*
*himself? . . . Is there not a necessity for deeply reflecting upon an*
*alteration of the system that breeds these crimes, instead of glorifying*
*the hangman who executes a lot of criminals to make room only for*
*the supply of new ones?*

*Karl Marx, "Capital Punishment,"*
*New York Daily Tribune, 18 February 1853*[1]

Philosophers have written at great length about the moral problems
involved in punishing the innocent—particularly as these problems
raise obstacles to an acceptance of the moral theory of Utilitarianism.
Punishment of an innocent man in order to bring about good social
consequences is, at the very least, not always clearly wrong on utilitarian principles. This being so, utilitarian principles are then to be
condemned by any morality that may be called Kantian in character.
For punishing an innocent man, in Kantian language, involves using
that man as a mere means or instrument to some social good and is

1. In a sense, my paper may be viewed as an elaborate commentary on this
one passage, excerpted from a discussion generally concerned with the efficacy
of capital punishment in eliminating crime. For in this passage, Marx (to the
surprise of many I should think) expresses a certain admiration for the classical
retributive theory of punishment. Also (again surprisingly) he expresses this
admiration in a kind of language he normally avoids—i.e., the moral language
of rights and justice. He then, of course, goes on to reject the applicability of
that theory. But the question that initially perplexed me is the following: what
is the explanation of Marx's ambivalence concerning the retributive theory; why
is he both attracted and repelled by it? (This ambivalence is not shared, for
example, by utilitarians—who feel nothing but repulsion when the retributive
theory is even mentioned.) Now except for some very brief passages in *The Holy
Family*, Marx himself has nothing more to say on the topic of punishment beyond what is contained in this brief *Daily Tribune* article. Thus my essay is in
no sense an exercise in textual scholarship (there are not enough texts) but is
rather an attempt to construct an assessment of punishment, Marxist at least in
spirit, that might account for the ambivalence found in the quoted passage. My
main outside help comes, not from Marx himself, but from the writings of the
Marxist criminologist Willem Bonger.

thus not to treat him as an end in himself, in accord with his dignity
or worth as a person.

The Kantian position on the issue of punishing the innocent, and
the many ways in which the utilitarian might try to accommodate
that position, constitute extremely well-worn ground in contemporary
moral and legal philosophy.[2] I do not propose to wear the ground
further by adding additional comments on the issue here. What I do
want to point out, however, is something which seems to me quite
obvious but which philosophical commentators on punishment have
almost universally failed to see—namely, that problems of the very
same kind and seriousness arise for the utilitarian theory with respect
to the punishment of the guilty. For a utilitarian theory of punishment
(Bentham's is a paradigm) must involve justifying punishment in
terms of its social results—e.g., deterrence, incapacitation, and rehabilitation. And thus even a guilty man is, on this theory, being punished
because of the instrumental value the action of punishment will have
in the future. He is being used as a means to some future good—e.g.,
the deterrence of others. Thus those of a Kantian persuasion, who see
the importance of worrying about the treatment of persons as mere
means, must, it would seem, object just as strenuously to the punishment of the guilty on utilitarian grounds as to the punishment of the
innocent. Indeed the former worry, in some respects, seems more
serious. For a utilitarian can perhaps refine his theory in such a way
that it does not commit him to the punishment of the innocent. However, if he is to approve of punishment at all, he must approve of
punishing the guilty in at least some cases. This makes the worry
about punishing the guilty formidable indeed, and it is odd that this
has gone generally unnoticed.[3] It has generally been assumed that if
the utilitarian theory can just avoid entailing the permissibility of
punishing the innocent, then all objections of a Kantian character to
the theory will have been met. This seems to me simply not to be
the case.

2. Many of the leading articles on this topic have been reprinted in *The Philosophy of Punishment*, ed. H. B. Acton (London, 1969). Those papers not included
are cited in Acton's excellent bibliography.

3. One writer who has noticed this is Richard Wasserstrom. See his "Why
Punish the Guilty?" *Princeton University Magazine* 20 (1964), pp. 14-19.

What the utilitarian theory really cannot capture, I would suggest, is the notion of persons having rights. And it is just this notion that is central to any Kantian outlook on morality. Any Kantian can certainly agree that punishing persons (guilty or innocent) may have either good or bad or indifferent consequences and that insofar as the consequences (whether in a particular case or for an institution) are good, this is something in favor of punishment. But the Kantian will maintain that this consequential outlook, important as it may be, leaves out of consideration entirely that which is most morally crucial —namely, the question of rights. Even if punishment of a person would have good consequences, what gives us (i.e., society) the moral right to inflict it? If we have such a right, what is its origin or derivation? What social circumstances must be present for it to be applicable? What does this right to punish tell us about the status of the person to be punished—e.g., how are we to analyze his rights, the sense in which he must deserve to be punished, his obligations in the matter? It is this family of questions which any Kantian must regard as morally central and which the utilitarian cannot easily accommodate into his theory. And it is surely this aspect of Kant's and Hegel's retributivism, this seeing of rights as basic, which appeals to Marx in the quoted passage. As Marx himself puts it: "What right have you to punish me for the amelioration or intimidation of others?" And he further praises Hegel for seeing that punishment, if justified, must involve respecting the rights of the person to be punished.[4] Thus Marx, like Kant, seems prepared to draw the important distinction between (a) what it would be good to do on grounds of utility and (b) what we have a right to do. Since we do not always have the right to do what it would be good to do, this distinction is of the greatest moral importance; and missing the distinction is the Achilles heel of all forms of Utilitarianism. For consider the following example: A Jehovah's Witness needs a blood

---

4. Marx normally avoids the language of rights and justice because he regards such language to be corrupted by bourgeois ideology. However, if we think very broadly of what an appeal to rights involves—namely, a protest against unjustified coercion—there is no reason why Marx may not legitimately avail himself on occasion of this way of speaking. For there is surely at least some moral overlap between Marx's protests against exploitation and the evils of a division of labor, for example, and the claims that people have a right not to be used solely for the benefit of others and a right to self-determination.

transfusion in order to live; but, because of his (we can agree absurd) religious belief that such transfusions are against God's commands, he instructs his doctor not to give him one. Here is a case where it would seem to be good or for the best to give the transfusion and yet, at the very least, it is highly doubtful that the doctor has a right to give it. This kind of distinction is elementary, and any theory which misses it is morally degenerate.[5]

To move specifically to the topic of punishment: How exactly does retributivism (of a Kantian or Hegelian variety) respect the rights of persons? Is Marx really correct on this? I believe that he is. I believe that retributivism can be formulated in such a way that it is the only morally defensible theory of punishment. I also believe that arguments, which may be regarded as Marxist at least in spirit, can be formulated which show that social conditions as they obtain in most societies make this form of retributivism largely inapplicable within those societies. As Marx says, in those societies retributivism functions merely to provide a "transcendental sanction" for the status quo. If this is so, then the only morally defensible theory of punishment is largely inapplicable in modern societies. The consequence: modern societies largely lack the moral right to punish.[6] The upshot is that a Kantian moral theory (which in general seems to me correct) and a Marxist analysis of society (which, if properly qualified, also seems to me correct) produces a radical and not merely reformist attack not merely on the scope and manner of punishment in our society but on the institution of punishment itself. Institutions of punishment constitute

5. I do not mean to suggest that under no conceivable circumstances would the doctor be justified in giving the transfusion even though, in one clear sense, he had no right to do it. If, for example, the Jehovah's Witness was a key man whose survival was necessary to prevent the outbreak of a destructive war, we might well regard the transfusion as on the whole justified. However, even in such a case, a morally sensitive man would have to regretfully realize that he was sacrificing an important principle. Such a realization would be impossible (because inconsistent) for a utilitarian, for his theory admits only one principle —namely, do that which on the whole maximizes utility. An occupational disease of utilitarians is a blindness to the possibility of genuine moral dilemmas—i.e., a blindness to the possibility that important moral principles can conflict in ways that are not obviously resolvable by a rational decision procedure.

6. I qualify my thesis by the word "largely" to show at this point my realization, explored in more detail later, that no single theory can account for all criminal behavior.

what Bernard Harrison has called structural injustices[7] and are, in the absence of a major social change, to be resisted by all who take human rights to be morally serious—i.e., regard them as genuine action guides and not merely as rhetorical devices which allow people to morally sanctify institutions which in fact can only be defended on grounds of social expediency.

Stating all of this is one thing and proving it, of course, is another. Whether I can ever do this is doubtful. That I cannot do it in one brief article is certain. I cannot, for example, here defend in detail my belief that a generally Kantian outlook on moral matters is correct.[8] Thus I shall content myself for the present with attempting to render at least plausible two major claims involved in the view that I have outlined thus far: (1) that a retributive theory, in spite of the bad press that it has received, is a morally credible theory of punishment—that it can be, H. L. A. Hart to the contrary,[9] a reasonable general justifying aim of punishment; and (2) that a Marxist analysis of a society can undercut the practical applicability of that theory.

### THE RIGHT OF THE STATE TO PUNISH

It is strong evidence of the influence of a utilitarian outlook in moral and legal matters that discussions of punishment no longer involve a consideration of the right of anyone to inflict it. Yet in the eighteenth and nineteenth centuries, this tended to be regarded as the central aspect of the problem meriting philosophical consideration. Kant, Hegel, Bosanquet, Green—all tended to entitle their chapters on punishment along the lines explicitly used by Green: "The Right of the State to Punish."[10] This is not just a matter of terminology but reflects, I think, something of deeper philosophical substance. These theorists, unlike the utilitarian, did not view man as primarily a maximizer of personal satisfactions—a maximizer of individual utilities. They were

7. Bernard Harrison, "Violence and the Rule of Law," in *Violence*, ed. Jerome A. Shaffer (New York, 1971), pp. 139-176.

8. I have made a start toward such a defense in my "The Killing of the Innocent," forthcoming in *The Monist* 57, no. 4 (October 1973).

9. H. L. A. Hart, "Prolegomenon to the Principles of Punishment," from *Punishment and Responsibility* (Oxford, 1968), pp. 1-27.

10. Thomas Hill Green, *Lectures on the Principles of Political Obligation* (1885), (Ann Arbor, 1967), pp. 180-205.

inclined, in various ways, to adopt a different model of man—man as a free or spontaneous creator, man as autonomous. (Marx, it may be noted, is much more in line with this tradition than with the utilitarian outlook.)[11] This being so, these theorists were inclined to view punishment (a certain kind of coercion by the state) as not merely a causal contributor to pain and suffering, but rather as presenting at least a prima facie challenge to the values of autonomy and personal dignity and self-realization—the very values which, in their view, the state existed to nurture. The problem as they saw it, therefore, was that of reconciling punishment as state coercion with the value of individual autonomy. (This is an instance of the more general problem which Robert Paul Wolff has called the central problem of political philosophy—namely, how is individual moral autonomy to be reconciled with legitimate political authority?)[12] This kind of problem, which I am inclined to agree is quite basic, cannot even be formulated intelligibly from a utilitarian perspective. Thus the utilitarian cannot even see the relevance of Marx's charge: Even if punishment has wonderful social consequences, what gives anyone the right to inflict it on me?

Now one fairly typical way in which others acquire rights over us is by our own consent. If a neighbor locks up my liquor cabinet to protect me against my tendencies to drink too heavily, I might well regard this as a presumptuous interference with my own freedom, no matter how good the result intended or accomplished. He had no right to do it and indeed violated my rights in doing it. If, on the other hand, I had asked him to do this or had given my free consent to his suggestion that he do it, the same sort of objection on my part would be quite out of order. I had given him the right to do it, and he had the right to do it. In doing it, he violated no rights of mine—even if, at the time of his doing it, I did not desire or want the action to be performed. Here then we seem to have a case where my autonomy may be regarded as intact even though a desire of mine is thwarted. For there is a sense in which the thwarting of the desire can be imputed to me

11. For an elaboration of this point, see Steven Lukes, "Alienation and Anomie," in *Philosophy, Politics and Society* (Third Series), ed. Peter Laslett and W. G. Runciman (Oxford, 1967), pp. 134-156.

12. Robert Paul Wolff, *In Defense of Anarchism* (New York, 1970).

(my choice or decision) and not to the arbitrary intervention of another.

How does this apply to our problem? The answer, I think, is obvious. What is needed, in order to reconcile my undesired suffering of punishment at the hands of the state with my autonomy (and thus with the state's right to punish me), is a political theory which makes the state's decision to punish me in some sense my own decision. If I have willed my own punishment (consented to it, agreed to it) then—even if at the time I happen not to desire it—it can be said that my autonomy and dignity remain intact. Theories of the General Will and Social Contract theories are two such theories which attempt this reconciliation of autonomy with legitimate state authority (including the right or authority of the state to punish). Since Kant's theory happens to incorporate elements of both, it will be useful to take it for our sample.

MORAL RIGHTS AND THE RETRIBUTIVE THEORY OF PUNISHMENT

To justify government or the state is necessarily to justify at least some coercion.[13] This poses a problem for someone, like Kant, who maintains that human freedom is the ultimate or most sacred moral value. Kant's own attempt to justify the state, expressed in his doctrine of the *moral title (Befugnis)*,[14] involves an argument that coercion is justified only in so far as it is used to prevent invasions against freedom. Freedom itself is the only value which can be used to limit freedom, for the appeal to any other value (e.g., utility) would under-

13. In this section, I have adapted some of my previously published material: *Kant: The Philosophy of Right* (London, 1970), pp. 109-112 and 140-144; "Three Mistakes About Retributivism," *Analysis* (April 1971): 166-169; and "Kant's Theory of Criminal Punishment," in *Proceedings of the Third International Kant Congress*, ed. Lewis White Beck (Dordrecht, 1972), pp. 434-441. I am perfectly aware that Kant's views on the issues to be considered here are often obscure and inconsistent—e.g., the analysis of "willing one's own punishment" which I shall later quote from Kant occurs in a passage the primary purpose of which is to argue that the idea of "willing one's own punishment" makes no sense! My present objective, however, is not to attempt accurate Kant scholarship. My goal is rather to build upon some remarks of Kant's which I find philosophically suggestive.

14. Immanuel Kant, *The Metaphysical Elements of Justice* (1797), trans. John Ladd (Indianapolis, 1965), pp. 35ff.

mine the ultimate status of the value of freedom. Thus Kant attempts to establish the claim that some forms of coercion (as opposed to violence) are morally permissible because, contrary to appearance, they are really consistent with rational freedom. The argument, in broad outline, goes in the following way. Coercion may keep people from doing what they desire or want to do on a particular occasion and is thus prima facie wrong. However, such coercion can be shown to be morally justified (and thus not absolutely wrong) if it can be established that the coercion is such that it could have been rationally willed even by the person whose desire is interfered with:

> Accordingly, when it is said that a creditor has a right to demand from his debtor the payment of a debt, this does not mean that he can *persuade* the debtor that his own reason itself obligates him to this performance; on the contrary, to say that he has such a right means only that the use of coercion to make anyone do this is entirely compatible with everyone's freedom, *including the freedom of the debtor*, in accordance with universal laws.[15]

Like Rousseau, Kant thinks that it is only in a context governed by social practice (particularly civil government and its Rule of Law) that this can make sense. Laws may require of a person some action that he does not desire to perform. This is not a violent invasion of his freedom, however, if it can be shown that in some antecedent position of choice (what John Rawls calls "the original position"),[16] he would have been rational to adopt a Rule of Law (and thus run the risk of having some of his desires thwarted) rather than some other alternative arrangement like the classical State of Nature. This is, indeed, the only sense that Kant is able to make of classical Social Contract theories. Such theories are to be viewed, not as historical fantasies, but as ideal models of rational decision. For what these theories actually claim is that the only coercive institutions that are morally justified are those which a group of rational beings could agree to adopt in a position of having to pick social institutions to govern their relations:

15. *Ibid.*, p. 37.
16. John Rawls, "Justice as Fairness," *The Philosophical Review* 67 (1958): 164-194; and *A Theory of Justice* (Cambridge, Mass., 1971), especially pp. 17-22.

The contract, which is called *contractus originarius*, or *pactum sociale* . . . need not be assumed to be a fact, indeed it is not [even possible as such. To suppose that would be like insisting] that before anyone would be bound to respect such a civic constitution, it be proved first of all from history that a people, whose rights and obligations we have entered into as their descendants, had *once upon a time* executed such an act and had left a reliable document or instrument, either orally or in writing, concerning this contract. Instead, this contract is a *mere idea* of reason which has undoubted practical reality; namely, to oblige every legislator to give us laws in such a manner that the laws *could* have originated from the united will of the entire people and to regard every subject in so far as he is a citizen as though he had consented to such [an expression of the general] will. This is the testing stone of the rightness of every publicly-known law, for if a law were such that it was impossible for an entire people to give consent to it (as for example a law that a certain class of subjects, by inheritance, should have the privilege of the *status of lords*), then such a law is unjust. On the other hand, if there is a mere *possibility* that a people might consent to a (certain) law, then it is a duty to consider that the law is just even though at the moment the people might be in such a position or have a point of view that would result in their refusing to give their consent to it if asked.[17]

The problem of organizing a state, however hard it may seem, can be solved even for a race of devils, if only they are intelligent. The problem is: "Given a multiple of rational beings requiring universal laws for their preservation, but each of whom is secretly inclined to exempt himself from them, to establish a constitution in such a way that, although their private intentions conflict, they check each other, with the result that their public conduct is the same as if they had no such intentions."[18]

17. Immanuel Kant, "Concerning the Common Saying: This May be True in Theory but Does Not Apply in Practice (1793)," in *The Philosophy of Kant*, ed. and trans. Carl J. Friedrich (New York, 1949), pp. 421-422.

18. Immanuel Kant, *Perpetual Peace* (1795), trans. Lewis White Beck in the Kant anthology *On History* (Indianapolis 1963), p. 112.

Though Kant's doctrine is superficially similar to Mill's later self-protection principle, the substance is really quite different. For though Kant in some general sense argues that coercion is justified only to prevent harm to others, he understands by "harm" only certain invasions of freedom and not simply disutility. Also, his defense of the principle is not grounded, as is Mill's, on its utility. Rather it is to be regarded as a principle of justice, by which Kant means a principle that rational beings could adopt in a situation of mutual choice:

> The concept [of justice] applies only to the relationship of a will to another person's will, not to his wishes or desires (or even just his needs) which are the concern of acts of benevolence and charity. . . . In applying the concept of justice we take into consideration only the form of the relationship between the wills insofar as they are regarded as free, and whether the action of one of them can be conjoined with the freedom of the other in accordance with universal law. Justice is therefore the aggregate of those conditions under which the will of one person can be conjoined with the will of another in accordance with a universal law of freedom.[19]

How does this bear specifically on punishment? Kant, as everyone knows, defends a strong form of a retributive theory of punishment. He holds that guilt merits, and is a sufficient condition for, the infliction of punishment. And this claim has been universally condemned—particularly by utilitarians—as primitive, unenlightened and barbaric.

But why is it so condemned? Typically, the charge is that infliction of punishment on such grounds is nothing but pointless vengeance. But what is meant by the claim that the infliction is "pointless"? If "pointless" is tacitly being analyzed as "disutilitarian," then the whole question is simply being begged. You cannot refute a retributive theory merely by noting that it is a retributive theory and not a utilitarian theory. This is to confuse redescription with refutation and involves an argument whose circularity is not even complicated enough to be interesting.

19. Immanuel Kant, *The Metaphysical Elements of Justice*, p. 34.

Why, then, might someone claim that guilt merits punishment? Such a claim might be made for either of two very different reasons. (1) Someone (e.g., a Moral Sense theorist) might maintain that the claim is a primitive and unanalyzable proposition that is morally ultimate—that we can just intuit the "fittingness" of guilt and punishment. (2) It might be maintained that the retributivist claim is demanded by a general theory of political obligation which is more plausible than any alternative theory. Such a theory will typically provide a technical analysis of such concepts as crime and punishment and will thus not regard the retributivist claim as an indisputable primitive. It will be argued for as a kind of theorem within the system.

Kant's theory is of the second sort. He does not opt for retributivism as a bit of intuitive moral knowledge. Rather he offers a theory of punishment that is based on his general view that political obligation is to be analyzed, quasi-contractually, in terms of reciprocity. If the law is to remain just, it is important to guarantee that those who disobey it will not gain an unfair advantage over those who do obey voluntarily. It is important that no man profit from his own criminal wrongdoing, and a certain kind of "profit" (i.e., not bearing the burden of self-restraint) is intrinsic to criminal wrongdoing. Criminal punishment, then, has as its object the restoration of a proper balance between benefit and obedience. The criminal himself has no complaint, because he has rationally consented to or willed his own punishment. That is, those very rules which he has broken work, when they are obeyed by others, to his own advantage as a citizen. He would have chosen such rules for himself and others in the original position of choice. And, since he derives and voluntarily accepts benefits from their operation, he owes his own obedience as a debt to his fellow-citizens for their sacrifices in maintaining them. If he chooses not to sacrifice by exercising self-restraint and obedience, this is tantamount to his choosing to sacrifice in another way—namely, by paying the prescribed penalty:

> A transgression of the public law that makes him who commits it unfit to be a citizen is called . . . a crime. . . .
>
> What kind and what degree of punishment does public legal justice adopt as its principle and standard? None other than the principle

of equality (illustrated by the pointer of the scales of justice), that is, the principle of not treating one side more favorably than the other. Accordingly, any undeserved evil that you inflict on someone else among the people is one you do to yourself. If you vilify him, you vilify yourself; if you steal from him, you steal from yourself; if you kill him, you kill yourself. . . .

To say, "I will to be punished if I murder someone" can mean nothing more than, "I submit myself along with everyone else to those laws which, if there are any criminals among the people, will naturally include penal laws."[20]

This analysis of punishment regards it as a debt owed to the law-abiding members of one's community; and, once paid, it allows re-entry into the community of good citizens on equal status.

Now some of the foregoing no doubt sounds implausible or even obscurantist. Since criminals typically desire not to be punished, what can it really mean to say that they have, as rational men, really willed their own punishment? Or that, as Hegel says, they have a right to it? Perhaps a comparison of the traditional retributivist views with those of a contemporary Kantian—John Rawls—will help to make the points clearer.[21] Rawls (like Kant) does not regard the idea of the social contract as an historical fact. It is rather a model of rational decision. Respecting a man's autonomy, at least on one view, is not respecting what he now happens, however uncritically, to desire; rather it is to respect what he desires (or would desire) as a rational man. (On Rawls's view, for example, rational men are said to be unmoved by feelings of envy; and thus it is not regarded as unjust to a person or a violation of his rights, if he is placed in a situation where he will envy another's advantage or position. A rational man

20. *Ibid.*, pp. 99, 101, and 105, in the order quoted.
21. In addition to the works on justice by Rawls previously cited, the reader should consult the following for Rawls's application of his general theory to the problem of political obligation: John Rawls, "Legal Obligation and the Duty of Fair Play," in *Law and Philosophy*, ed. Sidney Hook (New York, 1964), pp. 3-18. This has been reprinted in my anthology *Civil Disobedience and Violence* (Belmont, Cal., 1971), pp. 39-52. For a direct application of a similar theory to the problem of punishment, see Herbert Morris, "Persons and Punishment," *The Monist* 52, no. 4 (October 1968): 475-501.

would object, and thus would never consent to, a practice where another might derive a benefit from a position at his expense. He would not, however, envy the position *simpliciter*, would not regard the position as itself a benefit.) Now on Kant's (and also, I think, on Rawls's) view, a man is genuinely free or autonomous only in so far as he is rational. Thus it is man's rational will that is to be respected.

Now this idea of treating people, not as they in fact say that they want to be treated, but rather in terms of how you think they would, if rational, will to be treated, has obviously dangerous (indeed Fascistic) implications. Surely we want to avoid cramming indignities down the throats of people with the offhand observation that, no matter how much they scream, they are really rationally willing every bit of it. It would be particularly ironic for such arbitrary repression to come under the mask of respecting autonomy. And yet, most of us would agree, the general principle (though subject to abuse) also has important applications—for example, preventing the suicide of a person who, in a state of psychotic depression, wants to kill himself. What we need, then, to make the general view work, is a check on its arbitrary application; and a start toward providing such a check would be in the formulation of a public, objective theory of rationality and rational willing. It is just this, according to both Kant and Rawls, which the social contract theory can provide. On this theory, a man may be said to rationally will X if, and only if, X is called for by a rule that the man would necessarily have adopted in the original position of choice—i.e., in a position of coming together with others to pick rules for the regulation of their mutual affairs. This avoids arbitrariness because, according to Kant and Rawls at any rate, the question of whether such a rule would be picked in such a position is objectively determinable given certain (in their view) noncontroversial assumptions about human nature and rational calculation. Thus I can be said to will my own punishment if, in an antecedent position of choice, I and my fellows would have chosen institutions of punishment as the most rational means of dealing with those who might break the other generally beneficial social rules that had been adopted.

Let us take an analogous example: I may not, in our actual society, desire to treat a certain person fairly—e.g., I may not desire to honor a contract I have made with him because so doing would adversely affect my own self-interest. However, if I am forced to honor the contract by the state, I cannot charge (1) that the state has no right to do this, or (2) that my rights or dignity are being violated by my being coerced into doing it. Indeed, it can be said that I rationally will it since, in the original position, I would have chosen rules of justice (rather than rules of utility) and the principle, "contracts are to be honored," follows from the rules of justice.

Coercion and autonomy are thus reconciled, at least apparently. To use Marx's language, we may say (as Marx did in the quoted passage) that one virtue of the retributive theory, at least as expounded by Kant and Hegel on lines of the General Will and Social Contract theory, is that it manifests at least a formal or abstract respect for rights, dignity, and autonomy. For it at least recognizes the importance of attempting to construe state coercion in such a way that it is a product of each man's rational will. Utilitarian deterrence theory does not even satisfy this formal demand.

The question of primary interest to Marx, of course, is whether this formal respect also involves a material respect; i.e., does the theory have application in concrete fact in the actual social world in which we live? Marx is confident that it does not, and it is to this sort of consideration that I shall now pass.

ALIENATION AND PUNISHMENT

What can the philosopher learn from Marx? This question is a part of a more general question: What can philosophy learn from social science? Philosophers, it may be thought, are concerned to offer a priori theories, theories about how certain concepts are to be analyzed and their application justified. And what can the mundane facts that are the object of behavioral science have to do with exalted theories of this sort?

The answer, I think, is that philosophical theories, though not themselves empirical, often have such a character that their intelligibility depends upon certain empirical presuppositions. For example, our moral language presupposes, as Hart has argued,[22] that we are vulnerable creatures—creatures who can harm and be harmed by each

22. H. L. A. Hart, *The Concept of Law* (Oxford, 1961), pp. 189-195.

other. Also, as I have argued elsewhere,[23] our moral language pre-supposes that we all share certain psychological characteristics—e.g., sympathy, a sense of justice, and the capacity to feel guilt, shame, regret, and remorse. If these facts were radically different (if, as Hart imagines for example, we all developed crustaceanlike exoskeletons and thus could not harm each other), the old moral language, and the moral theories which employ it, would lack application to the world in which we live. To use a crude example, moral prohibitions against killing presuppose that it is in fact possible for us to kill each other.

Now one of Marx's most important contributions to social philoso-phy, in my judgment, is simply his insight that philosophical theories are in peril if they are constructed in disregard of the nature of the empirical world to which they are supposed to apply.[24] A theory may be formally correct (i.e., coherent, or true for some possible world) but materially incorrect (i.e., inapplicable to the actual world in which we live). This insight, then, establishes the relevance of empirical research to philosophical theory and is a part, I think, of what Marx meant by "the union of theory and practice." Specifically relevant to the argument I want to develop are the following two related points:

(1) The theories of moral, social, political and legal philosophy presuppose certain empirical propositions about man and society. If these propositions are false, then the theory (even if coherent or formally correct) is materially defective and practically inapplicable. (For example, if persons tempted to engage in criminal conduct do not in fact tend to calculate carefully the consequences of their ac-tions, this renders much of deterrence theory suspect.)

23. Jeffrie G. Murphy, "Moral Death: A Kantian Essay on Psychopathy," *Ethics* 82, no. 4 (July 1972): 284-298.

24. Banal as this point may seem, it could be persuasively argued that all Enlightenment political theory (e.g., that of Hobbes, Locke and Kant) is built upon ignoring it. For example, once we have substantial empirical evidence concerning how democracies really work in fact, how sympathetic can we really be to classical theories for the justification of democracy? For more on this, see C. B. Macpherson, "The Maximization of Democracy," in *Philosophy, Politics and Society* (Third Series), ed. Peter Laslett and W. G. Runciman (Oxford, 1967), pp. 83-103. This article is also relevant to the point raised in note 11 above.

Marxism and Retribution

(2) Philosophical theories may put forth as a necessary truth that which is in fact merely an historically conditioned contingency. (For example, Hobbes argued that all men are necessarily selfish and competitive. It is possible, as many Marxists have argued, that Hobbes was really doing nothing more than elevating to the status of a necessary truth the contingent fact that the people around him in the capitalistic society in which he lived were in fact selfish and competitive.)[25]

In outline, then, I want to argue the following: that when Marx challenges the material adequacy of the retributive theory of punishment, he is suggesting (a) that it presupposes a certain view of man and society that is false and (b) that key concepts involved in the support of the theory (e.g., the concept of "rationality" in Social Contract theory) are given analyses which, though they purport to be necessary truths, are in fact mere reflections of certain historical circumstances.

In trying to develop this case, I shall draw primarily upon Willem Bonger's *Criminality and Economic Conditions* (1916), one of the few sustained Marxist analyses of crime and punishment.[26] Though I shall not have time here to qualify my support of Bonger in certain necessary ways, let me make clear that I am perfectly aware that his analysis is not the whole story. (No monolithic theory of anything so diverse as criminal behavior could be the whole story.) However, I am convinced that he has discovered part of the story. And my point is simply that insofar as Bonger's Marxist analysis is correct, then to that same degree is the retributive theory of punishment inapplicable in modern societies. (Let me emphasize again exactly how this objection

25. This point is well developed in C. B. Macpherson, *The Political Theory of Possessive Individualism* (Oxford, 1962). In a sense, this point affects even the formal correctness of a theory. For it demonstrates an empirical source of corruption in the analyses of the very concepts in the theory.

26. The writings of Willem Adriaan Bonger (1876-1940), a Dutch criminologist, have fallen into totally unjustified neglect in recent years. Anticipating contemporary sociological theories of crime, he was insisting that criminal behavior is in the province of normal psychology (though abnormal society) at a time when most other writers were viewing criminality as a symptom of psychopathology. His major works are: *Criminality and Economic Conditions* (Boston, 1916); *An Introduction to Criminology* (London, 1936); and *Race and Crime* (New York, 1943).

to retributivism differs from those traditionally offered. Traditionally, retributivism has been rejected because it conflicts with the moral theory of its opponent, usually a utilitarian. This is not the kind of objection I want to develop. Indeed, with Marx, I have argued that the retributive theory of punishment grows out of the moral theory—Kantianism—which seems to me generally correct. The objection I want to pursue concerns the empirical falsity of the factual presuppositions of the theory. If the empirical presuppositions of the theory are false, this does indeed render its application immoral. But the immorality consists, not in a conflict with some other moral theory, but immorality in terms of a moral theory that is at least close in spirit to the very moral theory which generates retributivism itself—i.e., a theory of justice.)[27]

To return to Bonger. Put bluntly, his theory is as follows. Criminality has two primary sources: (1) need and deprivation on the part of disadvantaged members of society, and (2) motives of greed and selfishness that are generated and reinforced in competitive capitalistic societies. Thus criminality is economically based—either directly in the case of crimes from need, or indirectly in the case of crimes growing out of motives or psychological states that are encouraged and developed in capitalistic society. In Marx's own language, such an economic system alienates men from themselves and from each other. It alienates men from themselves by creating motives and needs that are not "truly human." It alienates men from their fellows by encouraging a kind of competitiveness that forms an obstacle to the development of genuine communities to replace mere social aggregates.[28] And in Bonger's thought, the concept of community is

27. I say "at least in spirit" to avoid begging the controversial question of whether Marx can be said to embrace a theory of justice. Though (as I suggested in note 4) much of Marx's own evaluative rhetoric seems to overlap more traditional appeals to rights and justice (and a total lack of sympathy with anything like Utilitarianism), it must be admitted that he also frequently ridicules at least the terms "rights" and "justice" because of their apparent entrenchment in bourgeois ethics. For an interesting discussion of this issue, see Allen W. Wood, "The Marxian Critique of Justice," *Philosophy & Public Affairs* 1, no. 3 (Spring 1972): 244-282.

28. The importance of community is also, I think, recognized in Gabriel de Tarde's notion of "social similarity" as a condition of criminal responsibility. See his *Penal Philosophy* (Boston, 1912). I have drawn on de Tarde's general account in my "Moral Death: A Kantian Essay on Psychopathy."

central. He argues that moral relations and moral restraint are possible only in genuine communities characterized by bonds of sympathetic identification and mutual aid resting upon a perception of
common humanity. All this he includes under the general rubric of
reciprocity.[29] In the absence of reciprocity in this rich sense, moral
relations among men will break down and criminality will increase.[30]
Within bourgeois society, then, crimes are to be regarded as normal,
and not psychopathological, acts. That is, they grow out of need,
greed, indifference to others, and sometimes even a sense of indignation—all, alas, perfectly typical human motives.

To appreciate the force of Bonger's analysis, it is necessary to read
his books and grasp the richness and detail of the evidence he provides
for his claims. Here I can but quote a few passages at random to give
the reader a tantalizing sample in the hope that he will be encouraged
to read further into Bonger's own text:

> The abnormal element in crime is a social, not a biological, element.
> With the exception of a few special cases, crime lies within the
> boundaries of normal psychology and physiology. . . .

> We clearly see that [the egoistic tendencies of the present economic
> system and of its consequences] are very strong. Because of these
> tendencies the social instinct of man is not greatly developed; they
> have weakened the moral force in man which combats the inclina-
> tion towards egoistic acts, and hence toward the crimes which are
> one form of these acts. . . . Compassion for the misfortunes of

29. By "reciprocity" Bonger intends something which includes, but is much
richer than, a notion of "fair trading or bargaining" that might initially be read
into the term. He also has in mind such things as sympathetic identification
with others and tendencies to provide mutual aid. Thus, for Bonger, reciprocity
and egoism have a strong tendency to conflict. I mention this lest Bonger's
notion of reciprocity be too quickly identified with the more restricted notion
found in, for example, Kant and Rawls.

30. It is interesting how greatly Bonger's analysis differs from classical deterrence theory—e.g., that of Bentham. Bentham, who views men as machines
driven by desires to attain pleasure and avoid pain, tends to regard terror as the
primary restraint against crime. Bonger believes that, at least in a healthy society, moral motives would function as a major restraint against crime. When
an environment that destroys moral motivation is created, even terror (as statistics tend to confirm) will not eradicate crime.

others inevitably becomes blunted, and a great part of morality consequently disappears. . . .

As a consequence of the present environment, man has become very egoistic and hence more *capable of crime*, than if the environment had developed the germs of altruism. . . .

There can be no doubt that one of the factors of criminality among the bourgeoisie is bad [moral] education. . . . The children—speaking of course in a general way—are brought up with the idea that they must succeed, no matter how; the aim of life is presented to them as getting money and shining in the world. . . .

Poverty (taken in the sense of absolute want) kills the social sentiments in man, destroys in fact all relations between men. He who is abandoned by all can no longer have any feeling for those who have left him to his fate. . . .

[Upon perception that the system tends to legalize the egoistic actions of the bourgeoisie and to penalize those of the proletariat], the oppressed resort to means which they would otherwise scorn. As we have seen above, the basis of the social feeling is reciprocity. As soon as this is trodden under foot by the ruling class the social sentiments of the oppressed become weak towards them. . . .[31]

The essence of this theory has been summed up by Austin J. Turk. "Criminal behavior," he says, "is almost entirely attributable to the combination of egoism and an environment in which opportunities are not equitably distributed."[32]

31. *Introduction to Criminology*, pp. 75-76, and *Criminality and Economic Conditions*, pp. 532, 402, 483-484, 436, and 407, in the order quoted. Bonger explicitly attacks Hobbes: "The adherents of [Hobbes's theory] have studied principally men who live under capitalism, or under civilization; their correct conclusion has been that egoism is the predominant characteristic of these men, and they have adopted the simplest explanation of the phenomenon and say that this trait is inborn." If Hobbists can cite Freud for modern support, Bonger can cite Darwin. For, as Darwin had argued in the *Descent of Man*, men would not have survived as a species if they had not initially had considerably greater social sentiments than Hobbes allows them.

32. Austin J. Turk, in the Introduction to his abridged edition of Bonger's *Criminality and Economic Conditions* (Bloomington, 1969), p. 14.

No doubt this claim will strike many as extreme and intemperate—a sample of the old-fashioned Marxist rhetoric that sophisticated intellectuals have outgrown. Those who are inclined to react in this way might consider just one sobering fact: of the 1.3 million criminal offenders handled each day by some agency of the United States correctional system, the vast majority (80 percent on some estimates) are members of the lowest 15-percent income level—that percent which is below the "poverty level" as defined by the Social Security Administration.[33] Unless one wants to embrace the belief that all these people are poor because they are bad, it might be well to reconsider Bonger's suggestion that many of them are "bad" because they are poor.[34] At any rate, let us suppose for purposes of discussion that Bonger's picture of the relation between crime and economic conditions is generally accurate. At what points will this challenge the credentials of the contractarian retributive theory as

33. Statistical data on characteristics of offenders in America are drawn primarily from surveys by the Bureau of Census and the National Council on Crime and Delinquency. While there is of course wide disagreement on how such data are to be interpreted, there is no serious disagreement concerning at least the general accuracy of statistics like the one I have cited. Even government publications openly acknowledge a high correlation between crime and socioeconomic disadvantages: "From arrest records, probation reports, and prison statistics a 'portrait' of the offender emerges that progressively highlights the disadvantaged character of his life. The offender at the end of the road in prison is likely to be a member of the lowest social and economic groups in the country, poorly educated and perhaps unemployed. . . . Material failure, then, in a culture firmly oriented toward material success, is the most common denominator of offenders" (*The Challenge of Crime in a Free Society*, A Report by the President's Commission on Law Enforcement and Administration of Justice, U. S. Government Printing Office, Washington, D.C., 1967, pp. 44 and 160). The Marxist implications of this admission have not gone unnoticed by prisoners. See Samuel Jorden, "Prison Reform: In Whose Interest?" *Criminal Law Bulletin* 7, no. 9 (November 1971): 779-787.

34. There are, of course, other factors which enter into an explanation of this statistic. One of them is the fact that economically disadvantaged guilty persons are more likely to wind up arrested or in prison (and thus be reflected in this statistic) than are economically advantaged guilty persons. Thus economic conditions enter into the explanation, not just of criminal behavior, but of society's response to criminal behavior. For a general discussion on the many ways in which crime and poverty are related, see Patricia M. Wald, "Poverty and Criminal Justice," *Task Force Report: The Courts*, U.S. Government Printing Office, Washington, D.C., 1967, pp. 139-151.

outlined above? I should like to organize my answer to this question around three basic topics:

1. *Rational Choice.* The model of rational choice found in Social Contract theory is egoistic—rational institutions are those that would be agreed to by calculating egoists ("devils" in Kant's more colorful terminology). The obvious question that would be raised by any Marxist is: Why give egoism this special status such that it is built, a priori, into the analysis of the concept of rationality? Is this not simply to regard as necessary that which may be only contingently found in the society around us? Starting from such an analysis, a certain result is inevitable—namely, a transcendental sanction for the status quo. Start with a bourgeois model of rationality and you will, of course, wind up defending a bourgeois theory of consent, a bourgeois theory of justice, and a bourgeois theory of punishment.

Though I cannot explore the point in detail here, it seems to me that this Marxist claim may cause some serious problems for Rawls's well-known theory of justice, a theory which I have already used to unpack some of the evaluative support for the retributive theory of punishment. One cannot help suspecting that there is a certain sterility in Rawls's entire project of providing a rational proof for the preferability of a certain conception of justice over all possible alternative evaluative principles, for the description which he gives of the rational contractors in the original position is such as to guarantee that they will come up with his two principles. This would be acceptable if the analysis of rationality presupposed were intuitively obvious or argued for on independent grounds. But it is not. Why, to take just one example, is a desire for wealth a rational trait whereas envy is not? One cannot help feeling that the desired result dictates the premises.[35]

35. The idea that the principles of justice could be proved as a kind of theorem (Rawls's claim in "Justice as Fairness") seems to be absent, if I understand the work correctly, in Rawls's recent *A Theory of Justice*. In this book, Rawls seems to be content with something less than a decision procedure. He is no longer trying to pull his theory of justice up by its own bootstraps, but now seems concerned simply to *exhibit* a certain elaborate conception of justice in the belief that it will do a good job of systematizing and ordering most of our considered and reflective intuitions about moral matters. To this, of course, the Marxist will want to say something like the following: "The considered and reflective in-

2. *Justice, Benefits, and Community.* The retributive theory claims
to be grounded on justice; but is it just to punish people who act out
of those very motives that society encourages and reinforces? If
Bonger is correct, much criminality is motivated by greed, selfishness,
and indifference to one's fellows; but does not the whole society encourage motives of greed and selfishness ("making it," "getting
ahead"), and does not the competitive nature of the society alienate
men from each other and thereby encourage indifference—even, perhaps, what psychiatrists call psychopathy? The moral problem here
is similar to one that arises with respect to some war crimes. When
you have trained a man to believe that the enemy is not a genuine
human person (but only a gook, or a chink), it does not seem quite
fair to punish the man if, in a war situation, he kills indiscriminately.
For the psychological trait you have conditioned him to have, like
greed, is not one that invites fine moral and legal distinctions. There
is something perverse in applying principles that presuppose a sense of
community in a society which is structured to destroy genuine community.[36]

Related to this is the whole allocation of benefits in contemporary

---

tuitions current in our society are a product of bourgeois culture, and thus any
theory based upon them begs the question against us and in favor of the status
quo." I am not sure that this charge cannot be answered, but I am sure that it
deserves an answer. Someday Rawls may be remembered, to paraphrase Georg
Lukács's description of Thomas Mann, as the last and greatest philosopher of
bourgeois liberalism. The virtue of this description is that it perceives the limitations of his outlook in a way consistent with acknowledging his indisputable
genius. (None of my remarks here, I should point out, are to be interpreted as
denying that our civilization derived major moral benefits from the tradition
of bourgeois liberalism. Just because the freedoms and procedures we associate
with bourgeois liberalism—speech, press, assembly, due process of law, etc.—are
not the only important freedoms and procedures, we are not to conclude with
some witless radicals that these freedoms are not terribly important and that the
victories of bourgeois revolutions are not worth preserving. My point is much
more modest and noncontroversial—namely, that even bourgeois liberalism requires a critique. It is not self-justifying and, in certain very important respects,
is not justified at all.)

36. Kant has some doubts about punishing bastard infanticide and dueling on
similar grounds. Given the stigma that Kant's society attached to illegitimacy
and the halo that the same society placed around military honor, it did not seem
totally fair to punish those whose criminality in part grew out of such approved
motives. See *Metaphysical Elements of Justice*, pp. 106-107.

society. The retributive theory really presupposes what might be called a "gentlemen's club" picture of the relation between man and society— i.e., men are viewed as being part of a community of shared values and rules. The rules benefit all concerned and, as a kind of debt for the benefits derived, each man owes obedience to the rules. In the absence of such obedience, he deserves punishment in the sense that he owes payment for the benefits. For, as rational man, he can see that the rules benefit everyone (himself included) and that he would have selected them in the original position of choice.

Now this may not be too far off for certain kinds of criminals—e.g., business executives guilty of tax fraud. (Though even here we might regard their motives of greed to be a function of societal reinforcement.) But to think that it applies to the typical criminal, from the poorer classes, is to live in a world of social and political fantasy. Criminals typically are not members of a shared community of values with their jailers; they suffer from what Marx calls alienation. And they certainly would be hard-pressed to name the benefits for which they are supposed to owe obedience. If justice, as both Kant and Rawls suggest, is based on reciprocity, it is hard to see what these persons are supposed to reciprocate for. Bonger addresses this point in a passage quoted earlier (p. 236): "The oppressed resort to means which they would otherwise scorn. . . . The basis of social feelings is reciprocity. As soon as this is trodden under foot by the ruling class, the social sentiments of the oppressed become weak towards them."

3. *Voluntary Acceptance.* Central to the Social Contract idea is the claim that we owe allegiance to the law because the benefits we have derived have been voluntarily accepted. This is one place where our autonomy is supposed to come in. That is, having benefited from the Rule of Law when it was possible to leave, I have in a sense consented to it and to its consequences—even my own punishment if I violate the rules. To see how silly the factual presuppositions of this account are, we can do no better than quote a famous passage from David Hume's essay "Of the Original Contract":

> Can we seriously say that a poor peasant or artisan has a free choice to leave his country—when he knows no foreign language or manners, and lives from day to day by the small wages which he ac-

quires? We may as well assert that a man, by remaining in a vessel, freely consents to the dominion of the master, though he was carried on board while asleep, and must leap into the ocean and perish the moment he leaves her.

A banal empirical observation, one may say. But it is through ignoring such banalities that philosophers generate theories which allow them to spread iniquity in the ignorant belief that they are spreading righteousness.

It does, then, seem as if there may be some truth in Marx's claim that the retributive theory, though formally correct, is materially inadequate. At root, the retributive theory fails to acknowledge that criminality is, to a large extent, a phenomenon of economic class. To acknowledge this is to challenge the empirical presupposition of the retributive theory—the presupposition that all men, including criminals, are voluntary participants in a reciprocal system of benefits and that the justice of this arrangement can be derived from some eternal and ahistorical concept of rationality.

THE upshot of all this seems rather upsetting, as indeed it is. How can it be the case that everything we are ordinarily inclined to say about punishment (in terms of utility and retribution) can be quite beside the point? To anyone with ordinary language sympathies (one who is inclined to maintain that what is correct to say is a function of what we do say), this will seem madness. Marx will agree that there is madness, all right, but in his view the madness will lie in what we do say—what we say only because of our massive (and often self-deceiving and self-serving) factual ignorance or indifference to the circumstances of the social world in which we live. Just as our whole way of talking about mental phenomena hardened before we knew any neurophysiology—and this leads us astray, so Marx would argue that our whole way of talking about moral and political phenomena hardened before we knew any of the relevant empirical facts about man and society—and this, too, leads us astray. We all suffer from what might be called the *embourgeoisment* of language, and thus part of any revolution will be a linguistic or conceptual revolution. We have grown accustomed to modifying our language or con-

ceptual structures under the impact of empirical discoveries in phys-
ics. There is no reason why discoveries in sociology, economics, or
psychology could not and should not have the same effect on entrenched patterns of thought and speech. It is important to remember,
as Russell remarked, that our language sometimes enshrines the
metaphysics of the Stone Age.

Consider one example: a man has been convicted of armed robbery. On investigation, we learn that he is an impoverished black
whose whole life has been one of frustrating alienation from the prevailing socio-economic structure—no job, no transportation if he could
get a job, substandard education for his children, terrible housing and
inadequate health care for his whole family, condescending-tardy-
inadequate welfare payments, harassment by the police but no real
protection by them against the dangers in his community, and near
total exclusion from the political process. Learning all this, would we
still want to talk—as many do—of his suffering punishment under the
rubric of "paying a debt to society"? Surely not. Debt for what? I do
not, of course, pretend that all criminals can be so described. But I
do think that this is a closer picture of the typical criminal than the
picture that is presupposed in the retributive theory—i.e., the picture
of an evil person who, of his own free will, intentionally acts against
those just rules of society which he knows, as a rational man, benefit
everyone including himself.

But what practical help does all this offer, one may ask. How should
we design our punitive practices in the society in which we now live?
This is the question we want to ask, and it does not seem to help
simply to say that our society is built on deception and inequity. How
can Marx help us with our real practical problem? The answer, I
think, is that he cannot and obviously does not desire to do so. For
Marx would say that we have not focused (as all piecemeal reform
fails to focus) on what is truly the real problem. And this is changing
the basic social relations. Marx is the last person from whom we can
expect advice on how to make our intellectual and moral peace with
bourgeois society. And this is surely his attraction and his value.

What does Bonger offer? He suggests, near the end of his book, that
in a properly designed society all criminality would be a problem "for
the physician rather than the judge." But this surely will not do. The

therapeutic state, where prisons are called hospitals and jailers are called psychiatrists, simply raises again all the old problems about the justification of coercion and its reconciliation with autonomy that we faced in worrying about punishment. The only difference is that our coercive practices are now surrounded with a benevolent rhetoric which makes it even harder to raise the important issues. Thus the move to therapy, in my judgment, is only an illusory solution—alienation remains and the problem of reconciling coercion with autonomy remains unsolved. Indeed, if the alternative is having our personalities involuntarily restructured by some state psychiatrist, we might well want to claim the "right to be punished" that Hegel spoke of.[37]

Perhaps, then, we may really be forced seriously to consider a radical proposal. If we think that institutions of punishment are necessary and desirable, and if we are morally sensitive enough to want to be sure that we have the moral right to punish before we inflict it, then we had better first make sure that we have restructured society in such a way that criminals genuinely do correspond to the only model that will render punishment permissible—i.e., make sure that they are autonomous and that they do benefit in the requisite sense. Of course, if we did this then—if Marx and Bonger are right—crime itself and the need to punish would radically decrease if not disappear entirely.

37. This point is pursued in Herbert Morris, "Persons and Punishment." Bonger did not appreciate that "mental illness," like criminality, may also be a phenomenon of social class. On this, see August B. Hollingshead and Frederick C. Redlich, *Social Class and Mental Illness* (New York, 1958). On the general issue of punishment versus therapy, see my *Punishment and Rehabilitation* (Belmont, Cal., forthcoming 1973).

# [4]

## The Moral Education
## Theory of Punishment

JEAN HAMPTON

> We ought not to repay injustice with injustice or
> to do harm to any man, no matter what we may
> have suffered from him.
>
> Plato, *Crito*, X, 49

There are few social practices more time-honored or more widely accepted throughout the world than the practice of punishing wrongdoers. Yet if one were to listen to philosophers discussing this practice, one would think punishment impossible to justify and difficult even to understand. However, I do not believe that one should conclude that punishment as a practice is morally unjustifiable or fundamentally irrational. Instead I want to explore the promise of another theory of punishment which incorporates certain elements of the deterrence, retributivist, and rehabilitation views, but whose justification for punishment and whose formula for determining what punishment a wrongdoer deserves are distinctive and importantly different from the reasons and formulas characterizing the traditional rival theories.

This view, which I call the moral education theory of punishment, is not new. There is good reason to believe Plato and Hegel accepted something like it,[1] and more recently, Herbert Morris and Robert Nozick have maintained that the moral education which punishment effects is at least part of punishment's justification.[2] I want to go further, however, and

---

1. See Hegel, *Philosophy of Right*, trans. T. Knox (Oxford: Clarendon Press, 1952), sections 90–104 (pp. 66–74); and see Plato, in particular the dialogues: *The Laws* (bks. 5 and 9), *Gorgias* (esp. pp. 474ff.), *Protagoras* (esp. pp. 323ff.) and Socrates's discussion of his own punishment in the *Apology*, and the *Crito*. I am not convinced that this characterization of either Hegel's or Plato's views is correct, but I do not have time to pursue those issues here. J. E. McTaggart has analyzed Hegel's position in a way that suggests it is a moral education view. See his "Hegel's Theory of Punishment," *International Journal of Ethics* 6 (1896), pp. 482–99; portions reprinted in *Philosophical Perspectives On Punishment*, ed. Gertrude Ezorsky (Albany, NY: State University of New York Press, 1972). In her *Plato on Punishment*, M. M. Mackenzie's presentation of Plato's position suggests it is not a strict moral education view.

2. Recently Morris has been explicitly advocating this view in "A Paternalistic Theory of Punishment," *American Philosophical Quarterly* 18, no. 4 (October 1981), but only as *one*

*The Moral Education*
                                   *Theory of Punishment*

suggest that by reflecting on the educative character of punishment we
can provide a full and complete justification for it. Hence my discussion
of the moral education theory in this paper is meant to develop it as a
complete justification of punishment and to distinguish it from its traditional rivals. Most of my discussion will focus on the theory's application
to the state's punishment of criminal offenders, but I will also be looking
at the theory's implications for punishment within other societal institutions, most notably the family.

I will not, however, be able to give an adequate development of the
theory in this paper. It is too complex, and too closely connected to many
difficult issues, including the nature of law, the foundation of ethical
reasoning, and the way human beings develop ethical concepts. Hence
what I shall do is simply to *introduce* the theory, sketching its outlines
in the first half, and suggesting what seem to be certain advantages and
drawbacks of the view in the second half. Much more work needs to be
done before anyone is in a position to embrace the view wholeheartedly,
hence I won't even attempt to argue in any detailed way here that it is
superior to the three traditional views. But I hope my discussion will show
that this theory is promising, and merits considerably more discussion
and study by the larger intellectual community.

## I. THE JUSTIFICATION

Philosophers who write about punishment spend most of their time worrying about whether the *state*'s punishment of criminals is justifiable, so
let us begin with that particular issue.

When does punishment by the state take place? The answer to this
question seems simple: the state carries out punishment upon a person
when he or she has broken a *law*. Yet the fact that the state's punishment
always follows the transgression of a law is surely neither coincidental
nor irrelevant to the understanding and justification of this practice. What

---

*aspect* of the justification of punishment. Morris argues that punishment is sufficiently
complicated to require a justification incorporating all of the justificatory reasons offered
by the traditional theories of punishment as well as by the moral education view. I do not
think this sort of patchwork approach to punishment will work and, in this article, I explore
the idea that the moral education view can, by itself, give an adequate justification of
punishment.

See also Nozick's recent book *Philosophical Explanations* (Cambridge: Harvard University Press, 1981), pp. 363–97.

is the nature of law? This is a thorny problem which has vexed philosophers for hundreds of years. For the purposes of this article, however, let us agree with Hart that there are (at least) two kinds of law, those which are power-conferring rules, for example, rules which specify how to make a contract or a will, and those which are "rules of obligation."[3] We are concerned with the latter kind of rule, and philosophers and legal theorists have generally analyzed the structure of this sort of law as "orders backed by threats" made by the state.

What is the subject matter of these orders? I will contend (consistent with a positivist account of law) that the subject matter *ought* to be (although it might not always be) drawn either from ethical imperatives, of the form "don't steal," or "don't murder," or else from imperatives made necessary for moral reasons, for example, "drive on the right"—so that the safety of others on the road is insured, or "advertise your university job in the professional journals"—so that blacks and women will not be denied an opportunity to secure the job.[4] The state makes these two kinds of commands not only to define a minimal set of duties which a human being in that community must follow in his or her dealings with others, but also to designate actions which, when followed by all members of the society, will solve various problems of conflict and coordination.[5]

And the threat? What role does it play? In the end, this is the central question for which we must have an adequate answer if we are to construct a viable theory of punishment.

The threat, which specifies the infliction of pain if the imperative is not obeyed, gives people a nonmoral incentive, that is, the avoidance of pain, to refrain from the prohibited action. The state hopes this incentive will block a person's performance of the immoral action whenever the ethical incentive fails to do so. But insofar as the threat given in the law is designed to play this kind of "deterring" role, carrying out the threat, that is, punishing someone when he or she has broken the law, is, at least in part, a way of "making good" on the threat. The threat will only deter the disobedience of the state's orders if people believe there is a good chance the pain will be inflicted upon them after they commit the

3. See Hart, *The Concept of Law* (Oxford: Clarendon Press, 1961), chaps. 5 and 6.
4. As stated, this is a positivist definition of law. However, with John Chipman Gray I am maintaining that morality, although not the same as law, should be the source of law. (See Gray's *The Nature and Source of Law* [New York: Macmillan, 1921], p. 84.)
5. See Edna Ullman-Margalit, *The Emergence of Norms* (Oxford: Clarendon Press, 1977) for a discussion of how law can solve coordination and conflict problems.

crime. But if the state punishes in order to make good on its threats, then the deterrence of future crime cannot be wholly irrelevant to the justification of punishment. And anyone, including Kant, who analyzes laws as orders backed by threats must recognize that fact.[6]

Moreover, I believe we must accept the deterrence theorist's contention that the justification of punishment is connected with the fact that it is a necessary tool for preventing future crime and promoting the public's well-being. Consider standard justifications of the state: philosophers from Plato to Kant to Hart have argued that because a community of people cannot tolerate violent and destructive behavior in its midst, it is justified in establishing a state which will coercively interfere in people's lives for publicly announced and agreed-upon reasons so that an unacceptable level of violence and harm can be prevented. Whereas we normally think the state has to respect its citizens' choices about how to live, certain choices, for example, choices to rape, to murder, or to steal, cannot be respected by a community which is committed to preserving and pursuing the well-being of its members. So when the state annexes punishment to these damaging activities, it says that such activities are not a viable option for anyone in that community.

But to say that the state's punishment is needed to prevent crime is not to commit oneself to the deterrence justification of punishment—it all depends on what one takes prevention to entail. And, as Hegel says, if we aimed to prevent wrongdoing only by deterring its commission, we would be treating human beings in the same way that we treat dogs.[7] Consider the kind of lesson an animal learns when, in an effort to leave a pasture, it runs up against an electrified fence. It experiences pain and is conditioned, after a series of encounters with the fence, to stay away from it and thus remain in the pasture. A human being in the same

---

6. Although Kant's position on punishment is officially retributive (see his *Metaphysical Elements of Justice*, trans. J. Ladd [Indianapolis: Bobbs-Merrill, 1965], p. 100, Academy edition, p. 331), his definition of law conflicts with his retributivist position. Note, for example, the deterrent flavor of his justification of law:

> if a certain use of freedom is itself a hindrance to freedom according to universal laws (that is, unjust), then the use of coercion to counteract it, inasmuch as it is the prevention of a hindrance to freedom according to universal laws, is consistent with freedom according to universal laws; in other words, this use of coercion is just (p. 36, Academy edition, p. 231; see also *Metaphysical Elements of Justice*, pp. 18–9, 33–45; Academy edition, pp. 218–21, 229–39).

7. Hegel, *Philosophy of Right*, addition to par. 99, p. 246.

pasture will get the same message and learn the same lesson—"if you want to avoid pain, don't try to transgress the boundary marked by this fence." But, unlike the animal in the pasture, a human being will also be able to reflect on the reasons for that fence's being there, to theorize about *why* there is this barrier to his freedom.

Punishments are like electrified fences. At the very least they teach a person, via pain, that there is a "barrier" to the action she wants to do, and so, at the very least, they aim to deter. But because punishment "fences" are marking *moral* boundaries, the pain which these "fences" administer (or threaten to administer) conveys a larger message to beings who are able to reflect on the reasons for these barriers' existence: they convey that there is a barrier to these actions *because* they are morally wrong. Thus, according to the moral education theory, punishment is not intended as a way of conditioning a human being to do what society wants her to do (in the way that an animal is conditioned by an electrified fence to stay within a pasture); rather, the theory maintains that punishment is intended as a way of teaching the wrongdoer that the action she did (or wants to do) is forbidden because it is morally wrong and should not be done for that reason. The theory also regards that lesson as public, and thus as directed to the rest of society. When the state makes its criminal law and its enforcement practices known, it conveys an educative message not only to the convicted criminal but also to anyone else in the society who might be tempted to do what she did.

Comparing punishments to electrical fences helps to make clear how a certain kind of deterrent message is built into the larger moral point which punishment aims to convey. If one wants someone to understand that an offense is immoral, at the very least one has to convey to him or her that it is prohibited—that it ought not to occur. Pain is the way to convey that message. The pain says "Don't!" and gives the wrongdoer a reason for not performing the action again; an animal shocked by a fence gets the same kind of message and the same kind of incentive. But the state also wants to use the pain of punishment to get the human wrongdoer to reflect on the moral reasons for that barrier's existence, so that he will make the decision to reject the prohibited action for *moral* reasons, rather than for the self-interested reason of avoiding pain.

If those who are punished (or who watch the punishment take place) reject the moral message implicit in the punishment, at least they will learn from it that there is a barrier to the actions they committed (or are

tempted to commit). Insofar as they choose to respond to their punishment (or the punishment of others) merely as a threat, it can keep them
within moral boundaries in the same way that fences keep animals in a
pasture. This deterrent effect of punishment is certainly welcome by the
state whose role is to protect its citizens, and which has erected a "punishment barrier" to certain kinds of actions precisely because those actions will seriously harm its citizens. But on the moral eduation view, it
is incorrect to regard simple deterrence as the aim of punishment; rather,
to state it succinctly, the view maintains that punishment is justified as
a way to prevent wrongdoing insofar as it can teach both wrongdoers and
the public at large the moral reasons for *choosing* not to perform an
offense.

I said at the outset that one of the reasons any punishment theory is
complicated is that it involves one in taking stands on many difficult
ethical and legal issues. And it should be quite clear already that particular
positions on the nature of morality and human freedom are presupposed
by the moral education view which distinguish the theory from its traditional rivals. Given that the goal of punishment, whether carried out
by the state on criminals or by parents on children, is the offender's (as
well as other potential offenders') realization of an action's wrongness,
the moral education view naturally assumes that there is a fact of the
matter about what is right and what is wrong. That is, it naturally rests
on ethical objectivism. Perhaps certain sophisticated subjectivists could
adapt the theory to accommodate their ontological commitments (punishment, they might say, teaches what society defines as right and wrong).
But such an accommodation, in my view, does real damage to the theory,
which purports to explain punishment as a way of conveying when an
action *is* wrong. Given that the theory holds that punishment is a way
of teaching ethical *knowledge*, if there is no such thing, the practice
seems highly suspect.

The theory also takes a strong stand on human freedom. It rests on
the idea that we can act freely in a way that animals cannot. If we were
only like animals, attempts at punishment would affect us in the way
that electrical fences affect animals—they would deter us, nothing more.
But this theory assumes that we are autonomous, that we can choose
and be held accountable for our actions. Thus it holds that punishments
must attempt to do more than simply deter us from performing certain
offenses; they must also, on this view, attempt to provide us with moral

reasons for our *choosing* not to perform these actions. Only creatures who are free to determine their lives according to their moral values can choose not to do an action because it is wrong. Insofar as the moral education view justifies punishment as a way of promoting that moral choice, it assumes that punishment is (and ought only to be) inflicted on beings who are free in this sense.[8] It might be that human beings who have lost their autonomy and who have broken a law can be justifiably treated in a painful way so as to deter them (even as we would deter dangerous animals) from behaving similarly in the future, but this theory would not call such treatment punishment.

Thus one distinction between the moral education view and the deterrence justification of punishment is that on the moral education view, the state is not concerned to use pain coercively so as to progressively eliminate certain types of behavior; rather, it is concerned to educate its citizens morally so that they choose not to engage in this behavior. Moreover, there is another important difference between the two views. On the deterrence view, the infliction of pain on certain individuals is justified as a way of promoting a larger social end. But critics of the deterrence view have pointed out that this is just to say that it is all right to *use* certain individuals to achieve a desirable social goal. The moral education theory, however, does not sanction the use of a criminal for social purposes; on the contrary, it attempts to justify punishment as a way to benefit the person who will experience it, a way of helping him to gain moral knowledge if he chooses to listen. Of course other desirable social goals will be achieved through his punishment, goals which include the education of the larger community about the immorality of the offense, but none of these ends is to be achieved at the expense of the criminal. Instead the moral good which punishment attempts to accomplish within the wrongdoer makes it something which is done *for* him, not *to* him.

There are also sharp differences between the moral education view and various rehabilitative theories of criminal "treatment." An advocate of the moral education view does not perceive punishment as a way of treating a "sick" person for a mental disease, but rather as a way of sending a moral message to a person who has acted immorally and who is to be

8. Kantians who see a close connection between autonomy and moral knowledge will note that this connection is suggested in these remarks.

held responsible for her actions.⁹ And whereas both theorists are concerned with the good which punishment can do for the wrongdoer, they
disagree about what that good is, one defining it as moral growth, the
other as the wrongdoer's acceptance of society's mores and her successful
operation in the community. In addition, as we shall discuss in Section
II, they disagree about what methods to use to achieve these different
ends.

Some readers might wonder how close the moral education view is to
the old retribution theory. Indeed references in the literature to a view
of this type frequently characterize it as a variant of retribution.¹⁰ Nonetheless, there are sharp and important differences between the two views,
which we will explore in more detail in Section II. Suffice to say now
that whereas retributivism understands punishment as performing the
rather metaphysical task of "negating the wrong" and "reasserting the
right," the moral education theorist argues that there is a concrete moral
*goal* which punishment should be designed to accomplish, and that goal
includes the benefiting of the criminal himself. The state, as it punishes
the lawbreaker, is trying to promote his moral personality; it realizes that
"[h]is soul is in jeopardy as his victim's is not."¹¹ Thus, it punishes him
as a way of communicating a moral message to him, which he can accept
or not, as he chooses.

Certain retributivists have also been very attracted to the idea that
punishment is a kind of speech act. For example, Robert Nozick in his
book *Philosophical Explanations* has provided a nice nine-point analysis
of punishment which presents it as a kind of communication and which
fits the account of meaning put forward by H. P. Grice.¹² Yet if punishment is a way of (morally) speaking with a wrongdoer, then why doesn't
this show that it is fundamentally justified *as a communication*, in virtue

9. Rehabilitationists disagree about exactly what disease criminals suffer from. See for
example the various psychiatric diagnoses of Benjamin Karpman in "Criminal Psychodynamics: A Platform," reprinted in *Punishment and Rehabilitation*, ed. J. Murphy (Belmont, CA: Wadsworth, 1973) as opposed to the behaviorist analysis of criminal behavior
offered by B. F. Skinner in *Science and Human Behavior* (New York: Macmillan, 1953),
pp. 182–93 and 446–49.

10. See for example Nozick's characterization of the view as "teleological retributivism,"
pp. 370–74 and Gertrude Ezorsky's use of that term in *Philosophical Perspectives on Punishment*.

11. Morris, "The Paternalistic Theory of Punishment," p. 268.

12. Nozick, pp. 369–80.

of what it is trying to communicate, rather than, in Nozick's view, as some kind of symbolic "linkage" of the criminal with "correct values"?[13]

Indeed, I would maintain that regarding punishment as a kind of moral communication is intuitively very natural and attractive. Consider, for example, what we say when we punish others: a father who punishes his child explains that he does so in order that the child "learn his lesson"; someone who has been physically harmed by another demands punishment "so that she will understand what she did to me"; a judge recently told a well-known user of cocaine that he was receiving a stiff sentence because his "matter-of-fact dabbling in cocaine . . . tells the whole world it is all right to use it."[14] These kinds of remarks accompanying our punishment efforts suggest that our principal concern as we punish is to get the wrongdoer to stop doing the immoral action by communicating to her that her offense was immoral. And the last remark by the judge to the cocaine user shows that when the state punishes it is important that these communications be public, so that other members of society will hear the same moral message. Even people who seem to be seeking revenge on wrongdoers behave in ways which show that they too want to make a moral point not only to the wrongdoer, but to anyone else who will listen. The hero seeking revenge in a Western movie, for example, never simply shoots the bad guy in the back when he finds him—he always confronts the bad guy first (usually in the presence of other people) and tells him *why* he is about to die. Indeed, the movie would be unsatisfying if he didn't make that communication. And surely, the hero's desire to explain his actions is linked with his desire to convey to the bad guy and to others in society that the bad guy had "done him wrong."[15]

Moreover, if one understands punishment as a moral message aimed at educating both the wrongdoer and the rest of society about the immorality of the offense, one has a powerful explanation (at least as powerful as the one offered by retributivism) of why victims so badly want

13. Ibid., pp. 374ff. The point is that if one is going to accept the idea that punishment is a communication, one is connecting it with human purposive activity, and hence the *purpose* of speaking to the criminal (as well as to the rest of society) becomes central to the justification of the communication itself. To deny this is simply to regard punishment as something fundamentally different from a species of communication (for example, to regard it as some kind of "value-linkage device") which Nozick seems reluctant to do.

14. *Los Angeles Times*, 30 July 1981, part 4, p. 1.

15. Nozick has also found the "communication" element in comic book stories about revenge; see *Philosophical Explanations*, pp. 368–69.

their assailants punished. If the point of punishment is to convey to the criminal (and others) that the criminal *wronged* the victim, then punishment is implicitly recognizing the victim's plight, and honoring the moral claims of that individual. Punishment affirms as a *fact* that the victim has been wronged, and as a *fact* that he is owed a certain kind of treatment from others. Hence, on this view, it is natural for the victim to demand punishment because it is a way for the community to restore his moral status after it has been damaged by his assailant.

Thus far, I have concentrated on how the state's punishment of criminals can be justified as an attempt at moral education. But I want to contend that punishment efforts by *any* institution or individual should be perceived as efforts at moral education, although the nature and extensiveness of the legitimate educative roles of these institutions and individuals might differ sharply. For example, I believe it is quite clear that parents want to make such a moral communication through their punishments.[16] Suppose for example, that a mother sees her daughter hitting another child. After stepping in to stop this violent behavior, the mother will reflect on what she can do to prevent its reoccurrence. If the mother chooses to try to do this by punishing her daughter, one of the things she "says" through the punishment is, "if you do this again, you will experience the same unpleasantness," and this message is directed at any other children in the family, as well as at this daughter. Hence, one of the things the mother is doing is introducing the incentive of avoiding pain into the children's "calculations" about how to act if and when they are tempted in the future to hurt each other. If a genuine concern for each other's well-being is absent from the children's minds, at least this incentive (as well as fear of losing her approval) might be strong enough to prevent them from hurting each other in the future.[17] But clearly the mother is also trying to get her children to appreciate that

16. Parental punishment can take many forms; although spanking and various kinds of corporal punishment are usually what spring to mind when one thinks of parental punishment, many parents punish through the expression of anger or disapproval, which can be interpreted by the child as a withdrawal of love or as the (at least temporary) loss of the parent's friendship. Such deprivations are in many ways far more serious than the momentary experience of bodily pain or the temporary loss of certain privileges, and hence, although they seem to be mild forms of punishment, they can in actuality be very severe. I am indebted to Herbert Morris for suggesting this point.

17. Because children are not completely responsible, rational beings, punishing them can also be justified as a way of encouraging in them certain kinds of morally desirable habits, insofar as it has "conditioning like" effects. Aristotle seems to regard punishment

there is a *moral* reason for prohibiting this action. The punishment is supposed to convey the message, "don't do this action again because it is *wrong*; love and not hatred or unwarranted violence is what one should display towards one another." The ultimate goal of the punishment is not merely to deter the child from performing the bad action in the future, but to deter her *by convincing her* (as well as the other children) to renounce the action because it is wrong. And the older and more ethically mature the child becomes, the less the parent will need to resort to punishment to make her moral point, and the more other techniques, like moral suasion, discussion, or debate, will be appropriate.

However, although both state and parental punishment should, according to this theory, be understood as efforts at moral communication and education, the theory does not regard the two kinds of punishment as exactly the same. While punishment should always be regarded as moral education, the "character" of that education can vary enormously, depending in particular on the nature of the institution or individual charged with inflicting the punishment. For example, a parent who is responsible for the full maturation and moral development of her child is naturally thought to be entitled to punish her children for many more offenses and in very different ways, than the children's schoolteacher, or the neighbor down the street. We also think of a university as having punishment rights over its students, but we certainly reject the idea that this sort of institution acts *in loco parentis* towards its students generally. Hence, the theory would not have us understand the punishment role of all institutions, and particularly governments, as the *same* as punishment by parents.[18] None of us, I believe, thinks that the state's role is to teach its citizens the entire content of morality—a role we might characterize as "moral paternalism." A variety of considerations are important in limiting the mode and extent of the state's punishment.

Nonetheless, some readers still might think the moral education theory implies a paternalistic theory of the state—after all, doesn't it maintain that the state can interfere in people's lives for their own good? But when such philosophers as John Stuart Mill have rejected paternalism, what

---

of children as, at least in part, playing this role. See for example *Nicomachean Ethics*, bk. I, chap. 4. I would not want to deny that aspect of parental punishment.

18. It is because I believe there are sharp and important differences between parental and state punishment that I eschew Herbert Morris's title for this type of punishment theory (that is, his title "the paternalistic theory of punishment").

they have rejected is a certain position on what should be law; specifically, they have rejected the state's passing any law which would restrict what an individual can do to *himself* (as opposed to what he can do to another). They have not objected to the idea that when the state justifiably interferes in someone's life *after* he has broken a law (which prohibited harm to another), it should intend good rather than evil towards the criminal. Now it is possible they might call this theory paternalistic anyway, not because it takes any stand on what should be law, but because it views the state's punishment as interference in his life plans without his consent for his own good. But why should paternalism in this sense be offensive? It would be strange indeed if philosophers insisted that the state should only try to prevent further harm to the community by actively intending to harm, or use, or at least be indifferent to, the people it punishes!

But, Mill might complain, if you are willing to allow the state to morally educate those who harm others, why not allow it to morally educate those who harm themselves? This is a good question, but one the moral education theory cannot answer. Indeed, answering it is the same as answering the question: What ought to be made law? Or, alternatively, what is the appropriate area for legislation? Though central to political theory, these questions are ones to which the moral education theory can give no answer, for while the theory maintains that punishment of a certain sort should follow the transgression of a law, it is no part of the theory to say *what* ethical reasons warrant the imposition of a law. Indeed, one of the advantages of the theory is that one can adopt it no matter what position one occupies on the political spectrum.

But, critics might insist, isn't this theory arguing that the state should be in the business of deciding and enforcing morality, overriding the autonomous moral decisions of its citizens? Yes, that is exactly the theory's point, the state *is* in that business in a very limited way. Imagine a murderer saying: "You, the state, have no right to tell me that my murder of this man is wrong," or a rapist protesting: "Who is the state to tell me that my rape of this woman is immoral?" These statements sound absurd, because we believe not merely that such actions are wrong, but that they are also heinous and morally appalling. The state is justified in punishing rapists and murderers because their choices about what to do betray a serious inability to make decisions about immoral and moral actions, which has resulted in substantial harm to some members of that community. And while some readers might find it offensive to contemplate the state presuming to morally educate anyone but serious felons, is this not exactly the kind of sentiment behind the libertarians' call for extensive constraints on the state's role and power?

Moreover, I wonder whether, by calling this theory paternalistic, one might not be irritated more by the thought of being governed than by the thought of what this particular theory says being governed involves. Yet, unless one is prepared to be an anarchist, one must admit that being governed is necessary as long as we, as human beings, are prone to immoral acts. We do not outgrow cruelty, or meanness, or the egoistic disregard for others when we reach the age of majority. On this view, the state exists because even adults need to be governed, although not in the way that children require governing by their parents. (Indeed, these ideas suggested by the theory form a germ of an argument against anarchism, which I can only pursue in another place.)

But, critics might insist, it is this theory's view of what governing involves that is objectionable. Who and what is the state, that it can presume to teach us a moral lesson? Yet I regard this question not as posing a challenge to the moral education view itself, but rather as posing a challenge *by* that theory to any existing state. Not only does the theory offer a partial explanation of the state's role, but it also proposes a view of what the state *ought* to be like if its punishment activities have any legitimacy. For example, insofar as the state should be morally educating when it punishes, this theory implies that the state's laws should be arrived at by reflection on what is right or wrong, and not on what is in the best interest of a particular class, or race, or sex. That this is not always true of the laws of our society is an indictment of our state, and punishments inflicted as a way of enforcing these biased laws cannot be justified. Moreover, if we accept the idea that the state is supposed to morally educate its citizens, it is natural to argue that all of its citizens should participate either directly or through representatives in the legislative branch of that institution in order to control and supervise its moral enforcement so that the resulting laws reflect the moral consensus of the community rather than the views of one class. Hence the moral education view can underlie an argument for the democratic structure of a state.

Finally, I would contend that the moral education theory illuminates better than any of its theoretical rivals the strategy of those who are civilly disobedient. Martin Luther King, Jr. wrote that it is critical for anyone who wants to be civilly disobedient to accept the penalty for his or her lawbreaking, not only to express "the very highest respect for law" but also "to arouse the conscience of the community over its injustice."[19] The moral education theory explains how both these objectives are achieved. The civilly disobedient person, when she accepts the penalty for law-breaking, is respecting the state's right to punish transgressors of its laws, but she is also forcing the state to commit itself, in full view of the rest of society, to the idea that her actions show she needs moral education. And when that person is protesting, as Gandhi or King did, offensive and unjust laws, she knows the state's punishment will appear morally outrageous and will arouse the conscience of anyone sensitive to the claims of justice. Therefore, the civilly disobedient person is, on this view, using the idea of what the state and its laws ought to be like if its punishment activities have legitimacy in order to effect moral improvement in the legal system.

## II. QUESTIONS AND CRITICISMS

Although I will not fully develop and defend the moral education view in this article, I now want to put some flesh on the skeletal presentation of the view just given by considering some questions which spring naturally to mind as one reflects on the theory.

*1. What is this theory's punishment formula?* Punishment formulas always follow directly from punishment justifications. If punishment is justified as a deterrent, then it follows from that justification that particular punishments should be structured so as to deter. But if punishment is justified as a way of morally educating the wrongdoer and the rest of society about the immorality of the act, then it follows that one should punish in ways that promote this two-part goal. But how do we go about structuring punishments that morally educate? And would this way of determining punishments yield intuitively more just punishments than those yielded by the formulas of the traditional theories?

One reason these formulas of all the traditional theories have been attacked as unjust is that all of them fail to incorporate an acceptable upper bound on what punishments can be legitimately inflicted on an

19. Martin Luther King, Jr., "Letter from a Birmingham Jail," from *Civil Disobedience*, ed. H. A. Bedau (New York: Pegasus, 1969), pp. 78–9.

offender. Consider that, once the deterrence theorist has defined his deterrence goal, any punishment that will achieve this goal is justified, including the most brutalizing. Similarly, the retributivist's *lex talionis* punishment formula (dictating that punishments are to be somehow equal to the crime) would seem to recommend, for example, torturing the torturer, murdering *all* murderers, and such recommendations cast serious doubt on the formula's moral adequacy.[20] Even the rehabilitation theory does not place strict limits on the kinds of "treatments" which can legitimately be given to offenders. If the psychiatric "experts" decide that powerful drugs, shock treatments, lobotomies or other similar medical procedures are legitimate and necessary treatments of certain criminals, why shouldn't they be used? The only upper bound on the treatments inherent in this theory derives from the consciences of psychiatrists and their consensus about what constitutes "reasonable" treatment, and many contend that history has shown such an upper bound to be far too high.[21]

The moral education theory, however, does seem to have the resources to generate a reasonable upper limit on how much punishment the state can legitimately administer. Because part of the goal of punishment is to educate the criminal, this theory insists that as he is educated, his autonomy must be respected. The moral education theorist does not want "education" confused with "conditioning." Shock treatments or lobotomies that would damage or destroy the criminal's freedom to choose are not appropriate educative techniques. On this view the goal of punishment is not to destroy the criminal's freedom of choice, but to persuade him to use his freedom in a way consistent with the freedom of others. Thus, any punishment that would damage the autonomy of the criminal is ruled out by this theory.

20. Some retributivists have tried to argue that the *lex talionis* needn't be regarded as a formula whose upper bound *must* be respected; see, for example, K. C. Armstrong, "The Retributivist Hits Back," *Philosophy of Punishment*, ed. H. B. Acton (London: Macmillan, 1969). However, critics can object that Armstrong's weaker retributivist position still does not *rule out* barbaric punishments (like torture) as permissible, nor does it explain why and when punishments which are less in severity than the criminal act can be legitimately inflicted.

21. Consider the START program used in a Connecticut prison to "rehabilitate" child molesters: electrodes were connected to the prisoner's skin, and then pictures of naked boys and girls were flashed on a screen while electric shocks were applied. The Federal Bureau of Prisons canceled this program just before they were about to lose a court challenge to the program's constitutionality (see David J. Rothman's discussion of this in "Behavior Modification in Total Institutions," *Hastings Center Report* 5, no. 1 [1975]: 22).

223                                    *The Moral Education*
                                      *Theory of Punishment*

In addition, it is important to remember that, on this view, punishments should be designed to convey to the criminal and to the rest of society the idea that the criminal's act was wrong. And it seems difficult if not impossible for the state to convey this message if it is carrying out cruel and disfiguring punishments such as torture or maiming. When the state climbs into the moral gutter with the criminal in this way it cannot credibly convey either to the criminal or to the public its moral message that human life must always be respected and preserved, and such actions can even undercut its justification for existing. Note that both of these considerations indicate this theory rules out execution as punishment.[22] (Of course, the moral education theory says nothing about whether the execution of criminals might be justified not as punishment but as a method of "legitimate elimination" of criminals who are judged to have lost all of their essential humanity, making them wild beasts of prey on a community that must, to survive, destroy them. Whether such a justification of criminal execution can be morally tolerable is something I do not want to explore here.)

But, the reader might wonder, how can inflicting *any* pain upon a criminal be morally educational? And why isn't the infliction of mild sorts of pains and deprivations also climbing into the moral gutter with the criminal? The moral education theorist must provide an explanation of why certain sorts of painful experiences (whose infliction on others we would normally condemn) may legitimately be inflicted in order to facilitate moral growth. But is such an explanation possible? And even if it is, would the infliction of pain always be the right way to send a moral message? If a criminal's psychological make-up is such that pain would not reform him, whereas "inflicting" a pleasurable experience would produce this reform, are we therefore justified only in giving him that pleasurable experience? Retributivists like Robert Nozick think the answer to this last question is yes, and thus reject the view as an adequate justification of punishment by itself.[23]

---

22. Apart from the fact that killing someone is hardly an appropriate technique for educating him, it is likely that this action sends a poor message to the rest of society about the value of human life. Indeed, in one of their national meetings, the Catholic bishops of the United States argued that repeal of capital punishment would send "a message that we can break the cycle of violence, that we need not take life for life, that we can envisage more human and more hopeful and effective responses to the growth of violent crime." ("Statement on Capital Punishment," *Origins* 10, no. 24 [27 November 1980]: 374.)

23. Nozick, pp. 373–74.

All three of these worries would be allayed if the moral education theorist could show that only the infliction of pain of a certain sort following a wrongdoing is *necessarily* connected with the promotion of the goal of moral education. In order to establish this necessary connection between certain sorts of painful experiences and moral growth, the moral education theorist needs an account of what moral concepts are, and an account of how human beings come to acquire them (that is, what moral education is). I cannot even attempt to propose, much less develop, answers to these central ethical issues here. But I will try to offer reasons for thinking that painful experiences of a particular sort would seem to be necessary for the communication of a certain kind of moral message.

It is useful to start our discussion by getting a good understanding of what actions count as punishment. First, if we see punishment from the offender's standpoint, we appreciate that it involves the loss of her freedom. This is obviously true when one is locked up in a penitentiary, but it is also true when, for example, parents stop their child's allowance (money that had previously been defined as hers is withheld—whether she likes it or not) or when they force her to experience a spanking or a lecture. I would argue that this loss of freedom is why (autonomous) human beings so dislike punishment. Second, whereas it is very natural to characterize punishment as involving pain or other unpleasant consequences, the infliction of what we intuitively want to call punishment might involve the wrongdoer in performing actions which one would not normally describe as painful or unpleasant. For example, a doctor who cheated the Medicare system and who is sentenced to compulsory weekend service in a state-supported clinic would not be undergoing what one would normally describe as a painful or unpleasant experience (he isn't being incarcerated, whipped, fined). Nonetheless, insofar as some of his free time is being taken away from him, the state is depriving him of his freedom to carry out his own plans and to pursue the satisfaction of his own interests. In this case, the state is clearly punishing an offender, but it sounds distorted to say that it is inflicting pain on him. Thus we need a phrase to describe punishment which will capture better than "infliction of pain" all of the treatments which we intuitively want to call punishment. For this purpose I propose the phrase "disruption of the freedom to pursue the satisfaction of one's desires," a phrase which is suitably general and which fits a wide variety of experiences that we want to call

225                                    *The Moral Education*
                                       *Theory of Punishment*


experiences of *punishment*. (It may well be *too* general, but I do not want
to pursue that issue here.)[24]

Thus I understand punishment as an experience which a wrongdoer
is forced by an authority to undergo in virtue of the fact that he has
transgressed (what ought to be) a morally derived rule laid down by that
authority, and which disrupts (in either a major or a minor way) the
wrongdoer's freedom to pursue the satisfaction of his desires. Given that
punishment is understood in this way, how do coercion and the disruption
of one's self-interested pursuits convey a *moral* message?

Before answering this question, it is important to make clear that punishment is only *one* method of moral education. Upon reflection, it is
clear, I think, that we choose to employ this method only when we're
trying to teach someone that an action is *wrong*, rather than when we
are trying to teach someone what (imperfect) moral duties he or she
ought to recognize. (We punish a child when he kicks his brother; we
don't punish him in order to get him to give Dad a present on Father's
Day.)

What is one trying to get across when one wants to communicate an
action's wrongness? The first thing one wants to convey is that the action
is forbidden, prohibited, "fenced off." Consider a mother who sees her
child cheating at solitaire. She might say to the child, "You mustn't do
that." Or if she saw her child putting his left shoe on his right foot, she
would likely say, "No, you mustn't dress that way." In both cases it would
be highly inappropriate for her to follow these words with punishment.
She is communicating to her child that what he is doing in these circumstances is inadvisable, imprudent, not playing by the rules, but she
is not communicating (and not trying to communicate) the idea that such
actions violate one's moral duty to others (or, for that matter, one's moral
duty to oneself). Now consider this mother seeing her son kick the neighbor's young daughter. Once again she might say, "You mustn't do that,"

24. George Fletcher, in *Rethinking Criminal Law* (Boston: Little, Brown, 1978), p. 410,
worries about defining punishment so that it doesn't include too much (for example, it
should not include the impeachment of President Nixon, despite the fact that it would be
a case of unpleasant consequences inflicted on Nixon by an authority in virtue of a wrongdoing). I do not have time here to consider how to hone my definition such that it will not
encompass impeachments, deportation, tort damages, and so forth. Indeed, perhaps the
only way one can do this is to bring into the definition of punishment its justification as
moral education.

to the child, but the "mustn't" in the mother's words here is unique. It is more than "you shouldn't" or "it isn't advisable" or "it's against the rules of the game." Rather, it attempts to convey the idea that the action is forbidden, prohibited, intolerable.

But merely telling the child that he "mustn't do that" will not effectively convey to the child that there is this profound moral boundary. Without punishment why shouldn't the child regard the "mustn't" in the parent's statement just as he did the "mustn't" in "You mustn't cheat at solitaire"? The mother needs to get across to the child the very special nature of the prohibition against this immoral act. How can she do this? Consider the fact that someone who (for no moral reason) violates a positive duty to others is not acting out of any interest in the other's well-being. A teenager who steals from a passer-by because she needs the money, a man who rapes a woman so that he can experience a sense of power and mastery—such people are performing immoral acts in order to satisfy their own needs and interests, insensitive to the needs and interests of the people they hurt. The way to communicate to such people that there is a barrier of a very special sort against these kinds of actions would seem to be to link performance of the actions with what such people care about most—the pursuit of their own pleasure. Only when disruption of that pursuit takes place will a wrongdoer appreciate the special force of the "mustn't" in the punisher's communication. So the only effective way to "talk to" such people is through the disruption of their own interests, that is, through punishment (which has been defined as just such a disruption).

What conclusions will a person draw from this disruption of his pleasure? At the very least he will conclude that his society (in the guise of the family, the state, the university, etc.) has erected a barrier to that kind of action, and that if he wants to pursue the satisfaction of his own desires, he won't perform that action again. So at the very least, he will understand his punishment as society's attempt to deter him from committing the action in the future. Such a conclusion does not have moral content. The person views his punishment only as a sign of society's condemnation of the act, not as a sign of the act's *wrongness*. But it is a start, and a *necessary first start*. If a wrongdoer has little or no conception of an action's wrongness, then the first thing one must do is to communicate to him that the action is prohibited. We must put up the electrical fence in an attempt to keep him out of a forbidden realm.

*The Moral Education*
                                    *Theory of Punishment*

But given that we want the offender to understand the moral reasons for the action's condemnation, how can punishment communicate those reasons? The punisher wants the wrongdoer to move from the first stage of the educative process initiated by punishment—the realization that society prohibits the action—to a second stage, where the moral reasons for the condemnation of the action are understood and accepted. Can punishment, involving the disruption of a person's self-interested pursuits, help an offender to arrive at this final moral conclusion, to understand, in other words, why this fence has been erected?

What is it that one wants the wrongdoer to see? As we noted before, someone who (for no moral reason) violates her (perfect) moral duty to others is not thinking about the others' needs and interests, and most likely has little conception of, or is indifferent to, the pain her actions caused another to suffer. Hence, what the punisher needs to do is to communicate to the wrongdoer *that* her victims suffered and how much they suffered, so that the wrongdoer can appreciate the harmfulness of her action. How does one get this message across to a person insensitive to others? Should not such a person be made to endure an unpleasant experience designed, in some sense, to "represent" the pain suffered by her victim(s)? This is surely the intuition behind the *lex talionis* but it best supports the concept of punishment as moral education. As Nozick admits,[25] it is very natural to regard the pain or unpleasantness inflicted by the wrongdoer as the punisher's way of saying: "This is what you did to another. You hate it; so consider how your victim felt." By giving a wrongdoer something like what she gave to others, you are trying to drive home to her just how painful and damaging her action was for her victims, and this experience will, one hopes, help the wrongdoer to understand the immorality of her action.

Of course, the moral education formula does not recommend that punishments be specifically *equal* to the crime—in many instances this doesn't even make sense. But what does the "representation" of the wrongful act involve, if not actual equality? This is a terribly difficult question, and I find I can only offer tentative, hesitant answers. One way the moral education theorist can set punishments for crimes is to think about "fit." Irrespective of how severe a particular crime is, there will sometimes be a punishment that seems naturally suited to it; for example, giving a

25. Compare Nozick's discussion of the content of the Gricean message of punishment, pp. 370–74.

certain youth charged with burglarizing and stealing money from a neighbor's house the punishment of supervised compulsory service to this neighbor for a period of time, or giving a doctor charged with cheating a government medical insurance program the punishment of compulsory unremunerated service in a state medical institution. And probably such punishments seem to fit these crimes because they force the offender to compensate the victim, and thus help to heal more effectively the "moral wound" which the offense has caused. Another way the moral education theorist can make specific punishment recommendations is to construct an ordinal scale of crimes, going from most offensive to least offensive, and then to link determinate sentences to each crime, respecting this ordinal comparison, and insuring proportionality between crime and punishment. But it is not easy to use either method to fashion a tidy punishment table because it is not easy to determine which painful experiences will be educative but not cruel, both proportional to the offense committed and somehow relevant to that offense. Indeed, our society has been notoriously unsuccessful in coming up with punishments that are in any way morally educative. And I would argue that it speaks in favor of this theory that it rejects many forms of incarceration used today as legitimate punishments, insofar as they tend to make criminals morally worse rather than better.

But even if this theory can tell us how to represent wrongdoing in a punishment, it must still handle other questions which I do not have time to pursue properly in this article. For example, how does that representation help the wrongdoer to understand and *accept* the fact that she did wrong and should do otherwise in the future? And if we want to send the most effective message possible in order to bring about this acceptance, should we try to tailor punishments to the particular psychological and moral deficiencies of the wrongdoer, or must considerations of equal treatment and fairness override this? Finally, does the view justify the state's punishing people who are innocent of any illegal act but who seem to need moral education?

The theory has a very interesting and complicated response to this last question. We have said that punishment is not the appropriate method to teach every sort of moral lesson, but only the lesson that a certain action is wrong. But on whom is the state justified in imposing such a lesson?—clearly, a person who has shown she needs the lesson by committing a wrong which the state had declared illegal, and clearly *not* a person who has shown she already understands this lesson (at least in some sense) by conscientiously obeying that law. We also believe that the state is justified in imposing this lesson on a person who has not broken that law but who has *tried* to do so. She might, for example, be punished for "attempted murder" or "attempted kidnapping." (And do we make the punishments for such attempts at wrongdoing less than for successful wrongdoings because we're not sure the attempts provide conclusive evidence that such people would have carried through?) But what about a person who has not broken a law or even attempted to do so but who has, say, talked about doing so publicly? Is that enough evidence that she needs moral education? Probably—by *some* person or institution, but not by the state. The point is that we believe the state should refrain from punishing immoral people who have nonetheless committed no illegal act, not because they don't need moral education but because the state is not the appropriate institution to effect that education. Indeed, one of the reasons we insist that the state operate by enacting laws is that doing so defines when it may coercively interfere in the lives of its citizens and when it may not; its legislation, in other words, defines the extent of its educative role (and there might exist constitutional rules guiding this legislation). So if the state were to interfere with its citizens' lives when they had not broken its laws, it would exceed its own legitimate role. In the end, the state may not punish immoral people who are innocent of any crime not because they don't need moral education, but because the state is not justified in giving it to them.

However, there is another question relevant to the issue of punishing the innocent. Given that I have represented the moral education theory as having a two-part goal—the moral education of the criminal and the moral education of the rest of society—it might be that a punishment which would achieve one part of this goal would not be an effective way of realizing the other part. Must we choose between these two objectives, or is it possible to show that they are inextricably linked? And if they are not, could it be that in order to pursue the goal of morally educating *society*, it would be necessary to punish an innocent person? More generally, could it be justifiable on this view to punish a wrongdoer much more (or much less) severely than her offense (if any) would seem to warrant if doing so would further society's moral education? If this were true, the theory would not preserve proportionality between crime and punishments. However, there are reasons for thinking that educating the criminal and educating the community are inextricably linked. For example, if the state aims to convey a moral lesson to the community about how other human beings should be treated, it will completely fail to do so if it inflicts pain on someone innocent of any wrongdoing—indeed, it would send a message exactly contrary to the one it had intended. But even if we suppose, for the sake of argument, that these educational objectives could become disengaged, we can preserve proportionality between a person's crime and her punishment by making the moral education of the criminal lexically prior to the moral education of the community (after all, we *know* she needs the lesson, we're less sure about the community).[26]

However, giving adequate arguments for solutions to any of the problems I have posed in this section requires a much more fully developed account of what moral education is and of how punishment would help to effect it. Some readers might think that developing such an account is simply an empirical rather than a philosophical task. But before we can know how to morally educate, we need a better theoretical understanding of what moral knowledge is, and why human beings do wrong. (Is it because, as Kant insists, we choose to defy the power of the moral law or because, as Socrates argues, we are morally ignorant?) Moreover, we need a better appreciation of the source and extent of the state's authority if we are to understand its legitimate role as moral educator. Further work on this theory has to come to grips with these issues in moral and political philosophy before we can know whether to embrace it. But I have tried to suggest in my remarks in this section that certain kinds of approaches to these issues are at least promising.

2. *Is the moral education of most criminals just a pipe dream?* How can we really expect hard-core criminals convicted of serious offenses to be able to change and morally improve? In answer to this last question, the moral education theorist will admit that the state can predict that many of the criminals it punishes will refuse to accept the moral message it delivers. As I have stressed, the moral education theory rests on the assumption of individual autonomy, and thus an advocate of this theory must not only admit but insist that the choice of whether to listen to the moral message contained in the punishment belongs to the criminal.

26. I have profited from discussions with Katherine Shamey on this point.

231                              *The Moral Education*
                                 *Theory of Punishment*


Thus it is very unlikely that society will be 100 percent successful in its
moral education efforts, no matter how well it uses the theory to structure
punishments.

   But at least the punishment the state delivers can have a deterrent
effect; even if the criminal refuses to understand the state's communication about why there is a barrier to his action, at least he will understand
*that* the barrier exists. Hegel once wrote that if a criminal is coerced by
a punishment, it is because he *chooses* to be so coerced; such a person
rejects the moral message and accepts instead the avoidance of pain as
his sole reason for avoiding the action.[27] In the end, punishments might
only have deterrent effects because that is all wrongdoers will let them
have.

   However, neither the state nor anyone else can determine who the
"losers" are. None of us can read another's mind, none of us knows the
pressures, beliefs, and concerns motivating another's actions and decisions. The state cannot, even with the help of a thousand psychiatrists,
*know for sure* who is a hopeless case and who isn't. Nor is this just a
simple epistemological problem. Insofar as the state, on this view, should
regard each person it punishes as autonomous, it is committed to the
view that the choice of whether to reform or not is a free one, and hence
one the state cannot hope to predict. Finally, the state's assumption that
the people it is entitled to punish are free means it must never regard
any one it punishes as hopeless, insofar as it is assuming that each of
these persons still has the ability to choose to be moral. Thus, as Hegel
puts it,[28] punishment is the criminal's "right" as a free person—to refuse
to punish him on the grounds that he has been diagnosed as hopeless is
to regard him as something other than a rational human being.

   But even if it seems likely that punishing some criminals will not effect
their moral growth, and may not even deter them, the moral education
of the community about the nature of their crimes can still be promoted
by their punishment. Indeed any victim of crime is going to be very
sensitive to this fact, insofar as he has been the one against whom the
wrong has been committed, and is the one who is most interested in
having the community acknowledge that what happened to him *shouldn't*
have happened. And as long as the person whom we punish is admitted
to be an autonomous human being, we cannot be convicted of using her

27. See Hegel, *Philosophy of Right*, sec. 91.
28. Ibid., sec. 100, p. 70.

as we educate the community about the wrongness of her offense, because we are doing something to her which is *for* her, which can achieve a great deal of good for her, if she will but let it.

3. *Shouldn't the moral education theory imply an indeterminate sentencing policy?* Throughout your discussion, rehabilitationists might complain, you have been assuming that punishment by the state should proceed from determinate sentences for specific crimes. But isn't indeterminate sentencing fairer? Why keep a criminal who has learned his moral lesson in jail just because his sentence has not run out, and why release a criminal who is unrepentant and who will probably harm the public again, just because his sentence has run out?

However, the moral education theorist has very good reasons, provided by the foundations of the theory itself, for rejecting the concepts of indeterminate sentencing and parole boards. First, this theorist would strongly disagree with the idea that a criminal should continue to receive "treatment" until his reform has been effected. Recall that it is an important tenet of the view that the criminals we punish are free beings, responsible for their actions. And you can't *make* a free human being believe something. In particular, you can't coerce people to be just for justice's sake. Punishment is the state's attempt to teach a moral lesson, but whether or not the criminal will listen and accept it is up to the criminal himself.

The moral education theorist takes this stand not simply because she believes one ought to respect the criminal's autonomy, but also because she believes one has no choice but to respect it. The fact that parole boards in this country have tried to coerce repentance is, from the standpoint of this theorist, a grave and lamentable mistake. (Consider James McConnell's claim, in an article in *Psychology Today*, that "Somehow we've got to *force* people to love one another, to force them to want to behave properly.")[29] Indeed, critics of present parole systems in the United States maintain that these systems only open the way for manipulation.[30] The parole board uses the threat of the refusal of parole to get the kind of behavior it wants from the criminal, and the criminal manipulates

29. From "Criminals Can be Brainwashed—Now," *Psychology Today*, April 1970, p. 14; also quoted in Rick Carlson's *The Dilemma of Corrections* (Lexington, MA: Lexington Books, 1976), p. 35.

30. See "The Crime of Treatment," American Friends Service Committee from *The Struggle for Justice*, chap. 6 (New York: Hill and Wang, 1971) reprinted in *Punishment: Selected Readings*, eds., Feinberg and Gross.

back—playing the game, acting reformed, just to get out. In the process, no moral message is conveyed to the criminal, and probably no real reformation takes place. The high recidivism rate in the United States tells the tale of how successful parole boards have been in evaluating the rehabilitation of prisoners. As one prisoner put it: "If they ask if this yellow wall is blue, I'll say, of course it's blue. I'll say anything they want me to say if they're getting ready to let me go."[31]

The moral education theorist doesn't want the state to play this game. A sentence for a crime is set, and when the criminal breaks a law, the sentence is inflicted on him as a way of teaching him that what he did was wrong. When the sentence is up, the criminal is released. The state hopes its message was effective, but whether it was or not is largely up to the criminal himself.

There is another important reason why the moral education theorist does not want to insist on repentance before release. Even a good state can make mistakes when it enacts law. It is not just possible but probable that the state at one time or another will declare a certain action immoral which some of its citizens will regard as highly moral. These citizens will often decide to disobey this "immoral" law, and while being punished, will steadfastly refuse to repent for an action they believe was right. Martin Luther King, Jr., never repented for breaking various segregation laws in the South while he was in jail; few draft resisters repented for refusing to go to Vietnam when they were in prison. By not insisting on the repentance of its criminals, the state is, once again, respecting the freedom of its citizens—particularly each citizen's freedom of conscience, and their right, as free beings, to disagree with its rulings. Hence, the moral education theorist doesn't want the state to insist on repentance because it doesn't want Solzhenitsyns rotting in jail until they have "reformed."[32]

How can the moral education theorist justify the punishment of a criminal who is already repentant prior to his sentencing, or who repents

31. Quoted by Carlson, p. 161; from David Fogel, *We Are the Living Proof* (Cincinnati: W. H. Anderson, n.d.).

32. Jeffrie Murphy has argued that instituting a rehabilitationist penal system would deny prisoners many of their present due process rights. See "Criminal Punishment and Psychiatric Fallacies," especially pp. 207–209, in *Punishment and Rehabilitation,* ed. J. Murphy. The American Friends Service Committee has also charged that the California penal system, which was heavily influenced by the rehabilitation theory, has in fact done this. See "The Crime of Treatment," pp. 91-93, in Feinberg et al.

before his sentence is completely served? The theorist's response to this question is complicated. Because it is difficult to be sure that a seemingly repentant criminal is *truly* repentant, and thus because a policy of suspending or shortening sentences for those who seem repentant to the authorities could easily lead the criminal to fake repentance before a court or a parole board, the moral education theorist would be very reluctant to endorse such a policy.

Moreover, it might well be the case that, prior to or during sentencing, a criminal's experience of repentance is produced in large part by the expectation of receiving the full punishment, so that the state's subsequent failure to inflict it could lead to a weakening of the criminal's renunciation of the action. Like a bad but repentant child who will conclude, if he is not punished by his parents, that his action must not have been so bad, the repentant criminal might well need to experience his complete sentence in order to "learn his lesson" effectively.

Finally, the lesson learning effected by punishment can also involve a purification process for a wrongdoer, a process of healing. As Herbert Morris has written, experiencing the pain of punishment can be a kind of catharsis for the criminal, a way of "burning out" the evil in his soul.[33] Novelists like Dostoevsky have explored the criminal's need, born of guilt and shame, to experience pain at the hands of the society he has wronged in order to be reconciled with them. Thus the rehabilitationist who would deny the criminal the experience of pain at the hands of the state would deny him what he may want and need to be forgiven—both by society and by himself. And punishment understood as moral education would explain how it could be perceived as a purification process. For how is it that one overcomes shame? Is it not by becoming a person *different* from the one who did the immoral action? The subsiding of shame in us seems to go along with the idea, "Given who I was, I did the action then, but I'm different now—I'm *better* now—and I wouldn't do the same act again." But how do we become different, how do we change, improve? Insofar as punishment is seen as a way of educating oneself about the offense, undergoing that experience is a way of changing for the better. It might well be the yearning for that change which drives a person like Raskolnikov towards his punishment.

Nonetheless, if there were clear evidence that a criminal was very

33. See Morris's discussion of certain wrongdoers' need to experience punishment in "The Paternalistic Theory of Punishment," p. 267.

235                                 *The Moral Education*
                                    *Theory of Punishment*

remorseful for his action and had already experienced great pain because of his crime (had "suffered enough"), this theory would endorse a suspension of his sentence or else a pardon (*not* just a parole). His moral education would have already been accomplished, and the example of his repentance would be lesson enough for the general public. (Indeed, punishment under these circumstances would make the state appear vindictive.) In addition, because the state conceives itself to be punishing a wrong, it is appropriate for it to allow certain sorts of excuses and mitigating circumstances to lessen the penalty normally inflicted for the crime in question.

   4. *Does the moral education theory actually presuppose the truth of retribution?* Retributivists have a very interesting criticism of the moral education theory available to them. Granted, they might maintain, that punishment is connected with moral education, still this only provides an additional reason for punishing someone—it does not provide the fundamental justification of punishment. That fundamental justification, they would argue, is retributive: wrongdoers simply *deserve* to experience pain for the sake of the wrong they have committed. As Kant has argued, however much good one intends one's punishment to effect,

> yet it must first be justified in itself as punishment, i.e. as mere harm, so that if it stopped there, and the person punished could get no glimpse of kindness hidden behind this harshness, he must yet admit that justice was done him, and that his reward was perfectly suitable to his conduct.[34]

Moreover, such modern retributivists as Walter Moberly have argued that it is only when the wrongdoer can assent to his punishment as already justified in virtue of his offense that the punishment can do him any good.[35]

   In a certain sense, Moberly's point is simply that a criminal will perceive his punishment as vindictive and vengeful unless he understands or accepts the fact that it is justified. But should the justification of punishment be cashed out in terms of the retributive concept of desert, given that it has been difficult for retributivists to say what they mean by the

34. Kant, *Critique of Practical Reason*, "The Analytic of Pure Practical Reason," Remark II. (Abbott trans. in *Kant's Theory of Ethics* [London: Longman, 1959], p. 127; Academy edition, p. 38.)

35. Walter Moberly, *The Ethics of Punishment*, (London: Faber & Faber, 1968), p. 141.

criminal's "deserving" punishment simply in virtue of his offense? Robert Nozick tries to cash out the retributive link between crime and "deserved" punishment by saying that the punishment represents a kind of "linkage" between the criminal and "right values."[36] But why is inflicting pain on someone a way of effecting this linkage? Why isn't the infliction of a pleasurable experience for the sake of the crime just as good a way of linking the wrongdoer with these right values? And if Nozick explains the linkage of pain with crime by saying that the pain is necessary in order to communicate to the criminal that his action was wrong, he has answered the question but lost his retributive theory. Other philosophers, like Hegel,[37] speak of punishment as a way of "annulling" or "canceling" the crime and hence "deserved" for that reason. But although Hegel's words have a nice metaphorical ring to them, it is hard to see how they can be given a literal force that will explain the retributivist concept of desert. As J. L. Mackie has written, insofar as punishment occurs after the crime, it certainly cannot cancel it—past events are not eliminated by later ones.[38]

It is partly because retributivists have been at a loss to explain the notion of desert implicit in their theory of punishment that I have sought to propose and explore a completely nonretributivist justification of punishment. But my reasons for rejecting retributivism are deeper. The retributive position is that it is somehow morally appropriate to inflict pain for pain, to take an eye for an eye, a tooth for a tooth. But how is it ever morally appropriate to inflict one evil for the sake of another? How is the society that inflicts the second evil any different from the wrongdoer who has inflicted the first? He strikes first, they strike back; why is the second strike acceptable but the first not? Plato, in a passage quoted at the start of this article, insists that both harms are wrong; and Jesus attacks retributivism[39] for similar reasons:

36. Nozick, pp. 374ff.

37. For example, see Hegel, *The Philosophy of Right*, sec. 101–103.

38. J. L. Mackie, "Morality and the Retributive Emotions," in *Criminal Justice Ethics* 1, no. 1 (Winter/Spring 1982): 3–10. In the face of the retributivists' failure to explain why punishment is deserved, Mackie wants to argue that our retributive intuitions spring from fundamental retributive emotions, which are part of a human being's fundamental moral make-up (and he gives a sketch of how our evolution as a species could have generated such emotions). But many retributivists, particularly the Kantian sort, would eschew such an explanation which, in any case, is hardly a *justification* of the retributive impulse itself.

39. Jesus rejected not only "negative retributivism," that is, the idea that we deserve bad

> You have learned that they were told, 'Eye for eye, tooth for tooth'. But
> what I tell you is this: Do not set yourself against the man who wrongs
> you. . . . You have heard that they were told 'Love your neighbor, hate
> your enemy'. But what I tell you is this: Love your enemy and pray for
> your persecutors; only so can you be children of your heavenly father,
> who makes the sun rise on good and bad alike, and sends the rain on
> the honest and dishonest. [Matt. 5:38–9, 43–6]

In other words, both reject retributivism because they insist that the only
thing human beings "deserve" in this life is *good*, that no matter what
evil a person has committed, no one is justified in doing further evil to
her.

But if one accepts the idea that no one can ever deserve ill, can we
hope to justify punishment? Yes, if punishment can be shown to be a
good for the wrongdoer. The moral education theory makes just such an
attempt to explain punishment as a good for those who experience it, as
something done *for* them, not to them, something designed to achieve a
goal that includes their own moral well-being. This is the justification of
punishment the criminal needs to hear so that he can accept it as legitimate rather than dismiss it as vindictive. Therefore, my interest in the
moral education theory is connected with my desire to justify punishment
*as a good* for those who experience it, and to avoid any theoretical justification of punishment that would regard it as a deserved evil.[40] Reflection on the punishment activities of those who truly love the people
they punish, for example, the infliction of pain by a parent on a beloved
but naughty child, suggests to me that punishment should not be justified
as a deserved evil, but rather as an attempt, by someone who cares, to
improve a wayward person.

Still, the moral education theory can incorporate a particular notion of
desert which might be attractive to retributivists. Anyone who is punished
according to this theory would know that his punishment is "deserved,"
that is, morally required, insofar as the community cannot morally tolerate
the immoral lesson that his act conveys to others (for example, the mes-

---

for doing bad, but also "positive retributivism," that is, the idea that we deserve good for
doing good, but I cannot go into that here.

40. Indeed, I believe that it is because retribution would justify punishment as a deserved
evil that it strikes many as much too close to revenge.

sage that raping a woman is all right if it gives one a feeling of self-mastery) and cannot morally allow that he receive no education about the evil of his act.

So the theory's point is this: Wrong occasions punishment not because pain deserves pain, but because evil deserves correction.

I have many people to thank for their help in developing the ideas in this paper; among them: Warren Quinn, Thomas Hill, Judith De Cew, Marilyn Adams, Robert Adams, Richard Healey, Christopher Morris, Norman Dahl, Julie Heath, George Fletcher, Robert Gerstein, David Dolinko, and especially Herbert Morris. I also want to thank the Editors of *Philosophy & Public Affairs* for their incisive comments, and members of my seminar on punishment at UCLA in the Spring of 1983 for their lively and helpful discussions of the theory. Portions of the article were also read, among other places, at the 1982 Pacific Division APA Meeting, at C.S.U. Northridge, and at the University of Rajasthan, Jaipur, India.

# [5]

## Justice, Civilization, and the Death Penalty: Answering van den Haag

JEFFREY H. REIMAN

On the issue of capital punishment, there is as clear a clash of moral intuitions as we are likely to see. Some (now a majority of Americans) feel deeply that justice requires payment in kind and thus that murderers should die; and others (once, but no longer, nearly a majority of Americans) feel deeply that the state ought not be in the business of putting people to death.[1] Arguments for either side that do not do justice to the intuitions of the other are unlikely to persuade anyone not already convinced. And, since, as I shall suggest, there is truth on both sides, such arguments are easily refutable, leaving us with nothing but conflicting intuitions and no guidance from reason in distinguishing the better from the worse. In this context, I shall try to make an argument for the abolition of the death penalty that does justice to the intuitions on both sides. I shall sketch out a conception of retributive justice that accounts for the justice of executing murderers, and then I shall argue that *though the death penalty is a just punishment for murder*, abolition of the death penalty is part of the civilizing mission of modern states. Before getting to this, let us briefly consider the challenges confronting those who would

This paper is an expanded version of my opening statement in a debate with Ernest van den Haag on the death penalty at an Amnesty International conference on capital punishment, held at John Jay College in New York City, on October 17, 1983. I am grateful to the Editors of *Philosophy & Public Affairs* for very thought-provoking comments, to Hugo Bedau and Robert Johnson for many helpful suggestions, and to Ernest van den Haag for his encouragement.

1. Asked, in a 1981 Gallup Poll, "Are you in favor of the death penalty for persons convicted of murder?" 66.25% were in favor, 25% were opposed, and 8.75% had no opinion. Asked the same question in 1966, 47.5% were opposed, 41.25% were in favor, and 11.25% had no opinion (Timothy J. Flanagan, David J. van Alstyne, and Michael R. Gottfredson, eds., *Sourcebook of Criminal Justice Statistics—1981*, U.S. Department of Justice, Bureau of Justice Statistics [Washington, D.C.: U.S. Government Printing Office, 1982], p. 209).

argue against the death penalty. In my view, these challenges have been most forcefully put by Ernest van den Haag.

## I. THE CHALLENGE TO THE ABOLITIONIST

The recent book, *The Death Penalty: A Debate*, in which van den Haag argues for the death penalty and John P. Conrad argues against, proves how difficult it is to mount a telling argument against capital punishment.[2] Conrad contends, for example, that "To kill the offender [who has committed murder in the first degree] is to respond to his wrong by doing the same wrong to him" (p. 60). But this popular argument is easily refuted.[3] Since we regard killing in self-defense or in war as morally permissible, it cannot be that we regard killing per se as wrong. It follows that the wrong in murder cannot be that it is killing per se, but that it is (among other things) the killing of an innocent person. Consequently, if the state kills a murderer, though it does the same physical act that he did, it does not do the wrong that he did, since the state is not killing an innocent person (see p. 62). Moreover, unless this distinction is allowed, all punishments are wrong, since everything that the state does as punishment is an act which is physically the same as an act normally thought wrong. For example, if you lock an innocent person in a cage, that is kidnapping. If the state responds by locking you in prison, it can hardly be said to be responding to your wrong by doing you a wrong in return. Indeed, it will be said that it is precisely because what you did was wrong that locking you up, which would otherwise be wrong, is right.[4]

2. Ernest van den Haag and John P. Conrad, *The Death Penalty: A Debate* (New York: Plenum Press, 1983). Unless otherwise indicated, page references in the text and notes are to this book.

3. Some days after the first attempt to execute J. D. Autry by lethal injection was aborted, an editorial in *The Washington Post* (14 October 1983) asked: "If the taking of a human life is the most unacceptable of crimes, can it ever be an acceptable penalty? Does an act committed by an individual lose its essential character when it is imposed by society?" (p. A26).

4. "Does fining a criminal show want of respect for property, or imprisoning him, for personal freedom? Just as unreasonable is it to think that to take the life of a man who has taken that of another is to show want of regard for human life. We show, on the contrary, most emphatically our regard for it, by the adoption of a rule that he who violates that right in another forfeits it for himself. . . ." (John Stuart Mill, "Parliamentary Debate on Capital Punishment Within Prisons Bill," in *Philosophical Perspectives on Punishment*, ed. Gertrude Ezorsky [Albany: State University of New York Press, 1972], p. 276; Mill made the speech in 1868.)

*Justice, Civilization, and*
                                                                   *the Death Penalty*

Conrad also makes the familiar appeal to the possibility of executing an innocent person and the impossibility of correcting this tragic mistake. "An act by the state of such monstrous proportions as the execution of a man who is not guilty of the crime for which he was convicted should be avoided at all costs. . . . The abolition of capital punishment is the certain means of preventing the worst injustice" (p. 60). This argument, while not so easily disposed of as the previous one, is, like all claims about what "should be avoided at all costs," neither very persuasive. There is invariably some cost that is prohibitive such that if, for example, capital punishment were necessary to save the lives of potential murder victims, there must be a point at which the number of saved victims would be large enough to justify the risk of executing an innocent—particularly where trial and appellate proceedings are designed to reduce this risk to a minimum by giving the accused every benefit of the doubt.[5] Since we tolerate the death of innocents, in mines or on highways, as a cost of progress, and, in wars, as an inevitable accompaniment to aerial bombardment and the like, it cannot convincingly be contended that, kept to a minimum, the risk of executing an innocent is still so great an evil as to outweigh all other considerations (see pp. 230–31).

Nor will it do to suggest, as Conrad does, that execution implies that offenders are incapable of change and thus presumes the offenders' "total identification with evil," a presumption reserved only to God or, in any case, beyond the province of (mere) men (p. 27; also, pp. 42–43). This is not convincing since no punishment, whether on retributive or deterrent grounds, need imply belief in the total evilness of the punishee—all that need be believed (for retribution) is that what the offender has done is as evil as the punishment is awful, or (for deterrence) that what he has done is awful enough to warrant whatever punishment will discourage others from doing it. "Execution," writes van den Haag, "merely presumes an identification [with evil] sufficient to disregard what good qualities the convict has (he may be nice to animals and love his mother). . . . No total identification with evil—whatever that means—is required; only a sufficiently wicked crime" (p. 35).

Thus far I have tried to indicate how difficult it is to make an argument

---

5. Mill argues that the possibility of executing an innocent person would be an "invincible" objection "where the mode of criminal procedure is dangerous to the innocent," such as it is "in some parts of the Continent of Europe. . . . But we all know that the defects of our [English] procedure are the very opposite. Our rules of evidence are even too favorable to the prisoner" (ibid., pp. 276–77).

for the abolition of the death penalty against which the death penalty advocate cannot successfully defend himself. But van den Haag's argument is not merely defensive—he poses a positive challenge to anyone who would take up the abolitionist cause. For van den Haag, in order to argue convincingly for abolition, one must prove either that "no [criminal] act, however horrible, justifies [that is, deserves] the death penalty," or that, if capital punishment were found to deter murder more effectively than life imprisonment, we should still "prefer to preserve the life of a convicted murderer rather than the lives of innocent victims, even if it were certain that these victims would be spared if the murderer were executed" (p. 275).

If van den Haag is right and the abolitionist cause depends on proving either or both of these assertions, then it is a lost cause, since I believe they cannot be proven for reasons of the following sort: If people ever deserve anything for their acts, then it seems that what they deserve is something commensurate in cost or in benefit to what they have done. However horrible executions are, there are surely some acts to which they are commensurate in cost. If, as Camus says, the condemned man dies two deaths, one on the scaffold and one anticipating it, then isn't execution justified for one who has murdered two people? if not two, then ten?[6] As for the second assertion, since we take as justified the killing of innocent people (say, homicidal maniacs) in self-defense (that is, when necessary to preserve the lives of their innocent victims), then it seems that we must take as justified the killing of *guilty* people if it is necessary to preserve the lives of innocent victims. Indeed, though punishment is not the same as self-defense, it is, when practiced to deter crimes, arguably a form of social defense—and parity of reason would seem to dictate that if killing is justified when necessary for self-defense, then it is justified when necessary for social defense.

It might be thought that injuring or killing others in self-defense is justifiable in that it aims to stop the threatening individual himself, but that punishing people (even guilty people) to deter others is a violation

6. "As a general rule, a man is undone by waiting for capital punishment well before he dies. Two deaths are inflicted on him, the first being worse than the second, whereas he killed but once" (Albert Camus, "Reflections on the Guillotine," in *Resistance, Rebellion and Death* [New York: Alfred A. Knopf, 1969], p. 205). Based on interviews with the condemned men on Alabama's death row, Robert Johnson presents convincing empirical support for Camus' observation, in *Condemned to Die: Life Under Sentence of Death* (New York: Elsevier, 1981).

*Justice, Civilization, and*
                            *the Death Penalty*


of the Kantian prohibition against using people merely as means to the well-being of others.[7] It seems to me that this objection is premised on the belief that what deters potential criminals are the individual acts of punishment. In that case, each person punished is truly being used for the benefit of others. If, however, what deters potential criminals is the existence of a functioning punishment system, then everyone is benefited by that system, including those who end up being punished by it, since they too have received the benefit of enhanced security due to the deterring of some potential criminals. Even criminals benefit from what deters other criminals from preying on them. Then, each act of punishment is done as a necessary condition of the existence of a system that benefits all; and no one is used or sacrificed *merely* for the benefit of others.

If I am correct in believing that the assertions that van den Haag challenges the abolitionist to prove cannot be proven, then the case for the abolition of the death penalty must be made while accepting that some crimes deserve capital punishment, and that evidence that capital punishment was a substantially better deterrent to murder than life imprisonment would justify imposing it. This is what I shall attempt to do. Indeed, I shall begin the case for the abolition of the death penalty by defending the justice of the death penalty as a punishment for murder.


## II. JUST DESERTS AND JUST PUNISHMENTS

In my view, the death penalty is a just punishment for murder because the *lex talionis*, an eye for an eye, and so on, is just, although, as I shall suggest at the end of this section, it can only be rightly applied when its implied preconditions are satisfied. The *lex talionis* is a version of retributivism. Retributivism—as the word itself suggests—is the doctrine that the offender should be *paid back* with suffering he deserves because of the evil he has done, and the *lex talionis* asserts that injury equivalent to that he imposed is what the offender deserves.[8] But the *lex talionis* is

7. Jeffrie G. Murphy, "Marxism and Retribution," *Philosophy & Public Affairs* 2, no. 3 (Spring 1973):219.
8. I shall speak throughout of retribution as paying back for "harm caused," but this is shorthand for "harm intentionally attempted or caused"; likewise when I speak of the death penalty as punishment for murder, I have in mind premeditated, first-degree murder. Note also that the harm caused by an offender, for which he is to be paid back, is not necessarily limited to the harm done to his immediate victim. It may include as well the suffering of

not the only version of retributivism. Another, which I shall call "proportional retributivism," holds that what retribution requires is not equality of injury between crimes and punishments, but "fit" or proportionality, such that the worst crime is punished with the society's worst penalty, and so on, though the society's worst punishment need not duplicate the injury of the worst crime.[9] Later, I shall try to show how a form of proportional retributivism is compatible with acknowledging the justice of the *lex talionis*. Indeed, since I shall defend the justice of the *lex talionis*, I take such compatibility as a necessary condition of the validity of any form of retributivism.[10]

---

the victim's relatives or the fear produced in the general populace, and the like. For simplicity's sake, however, I shall continue to speak as if the harm for which retributivism would have us pay the offender back is the harm (intentionally attempted or done) to his immediate victim. Also, retribution is not to be confused with *restitution*. Restitution involves restoring the *status quo ante*, the condition prior to the offense. Since it was in this condition that the criminal's offense was committed, it is this condition that constitutes the baseline against which retribution is exacted. Thus retribution involves imposing a loss on the offender measured from the status quo ante. For example, returning a thief's loot to his victim so that thief and victim now own what they did before the offense is *restitution*. Taking enough from the thief so that what he is left with is less than what he had before the offense is *retribution*, since this is just what he did to his victim.

9. "The most extreme form of retributivism is the law of retaliation: 'an eye for an eye' " (Stanley I. Benn, "Punishment," *The Encyclopedia of Philosophy* 7, ed. Paul Edwards [New York: Macmillan, 1967], p. 32). Hugo Bedau writes: "retributive justice need not be thought to consist of *lex talionis*. One may reject that principle as too crude and still embrace the retributive principle that the severity of punishments should be graded according to the gravity of the offense" (Hugo Bedau, "Capital Punishment," in *Matters of Life and Death*, ed. Tom Regan [New York: Random House, 1980], p. 177). See also, Andrew von Hirsch, "Doing Justice: The Principle of Commensurate Deserts," and Hyman Gross, "Proportional Punishment and Justifiable Sentences," in *Sentencing*, eds. H. Gross and A. von Hirsch (New York: Oxford University Press, 1981), pp. 243–56 and 272–83, respectively.

10. In an article aimed at defending a retributivist theory of punishment, Michael Davis claims that the relevant measure of punishment is not the cost to the offender's victim ("property taken, bones broken, or lives lost"), but the "value of the unfair advantage he [the offender] takes of those who obey the law (even though they are tempted to do otherwise)" (Michael Davis, "How to Make the Punishment Fit the Crime," *Ethics* 93 [July 1983]:744). Though there is much to be said for this view, standing alone it seems quite questionable. For example, it would seem that the value of the unfair advantage taken of law-obeyers by one who robs a great deal of money is greater than the value of the unfair advantage taken by a murderer, since the latter gets only the advantage of ridding his world of a nuisance while the former will be able to make a new life without the nuisance and have money left over for other things. This leads to the counterintuitive conclusion that such robbers should be punished more severely (and regarded as more wicked) than murderers. One might try to get around this by treating the value of the unfair advantage as a function of the cost imposed by the crime. And Davis does this after a fashion. He takes the value of such advantages to be equivalent to the prices that licenses to commit crimes

*Justice, Civilization, and*
                                  *the Death Penalty*

There is nothing self-evident about the justice of the *lex talionis* nor, for that matter, of retributivism.[11] The standard problem confronting those who would justify retributivism is that of overcoming the suspicion that it does no more than sanctify the victim's desire to hurt the offender back. Since serving that desire amounts to hurting the offender simply for the satisfaction that the victim derives from seeing the offender suffer, and since deriving satisfaction from the suffering of others seems primitive, the policy of imposing suffering on the offender for no other purpose than giving satisfaction to his victim seems primitive as well. Consequently, defending retributivism requires showing that the suffering imposed on the wrongdoer has some worthy point beyond the satisfaction of victims. In what follows, I shall try to identify a proposition—which I call the *retributivist principle*—that I take to be the nerve of retributivism. I think this principle accounts for the justice of the *lex talionis* and indicates the point of the suffering demanded by retributivism. Not to do too much of the work of the death penalty advocate, I shall make no extended argument for this principle beyond suggesting the considerations that make it plausible. I shall identify these considerations by drawing, with considerable license, on Hegel and Kant.

I think that we can see the justice of the *lex talionis* by focusing on the striking affinity between it and the *golden rule*. The *golden rule* mandates "Do unto others as you would have others do unto you," while the *lex talionis* counsels "Do unto others as they have done unto you." It would not be too far-fetched to say that the *lex talionis* is the law enforcement arm of the golden rule, at least in the sense that if people were actually treated as they treated others, then everyone would necessarily follow the golden rule because then people could only willingly act toward others as they were willing to have others act toward them. This is not to suggest that the *lex talionis* follows from the golden rule, but rather that the two share a common moral inspiration: the equality

---

would bring if sold on the market, and he claims that these prices would be at least as much as what non-licenseholders would (for their own protection) pay licensees not to use their licenses. Now this obviously brings the cost to victims of crime back into the measure of punishment, though only halfheartedly, since this cost must be added to the value to the licensee of being able to use his license. And this still leaves open the distinct possibility that licenses for very lucrative theft opportunities would fetch higher prices on the market than licenses to kill, with the same counterintuitive result mentioned earlier.

11. Stanley Benn writes: "to say 'it is fitting' or 'justice demands' that the guilty should suffer is only to affirm that punishment is right, not to give grounds for thinking so" (Benn, "Punishment." p. 39).

of persons. Treating others as you *would* have them treat you means treating others as equal to you, because adopting the golden rule as one's guiding principle implies that one counts the suffering of others to be as great a calamity as one's own suffering, that one counts one's right to impose suffering on others as no greater than their right to impose suffering on one, and so on. This leads to the *lex talionis* by two approaches that start from different points and converge.

I call the first approach "Hegelian" because Hegel held (roughly) that crime upsets the equality between persons and retributive punishment restores that equality by "annulling" the crime.[12] As we have seen, acting according to the golden rule implies treating others as your equals. Conversely, violating the golden rule implies the reverse: Doing to another what you would *not* have that other do to you violates the equality of persons by asserting a right toward the other that the other does not possess toward you. Doing back to you what you did "annuls" your violation by reasserting that the other has the same right toward you that you assert toward him. Punishment according to the *lex talionis* cannot heal the injury that the other has suffered at your hands, rather it rectifies the indignity he has suffered, by restoring him to equality with you.

"Equality of persons" here does not mean equality of concern for their happiness, as it might for a utilitarian. On such a (roughly) utilitarian understanding of equality, imposing suffering on the wrongdoer equivalent to the suffering he has imposed would have little point. Rather, equality of concern for people's happiness would lead us to impose as little suffering on the wrongdoer as was compatible with maintaining the happiness of others. This is enough to show that retributivism (at least

---

12. Hegel writes that "The sole positive existence which the injury [i.e., the crime] possesses is that it is the particular will of the criminal [i.e., it is the criminal's intention that distinguishes criminal injury from, say, injury due to an accident]. Hence to injure (or penalize) this particular will as a will determinately existent is to annul the crime, which otherwise would have been held valid, and to restore the right" (G.W.F. Hegel, *The Philosophy of Right*, trans. by T. M. Knox [Oxford: Clarendon Press, 1962; originally published in German in 1821], p. 69, see also p. 331n). I take this to mean that the right is a certain equality of sovereignty between the wills of individuals, crime disrupts that equality by placing one will above others, and punishment restores the equality by annulling the illegitimate ascendance. On these grounds, as I shall suggest below, the desire for revenge (strictly limited to the desire "to even the score") is more respectable than philosophers have generally allowed. And so Hegel writes that "The annulling of crime in this sphere where right is immediate [i.e., the condition prior to conscious morality] is principally revenge, which is just in its content in so far as it is retributive" (ibid., p. 73).

*Justice, Civilization, and*
                                       *the Death Penalty*

in this "Hegelian" form) reflects a conception of morality quite different from that envisioned by utilitarianism. Instead of seeing morality as administering doses of happiness to individual recipients, the retributivist envisions morality as maintaining the relations appropriate to equally sovereign individuals. A crime, rather than representing a unit of suffering added to the already considerable suffering in the world, is an assault on the sovereignty of an individual that temporarily places one person (the criminal) in a position of illegimate sovereignty over another (the victim). The victim (or his representative, the state) then has the right to rectify this loss of standing relative to the criminal by meting out a punishment that reduces the criminal's sovereignty in the degree to which he vaunted it above his victim's. It might be thought that this is a duty, not just a right, but that is surely too much. The victim has the right to forgive the violator without punishment, which suggests that it is by virtue of having the right to punish the violator (rather than the duty), that the victim's equality with the violator is restored.

I call the second approach "Kantian" since Kant held (roughly) that, since reason (like justice) is no respecter of the sheer difference between individuals, when a rational being decides to act in a certain way toward his fellows, he implicitly authorizes similar action by his fellows toward him.[13] A version of the golden rule, then, is a requirement of reason: acting rationally, one always acts as he would have others act toward him. Consequently, to act toward a person as he has acted toward others is to treat him as a rational being, that is, as if his act were the product of a rational decision. From this, it may be concluded that we have a duty to do to offenders what they have done, since this amounts to according them the respect due rational beings.[14] Here too, however, the assertion

13. Kant writes that "any undeserved evil that you inflict on someone else among the people is one that you do to yourself. If you vilify him, you vilify yourself; if you steal from him, you steal from yourself; if you kill him, you kill yourself." Since Kant holds that "If what happens to someone is also willed by him, it cannot be a punishment," he takes pains to distance himself from the view that the offender *wills* his punishment. "The chief error contained in this sophistry," Kant writes, "consists in the confusion of the criminal's [that is, the murderer's] own judgment (which one must necessarily attribute to his reason) that he must forfeit his life with a resolution of the will to take his own life" (Immanuel Kant, *The Metaphysical Elements of Justice, Part I of The Metaphysics of Morals,* trans. by J. Ladd [Indianapolis: Bobbs-Merrill, 1965; originally published in 1797], pp. 101, 105–106). I have tried to capture this notion of attributing a judgment to the offender rather than a resolution of his will with the term 'authorizes.'

14. "Even if a civil society were to dissolve itself by common agreement of all its members

of a duty to punish seems excessive, since, if this duty arises because doing to people what they have done to others is necessary to accord them the respect due rational beings, then we would have a duty to do to all rational persons *everything*—good, bad, or indifferent—that they do to others. The point rather is that, by his acts, a rational being *authorizes* others to do the same to him, he doesn't *compel* them to. Here too, then, the argument leads to a right, rather than a duty, to exact the *lex talionis*. And this is supported by the fact that we can conclude from Kant's argument that a rational being cannot validly complain of being treated in the way he has treated others, and where there is no valid complaint, there is no injustice, and where there is no injustice, others have acted within their rights.[15] It should be clear that the Kantian argument also rests on the equality of persons, because a rational agent

---

..., the last murderer remaining in prison must first be executed, so that everyone will duly receive what his actions are worth" (Kant, ibid., p. 102). Interestingly, Conrad calls himself a retributivist, but doesn't accept the strict Kantian version of it. In fact, he claims that Kant "did not bother with justifications for his categorical imperative ..., [but just] insisted that the Roman *jus talionis* was the reference point at which to begin" (p. 22). Van den Haag, by contrast, states specifically that he is "not a retributionist" (p. 32). In fact he claims that "retributionism" is not really a *theory* of punishment at all, just "a feeling articulated through a metaphor presented as though a theory" (p. 28). This is so, he maintains, because a theory "must tell us what the world, or some part thereof, is like or has been or will be like" (ibid.). "In contrast," he goes on, "deterrence theory is, whether right or wrong, a theory: It asks what the effects are of punishment (does it reduce the crime rate?) and makes testable predictions (punishment reduces the crime rate compared to what it would be without the credible threat of punishment)" (p. 29). Now, it should be obvious that van den Haag has narrowed his conception of "theory" so that it only covers the kind of things one finds in the empirical sciences. So narrowed, there is no such thing as a theory about what justifies some action or policy, no such thing as a Kantian theory of punishment, or, for that matter, a Rawlsian theory of jusice—that is to say, no such thing as a *moral* theory. Van den Haag, of course, could use the term 'theory' as he wished, were it not for the fact that he appeals to deterrence theory not merely for predictions about crime rates but also (indeed, in the current context, primarily) as a theory about what justifies punishment—that is, as a *moral* theory. And he must, since the fact that punishment reduces crime does not imply that we should institute punishment unless we *should* do whatever reduces crime. In short, van den Haag is about moral theories the way I am about airplanes: He doesn't quite understand how they work, but he knows how to use them to get where he wants to go.

15. "It may also be pointed out that no one has ever heard of anyone condemned to death on account of murder who complained that he was getting too much [punishment] and therefore was being treated unjustly; everyone would laugh in his face if he were to make such a statement" (Kant, *Metaphysical Elements of Justice*, p. 104; see also p. 133).

*Justice, Civilization, and*
*the Death Penalty*

only implicitly authorizes having done to him action similar to what he has done to another, if he and the other are similar in the relevant ways.

The "Hegelian" and "Kantian" approaches arrive at the same destination from opposite sides. The "Hegelian" approach starts from the victim's equality with the criminal, and infers from it the victim's right to do to the criminal what the criminal has done to the victim. The "Kantian" approach starts from the criminal's rationality, and infers from it the criminal's authorization of the victim's right to do to the criminal what the criminal has done to the victim. Taken together, these approaches support the following proposition: The equality and rationality of persons implies that an offender deserves and his victim has the right to impose suffering on the offender equal to that which he imposed on the victim. This is the proposition I call the *retributivist principle*, and I shall assume henceforth that it is true. This principle provides that the *lex talionis* is the criminal's just desert and the victim's (or as his representative, the state's) right. Moreover, the principle also indicates the point of retributive punishment, namely, it affirms the equality and rationality of persons, victims and offenders alike.[16] And the point of this affirmation is, like any moral affirmation, to make a statement, to the criminal, to impress upon him his equality with his victim (which earns him a like fate) and his rationality (by which his actions are held to authorize his fate), and to the society, so that recognition of the equality and rationality of persons becomes a visible part of our shared moral environment that none can ignore in justifying their actions to one another.

When I say that with respect to the criminal, the point of retributive punishment is to impress upon him his equality with his victim, I mean to be understood quite literally. If the sentence is just and the criminal rational, then the punishment should normally *force* upon him recognition of his equality with his victim, recognition of their shared vulnerability to suffering and their shared desire to avoid it, as well as recognition of the fact that he counts for no more than his victim in the eyes of their fellows. For this reason, the retributivist requires that the offender be

16. Herbert Morris defends retributivism on parallel grounds. See his "Persons and Punishment," *The Monist* 52, no. 4 (October 1968):475–501. Isn't what Morris calls "the right to be treated as a person" essentially the right of a rational being to be treated only as he has authorized, implicitly or explicitly, by his own free choices?

sane, not only at the moment of his crime, but also at the moment of his punishment—while this latter requirement would seem largely pointless (if not downright malevolent) to a utilitarian. Incidentally, it is, I believe, the desire that the offender be forced by suffering punishment to recognize his equality with his victim, rather than the desire for that suffering itself, that constitutes what is rational in the desire for revenge.

The retributivist principle represents a conception of moral desert whose complete elaboration would take us far beyond the scope of the present essay. In its defense, however, it is worth noting that our common notion of moral desert seems to include (at least) two elements: (1) a conception of individual responsibility for actions that is "contagious," that is, one which confers moral justification on the punishing (or rewarding) reactions of others; and (2) a measure of the relevant worth of actions that determines the legitimate magnitude of justified reactions. Broadly speaking, the "Kantian" notion of authorization implicit in rational action supplies the first element, and the "Hegelian" notion of upsetting and restoring equality of standing supplies the second. It seems, then, reasonable to take the equality and rationality of persons as implying moral desert in the way asserted in the retributivist principle. I shall assume henceforth that the retributivist principle is true.

The truth of the retributivist principle establishes the justice of the *lex talionis*, but, since it establishes this as a right of the victim rather than a duty, it does not settle the question of whether or to what extent the victim or the state should exercise this right and exact the *lex talionis*. This is a separate moral question because strict adherence to the *lex talionis* amounts to allowing criminals, even the most barbaric of them, to dictate our punishing behavior. It seems certain that there are at least some crimes, such as rape or torture, that we ought not try to match. And this is not merely a matter of imposing an alternative punishment that produces an equivalent amount of suffering, as, say, some number of years in prison that might "add up" to the harm caused by a rapist or a torturer. Even if no amount of time in prison would add up to the harm caused by a torturer, it still seems that we ought not torture him even if this were the only way of making him suffer as much as he has made his victim suffer. Or, consider someone who has committed several murders in cold blood. On the *lex talionis*, it would seem that such a criminal might justly be brought to within an inch of death and then revived (or to within a moment of execution and then reprieved) as many times as he has killed (minus one), and then finally executed. But surely this is a degree of cruelty that would be monstrous.[17]

Since the retributivist principle establishes the *lex talionis* as the victim's right, it might seem that the question of how far this right should be exercised is "up to the victim." And indeed, this would be the case in the state of nature. But once, for all the good reasons familiar to readers of John Locke, the state comes into existence, public punishment replaces private, and the victim's right to punish reposes in the state. With this, the decision as to how far to exercise this right goes to the state as well. To be sure, since (at least with respect to retributive punishment) the victim's right is the source of the state's right to punish, the state must exercise its right in ways that are faithful to the victim's right. Later, when I try to spell out the upper and lower limits of just punishment, these may be taken as indicating the range within which the state can punish and remain faithful to the victim's right.

I suspect that it will be widely agreed that the state ought not administer punishments of the sort described above even if required by the letter of the *lex talionis*, and thus, even granting the justice of *lex talionis*, there are occasions on which it is morally appropriate to diverge from its requirements. We must, of course, distinguish such morally based divergence from that which is based on practicality. Like any moral principle, the *lex talionis* is subject to "ought implies can." It will usually be impossible to do to an offender exactly what he has done—for example, his offense will normally have had an element of surprise that is not possible for a judicially imposed punishment, but this fact can hardly free him from having to bear the suffering he has imposed on another. Thus, for reasons of practicality, the *lex talionis* must necessarily be qualified to call for doing to the offender *as nearly as possible* what he has done to his victim. When, however, we refrain from raping rapists or torturing torturers, we do so for reasons of morality, not of practicality. And, given the justice of the *lex talionis*, these moral reasons cannot amount to claiming that it would be *unjust* to rape rapists or torture torturers. Rather

17. Bedau writes: "Where criminals set the limits of just methods of punishment, as they will do if we attempt to give exact and literal implementation to *lex talionis*, society will find itself descending to the cruelties and savagery that criminals employ. But society would be deliberately authorizing such acts, in the cool light of reason, and not (as is often true of vicious criminals) impulsively or in hatred and anger or with an insane or unbalanced mind. Moral restraints, in short, prohibit us from trying to make executions perfectly retributive" (Bedau, "Capital Punishment," p. 176).

the claim must be that, even though it would be just to rape rapists and torture torturers, other moral considerations weigh against doing so.

On the other hand, when, for moral reasons, we refrain from exacting the *lex talionis*, and impose a less harsh alternative punishment, it may be said that we are not doing full justice to the criminal, but it cannot automatically be the case that we are doing an *injustice* to his victim. Otherwise we would have to say it was unjust to imprison our torturer rather than torturing him or to simply execute our multiple murderer rather than multiply "executing" him. Surely it is counterintuitive (and irrational to boot) to set the demands of justice so high that a society would have to choose between being barbaric or being unjust. This would effectively price justice out of the moral market.

The implication of this is that there is a range of just punishments that includes some that are just though they exact less than the full measure of the *lex talionis*. What are the top and bottom ends of this range? I think that both are indicated by the *retributivist principle*. The principle identifies the *lex talionis* as the offender's desert and since, on retributive grounds, punishment beyond what one deserves is unjust for the same reasons that make punishment of the innocent unjust, the *lex talionis* is the upper limit of the range of just punishments. On the other hand, if the retributivist principle is true, then denying that the offender deserves suffering equal to that which he imposed amounts to denying the equality and rationality of persons. From this it follows that we fall below the bottom end of the range of just punishments when we act in ways that are incompatible with the *lex talionis* at the top end. That is, we fall below the bottom end and commit an injustice to the victim when we treat the offender in a way that is no longer compatible with sincerely believing that he deserves to have done to him what he has done to his victim. Thus, the upper limit of the range of just punishments is the point after which more punishment is unjust to the offender, and the lower limit is the point after which less punishment is unjust to the victim. In this way, the range of just punishments remains faithful to the victim's right which is their source.

This way of understanding just punishment enables us to formulate proportional retributivism so that it is compatible with acknowledging the justice of the *lex talionis*: If we take the *lex talionis* as spelling out the offender's just deserts, and if other moral considerations require us to refrain from matching the injury caused by the offender while still allowing us to punish justly, then surely we impose just punishment if we impose the closest morally acceptable approximation to the *lex tal̲ionis*. Proportional retributivism, then, in requiring that the worst crime be punished by the society's worst punishment and so on, could be understood as translating the offender's just desert into its nearest equivalent in the society's table of morally acceptable punishments. Then the two versions of retributivism (*lex talionis* and proportional) are related in that the first states what just punishment would be if nothing but the offender's just desert mattered, and the second locates just punishment at the meeting point of the offender's just deserts and the society's moral scruples. And since this second version only modifies the requirements of the *lex talionis* in light of other moral considerations, it is compatible with believing that the *lex talionis* spells out the offender's just deserts, much in the way that modifying the obligations of promisers in light of other moral considerations is compatible with believing in the binding nature of promises.

Proportional retributivism so formulated preserves the point of retributivism and remains faithful to the victim's right which is its source. Since it punishes with the closest morally acceptable approximation to the *lex talionis*, it effectively says to the offender, you deserve the equivalent of what you did to your victim and you are getting less only to the degree that *our* moral scruples limit us from duplicating what you have done. Such punishment, then, affirms the equality of persons by respecting *as far as is morally permissible* the victim's right to impose suffering on the offender equal to what he received, and it affirms the rationality of the offender by treating him as authorizing others to do to him what he has done though they take him up on it only *as far as is morally permissible*. Needless to say, the alternative punishments must in some convincing way be comparable in gravity to the crimes which they punish, or else they will trivialize the harms those crimes caused and be no longer compatible with sincerely believing that the offender deserves to have done to him what he has done to his victim and no longer capable of impressing upon the criminal his equality with the victim. If we punish rapists with a small fine or a brief prison term, we do an injustice to their victims, because this trivializes the suffering rapists have caused and thus is incompatible with believing that they deserve to have done to them something comparable to what they have done to their victims. If, on the other hand, instead of raping rapists we impose on them some grave penalty, say a substantial term of imprisonment, then we do no injustice even though we refrain from exacting the *lex talionis*.

To sum up, I take the *lex talionis* to be the top end of the range of just punishments. When, because we are simply unable to duplicate the criminal's offense, we modify the *lex talionis* to call for imposing on the offender as nearly as possible what he has done, we are still at this top end, applying the *lex talionis* subject to "ought implies can." When we do less than this, we still act justly as long as we punish in a way that is compatible with sincerely believing that the offender deserves the full measure of the *lex talionis*, but receives less for reasons that do not undermine this belief. If this is true, then it is not unjust to spare murderers as long as they can be punished in some other suitably grave way. I leave open the question of what such an alternative punishment might be, except to say that it need not be limited to such penalties as are currently imposed. For example, though rarely carried out in practice, a life sentence with no chance of parole might be a civilized equivalent of the death penalty—after all, people sentenced to life imprisonment have traditionally been regarded as "civilly dead."[18]

It might be objected that no punishment short of death will serve the point of retributivism with respect to murderers because no punishment short of death is commensurate with the crime of murder since, while some number of years of imprisonment may add up to the amount of harm done by rapists or assaulters or torturers, no number of years will add up to the harm done to the victim of murder. But justified divergence from the *lex talionis* is not limited only to changing the form of punishment while maintaining equivalent severity. Otherwise, we would have to torture torturers rather than imprison them if they tortured more than could be made up for by years in prison (or by the years available to them to spend in prison, which might be few for elderly torturers), and we would have to subject multiple murderers to multiple "executions." If justice allows us to refrain from these penalties, then justice allows punishments that are not equal in suffering to their crimes. It seems to me that if the objector grants this much, then he must show that a punish-

18. I am indebted to my colleague Robert Johnson for this suggestion, which he has attempted to develop in "A Life for a Life?" (unpub. ms.). He writes that prisoners condemned to spend their entire lives in prison "would suffer a civil death, the death of freedom. The prison would be their cemetery, a 6′ by 9′ cell their tomb. Their freedom would be interred in the name of justice. They would be consigned to mark the passage of their lives in the prison's peculiar dead time, which serves no purpose and confers no rewards. In effect, they would give their civil lives in return for the natural lives they have taken."

*Justice, Civilization, and*
*the Death Penalty*

ment less than death is not merely incommensurate to the harm caused by murder, but so far out of proportion to that harm that it trivializes it and thus effectively denies the equality and rationality of persons. Now, I am vulnerable to the claim that a sentence of life in prison that allows parole after eight or ten years does indeed trivialize the harm of (premeditated, coldblooded) murder. But I cannot see how a sentence that would require a murderer to spend his full natural life in prison, or even the lion's share of his adult life (say, the thirty years between age twenty and age fifty), can be regarded as anything less than extremely severe and thus no trivialization of the harm he has caused.

I take it then that the justice of the *lex talionis* implies that it is just to execute murderers, but not that it is unjust to spare them as long as they are systematically punished in some other suitably grave way. Before developing the implications of this claim, a word about the implied preconditions of applying the *lex talionis* is in order.

Since this principle calls for imposing on offenders the harms they are responsible for imposing on others, the implied preconditions of applying it to any particular harm include the requirement that the harm be one that the offender is fully responsible for, where responsibility is both psychological, the capacity to tell the difference between right and wrong and control one's actions, and social. If people are subjected to remediable unjust social circumstances beyond their control, and if harmful actions are a predictable response to those conditions, then those who benefit from the unjust conditions and refuse to remedy them share responsibility for the harmful acts—and thus neither their doing nor their cost can be assigned fully to the offenders alone. For example, if a slave kills an innocent person while making his escape, at least part of the blame for the killing must fall on those who have enslaved him. And this is because slavery is unjust, not merely because the desire to escape from slavery is understandable. The desire to escape from prison is understandable as well, but if the imprisonment were a just sentence, then we would hold the prisoner, and not his keepers, responsible if he killed someone while escaping.

Since I believe that the vast majority of murders in America are a predictable response to the frustrations and disabilities of impoverished social circumstances,[19] and since I believe that that impoverishment is

19. "In the case of homicide, the empirical evidence indicates that poverty and poor economic conditions are systematically related to higher levels of homicide" (Richard M. McGahey, "Dr. Ehrlich's Magic Bullet: Economic Theory, Econometrics, and the Death

132                              *Philosophy & Public Affairs*

a remediable injustice from which others in America benefit, I believe
that we have no right to exact the full cost of murders from our murderers
until we have done everything possible to rectify the conditions that
produce their crimes.[20] But these are the "Reagan years," and not many—
who are not already susceptible—will be persuaded by this sort of argument.[21] This does not, in my view, shake its validity; but I want to

---

Penalty," *Crime & Delinquency* 26, no. 4 [October 1980]:502). Some of that evidence can
be found in Peter Passell, "The Deterrent Effect of the Death Penalty: A Statistical Test,"
*Stanford Law Review* (November 1975):61–80.

20. A similar though not identical point has been made by Jeffrie G. Murphy. He writes
"I believe that retributivism can be formulated in such a way that it is the only morally
defensible theory of punishment. I also believe that arguments, which may be regarded as
Marxist at least in spirit, can be formulated which show that social conditions as they obtain
in most societies make this form of retributivism largely inapplicable within those societies"
(Murphy, "Marxism and Retribution," p. 221). Though my claim here is similar to Murphy's,
the route by which I arrive at it differs from his in several ways. Most important, a key
point of Murphy's argument is that retributivism assumes that the criminal freely chooses
his crime while, according to Murphy, criminals act on the basis of psychological traits
that the society has conditioned them to have: "Is it just to punish people who act out of
those very motives that society encourages and reinforces? If [Willem] Bonger [a Dutch
Marxist criminologist] is correct, much criminality is motivated by greed, selfishness, and
indifference to one's fellows; but does not the whole society encourage motives of greed
· and selfishness ('making it,' 'getting ahead'), and does not the competitive nature of the
society alienate men from each other and thereby encourage indifference—even, perhaps,
what psychiatrists call psychopathy?" (ibid., p. 239). This argument assumes that the
criminal is in some sense unable to conform to legal and moral prohibitions against violence,
and thus, like the insane, cannot be thought responsible for his actions. This claim is rather
extreme, and dubious as a result. My argument does not claim that criminals, murderers
in particular, cannot control their actions. I claim rather that, though criminals can control
their actions, when crimes are predictable responses to unjust circumstances, then those
who benefit from and do not remedy those conditions bear some responsibility for the
crimes and thus the criminals cannot be held *wholly* responsible for them in the sense of
being legitimately required to pay their full cost. It should be noted that Murphy's thesis
(quoted at the beginning of this note) is stated in a somewhat confused way. Social conditions that mitigate or eliminate the guilt of offenders do not make retributivism *inapplicable*. Retributivism is applied both when those who are guilty because they freely chose
their crimes are punished *and* when it is held wrong to punish those who are not guilty
because they did not freely choose their crimes. It is precisely by the application of retributivism that the social conditions referred to by Murphy make the punishment of criminals
unjustifiable.

21. Van den Haag notes the connection between crime and poverty, and explains it and
its implications as follows: "Poverty," he holds, "does not compel crime; it only makes it
more tempting" (p. 207). And it is not absolute poverty that does this, only relative deprivation, the fact that some have less than others (p. 115). In support of this, he marshals
data showing that, over the years, crime has risen along with the standard of living at the
bottom of society. Since, unlike absolute deprivation, relative deprivation will be with us

*Justice, Civilization, and*
*the Death Penalty*

make an argument whose appeal is not limited to those who think that
crime is the result of social injustice.²² I shall proceed then, granting not
only the justice of the death penalty, but also, at least temporarily, the
assumption that our murderers are wholly deserving óf dying for their
crimes. If I can show that it would still be wrong to execute murderers,

---

no matter how rich we all become as long as some have more than others, he concludes
that this condition which increases the temptation to crime is just an ineradicable fact of
social life, best dealt with by giving people strong incentives to resist the temptation. This
argument is flawed in several ways. First, the claim that crime is connected with poverty
ought not be simplistically interpreted to mean that a low absolute standard of living itself
causes crime. Rather, what seems to be linked to crime is the general breakdown of stable
communities, institutions and families, such as has occurred in our cities in recent decades
as a result of economic and demographic trends largely out of individuals' control. Of this
breakdown, poverty is today a sign and a cause, at least in the sense that poverty leaves
people with few defenses against it and few avenues of escape from it. This claim is quite
compatible with finding that people with lower absolute standards of living, but who dwell
in more stable social surroundings with traditional institutions still intact, have lower crime
rates than contemporary poor people who have higher absolute standards of living. Second,
the implication of this is not simply that it is relative deprivation that tempts to crime, since
if that were the case, the middle class would be stealing as much from the rich as the poor
do from the middle class. That this is not the case suggests that there is some threshold
after which crime is no longer so tempting, and while this threshold changes historically,
it is in principle one all could reach. Thus, it is not merely the (supposedly ineradicable)
fact of having less than others that tempts to crime. Finally, everything is altered if the
temptation to crime is not the result of an ineradicable social fact, but of an injustice that
can be remedied or relieved. Obviously, this would require considerable argument, but it
seems to me that the current distribution of wealth in America is unjust whether one takes
utilitarianism as one's theory of justice (given the relative numbers of rich and poor in
America as well as the principle of declining marginal returns, redistribution could make
the poor happier without an offsetting loss in happiness among the rich) or Rawls's theory
(the worst-off shares in our society could still be increased, so the difference principle is
not yet satisfied) or Nozick's theory (since the original acquisition of property in America
was marked by the use of force against Indians and blacks, from which both groups still
suffer).

22. In arguing that social injustice disqualifies us from applying the death penalty, I am
arguing that unjust discrimination in the *recruitment* of murderers undermines the justice
of applying the penalty under foreseeable conditions in the United States. This is distinct
from the argument that points to the discriminatory way in which it has been *applied* to
murderers (generally against blacks, particularly when their victims are white). This latter
argument is by no means unimportant, nor do I believe that it has been rendered obsolete
by the Supreme Court's 1972 decision in *Furman v. Georgia* that struck down then-existing
death penalty statutes because they allowed discriminatory application, or the Court's 1976
decision in *Gregg v. Georgia*, which approved several new statutes because they supposedly
remedied this problem. There is considerable empirical evidence that much the same pattern
of discrimination that led to *Furman* continues after *Gregg*. See for example, William J.
Bowers and Glenn L. Pierce, "Arbitrariness and Discrimination in Post-*Furman* Capital

I believe I shall have made the strongest case for abolishing the death penalty.

## III. CIVILIZATION, PAIN, AND JUSTICE

As I have already suggested, from the fact that something is justly deserved, it does not automatically follow that it should be done, since there may be other moral reasons for not doing it such that, all told, the weight of moral reasons swings the balance against proceeding. The same argument that I have given for the justice of the death penalty for murderers proves the justice of beating assaulters, raping rapists, and torturing torturers. Nonetheless, I believe, and suspect that most would agree, that it would not be right for us to beat assaulters, rape rapists, or torture

---

Statutes," *Crime & Delinquency* 26, no. 4 (October 1980):563–635. Moreover, I believe that continued evidence of such discrimination would constitute a separate and powerful argument for abolition. Faced with such evidence, van den Haag's strategy is to grant that discrimination is wrong, but claim that it is not "inherent in the death penalty"; it is a characteristic of "its distribution" (p. 206). Thus discrimination is not an objection to the death penalty itself. This rejoinder is unsatisfactory for several reasons. First of all, even if discrimination is not an objection to the death penalty *per se*, its foreseeable persistence is—as the Court recognized in *Furman*—an objection to instituting the death penalty *as a policy*. Moral assessment of the way in which a penalty will be carried out may be distinct from moral assessment of the penalty itself, but, since the way in which the penalty will be carried out is part of what we will be bringing about if we institute the penalty, it is a necessary consideration in any assessment of the morality of instituting the penalty. In short, van den Haag's strategy saves the death penalty in principle, but fails to save it in practice. Second, it may well be that discrimination is (as a matter of social and psychological fact in America) inherent in the penalty of death itself. The evidence of its persistence after *Furman* lends substance to the suspicion that something about the death penalty—perhaps the very terribleness of it that recommends it to van den Haag—strikes at deep-seated racial prejudices in a way that milder penalties do not. In any event, this is an empirical matter, not resolved by analytic distinctions between what is distributed and how it is distributed. Finally, after he mounts his argument against the discrimination objection, van den Haag usually adds that those who oppose capital punishment "because of discriminatory application are not quite serious . . . , [since] they usually will confess, if pressed, that they would continue their opposition even if there were no discrimination whatsoever in the administration of the death penalty" (p. 225). This is preposterous. It assumes that a person can only have one serious objection to any policy. If he had several, then he would naturally continue to oppose the policy *quite seriously* even though all his objections but one were eliminated. In addition to discrimination in the *recruitment* of murderers, and in the *application* of the death penalty among murderers, there is a third sort that affects the justice of instituting the penalty, namely, discrimination in the *legal definition* of murder. I take this and related issues up in *The Rich Get Richer and the Poor Get Prison: Ideology, Class, and Criminal Justice*, 2nd ed. (New York: John Wiley, 1984).

*Justice, Civilization, and*
                               *the Death Penalty*

torturers, *even though it were their just deserts*—and even if this were the only way to make them suffer as much as they had made their victims suffer. Calling for the abolition of the death penalty, though it be just, then, amounts to urging that as a society we place execution in the same category of sanction as beating, raping, and torturing, and treat it as something it would also not be right for us to do to offenders, *even if it were their just deserts.*

To argue for placing execution in this category, I must show what would be gained therefrom; and to show that, I shall indicate what we gain from placing torture in this category and argue that a similar gain is to be had from doing the same with execution. I select torture because I think the reasons for placing it in this category are, due to the extremity of torture, most easily seen—but what I say here applies with appropriate modification to other severe physical punishments, such as beating and raping. First, and most evidently, placing torture in this category broadcasts the message that we as a society judge torturing so horrible a thing to do to a person that we refuse to do it even when it is deserved. Note that such a judgment does not commit us to an absolute prohibition on torturing. No matter how horrible we judge something to be, we may still be justified in doing it if it is necessary to prevent something even worse. Leaving this aside for the moment, what is gained by broadcasting the public judgment that torture is too horrible to inflict even if deserved?

I think the answer to this lies in what we understand as civilization. In *The Genealogy of Morals*, Nietzsche says that in early times "pain did not hurt as much as it does today."[23] The truth in this puzzling remark is that progress in civilization is characterized by a lower tolerance for one's own pain and that suffered by others. And this is appropriate, since, via growth in knowledge, civilization brings increased power to prevent or reduce pain and, via growth in the ability to communicate and interact with more and more people, civilization extends the circle of people with whom we emphathize.[24] If civilization is characterized by lower tolerance

23. Friedrich Nietzsche, *The Birth of Tragedy and The Genealogy of Morals* (New York: Doubleday, 1956), pp. 199–200.

24. Van den Haag writes that our ancestors "were not as repulsed by physical pain as we are. The change has to do not with our greater smartness or moral superiority but with a new outlook pioneered by the French and American revolutions [namely, the assertion of human equality and with it 'universal identification'], and by such mundane things as the invention of anesthetics, which make pain much less of an everyday experience" (p. 215; cf. van den Haag's *Punishing Criminals* [New York: Basic Books, 1975], pp. 196–206).

for our own pain and that of others, then publicly refusing to do horrible things to our fellows both signals the level of our civilization *and, by our example, continues the work of civilizing.* And this gesture is all the more powerful if we refuse to do horrible things to those who deserve them. I contend then that the more things we are able to include in this category, the more civilized we are and the more civili*zing.* Thus we gain from including torture in this category, and if execution is especially horrible, we gain still more by including it.

Needless to say, the content, direction, and even the worth of civilization are hotly contested issues, and I shall not be able to win those contests in this brief space. At a minimum, however, I shall assume that civilization involves the taming of the natural environment and of the human animals in it, and that the overall trend in human history is toward increasing this taming, though the trend is by no means unbroken or without reverses. On these grounds, we can say that growth in civilization generally marks human history, that a reduction in the horrible things we tolerate doing to our fellows (even when they deserve them) is part of this growth, and that once the work of civilization is taken on consciously, it includes carrying forward and expanding this reduction.

This claim broadly corresponds to what Emile Durkheim identified, nearly a century ago, as "two laws which seem . . . to prevail in the evolution of the apparatus of punishment." The first, the law of quantitative change, Durkheim formulates as:

> *The intensity of punishment is the greater the more closely societies approximate to a less developed type—and the more the central power assumes an absolute character.*

And the second, which Durkheim refers to as the law of qualitative change, is:

> *Deprivations of liberty, and of liberty alone, varying in time according to the seriousness of the crime, tend to become more and more the normal means of social control.*[25]

Several things should be noted about these laws. First of all, they are not two separate laws. As Durkheim understands them, the second exem-

25. Emile Durkheim, "Two Laws of Penal Evolution," *Economy and Society* 2 (1973):285 and 294; italics in the original. This essay was originally published in French in *Année Sociologique* 4 (1899–1900). Conrad, incidentally, quotes Durkheim's two laws (p. 39), but does not develop their implications for his side in the debate.

*Justice, Civilization, and*
                                    *the Death Penalty*

plifies the trend toward moderation of punishment referred to in the
first.[26] Second, the first law really refers to two distinct trends, which
usually coincide but do not always. That is, moderation of punishment
accompanies *both* the movement from less to more advanced types of
society *and* the movement from more to less absolute rule. Normally
these go hand in hand, but where they do not, the effect of one trend
may offset the effect of the other. Thus, a primitive society without absolute rule may have milder punishments than an equally primitive but
more absolutist society.[27] This complication need not trouble us, since
the claim I am making refers to the first trend, namely, that punishments
tend to become milder as societies become more advanced; and that this
is a trend in history is not refuted by the fact that it is accompanied by
other trends and even occasionally offset by them. Moreover, I shall close
this article with a suggestion about the relation between the intensity of
punishment and the justice of society, which might broadly be thought
of as corresponding to the second trend in Durkheim's first law. Finally,
and most important for our purposes, is the fact that Durkheim's claim
that punishment becomes less intense as societies become more advanced
is a generalization that he supports with an impressive array of evidence
from historical societies from pre-Christian times to the time in which
he wrote—and this in turn supports my claim that the reduction in the
horrible things we do to our fellows is in fact part of the advance of
civilization.[28]

Against this it might be argued that many things grow in history, some

26. Durkheim writes that "of the two laws which we have established, the first contributes
to an explanation of the second" (Durkheim, "Two Laws of Penal Evolution," p. 299).

27. The "two causes of the evolution of punishment—the nature of the social type and
of the governmental organ—must be carefully distinguished" (ibid., p. 288). Durkheim
cites the ancient Hebrews as an example of a society of the less developed type that had
milder punishments than societies of the same social type due to the relative absence of
absolutist government among the Hebrews (ibid., p. 290).

28. Durkheim's own explanation of the progressive moderation of punishments is somewhat unclear. He rejects the notion that it is due to the growth in sympathy for one's
fellows since this, he maintains, would make us more sympathetic with victims and thus
harsher in punishments. He argues instead that the trend is due to the shift from understanding crimes as offenses against God (and thus warranting the most terrible of punishments) to understanding them as offenses against men (thus warranting milder punishments). He then seems to come round nearly full circle by maintaining that this shift works
to moderate punishments by weakening the religious sentiments that overwhelmed sympathy for the condemned: "The true reason is that the compassion of which the condemned
man is the object is no longer overwhelmed by the contrary sentiments which would not
let it make itself felt" (ibid., p. 303).

good, some bad, and some mixed, and thus the fact that there is some historical trend is not a sufficient reason to continue it. Thus, for example, history also brings growth in population, but we are not for that reason called upon to continue the work of civilization by continually increasing our population. What this suggests is that in order to identify something as part of the work of civilizing, we must show not only that it generally grows in history, but that its growth is, on some independent grounds, clearly an advance for the human species—that is, either an unmitigated gain or at least consistently a net gain. And this implies that even trends which we might generally regard as advances may in some cases bring losses with them, such that when they did it would not be appropriate for us to lend our efforts to continuing them. Of such trends we can say that they are advances in civilization except when their gains are outweighed by the losses they bring—and that we are only called upon to further these trends when their gains are *not* outweighed in this way. It is clear in this light that increasing population is a mixed blessing at best, bringing both gains and losses. Consequently, it is not always an advance in civilization that we should further, though at times it may be.

What can be said of reducing the horrible things that we do to our fellows even when deserved? First of all, given our vulnerability to pain, it seems clearly a gain. Is it however an unmitigated gain? That is, would such a reduction ever amount to a loss? It seems to me that there are two conditions under which it would be a loss, namely, if the reduction made our lives more dangerous, or if not doing what is justly deserved were a loss in itself. Let us leave aside the former, since, as I have already suggested and as I will soon indicate in greater detail, I accept that if some horrible punishment is necessary to deter equally or more horrible acts, then we may have to impose the punishment. Thus my claim is that reduction in the horrible things we do to our fellows is an advance in civilization *as long as our lives are not thereby made more dangerous*, and that it is only then that we are called upon to extend that reduction as part of the work of civilization. Assuming then, for the moment, that we suffer no increased danger by refraining from doing horrible things to our fellows when they justly deserve them, does such refraining to do what is justly deserved amount to a loss?

It seems to me that the answer to this must be that refraining to do what is justly deserved is only a loss where it amounts to doing an injustice. But such refraining to do what is just is not doing what is unjust,

*Justice, Civilization, and*
                                           *the Death Penalty*

unless what we do instead falls below the bottom end of the range of just punishments. Otherwise, it would be unjust to refrain from torturing torturers, raping rapists, or beating assaulters. In short, I take it that if there is no injustice in refraining from torturing torturers, then there is no injustice in refraining to do horrible things to our fellows generally, when they deserve them, as long as what we do instead is compatible with believing that they do deserve them. And thus that if such refraining does not make our lives more dangerous, then it is no loss, and given our vulnerability to pain, it is a gain. Consequently, reduction in the horrible things we do to our fellows, when not necessary to our protection, is an advance in civilization that we are called upon to continue once we consciously take upon ourselves the work of civilization.

To complete the argument, however, I must show that execution is horrible enough to warrant its inclusion alongside torture. Against this it will be said that execution is not especially horrible since it only hastens a fate that is inevitable for us.[29] I think that this view overlooks important differences in the manner in which people reach their inevitable ends. I contend that execution is especially horrible, and it is so in a way similar to (though not identical with) the way in which torture is especially horrible. I believe we view torture as especially awful because of two of its features, which also characterize execution: intense pain and the

---

29. Van den Haag seems to waffle on the question of the unique awfulness of execution. For instance, he takes it not to be revolting in the way that earcropping is, because "We all must die. But we must not have our ears cropped" (p. 190), and here he cites John Stuart Mill's parliamentary defense of the death penalty in which Mill maintains that execution only *hastens* death. Mill's point was to defend the claim that "There is not . . . any human infliction which makes an impression on the imagination so entirely out of proportion to its real severity as the punishment of death" (Mill, "Parliamentary Debate," p. 273). And van den Haag seems to agree since he maintains that, since "we cannot imagine our own nonexistence . . . , [t]he fear of the death penalty is in part the fear of the unknown. It . . . rests on a confusion" (pp. 258–59). On the other hand, he writes that "Execution sharpens our separation anxiety because death becomes clearly foreseen. . . . Further, and perhaps most important, when one is executed he does not just die, he is put to death, forcibly expelled from life. He is told that he is too depraved, unworthy of living with other humans" (p. 258). I think, incidentally, that it is an overstatement to say that we cannot imagine our own nonexistence. If we can imagine any counterfactual experience, for example, how we might feel if we didn't know something that we do in fact know, then it doesn't seem impossible to imagine what it would "feel like" not to live. I think I can arrive at a pretty good approximation of this by trying to imagine how things "felt" to me in the eighteenth century. And, in fact, the sense of the awful difference between being alive and not that enters my experience when I do this, makes the fear of death—not as a state, but as the absence of life—seem hardly to rest on a confusion.

spectacle of one human being completely subject to the power of another. This latter is separate from the issue of pain since it is something that offends us about unpainful things, such as slavery (even voluntarily entered) and prostitution (even voluntarily chosen as an occupation).[30] Execution shares this separate feature, since killing a bound and defenseless human being enacts the total subjugation of that person to his fellows. I think, incidentally, that this accounts for the general uneasiness with which execution by lethal injection has been greeted. Rather than humanizing the event, it seems only to have purchased a possible reduction in physical pain at the price of increasing the spectacle of subjugation—with no net gain in the attractiveness of the death penalty. Indeed, its net effect may have been the reverse.

In addition to the spectacle of subjugation, execution, even by physically painless means, is also characterized by a special and intense psychological pain that distinguishes it from the loss of life that awaits us all. Interesting in this regard is the fact that although we are not terribly squeamish about the loss of life itself, allowing it in war, self-defense, as a necessary cost of progress, and so on, we are, as the extraordinary hesitance of our courts testifies, quite reluctant to execute. I think this is because execution involves the most psychologically painful features of deaths. We normally regard death from human causes as worse than death from natural causes, since a humanly caused shortening of life lacks the consolation of unavoidability. And we normally regard death whose coming is foreseen by its victim as worse than sudden death, because a foreseen death adds to the loss of life the terrible consciousness of that impending loss.[31] As a humanly caused death whose advent is foreseen by its victim, an execution combines the worst of both.

Thus far, by analogy with torture, I have argued that execution should be avoided because of how horrible it is to the one executed. But there

---

30. I am not here endorsing this view of voluntarily entered slavery or prostitution. I mean only to suggest that it is *the belief* that these relations involve the extreme subjugation of one person to the power of another that is at the basis of their offensiveness. What I am saying is quite compatible with finding that this belief is false with respect to voluntarily entered slavery or prostitution.

31. This is no doubt partly due to modern skepticism about an afterlife. Earlier peoples regarded a foreseen death as a blessing allowing time to make one's peace with God. Writing of the early Middle Ages, Phillippe Aries says, "In this world that was so familiar with death, sudden death was a vile and ugly death; it was frightening; it seemed a strange and monstrous thing that nobody dared talk about" (Phillippe Aries, *The Hour of Our Death* [New York: Vintage, 1982], p. 11).

141                              *Justice, Civilization, and*
                                  *the Death Penalty*

are reasons of another sort that follow from the analogy with torture. Torture is to be avoided not only because of what it says about *what* we are willing to do to our fellows, but also because of what it says about *us* who are willing to do it. To torture someone is an awful spectacle not only because of the intensity of pain imposed, but because of what is required to be able to impose such pain on one's fellows. The tortured body cringes, using its full exertion to escape the pain imposed upon it— it literally begs for relief with its muscles as it does with its cries. To torture someone is to demonstrate a capacity to resist this begging, and that in turn demonstrates a kind of hardheartedness that a society ought not parade.

And this is true not only of torture, but of all severe corporal punishment. Indeed, I think this constitutes part of the answer to the puzzling question of why we refrain from punishments like whipping, even when the alternative (some months in jail versus some lashes) seems more costly to the offender. Imprisonment is painful to be sure, but it is a reflective pain, one that comes with comparing what is to what might have been, and that can be temporarily ignored by thinking about other things. But physical pain has an urgency that holds body and mind in a fierce grip. Of physical pain, as Orwell's Winston Smith recognized, "you could only wish one thing: that it should stop."[32] Refraining from torture in particular and corporal punishment in general, we both refuse to put a fellow human being in this grip *and* refuse to show our ability to resist this wish. The death penalty is the last corporal punishment used officially in the modern world. And it is corporal not only because administered via the body, but because the pain of foreseen, humanly administered death strikes us with the urgency that characterizes intense physical pain, causing grown men to cry, faint, and lose control of their bodily functions. There is something to be gained by refusing to endorse the hardness of heart necessary to impose such a fate.

By placing execution alongside torture in the category of things we will not do to our fellow human beings even when they deserve them, we broadcast the message that totally subjugating a person to the power of others *and* confronting him with the advent of his own humanly administered demise is too horrible to be done by civilized human beings to their fellows even when they have earned it: too horrible to do, and

32. George Orwell, *1984* (New York: New American Library, 1983; originally published in 1949), p. 197.

too horrible to be capable of doing. And I contend that broadcasting this message loud and clear would in the long run contribute to the general detestation of murder and be, to the extent to which it worked itself into the hearts and minds of the populace, a deterrent. In short, refusing to execute murderers though they deserve it both reflects and continues the taming of the human species that we call civilization. Thus, I take it that the abolition of the death penalty, though it is a just punishment for murder, is part of the civilizing mission of modern states.

## IV. CIVILIZATION, SAFETY, AND DETERRENCE

Earlier I said that judging a practice too horrible to do even to those who deserve it does not exclude the possibility that it could be justified if necessary to avoid even worse consequences. Thus, were the death penalty clearly proven a better deterrent to the murder of innocent people than life in prison, we might have to admit that we had not yet reached a level of civilization at which we could protect ourselves without imposing this horrible fate on murderers, and thus we might have to grant the necessity of instituting the death penalty.[33] But this is far from proven. The available research by no means clearly indicates that the death penalty reduces the incidence of homicide more than life imprisonment does. Even the econometric studies of Isaac Ehrlich, which purport to show that each execution saves seven or eight potential murder victims, have not changed this fact, as is testified to by the controversy and objections from equally respected statisticians that Ehrlich's work has provoked.[34]

33. I say "might" here to avoid the sticky question of just how effective a deterrent the death penalty would have to be to justify overcoming our scruples about executing. It is here that the other considerations often urged against capital punishment—discrimination, irrevocability, the possibility of mistake, and so on—would play a role. Omitting such qualifications, however, my position might crudely be stated as follows: *Just desert limits what a civilized society may do to deter crime, and deterrence limits what a civilized society may do to give criminals their just deserts.*

34. Isaac Ehrlich, "The Deterrent Effect of Capital Punishment: A Question of Life or Death," *American Economic Review* 65 (June 1975):397–417. For reactions to Ehrlich's work, see Alfred Blumstein, Jacqueline Cohen, and Daniel Nagin, eds., *Deterrence and Incapacitation: Estimating the Effects of Criminal Sanctions on Crime Rates* (Washington, D.C.: National Academy of Sciences, 1978), esp. pp. 59–63 and 336–60; Brian E. Forst, "The Deterrent Effect on Capital Punishment: A Cross-State Analysis," *Minnesota Law Review* 61 (May 1977):743–67, Deryck Beyleveld, "Ehrlich's Analysis of Deterrence," *British Journal of Criminology* 22 (April 1982):101–23, and Isaac Ehrlich, "On Positive Methodology, Ethics and Polemics in Deterrence Research," *British Journal of Criminology* 22

*Justice, Civilization, and
the Death Penalty*

Conceding that it has not been proven that the death penalty deters more murders than life imprisonment, van den Haag has argued that neither has it been proven that the death penalty does *not* deter more murders,[35] and thus we must follow common sense which teaches that the higher the cost of something, the fewer people will choose it, and therefore at least some potential murderers who would not be deterred by life imprisonment will be deterred by the death penalty. Van den Haag writes:

> . . . our experience shows that the greater the threatened penalty, the more it deters.
>
> . . . Life in prison is still life, however unpleasant. In contrast, the death penalty does not just threaten to make life unpleasant—it threatens to take life altogether. This difference is perceived by those affected. We find that when they have the choice between life in prison and execution, 99% of all prisoners under sentence of death prefer life in prison. . . .

From this unquestioned fact a reasonable conclusion can be drawn in favor of the superior deterrent effect of the death penalty. Those who have the choice in practice . . . fear death more than they fear life in prison. . . . If they do, it follows that the threat of the death penalty, all other things equal, is likely to deter more than the threat of life in prison. One is most deterred by what one fears most. From which it

---

(April 1982):124–39. Much of the criticism of Ehrlich's work focuses on the fact that he found a deterrence impact of executions in the period from 1933–1969, which includes the period of 1963–1969, a time when hardly any executions were carried out and crime rates rose for reasons that are arguably independent of the existence or nonexistence of capital punishment. When the 1963–1969 period is excluded, no significant deterrent effect shows. Prior to Ehrlich's work, research on the comparative deterrent impact of the death . penalty versus life imprisonment indicated no increase in the incidence of homicide in states that abolished the death penalty and no greater incidence of homicide in states without the death penalty compared to similar states with the death penalty. See Thorsten Sellin, *The Death Penalty* (Philadelphia: American Law Institute, 1959).

35. Van den Haag writes: "Other studies published since Ehrlich's contend that his results are due to the techniques and periods he selected, and that different techniques and periods yield different results. Despite a great deal of research on all sides, one cannot say that the statistical evidence is conclusive. Nobody has claimed to have *disproved* that the death penalty may deter more than life imprisonment. But one cannot claim, either, that it has been proved statistically in a conclusive manner that the death penalty does deter more than alternative penalties. This lack of proof does not amount to disproof" (p. 65).

follows that whatever statistics fail, or do not fail, to show, the death penalty is likely to be more deterrent than any other. [Pp. 68–69][36]

Those of us who recognize how common-sensical it was, and still is, to believe that the sun moves around the earth, will be less willing than Professor van den Haag to follow common sense here, especially when it comes to doing something awful to our fellows. Moreover, there are good reasons for doubting common sense on this matter. Here are four:

1. From the fact that one penalty is more feared than another, it does not follow that the more feared penalty will deter more than the less feared, unless we know that the less feared penalty is not fearful enough to deter everyone who can be deterred—and this is just what we don't know with regard to the death penalty. Though I fear the death penalty more than life in prison, I can't think of any act that the death penalty would deter me from that an equal likelihood of spending my life in prison wouldn't deter me from as well.[37] Since it seems to me that whoever

---

36. An alternative formulation of this "common-sense argument" is put forth and defended by Michael Davis in "Death, Deterrence, and the Method of Common Sense," *Social Theory and Practice* 7, no. 2 (Summer 1981):145–77. Davis's argument is like van den Haag's except that, where van den Haag claims that people *do* fear the death penalty more than lesser penalties and *are* deterred by what they fear most, Davis claims that it is *rational* to fear the death penalty more than lesser penalties and thus *rational* to be more deterred by it. Thus, he concludes that the death penalty is the most effective deterrent *for rational people*. He admits that this argument is "about rational agents, not actual people" (ibid., p. 157). To bring it back to the actual criminal justice system that deals with actual people, Davis claims that the criminal law makes no sense unless we suppose the potential criminal to be (more or less) rational" (ibid., p. 153). In short, the death penalty is the most effective deterrent because it would be rational to be most effectively deterred by it, and we are committed by belief in the criminal law to supposing that people will do what is rational. The problem with this strategy is that a deterrence justification of a punishment is valid only if it proves that the punishment actually deters actual people from committing crimes. If it doesn't prove that, it misses its mark, no matter what we are committed to supposing. Unless Davis's argument is a way of proving that the actual people governed by the criminal law will be more effectively deterred by the death penalty than by lesser penalties, it is irrelevant to the task at hand. And if it is a way of proving that actual people will be better deterred, then it is indistinguishable from van den Haag's version of the argument and vulnerable to the criticisms of it which follow.

37. David A. Conway writes: "given the choice, I would strongly prefer one thousand years in hell to eternity there. Nonetheless, if one thousand years in hell were the penalty for some action, it would be quite sufficient to deter me from performing that action. The additional years would do nothing to discourage me further. Similarly, the prospect of the death penalty, while worse, may not have any greater deterrent effect than does that of life imprisonment" (David A. Conway, "Capital Punishment and Deterrence: Some Considerations in Dialogue Form," *Philosophy & Public Affairs* 3, no. 4 [Summer 1974]:433).

*Justice, Civilization, and
the Death Penalty*

would be deterred by a given likelihood of death would be deterred by an *equal* likelihood of life behind bars, I suspect that the common-sense argument only seems plausible because we evaluate it unconsciously assuming that potential criminals will face larger likelihoods of death sentences than of life sentences. If the likelihoods were equal, it seems to me that where life imprisonment was improbable enough to make it too distant a possibility to worry much about, a similar low probability of death would have the same effect. After all, we are undeterred by small likelihoods of death every time we walk the streets. And if life imprisonment were sufficiently probable to pose a real deterrent threat, it would pose as much of a deterrent threat as death. And this is just what most of the research we have on the comparative deterrent impact of execution versus life imprisonment suggests.

2. In light of the fact that roughly 500 to 700 suspected felons are killed by the police in the line of duty every year, and the fact that the number of privately owned guns in America is substantially larger than the number of households in America, it must be granted that anyone contemplating committing a crime *already* faces a substantial risk of ending up dead as a result.[38] It's hard to see why anyone *who is not already deterred by this* would be deterred by the addition of the more distant risk of death after apprehension, conviction, and appeal. Indeed, this suggests that people consider risks in a much cruder way than van den Haag's appeal to common sense suggests—which should be evident to anyone who contemplates how few people use seatbelts (14% of drivers, on some estimates), when it is widely known that wearing them can spell the difference between life (outside prison) and death.[39]

3. Van den Haag has maintained that deterrence doesn't work only by means of cost-benefit calculations made by potential criminals. It works also by the lesson about the wrongfulness of murder that is slowly learned in a society that subjects murderers to the ultimate punishment (p. 63). But if I am correct in claiming that the refusal to execute even those who deserve it has a civilizing effect, then the refusal to execute also teaches a lesson about the wrongfulness of murder. My claim here is

38. On the number of people killed by the police, see Lawrence W. Sherman and Robert H. Langworthy, "Measuring Homicide by Police Officers," *Journal of Criminal Law and Criminology* 70, no. 4 (Winter 1979):546–60; on the number of privately owned guns, see Franklin Zimring, *Firearms and Violence in American Life* (Washington, D.C.: U.S. Government Printing Office, 1968), pp. 6–7.

39. *AAA World* (Potomac ed.) 4, no. 3 (May–June 1984), pp. 18c and 18i.

admittedly speculative, but no more so than van den Haag's to the contrary. And my view has the added virtue of accounting for the failure of research to show an increased deterrent effect from executions *without having to deny the plausibility of van den Haag's common-sense argument that at least some additional potential murderers will be deterred by the prospect of the death penalty*. If there is a deterrent effect from *not executing*, then it is understandable that while executions will deter some murderers, this effect will be balanced out by the weakening of the deterrent effect of not executing, such that no net reduction in murders will result.[40] And this, by the way, also disposes of van den Haag's argument that, in the absence of knowledge one way or the other on the deterrent effect of executions, we should execute murderers rather than risk the lives of innocent people whose murders might have been deterred if we had. If there is a deterrent effect of not executing, it follows that we risk innocent lives either way. And if this is so, it seems that the only reasonable course of action is to refrain from imposing what we know is a horrible fate.[41]

40. A related claim has been made by those who defend the so-called brutalization hypothesis by presenting evidence to show that murders *increase* following an execution. See, for example, William J. Bowers and Glenn L. Pierce, "Deterrence or Brutalization: What is the Effect of Executions?" *Crime & Delinquency* 26, no. 4 (October 1980):453–84. They conclude that each execution gives rise to two additional homicides in the month following, and that these are real additions, not just a change in timing of the homicides (ibid., p. 481). My claim, it should be noted, is not identical to this, since, as I indicate in the text, what I call "the deterrence effect of not executing" is not something whose impact is to be seen immediately following executions but over the long haul, and, further, my claim is compatible with finding no net increase in murders due to executions. Nonetheless, should the brutalization hypothesis be borne out by further studies, it would certainly lend support to the notion that there is a deterrent effect of not executing.

41. Van den Haag writes: "If we were quite ignorant about the marginal deterrent effects of execution, we would have to choose—like it or not—between the certainty of the convicted murderer's death by execution and the likelihood of the survival of future victims of other murderers on the one hand, and on the other his certain survival and the likelihood of the death of new victims. I'd rather execute a man convicted of having murdered others than put the lives of innocents at risk. I find it hard to understand the opposite choice" (p. 69). Conway was able to counter this argument earlier by pointing out that the research on the marginal deterrent effects of execution was not *inconclusive* in the sense of *tending to point both ways*, but rather in the sense of *giving us no reason to believe that capital punishment saves more lives than life imprisonment*. He could then answer van den Haag by saying that the choice is not between risking the lives of murderers and risking the lives of innocents, but between killing a murderer with no reason to believe lives will be saved, and sparing a murderer with no reason to believe lives will be lost (Conway, "Capital Punishment and Deterrence," pp. 442–43). This, of course, makes the choice to spare the

147 *Justice, Civilization, and*
*the Death Penalty*

4. Those who still think that van den Haag's common-sense argument for executing murderers is valid will find that the argument proves more than they bargained for. Van den Haag maintains that, in the absence of conclusive evidence on the relative deterrent impact of the death penalty versus life imprisonment, we must follow common sense and assume that if one punishment is more fearful than another, it will deter some potential criminals not deterred by the less fearful punishment. Since people sentenced to death will almost universally try to get their sentences changed to life in prison, it follows that death is more fearful than life imprisonment, and thus that it will deter some additional murderers. Consequently, we should institute the death penalty to save the lives these additional murderers would have taken. But, since people sentenced to be tortured to death would surely try to get their sentences changed to simple execution, the same argument proves that death-by-torture will deter still more potential murderers. Consequently, we should institute death-by-torture to save the lives these additional murderers would have taken. Anyone who accepts van den Haag's argument is then confronted with a dilemma: Until we have conclusive evidence that capital punishment is a greater deterrent to murder than life imprisonment, he must grant *either* that we should not follow common sense and not impose the death penalty; *or* we should follow common sense and torture murderers to death. In short, either we must abolish the electric chair or reinstitute the rack. Surely, this is the *reductio ad absurdum* of van den Haag's common-sense argument.

## Conclusion: History, Force, and Justice

I believe that, taken together, these arguments prove that we should abolish the death penalty though it is a just punishment for murder. Let me close with an argument of a different sort. When you see the lash fall upon the backs of Roman slaves, or the hideous tortures meted out in the period of the absolute monarchs, you see more than mere cruelty at work. Surely you suspect that there is something about the injustice of imperial slavery and royal tyranny that requires the use of extreme

---

murderer more understandable than van den Haag allows. Events, however, have overtaken Conway's argument. The advent of Ehrlich's research, contested though it may be, leaves us in fact with research that tends to point both ways.

force to keep these institutions in place. That is, for reasons undoubtedly related to those that support the second part of Durkheim's first law of penal evolution, we take the amount of force a society uses against its own people as an inverse measure of its justness. And though no more than a rough measure, it is a revealing one nonetheless, because when a society is limited in the degree of force it can use against its subjects, it is likely to have to be a juster society since it will have to gain its subjects' cooperation by offering them fairer terms than it would have to, if it could use more force. From this we cannot simply conclude that reducing the force used by our society will automatically make our society more just—but I think we can conclude that it will have this tendency, since it will require us to find means other than force for encouraging compliance with our institutions, and this is likely to require us to make those institutions as fair to all as possible. Thus I hope that America will pose itself the challenge of winning its citizens' cooperation by justice rather than force, and that when future historians look back on the twentieth century, they will find us with countries like France and England and Sweden that have abolished the death penalty, rather than with those like South Africa and the Soviet Union and Iran that have retained it—with all that this suggests about the countries involved.

# [6]

# CIVIL DISQUALIFICATIONS ATTENDING CONVICTION: A SUGGESTED CONCEPTUAL FRAMEWORK*

Andrew von Hirsch[†]
Martin Wasik[‡]

## I. Introduction

A PERSON convicted of a crime suffers punishment—a fine, a community sentence, or perhaps a custodial term. In addition to that sanction, however, conviction of the crime may trigger a variety of disqualifications. The offender may be barred from holding public office, or from serving on a jury. He may be precluded from certain types of employment, or be prevented from driving a vehicle. These consequences may considerably restrict the person's prospects for earning a living or his mobility. Yet the visibility of these measures is low: provisions authorising various disqualifications are scattered throughout the statute books, and are not easy to find. While there is now a considerable body of jurisprudence on sentencing,[1] the principles which should inform the proper use of disqualifications have received little serious attention.[2]

One reason for this topic's neglect has been the perception that civil disqualifications attendant upon conviction have become much less onerous than they used to be. A person convicted of a crime—or at least, of a felony—once forfeited such basic civil rights as the capacity to acquire or transfer property, or to bring suit or testify in the courts. Many of the sweeping disabilities of earlier times have been abolished, and only a few disqualifications remain which flow automatically from the fact of conviction. An example of these surviving disqualifications is loss of the right to vote for the duration

---

* The authors benefited from comments received at a guest seminar held on 1 November 1996 at the Law Faculty of the University of Birmingham. We are grateful also for extensive comments provided by Antony Duff, John Kleinig, and Stephen Shute—as well as for the suggestions of numerous other colleagues who read earlier versions of this article.
† Honorary Professor of Penal Theory and Penal Law, and Fellow of Fitzwilliam College, University of Cambridge.
‡ Professor of Law at the University of Manchester; British Academy/Leverhulme Trust Senior Research Fellow 1997–98.

[1] See, *e.g.*, A. Ashworth, *Sentencing and Criminal Justice*, 2nd ed. (1995); A. von Hirsch, *Censure and Sanctions* (1993); A. von Hirsch & A. Ashworth (eds.), *Principled Sentencing* (1992).
[2] A short discussion can be found in Advisory Council on the Penal System, *Non-Custodial and Semi-Custodial Penalties* (1970), Chap. 6.

of a custodial sentence. Other kinds of disabilities, however, are not disappearing and, indeed, are expanding in scope. This is most clearly the case for employment disqualifications. Conviction for certain offences may result in the offender being barred by the sentencing judge, or being prevented by a licensing authority, from engaging or continuing to engage in various professions or occupations. Such disqualifications can often have a greater adverse impact on the defendant than the formal punishment administered on sentence.[3]

Should disqualifications be considered as a species of punishment?[4] Or should they be seen as civil measures ancillary to punishment, concerned with preventing certain kinds of risk?[5] If they have this civil character, should they be exempted from the limitations applicable to punishments—in particular, the requirements of proportionality and desert? What alternative restrictions should then be applicable, and by what test can disqualifications properly be distinguished from penal sanctions? The present article addresses these questions.

The article has certain limitations of scope. First, it addresses only *disqualifications*, by which we mean legal requirements that the defendant desist from certain occupations or activities. Requirements that the defendant take affirmative steps (such as registering with the police after the expiration of sentence and possibly notifying to them his whereabouts[6]) will not be addressed; these are more complicated matters, as such measures' appropriateness would depend on the character and onerousness of those required steps. Second, we deal only with *state-imposed* disqualifications—imposed by statute, by a judge at the time of sentence, or by an official licensing authority. We do not discuss loss of employment opportunities and other disadvantages which convicted persons incur at the hands of private firms or individuals;[7] these raise different problems, since they relate not to governmental action but to dealings among private parties.

We begin with a brief survey of state-imposed disqualifications.

---

[3] Occasionally such consequences appear starkly in sentencing cases. In *Lowery* (1993) 14 Cr. App. R. (S.) 485 the defendant, in consequence of his conviction for fraud, forfeited his employment, lost his home (which came with the job), and his pension rights were frozen. For the relevance of such consequences to the sentence to be imposed, see Ashworth, *op. cit.* n. 1 above, pp. 142–144.

[4] N. Walker, in *Why Punish?* (1991), p. 1, comments that "a shared conception of punishment" involves the infliction of something assumed to be unwelcome to the recipient, such as "the inconvenience of a disqualification, the hardship of incarceration . . . " etc. In *Young* (1990) 12 Cr. App. R. (S.) 262 the Court of Appeal said that the offender's disqualification from acting as a company director for two years was "unquestionably a punishment".

[5] Texts on sentencing tend to treat disqualifications as a form of ancillary order, distinct from punishments. See D. Thomas, *Current Sentencing Practice*, Part H, and M. Wasik, *Emmins on Sentencing*, 2nd ed. (1993), Chap. 10.

[6] Sex Offenders Act 1997, Part I. State laws in the US require released sex offenders to register with the police, who may inform local residents of the nature of the offender's crime, and his address. These laws have survived challenge in the courts: see *State* v. *Ward*, 123 Wn. 2d. 488 (1994) (Washington) and *State* v. *Noble*, 171 Ariz. 171, 829 P. 2d. 1217 (1992) (Arizona).

[7] On which see J.P. Martin and D. Webster, *The Social Consequences of Conviction* (1971) and N. Walker, *Punishment, Danger and Stigma* (1980).

This is followed by the main part of the article, which attempts to sketch a theory of when, why, and with what limitations disqualifications imposed by the state upon convicted offenders should be permissible. Our theory is meant to be normative rather than descriptive: we are offering a conception of how disqualifications *should* be dealt with, rather than a doctrine that purports to account for existing law. In our final section, we recommend some remedial steps, based on our theory.

Our theory, in a nutshell, treats disqualifications not as supplemental punishments, but as civil measures dealing with risks of certain kinds. This perspective, however, calls for careful limitation and targeting of the measures: they should be used only when the occupation or activity is especially sensitive to abuse, and when the defendant's criminal conduct is of a kind that is indicative of risk of that kind of abuse. We argue also that certain basic rights and interests—such as those of liberty, or of access to the more common-place sorts of employment—should not be subject to civil disqualifications. And we also suggest why proposals to convert disqualifications into criminal penalties—such as schemes to remove offenders' driving licences for crimes not involving misuse of a vehicle—are not desirable.

## II. TYPES OF DISQUALIFICATION

Conducting a survey of state-imposed disqualifications is no easy matter. The authorising provisions are found in diverse places throughout the statute book, and vary considerably across different jurisdictions. A convicted person may face difficulty simply in finding out what activities he is supposed to avoid. Disqualifications do, however, seem to fall into three main types: (1) those that take effect automatically on conviction, (2) those that may be imposed by the sentencing judge, and (3) those imposed by regulatory agencies.

### 1. Disqualifications automatic upon conviction

In earlier times, there were many such incidents of conviction, involving extensive loss of civil rights. Convicted persons would incur "civil death", losing the right to hold or transfer property, to vote, to bring suit in the courts, or even to make public statements or to visit certain places.[8] Now, there are few such deprivations, although they have not disappeared altogether. In England and Wales, a convicted person

---

[8] For detailed reviews see H.R.S. Ryan, "Loss of Civil and Political Rights on Conviction of a Criminal Offence" (1963) 5 *Criminal Law Quarterly* 470; M.R. Damaska, "Adverse Legal Consequences of Conviction and Their Removal: A Comparative Survey" (1968) 59 *Journal of Criminal Law, Criminology and Police Science* 347 & 542; and (Special Issue) "The Collateral Consequences of a Criminal Conviction" (1970) 23 *Vanderbilt Law Review* 929.

602 *The Cambridge Law Journal* [1997]

sentenced to imprisonment loses the right to vote for the duration of the sentence.[9] In some American states a person convicted of any imprisonable offence loses the right to vote until completion of sentence, even if he has not been incarcerated.[10] In England and Wales, a convicted person who has at any time served a custodial sentence of five years or more, or within the preceding 10 years has served a custodial sentence of any length, or received a sentence of community service or probation, is ineligible to serve as a juror.[11] A person given a custodial sentence of three years or more is prohibited from possessing or acquiring any firearm or ammunition.[12] Conviction can also entail automatic employment disqualification: in the State of Washington, for example, conviction for any felony means that the person is debarred for life from holding any public office.[13]

## 2. Disqualifications imposed at sentencing stage

A range of disqualificatory powers are conferred upon the sentencing judge by statute. Some such disqualifications are mandatory, such as driving disqualification wherever a person has been convicted of certain serious driving offences,[14] or has been convicted of a series of less serious driving offences.[15] More typically, however, the sentencer is given discretion to disqualify those who have been convicted of certain crimes, in respect of various particular activities and employments. Driving disqualifications are discretionary in a range of cases where they are not mandatory.[16] Offending drivers can be banned for life, or for a specified period, or until they re-take and pass their driving test.[17] Offenders convicted of certain kinds of financial frauds may be disqualified from holding office as a company director for a specified period of years.[18] Conviction for an offence involving corruption may result in forfeiture of any public office held and disqualification from holding public office for a specified period of time.[19] Offenders may be barred from holding a licence to sell liquor[20]

---

[9] Representation of the People Act 1983, s. 3(1).
[10] *E.g.* Constitution of the State of Washington, Art. VI, para. 3.
[11] Juries Act 1974, sched. I, part II.
[12] Firearms Act 1968, s. 21. We do not address firearms legislation in this article, in view of the extensive literature on this special subject, and the controversy over whether even ordinary, unconvicted citizens should be allowed to possess firearms.
[13] R.C.W. 9.92.120; see further D. Boerner, *Sentencing in Washington* (1985).
[14] Road Traffic Offenders Act 1988, s. 34 (obligatory disqualification subject to "special reasons").
[15] Road Traffic Offenders Act 1988, s. 35 (subject to "mitigating grounds").
[16] Currently the Crown Court on sentence may disqualify from driving a person who has used a motor vehicle to commit a non-motoring offence: Powers of Criminal Courts Act 1973, s. 44. The Crime (Sentences) Act 1997 authorises the banning of convicted offenders from driving even where no vehicle was used in commission of the offence. This measure is addressed more fully in Part VI.
[17] Road Traffic Offenders Act 1988, s. 36.
[18] Company Directors Disqualification Act 1986, s. 1 & s. 2.
[19] Public Bodies Corrupt Practices Act 1889, s. 2
[20] Licensing Act 1984, s. 100 & s. 101.

or a betting or gaming licence.[21] They may be barred from entering public houses[22] or from attending football matches.[23] A person may be banned from keeping animals, for life or for a specified period.[24]

### 3. Disqualification by regulatory authority

A wide range of employment disqualifications can be imposed by regulatory authorities. These disqualifications may either bar the person from applying for a particular employment, or result in termination of an employment which he or she already has. Wide discretion is granted in the exercise of these powers, with which the courts will rarely interfere.[25] The bodies having these powers range from professional associations, such as the Law Society[26] and the General Medical Council,[27] through local authorities which regulate the employment of teachers, social workers, child minders,[28] and taxi drivers[29] in their area, to smaller trade associations, which are authorised to regulate building workers, and others engaged in various trades. While some of these bodies are private associations, their power to disbar offenders is conferred by statute, thus making such disqualifications (at least indirectly) state-imposed.

Some general points should be made about the three categories identified above. Although the first group (automatic disqualification on conviction) may perhaps be regarded as a residual category, it still gives rise to some important concerns. The Prison Reform Trust, for example, is campaigning for the right to vote to be extended to all prisoners in England, in line with practice in many other countries.[30] The second and third categories are in no sense residual, and the clear trend in recent years has been for them to increase in number and complexity. A range of new forms of court-ordered disqualifications has been created in recent years, and more are planned. There is a

---

[21] Gaming Act 1968, s. 24 & s. 25

[22] Licensed Premises (Exclusion of Certain Persons) Act 1980, s. 1.

[23] Public Order Act 1986, s. 30; Football Spectators Act 1989, part II.

[24] Protection of Animals Act 1911, s. 3; Protection of Animals (Amendment) Act 1954, s. 1.

[25] See B. Harris, *Law and Practice of Disciplinary and Regulatory Proceedings* (1995). The leading decisions are *Faramus* v. *Film Artistes' Association* [1964] A.C. 925 and *McInnis* v. *Onslow Fane and Another* [1978] 3 All E. R. 211. In the former case the House of Lords upheld the Association's rule prohibiting membership to anyone who had *ever* been convicted of a non-motoring offence.

[26] The Solicitors Act 1974; Courts and Legal Services Act 1990; The Solicitors' (Disciplinary) Proceedings) Rules 1994 (S.I. 1994, No. 228). See further *Bolton* v. *Law Society* [1994] 2 All E.R. 486.

[27] The Medical Act 1983; The General Medical Council (Procedure) Rules 1988 (S.I. 1988, No. 2255). See further *Libman* v. *G.M.C.* [1972] 1 All E.R. 798. Other examples are the Nurses, Midwives and Health Visitors Act 1997, the Pharmacy Act 1954 and the Architects Act 1997.

[28] Children Act 1989; The Disqualification from Caring for Children Regulations (S.I. 1991, No. 2094).

[29] Local Government (Miscellaneous Provisions) Act 1976, as amended by Road Traffic Act 1991, s. 47.

[30] Prison Reform Trust, *Fair Votes for Prisoners* (1996).

veritable forest of regulatory disqualifications,[31] found throughout the law.

Over the years and across different jurisdictions, it has been recognised that these various forms of disqualification, particularly those which affect employment prospects, often have a serious debilitating impact upon convicted persons. Efforts have been made to counteract some of these effects. The remedial legislation affects both state-imposed disqualifications and those imposed by private parties. One approach has been to adopt a sentencing rule whereby certain convictions imposed by a criminal court are deemed by statute not to count as convictions, and thereby not to attract the normal disabling consequences of conviction.[32] A second approach has been the creation of statutory expungement provisions. These have the effect that, after the passage of a period of time, the relevant disqualifications cease to have effect.[33] In some jurisdictions the passage of time triggers this effect automatically. In others, the convicted person is required to make application to a court or other authoritative body, which may then exercise its discretion to expunge the conviction.[34] The practical effect of expungement is that the convicted person may then omit reference to the conviction (on an employment application form, for instance).

With this brief descriptive survey of disqualifications, let us turn to our main question: their justifiability. To what extent, and on what grounds should disqualifications such as those just described be retained?

### III. The Need for Sparing Use of Disqualifications

Before considering what specific functions disqualifications might have, we want first to suggest some general reasons for subjecting *all* such disabilities to careful scrutiny. It surely is desirable to give offenders the opportunity to lead normal lives after they have completed their punishments. The more one precludes former convicts

---

[31] There is also a mass of regulation relating to the disclosure of criminal records to prospective employers for vetting purposes, much of it contained in delegated legislation and Home Office Circulars. For discussion see B. Hebenton and T. Thomas, *Criminal Records* (1993), Chap 5. Part V of the Police Act 1997 now requires a job applicant, on request, to furnish a prospective employer with a "criminal conviction certificate", to be obtained by the applicant from the Criminal Records Agency on payment of a fee. See further Home Office, *On The Record*, Cm. 3308, 1996.

[32] Powers of Criminal Courts Act 1973, s. 1C. See further M. Wasik, "Discharge Provisions and the Restricted Meaning of 'Conviction'" (forthcoming in the *Law Quarterly Review*).

[33] Rehabilitation of Offenders Act 1974, s. 7(1)(d).

[34] See B. Kogon and D. Loughery, "Sealing and Expungement of Criminal Records" (1970) 61 *Journal of Criminal Law, Criminology and Police Science* 378 and J.S. Leon, "Post-Sentencing Problems: Some Consequences of a Finding of Guilt in Criminal Cases" (1978) 20 *Criminal Law Quarterly* 318.

from pursuing legitimate occupations or activities, the more one is restricting the opportunities for them to live normal lives. The risk of over-broad restriction is all the greater because disqualifications often are adopted piecemeal and tend to cumulate: securities regulators want to exclude ex-offenders from the securities industry, plumbers want a similar exclusion for ex-offenders as plumbers, and so forth.

Why is it important to safeguard ex-offenders' prospects for living normal lives? Part of the concern is one of criminal policy—that former offenders should retain opportunities to re-settle in their communities and to lead law-abiding existences. The Court of Appeal thus has stated recently that "[I]t is in the public interest that persons should renounce a life of crime and that they should take up honest work and live a proper life . . .".[35] This aim also receives tacit recognition in the various English provisions on community sentences, which require that their performance by the offender be arranged, so far as possible, so as not to disrupt the offender's existing education and employment commitments.[36] The more that convicted persons are restricted by law from pursuing legitimate occupations, the fewer opportunities they will have for remaining law abiding.[37] While there is no simple correlation between unemployment and criminality, a lack of employment opportunities can increase the economic incentives to commit crime.[38]

There is, however, a more fundamental reason for giving careful scrutiny to disqualifications: namely, that former convicts should not be relegated to second-class citizenship. A fair system of punishment is one in which the offender is subjected to specified penal restrictions, which bear a reasonable relation to the gravity of the crime, and which are operative only for a specified time. A corollary to this assumption is that civil disqualifications—which may take effect or continue even after completion of sentence—should be imposed parsimoniously, with appropriate restrictions of purpose, duration, and scope. The wider the range and intrusiveness of such deprivations, the closer they come to creating a status of second-class citizenship for those who have been convicted and punished.

These arguments should suffice to support repeal of a number of

---

[35] *Meyers* [1996] 1 Cr. App. R (S.) 249 at p. 251.

[36] Powers of Criminal Courts Act 1973, s. 15(3) (community service orders); Criminal Justice Act 1982, s. 17(8) (attendance centre orders); Criminal Justice Act 1991, s. 12(3) (curfew orders).

[37] See Council of Europe, *The Criminal Record and Rehabilitation of Convicted Persons* (1984), p. 31: ". . . if one is to prevent a convicted person from committing further offences, their social reintegration must be made as easy as possible". The Court of Appeal has held that, in general, when imposing a driving ban the court should have regard to the offender's employment prospects (*Weston* (1982) 4 Cr. App. R. (S.) 51), and has noted that a long driving ban can be counter-productive, by in effect inviting the offender to commit further offences (*Matthews* (1987) 9 Cr. App. R. (S.) 1) or otherwise handicapping the offender in trying to rehabilitate himself (*West* (1986) 8 Cr. App. R. (S.) 266).

[38] See, for example, T. Bennett and R. Wright, *Burglars on Burglary* (1984), p. 31.

existing disqualifications. The loss of the right to vote is an example. Voting is an important civil right and, notwithstanding occasional rhetoric about "safeguarding the purity of the ballot box", it is not apparent how or why permitting prisoners to vote would undermine the democratic process. The franchise is a fundamental right of citizenship, and its removal denies convicted persons the opportunity to promote their own legitimate interests through the political process. Disenfranchising prisoners would also appear to be discriminatory, given the over-representation of ethnic minority groups in custody.[39] Claims that it is impractical to make arrangements for prisoners to vote are unconvincing. In Australia all citizens must vote, and that includes prisoners.

Other forms of disqualification, however, are less implausible. It does seem to make sense to bar the convicted dangerous driver from driving again, at least for a period of time, or to ensure that the convicted embezzler does not become a bank director. Even so, these disqualifications require examination. How, precisely, can such disabilities be justified? What are the scope and limits of their justification?

## IV. Disqualifications as Risk-Prevention Measures

### 1. The basis for intervention: risk prevention

We think that disqualifications (to the extent that they are supportable at all) should ordinarily be viewed as being civil risk-prevention measures. While such disabilities are triggered by a conviction, they properly should function as methods of forestalling certain risks in the context of a specified occupation or activity,[40] rather than as ancillary penalties. Barring the convicted fraudster from acting as a solicitor or banker serves to prevent him from misusing these sensitive positions to perpetrate further frauds; banning the convicted dangerous driver from driving for a period of time addresses the risks which he poses on the roads. If disqualifications thus serve as civil risk-prevention measures, their use and the limitations applying to them should be governed by concerns about risk. The issue becomes: when do the concerns about risk warrant depriving a convicted person of his normal opportunities to carry on certain occupations, or to engage in certain activities? Often, disqualification consequent upon conviction

---

[39] See R. Hood, *Race and Sentencing* (1992).
[40] In *Cobbey* (1993) 14 Cr. App. R. (S.) 82, the Court of Appeal said that the purpose of a company director disqualification order was ". . . to prevent [the offender] from using a corporate vehicle to defraud others in the way that he has done here, through dishonesty and no doubt also incompetence . . .". Contrast the comment cited in n. 4 above.

is only part of the state's machinery for regulating more generally the occupation or activity involved. Disbarring the convicted solicitor from practising law can be seen as part of a broader scheme for regulating that profession, in the interests of clients and the public.

## 2. Sparing intervention on grounds of risk

Disqualifications, when viewed as civil risk-prevention measures, possess two worrisome features. One is the tendency to overprediction of forecasts of offending: where predictions of more serious infractions are concerned, the majority of those classified as bad risks will not, in fact, be found to engage in the predicted behaviour.[41] The character of any single criminal act, moreover, tends to be a weak predictor—weaker, for example, than the offender's full criminal history. If someone has committed an offence involving a given activity, that information alone does not provide a strong basis for inferring that he is likely to offend again, still less that (should he offend again) his offence would involve that kind of activity.[42] Risk-based judgments also tend to switch attention from the interests of individuals to the management of collectives: it is simply more convenient to exclude all members of any given group whose members include higher-than average risks.[43] Such tendencies can easily lead to inappropriate and over-broad risk-avoidance postures, such as the assumption that virtually *no* degree of risk can be tolerated.

Another, more basic concern relates to notions of human agency. If an intending airline pilot is barred from flying because he cannot pass his tests, the basis of that decision is the person's capacity—he is thought to lack the skills needed to fly safely. When a businessman is barred from serving as a company director on account of a fraud conviction, however, this relates not to capacity[44] but to his future choices: it is feared that he may commit another fraud. Where the future decisions of a person (rather than his existing capacities) are at issue, our legal tradition has shown, quite correctly, a reluctance to intervene before the fact—we do not normally try to restrain the person from offending before he has actually committed the offending act or taken significant steps toward committing it. Such forbearance reflects the assumption that persons are agents, not beasts—beings who are capable of deciding whether or not to act, and of considering

---

[41] For references, see A. von Hirsch and A. Ashworth, "Protective Sentencing under Section 2(2)(b): The Criteria for Dangerousness" [1996] *Criminal Law Review* 175, particularly p. 176 and nn. 5–8.

[42] G.J.O. Phillpotts and L.B. Lancucki, *Previous Convictions, Sentence and Reconvictions* (1979), Home Office Research Study No. 53.

[43] See M. Feeley and J. Simon, "Actuarial Justice: The Emerging New Criminal Law" in D. Nelken (ed.), *The Futures of Criminology* (1994), p. 173.

[44] Though see 5 below.

reasons (both of a moral and of a prudential character) in so deciding. Refraining from pre-emptive intervention also ensures that the person will be left alone, so long as he does not offend. While such forbearance calls for accepting a degree of risk, it gives the person the option of complying and thus perserving his freedom from intrusion.[45]

Penal sanctions are not primarily pre-emptive interventions: the offender is punished in consequence of having chosen already to offend, and the extent of his punishment should depend in important part on the degree of wrongfulness of that past choice.[46] Disqualifications as civil measures, however, are addressed to the offender's future behaviour: the dishonest company director is barred from serving in that capacity to prevent him from commiting further frauds; and his conviction serves just to establish that he has been dishonest—and thus may continue to be so in future. If prevention of future misconduct is the mission, this comes into tension with the notion of agency just mentioned: the disbarred director is prevented from continuing to sit on company boards in advance of a choice on his part to offend again in this capacity.

These concerns about overprediction and about human agency should, in our view, dictate parsimony in the use of disqualifications: such measures should be invoked on risk-prevention grounds only where the case for them is strong. When might that be? Two considerations seem to be relevant here. The first is the specially vulnerable character of the occupation or activity involved, and the second is the bearing of the conviction on that particular risk. Let us consider these, in turn.

### 3. *Special vulnerability of the occupation or activity*

The case for disqualification seems strongest when the occupation or activity involved is one that is especially vulnerable to abuse and where that abuse, if it occurred, would involve substantial harm. So, the reasons why the particular occupation or activity is so sensitive need to be made explicit.

One might start with traditionally regulated professions, such as those of medicine and the law. These activities require special professional skills, and tend to be fiduciary in character. Why does a

---

[45] For application of this argument to criminal sanctions, see H.L.A. Hart, *Punishment and Responsibility* (1968), Chaps. 1 & 7.
[46] English sentencing law thus generally calls for observance of proportionality in deciding the severity of sentence; see Criminal Justice Act 1991, ss. 2(2)(a) and 6(2)(b). An exception is made under s. 2(2)(b) of the Act permitting longer-than-proportionate sentences but only in cases of special danger rather than of ordinary risks of recidivism. See von Hirsch & Ashworth *op. cit.* n. 41 above. For more on the role of proportionality in punishment, and on the extent to which risk may be considered in deciding penal sanctions, see pp. 611–612 and 616–617 below at nn. 51–53 and 67–70 respectively.

power to impose conviction-based disqualifications seem appropriate to these professions? The power to disqualify is part of wider powers to regulate the profession in the public interest. The vulnerability of those served by the professions is also great: solicitors occupy a position of trust *vis-à-vis* their clients, who may lack the expertise to determine whether they are being served competently and honestly. Dishonesty or incompetence may well adversely affect the clients' vital interests—even their livelihood. Given this vulnerability, it is thought wise to err on the side of caution when deciding who may pursue or continue in the profession. That is why the solicitor convicted of fraud may be disbarred to forestall the risk of further dishonesty at the expense of clients—even though, as just noted, such judgments of risk entail overbreadth and bypass personal agency.[47]

The solicitor provides the paradigm case, as this involves (i) an established profession, involving (ii) special skills, subject to (iii) licensing and extensive regulation, with (iv) services having a fiduciary character, and (v) a clientele having substantial vulnerability. In other kinds of work, some of these elements may be lacking, but there may remain special reasons for considering the activity unusually sensitive to abuse. Consider these three examples:

— Acting as a company director is not a profession in the established sense, in that no special formal qualifications may be involved. Nevertheless, an extensive system of state regulation is in place, and a company director acts in a fiduciary capacity in relation to the interests of the company and its shareholders. The director's powers and "insider" position place him or her in a position to do a great deal of harm to those interests.

— Serving as an attendant in a nursing home, hospital or children's home may involve unskilled labour, and these are activities that only recently have come under state supervision. Nevertheless, there remains a specially vulnerable clientele not in a position to protect itself, and abuse of the position entails the potential of an unusual degree of harm.

— Driving a vehicle is not in itself a job or profession, but rather an activity in which a large number of persons engage. Drivers do not act in a fiduciary capacity (except, perhaps, with respect to other occupants of the vehicle). Driving does, however, call for special skills and has long been subject to licensing and an elaborate scheme of regulation. It involves substantial hazards,

---

[47] See the comments of Sir Thomas Bingham M.R. in *Bolton* v. *Law Society* [1994] 2 All E.R. 486, at p. 492, that the reasons for disqualifying a solicitor include that of denying the opportunity of re-offending.

with regard to the likelihood of accidents occurring, and to their potential seriousness when they do.

When, then, may an activity be deemed so sensitive as to overcome our general principle of sparing intervention? We can offer no hard-and-fast dividing line, but the case for intervention is strongest when *all* of the elements (i) to (v) described above are present—an established profession, special skills, a comprehensive licensing system, work of a fiduciary character, and special vulnerability of the clientele. If the occupation or activity involves fewer of these elements, then we move away from the paradigm. It is the fifth and final element, however, which remains indispensable—the activity has to be one of special vulnerability, in that its risks need to be of a substantially greater magnitude than the routine hazards of everyday dealings with other persons.

### 4. Germaneness of the conviction to the risk

Where the activity qualifies as specially vulnerable for the reasons just outlined, there remains the question whether the conviction is sufficiently germane to the risks which are sought to be avoided. This is an area in which current practice is often deficient. Even where disqualifications are imposed as part of the sentencing process, rather than coming into effect automatically on conviction, attention is seldom directed to the particulars of type, extent and duration of risk. Disqualificatory powers which are operational on sentence often confer a wide and unfettered discretion on duration of the ban,[48] and (driving disqualifications apart[49]) there is very little appellate guidance on their appropriate use. Courts and administrative agencies may all too easily be tempted to impose blanket disqualifications on offenders whenever they have been convicted of certain types of crime.

What is required, as a precondition for imposing a disqualification, is a careful analysis of what kind of risks a conviction of a given type suggests. We need to identify what it is about a particular occupation or activity that makes it sensitive to abuse, and what kind of potential abuse is involved. The occupation of banker or broker carries with it a special risk of dishonesty, but not other risks (such as those of violence). Even with dishonesty, it may be that certain forms of bank employment carry this sensitivity, but surely not all. One then needs to consider whether, and to what extent, the circumstances of the particular conviction indicates a strong potential for future abuse of that kind. If dishonesty to clients is the concern, a fraud conviction

---

[48] For example, under the Protection of Animals (Amendment) Act 1954, s. 1, disqualification from keeping animals may relate to *all* animals, or animals of any particular kind, and may be "for such period as the court thinks fit". See also n. 99 below.

[49] For the relevant cases, see D. Thomas, *Current Sentencing Practice*, Part H.

may well suggest that risk, but a conviction for, say, drug abuse, would not. Finally, the duration of the risk has to be considered. For how long can the forecast of risk be sustained with a modicum of confidence? Disqualifications of indefinite duration should always be deemed suspect.

## 5. Considerations ulterior to risk?

Are there any considerations ulterior to risk that might be the basis for disqualifications? In a narrow class of cases, a conviction might be indicative of *incapacity*. Take the case of a high-ranking judge who has been convicted of a serious domestic assault. According to the risk criteria we have just set forth, there would be no case for disqualification. Whilst high judicial office is clearly an activity vulnerable to fraud or other abuse of position, it is not specially sensitive to acts of physical aggression—so that a conviction for domestic assault provides little basis for supposing that the judge would misuse his public office. The problem, however, is that a conviction of this kind could so greatly diminish the public standing and authority of the judge as to undermine his ability to perform his duties. The criterion in cases such as these is not risk, but incapacity—whether the conviction renders the person incapable of carrying out his or her duties.

Disqualification from office for this reason of incapacity should, we think, be employed only in a narrow range of cases. If the suggested ground for incapacity is diminished public authority, as in the case just referred to, then it needs to be shown that the person's position is one in which a high public standing and authority is essential, and it also needs to be shown why that conviction would undermine that standing.[50] How these cases should be dealt with is also dependent on the criteria for discharge on grounds of incapacity—a matter which we shall not explore further here.

## V. THE SEVERITY OF DISQUALIFICATIONS: PROPORTIONALITY LIMITS

### 1. Desert-based proportionality constraints are generally inapplicable

Desert-based proportionality constraints derive from the censuring implications of punishment. It is because the penal sanction condemns—and because its severity connotes the degree of implicit censure—that penalties' severity should fairly reflect the degree of blameworthiness (*i.e.*, the seriousness) of the criminal conduct.[51] This

---

[50] In recent years there have been examples of judges being convicted of drunk-driving who have not been required to leave office.

[51] See von Hirsch *op. cit.* n. 1, Chap. 2. For the relative weight that should be given to desert against other factors in sentencing, see *ibid.*, Chap. 6; see also pp. 616–618 below.

reasoning, however, does not extend to disqualifications functioning as civil deprivations: they lack the explicit censuring implications of penal sanctions. That is why disqualifications may legitimately look chiefly to risk, rather than to the gravity of past criminal choices.[52] When the solicitor offends, it is his punishment—the fine, prison term, or whatever—that should comport reasonably with the seriousness of his offence; whether he is also to be disbarred should depend, instead, on the risk of further professional misconduct involved. Our conclusion regarding the inapplicability of ordinary desert constraints may seem surprising, considering our strong advocacy of desert principles in other writings, and our voiced scepticism about incapacitative sentencing policies.[53] Disqualifications, however, operate according to a different logic from punishments—and that difference should be recognised.

## 2. Are there "outer" proportionality constraints?

Although, as we have just argued, normal desert-based constraints do not apply to disqualifications, the question remains whether any partial or residual limitations akin to proportionality still should apply. Would it, for instance, be appropriate for conviction for a minor offence to lead to lengthy and onerous disqualifications if the risk considerations so indicate? Or should there be a minimum of commensurability between the gravity of the offence and the burdensomeness of the disqualification?

The Court of Appeal has suggested that there should be such limits, in relation to disqualification of a company director. In *Millard*[54] the Court identified an "upper bracket" of disqualification for more than ten years, which they said should be reserved for particularly serious cases, and a "middle bracket" of six to ten years for a director who has been convicted of somewhat lesser violations. Magistrates' courts, which deal with less serious offences still, should not exceed a maximum of five years' disqualification. We agree with the Court's general approach. What needs to be explained, however, is the rationale: *why* should we observe such outer "proportionality" constraints for disqualifications? If the censure-based argument supporting desert constraints cannot be invoked for disqualifications, what other arguments might be available, and what kind of limitations would these point to?

---

[52] Thus in *Buckley* (1988) 10 Cr. App. R. (S.) 477 the Court of Appeal explained that disqualifying a driver until he re-takes and passes the driving test ". . . is not to be exercised as an additional punishment . . .".

[53] Von Hirsch *op. cit.*, n. 1; M. Wasik and A. von Hirsch, "Section 29 Revised: Previous Convictions in Sentencing" [1994] *Criminal Law Review* 409.

[54] (1994) 15 Cr. App. R. (S.) 445. These periods are the same as those applicable in civil proceedings for disqualification: *In Re Sevenoaks Stationers (Retail) Ltd.* [1991] Ch. 164.

Human-rights jurisprudence operates with a non-desert notion of "proportionality", involving the idea of suitability of means to ends: drastic interventions in people's lives ought not to be resorted to in order to achieve relatively unimportant goals.[55] This means that burdensome restrictions may not be imposed in order to prevent relatively trivial risks—but this is something that our analysis of risk has suggested in any event.[56] This notion of "proportionality" is actually concerned with the magnitude of the *future* risks to be prevented, rather than with the gravity of the past crime of conviction. The latter issue, however, is the one with which we are concerned here: what should be the relationship between the seriousness of the (past) offence and the degree of (future) restriction?

One possible argument for outer proportionality-limits is an empirical one. We know that the best predictor of future misconduct tends to be the offender's past behaviour. When someone has been convicted of a lesser crime, there is little reason to anticipate that he will engage in major forms of lawbreaking in the future, so that onerous disqualifications would make little sense. Standing alone, however, this argument has the limitation of all such empirical claims. While it is doubtless true that petty crimes ordinarily are indifferent predictors of substantial future misconduct, there might be exceptional cases where the crime of conviction, taken together with other indicia of risk, could suggest a more substantial danger. Nevertheless, we think that the empirical argument does provide some support for outer severity constraints. We mentioned earlier the tendency of risk judgments to overbreadth: it is too easy to adopt a "no-risk" posture in which a minor infraction leads to permanent disbarment. Requiring long-term disqualifications to be supported by conviction of a crime of a substantial nature helps to constrain this tendency.

Outer proportionality requirements also serve another function, however—that of protecting people from their own imprudence. The solicitor who participates in a substantial financial fraud has little to complain of if, in addition to the criminal penalties he suffers, he is disbarred. For it is not only the law's threats, but his own conscience and sense of the profession, that should have counselled strongly against such conduct, and should have brought to mind its inconsistency with the responsibilities of being a lawyer. By contrast, consider the rule that existed in many US states some years ago, according to which a person convicted of possession of a small amount of marijuana could be barred permanently from practising law. Ostensibly, the

---

[55] D.J. Harris, M. O'Boyle and C. Warbrick, *The Law of the European Convention on Human Rights* (1995), pp. 11–12. This notion of "non-excess" is one aspect of the suitability of means to ends. The other aspect is fitness: the means pursued must be ones that help promote the ends in view.

[56] See Part IV, 3 (special vulnerability), above.

reason for this was that the person has shown himself unsuited for carrying out an attorney's duties of upholding the law. The effect, however, was that a law student, or young lawyer, could find his career destroyed because of a small transgression. One objection to such a policy relates to the risk principles discussed already: it is doubtful whether a conviction of this kind suggests any significant risk that the lawyer will engage in professional malpractice.[57] But there is a further objection which relates to the present concern about excessiveness. Marijuana possession for personal use is venial misconduct, at most. Its minor character means that ordinary persons cannot be expected to have the kind of inhibitions against engaging in it that they have for more substantial crimes. If conviction for such lesser misconduct can lead to the drastic consequence of permanent disbarment, the law becomes a trap for the thoughtless or imprudent.[58] The underlying principle here, we think, is that of giving persons fair opportunity to avoid legal consequences, especially those of a drastic character. The most obvious application of this idea is the fair-notice principle—that the rules which provide for the legal consequences must be announced in advance. But we think that such protections should extend beyond bare notice requirements. Where the misconduct is of a lesser character, ordinarily-fallible human beings may too easily be tempted to commit those acts notwithstanding legal prohibitions; and would have little moral understanding of why harsh impositions could appropriately ensue. Concerns with fair opportunity of avoidance thus militate against such sanctions. In illustration, consider *Barnsley Metropolitan Borough Council, ex p. Hook,*[59] involving Harry Hook, a market trader in Barnsley operating under a licence granted by the local authority. At 6.30 p.m. one evening after the market had closed Hook was seen urinating in a side street and was reported by two council workers to whom he had spoken in abusive terms. His licence to trade was terminated by the council. The Divisional Court upheld the council's decision, but the Court of Appeal subsequently reinstated the licence. The main ground for the decision was that the manner in which the council had proceeded against Hook amounted to a breach of natural justice. Lord Denning, however, added the further ground that it was disproportionate and "quite wrong" for the council to have "deprive[d] Hook of his livelihood" for an offence for which "some small fine might have been inflicted" by the magistrates.[60]

[57] See Part IV, 4.
[58] This is quite different from barring the prospective solicitor who cannot pass his examinations. Being a solicitor requires (and is widely understood as requiring) certain skills, and so it is no "trap" to deny access to the profession to one whose examination failure demonstrates a lack of those skills.
[59] [1976] 1 W.L.R. 1052.
[60] At pp. 1057–1058.

The arguments we have just advanced do *not* amount to a requirement that disqualifications should be made subject to the systematic scaling requirements of desert—since, we have argued, disqualifications are not penal sanctions. What is required are only broad upper "proportionality" limits—constraining the use of harsh civil disqualifications in response to conviction for lesser offences. Unlike desert requirements for penal sanctions, however, no converse lower limits are implied: in the absence of the requisite degree and kind of risk, no disqualification need be imposed—even on someone convicted of serious misconduct. The requirements of adequate punishment[61] for serious offending apply to penalties imposed on sentence, but they do not apply to collateral civil consequences.

## VI. MIGHT DISQUALIFICATIONS BE RECONSTITUTED AS PUNISHMENTS?

Disqualifications deprive offenders of certain interests that they would otherwise have while living in the community, such as holding a particular job or driving a car. Could such deprivations explicitly be made to serve as community punishments? Requiring an offender to perform community service, or placing him under curfew, are now prescribed as community sentences.[62] What, then, would be wrong with "punishing" a convicted thief by, say, disqualifying him from driving?

There have been some legislative enactments of this kind. In the 1960s, the State of New York enacted a statute barring persons convicted under the Smith Act (which punished certain kinds of seditious advocacy) from holding a state driving licence. The aim was to enhance the penalties suffered by convicted Communists, by denying them after release from prison the normal citizen's privilege of driving a vehicle.[63] At the Annual Conservative Party Conference in October 1996, the former Home Secretary, Michael Howard, proposed a comparable (albeit more sweeping) measure: that sentencing courts should be given broad authority to ban convicted offenders from driving, even if no vehicle was used in the commission of their offence.[64] This proposal became part of the Crime (Sentences) Act 1997;[65] and the present Home Secretary, Jack Straw, has announced

---

[61] See Ashworth *op. cit.*, n. 1, Chap. 9.
[62] See Criminal Justice Act 1991, s. 6.
[63] The statute and its aims are described in J. Feinberg, "The Expressive Function of Punishment", in J. Feinberg (ed.), *Doing and Deserving* (1970), pp. 95–110.
[64] The seeds of the proposal can be found in the Report of the Advisory Council on the Penal System (1970), at p. 43.
[65] Crime (Sentences) Act 1997, s. 39: ". . . [T]he court by or before which a person is convicted of an offence may, in addition to or instead of dealing with him in any other way, order him to be disqualified, for such period as it thinks fit, for [sic] holding or obtaining a driving licence."

616                     *The Cambridge Law Journal*                    [1997]

(just as this article went to press) that the provision will be brought into force on 1 January 1998.

It is significant that none of the disqualifications discussed in this article (including driving bans) are treated as punishments in the general provisions of law regulating sentencing. Section 6(4) of the Criminal Justice Act of 1991 lists a variety of community sanctions— probation, community service, curfews, and so forth—as sentences which a court may impose. These sentences are all made subject to the proportionality and "suitability" requirements set out in section 6(2) of that Act. Disqualifications are not included in this list,[66] and the legislative provisions enacting the new motoring ban do not place this measure within the framework of Section 6. There thus are no explicit criteria by which a sentencing court can determine whether such a ban should be imposed upon a convicted thief as an additional penalty or what the duration of such a ban should be. The ban will not be a true disqualification either, since it can be imposed by a sentencer regardless of the existence of *any* relevant risk.

Notwithstanding these defects, however, this legislation raises an interesting question: whether it should ever be permissible to use disqualifications as penalties. It does not seem obvious that disqualifications and punishments must always and necessarily be mutually exclusive categories. Nevertheless, employment bans, and broad-gauge driving prohibitions of the kind just mentioned, are poorly suited to serve as penal sanctions. To see why, we need to consider briefly the desiderata for punishments—what features fit sanctions to a penal role.

*1. The desiderata for punishments*

A central function of the criminal sanction is to convey censure—that is, formal disapproval of the criminal conduct—in a manner that comports fairly with the seriousness of the offending behaviour.[67] To serve that function, punishments need to be reasonably capable of being calibrated to reflect the gravity of the offence. This concern about comparability and calibration does not require an assumption that "just deserts" is the only legitimate sentencing concern. We ourselves have suggested elsewhere that ulterior penal aims may properly be considered in deciding among penalties of approximately equivalent severity.[68] Other penal theorists have suggested that such

---

[66] A distinction needs to be drawn between the ancillary sentencing powers which we are describing and other sentencing powers, such as a forfeiture order made under the Powers of Criminal Courts Act 1973, s. 43. That section enables the court to deprive the offender of his rights in property which he used in the commission of the offence, and it is properly regarded as a financial penalty—a fine *in specie*. See *Buddo* (1982) 4 Cr. App R. (S.) 268. Also distinct are measures designed to confiscate the accumulated profits of offending; see, *e.g.*, Drug Trafficking Act 1994.

[67] See von Hirsch *op. cit.* n. 1, Chaps. 2 & 7.

[68] *Ibid.*, Chap. 7; see also M. Wasik and A. von Hirsch, "Non-custodial Penalties and the Principles of Desert" [1988] *Criminal Law Review* 555.

ulterior aims may legitimately be considered within an appropriate range or band of penal severity, without desert-equivalence being required;[69] or that desert constraints may be exceeded for certain categories of exceptional danger.[70] But such conceptions all presuppose, notwithstanding their differences, that the gravity of the offence is an important consideration and that the severity of the sanction should, to a substantial degree, be commensurate with it. If a sanction can only poorly be calibrated, it comports badly with this conception of punishment.

Consider that traditional and widely-used non-custodial sanction, the fine. Financial penalties' quantitative character lends itself to grading. The problem has been to achieve a modicum of *de facto* even-handedness in the sanction's operation. The device of the unit fine is an attempt at even-handed application: given inequalities in people's earnings, fining individuals on the basis of units of earnings is more equitable than fining on the basis of flat amounts. The unit fine was introduced in England in 1991 and (with little apparent justification) abolished again in 1993.[71] Other European countries make extensive use of this device, and England does retain the kernel of the idea in requiring sentencers to consider the offender's means when setting the level of a fine.[72]

Certain types of penal sanctions, such as probation, have dual functions: they are meant both to punish, and to reduce the offender's propensity for reoffending.[73] These sentences can be made to operate so that proportionality requirements constrain the sanction's preventative aims. Under English law, the degree of onerousness of any community sentence, including a probation order, should be set in accordance with the gravity of the offence.[74] Within the limits of proportionality, however, the particular requirements to be written into the order can be decided according to the offender's needs.[75]

With sanctions such as these, the preventative element stands in some degree of tension with the proportionality-based concern for ease of calibration. For a probation order, for example, the duration of the period of supervision can be set according to the gravity of the offence; but the severity of the sanction depends also on the intensity

---

[69] For discussion of such "band" approaches, see von Hirsch *op. cit.* n. 1, Chap. 6; and from a different perspective, see M. Tonry, *Sentencing Matters* (1996), Chaps. 1 & 8.

[70] For description and analysis of such views, see von Hirsch *op. cit.* n. 1, Chap. 6.

[71] For a thoughtful analysis of the events leading to abolition, see Lord Windlesham, *Responses to Crime*, Vol. 3 (1996), Chap. 1.

[72] Criminal Justice Act 1991, s. 18.

[73] The Powers of Criminal Courts Act 1973, s. 2(1) indicates that a probation order is an appropriate sentence where supervision will assist in "securing the rehabilitation of the offender" or "protecting the public from harm from him or preventing the commission by him of further offences".

[74] Criminal Justice Act 1991, s. 6.

[75] *Ibid.*; Powers of Criminal Courts Act 1973, s. 3 and Sched. 1A. See also Ashworth *op. cit.* n. 1, Chap. 10.

or onerousness of any treatment or activities the probationer is required to undertake, and this is less easy to assess. Some loss of ease of calibration is deemed worthwhile, however, in the interests of promoting the offender's return to a law-abiding life.

Another desideratum concerns the way in which the sanction can be enforced. Where the defendant has sufficient assets or earnings, a fine can be enforced through a variety of techniques, including attachment of earnings, seizure of assets and the like—and, as a last resort, penalising defendants who wilfully refuse to pay. There are obvious problems of enforcement with respect to indigent defendants, but these may be met by imposing an alternative sanction of roughly comparable severity.

The third desideratum is the by-now-familiar theme of avoiding counter-productiveness. Penal measures should not be of a character that significantly increases offenders' incentives to recidivate.[76]

### 2. Driving and employment bans as penal sanctions

Driving bans imposed for offences unrelated to driving, and employment bans imposed simply as punishments, would not achieve the foregoing desiderata well. To begin with, such sanctions cannot be sustained as probation can, as a measure addressed in part to risk-related concerns—for, *ex hypothesi*, these disqualifications would apply to persons whose crimes suggest no special risks regarding the activity which is the subject of the ban.

These disqualifications would, therefore, have to be treated as penalties of general applicability, comparable to the fine. Thus viewed, they fare badly. Consider calibration and even-handedness, first. The duration of a driving ban might be adjusted according to the gravity of the offence, but the ban's actual impact would be very variable. Persons living in areas well served by public transport, such as London, could manage without a car with little serious inconvenience. Those living outside such areas would suffer more, but there could be very significant differences depending, for example, on the distance from home of the person's place of work, and the extent to which a vehicle is used in his employment,[77] or in his other everyday activities. There would be no easy way of compensating for these inequalities, akin to the unit-fine device for fines. Comparable or greater difficulties would apply to professional disqualifications, if used as punishments: the

---

[76] Sometimes, the concern about avoiding counter-productiveness has to be disregarded because of the absence of alternatives: the prison appears to have criminogenic effects for some types of offenders, but there appears to be no other acceptable sanctions suited to the most serious crimes (see A. von Hirsch, *Doing Justice* (1976), Chap 13). We are speaking here, however, of non-custodial sanctions, where alternatives do exist.

[77] Note, however, the unadopted suggestion of the Advisory Council on the Penal System (1970) at p. 45 that courts might be given power to disqualify offenders from driving at weekends.

impact of the disqualification would vary according to whether the defendant was an active member of the profession or not, and upon how easy it would be for him to find alternative work.

Enforcement of such bans would also be troublesome, and potentially intrusive into the interests of third parties. Enforcing the driving ban with any degree of vigour would require the police to stop vehicles, and ask drivers to produce their licences. With existing, risk-based driving bans, the police can make stops based on indicia of poor driving. But since a comprehensive driving ban would be unrelated to risk, the banned drivers would drive no worse than ordinary citizens. To achieve any effective level of enforcement, therefore, the authorities would have to resort to suspicionless stops—where the majority of those affected would be ordinary non-convicted drivers.[78]

Finally, the counterproductivity argument[79] applies strongly. Many persons' employment opportunities depend on access to a vehicle. To ban convicted persons from driving, therefore, may significantly diminish their work opportunities, and thereby, their prospects for living law-abiding lives.[80] Why create such perverse incentives, when the defendant's use of the vehicle poses no special risk of accident? The counterproductivity argument applies *a fortiori* to employment bans: these clearly impede the ability of the offender to return to a normal existence. Making it harder for the ex-offender to return to making his living, where he poses no special risks in that line of work, seems strange indeed.

If the newly authorised driving ban cannot be justified as a workable penal sanction, and if it makes no sense as a civil disqualificatory measure, what is its real aim? It is, in our judgment, simply a reversion to the idea of demoting convicted persons to second-class citizenship.[81] We hope that English judges will make use of this provision sparingly.

The comprehensive driving ban just discussed is, of course, an extreme version of using disqualifications as penalties: the ban is to be imposed on those whose crimes have nothing to do with driving. What

---

[78] Indeed, the new law expressly expands the power of the police to stop motorists. Such interventions would be more problematic than routine stops of drivers to administer breathalyser tests—a measure addressed to the the special dangers of driving under the influence of alcohol. Here, there would be no special danger to be dealt with, and the only reasons for the stops would be to enforce a sanction that could be replaced by other, more suitable and easily enforced ones.

[79] See Part III, above.

[80] The measure is also counter-productive in the sense that it is bound to result in more unlicensed (and thus uninsured) drivers on the road.

[81] See Part III, above. See also Feinberg's discussion of New York's driving ban against convicted Communists, n. 63 above. The populist law-and-order stance, which this proposal exemplifies, is in part characterised by giving offenders this reduced status: convicts are to be dealt with as virtually a species apart, with whom ordinary persons need have no sympathy. Deprivations such as these would serve as a mark of such persons' separate and inferior status. See further D. Garland, "The Limits of the Sovereign State: Strategies of Crime Control in Contemporary Society" (1996) 36 *British Journal of Criminology* 445, at pp. 459–461.

620              *The Cambridge Law Journal*              [1997]

of less bizarre schemes—such as adopting a schedule of driving-ban sanctions on those convicted of bad driving? For certain driving offences, mandatory driving bans are provided by statute; in other instances, magistrates impose such bans routinely as a form of tariff.[82] The acceptability of these bans, and whether they should be classified as civil disqualifications or criminal penalties, would depend on how these schemes are structured and operate. If the duration of the ban is graded according to the gravity of the driving offence, the scheme seems more like a punishment. (There remain the difficulties, referred to above, of calibrating such penalties precisely;[83] but since the sanction to some degree also addresses risks of further bad driving, it would seem to resemble dual-purpose penalties such as probation—where we suggested that some loss of ease of calibration might be deemed worthwhile in the interest of the sanction's preventative features.[84]) If, however, the duration of driving prohibitions is not graded primarily according to the seriousness of the current offence, but the measure is well targeted to risk, it may be regarded as a civil disqualification.[85] The scheme becomes questionable, however, if it fits neither criterion well—that is, it neither reflects the proportionality requirements appropriate for punishments, nor addresses risk in the way in which we have suggested a disqualification should.[86]

### VII. THE REACH OF DISQUALIFICATIONS: WHAT KINDS OF DEPRIVATIONS SHOULD NOT BE IMPOSED AS CIVIL MEASURES?

Having thus addressed the possibility of treating disqualifications as punishments, we need now also consider the reverse: whether the impositions that commonly serve as punishments might be redesignated as civil disqualifications. Were this permissible, it would raise the disturbing possibility of various deprivations of liberty being imposed on simple risk grounds: what, for example, would prevent curfews, or even periods of confinement, from being used as "disqualifications" ancillary to conviction, if sufficient crime-preventative grounds so indicated? To deal with such questions, we need to consider whether there might be certain interests which ought never be taken away as civil disqualifications.

Consider the curfew. Under the provisions of the Criminal Justice Act 1991, this measure can be imposed as a community sentence, but

---

[82] See, R. Hood, *Sentencing the Motoring Offender* (1972), at p. 80 et. seq. See also p. 602 above, at nn. 14–17.
[83] See p. 618 above, at n. 77.
[84] See the discussion on pp. 617–618 above, at nn. 73–75.
[85] This might be true, for example, if the duration of the ban is based on a cumulative score which depends less on the current offence than on the driver's previous record of bad driving.
[86] See Part IV, 3 & 4.

is subject to the proportionality constraints which that Act prescribes.[87] Without the justification supplied by the conviction, however, such restrictions of liberty would not be appropriate. The point is clear enough with respect to liberty-deprivations imposed independently of any conviction: whatever the conceivable merits (and we think them dubious) of putting children under general curfews,[88] it would seem plainly improper to impose curfews on sane adults solely on grounds of risk, without a conviction first having been secured. The same logic, we think, extends to imposing such restrictions collaterally to a conviction: this likewise is problematic, if such measures function as civil risk-control methods and are treated as exempt from the limiting principles applicable to punishments. This should hold even were such constraints capable of meeting risk criteria analogous to those we outlined earlier for employment disqualifications.[89]

Why is it that a criminal conviction is essential in principle to the deprivation of liberty? It stems from the idea of liberty as a fundamental right—one so important as to take precedence over ordinary societal interests. This idea has sometimes been expressed in the formulation that the right to liberty should "trump" concerns about the general welfare.[90] It is debatable, of course, *which* interests should be given this degree of precedence; but we think that certain basic liberties— including the entitlement to freedom of movement—should be accorded this importance.

Risk considerations, *par excellence*, are concerned with social and preventative interests.[91] To treat freedom of movement as a right, then, implies that it ordinarily should not be taken away solely upon grounds of risk. Granted, there are exceptions, but they should be narrow ones. Quarantine measures represent a special and limited exception, where the magnitude of the risk of pandemic disease to the populace is so great as to override normal presumptions about liberty.[92] Pre-trial detention is another exception—based upon its limited duration and the absence of practicable alternatives: the justice system will fail to function if it cannot secure the presence of defendants.[93] Other

---

[87] Criminal Justice Act 1991, s. 6; see also Ashworth *op. cit.* n. 1, Chap. 10.

[88] The present Home Secretary has suggested the possibility of imposing night-time curfews on certain young children.

[89] See Part IV, 3 & 4.

[90] See R. Dworkin, *Taking Rights Seriously* (1977), Chap 7; but see J. Raz, *The Morality of Freedom* (1986), Chaps. 7 & 8.

[91] For more discussion on why such risk considerations should be seen as societal interests, rather than rights-based claims that compete with a person's right of liberty of movement, see von Hirsch *op. cit.* n. 1, p. 51n.

[92] See *ibid.*, pp. 49–50, for discussion of the status of risks of extraordinary gravity.

[93] See, von Hirsch *Doing Justice* (1976), p. 130. Pre-trial detention to prevent bail crimes, however, is considerably more controversial—precisely because such restraint is not necessary for preserving a system of trials. A corollary to the power of pre-trial detention is the power to restrict the defendant's movements in the community before trial, in lieu of confining him. Conditions restricting liberty, such as a curfew or a requirement not to enter a certain area, may thus be

narrowly-drawn exceptions might conceivably be defensible, if the dangers to be prevented are of extraordinary magnitude, or the intrusion on liberty of movement is restricted in scope and duration. But in normal circumstances, a competent adult ought to lose his liberty only when that deprivation is justified as a penal sanction. The conviction, in this situation, does not merely provide evidentiary support for an assessment of risk; rather, it is essential to the loss of the person's claim against the general interest—he may be deprived of his liberty because that deprivation is an appropriate penal response to having offended. The limitations of proportionality thus apply to that sanction—and risk considerations may enter only to such extent as the principles of punishment permit.[94] So, imprisoning an offender, or subjecting his movements to a curfew, should be penal impositions. Such deprivations would be seriously problematic in civil-liberties terms if imposed as civil disabilities collateral to conviction.[95]

Another category of basic right which should not be taken away by disqualification, we think, is access to the general employment market. Whilst the convicted solicitor may appropriately be barred from legal work, the factory worker convicted of assault in the workplace should not be prevented by law from working in factories. The class of occupations from which a convicted defendant may be barred should be narrow enough so that the remainder—non-excludable work—leaves him or her reasonable opportunities to find employment. Two reasons for this have been mentioned earlier. The first is that the criteria sketched previously would not support broad employment exclusions.[96] The second is the counter-productivity argument—that the more comprehensive the exclusion from working life, the harder it will be for the offender to live a law-abiding existence.[97] A further ground derives, however, from what we are speaking of here: that access to employment constitutes an important civil right.[98] Exclusion from a limited class of sensitive occupations may be consistent with such a right, but comprehensive disqualifications would not be. (Concededly, employment rights have not been so

---

imposed as a condition of bail: Bail Act 1976, Sched I. As measures based on the pre-trial dentention power, however, these conditions must terminate on acquittal even if there is reason to think that the person still would represent a risk. See also A. Samuels, "No Driving as a Requirement or Condition of Bail" [1988] *Criminal Law Review* 739.

[94] See von Hirsch *op. cit.* n. 1, and pp. 616–617 above at nn. 67–70.

[95] Indeed, confining an adult merely on grounds of risk would raise serious questions under Article 5 of the European Convention on Human Rights.

[96] See Part IV, 3 & 4, above.

[97] See Part III, above.

[98] The E.C. Charter of the Fundamental Social Rights of Workers, Title I, para. 4 states that "Every individual shall be free to choose and engage in an occupation according to the regulations governing each occupation." See also the International Covenant on Economic, Social and Cultural Rights (1966), Article 6: "The States Parties to the present Covenant recognise the right to work, which includes the right of everyone to the opportunity to gain his living by work which he freely chooses or accepts, and will take appropriate steps to safeguard this right."

deeply entrenched in civil-liberties thinking as rights to freedom of movement—so the case here is less clear than it is with curfews; nevertheless, we think it strong enough to warrant ruling out broad-based employment bans.)

A rule-of-thumb that might be useful in this area is whether the purported disqualification could be supportable on grounds of risk alone, independently of a conviction. This is a matter of principle rather than one which turns upon the particular provisions of current law. If a conviction is legally required before a particular disqualification may be imposed, it should be asked why this is the case. Is it simply a matter of there being no other readily available evidence of the relevant risk?[99] Or is it the more fundamental consideration, that the interest is of such importance that it would be wrong to deprive a responsible adult of it solely upon grounds of risk? We shall not try here to offer further examples of rights or interests which are "basic" in the foregoing sense and hence are not appropriate for disqualifications. What is important for our purposes is to identify the principle: namely, whether the right or interest is one which is fundamental in a rights-respecting society.

## VIII. SOME REMEDIAL STEPS

In this article, we have sketched a conceptual framework concerning the use of disqualifications—this being an area of law in which little theory has hitherto developed. We have argued that state-imposed disqualifications ordinarily should not be regarded as being penal sanctions; where justifiable, these measures should be based on concerns about risk. We have proposed[100] that a disqualification should only operate for certain types of occupations or activities which are especially sensitive to abuse of a sort involving substantial potential harm—and where the defendant's crime is indicative of risk of the kind relating to that vulnerability to abuse. Application of these qualifying conditions would entail a significant diminution in the use of state-imposed disqualifications and, for those bans remaining, a narrowing of their permissible scope. We have suggested certain additional limitations: for example, that certain basic rights—such as

[99] Consider the English law on the keeping of domestic animals. At present, a person may keep domestic animals without a licence, if not in the business of doing so (say, as operator of a kennel or riding establishment). The only ground for barring such a person from keeping animals is a conviction for cruelty or mistreatment of animals. However, it would not seem problematic in principle to ban a person from keeping an animal without first requiring a conviction. Dog breeders may lose their licence to operate kennels if inspection by the local authority shows that the dogs are cruelly treated, without the need to obtain a conviction. Conceivably, such a rule might reasonably be extended to the non-commercial keeping of animals.

[100] In Part IV, 3 & 4.

those of liberty, or general access to the employment market—should not be taken away as civil disqualifications.[101] Given this framework, what changes should be made to the existing law regarding disqualifications? We would propose the following remedial steps:

(1) Application of our analysis would result in the immediate repeal of existing disqualifications which have little or no bearing upon risk,[102] but which merely relegate those convicted to the condition of second-class citizenship. Restrictions on the rights of convicted persons to vote are, we think, a clear example.[103] Driving disqualifications employed in circumstances involving no risk of misuse of a vehicle are also objectionable on this ground.[104] Disqualifications of this kind are equally problematic, whether they come into effect automatically upon conviction or as a result of judicial order upon sentence.[105]

(2) Those disqualifications which can, at least in some cases, be justified on grounds of risk should be made subject to a proper procedural assessment as to whether their imposition can thus be sustained. Since disqualifications which take effect automatically upon conviction permit no such procedural assessment, and lack any element of targeting, there must be a strong presumption against them. To be sustainable, such automatic disqualifications would have to fulfil our proposed requirements in virtually every case—and that is unlikely to be so.

(3) When disqualifications are imposed as part of the sentencing process, this does permit an analysis of risk to be made, subject to appropriate procedural safeguards. Counsel can argue whether the particular disqualification was justified in the circumstances of the case, and the imposition of a disqualification can (and should in every case) be subject to the defendant's right to challenge on appeal. We think, however, that the criteria for the exercise of disqualificatory powers on sentence should be more circumscribed than they are at present, to ensure that sentencing judges exercise these powers in the manner which we have proposed. At present, judicial discretion to use disqualificatory powers is largely unfettered, both as to the appropriate use of a particular disqualification, and as to its duration. For example, the only statutory limitation on the power to disqualify a person from acting as a company director is that such person must have been convicted of an indictable offence "in connection with the promotion, formation, management or liquidation of a company . . .".[106] The

---

[101] See Part VII.
[102] But see the one type of exception discussed in Part IV, 5.
[103] See Part III.
[104] See Part VI, 2.
[105] In France and in the Netherlands deprivation of civil rights, including the right to vote, may be imposed upon a convicted offender at the discretion of the sentencing judge: Prison Reform Trust (1996).
[106] Company Directors Disqualification Act 1986, s. 2(1).

phrase "in connection with" has been given the broadest possible interpretation by the courts.[107] Our analysis would call for the more restrictive approach embodied in our suggested criteria regarding risk.[108]

Although we do not perceive disqualifications as being penal sanctions, we have argued[109] that conviction for lesser offences should not lead to lengthy and burdensome disqualifications. This is the approach adopted in *Millard*[110] on disqualification of company directors, and we think that it should be extended to other forms of disqualification as well.

(4) A judge cannot be expected to specify, at the time of sentence, every form of employment in respect of which a convicted person would represent a substantial risk, and thus there would be little point giving sentencers wide general powers to list forms of employment from which the offender should be banned.[111] Inevitably, professional bodies and regulatory agencies will be needed to exercise a second tier of control over those who would present serious risks if they were admitted to that particular sphere of specialised activity, or were permitted to continue in such activities. We think, however, that the criteria for the exercise of discretion by such regulatory agencies should be tightened, so as to make the risk principles which we have identified above explicit, and central to their decision-making. Currently, the exercise of discretion to exclude from employment those who have been convicted is far too broad, and is not made subject to the appropriate risk indicia. The High Court is prepared to interfere with disqualification decisions made by disciplinary bodies only on grounds of denial of natural justice.[112] The cases show that the Court will hardly ever overturn an employment ban, since ". . . the disciplinary committee are the best possible people for weighing the seriousness of the professional misconduct".[113] The remedy of judicial review would not, in any event, be available in respect of the smaller trade associations. Article 6 of the European Convention on Human Rights (concerning rights to fair hearing) has some relevance in this

---

[107] It is only necessary that the offence ". . . must have some relevant factual connection with the management of the company": *Goodman* (1992) 14 Cr. App. R. (S.) 147. There is no need to show actual misconduct in the company's affairs: *Georgiou* (1988) 10 Cr. App. R. (S.) 137.

[108] See Part IV, 3 & 4.

[109] For the reasons set out in Part V.

[110] (1994) 15 Cr. App. R. (S.) 445; see pp. 612–614 above.

[111] See, however, the provisions of the US Federal Sentencing Guidelines, para. 5F5.5, authorising a variety of "occupational restrictions". See also the unadopted suggestion of the Advisory Council on the Penal System (1970), at p. 46, that sentencers should have power to pass a "prohibited employment order".

[112] P.P. Craig, *Administrative Law*, 3rd ed. (1994), Part II, especially pp. 317–320.

[113] *Per* Lord Goddard C.J. in *Re A Solicitor* [1956] 3 All E. R. 516 at p. 517, ringingly endorsed by Sir Thomas Bingham M.R. in *Bolton* v. *Law Society* [1994] 2 All E. R. 486 at p. 490.

context,[114] but again the emphasis is upon procedural propriety rather than the substantive merits of disbarment on the facts of the case.[115] What is lacking, in our view, is an appropriate power of review to challenge disqualification on the ground that the appropriate risk requirements have not been satisfied.

(5) In this article we have been concerned to discuss the legitimate scope of "state-imposed" disqualifications. Our proposals, if implemented, would have only limited effect upon private employment rights. Even when a convicted person has not officially been disqualified from his employment, it still remains largely open to a private employer to fire him, or to refuse to hire an applicant who has a conviction.[116] Under English law an employer is entitled to dismiss an employee after commission of an offence, whether or not the offence was committed at work or had any connection with the employment, if the employer thinks that the person's remaining in employment might damage the employer's reputation or be unacceptable to fellow employees.[117] It is at least arguable, however, that it is discriminatory to fire (or refuse to hire) a convicted person in circumstances where his or her employment would represent no demonstrable risk, and that such practices should be prohibited or restricted.[118] Under current English law it is unlawful to refuse employment on the basis that the defendant has a *spent* conviction.[119] It seems to us that other indicia of risk apart from staleness of conviction, such as the magnitude of the risk and the germaneness of the conviction to the type of employment being considered, ought also to be relevant to private employment decisions. However, exploration of this issue is beyond the scope of the present article.

---

[114] See *Le Compte, Van Leuwen and De Meyere* v. *Belgium* (1982) 5 E.H.R.R. 183 and *Konig* v. *Germany* (1984) 2 E.H.R.R. 170, both cases of doctors disqualified from practice.

[115] See further Harris *op. cit.* n. 25, Chap 2.

[116] "Outside . . . areas of statutory intervention . . . an employer is free to refuse to hire a person for any reason, no matter how capricious, or for no reason at all.": S. Deakin and G.S. Morris, *Labour Law* (1995), p. 136.

[117] See *ibid.*, p. 422: "Dismissal for a conviction . . . will almost certainly be a potentially fair reason." In *Shan* v. *Croydon Area Health Authority* (1975) 13630/75/D (cited in M. Whincup, *The Right to Dismiss* (1982), p. 94), the defendant was a doctor, who was convicted of stealing a bag from a shop. She was fined £50. Dismissal from her employment was upheld.

[118] Several Human Rights Codes in Canadian provinces prohibited the refusal of employment, or the refusal of association membership, where the applicant's conviction did not "relate to the occupation, employment or membership": Human Rights Code of British Columbia, ss. 8 & 9, discussed by Leon *op. cit.* n. 34, pp. 326–327. Unfortunately, even this basic step has not been adopted in the Canadian Charter of Civil Rights and Freedoms.

[119] Rehabilitation of Offenders Act 1974, s. 4. There are, however, numerous exceptional employments where convictions must be revealed although spent; see Rehabilitation of Offenders Act 1974 (Exceptions) Order 1975 (S.I. 1975, No. 1023). See further *Torr* v. *British Railways Board* [1977] I.R.L.R. 184.

# Part II
# Punishment and Imprisonment

# [7]

# Imprisonment

ANTHONY O'HEAR

> Morals reformed—health preserved—industry invigorated—
> instruction diffused—public burthens lightened—economy seated
> as it were upon a rock—the gordian knot of the Poor Laws not cut
> but untied—all by a simple idea of Architecture.
>
> Jeremy Bentham, Panopticon, p. 39

It is appropriate that a lecture in a series on 'Philosophy and Practice' should open by considering Bentham's ideas on imprisonment. For Bentham, incontestably a philosopher, was equally incontestably a practical reformer. This, indeed, is a received idea among philosophers; that is to say, most philosophers know that Bentham designed 'a model prison of novel design' (Mary Warnock), but few have actually considered the design, its implications or its effects. Most are content, like Warnock, with observing that the panopticon plan was formally rejected, before passing on to the abstraction of Bentham's felicific calculus, his notion of utility, and his ideas about the foundations of law. Yet, strange as it may seem, the underlying idea of the panopticon has never been completely abandoned. One aspect of the idea pervades penal thinking, even while prison practice is still influenced by Bentham's practical proposals; moreover, the panoptic ideal has taken root far beyond the walls of actual prisons. Here is philosophy in practice, and yet, in many ways, practically and intellectually a failure.

To understand the nature of the failure, we shall have to go beyond and behind philosophical abstraction. We will have to see why Bentham's hopes for prisons failed in practice. But, that they and similar ideas had failed and were perhaps bound to fail has been widely recognized since 1830 at least. Yet Benthamite ideas and practice continue to pervade penal practice. So this leads us to ask why such overtly inefficacious ideas should still be so influential. So we have to go behind the ideas to the underlying social reality. And in doing this, we shall be led to go beyond ideas about prisons, because, as I shall argue, prisons as we have them cannot be considered in abstraction from the criminal justice system as a whole, and our ways of social stratification and organization generally.

Prison, as we know it today, is a recent phenomenon. It seems so natural that talk of alternatives to imprisonment can be made to sound quite radical. Yet prison was itself a radical alternative for dealing with crime only 200 years ago. It was a radical alternative to

**Anthony O'Hear**

punishment by public torture and execution, by public humiliation, by transportation: in 1776 in John Howard's survey of English prisons, those prisons that did exist contained debtors rather than felons, and the felons that were incarcerated were in the main people awaiting trial or sentence of death or transportation. Anyone in a prison could bring families and friends in, or indeed prostitutes if they could afford it. Better-off prisoners could secure all sorts of privileges from the keepers who were private contractors, unsupervised by higher authority. Food and drink had to be bought from the keepers. Discipline was arbitrary and capricious. To a large extent, prisons were self-governing, with a flourishing subculture, including mock trials and punishments conducted by the inmates themselves. Disease, disorder, brutality and corruption were rife, and these were the features of prison life that shocked the reformers of the eighteenth and early nineteenth centuries. These were men like John Howard, motivated by religious ideals, or men like Bentham, shocked by the obvious and multiple inutility of contemporary institutions of punishment. Reformers from both religious and rationalistic-cum-utilitarian standpoints hoped to replace the brutal unequally applied and ineffective system of criminal justice that existed in the eighteenth century with a system of fixed and equally distributed penalties, which combined correction of the mind with correction of the body, which produced bodily health rather than disease, and which sent formerly dishonest men out honest, either through having come to terms with God and their conscience or through having been (in Bentham's phrase) 'ground honest' by the prison machine.

People often write as if there is something inconsistent with punishing somebody and hoping to reform him at the same time. Maybe there is, and maybe all that imprisonment can achieve is a system of 'humane containment', to use a characteristically weaselly phrase that was current in Home Office jargon in the 1970s. But, if that is so, a re-thinking of the style of imprisonment currently practised is called for, because the types of rules and structures that currently govern penal practice are inherently panoptic in Bentham's sense and hence, in aim, reformatory. Some people may think that our present system of imprisonment is disordered and corrupt, and that there is therefore not much difference between Newgate in the 1760s and Wormwood Scrubs in the 1980s. But they would be wrong in two vital respects, respects which take us to the essence of Bentham's panopticism. In the first place, the only rules or work or timetables which obtained in an eighteenth-century prison were at the discretion of the keepers, the upshot being that they were more honoured in the breach than in the observance. But then, secondly,

## Imprisonment

and more crucially, in Newgate in the 1760s, there was 'roughly one turnkey, officer or watchman for every hundred prisoners'. Hence the flourishing of inmate subculture. By 1830 panoptical reforming zeal had produced a ratio of one officer to eighteen prisoners in Coldbath Fields House of Correction. I have recently read that the current inmate/staff ratio in British prisons is 1:1·74, and there are 19,695 prison officers alone for 44,000 prisoners (*Social Trends*, 1983). At Grendon Underwood, about which I will say more later, the ratio is 1:1. 'Humane containment' surely does not require such ratios. Has panopticism then triumphed in a way unsuspected even by Bentham, who thought that one of the advantages of his plan was that the many could be surveyed by the few?

Panopticism is the principle that everyone in an institution is constantly visible to someone, although not everyone is visible to anyone. In Bentham's panopticon (which could be used as a factory or a workhouse, as much as a prison), there is an observation tower at the centre and, surrounding it, a ring-like structure divided into storeys and individual cells. The cells are backlit, while the tower's windows are covered by venetian blinds, so that all that is happening in each cell is visible from the tower, although the inmates of the cells will be unable to see what is happening in the control tower. The aim of the structure is to ensure that each prisoner or worker or intermediate guard or supervisor can be seen from the control tower and realizes that this is so, but that they should not know when or even if they are actually being observed.

Bentham was, as just suggested, well aware that the guards themselves needed supervising and guarding. In this, he was at one with Howard and the other reformers, both religious and radical, one of whose main complaints about eighteenth-century prisons had been the disorderly and corrupt lives led by prisoners and guards alike. To remedy this, and to produce the circumstances of observation and control in which rogues might be rehabilitated through the extinction of anti-social traits and the reinforcement of positive social attitudes, by a careful blending of pleasure and pain, the lives of everyone in a modern prison were to be regulated by rule and a detailed discipline, dividing the day up into segments for work, for eating, for sleeping, for solitary meditation, and so on. Staff and inmates alike were to be bound by discipline and rule, segregated from each other and from potentially disruptive influences of the outside world and would alike be overseen by the unseen eyes in the inspection tower. As Michael Ignatieff sums it up, rules

had a double meaning for the reformers. They were an enumeration of the inmates' deprivation, but also a charter of their rights.

**Anthony O'Hear**

> They bound both sides of the institutional encounter in obedience
> to an impartial codes enforced from outside. As such they
> reconciled the interests of the state, the custodians and the
> prisoners alike (1978, p. 78).

But who, it will be asked, oversaw the superior controller in his
inspection tower which is also to be his house? Bentham thought that
his inspection-machine could be operated by anyone, by the governor's family or friends, for whom the scene from their lodge would
be 'very various' and 'not altogether unamusing'. More than that, the
general public would be allowed to visit the inspection tower to
observe human behaviour in laboratory conditions. Their motivation
for these visits would not matter, whether it was out of anxiety for
the internees or out of general curiosity. The governor would still be
judged by his institution being open and visible to the public—to the
'great open committee of the tribunal of the world' as Bentham put
it—as much as it is to him. More than that, as the regulator and
observer of what goes on in his institution, and enclosed in the
middle of it he will himself be the first victim of any disaster within,
such as an epidemic or revolt, a hostage in his own hands, as
Bentham says, for the salubrity of the whole.

Modern prisons, whether their architecture be nineteenth or
twentieth century, preserve in essence many of the most significant
features of Bentham's panopticon. This is hardly surprising as,
despite the formal rejection of the panoticon project, prison
architecture and planning in the early nineteenth century followed
Bentham's ideas, except that the state prisons were not, like
Bentham's to be privately run to make a profit for the governing
entrepreneurs. To quote Ignatieff again, in both the Panopticon and
the prison regimes actually established in the nineteenth century,

> the pain of intention (was substituted) for the pain of neglect, the
> authority of rules for the authority of custom, the regimes of hard
> labour for the disorder of idleness. In both the criminal was
> separated from the outside world by a new conception of social
> distance, epitomized by uniforms, walls and bars. The ruling
> image in both was the idea of the eye of the state—impartial
> humane and vigilant—holding the 'deviant' in the thrall of its
> omniscient gaze (1978, p. 113).

It is especially relevant in this last respect that current penal practice
follows Bentham in spirit, if not in architecture. The modern
'psychiatric' prison, Grendon Underwood, may look more like a
college than Pentonville, but Bentham would surely have recognized
this 'very human and humane institution' as it has been described by

**Imprisonment**

a one-time director of Prison Medical Services, as a laboratory of scrutiny and reform, just as much as his own panopticon, that manufactory of reformation, from which convicts would not be released until they had given satisfactory proof of their reform. Only the modality has changed. Tony Parker was told by one of the psychologists employed at Grendon that

> perhaps one of the things that can be said in favour of Grendon is that we do have a certain amount of freedom here, more so than one would in other prisons, to contemplate the possibilities of, and sometimes to carry out, brief experimental work (1970, p. 130).

He was also told by several of the inmates that they were simply playing the system, making the 'right' responses to the therapy and so on, so as to stay on in the pleasant surroundings of Grendon until they achieved remission or parole, in exactly the same way as nineteenth-century reports show prison chaplains constantly being deceived by hypocritical professions of reform. He was also told by one prisoner that 'I don't think I could exist for very long without someone watching over me'.

Surveillance and institutionalization, whether inspired by commercial–utilitarian ideas (Bentham), religion (Howard), or the psycho-sciences (Grendon Underwood), these are the key features of the modern penitentiary, although, in contrast to Benthamite panopticism, surveillance in contemporary prisons is strictly one way. The prison service operates under conditions of great secrecy. The public are not able to observe what goes on in prisons, except with the permission of the Home Office and under strictly regulated conditions. Journalists visiting prisons, for example, have to sign a statement agreeing not to publish any information they learn during their visit. Prisoners themselves, like the public generally, are not allowed to know the Standing Orders for prisons, although they are liable to punishment for any breach of these orders. Their rights to consult solicitors over grievances and to be legally represented when they are themselves tried on disciplinary charges are strongly restricted. Not surprisingly, there has been a crop of cases recently to the European Commission on Human Rights on such matters, and the Home Office always seems to oppose any attempt to grant prisoners the most elementary legal rights of defence, representation, and appeal to independent arbitration. It is, in fact, almost impossible for a prisoner to establish misconduct against him by prisoner officers, particularly with the apparently growing use of riot squads made up of unidentifiable officers from other prisons to quell incidents in prisons. Moreover prisoners are not allowed to check or comment on the records being compiled on them by their warders,

**Anthony O'Hear**

records on which their chance of parole depends. In other words, the most elementary safeguards against the abuse of the Benthamite type of prison—foreseen by the reformers themselves—have not been implemented. In any impartial assessment of the relationship between imprisonment and the crime rate, the crimes committed in prison against the inmates will have to be included.

It is clear that the natural momentum of the institution to preserve discipline in what may be circumstances of considerable degradation to inmates and staff alike, when combined with the veil of official secrecy, makes it all too easy for a man in prison to be deprived of natural justice. The reforms, so boldly entered on in the nineteenth century have failed to produce the intended effect of dispensing with a need for guards to guard the guards, though it might be argued that this is because in this respect the reforms have never really been put into practice. However, where the reformers are more directly open to criticism is in their assumption that human nature is so malleable that a prison machine could be devised so as to grind rogues honest. Bentham's metaphor of grinding rogues is in its way more revealing than much of the talk of reformers since his time. One of the few members of the medical staff from Grendon who would speak to Tony Parker spoke of the way in which large numbers of people in prison are dangerous to themselves:

> they go through life determined to find trouble and be punished; and this is a very serious state of mind for anyone to be in. Something has to be done about it ... (1970, p. 214),

for their own good, presumably. Of course, this was Bentham's idea too, and Howard's in their own ways. The reforming trick is always to make controlling a man appear as if it is in his own best interests, and the reforming itself a favour done to him. But prison cannot be a favour. Nor can it reform, except indirectly, as perhaps in the Barlinnie special unit, by producing the conditions in which a man might discover some constructive talents or interests he was formerly unaware of. But reform is not going to be achieved by seclusion, discipline, exhortation or 'therapy', all of which will tend to alienate an individual from the controlling authority, to separate him in mind and spirit from the rest of mankind, and to instil in him a dependence on institutional structures from which he will find it hard to break out.

All the evidence points to this, and it was recognized at a very early stage of the prison reform movement, as has been documented by Michel Foucault (1977, pp. 264–268) with a host of references to and quotations from writers of the 1830s and 1840s. Among points made are that prison itself produces delinquents by throwing

208

**Imprisonment**

anti-social individuals together, by exacerbating their anti-social propensities by condemning them to 'an unnatural, useless and dangerous existence', by laying them open to assaults by warders or by other prisoners, by the use of the parole system once they leave prison, which makes it hard for them to find honest work, and which keeps them under constant surveillance, and which, by throwing their families into destitution, produces further delinquency. What we have had since the 1830s has in fact been a realization of the failure of prison as a reformatory, but this is usually attributed to internal failures of technique or of severity. Both these responses seem to me to be fundamentally dishonest. As William Godwin pointed out in 1793 in his *Enquiry Concerning Political Justice,* coercion is 'no argument: it begins with producing the sensation of pain, and the sentiment of distaste. It begins with violently alienating the mind from the truth with which we wish it to be impressed.' And penal technique and its context is bound to be coercive. On the other hand, making prison more severe will not reform convicts in any fundamental sense, and greater brutality in prisons generally brings about public disquiet, as it did with Howard and Bentham. Indeed, prison officers do not like working in 'penal dustbins', nor do governors like presiding over them, apparently. And so the movement for something useful to be done *in* prisons *to* prisoners gets further impetus, and the failure of the penitentiary to reform represented as a mere failure of technique.

But if the hope that prison might be able, by some technique or other, to reform criminals is a forlorn one, involving now a certain amount of naivety or bad faith on the part of those who advocate it, this does not mean that prisons might not be necessary to society, and justifiable on other grounds. As noted earlier, they replaced a whole range of other penalties and any society needs some way of dealing with those who break its laws. A legal system without sanctions of any sort is unlikely to be very effective; the overall social good to be gained from having an ordered and generally beneficial state will undoubtedly outweigh a certain amount of pain and loss of freedom for those who offend, if such is indeed the cost of protecting the rights and freedom of the majority. But in saying this, we still have to determine how the pain and loss of freedom is to be construed, and what form it should take.

One view of punishment that is currently quite fashionable is that the state or society has a right or even a duty to express its disapproval of law-breakers in a ritual or symbolic way causing them pain. This view has the advantage over some others in that we do not now have to justify punishment in terms of its effects: if punishment does not reform or deter, that does not matter, because that is not its

**Anthony O'Hear**

point. In a way this 'expressive' view of punishment takes us back to the pre-nineteenth century theatre of public humiliations and executions, which, interestingly were, on occasion counter-productive for the authorities, in that they gave the criminal a chance to become a popular hero (as often happened in public executions). This aside, however, two awkward problems remain for the idea of punishment as expression of outrage. First, we surely cannot justify depriving someone of life or liberty simply because we disapprove of them. The onus will be on us to show that depriving them of life or liberty is either deserved on other grounds or the only means to some overriding social good. In other words, if our expression of social disapproval is to be through the pain or death of someone else, then we have to show an independent justification for inflicting pain or death on them. No doubt legal punishments do express social disapproval, but they also need some further justification. We are now beyond the stage at which the demands of ritual alone would appear to justify the killing of a goat or a cat, yet the expressive justification of punishment says in effect that men can be killed or imprisoned for purely symbolic reasons. Then, secondly, the expressive function of punishment is not well served by shutting people from public view and rendering them effectively incommunicado. Roger Scruton, an advocate of the view that punishment should 'express and propitiate outrage' is not afraid to draw this conclusion:

> The healthiest form of punishment will be immediate, intelligible, even violent, conceived by the citizen as a natural retaliation...

and he goes on to say that imprisonment is not the best way to convey to either public or criminal 'an adequate sense of punishment as a *response* to crime, in the way that a human action may constitute a response' (1980, pp. 82–84). While this is true, it is not true that an expressive response to crime, in the form, presumably of flogging, mutilation or public execution, can be justified simply in terms of the expression of natural outrage at offence. Indeed, civilized society and the law itself since the time of the Orestia can be seen as an attempt to sublimate and redirect in a more positive way the feelings that fuelled the natural and fruitlessly repetitive cycles of revenge that characterize earlier societies.

It will perhaps be said at this point that the criminal does not simply bear the brunt of our outrage. Rather, he deserves retribution for his offence. Through his own suffering he must repay his debt to society, whether in doing so any further good is achieved or not. This view is usually known as retributivism, and despite its familiarity and what I shall later suggest is a grain of truth in its implication that it would be just to punish only where offences exist, I

210

## Imprisonment

must confess to some difficulty in understanding it as a justification for merely inflicting a surplus of pain on an offender. It is quite unclear to me how simply sending someone to prison or punishing him in some other way repays his crime, his victim or society itself. How, except by a mysterious 'moral alchemy' (to use a phrase of H. L. A. Hart) are offences repaid or cancelled out just by inflicting suffering on the perpetrator of the offence? In addition, retributivism when combined with imprisonment leads us, as Scruton points out, to engage in 'an absurd mathematics of crime, according to which it seems the robbery of a mail train is roughly four times as bad as premeditated murder—a result which is deeply repugnant 'to the normal conscience'. The repugnance is in some measure due to the incoherence of thinking that there could be a single currency of desert, whereby crimes of vastly different sorts all paid for in years, months and days. But this incoherence is inherent in the very idea of retributivism, and compounded by its being cashed out in terms of imprisonment. Small wonder that judges in sentencing appear to place more stress on the degree of outrage they work up for a crime, or on the supposed deterrent effect of a sentence than on anything like a strict calculus of penalty.

Expressive and retributive justifications of punishment, then, are of doubtful validity in themselves, and, in addition fit better with more overtly barbaric penalties than imprisonment. It is, however, possible to view retribution in a somewhat different light from the traditional one of the offender's pain in itself cancelling out his debt to society, and to see it as a demand that an offender repay or make reparation in some way to his victim. With this there can surely be no quarrel, nor with the idea that such compensation be organized by the state according to standard procedures of investigation and enforcement. If one of the main reasons for a state at all is to provide security for its members, it is not unreasonable to see the provision of compensation for victims as one of its duties. What is *prima facie* surprising is that neither states, nor philosophers come to that (though cf. Day, 1978), have paid much attention to the idea of victims being compensated through the efforts of their injures. A system of enforced controlled reparation as a punishment for small property crimes might well be practicable and would make far more sense from everyone's point of view, including the victim's than the costly and frequently counter-productive imprisonment of petty thieves. One-third of the prison population is apparently behind bars because of petty theft. The removal of such people from the prison system and of petty theft from the category of imprisonable crime would be a major practical improvement to our system of criminal justice. In saying this, however, I am reversing the arguments of the

## Anthony O'Hear

eighteenth- and nineteenth-century reformers who argued very strongly in favour of imprisoning petty criminals, where previously they might have gone free, and of those who nowadays advocate short sharp shocks to such people, in order to prevent them becoming bigger criminals. All the evidence, of course, points the other way, that prison itself makes one-time petty criminals into bigger and persistent ones, and that keeping them out of the prison system is the best way of preventing this downward spiral.

Of course, there are plenty of crimes which are not petty thefts or small burglaries, and where the idea of reparation to victims, or some sort of mediation between victim and offender is inappropriate. We want to deter such crimes. How should society set about doing this? Moreover, can we be sure that a system of reparation and mediation would actually deter the petty crimes which are not actually committed, but which the present system of imprisonment, it is claimed, does deter?

To deal with these questions and the whole idea of deterrent sentencing satisfactorily, we desperately need information of an empirical sort, but it is in fact extremely hard to discover the truth in assessing the deterrent effects of legal sanctions, once we get beyond the limiting cases of having no sanctions at all or of punishing every wrongdoer with some extremely severe penalty. But the latter would be impossible without total supervision of everyone all the time, which is in itself impossible and surely unacceptable anyway on ethical grounds. So, in practice, we have to consider what to do to deter crime in a world in which the vast majority of actual crimes are going to go undetected. (The Metropolitan Police are proud of a clear-up rate on reported crime of 17 per cent, which is probably nearer 5 per cent in fact if we take unreported crime into account.) Research studies have shown that well-directed blitzes on specific offences, with heavy policing and heavy penalties, can have some temporary effect on the incidence of those offences, but for normal circumstances, the conclusion of the studies on the effect of deterrence is in conclusive.

In the words of Deryck Beyleveld, in his review of the relevant studies,

> there exists no scientific basis for expecting that a general deterrence policy, which does not involve an unacceptable interference with human rights, will do anything to control the crime rate (1979, p. 136).

Beyleveld does point out that most studies in this area claim to have discovered significant correlations between probability of sanctions and offence-rates, though no correlation between severity of sanc-

## Imprisonment

tions and offence-rates, but he is highly critical of the methodological assumptions of the studies. He thinks we are just as much in the dark on the deterrent effect on the crime rate of increasing police manpower as we are on the effect of increasing fines or sentences. What, however, is not in doubt is that at any given time in Holland 1·3 per 10,000 of the population is in prison, compared with 8 per 10,000 in Britain, while the crime rates of the two countries are roughly comparable. (The figures for Italy, France, Denmark, Luxembourg and Germany are 2·2, 3·9, 4·5, 5·9 and 6·7, respectively.) It seems likely that a lot less imprisonment and far shorter sentences will not by themselves decrease the deterrent effect of legal sanctions, which can be other than imprisonment, as I have already suggested in connection with reparations for petty crime. In view of the uncertainty surrounding the deterrent effect of sentencing policy, one is led to the conclusion that imprisonment—itself a great evil to the person imprisoned, highly costly and wasteful of all sorts of resources, and a contributing cause to further offences both inside and outside the prison—should not be used in the mere hope that it might deter people, except in the case of major offences, whose harm greatly outweighs the evils of imprisoning a man against his will. In fact, this whole area is one where far more empirical knowledge is required before sensible conclusions can be drawn.

However, even supposing we had more evidence that other people would be deterred from some major crime by your being in prison, would thus justify you being put there, as a public utility, so to speak? According to D. D. Raphael it would, if you had committed a crime:

> where however a person is guilty of having wilfully done wrong, he has thereby forfeited part of his claim to be treated as an end in himself: in acting as a non-moral being he leaves it open to his fellows to use him as such (1955, p. 71).

This is surely going too far; apart from anything else, no one could claim the right to be treated as an end on this basis. Nor can I agree with Rousseau's claim in the *Social Contract* (Bk 1, Ch. IV) that the criminal, by declaring war on the state from within, places himself outside the state and morality. Nevertheless, it might be possible in cases of crimes where direct reparation is impossible because, for example, the harm done is too great, or too personal, to be repaired to see one's enforced reparation on being convicted in terms of the deterrent effect on potential wrongdoers, thereby saving their potential victims. Imprisonment could then be seen as a sort of proxy-reparation, helping not one's own victims but other potential sufferers from similar offences.

**Anthony O'Hear**


In addition to possibly providing the means for some people to make reparation for wrongs that cannot be directly righted imprisonment could also be justified as a means of taking some types of dangerously anti-social people out of circulation for a time, at least. We all have our favourite examples of candidates for this role, hit men for organized crime, terrorists, drug racketeers, men who prey violently on women, and the like. Talk of dangerous crime and dangerous criminals, however, raises a number of difficulties. Would we, for example, be justified in detaining people who are merely potentially dangerous, or continuing to detain people who have been convicted of a dangerous offence, after the completion of their sentence on the grounds that they are likely to offend again? One would feel a lot happier here if dangerousness were far more clearly defined and predictable than it actually is. What evidence there is suggests that of people predicted on psychological or medical grounds to be dangerous, only one in three or one in four will actually commit a dangerous crime. In these circumstances, we could hardly be justified in detaining for an indefinite period even on strict utilitarian calculations all those whom are potentially dangerous according to the available criteria. Moreover, if we were able to predict with considerable accuracy that certain people will definitely commit a violent crime, we would hardly be justified in inflicting any surplus of pain on them beyond some sort of supervision over them, because our ability to make such predictions itself testifies to their inability to do otherwise.

I am suggesting that if imprisonment of convicted serious criminals is a way of deterring others from serious crime, and if it is the only way of stopping actually dangerous people from continuing their activities, then it will be right to punish them by means of set terms of imprisonment. My reasoning here, as in my suggestion regarding reparation is broadly utilitarian, in that the justification if institutional reparation and imprisonment, where appropriate, would be in terms of their generally beneficial effects; in the case of imprisonment, this would be in terms of any discoverable deterrence and prevention. To make these proposals for punishment by means of reparation or imprisonment consistent with our intuitions of natural justice and our beliefs about human responsibility for actions, we would also have to ensure that people should not be put in prison except when they had done wrong. This is the grain of truth at the heart of retributivism, that we should punish only when wrong has been intentionally done, and in some way proportionate to the wrong done. But this provides only the conditions in which any question of punishment can arise. It does not, I have argued, justify particular institutions of punishment or applications of it. To assess

214

## Imprisonment

these questions we need to look to further goods that punishing might plausibly secure, such as restoration of what is owing, deterrence and prevention of wrong-doing. Nevertheless our retributivist intuitions regarding just punishment rule out detaining people just because they might be dangerous. Apart from the other reasons I have given, sentencing for this reason would be far too open to abuse and would involve an unacceptable degree of surveillance over and pseudo-medical interference with people in prison and in the population as a whole. Further, the prisons that would be needed in order to deter and interrupt major crime should not attempt to treat or reform the individuals in them, for the reasons given earlier in the paper. The discipline within the prisons, then, would not need to be structured as if to reform. Indeed, in the words of Mountbatten's recommendations for maximum security prisons it should be 'as liberal and constructive as possible' inside, including opportunities to study and work for a fair wage, and the prison as secure as necessary without. Given that those inside will be let out sometime, visits and contact with the world outside should be maximized consistent with security, and prisoners should be accorded full legal rights.

What I have been suggesting in the preceding paragraph is in some ways in line with Mountbatten's proposals of 1966 for maximum security prisons, which were never put into effect for political reasons. The difference between my suggestion and the Mountbatten report is that I do not think that there should be any other prisons at all, and that given the failure of prison and our lack of knowledge in these areas, we should experiment boldly with alternatives to imprisonment. Prisons in the modern sense were introduced as an experiment in the reformation of human beings, and this experiment has failed. I point this out against the background of a current daily prison population of 44,000 compared with 10,000 in 1928 and 1938, 20,000 in 1956 and 29,000 in 1964: the population is to rise to 52,000 by 1990 when ten new prisons are ready, or so the Home Office believes. More prisons simply produce more prisoners, because the courts, urged on by the media and populist politicians, make sure all the available places are filled, splitting families, wrecking lives.

Who, in any case, are these 44,000? Are they people who have split families or wrecked live? In large measure it appears that those who are in prison are more sinned against than sinning. While it is extremely difficult to get figures on categories of people in prison—there are, for example, no statistics on the class breakdown of those in prison—it is clear that large numbers of people in prison are either petty criminals or mentally disordered or both. Many are in prison because of small debts, fine defaulting, vagrancy, drunkenness, homelessness or prostitution and the homosexual offences of impor-

**Anthony O'Hear**

tuning or having sex with people between the ages of eighteen and twenty-one. I can see no justification for any of those categories being in prison, nor is it right that so many people should be held on remand for so long especially when up to half of them will eventually be found innocent or, even under present practice, given non-custodial sentences. (48,000 were held on remand in 1982 of whom 2,000 were eventually found innocent and 16,000 given non-custodial sentences.)

A survey of a sample of the population of male prisoners in the South-East was done in 1972, however, and published in the *Home Office Research Bulletin* in 1978. It deserves wide publicity, and our democratic responsibility regarding what is being done in our name requires us to pierce the veil of Home Office secrecy and apathy to see whether its results are characteristic of the penal system generally. The following figures stand out. Eighty-two per cent of the survey were manual, semi-skilled or unskilled workers in their usual jobs, compared with sixty-two per cent in the population as a whole. Twenty-one per cent were classified as mentally disordered, and of those convicted of serious offences against the person thirty-nine per cent were mentally disordered. Only one-third of the total had been convicted of 'serious' offences. About forty per cent of the total survey were either homeless or mentally disordered or both. Many of those not actually classified as mentally disordered were regarded as unstable, and only thirty-three per cent were mentally 'apparently normal'. About one-third were regarded by the researchers as 'divertible' from prison, having committed no serious offence against the person, having made no great gains from crime, and having shown no great competence in their criminal activities. Yet over half of these were serving sentences of more than one year. Fifty-four per cent of those released from short- or medium-term sentences were reconvicted within two years while the proportion of homeless and disordered prisoners reconvicted within two years was seventy-two per cent; fifty-nine per cent of those reconvicted were sentenced to further terms of imprisonment. The picture given by this report is amplified by a National Association for the Care and Resettlement of Offenders report which shows that on 30 June 1982 there were 44,002 people in custody. Seventeen per cent were awaiting trial or sentence, twenty-five per cent were under twenty-one, forty-nine per cent were serving sentences of eighteen months or less, and over half were detained for non-payment of fines, burglary and theft (not including crimes against the person).

The conclusion from these sets of figures is that a very large proportion of those in prison are petty and incompetent delinquents, socially and mentally disadvantaged. Sending them to prison is not

## Imprisonment

only, in many cases, cruel and unnecessary; it also makes it highly likely that they will return. Prison, far from solving any problems, actually creates crime and makes criminals. Why then do we tolerate it? Answering this question takes us back to the origins of the prison and forward to the social role of crime and its current definition.

The growth of the modern prison coincided not simply with the work of the reformers but also with a period of considerable social change. It coincided with the massive enclosing of common land and the suppression of the customary rights of the poor over game, wood, deadfall and the like, with the increasing use of casual, seasonal labour on the land, and hence high rural unemployment, and, increasingly, with the growth of industrial towns. All those phenomena meant that there were large numbers of small thieves and vagrants, victims of the new social conditions in that survival within the law was hard for them, who, it seemed to the propertied classes, had to be controlled in the interests of stability and of property. By the 1840s, we are told, 'summary offenders (vagrants, poachers, petty theives, disorderlies, and public drunkards) accounted for more than half of the prison population', and a further quarter were debtors or deserters (cf. Ignatieff, 1978, p. 179). Then, as now, the criminal justice system was largely directed at small game, against the deprived and the dispossessed. One can hardly maintain that the middle and upper classes are so much more moral and honest than the rest of society as the prison population suggests or that things done by the middle and upper classes do not cause equal or greater measures of human suffering than the petty crimes of the working classes, yet our system of criminal justice—police, courts and prisons—appears to concentrate most of its efforts into fighting the working class petty offender and to proffer a high degree of tolerance towards the makers of lethal products such as asbestos, unsafe cars, thalidomide, and so on, as well as towards usury and property speculation, ²industrial pollution and dubious banking, insurance, legal and stock-market practices. Perhaps we should recall that Bentham saw his panopticon untying the Gordian knot of the Poor Laws.

We need to ask what function prisons and the criminal justice system as a whole performs in our society, given that it is so lopsided and so inefficacious and so many ways. Why does it carry on as it does? The answer supplied by Michel Foucault has considerable plausibility: prison in one obvious sense a failure, is in another sense a great success:

For the observation that prison fails to eliminate crime one should perhaps substitute the hypothesis that prison has succeeded

217

**Anthony O'Hear**

extremely well in producing delinquency, a specific type, a politically or economically less dangerous — and, on occasion, usable — form of illegality: in producing delinquents, in an apparently marginal, buy in fact centrally supervised milieu; in producing the delinquent as a pathologized subject (1977, p. 277).

Prisons are filled with delinquents, people who resist the disciplinary normalization of school and work, who are processed in such a way that they can hardly fail to repeat the cycle of delinquency and imprisonment over and over again. This delinquency in turn presents itself as a rising tide of crime, and justifies a greater and greater police surveillance of the milieu of the delinquents. The delinquents themselves are the subjects of massive surveillance, which, of course, naturally takes in their families, friends and neighbours. Delinquency itself is typically fragmented and marginalized, infinitely less dangerous and politically potent than the bands of vagrants and vagabonds that swarmed the country in earlier times; the delinquent himself is denied the opportunity to make common cause with his own kind, but taken up into a hierarchical network of punishment and surveillance. Moreover, despite middle-class fears, the principal victims of working classes delinquency are members of the working classes. The effect of this, of course, is to produce demands within the working classes themselves for greater policing. Prison was conceived as a panoptic structure; its logic and effect is to extend panopticism outside the prisons themselves into the heart of the potentially dangerous under-classes of society.

I would suggest further that we are extremely intolerant of those who deviate socially if they are members of the lower classes. You have to learn and you have to work in the disciplined way laid down by authority. Failure to fit in to the accepted schedules of education and work almost inevitably leads to delinquency. In this paper, I have argued that delinquents should not be sent to prison, but the deeper question is whether we are prepared to tolerate deviance—the refusal or mere inability to fit into the disciplines of society—without forcing the deviant into delinquency. The panopticism of the prison will not necessarily disappear just because we empty our prisons of delinquents, and get them to make reparation for the damage they have done, or refer the mentally disordered offender for more appropriate treatment than prison. Indeed, it might increase, with the corresponding increase of probation services, psychiatric care and the like. From the humanitarian point of view, we surely should aim to get individual petty offenders and the like out of prison, and to keep them out, as well as attempting to redress the wrongs done to the victims of petty crime. But we should also ask ourselves why

**Imprisonment**

petty crime concerns us so much, why people take it up as a way of life, and whether we are prepared to go on tolerating the distributions of social goods and processes of normalization which seem inevitably produce it, and the extent of the surveillance that is invoked to control it. The following words of Ignatieff, may stand as counterpoint to my opening quotation from Bentham:

> Toleration (towards the lawbreaker) does not appear to increase with the consolidation of social order. Despite the fact that the modern state has appropriated to itself a degree of power that would have thoroughly terrified our eighteenth century ancestors, public discussion about social control in Western society conveys the impression of a state barely able to hold the line against criminality and terrorism. This alarmism, which seems so exaggerated if looked at from the vantage point of a Londoner of the riotous 1770s, acts to legitimize ever more intrusive police deployment.... The historical consolidation by the 1860s of a structure of total institutions and policing did not succeed in quieting fears of disorder but only exacerbated them. Apparently, order breeds not peace of mind but greater anxiety and recurring demands for more order. It is a need that knows no satisfaction, at least not in this type of society (1978, p. 218).

I am aware that in writing about prisons I have gone far beyond abstract philosophical considerations, and also beyond the subject of prison itself. But I will end with a speculation that is more abstract and philosophical: as to whether the Benthamite philosophy, and the whole calculus approach to questions of politics and value, whose application we see in the prison system, may not be a product of a cast of mind and a society that finds human disorderliness intolerable, and is determined to push it to the margins, socially and economically. Bentham, it will be remembered, thought that the panopticon could also be used as a school, a hospital, a madhouse, a workhouse, a factory, anywhere, in fact, where 'the more constantly the persons to be inspected are under the eyes of the persons who should inspect them, the more perfectly will the purpose of the establishment have been attained' (1787, p. 40).

**Bibliography**

*Note*: I have drawn heavily on Foucault and Ignatieff on the historical background to the current prison system, while Martin Wright's *Making Good* is a comprehensive study of the present state of the prison system.

219

**Anthony O'Hear**

J. Bentham *Panopticon* (Collected Works), J. Bowring (ed.), Vol. IV (1787).

D. Beyleveld, 'Deterrence Research as a Basis for Deterrence Policies', *Howard Journal* **18,** (1979), 135–149.

J. P. Day, 'Retributive Punishment', *Mind* **87,** (1978), 498–516.

M. Foucault, *Discipline and Punish* (London: Allen Lane, 1977).

R. Hattersley, 'Criminal Justice in the 1980s', *Howard Journal* **22** (1983), 1–7.

M. Ignatieff, *A Just Measure of Pain* (London: Macmillan, 1978).

T. Parker, *The Frying Pan* (New York: Harper and Row, 1970).

D. Raphael, *Moral Judgement* (London: George Allen and Unwin, 1955).

R. Scruton, *The Meaning of Conservatism* (Hamondsworth: Penguin Books, 1980).

J. E. Thomas & R. Pooley, *The Exploding Prison* (London: Junction Books, 1980).

M. Wright, *Making Good* (London: Burnett Books, 1982).

# [8]

# RETRIBUTION AND INCARCERATION

## Richard L. Lippke

Incarceration is widely assumed to be the legal punishment of choice for serious criminal offenders. Yet this assumption is not often or carefully defended. Those who support the crime reduction approach to the justification of legal punishment would seem to face a relatively easy task in defending this assumption. Imprisonment obviously incapacitates offenders and, perhaps a bit less obviously, deters would-be offenders. Still, numerous questions would need to be addressed by those who defend incarceration on these grounds: For what crimes should it be used if we are to achieve the maximum and most cost-effective crime reduction effects? What should the lengths of prison sentences be for the various criminal offenses if we are to maximize crime reduction and minimize the social and personal costs of incarceration? And which conditions of incarceration are most apt to reduce crime at the least overall cost to society and to offenders? These are all difficult questions and there appear to be few systematic attempts by those who favor the crime reduction approach to address them.

It is even less clear how those who defend punishment on retributive grounds support the use of incarceration. In defending its use, retributivists cannot cite the social benefits of detaining serious offenders or dissuading individuals tempted to commit harmful acts. Standard retributive appeals to restoring justice or depriving offenders of the unfair advantages gained by their acts may only justify the imposition of some losses or other on them. Such appeals fall well short of justifying the specific kinds of losses imposed by incarceration. Like their crime reduction counterparts, retributivists must address other questions regarding the use of incarceration: Which offenses merit imprisonment as a sanction? What prison terms are appropriate for the various types of criminal offenses? And what is the requisite character of incarceration—what conditions must imprisonment satisfy for it to perform its role within a retributive theory of punishment? Again, in the voluminous literature on punishment generally, and on retributivism specifically, there are relatively few attempts to address systematically these sorts of questions.[1]

Given the number and difficulty of the questions raised by the use of incarceration as a legal sanction, this essay will focus only on developing a retributive account of the answers to them. Even limiting its focus in this way will not permit us to get much beyond making claims that in many places are little more than tentative and programmatic in character. These are difficult questions. It is easy to harbor doubts about retributivism's ability to address them adequately, but we might have similar doubts about any theory's ability to address them adequately. But retributivism, in particular, has been criticized on the grounds that it has little to say about sentencing beyond the vague nostrum that offenders ought to be punished proportionally with their ill deserts.[2] This essay argues that such criticism is unfounded, though it must be conceded that those interested in defending the theory have not spent enough time discussing its implications for sentencing. A retributive defense of incarceration has much to offer, some of which is predictable and some of which is quite surprising given the theory's sometimes formidable reputation.

## Choosing A Version of Retributivism

The first difficulty to be faced is that there are numerous versions of retributivism defended in the literature on punishment and they do not all have the same implications for sentencing generally and for an account of the role of incarceration specifically.[3] Discussion of these different retributive theories would take us too far afield. What most of them have in common is the notion that all and only those who violate certain moral standards ought to be punished commensurately with the seriousness of their violations. Typically, retributivists require that the relevant moral standards be ones codified and enforced by the law, so that individuals are put on notice regarding the consequences of their violation and so that carefully circumscribed procedures are used to detect and try suspected wrongdoers. Still, some defend retributive punishment in the state of nature.[4] The seriousness of violations is usually conceived by retributivists as a function of both the extent of harm done (or threatened) to victims and the degree of culpability offenders exhibit in causing those harms. Let us suppose that the harm done (or threatened) to victims is to be gauged by considering two things—the moral importance of the interests invaded by an offense and the extent to which they are invaded. This yields a type of moral retributivism according to which punishment is deserved only if it is a response to the commission of certain moral wrongs (which are also, presumably, prohibited by the criminal law).[5] This contrasts with legal retributivism, which construes deserved punishment as a response to the violation of legal standards that may or may not be defensible on moral grounds.

## RETRIBUTION AND INCARCERATION 31

Which interests are morally important enough to merit legal protection and how we are to rank order such interests are two questions that a theory of moral rights is supposed to help us answer. But here also, there are many such theories available. It can be argued that such diversity is not a problem for retributivism so long as the theory can accommodate most of these theories, something which it appears it can do. What this means is that a retributive approach to punishment can be grafted onto competing accounts of what interests the law should aim to protect and in what order of importance.

There are also differences among legal theorists about the nature and constituents of the other component of crime seriousness—namely, criminal culpability. Again, it can be argued that these differences do not pose insuperable difficulties for retributivism, though they may lead to slightly different accounts of crime seriousness. For purposes of discussion, let us assume that culpability for criminal harms is greatest where offenders, with premeditation, freely and intentionally act to invade those interests of persons that the law (according to some theory of moral rights) ought to protect. In such cases, the resulting harms can most fully be imputed to offenders, rather than to chance or the projects of other agents. Indeed, in the clearest cases of full culpability, offenders work assiduously to harm others, attempting to counter the workings of chance or other agents. Culpability decreases where interest invasions are the result of reckless or negligent conduct, or where offenders have diminished responsibility due to age, mental illness or the presence of things like provocation or duress. Harm to victims can only partially be imputed to offenders and their projects where chance (in cases of recklessness or negligence), the projects of other agents (in cases of provocation or duress), or deficiencies in the ability to act responsibly (in cases of children) play some role in producing it.

According to retributive theory, punishment is justified as a way of restoring the just status quo ante that was disrupted by the offender.[6] How punishment performs this task remains a matter of some controversy among retributive theorists. Though the view cannot be defended here, a plausible interpretation of how the state performs this task says that legal punishment involves state efforts to restore the equality of condition that, at least in those respects designated by basic moral rights, all citizens are entitled to. All citizens are entitled to have their lives, bodies, psychological integrity, and justly held property respected and defended by the law. In these respects, at least, the state should act to ensure their equality. Whether it should act in other ways to ensure equality among citizens is, of course, a matter of considerable controversy, though this is not a controversy the resolution of which may have significant implications for the core areas of the criminal law.

Criminal offenders act in (legally prohibited) ways that deprive victims of some or all of the equality of condition victims are entitled to. There are, it must be admitted, various ways in which the state might attempt to restore the requisite equality of condition. But with most serious crimes it can arguably be shown that the imposition of penal losses is the only appropriate equalizing response by the state. In particular, where victims cannot be made whole again by offender compensation or restitution, the state must respond by imposing penal losses or deprivations on offenders that are commensurate with their ill deserts. By doing so the state diminishes the life-prospects of offenders in ways comparable with the ways in which offenders diminished the life-prospects of their victims.

There are many questions raised by this brief account of retributivism that will not be addressed.[7] It or something like it seems the core of retributivism—that legal punishment is not designed to incapacitate, deter, or rehabilitate, but to impose penalties on offenders that reflect the seriousness of their offenses. Let us consider what such an account suggests about the use of incarceration as a penal sanction.

## WHY INCARCERATE?

At a minimum, incarceration drastically restricts the freedom of movement and freedom of association of offenders, and deprives them of much of their privacy. As such, it imposes losses on offenders that may bear little resemblance to the harms offenders imposed on their victims. Also, there are other kinds of losses or deprivations the state might, in theory, inflict on criminal offenders if its aim is to diminish their life-prospects commensurately with their ill deserts. Among these other kinds of losses or deprivations are corporal punishment, banishment, public denunciation, forfeiture of rights to employment or travel, or a requirement that other citizens shun offenders. What is it, then, about incarceration that makes it particularly suitable for use as an equalizing criminal sanction, especially in relation to serious offenders?

The answer can be discerned if we return to the notion that the criminal law ought to be concerned with securing certain vital interests of individuals, ones typically conceived of as moral rights. Since there exist numerous theories about what rights are and which ones persons possess, the strategy in this essay will be to choose one theory and use it to construct a model specification of the retributive approach to justifying incarceration. Arguably this model specification is fairly representative in the sense that competing theories of rights would, when combined with a retributive approach to punishment, yield similar accounts of the role incarceration plays in restoring just status quo antes.

## RETRIBUTION AND INCARCERATION 33

One plausible account of moral rights is that they designate a group of capabilities whose role is to enable persons to live decent lives shaped by their autonomous choices.[8] Life, physical and psychological integrity, and freedom from a range of interferences are among the things persons must have if they are to shape and enjoy their own lives. Serious crimes defeat these capabilities in numerous ways and to varying degrees. In some cases they deprive victims of their lives entirely; in others they leave victims physically or psychologically shattered so that, for some period of time, it is difficult for them to have decent lives shaped by their own choices.

Let us assume that retributivists must eschew sentencing approaches such as *lex talionis* that require the state to impose losses or deprivations on offenders that are of the same type as those offenders inflicted on their victims (e.g., blinding those offenders who blinded their victims). The difficulties raised by such approaches are well-known and appear insurmountable.[9] But if retributivists reject a strict equalizing approach to sentencing, they must provide some alternative organizing idea around which to develop a theory. One such organizing idea is that of the capabilities required to live a decent life shaped by one's autonomous choices. Criminal offenses intrude upon these capabilities and penal sanctions might be designed with an eye toward matching the extent of the intrusions, though also taking into account the degree of offender culpability for the intrusion. Incarceration might thus be regarded by retributivists as an especially suitable penal response to those serious offenses that defeat or diminish in significant ways the capabilities of victims to live decent lives of their own choosing. There seems little doubt that those incarcerated suffer severe losses to such capabilities. Imprisonment cramps and truncates the lives of offenders, at least for the duration of their sentences. As such it does something to serious offenders that is comparable, if not exactly equivalent, to what many of them have done to their victims.[10] At the same time, if efforts are made to minimize the degrading and inhumane aspects of imprisonment, its use as a sanction for serious offenders arguably does not run afoul of the retributive requirement that legal punishment be structured so that it treats offenders as moral beings capable of rational and responsible conduct. Imprisonment does significantly diminish the abilities of offenders to live rich and autonomous lives. Yet it need not wholly deprive them of their physical and psychological health, work and interaction with others, or opportunities to enjoy or entertain themselves. Nor need it erode the capacities constitutive of moral personhood. Prisoners can be treated in ways that preserve their ability and willingness to comprehend and respond constructively to the reasons for which they are being punished.

In contrast, other penalties that we might impose on serious offenders do not, in most cases, inflict appropriate kinds of losses on them, are impractical, or are inconsistent with treating them as beings capable of comprehending their wrongs and the justice of their punishment. Banishment of offenders, in addition to being impractical, would only disrupt offenders' lives if they were assigned to locales where living decent lives on their own terms would be difficult. Corporal punishment may not inflict commensurate losses if it is relatively brief in duration. On the other hand, if it goes on for longer periods of time or is repeated on numerous occasions, its long-term effects may be so traumatizing that they exceed proportionality limits. There is also Jeffrie Murphy's contention that corporal punishment does not treat offenders as moral beings because, for the duration of its infliction, they are reduced to little more than suffering animals.[11] Public condemnation will only disrupt the lives of offenders who are sensitive to social perceptions of their conduct. While we can imagine societies where public condemnation would be devastating to the life-prospects of offenders, most of us do not live in such societies. Many offenders are apt to simply go on about their business indifferent to what the state has said about their conduct.

Importantly, retributivists need not insist that incarceration of serious offenders is necessarily the only sanction that imposes the appropriate kinds of losses on them. If there are other sanctions that would function in comparable ways to defeat or diminish the capabilities of serious offenders to live decent lives on their own terms, then retributivists might be open to their use. Retributive theorists need only make the more modest claim that incarceration is one type of sanction that serves the requisite equalizing purpose of punishment. They might be skeptical about other sanctions doing so, but that is all they need be.

Two objections to the retributive account of incarceration developed so far might be made. First, it might be argued that the effects of many crimes on the abilities of victims to live decent lives shaped by their own choices are apt to be quite different than the effects of incarceration on offenders. For instance, rape victims suffer not only assaults on their bodily integrity and dignity but also the fears, anxieties, and inability to trust others that typically result from severe victimization. These harms may stunt or deform victims' abilities to live decent lives of their own choosing in myriad ways and for lengthy periods of time. It might reasonably be asked how incarcerating rapists imposes any sort of equivalent loss on them. Keep in mind, however, that the losses imposed by punishment need not, on the account developed in this essay, be strictly equivalent to those suffered by the victims of crime. It is enough if the effects of punishment interfere commensurately with the capabilities of offenders to live decent lives of their own choosing. And arguably imprisonment does this especially if the lengths of sentences are made to reflect the extent to which crimes diminish the life prospects of victims. Prison does deprive individuals of significant control over their lives, even over their bodies. It also puts individuals in circumstances where they are very likely to experience fears about their safety and future, anxieties about how others will perceive or react to them, and loss of connection with those they love or care about. More would have to be said to show that incarceration diminishes the abilities of other serious offenders to live decent lives of their own choosing in ways comparable to the ways in which their crimes harmed their victims. But hopefully enough has been said here to indicate how the argument would proceed.

This brings us to the second objection. It is seems likely that the effects of whatever physical, psychological, or financial losses most crime victims suffer taper off over time. Most victims eventually resume their lives and are progressively less debilitated by their victimization. Yet it might be argued that imprisonment and its effects are more all or nothing. Its debilitating effects do not taper off, at least so long as offenders are behind bars. Hence it might be argued that incarceration debilitates more than crime does. Yet this objection ignores the ways in which the punishment of serious offenders can also be tapered off. Those imprisoned for their crimes can gradually be granted more privileges or opportunities within prisons, can be assigned to work release programs or to halfway houses, or can be released on parole. In these and other ways they too can be eased back into circumstances where they slowly regain control over their lives and enjoy improved living conditions.

## For Which Crimes is Incarceration Appropriate?

Most modern legal systems utilize a range of penal sanctions, assigning the most severe ones like incarceration to crimes above a certain level of seriousness. This seems entirely appropriate given the various ways in which crimes harm their victims. The question we now face is whether retributivism offers any insight into determining the level of seriousness at which incarceration becomes an appropriate sanction.

All criminal sanctions can be understood as diminishing, to a greater or lesser extent, the capabilities of offenders to live decent lives shaped by their autonomous choices. So-called intermediate sanctions, which include electronic monitoring, confinement to one's house or apartment, requirements to report to probation officers or other officials on a regular (even daily) basis, and community service, can be quite disruptive to offenders' lives, especially if combined with fines or requirements to pay restitution to victims. Collectively, sanctions short of imprisonment might be very burdensome to offenders in terms of disrupting their abilities to live their lives as they choose—as much if not more so than relatively short prison sentences. Also, prisons vary from minimum to maximum security facilities, with the latter imposing more extensive restrictions on the activities of inmates.

As Andrew von Hirsch and Nils Jareborg have argued, criminal offenses impose losses of diverse kinds on victims and do so to greater or lesser degrees.[12] We are not likely to find any clear line separating lesser and greater offenses, though it is possible to classify crimes by reference to the standard kinds of harm they inflict. This continuum of offenses and the harms they inflict mirrors the continuum of penal sanctions that imposes minor to quite substantial losses on offenders. All of this suggests that a retributive approach to sentencing is unlikely to ground any sharp line separating offenses for which incarceration is appropriate and ones for which some combination of intermediate or other sanctions is sufficient. This does not mean, however, that a retributive approach to sentencing tells us nothing about the sorts of crimes for which incarceration seems a commensurate penal sanction.

Given the extent to which incarceration diminishes the capabilities of offenders to live decent lives on their own terms, it follows that a retributive approach to sentencing would only justify its use in relation to offenses that, with at least moderate levels of culpability, do substantial harm to victims. The clearest cases of offenses for which incarceration would be appropriate are those causing loss of life, significant physical or psychological injuries, or significant loss or damage to property that individuals rely upon for material comfort and support. In these cases the harms to victims are apt to undermine (for some period of time) or destroy their capabilities of living decent lives of their own choosing. Those who inflict such harms should be made to endure significant losses to their own similar capabilities for some appropriate period of time. Where harms to victims are mild to moderate, or where offender culpability is lower, the retributive case for incarceration (as opposed to the infliction of other penal sanctions) is weaker. For instance, many property crimes impose inconveniences of various kinds on their victims, but these are often short-lived and in some cases ameliorated by the availability of insurance that allows victims to quickly replace their stolen property. A retributive approach may not therefore support the use of prison sentences for a whole range of minor to moderately serious property crimes.[13]

A retributive defense of incarceration may also not support the use of incarceration for crimes that are victimless or involve some degree of victim cooperation.[14] For instance, many drug crimes either have no clear victims or, if they have them, have victims who are somewhat complicit in producing the harms that befall them. Of course, depending on the substantive theory of moral rights used to ground a retributive approach to punishment, there may be little justification available for having drug possession and use laws in the first place. Some might wish to defend enforcement of such laws so long as they are duly enacted by democratic majorities. Others will argue against their enforcement on the grounds that individuals have basic moral rights to determine what substances they ingest or inject into themselves. But even if there is reason to have and enforce such laws, a retributive approach may not support incarcerating those who violate them. Incarceration should be reserved for offenses that culpably cause clear and substantial harms to victims. It should not be used to discourage minor offenses that the public, perhaps unaccountably, cares a great deal about.

Some will still regard the retributive approach to determining the criminal offenses for which incarceration is an appropriate sanction as hopelessly vague. It is, admittedly, indeterminate, though perhaps not hopelessly so. The question is whether any other approach to the justification of legal punishment is likely to give us more precise guidance in determining when incarceration is to be employed. Again, offenses differ by degree in their impact on victims and sanctions differ by degree in their impact on offenders. It seems a dubious proposition to believe that there is any sort of bright line separating imprisonable offenses from ones for which other sanctions are appropriate.

## How Long to Incarcerate?

Critics of retributivism charge that the theory is unhelpful when it comes to assigning determinate sentences to crimes. Specifically, it is claimed that talk about sentences being proportional to or commensurate with the seriousness of crimes at best sets lower and upper limits to sentences without telling us much at all about how to fix sentences within what is likely to be a fairly broad range. To some extent it must be admitted that the retributive account sketched below will only be capable of fixing sentences for the various crimes within some determinate range. For the most part this is because the harms inflicted on victims by crimes and the losses imposed on offenders by punishment cannot be quantified or compared along some common metric. Only rough estimates of the extent to which each of these interferes with individuals' lives can be made and compared against one another. There may be room within a comprehensive theory of sentencing for crime reduction considerations to play some role in helping us to specify sentence lengths more precisely, especially so long as employing such considerations does not take us outside the parameters set by retributive considerations.[15] On the other hand, there is reason to doubt that crime reduction approaches to sentencing can themselves provide us with highly determinate sentences for crimes.[16] It may be that no approach to the justification of punishment is capable of giving us more than broad contours for determining sentence lengths.

Retributivism treats the seriousness of crimes as a function of both the harms they cause (or threaten to cause) victims and the degree of culpability offenders exhibit in causing those harms. Our model specification of a retributive approach holds that the extent of harm is to be gauged by determining how far crimes interfere with the capabilities of victims to live decent lives shaped by their autonomous choices. Yet one question raised by this model specification has to this point been ignored. Should we measure harm by reference to an account of the standard harms the various types of crimes cause their victims, or by examining the actual harms crimes cause their victims in each instance? The latter, more individualized approach, would require us to carefully investigate victim losses in each case to determine how serious an offense was. The former approach focuses on the harms types of offenses tend to cause their victims, with less attention to the specific details of each offense.

Von Hirsch and Jareborg suggest a plausible compromise, where criminal harm is gauged by focusing on the standard harms caused by the various types of offenses, while permitting the introduction of aggravating or mitigating factors in specific cases that either raise or lower assessments of the extent of harm.[17] This suggests that legislators ought to assign a range of sentences for any given type of crime and then allow the courts to make the final determination of the sanctions to be imposed in particular cases. Doing so would satisfy the twin retributive desiderata of maintaining proportionality in sentencing and providing would-be offenders with prior notice of the sanctions they face for lawbreaking.

Von Hirsch and Jareborg argue that criminal acts intrude upon four main kinds of interests: physical integrity, material support and amenity, freedom from humiliation, and privacy/autonomy.[18] They then provide analyses of a range of serious crimes and the extent to which they intrude upon one or more of these four interests. As von Hirsch and Jareborg make clear, the assessment of harms to victims involves both empirical and value judgments about which disagreement is possible. It involves empirical judgments because we must determine which interests crimes intrude upon and to what extent. It involves value judgments because we must determine how significant those intrusions are, especially in relation to their impact on the capabilities of persons to live decent lives of their own choosing. Though there is room for disagreement in making these judgments, it is not hard to anticipate a rough ordering of offenses according to the extent of harm they threaten or inflict. The most serious crimes will be ones inflicting (or threatening) loss of life, significant physical disability or impairment of health, loss of property to the extent that continued material support and amenity are jeopardized, or significant humiliation and loss of privacy. Lesser crimes will be ones that inflict (or threaten) some modest or small loss of property or freedom of action, or which violate privacy or dignity in relatively minor ways.

Even if by using this approach we are able to flesh out a rough ranking of crimes, two problems remain. First, we need some account of how to factor offender culpability into the determination of crime seriousness. Second, we need some account of how to link up prison sentences of different lengths to serious offenses of various kinds. These are both daunting problems and this essay will do little more than gesture in the direction of solving them.

With regard to the former problem, a distinction currently employed by the criminal law might usefully be incorporated into a retributive theory of sentencing. The law prohibits acting in ways that might cause certain sorts of harms and acting with certain types of intentions. The former, which George Fletcher calls "crimes of harmful consequences," include offenses such as homicide, battery, and arson.[19] These are offenses where there is a conceptual gap between the action and the consequence. It is possible to cause death, injury, or to burn down buildings in numerous ways—intentionally, recklessly, negligently, or accidentally. On the other hand, with what Fletcher terms "crimes of harmful actions," it is not possible to commit them negligently or accidentally.[20] Such crimes include rape, larceny, and burglary. In these cases the crimes are defined as actions with certain types of intentions or purposes. Factoring culpability into the scale of crime seriousness is more of a problem with crimes of harmful consequences than with crimes of harmful actions. The latter are all done deliberately and thus agent culpability for the harms wrought by them is fairly high. The seriousness of such offenses will, on a retributive approach, mostly be a function of the harms they inflict or threaten. Of course, we may still need to discount the seriousness of such offenses where the agents committing them are young, mentally unstable, or subject to some form of duress.[21]

40                    PUBLIC AFFAIRS QUARTERLY

With crimes of harmful consequences, the task of factoring culpability into a determination of their seriousness might begin with comparing
cases where agents inflict similar harms and are distinguished only by
the extent of their blameworthiness in doing so. With harms caused
purposefully, the seriousness of the offense will be a fairly straightforward function of the harms inflicted. But compare offenses involving
the purposeful infliction of harms with ones where offenders act knowing that they are likely to harm others while lacking any intention to
inflict such harms. The difference in culpability between such cases
seems slight. While those who purposefully cause harm are most highly
culpable, those who knowingly do so, even if they can correctly claim
that they do not intend to harm their victims, nonetheless are highly
blameworthy. For those who knowingly cause harm are aware that potential victims stand in the paths of their dangerous conduct and do
nothing to avert the harms apt that result. Indeed, it would not be unusual for us to wonder how those who knowingly harm others could
have acted as they did without intending to cause them harm. Such a
degree of indifference to the harms they threaten is hard to understand
without supposing them to be actively malevolent in ways similarly to
those who purposefully cause harm. Hence, while we may think it appropriate to discount the seriousness of offenses where harm is knowingly
rather than purposefully caused, the discount should not be a large one.
Perhaps knowingly causing harms is only seventy to ninety percent as
serious as purposefully causing them, but it is surely more than thirty
to fifty percent as serious. If a ten-year prison term is just in relation to
the deliberate causation of certain harms, then something on the order
of a seven-to-nine-year sentence seems just in relation to the knowing
causation of similar harms.

The next step in this process would be to compare those who knowingly cause harm with those who recklessly do so. Then we would have
to compare those who recklessly cause harm with those who negligently
do so. It may be that the difference in culpability between each of these
pairs is not constant—that there is, for instance, a larger culpability
gap between those who negligently and recklessly cause harm than there
is between those who knowingly and purposefully cause harm. All of
this would have to be discussed further. But it does not seem implausible to think that we could arrive at some rough scale of crime seriousness
that could be used to assist legislators in the task of assigning terms of
incarceration to those who inflict similar harms with differing degrees
of culpability.

This brings us to the problem of linking serious crimes up with appropriate prison sentences—a problem that is usually referred to as one
of "anchoring" the scale of punishment.[22] Just as evaluating the impact

of crimes on victims involves making empirical and value judgments, so assessing the impact of criminal sanctions such as incarceration upon offenders requires both empirical and value judgments. According to our model specification of retributivism, we are to make the effects of crime and the effects of punishment roughly comparable. Hence we must, it seems, be prepared to investigate how and to what extent confinement affects offenders and evaluate its impact on their capabilities of living decent lives of their own choosing. A retributive approach to sentencing has significant empirical dimensions on both the victim and offender side of the equation. The task of determining the effects of incarceration on offenders will be complicated by the fact that the character of prisons varies to a considerable extent. Some are harsher or more austere places than others. Hence, some prisons may be more or more quickly debilitating to prisoners than others. The implications of these variations in prison environments for a retributive theory of sentencing will be discussed more fully in the next section.

One place to anchor the sanction and crime seriousness scales is at the top, so to speak. We might first focus on crimes that, with a high degree of culpability, cause death. First degree murder, for instance, wholly deprives victims of their capabilities of living decent lives of their own choosing, and those who commit it are fully responsible for this deprivation. It seems that on retributive grounds, a very lengthy prison sentence or perhaps the death penalty, are, in this case, the only sanctions that impose commensurate losses on offenders.[23] Loss of life is the most grave one individuals can suffer, and where they suffer it due to acts for which offenders are fully culpable, then offenders must suffer some comparably weighty loss. As we hold the loss caused victims constant and scale down the degree of offender culpability, the length of appropriate prison sentences should be reduced accordingly. Surprisingly, perhaps, when we turn to serious offenses that cause harms other than loss of life, the retributive case for lengthy prison terms is weaker. Crimes like rape or aggravated assault can cause their victims significant, long-term physical and psychological injuries that impair their capabilities to live decent lives of their own choosing. But imprisonment also imposes significant losses on offenders. It is hard to see how, in most cases, prison sentences of more than five to ten years would be needed to impose commensurate losses on those guilty of such crimes. Indeed, it might be argued that shorter prison terms are commensurable in many cases of rape or aggravated assault. As we move away from personal crimes to property crimes, the retributive case for lengthy imprisonment appears weaker still. As noted earlier, most victims of property crimes seem likely to recover from their victimization in relatively short periods of time, even if we include resulting harms

such as invasion of privacy or emotional trauma. Except in special circumstances, it is hard to see how incarceration for lengthy terms would
be needed to impose commensurate losses on offenders who commit
property crimes.

Much more would have to be said here to fill out and defend this
outline of a retributive approach to determining the lengths of prison
sentences. Also, two further problems should be mentioned. First, how
would our model specification address crimes with multiple victims? At
least three options are available. We could view a crime with multiple
victims as actually consisting of a series of crimes, each with its own
victim. This would suggest that the offender should be punished with
consecutive sentences where each sentence is determined with an eye to
the harms inflicted on individual victims. The downside to this approach
is that in cases of offenses that impose small or modest losses on multiple victims, the offender might wind up with consecutive sentences
imposing collective losses that exceed, perhaps significantly, those inflicted on any one victim. Alternatively, we could punish offenders whose
crimes have multiple victims with concurrent sentences. Perhaps the
offender would have to actually serve the sentence that was appropriate
given the worst harm his actions inflicted. The downside to this approach is that, in some sense, the offender would not really be punished
for the losses inflicted on second, third, etc. victims. The third option
would be to consider crimes with multiple victims to be somewhat more
serious than those with single victims but not as serious as straightforward aggregation of victim harms would suggest. This approach suggests
that we should punish crimes with multiple victims more harshly than
ones with single victims. Here again, the downside is that the losses
imposed on the second, third, etc. victims are not adequately matched
by the sanction imposed on the offender.

This essay contends that retributivists should support the first approach, in spite of its potential for imposing aggregate losses on offenders
that exceed the harms imposed on any single victim.[24] The argument in
support of this contention is simple enough. If offenders over time commit several crimes, each with its own victim, retributivism requires that
the punishment imposed in each case be commensurate with the seriousness of the offense. It would not be appropriate to reduce an
offender's sentence in a current case just because she had been punished
previously for a similar offense. We would view each offense, with its
victim, as a separate crime meriting punishment. It is not clear, then,
why we should view single crimes with multiple victims any differently. Of course, it may be that an offender intended to harm only one
individual and others were inadvertently harmed by her act. This might

give us grounds for believing her less culpable for the harms she inadvertently caused. But it would not be grounds for punishing her less harshly just because they were second, third, etc. victims.

Second, there is the problem whether a retributive approach would support the assignment of harsher sanctions to those who have previously been convicted of serious crimes. In other words, should there be a recidivist premium? Or would a retributive approach to sentencing instead assign sentences to offenders based solely on the crimes for which they have recently been convicted, ignoring their past criminal records? Given the importance within retributive theory of imposing sentences on offenders that are commensurate with the seriousness of their crimes, there seem few grounds to impose a recidivist premium.[25] One suspects that such premiums are more easily defended by those supporting punishment's crime reduction aims. Still, Martin Wasik and Andrew von Hirsch argue persuasively that recidivism does provide us with clearer evidence of the culpability of offenders.[26] With first or second time offenders, we might be convinced that their engagement in criminal activity was the result of youth, temporary bad judgment, or undue influence by others. Thus we might be led to reduce the sentences of such offenders in some cases. But once it is clear that individuals are determined to continue their criminal careers, any doubts about the extent of their culpability become difficult to sustain. A retributive approach to sentencing may only provide us with enough guidance to determine a range of sentences for any given crime. It will then be up to judges or juries to make more fine-grained assessments about such things as offender culpability before a penalty within the relevant range is assigned. With repeat offenders a retributive approach would presumably support the assignment of penalties at or near the top of the relevant range.

## The Character of Incarceration

Retributivism insists that legal punishment be structured so that, at a minimum, it is consistent with treating offenders as moral beings capable of understanding the wrongs they have committed and the fairness of the penal sanctions imposed on them by the state in response to those wrongs. Offenders do not, of course, have to accept the justification proffered by the state in defense of it imposition of legal sanctions; nor should steps be taken to force offenders to come to such an acceptance. Given this constraint on the structure and content of criminal sanctions, there is nonetheless room for debate about the kinds of prison conditions

capable of satisfying it. It may help to conceive of prison conditions
along a continuum. At one extreme would be very harsh prison conditions that deprived offenders of all freedom of movement and association
within prisons, work, contact with the outside world, exercise, recreation, and entertainment. Prison conditions in many of the new supermax
facilities springing up around the country approach this extreme.[27] Such
facilities confine inmates to their cells for twenty-two to twenty-three
hours of each day, permit them very little interaction with fellow inmates or guards, provide extremely limited access to recreation or
entertainment, and completely deny inmates access to work. At the other
extreme would be prison conditions that permitted inmates some freedom of movement and association within the facility, ready access to
paid labor, frequent contact with the outside world, and generous levels
of access to recreation, exercise, and entertainment.

Prison conditions at the harsh extreme appear to run afoul of retributive constraints on punishment. For one thing, such prison conditions
would leave inmates with few opportunities to act as independent agents.
As John Kleinig has noted, prison life can be austere and difficult without depriving inmates of all avenues along which they can develop and
exercise their individuality.[28] If we are not to degrade inmates—that is,
if we are to allow them some room within which to exercise their capacities as rational, purposive agents—then we cannot subject them to
conditions that wholly truncate their choices and actions. In addition,
prison conditions at the harsh extreme might erode the capacities and
dispositions constitutive of moral personhood. These are capacities and
dispositions that need to be regularly exercised if they are not to be
lost. Intuitively it seems that prison conditions imposing isolation and
passivity on inmates will gradually chip away at whatever practical reasoning skills and motivations they had, and cause further atrophy of
what may have already been weak capacities to identify with and feel
for others. Indeed, there is empirical evidence that goes some way toward confirming this intuition.[29] This suggests that retributivists would
support the establishment and maintenance of prison conditions that
are, at the very least, toward the middle of the above continuum.

It might be argued that retributivists ought to support the establishment and maintenance of prison conditions that are closer to the more
generous extreme. After all, many legal offenders got into trouble in
the first place because their moral capacities were weak or underdevel-
oped in various ways. To the extent that these moral failings can be
traced to unjust social conditions which offenders had to endure, it could
be claimed that prisons ought to do more than not cause the further
deterioration of offenders' moral capacities. They should, instead, see

to the improvement of offenders' moral, social, and work skills. However, judgments about the justice of broader social conditions and their impact on criminal offending are notoriously dependent on assumptions about the nature of social justice and individual responsibility. Hence, depending on their views about these matters, retributivists might or might not be attracted to the idea that the state has some positive responsibility to undertake efforts to enhance (as opposed to not causing the deterioration of) offenders' moral capacities.

There is another reason why retributivists should concern themselves with the character of imprisonment. The extent to which incarceration deprives offenders of decent lives lived on their own terms varies both with the duration and conditions of their incarceration. Prison conditions that are exceedingly harsh will be harmful to the physical, mental, or moral health of inmates in relatively short order, and devastating to them over an extended period of time. Not only will such conditions threaten the moral capacities of inmates, they might, if imposed for too long, inflict losses on offenders that are disproportional with the seriousness of their crimes. Retributivists cannot support prison conditions that are so harsh as to leave offenders emotionally or otherwise crippled, especially once they have served their terms. To do so would be to support the infliction of penal losses that are excessive. This raises the further question whether retributivists should urge reductions in prison sentences for offenders who are made to endure prison conditions tending toward the harsh extreme sketched above. We may suspect that the answer is "yes," but this is an issue best left for further discussion.

## CONCLUDING REMARKS

It may be that a comprehensive approach to sentencing must combine retributive, crime reduction, and other justifying aims of punishment. The aim of this discussion has not been to demonstrate the exclusive importance of the retributive approach. Nor has it been to show its priority in a comprehensive theory of sentencing, though perhaps this can and should be shown. The aim instead has been to say enough about the retributive approach to justifying incarceration to show that it is a fruitful one. Much work obviously remains to be done in developing it. Again, those who favor other approaches to sentencing also have a lot of work to do in explaining why, when, for how long, and under what conditions we should incarcerate serious offenders. There is no reason to believe that these tasks will be any easier for them to accomplish than they are for retributivists.

*James Madison University*

46                    PUBLIC AFFAIRS QUARTERLY

## NOTES

1. Andrew von Hirsch and Nils Jareborg offer an illuminating account of the harm component of crime seriousness, one on which this essay draws. See their "Gauging Criminal Harm: A Living-Standard Analysis," *Oxford Journal of Legal Studies*, vol. 11 (1991), pp. 1–38. Others who discuss the retributive approach to sentencing include Michael Davis in *To Make the Punishment Fit the Crime: Essays in the Theory of Criminal Justice* (Boulder, Colo.: Westview, 1992), especially pp. 69–97, and Don E. Scheid, "Constructing a Theory of Punishment, Desert, and the Distribution of Punishments," *Canadian Journal of Law and Jurisprudence*, vol. 10 (1997), pp. 441–506.

2. See Russ Shafer-Landau, "The Failure of Retributivism," *Philosophical Studies*, vol. 82 (1996), pp. 289–316, especially pp. 298–304, for a clear account of the difficulties facing a retributive approach to sentencing.

3. There are both unfair advantage versions of retributivism and communicative versions of it. On the former, see Wojciech Sadurski, *Giving Desert Its Due* (Dordrecht, Netherlands: D. Reidel, 1985), pp. 221–258; George Sher, *Desert* (Princeton, N.J.: Princeton University Press, 1987), pp. 69–90; and Herbert Morris, "Persons and Punishment," *Monist*, no. 52 (1968), pp. 475–501. On the latter, see Jean Hampton, "A New Theory of Retributivism," in *Liability and Responsibilitiy: Essays in Law and Morals*, ed. R. G. Frey and Christopher W. Morris (Cambridge: Cambridge University Press, 1991), pp. 377–414; and Jami L. Anderson, "Annulment Retributivism: A Hegelian Theory of Punishment," *Legal Theory*, vol. 5 (1999), pp. 363–388.

4. See Robert Nozick, *Anarchy, State, and Utopia* (New York: Basic Books, 1974).

5. The distinction between moral and legal retributivism is elaborated by Kathleen Dean Moore in *Pardons: Justice, Mercy, and the Public Interest* (New York: Oxford University Press, 1989), pp. 99–121.

6. Notoriously, problems arise in using the theory to justify punishment where status quo antes are unjust. See Jeffrie Murphy, "Marxism and Retribution," *Philosophy and Public Affairs* 2 (1973) 217–243. See also the essays in *From Social Justice to Criminal Justice: Poverty and the Administration of the Criminal Law*, ed. William C. Heffernan and John Kleinig (New York: Oxford University Press, 2000).

7. This version of retributivism is developed in my "Victim-Centered Retributivism," *Pacific Philosophical Quarterly*, forthcoming.

8. See von Hirsch and Jareborg in "Gauging Criminal Harm." Von Hirsch and Jareborg, in turn, draw on Amartya Sen's work, in particular his *The Standard of Living* (Cambridge: Cambridge University Press, 1987).

9. For discussion of these difficulties, see Shafer-Landau, "The Failure of Retributivism," pp. 308–309. But see Jeremy Waldron's skillful defense of an abstract version of *lex talionis*, in "Lex Talionis," *Arizona Law Review*, vol. 34 (1992), pp. 25–51.

RETRIBUTION AND INCARCERATION 47

10. Admittedly, some offenders might, unexpectedly, flourish under conditions of incarceration. It is not obvious what we can or should do about this from a retributive perspective. Legal sanctions must be set with an eye to the typical reactions of humans, and incarceration will surely be an unpleasant experience for the vast majority of offenders.

11. Jeffrie G. Murphy, "Cruel and Unusual Punishments," in *Law, Morality, and Rights*, ed. M. A. Steward (Dordrecht, Netherlands: D. Reidel, 1983), pp. 387.

12. Von Hirsch and Jaresborg, "Gauging Criminal Harm," especially pp. 19–23.

13. A point made famous by Alan Goldman in "The Paradox of Punishment," *Philosophy and Public Affairs*, vol. 9 (1979), pp. 42–58. Goldman argues that the retributive approach may therefore not support prison sentences for property crimes sufficient to deter many would-be offenders. Whether this claim is plausible will not be addressed.

14. Cf. Von Hirsch and Jaresborg, "Gauging Criminal Harm," pp. 33–34. It must be admitted, however, that the line between crimes with victims and those without is none too precise.

15. In particular, criminal attempts appear to pose serious difficulties for retributive approaches keyed to punishing offenders commensurately with the harms caused the victims of crimes. Where no one is injured by an attempted crime, it is not clear how such retributive approaches can justify punishment of those who make the attempt. Here crime reduction considerations may need to be brought in to justify punishment, though arguably the sanctions imposed for attempts should take into account the harms likely to be caused if the attempts succeeded.

16. Crime reduction approaches to sentencing would require the acquisition and evaluation of enormous amounts of information about the incapacitation and deterrence effects of various sentences for each type of crime. We might reasonably doubt whether that information is available or could be evaluated by human beings. In addition, the crime reduction approach to sentencing would require us to weigh and balance the myriad beneficial and harmful consequences likely to result from different sentences for each type of crime. Not only would such weighing and balancing be extraordinarily complex, it would involve comparisons among interests that are apt to be quite diverse and, some would argue, incommensurable.

17. Von Hirsch and Jaresborg, "Gauging Criminal Harm," pp. 4–5.

18. Von Hirsch and Jaresborg exclude psychological harms from their typography of criminal harms because they believe some such harms are already captured in other ways by their typography (e.g., a sense of shame or debasement fits under their heading of freedom from humiliation) or are of dubious merit (e.g., they may be based on irrational fears). See "Gauging Criminal Harm," 23. Yet victimization studies regularly point to various kinds of psychological harms suffered by crime victims which, whether rational or not, diminish the quality of their lives for some period of time. See, for instance, Patricia A. Resick, "Psychological Effects of Victimization: Implications for the Criminal Justice System," *Crime and Delinquency* 33 (1987): 468–478. I believe a case can be made for including a broader array of psychological harms in an account of criminal harm than von Hirsch and Jaresborg include in their account.

19. George P. Fletcher, *Rethinking Criminal Law* (Boston: Little, Brown, 1978), p. 113.

20. Though as Fletcher notes, there can be mistaken thefts or sexual penetrations. See *Rethinking Criminal Law*, p. 114.

21. There is also a case to be made for discounting the culpability of offenders who have suffered severe social deprivation in the formative years of their lives on the grounds that their capacities for moral responsibility may have been significantly compromised. For an interesting discussion of this possibility, see R. Jay Wallace, *Responsibility and the Moral Sentiments* (Cambridge, Mass.: Harvard University Press, 1996), pp. 231–233.

22. See Andrew von Hirsch, *Censure and Sanctions* (Oxford: Clarendon Press, 1993), pp. 36–46.

23. The debate about whether retributivism either requires or permits the death penalty for the most serious crimes is beyond the scope of this essay.

24. There is also the practical problem that an offender might die before serving a series of consecutive sentences for a crime with multiple victims.

25, But see Davis, *To Make the Punishment Fit the Crime*, pp. 121–148.

26. Martin Wasik and Andrew von Hirsch, "Section 29 Revised: Previous Convictions in Sentencing," *Criminal Law Review* (1994), pp. 409–418.

27. For a description and analysis of supermax prison conditions, see Leena Kurki and Norval Morris, "The Purposes, Practices, and Problems of Supermax Prisons," in *Crime and Justice: A Review of Research*, vol. 28, ed. Michael Tonry (Chicago: University of Chicago Press, 2001), pp. 385–424.

28. John Kleinig, "The Hardness of Hard Treatment," in *Fundamentals in Sentencing Theory*, ed. Andrew Ashworth and Martin Wasik (Oxford: Clarendon Press, 1998), pp. 286–288.

29. See Craig Haney and Mona Lynch, "Regulating Prisons of the Future: A Psychological Analysis of Supermax and Solitary Confinement," *New York University Review of Law & Social Change*, vol. 23 (1997), pp. 477–570.

# Part III
# The Restorative Challenge
# and Challenges in Restoration

# [9]

# REASON FOR EMOTION: REINVENTING JUSTICE WITH THEORIES, INNOVATIONS, AND RESEARCH—THE AMERICAN SOCIETY OF CRIMINOLOGY 2002 PRESIDENTIAL ADDRESS*

LAWRENCE W. SHERMAN
University of Pennsylvania

*Criminology was born in the age of reason to apply "reason" to justice, tempering the expression of moral indignation with the economics of deterrence. Modern criminology is now poised for reinventing justice around the emotions of victims, offenders, and society. One prime example is restorative justice. Others include wider use of biomedical mental health treatments for offenders, programs to make justice officials more aware of the emotional impact of their words on citizens, and programs to help justice officials manage their own emotions. Research can advance theory and innovations as a basis for a new paradigm of "emotionally intelligent justice."*

". . .he that will not apply new remedies must expect new evils: for time is the greatest innovator; and if time of course alter things to the worse, and wisdom and counsel shall not alter them to the better, what shall be the end?"
—Francis Bacon, "Of Innovations" (1625)

---

* Delivered at the presentation of the ASC Presidential Award for Distinguished Contributions to Justice to the Rt. Hon. Lord Harry Woolf, the Lord Chief Justice of England and Wales. This writing was made possible by the support of Jerry and Ellen Lee and the Jerry Lee Foundation, the Albert M. Greenfield Chair of Human Relations and the School of Arts and Sciences at the University of Pennsylvania. The new empirical findings reported in this address are the joint product of a collaboration with Heather Strang, Geoffrey Barnes, Daniel J. Woods, and others associated with the RISE project at Australian National University, Research School of Social Sciences. That work was supported in part by the Australian Criminology Research Council, the Australian Department of Health, the Australian Department of Transport and Communications, the Australian National University, the Smith Richardson Foundation, and Grant No. JUST98JCX-003 awarded to the University of Maryland from the National Institute of Justice, U.S. Department of Justice, under the Omnibus Crime Control and Safe Streets Act of 1968, as amended. Points of view or opinions expressed in this article are those of the author and do not necessarily represent the official positions or policies of the U.S. Department of Justice. The author is grateful for comments on earlier drafts provided by Charles Wellford, Jeffrey A. Roth, John Braithwaite, and Heather Strang.

2                              SHERMAN

"Punishment is so complicated by our emotions."
                                    —Scott Turow (2002)

What is the reason for criminology? For three centuries, criminology has tried to make reason, rather than emotion, the primary method of justice. The results so far are modest, blocked by a paradox in social policy: *we presume that criminals are rational, but justice should be emotional.* Democracies require punishments to express public emotions about crime, while assuming that crime itself is a rational choice of rational actors. The promise of criminology is to reverse these positions: to use reason for emotion, rather than emotion against alleged reason. The reason for criminology can then be to make justice more rational about its effects on the emotional causes and prevention of crime.

The "Age of Reason" (Paine, 1794) that gave birth to criminology (Radzinowicz, 1966) offers many lessons for reinventing justice. In a century in which Thomas Paine wrote that "We have it in our power to begin the world over again" (quoted in Foner, 2002), Cesare Beccaria's 1764 essay on crime and punishment did just that—eventually leading Europe to abolish the death penalty, torture, and secret trials. Since then, both justice and criminology have misplaced the Enlightenment vision of reinvention, keeping it at the margins rather than at the center of each enterprise. But a new window of opportunity is opening for criminology to reinvent justice, fueled by widespread dissatisfaction with current practices and their costs (Butterfield, 2002). The time may be ripe for criminology to advance a new paradigm of justice, one that works far better than our muddled legacy of Bentham and Lombroso. The most promising approach to such a paradigm would address what Massey (2002:2) describes as the interplay between rational and emotional causes of human behavior, a paradigm we might call *emotionally intelligent justice*: the explicit recognition and management of the effects of emotions in causing the behavior of both officials and offenders.

## REINVENTING JUSTICE

The hope that criminology might build a new paradigm of justice comes from many sources, most notably the Lord Chief Justice of England and Wales (Woolf, 1998, 2002). Writing that the British penal system has "lost its way," he invites criminology to replace the "tattered remedies which are being currently deployed" by criminal justice. Rather than just addressing narrowly limited questions about crime, Lord Woolf (1998: xi–xii) suggests criminology could help develop a "radical alternative," or what many would call a new paradigm of justice (Kuhn, 1964). Because the punitive approach imposing ever tougher jail sentences has failed, he says, society needs criminology to develop a vision for a more "holistic" approach to justice, with community-based penalties, restorative justice, drug treatment and rehabilitation (Woolf, 2002).

Many Americans support Lord Woolf's view. A 1998 poll of 4,000 people in nine northeastern states found that 75% wanted to revamp the entire criminal justice system, without even knowing how that would be done (Boyle, 1999). When asked what the most important outcome of justice would be for drug addicts who burglarized or robbed them at gunpoint, only 38% said that going to jail would be the most important result for burglars, and only 49% for armed robbers. Sixty percent said that drug-addicted criminals should be put into drug treatment, regardless of whether they went to jail. Three-fifths (59%) thought decisions about penalties for nonviolent crimes should be made by local community boards of citizens. More than three quarters (77%) said that victims should have an opportunity to meet with the offender to talk about the reasons for the crime and whether the offender accepted responsibility for it. In a 1996 national survey of 1,085 Americans, 79% of respondents said that they thought restitution would be effective as an alternative to prison at protecting citizens from crime (Maguire and Pastore, 1998:137).

Accepting Lord Woolf's challenge to reinvent justice in the ways many Americans support would take criminologists back to our roots. Criminology was founded for the purpose of reinventing justice, by using both normative and empirical tools. Beccaria devised a blueprint for justice in democracies just in time for democracy itself to be invented. His 1764 treatise influenced John Adams and Thomas Jefferson (McCullough, 2001; Wolfgang, 1996), as well as the U.S. Constitution. It is hard to overstate the beneficial effects of Beccaria's work on the reduction of human misery (Phillipson, 1923; Radzinowicz, 1966; Wolfgang, 1996).

Beccaria accomplished nothing less than reinventing justice in the North Atlantic world. At a time when torture and execution were widespread, when trials were often held in secret, when judges could make up law on the spot, Beccaria lit a match that shed light on these horrors. That match ignited a conflagration, as Gladwell (2000) has described such "tipping points," which burned away the moral justification for much of the retributive paradigm of justice. From Russia's Empress Catherine II to New York's Governor Cuomo (1996), Beccaria's moral arguments were widely, if not completely, accepted by those who governed. The central plank in his thesis was that the only morally acceptable justification for punishment is crime prevention, with no room at all for retribution. This view contributed greatly to the reduction of severity in punishment. It also fostered the later development of deterrence as a new, "rational" paradigm for justice (Bentham, 1789) that competed with, but never defeated, the emotionally expressive premises of retribution.

Yet for all the good he did to humanity, Beccaria left a kind of curse on

4                          SHERMAN

criminology. That curse is the confusion of moral and causal truth, the pre-scientific idea that reasoning alone can establish what is true even without experimental tests. The moral Enlightenment of Beccaria (1764) did not fully connect with the scientific Enlightenment of Francis Bacon (1620), whose method of testing hypotheses with empirical, and preferably experimental, evidence is the cornerstone of modern science.[1] If Beccaria had only extended his framework of *moral* theory to include Bacon's roadmap of an experimentally testable *causal* theory of punishment effects, the history of criminology and justice could have been very different—and he may have accomplished his own goals for even milder punishments. As it happened, his readers interpreted the deterrent effect of punishment as a logical-moral truth, rather than as an empirically falsifiable hypothesis. Now virtually every criminal law code in the world carries the "domain assumption" (Gouldner, 1970) that painful punishment deters crime (Morris, 1966), posing a huge (if not insurmountable) obstacle to scientific testing of criminal sanction effects. Beccaria reinvented the values of justice as *more deterrent than retributive*, but failed to open the values of justice to the methods of experimental science.

Our salvation from Beccaria's curse may lie in his strong emphasis on human rights, a source of the Eighth Amendment ban on cruel and unusual punishment. This ban creates a constraint on deterrence that has steadily increased in cost. Torture and hanging were cheap, prison is more expensive, and decent prisons have become even more expensive. As the standards of decent prison treatment rise with general social standards of decency through the civilizing process (Elias, 1994), the cost of the alleged benefits of deterrence rise apace. The democratic pressure to limit taxes thus acts as a counterweight to prison population size, which might otherwise grow endlessly. The rapid growth of prison populations in the United States and the United Kingdom in recent years had the unintended consequence of raising many questions about the deterrence doctrine. Whether the cost of prison is measured in the human misery of overcrowding, or by the cuts in educational and other government services in order to pay for prisons, there is a rising chorus of voices asking what we really get from so much incarceration (Zimring et al., 2001). Some governors are even releasing prison inmates early or laying off prison guards for the sole purpose of reducing state deficits (Butterfield, 2002).

These constraints on costs and rights create an open window for inventions that can reduce the number of prisoners (and executions) without

---

1.  Although Beccaria opens his essay with a quote from Bacon's (1625) literary essays, and while Beccaria uses his "observations" to argue that the death penalty is ineffective, he fails to employ the systematic methods Bacon (1620) suggests are needed to test hypotheses in a way that differs from ordinary experience.

## REINVENTING JUSTICE 5

increasing crime. Such inventions require the empirical methods of Bacon married to the moral vision of Beccaria, as exemplified by Benjamin Franklin. While "Franklin the inventor" is remembered mostly for his stove, his eyeglasses and the lightning rod, Franklin's most influential inventions were social institutions. The free library, the public fire department, and even the invention of constitutional democracy were driven by both his normative and causal theories, as well as by observations (Franklin, 1790). That is how the penitentiary itself was invented, and that is how its task can be reinvented by contemporary criminology. Charting a course to accomplish that goal can be aided by reflections on 1) the social capital needed for inventions, 2) the paradigms of justice we would replace, 3) the development of restorative justice as an example of the cyclical process of theories affecting innovations which affect research, 4) the results of the development of restorative justice so far, and 5) the benefits of becoming even bolder in our inventions and experiments.

## INVENTIONS AND SOCIAL CAPITAL

The evidence from both Beccaria and Franklin suggests that the key to successful inventions is social capital rather than lone scholarship. Like the coinventors of the steam engine (Uglow, 2002), of major philosophies (Collins, 1998), of the polio vaccine (Smith, 1990) and of other major innovations, both Beccaria and Franklin were deeply embedded in a social network of collaborators. Beccaria was the product of a network of thinkers at a private salon (the Accademia dei Pugni) in Milan that had actually assigned him to write about crime and punishment, given him many ideas, and edited his work (Phillipson, 1923:6). Franklin was the founder of both a moral-political-scientific weekly discussion group ("The Junto") and later "the American Philosophical Society held at Philadelphia for Promoting Useful Knowledge," the first learned society in North America, which he consulted with on most major projects (Brands, 2000:92, 169).

Similarly, all modern inventors in criminology appear linked to coinventors, especially practitioners, who construct new institutional designs so they can be evaluated. David Olds has invented a highly successful crime prevention strategy in collaboration with registered nurses making home visits to at-risk mothers of newborn children (Olds et al., 1986, 1998). Ronald Clarke (1997) has collaborated with a wide network of public and private organizations, as well as other criminologists, to invent new forms of situational crime prevention. Denise and Gary Gottfredson have worked in partnership with school principals and a wide network of their students to reinvent schools as more effective crime prevention institutions. The Vera Institute of Justice, founded by Herbert

6                                    SHERMAN

Sturz, has invested four decades in building bridges with New York City justice agencies for testing new ideas to help minimize the use of prison.

Perhaps the network of coinventors working most directly to meet Lord Woolf's challenge is the Regulatory Institutions Network (REGNET), led by John Braithwaite at the Australian National University. Collectively, this global update of Beccaria's academy is constructing normative and empirical theories of restorative justice (Ahmed et al., 2001; Braithwaite, 2002; Strang and Braithwaite, 2000, 2001, 2002), working with practitioners to design and implement innovations based on those theories (McDonald and Moore, 2001; Morrison, 2001; Pollard, 2001; Ritchie and O'Connell, 2001), doing both basic and evaluation research to understand how the innovations work (Harris, 2001), their effectiveness at reducing crime (Sherman et al., 2003) and helping victims (Strang, 2002). REGNET provides a prime example of how criminology can reinvent justice through a cycle of theory, innovations, and research.

The REGNET agenda is building what could become one major component of a broader emotional intelligence paradigm of justice. Such a paradigm would indeed be a radical alternative to current practice, as well as a return to the ancient institutions of justice that lasted some 500 generations (Braithwaite, 1998, 2002). It would also be fueled by the explosion of basic research in the neuroscience (Ledoux, 1996) and social science of emotions (Katz, 1999; Scheff and Retzinger, 1991), including the discovery of biosocial interactions between the MAOA gene and child abuse in causing adult violence (Caspi et al., 2002), the discovery that the GPR gene conditions fear and memory of punishment (Shumyatsky et al., 2002), and the growing criminology of emotions (Karstedt, 2002), with theories making emotions far more explicit (Agnew, 1992, 2001) and innovations based on managing emotions (e.g., Josi and Sechrest, 1999). The importance of these scientific developments is underscored by the discovery that the emotional center of the brain (the limbic system) has far more connections sending messages to the rational center of the brain (the pre-frontal cortex) than vice versa (Massey, 2002:17), showing why emotional impulses so often overwhelm rational cognition. The fact that rationality is a recent arrival in human evolution, while emotional forces have long dominated behavior, suggests the limitation of a paradigm that presumes rationality of either criminals or justice officials. These facts reveal the challenge of developing a paradigm of emotionally intelligent justice, in which the central tools will be inventions for helping offenders, victims, communities, and officials manage each others' emotions to minimize harm. That paradigm would be a substantial departure from justice paradigms of recent centuries.

REINVENTING JUSTICE 7

## FOUR PARADIGMS OF JUSTICE

Since the dawn of the modern era (Barzun, 2000), two paradigms of justice have competed for primacy. One is based on punishment as a symbolic *expression* of the emotions of anger and outrage by the state and society at the act of a criminal. The other is based on punishment making the decision-making *economics* of crime more favorable to law-abiding than to law-breaking. The competition has resulted in a compromise third paradigm that dominates current practice and amounts to *expressive economics*. Each of these paradigms places the state and the offender in different positions on a dimension of rational to emotional bases of conduct (Figure 1), which logically suggest a fourth paradigm that criminology is poised to develop: *emotional intelligence*.

### Figure 1  Paradigms of Justice

| | Offender Rational | Offender Emotional |
|---|---|---|
| Law Emotional | 1. Expressive Economics | 2. Expression |
| Law Rational | 3. Economics | 4. Emotional Intelligence |

1. The prevailing *expressive economics* paradigm of justice combines the expressive (Feinberg, 1994) and economic (Wilson, 1983) paradigms, in which the state acts *emotionally* towards *rational* offenders.
2. In the *expression* paradigm (Durkheim, 1893:98; Ranulf, 1938), the state is morally obliged to take an explicitly *emotional* stance towards a presumably *emotional* offender, without regard for harm to the state's self-interest in the effect of its action on the offender's future behavior.
3. In the *economics* paradigm, the state takes an explicitly *rational*

8                        SHERMAN

stance towards a presumptively *rational* offender, trying to maximize the self-interest of both in reducing criminal conduct (Bentham, 1789).

4.  In a new paradigm of *emotional intelligence*, the state would try to
    make its officials control their own emotions (Beccaria, 1764:17)
    in order to adopt a *rational* stance towards a presumably *emo-
    tional* offender, as well as towards the emotions of victims and
    communities, in order to persuade all citizens to comply with the
    law (Tyler and Huo, 2002) and repair the harm caused by past
    crime (Braithwaite, 2002).

The prevailing compromise of *expressive economics* creates the fundamental paradox that causes so much frustration with modern criminal justice: the use of emotion against reason. Few of us expect much justice
from an expressive state that dramatizes its outrage at a rational offender
who coolly calculates costs and benefits. While academics debate the merits of one side or other of the compromise in the abstract, the daily fusion
of the two makes no one happy. Nor is the paradigm vulnerable to
research and development, given its non-falsifiable moral content from the
expression paradigm.

The pure version of the *expression* paradigm of justice is a moral obligation in such Puritan theologies as those found in the fundamentalist Prot-
estantism (Applegate et al., 2000) of John Calvin's Geneva, where a child
was beheaded in 1568 for hitting its parents (Carpenter, 1917:151). The
demand for such moral expression may rise in direct proportion to economic strains of income inequality for the lower middle classes (Ranulf,
1938), which may explain why prison populations have grown in the
United States and United Kingdom so much in recent decades as income
inequality has risen (Barbelet, 2002). Punishment in this paradigm is a
righteous, even painful, duty that ethically cannot be avoided (Van den
Haag, 1975). Beccaria's attacks on expressive punishment as immoral
helped abolish the death penalty. But they could not stop the widespread
use of prison even in abolitionist countries like England, where one criminologist recently defended the duty of justice to express emotions even
when the effect may be to cause more crime:

> "Even if. . .formal justice. . .sanctions make people more. . .brutal, out
> for revenge on the person who reported them to the police. . .even if
> [other]. . .programmes can be shown to be more effective in reducing
> reoffending, there remains the demand for authoritative condemna-
> tion of the class of behaviours of which the incident is a part" (Hud-
> son, 2002:629).

These demands to punish for punishment's sake persist as almost a "bread
and circuses" spectacle for a distant audience, as Karstedt (2002:310)

## REINVENTING JUSTICE                                      9

describes it, remote from the people involved in a crime, even though victims and others close to an offense feel more restrained by emotions of empathy and sympathy for offenders. What *is* falsifiable in this paradigm is the idea that expressive punishment is what victims deserve to have because they want it—since many do not (Strang, 2002). As one inner-city victim of violence told Jones (2002), "I mean you go to court, you're getting them locked up—you know what I'm saying—for what they did to you, but like that ain't no satisfaction."

The *economics* paradigm of justice, in contrast, is eminently falsifiable. If prison does not reduce crime, then Bentham's (1789) principles would imply that prison should be abandoned. Criminologists have not only compiled a large record of evidence of deterrence failures (Sherman, 1993), but also can show that the basic mechanisms of deterrence only work on some people and backfire on others. The deterrence paradigm's implicit premise that tastes and preferences are fixed (Massey, 2002:21) and universal, including the distaste for prison, is demonstrably false (Duncan, 1996). Some offenders apparently offend in hopes that they can humiliate authority, as in the American Indian parable of the "duck in a noose" who drags a would-be captor to death (as cited by Washington sniper John Allen Muhammed; see Bohlen, 2002:A31). The justice-as-economics paradigm may also overestimate the cost of prison to an offender's reputation in communities where imprisonment is so common it may become a badge of honor. The much greater failure of deterrence among socially marginalized communities (Marciniak, 1994) and individuals (Berk et al., 1992; Pate and Hamilton, 1992; Sherman and Smith, 1992) makes an alternative to the economic paradigm more urgent as such communities grow in population size.

A new paradigm of *emotionally intelligent justice* would also be falsifiable, but arguably more promising than our current "tattered remedies" of retribution and deterrence. Such a paradigm would not assume, as Bentham did (unlike Beccaria, 1764:51), that all people will have the same emotional reactions to justice processes. This was the mistake made by the first modern attempt to achieve emotionally intelligent justice, the Quakers' penitentiary, in which all offenders were assumed to derive equal benefit from the chance to read the Bible in solitary confinement. The lesson of hundreds of studies of rehabilitation is that different ways of trying to shape offenders' emotions will be effective for different kinds of offenders (MacKenzie, 2002), and that a "one size fits all" strategy should be discarded in favor of Beccaria's (1764:10) "geometric" precision in sanctioning. Tyler's research on procedural justice also shows that, for example, minority group members may have different reactions to contacts with the criminal justice system, given the different emotional context and history of legal treatment of minorities compared to majority

10                              SHERMAN

group citizens (Tyler and Huo, 2002:Part IV). An emotionally intelligent justice system, like an emotionally intelligent political campaign or product marketing plan, is likely to employ disaggregated strategies based on research evidence about what messages or methods work best for each type of audience (Massey, 2002).

SHAME, REMORSE, AND EMPATHY.

Many recent proposals for an alternative paradigm of justice to engage with offenders' emotions have focused on the use of shame. Braithwaite (1989) focused his proposals on reintegrative shaming, in which only the crime and not the criminal would be subject to shame. Kahan (1996, 1998) focused on stigmatic shaming, in which the offender would be deterred not by prison but by the prospect of humiliation in public. Empirical evidence on both kinds of shame may prove them ineffective at shaping offender attitudes about compliance with law, as Braithwaite and his colleagues have recently reported (Ahmed et al., 2001). These and other research results have prompted some theorists (Karstedt, 2002; Van Stokkom, 2002) to suggest that remorse should be the principal emotion engaged in justice. Others suggest that offender empathy for victims, as well as victim empathy for offenders, may be the primary emotional tools for preventing future crime (Strang, 2002).

Whatever emotions may prove most effective in achieving compliance with the law, there is a major issue of how justice can most effectively gain emotional intelligence. Although judges and juries have long been allowed to measure remorse, for example, and even to make remorse a legally decisive factor in whether to execute U.S. citizens (Liptak, 2002), there is scant evidence that court processes are effective in creating remorse, shame, or any other emotion except anger. What seems more likely is that such emotions are best created outside of court, with alternative (or supplementary) justice processes designed to allow a wide range of unstructured dialogue. Such out-of-court justice, with or without a return to court for further decisions, is at the center of the ANU REGNET's efforts to build the invention of restorative justice.

## RESTORATIVE JUSTICE

Restorative justice is a broad category of inventions embracing many specific programs (Braithwaite, 1998, 1999, 2002), old and new. An inductive definition derived from surveying the current field of ideas might include the following list of elements:

**Purpose:** To repair the harm of the crime under discussion, and prevent further crimes by the offenders, victims, or supporters of either.

## REINVENTING JUSTICE                              11

**Responsibility:** Offenders must first accept responsibility for having caused harm, and not dispute the factual claim that they are guilty, regardless of whether they formally plead guilty.

**Method:** Any means that can produce reconciliation between victims, offenders and their supporters, minimizing anger and leaving all satisfied that they have been treated fairly while justice has been done. (Face-to-face conferences among stakeholders in a crime, led by a disinterested third party, are the most widely tested method.)

**Decisions:** To the extent possible, decisions about what should happen next to repair harm and prevent future crime are made collectively and consensually by all the individual participants in the process who were closest to the crime, as a form of justice ratified or supplemented by decisions of courts.

**Emotional Power:** The power of the process comes from the engine of emotional engagement of the participants, in contrast to the suppression of participants' emotions in court determinations of guilt (prior to courts' expressions of broader public emotions when punishing crimes).

**Emotions to Engage:** Remorse, guilt, shame, empathy, hope.

**Emotions to Avoid:** Anger, humiliation, fear, disgust.

**Outcome:** Offenders repair harm as feasible, given the nature of the crime.

These elements suggest that modern programs for restorative justice pose a kind of "back to the future" innovation that recreates what may have been the predominant form of justice in human history. Before the rise of nation-states in Europe, Germanic and Mediterranean tribes widely practiced the model described above (Weitekamp, 1989). Restorative justice never stopped among certain groups of South Asians, Pacific Islanders, American Indians, Middle Eastern (Blumenfeld, 2002:302–307) and African (Huxley, 1939:196) villages. The Wergild (man-price) system specified tariffs to be paid by offenders' families to victims' families for the loss of different limbs in violent quarrels. These payments, whether in precious metals, animals, or other forms of exchange, were called "blood money" because they were supposed to *prevent* bloodshed by managing victims' emotions (Pollock and Maitland, 1898a:46–48).

Payments symbolize the fact that the victims hold the moral high ground, just as modern retributivists think that court condemnation is needed to symbolize the evil of a crime. Failure to make such payments

12                                  SHERMAN

was expected to lead to blood feuds or retaliation, such as chopping off an offender's hand (Blumenfeld, 2002:307). The historical emphasis on tariffs leads many modern officials to think that restorative justice is primarily about compensation, as in civil court, yet historical and contemporary evidence suggests that emotions, and not payments, drive restorative justice. Victims given the opportunity to confront their offenders seem more interested in apologies and explanations than they are in money (Strang, 2002). Thus monetary incentives for reconciliation prove very helpful to get parties into a meeting, after which the emotional dynamics of face-to-face dialogue make the utility of cash value less important than sincere expressions of regret, remorse, apologies, and forgiveness.

Restorative justice disappeared in the North Atlantic world when kings found it profitable to establish a "king's peace," paid for by the compensation that formerly went to victims. As Christie (1977) has suggested, kings "stole" crimes from victims long before kings could offer much protection in return. Restorative justice was the predominant form of English justice until the 12th century, when the Norman kings made the crown the victim of most felonies (Pollock and Maitland, 1898a:138, 153–156, 525; 1898b:455, 458–460). Restorative justice was eventually followed by a terrible rise in the cruelty of kings' punishments (Durant and Durant, 1965:72). The logic of justice was converted from reconciliation to repression, with fear the primary emotion to be engendered and outrage the main emotion to be expressed. The decisions to effect these changes were never democratic, but the retributive legacy of tyrannical monarchs has long been accepted as more natural than the restorative justice it replaced.

Recent efforts to rebuild restorative justice have engaged criminologists in a cyclical pattern that could be used to invent any other new approach to justice. That pattern consists of

    A.  THEORIES. Developing theories, both normative and empirical, about how justice can work more humanely, fairly and effectively than it does at present.

    B.  INNOVATION. Developing and implementing innovations that are guided by the theories.

    C.  RESEARCH. Performing quantitative and qualitative tests of hypotheses to inform and refine theories, and to measure the effects of innovations applying the theories.

The case of restorative justice provides ample illustration of how these steps proceed in cycle, with research informing theories, changes in theories guiding changes in innovations, and research on innovations leading to further modification of theories.

REINVENTING JUSTICE 13

Figure 2  Reinventing Justice

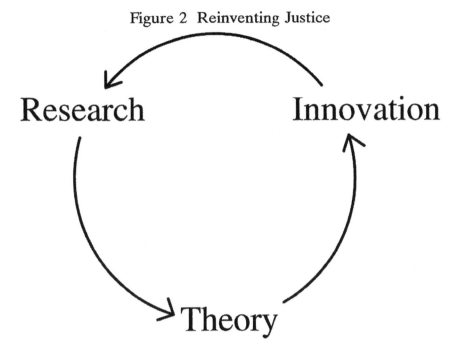

THEORIES

The normative theories of restorative justice may be found in many the-ological and philosophical sources, such as Gandhi's famous dictum that "an eye for an eye leaves everyone blind." Judaism, Christianity, and Islam all offer texts that stress the value of atonement and forgiveness, as do most other religious traditions. Recent normative work attacks victims' exclusion from criminal process and the state's disregard for victims' voices (Reiff, 1979; Rock, 1986). Normative preference for deliberative democracy at a local, face-to-face level also supports the idea of important decisions about offenders being made by those most affected by a crime (Braithwaite, 2002), although with fairer procedures and controls than manifested by such grass roots groups as the Ku Klux Klan or vigilante posses. Finally, many restorative justice scholars object to the brutality and rape found in prison, leading them to seek alternatives to imprison-ment (Sherman, 2000).

The empirical theories supporting restorative justice are grounded in basic research on offending and desistance over the life course (e.g., Gior-dano et al., 2002; Laub and Sampson, 2001; Maruna, 2001). Different the-ories of desistance emphasize different aspects of change over the life course, from externally structured turning points such as marriage and

14                         SHERMAN

employment, to internally generated cognition and identity building. Some evidence suggests that desistance may occur through epiphanies, or sudden realization of the emotional costs of offending and the benefits of compliance with law (Laub and Sampson, 2001:49). Other accounts chart more gradual changes in identity (Maruna, 2001) or more cumulative processes (Giordano et al., 2002). No theory appears inconsistent with the hypothesis that justice processes could help manufacture an epiphany, or that a restorative justice agreement could create conditions fostering the adoption of a new identity for "going straight." Further advances in desistance theory will continue to help inform emotionally intelligent justice innovations on how to accelerate naturally occurring patterns.

Restorative justice is also closely linked to procedural justice theory (Tyler, 1990). This major breakthrough in the science of justice shows the emotional consequences of how justice officials speak to suspects, defendants, and offenders, as more important for compliance than the content of the decisions officials make. The most profound implication of procedural justice is that every judge and police officer is a sales agent for legal compliance, and that many of them have a poor sales record. The theory and its research base suggest that the manners and emotional overtones of justice officials affect future offending rates as much or more than the formal decisions and severity of punishments (Tyler and Huo, 2002). Because legal officials are widely seen as disrespectful of citizens' dignity in the manner officials adopt, far more crime occurs than would if official manners were guided by research evidence on making citizens feel that the law is legitimate (Tyler, 1998). Rather than trying to change recruitment and training patterns for the entire criminal justice system, innovations based on this theory may be most readily created by inserting new procedures that build legitimacy among citizens. Merely offering counsel to indigent defendants at bail hearings, for example, substantially reduces their perception that judges are rude to them (Colbert et al., 2002:1760).

All of these theories add up to falsifiable hypotheses that restorative justice practices will be more effective than conventional justice in reducing repeat offending, helping victims, and in building legitimacy of the law. In more detailed terms, the theories imply that an intense discussion of a crime by legitimately concerned parties for some 90 minutes can prompt or enhance a process of an offender desisting from crime for years afterwards. Finally, this claim is made relative to non-restorative justice so that high failure rates can still be expected, as long as they are substantially lower than the failure rates of conventional justice.

## INNOVATION

The modern revival of restorative justice is less than three decades old, but it has long passed a "tipping point" of cascading innovations. In 1989,

New Zealand replaced its U.S.-style juvenile court with a system of restorative justice based on indigenous Maori practices that had remained intact since British colonization. By 1992 Australian police in New South Wales were adopting similar practices for diverting juvenile cases from prosecution in court. By 1995 Australian Federal Police in Canberra were testing restorative justice conferences as a diversion for violent crimes, juvenile shoplifting and other property crimes, and adult drunk driving (Sherman et al., 2003). Related programs spread around Australia, although without randomized trials, incorporating more serious juvenile offenses and even some in-prison conferences with murderers and others. On other continents, Minnesota corrections officials began using restorative justice with inmates, Canadian justice adopted indigenous practices such as "sentencing circles," and police in Thames Valley, England, began using restorative practices for juvenile cautions (Kurki, 2000).

By 1995 the Indianapolis Police had visited the Canberra experiments and started testing restorative justice (RJ) on very young offenders aged 7–14 (McGarrell et al., 2000). Bethlehem (PA) police conducted a similar experiment under NIJ support (McCold and Wachtel, 1998). In 1998 the British Parliament reformed all juvenile justice under largely restorative principles with the creation of the Youth Justice Board for England and Wales, and by 2002 the Home Office was supporting tests of RJ for serious adult offending as a supplement to sentencing, probation and resettlement of prison inmates (Sherman et al., 2002).

While the theoretical roots of these innovations varied, most of them had strong links to Braithwaite's (1989) theory of reintegrative shaming. As the practitioners encountered cultural resistance by offenders and victims to the concept of "shame," both the emotional overtones and the substantive concept of "shaming" rapidly disappeared from the practitioners' vocabulary over the decade after the theory was published. In contrast, the values of respect and redemption inherent in the theory were well received, and flourished in both rhetoric and action.

## RESEARCH

The RJ innovations stand alone in criminology for the volume of randomized controlled trials (RCTs) linked to the innovations. The Campbell Crime and Justice Group registry of RJ trials currently stands at 14 worldwide, with more in planning or prospect. All of these trials test one form of RJ, sometimes called "family group conferences," even though no family member may be present. The common feature of these conferences is an attempt to bring victims, offenders and supporters into the same room to discuss, face-to-face, three key questions: what happened, who was affected by it, and how the offender can help repair the harm. The process of democratic deliberation gives equal say to all participants, and seeks a

16                              SHERMAN

consensus on an "outcome agreement" that generally specifies what the offender will do in the future. All 14 randomized trials of these conferences have tested conferences led by police or other facilitators trained by practitioners associated with the ANU's REGNET. These trials include the Bethlehem (PA) trial of diversion to RJ for juveniles accused of violent crimes (RCT #1) and of property crimes (RCT #2) (McCold and Wachtel, 1998); the Indianapolis test of judicial sentences to RJ with a combined sample of 7- to 14-year-old offenders accused of a range of crimes including property and minor violence (RCT #3) (McGarrell et al., 2000), the Canberra RISE tests of diversionary RJ for violence up to age 29 (RCT #4), juvenile property crimes with personal victims (RCT #5), juvenile shoplifting against large corporations (RCT #6), and mostly adult driving over the prescribed limits of alcohol concentration in the bloodstream (RCT #7) (Sherman et al., 2003). All seven of these trials have now reported at least some results on recidivism effects of up to two years.

In mid-2002, seven more RCTs began in England under support from the Home Office Research, Development and Statistics Directorate. In London, Metropolitan Police officers are testing RJ after guilty pleas, but before sentencing in Crown Court, for adults committing robbery-street crime (RCT #8) and burglary (RCT #9). In Northumbria, police officers are testing RJ after guilty pleas, but before sentencing in Magistrates' Courts, for adult assault (RCT #10) and property crimes with personal victims (RCT #11). They are also testing RJ as a form of "final warning" of juveniles for most offenses except shoplifting (RCT #12). In the National Probation Service-Thames Valley, probation officers, prison staff and professional mediators are testing RJ as a prelude to inmates leaving prison after serving terms for violent crimes (RCT #13) and as a form of community sentence (RCT #14). Whatever conclusions may be reached from the first seven RCTs about diverting cases from formal justice, the conclusions will be further informed by the results of the English RCTs inserting RJ into formal justice. The latter will illuminate the effects of RJ for more serious offenses involving a much broader range of points in the formal justice process, with rich admixtures of deterrence, retribution, and emotional engagement not found in the first seven RCTs.

These quantitative RCTs comprise only a tiny fraction of the research that criminology can contribute to reinventing justice in this way. "Experimental ethnography," or the linkage of qualitative field work on desistance (Maruna, 2001) to experimental designs, as well as to offenders and victims who refuse to participate in RJ, would provide enormous qualitative insight to the emotions generated by these innovations. Long-term cohort studies of the lifecourse of offenders and victims asked to participate in RJ, using interviews and official data (e.g., Sampson and Laub,

1993), could also provide much firmer understanding. Even more historical and comparative research on restorative processes is needed to reveal macro-level questions about the paradigm.

Moreover, the general prevention questions about restorative justice have yet to be framed. Whether people who have never committed a crime would be more or less likely to do so if restorative justice was in widespread use is an important empirical question. It can only be answered with experimental results, but such experiments will not be possible until some jurisdictions have actually developed widespread use of RJ. Ideally, quasi-experiments and even RCTs introducing RJ on a large scale in some communities and not others can be implemented to address the general prevention issues.

## RESULTS SO FAR

The first seven RCTs provide some surprising (Bottoms et al., 2001:229) results on the effects of RJ on victims and offenders. Rather than supporting predictions that restorative justice would work better for minor offenses, the research tends to show just the opposite. While the experiments vary in the success of their implementation, they show greater reduction in repeat offending—and in victim desire for revenge—with samples including violent crimes than with samples of property or less serious crime.

### VICTIM EFFECTS

Strang (2002:139) reports that RJ has a large effect on preventing victim desire to harm offenders after violent crimes, but not after property crimes. These and other results come from her interviews with 232 victims whose cases were randomly assigned to either conventional prosecution or diversion to restorative justice in Canberra. The comparisons show substantial evidence of emotional benefits for victims invited to meet with their offenders and deliberate on the outcome agreement, relative to victims not offered that chance. (These included such varied arrangements as direct restitution to victims, offender donations to charities named by the victim, hundreds of hours of community service, agreements that offenders would seek drug or alcohol treatment, or other services helping them to desist from crime.) Attending conferences generally made victims less fearful of the offender and of crime in general. But the results also revealed a risk of RJ in day-to-day practice: victims who were promised an RJ conference, but never received one, were more dissatisfied with the way their cases were treated than victims who were never promised one at all.

Despite the dissatisfaction of victims who did not receive their promised

18                              SHERMAN

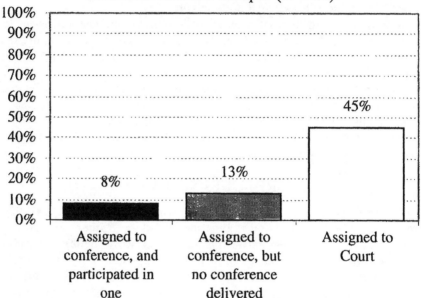

Figure 3  Victim Would Harm Offender
Canberra Violence Sample (N = 81)

RJ conference, even the promise of restorative justice seemed to reduce the desire for revenge against offenders among victims of violent crime (Figure 3). This finding suggests that it may be the idea of court itself, shutting victims out, that increases victim desire for physical vengeance relative to a process that treats their views as important enough to even plan a conference with them, but this benefit is also found only for violent crime.

RECIDIVISM EFFECTS

The effects of RJ on recidivism also vary by type of crime. In the four Canberra tests, only the violent crime RCT produced a reduction in repeat offending. RJ had no significant effects on recidivism after adult drunk driving, juvenile shoplifting, and juvenile property crimes, but it reduced recidivism after violent crimes by 41% (Sherman et al., 2003). Figure 4 shows the four-year trend in apprehensions (arrests) per year per offender, starting two years before the date of random assignment, expressed in percentage difference from the baseline year before random assignment. The fact that the beneficial effects actually increased, rather than decayed, over time is encouraging evidence for the hypothesis that the emotional memory (Massey, 2002) of an RJ conference is powerful and long-lasting. The only other test of RJ on a sample including violent

## REINVENTING JUSTICE 19

## Figure 4 Relative Percent Change in Yearly Crime Frequency* by Assigned Treatment (Violent Crime, N = 121)

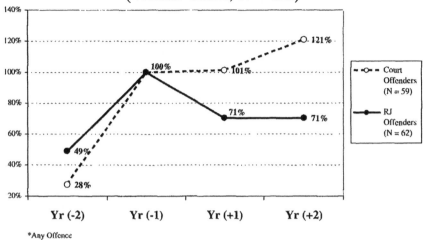

*Any Offence

crime—Indianapolis juveniles—also reports a reduction in recidivism (at 6 months) (McGarrell et al., 2000).

The evidence on RJ for nonviolent crime is consistently more negative than it is for violent crimes. While the Indianapolis data combined property and violent crime, the Bethlehem and Canberra RCTs separated them. None of the four tests of RJ on juvenile property crime in Bethlehem and Canberra have shown any significant differences in repeat offending between randomly assigned offers of RJ and standard court treatment, nor did the Canberra test of RJ on half of the 900 drivers caught driving under the influence of alcohol. The latter experiment actually produced a small increase among the RJ cases in the frequency of repeat arrest for all offense types in the first year after random assignment (Sherman et al., 2000), which disappeared by the end of the second year (Sherman et al., 2003).

Although the difference in the effects of RJ on violence and other crimes may or may not persist with the seven new RCTs underway, it invites explanations based on the emotional dynamics of the conferences. Ongoing analysis of the observational data on the four Canberra RCTs may help provide insights. So might basic research in neuroscience, which has recently reported large differences in neural measures of stress response by parolees convicted of violent crimes versus property crimes (Cherek et al., 1999). Whatever the reason, the findings to date suggest potential for RJ to be effective with more, rather than less, serious

20                          SHERMAN

offenses. Testing RJ on such offenses raises the possibility of it becoming an alternative to imprisonment.

EFFECTS ON INCARCERATION

The seven RCTs reported so far can say little about the effects of an RJ option on the use of incarceration because of the extremely rare use of incarceration in the control groups. In England, where the prison population is rising at a rapid rate, the idea of restorative justice has been seriously considered as an alternative to prison, but not without controversy. The Lord Chief Justice of England and Wales (Woolf, 2001, 2002) has repeatedly called for judges to consider restorative justice as an alternative to at least short prison sentences. More recently, the chair of a committee of the Association of Chief Police Officers, the Chief Constable of Thames Valley, proposed diversion of offenders arrested for burglary to restorative conferences combined with close community supervision and intensive rehabilitation. This proposal for an alternative to prosecution for arrested burglars, most of whom escape punishment because the charges are dropped in any case, was reported by The Sunday Times of London with scornful headlines (Leppard, 2002), but it is not very distant from what judges may do already in sentencing burglars, and such conditional cautions could well reduce recidivism. Four of the English RCTs will be able to measure, among other things, what effect the occurrence of an RJ conference has on judges' decisions to sentence offenders to prison.

In the long run, the willingness to use RJ as a substitute for prison, rather than as a supplement to it, may depend on the capacity of inventors to demonstrate that RJ is just as effective as prison in preventing crime, or that RJ combined with shorter prison terms can be just as effective as longer (more expensive) sentences without RJ. Demonstrating such results may depend on the boldness of inventors in using the emotions of the 90-minute encounter to mobilize longer-term, powerful strategies to prevent repeat offending.

## EMOTIONALLY INTELLIGENT JUSTICE

Inventors face two major tasks in making justice more emotionally intelligent. One task is to develop better capacity for the justice system to process cases without angering defendants, victims, and others so much that they become more likely to commit crime. The second is to develop bolder experiments with a broader range of tools for helping people obey the law—besides the threat to lock them up. Both tasks can proceed in tandem to help develop emotionally intelligent systems of justice, not just disconnected programs. Keeping the process of inventing such systems alive, however, will require open minds and a license to produce more failures than successes, just as in every other process of invention.

## JUSTICE TALKING FOR PREVENTION

The Canberra findings that superficially similar justice processes produce different or opposite recidivism effects raise profound questions about conventional justice. If slight variations in the emotional content of a justice "encounter" can produce long-lasting effects on repeat offending, what may be the result of differences in the ways police speak to motorists (Tyler, 1990), IRS agents speak to taxpayers (Kinsey, 1992), or the ways judges speak to offenders? The word "scolding" ("rebuking in ill temper justly or unjustly"—Webster's, 1985:1052) may be most useful in understanding the emotional messages that may or may not be conveyed in the course of administering justice, and describes what community representatives often did in Canberra drinking-driving conferences.

Research in other settings also suggests that talking (and listening) can have major emotional effects on future criminal behavior matters. Judges in Germany, for example, vary in the frequency with which they administer scoldings to convicted defendants. Pfeiffer (1994) reports that cases randomly assigned to judges who regularly scold offenders at sentencing produce significantly higher rates of repeat offending than cases assigned to judges who scold offenders only rarely. In the Milwaukee domestic violence arrest experiment, people arrested for domestic violence did not get scolded by police during the arrest process, but they were often ignored. Based on interviews with offenders in jail immediately after arrest, it appears that simply not listening to a suspect's version of events during an arrest process may increase repeat offending, in contrast to police listening to the suspect's account of what happened (Paternoster et al., 1997).

Teaching judges, police, and other officials to speak and listen to all offenders more in sorrow than in anger may well be a path to reduced recidivism and lower crime rates. The problem is to implement such a major change in the conduct, let alone the autonomy, of justice officials. Inventors may find the path to the goal less difficult if they create different procedures, such as restorative justice conferences, than are currently in use. For example, a judge could discuss a sentence with an offender and his family in chambers, and the results for repeat offending can be tested in an RCT using formal courtroom sentencing as the control group. Police pondering the findings that how they speak to offenders during arrest affects recidivism (Paternoster et al., 1997) could introduce a "suspect briefing" phase during the arrest process: orienting the suspect to what is going to happen next and why, allowing questions to be asked and answered. These and other procedural add-ons might have powerful effects on offender emotions and compliance.

22                          SHERMAN

BOLDER INVENTIONS

Although changing the way officials talk to citizens may be important, it may be even more important to test bolder inventions that go far beyond talk to affect emotions. These inventions include three possible types. One is the enhancement of the social support for law-abiding conduct that basic research (Laub and Sampson, 2001) suggests can foster desistance. A second is the use of medical and nutritional interventions that are already shown to foster compliance with law. The third, and theoretically most potent, would be combinations of the two approaches.

Given the high costs of incarceration, there is a wide open window for intensive but still less expensive (than prison) programs that could be as effective as prison in total crime prevention benefits. Note that such benefits can only be calculated fairly after a control group *in* prison *leaves* prison, with a long enough follow-up period to compare total offenses committed by out-of-prison experimental program cases and in-prison control cases. The illusory gain of "perfect" crime prevention during incarceration may well disappear in a comparison of the lifetime prevention benefits of keeping people out of prison, which can never be estimated simply on the basis of the offending rate during alternatives to incarceration. The randomized field experiment comparing community service work to short prison terms in Switzerland (Killias et al., 2000) is a model approach to such evaluations and evidence that offenders feel much more positive emotions towards law and work if they are spared even 14 days behind bars—without any measurable increase in offending rates.

INTENSIVE SOCIAL SUPPORT

The idea of using a more intensive form of support with offenders after they are released from incarceration makes theoretical sense, but has been hard to achieve in practice (MacKenzie, 2002). Program integrity at delivering more services is a widespread issue and a prime example of how "engineering" is a key component of the innovation phase of the reinvention process. Where program integrity of delivering such services as job training, drug treatment, and literacy education appears strong, the approach has generally been found to prevent crime (e.g., Fonagy and Kurtz, 2002:163, 180). English officials also report frequent failures of offenders to keep appointments with social services. The use of restorative justice to emotionally engage offenders and increase their commitment to these programs may be one way to reinvent them for even greater success with any in-prison, post-prison, or instead-of-prison program for "going straight" (Social Exclusion Unit, 2002).

# REINVENTING JUSTICE 23

## MEDICAL AND NUTRITIONAL PROGRAMS

Convicted offenders suffer high levels of mild to serious forms of mental illness (Farah, 2002) and nutritional deprivation (Gesch et al., 2002). The potential for improving the emotional state of offenders by treating these risk factors seems substantial, despite the considerable normative debate that such ideas may evoke. Depression, for example, is highly linked to dysfunctions in the brain's processing of serotonin, a major neurotransmitter, which is in turn linked to aggressive (Walsh and Dinan, 2001:86) and violent (Farah, 2002:1125) behavior. Emotionally, this condition makes people irritable and anger-prone. Three independent double-blind, placebo-controlled RCTs of Selective Serotonin Reuptake Inhibitors, including fluoxetine (marketed as Prozac), have shown reduced aggression in patients with personality disorder (Farah, 2002:1125). A meta-analysis of studies encompassing 2615 Prozac patients and 1377 patients on placebo pills found that the rate of violent or aggressive incidents reported among the patients taking Prozac was 75% lower than it was in the placebo group (Walsh and Dinan, 2001).

Nutrition is another avenue to the emotions generally ignored in both criminology and justice, despite ample evidence (and parental advice) that diet can affect emotions and behavior. In a double-blind, placebo-controlled trial in a young offenders' prison, a daily dose of supplementary vitamins and minerals had a substantial effect on reducing disciplinary misconduct within the institution (Gesch et al., 2002). The challenge of taking this idea beyond prison and into the community would be to engineer high rates of offender cooperation with taking the nutritional supplements.

Compliance with community-based drug treatment regimens has been enhanced by court-ordered supervision in drug courts in ways that reduced repeat offending (Gottfredson and Exum, 2002), and could serve as a model for other kinds of treatments. The treatment of depression may also become easier with the development of a new "patch" form of delivery of the monamine oxidase (MAO) inhibitor selegiline (Bodkin and Amsterdam, 2002), which raises compliance with daily dosage intake to 94%.[2] This and other approaches to community-based management of mentally ill offenders can be developed by the new "Mental Health Courts," modeled on drug courts, that have been established in Georgia, New Jersey, and elsewhere (Wolff, 2002). There are major "engineering" questions in the design and operation of such courts, including the critical questions of diagnosis, eligibility, and diversion from criminal justice

---

2. While MAO inhibitors have not apparently been tested against the criterion of violence (unlike SSRIs), MAO inhibitors are very successful at treating depression, and may therefore also help to prevent violence against others or self.

24                          SHERMAN

processses, but the fact that the majority of New Jersey jails provide no aftercare for 90% of seriously mentally ill offenders (Wolff et al., 2002) suggests that new systems should at least be tested.

The normative capacity of criminology can be profitably engaged in the question of what to do about such research findings. Courts and probation officers routinely require offenders to take anger management classes without arousing controversy, even though they have yet to be tested by randomized trials (Fonagy and Kurtz, 2002:163). Suggesting that anger might be managed through a court-ordered pill seems to evoke much deeper emotion (Farah, 2002), on the shared premise that pills might actually work better than talk, with deeper implications for personal freedom. Drug courts require offenders to take medicines as a condition of personal liberty, but when the underlying condition also involves drugs, the normative debate seems less emotional. The fact that drug abuse and depression may often be related may mean that drug courts could order treatment for depression, while depression without proven drug abuse would remain untreated. Other conditions could also be diagnosed and treated by psychiatrists working under court supervision, such as childhood exposure to violence. Such life experience is a major risk factor for post-traumatic stress disorder (PTSD), and is seven times higher among elite college students from segregated minority group areas than among those raised in white or integrated neighborhoods (Massey, 2002:24). Drug treatments for PTSD could also be a part of the toolbox for mental health courts or their staff physicians under a new paradigm of emotionally intelligent justice.

Emotional intelligence also requires attention to legitimacy of justice. The legitimacy of drug treatments for mental health may be much greater when there is truly voluntary agreement by offenders, as opposed to the coercion that is at the core of drug courts. Here again, the deliberative democracy of restorative justice may be a useful tool. In the course of a restorative justice conference in London, for example,

> a young adult woman who had pled guilty on an ATM robbery at knifepoint met with her victim, her victim's family, and her foster parents with a New Scotland Yard police officer facilitating the discussion. She was of borderline IQ and diagnosed schizophrenic. She had stopped taking her medications at the time of the robbery because she had been told the pills would make her fat. After a three hour discussion of the pain her crime had caused to the victim and the victim's family, the question of what should be done to repair the harm was put to the offender. The offender then voluntarily promised to take her "meds" faithfully in the future. When her signed agreement to do that was submitted to the sentencing judge in Crown Court, the judge decided not to send the offender to prison, which would have been

## REINVENTING JUSTICE 25

the customary treatment for the offense. Instead, the offender was given a community sentence under the supervision of the Probation Service (Bennett, 2002).

In the course of RJ conferences, victims often focus on offenders' self-improvement as the best way to repair the harm the crime has caused. Offenders in RJ often propose to provide material payback to victims, but are emotionally moved by the victim's desire to see the offender turn her life around. If by making voluntary undertakings to comply with medical or even nutritional treatments, offenders could achieve reduced offending *and* a substantial reduction in the use of imprisonment, a normative debate on such justice would have important facts to consider. Is a world with more pharmacology and less prison better or worse than a world with more prison but less pharmacology? That may not be the only choice, but it could be very important for criminology to find out.

BIOSOCIAL BOLDNESS

Perhaps the most promising line of invention would be to combine the biomedical treatment of crime risk factors with social support. One major normative objection to biomedical treatment is that it ignores the social risk factors of crime, including criminogenic families, friendships, and neighborhoods. The objection is framed as if the two strategies were mutually exclusive. This need not be so. There is no reason in principle why new responses to crime could not include interventions in both the biomedical and social risk factors. For example, someone coming out of prison who agrees to treatment for mild depression could also be given financial support to move to a new neighborhood in a lower crime area, given help getting (and keeping) a job, and could attend drug treatment or literacy classes (etc.) as indicated. The use of restorative justice to obtain agreement to this plan and to enhance the offender's emotional commitment to it might be the glue that makes it stick together. Theory and research so far suggest that such a combination is well worth a test. The clear benefits of a biosocial approach to early childhood visits to parents by registered nurses (Olds et al., 1986, 1998) for example, is one of many lessons that the criminology of "primary" prevention can inform the criminology of justice.

EMOTIONALLY INTELLIGENT SYSTEMS

The new paradigm criminology could build is one in which a justice *system* becomes emotionally intelligent in all of its interactions with suspected, accused, and convicted offenders, as well as with victims, their families and communities. Although this concept has been developed by psychologists at the individual level, criminology can also invent ways to

26                    SHERMAN

foster such intelligence at the level of social systems. With a little adaptation from the individual-level constructs proposed by Gardner, Salovey, and others, the elements of an emotionally intelligent justice system would be these (Goleman, 1995):

KNOWING THE SYSTEM'S EMOTIONS.

Justice officials from police to judges to prison and probation officers who are aware of their own emotional forces may be able to manage those emotions more effectively. Police agencies training officers not to express emotions, for example, may be better off training officers to acknowledge their emotions, and take appropriate steps to deal with them. Emotional "hot spots" of justice activity could be mapped and studied, including arrests, high-speed chases, sentencing decisions, the first day's release from prison. Experimental interventions promoting more self-awareness of the justice system's emotions could be tested for their effectiveness in reducing repeat offending.

RECOGNIZING EMOTIONS IN VICTIMS AND OFFENDERS

Similar innovations could be developed for making justice officials more aware of the emotional state of the citizens involved with the justice system. While some tools, such as pre-sentence reports, are already designed to do this, they could be enhanced with more precise and comprehensive emotional and mental health assessments. Controlled tests of greater investment in such "intelligence" about citizen emotions could reveal its value for reducing crime, and justify greater investment in gaining better intelligence.

MANAGING EMOTIONS

Most important is accurate predictions about the effects of decisions—and manners of administering the decisions—on the long-term emotional states of offenders and victims. Understanding how to *avoid* provoking such emotions as defiance, anger, and humiliation may be more important than understanding how to instill a desire to obey the law. Justice systems may have even more opportunity to avoid doing harm than to achieve positive good.

## SUSTAINING INVENTIVENESS

In order to find enough successful inventions to build a paradigm of emotionally intelligent justice, it is essential to ask the right questions. The right question about restorative justice, procedural justice, or other inventions, is not whether they work in general. Rather, the key question for inventors is what effects on crime different versions of such inventions

# REINVENTING JUSTICE 27

may have under different circumstances. For restorative justice, the questions are now focused on what effects it may have on different kinds of offenses and offenders in different social settings. "What works for whom (Fonagy et al., 2002), when, and where" is the standard question for an emotionally intelligent system to answer.

Differentiation of effects under different conditions can only be achieved by finding that something does not work for someone. Learning such lessons is a research success, but it may be misinterpreted as a policy failure. Expectations set too high may lead to overreaction to any one negative result, but success is gained just as much from negative results as from positive ones, especially in the avoidance of harm. Penicillin may work with most people, for example, but knowing that some people are allergic may save lives.

Dismissing an entire line of theoretically promising research on the basis of a few negative results would deny the historical record of how inventions are created, not to mention Baconian principles of science (Bacon, 1620). The expectation from history is that most versions of an invention will fail, until one or two of them succeed to a reasonable degree. The lightbulb, the airplane, automobile, and even police departments (Miller, 1977) all followed that trajectory. RCTs are not for vote counting, and negative research results should not doom future refinements and enhancements. In chemotherapy for cancer, 500,000 substances were tested in order to find 10 that worked (Oldham, 1987). The important point is not the tests that fail, but replicating and extending the tests that succeed.

The reasons for criminology, of course, will always be far broader than reinventing justice. All kinds of criminology, such as ethnography (e.g., Anderson, 1978), life-course research (Nagin et al., 1995), and evaluations of primary prevention programs (e.g., Olds et al., 1986, 1998), are ultimately necessary for the advancement of knowledge about crime. The primary reason for criminology in democracies may be that justice is an emotional hot spot of our field, one that will always be at the core of public discourse on crime. While this fact implies that we should therefore give justice far more empirical and experimental attention than we have done in recent years, the application of reason for emotion in justice requires the most comprehensive and diverse approach to criminology we can build.

It is too soon to tell whether criminology can develop an emotionally intelligent paradigm of justice. Whatever focus future justice inventions may take, more work with emotions may allow us to reduce the cruelty of both offenders and of the justice system. The window of opportunity posed by the desire to restrain public expenditure may not last, if Ranulf's (1938) grim forecast about punishment and income inequality is correct.

28                          SHERMAN

Inventiveness might even solve that problem, making less cruel forms of penalty more emotionally attractive to those demanding punishment (cf. Boyle, 1999). The system response to intelligence on public emotions about fairness is already manifested in the 32% drop in U.S. executions from 2000 to 2001, as concerns about wrongful conviction increased with DNA testing of death row inmates (McCaffrey, 2002). Criminology in the Age of Information may benefit from the same kind of turmoil over government that helped Beccaria and his colleagues in the Age of Reason. They made the most of their opportunity. Let us see what we can do with ours.

## REFERENCES

Ahmed, Eliza, Nathan Harris, John Braithwaite, and Valerie Braithwaite
    2001    Shame Management Through Reintegration. Cambridge: Cambridge University Press.

Agnew, Robert
    1992    Foundations for a general strain theory of crime and delinquency. Criminology 30:47–87.
    2001    Building on the foundation of general strain theory: Specifying the types of strain most likely to lead to crime and delinquency. Journal of Research in Crime and Delinquency 38:319–361.

Anderson, Elijah
    1978    A Place on the Corner. Chicago: University of Chicago Press.

Applegate, Brandon K., Francis T. Cullen, Bonnie S. Fisher, and Thomas Vander Ven
    2000    Forgiveness and fundamentalism: Reconsidering the relationship between correctional attitudes and religion. Criminology 38:719–753.

Bacon, Francis
    1620    Novum Organum, translated and edited by Peter Urbach and John
    [1994]   Gibson. Chicago: Open Court.
    1625    The Essayes or Counsels, Civill and Morall, of Francis Lo. Verulam
    [1985]   Viscount St. Alban. London, edited by M. Kiernan and reprinted at The Clarendon Press, Oxford, U.K. (1985).

Barbelet, J.M.
    2002    Moral indignation, class inequality and justice: An exploration and revision of Ranulf. Theoretical Criminology 6:279–297.

Barzun, Jacques
    2000    From Dawn To Decadence: 500 Years of Western Cultural Life. N.Y.: HarperCollins.

Beccaria, Cesare
    1764    Of Crimes and Punishments. N.Y.: Marsilio Publishers.
    [1996]

Bennett, Sarah
    2002    Personal Communication.

# REINVENTING JUSTICE 29

Blumenfeld, Laura
2002 Revenge. A Story of Hope. N.Y.: Simon and Schuster.

Bentham, Jeremy
1789 Principles of Morals and Legislation, edited by J.H. Burns and H.L.A.
[1970] Hart. London: Athlone.

Berk, Richard A., Alec Campbell, Ruth Klap, and Bruce Western
1992 The deterrent effect of arrest in incidents of domestic violence: A
Bayesian analysis of four field experiments. American Sociological
Review 57:698–708.

Bodkin, J. Alexander and Jay D. Amsterdam
2002 Transdermal selegiline in major depression: A double-blind, placebo-
controlled, parallel-group study in outpatients. The American Journal of
Psychiatry 159:1869–1875.

Bohlen, Celestine
2002 A Phrase Explained: 'Duck in a Noose' is Traced to a Folk Tale. New
York Times, 25 October.

Bottoms, Anthony, Loraine Gelsthorpe, and Sue Rex
2001 Concluding reflections. In Anthony Bottoms, Loraine Geslthorpe, and
Sue Rex, (eds.). Community Penalties: Change and Challenges. Cullompton, Devon, U.K.: Willan Publishing.

Boyle, John M.
1999 Crime Issues in the Northeast: Statewide Surveys of the Public and Crime
Victims in Connecticut, Delaware, Maine, Massachusetts, Vermont, New
Hampshire, New Jersey, New York, and Rhode Island. Conducted for
Council of State Governments. Silver Spring, Md.: Schulman, Ronca and
Bucuvalas, Inc.

Braithwaite, John
1989 Crime, Shame and Reintegration. Cambridge, U.K.: Cambridge University Press.
1998 Restorative justice. In Michael Tonry (ed.), The Handbook of Crime and
Punishment. Oxford, U.K.: Oxford University Press.
1999 Restorative justice: Assessing optimistic and pessimistic accounts. In
Michael Tonry (ed.), Crime and Justice: A Review of Research, Vol. 25.
Chicago: University of Chicago Press.
2002 Restorative Justice and Responsive Regulation. Oxford, U.K.: Oxford
University Press.

Brands, H.W.
2000 The First American: Life and Times of Benjamin Franklin. N.Y.:
Doubleday.

Butterfield, Fox
2002 Inmates Go Free to Reduce Deficits: States Can't Pay Tab on Years of
Tough Law Enforcement. New York Times, 19 December, p. A1.

Carpenter, Sanford N.
1917 The Reformation in Principle and Action. Philadelphia: The Lutheran
Publication Society.

Cherek, Don R., F. Gerard Moeller, F. Khan-Dawood, Allan Swann, and Scott D.
Lane

30 SHERMAN

1999      Prolactin response to Buspirone was reduced in violent compared to nonviolent parolees. Psychopharmacologia 142 (2):144–148.

Caspi, Avshalom, Joseph McClay, Terrie E. Moffitt, Jonathan Mill, Judy Martin, Ian W. Craig, Alan Taylor, and Richie Poulton
2002      Role of genotype in the cycle of violence in maltreated children. Science Magazine 297 (5582):851–854.

Christie, Nils
1977      Conflicts as property. British Journal of Criminology 17:1–15.

Clarke, Ronald V. (ed.)
1997      Situational Crime Prevention. Albany, N.Y.: Harrow and Heston.

Colbert, Douglas L., Ray Paternoster, and Shawn Bushway
2002      Do attorneys really matter? The empirical and legal case for the right of counsel at bail. Cardozo Law Review 23:1719–1793.

Collins, Randall
1998      The Sociology of Philosophies: A Global Theory of Intellectual Change. Cambridge, Mass.: Harvard University Press.

Cuomo, Mario
1764      Foreword in Cesare Beccaria, Of Crimes and Punishments (1764). N.Y.:
[1996]    Marsilio.

Duncan, Martha Grace
1996      Romantic Outlaws, Beloved Prisons. N.Y.: New York University Press.

Durant, Will and Ariel Durant
1965      The Story of Civilization: Part IX. The Age of Voltaire. N.Y.: Simon and Schuster.

Durkheim, Emile
1893      The Division of Labor in Society. N.Y.: Free Press.
[1964]

Elias, Norbert
1994      The Civilizing Process: Sociogenetic and Psychogenetic Investigations. Translated by Edmund Jephcoft. Revised edition, 2000. Oxford, U.K.: Basil Blackwell.

Farah, Martha
2002      Emerging ethical issues in neuroscience. Nature Neuroscience 5:1123–1129.

Feinberg, Joel
1994      The expressive function of punishment. In Antony Duff and David Garland (eds.), A Reader on Punishment. Oxford, U.K.: Oxford University Press.

Fonagy, Peter and Arabella Kurtz
2002      Conduct disorder. In Peter Fonagy, Mary Target, David Cottrell, Jeannette Phillips, and Zarrina Kurtz, (eds.), What Works for Whom? A Critical Review of Treatments for Children and Adolescents. N.Y.: The Guilford Press.

Fonagy, Peter, Mary Target, David Cottrell, Jeanette Phillips, and Zarinna Kurtz (eds.)

2002     What Works for Whom? A Critical Review of Treatments for Children and Adolescents. N.Y.: The Guilford Press.

Foner, Eric
2002     Thomas Paine. American National Biography Online, downloaded Nov. 29.

Franklin, Benjamin
1790     Autobiography. Mineola, N.Y.: Dover Publications.
[1996]

Gesch, C. Bernard, Sean M. Hammond, Sarah E. Hampson, Anita Eves, and Martin J. Crowder
2002     Influence of supplementary vitamins, minerals and essential fatty acids on the antisocial behaviour of young adult prisoners: Randomised, placebo-controlled trial. The British Journal of Psychiatry 181:22–28.

Giordano, Peggy, Stephen A. Cernkovich, and Jennifer L. Rudolph
2002     Gender, crime and desistance: Toward a theory of cognitive transformation. American Journal of Sociology 107:990–1064.

Gladwell, Malcolm
2000     The Tipping Point. Boston: Little, Brown & Co.

Goleman, Daniel
1995     Emotional Intelligence. N.Y.: Bantam.

Gottfredson, Denise and M. Lyn Exum
2002     The Baltimore city drug treatment court: One-year results from a randomized study. Journal of Research in Crime and Delinquency 39:337–356.

Gouldner, Alvin W.
1970     The Coming Crisis of Western Sociology. London: Heinemann.
[1972]

Harris, Nathan
2001     Shaming and shame: Regulating drink-driving. In Eliza Ahmed, Nathan Harris, John Braithwaite, and Valérie Braithwaite, Shame Management Through Reintegration. Cambridge U.K.: Cambridge University Press.

Hudson, Barbara
2002     Restorative justice and gendered violence: Diversion or effective justice? British Journal of Criminology 42:616–634.

Huxley, Elspeth
1939     Red Strangers. London: Penguin.
[1999]

Jones, Nikki
2002     Context of violence in lives of at-risk inner-city girls. Paper presented to the American Society of Criminology.

Josi, Don A. and Dale K. Sechrest
1999     A pragmatic approach to parole aftercare: Evaluation of a community reintegration program for high-risk youthful offenders. Justice Quarterly 16:51–79.

32                           SHERMAN

Kahan, Daniel
   1996      What do alternative sanctions mean? University of Chicago Law Review
             63:591–653.
   1998      The anatomy of disgust in criminal law. University of Michigan Law
             Review 69:1621–1657.

Karstedt, Susanne
   2002      Emotions and criminal justice. Theoretical Criminology 6:299–318.

Katz, Jack
   1999      How Emotions Work. Chicago: University of Chicago Press.

Killias, Martin, Marcelo F. Aebi, and Denis Ribeaud
   2000      Learning through controlled experiments: Community service and heroin
             prescription in Switzerland. Crime and Delinquency 46:233–251.

Kinsey, Karyl
   1992      Deterrence and alienation effects of IRS enforcement: An analysis of
             survey data. In Joel Slemrod (ed.), Why People Pay Taxes. Ann Arbor,
             Mich.: University of Michigan Press.

Kuhn, Thomas S.
   1964      The Structure of Scientific Revolutions. Chicago: University of Chicago
             Press.

Kurki, Leena
   2000      Restorative and community justice in the United States. In Michael Tonry
             (ed.), Crime and Justice: A Review of Research, Vol. 27. Chicago:
             University of Chicago Press.

Laub, John H. and Robert J. Sampson
   2001      Understanding desistance from crime. In Michael Tonry (ed.), Crime and
             Justice: A Review of Research, Vol. 28.

LeDoux, Joseph
   1996      The Emotional Brain: The Mysterious Underpinnings of EmotionalLife.
             N.Y.: Simon and Schuster.

Leppard, David
   2002      Don't Jail Burglars, Make Them Say Sorry, Urge Police Chiefs. The
             Sunday Times (London), 27 October, p. 1.

Liptak, Adam
   2002      Not at All Remorseful, But Not Guilty Either. New York Times, 3
             November, Week in Review, p. 4.

MacKenzie, Doris Layton
   2002      Reducing the criminal activities of known offenders and delinquents:
             Crime prevention in the courts and corrections. In Lawrence W.
             Sherman, David P. Farrington, Brandon C. Welsh, and Doris Layton
             MacKenzie (eds.), Evidence Based Crime Prevention. London: Routledge.

Maguire, K. and Ann L. Pastore
   1998      Sourcebook of Criminal Justice Statistics 1997. Washington, D.C.: Bureau
             of Justice Statistics, U.S. Department of Justice.

# REINVENTING JUSTICE      33

Marciniak, Elizabeth
  1994      Community Policing of Domestic Violence: Neighborhood Differences in the Effect of Arrest. Ph.D. Dissertation, University of Maryland-College Park.

Maruna, Shadd
  2001      Making Good: How Ex-Offenders Reform and Reclaim Their Lives. Washington, D.C.: American Psychological Association Press.

Massey, Douglas
  2002      2001 Presidential address. A brief history of human society: The origin and role of emotion in social life. American Sociological Review 67:1–29.

McCaffrey, Shannon
  2002      On U.S. Death Row, There's Less Company. Philadelphia Inquirer, 16 December, A2.

McCold, Paul and Ben Wachtel
  1998      Restorative Police Experiment: The Bethlehem Pennsylvania Police Family Group Conferencing Project. Pipersville, PA: Community Service Foundation.

McCullough, David
  2001      John Adams. N.Y.: Simon and Schuster.

McGarrell, Edmund F., Kathleen Olivares, Kay Crawford, and Natalie Kroovand
  2000      Returning Justice to the Community: The Indianapolis Juvenile Restorative Justice Experiment. Indianapolis: Hudson Institute.

McDonald, John and David Moore
  2001      Community conferencing as a special case of conflict transformation. In Heather Strang and John Braithwaite (eds.), Restorative Justice and Civil Society. Cambridge U.K.: Cambridge University Press.

Miller, Wilbur
  1977      Cops and Bobbies. Chicago: University of Chicago Press.

Morris, Norval
  1966      Impediments to Penal Reform. University of Chicago Law Review 33:627–656.

Morrison, Brenda
  2001      The school system: Developing its capacity in the regulation of a civil society. In Heather Strang and John Braithwaite (eds.), Restorative Justice and Civil Society. Cambridge, U.K.:Cambridge University Press.

Nagin, Daniel S., David P. Farrington, and Terrie E. Moffitt
  1995      Life-course trajectories of different types of offenders. Criminology 33:111–140.

Oldham, Robert K.
  1987      Patient-funded cancer research. New England Journal of Medicine 316:46–47.

Olds, David, Charles R. Henderson, Robert Chamberlin, and R. Tatelbaum
  1986      Preventing child abuse and neglect: A randomized trial of nurse home visitation. Pediatrics 78:65–78.

Olds, David, Charles R. Henderson, Robert Cole, John Eckenrode, Harriet Kitzman, Dennis Luckey, Lisa Pettitt, Kimberly Sidora, Pamela Morris, and Jane Powers

34                    SHERMAN

1998      Long-term effects of nurse home visitation on children's criminal and
          anti-social behavior: 15-year follow-up of a randomized controlled trial.
          Journal of the American Medical Association 280:1238–1244.

Paine, Thomas
1794      The Age of Reason. London. Reprinted at Putnam, N.Y.
[1924]

Pate, Antony M. and Edwin E. Hamilton
1992      Formal and informal deterrents to domestic violence: The Dade County
          spouse assault experiment. American Sociological Review 57:691–697.

Paternoster, Raymond, Bobby Brame, Ronet Bachman, and Lawrence W. Sherman
1997      Do fair procedures matter? The effect of procedural justice on spouse
          assault. Law and Society Review 31:163–204.

Pfeiffer, Christian
1994      Personal Communication summarizing his German language Ph.D. thesis.

Phillipson, Coleman
1923      Three Criminal Law Reformers: Beccaria, Bentham, Romilly. Reprinted
[1975]    at Montclair, N.J.: Patterson Smith.

Pollard, Charles
2001      If your only tool is a hammer, all your problems will look like nails. In
          Heather Strang and John Braithwaite (eds.), Restorative Justice and Civil
          Society. Cambridge, U.K.: Cambridge University Press.

Pollock, Sir Frederick and Frederic William Maitland
1898      The History of English Law, 2d ed. Reissued 1968. Cambridge U.K.:
          Cambridge University Press.
1898a     Volume I.
1898b     Volume II.

Radzinowicz, Leon
1966      Ideology & Crime: A Study of Crime in Its Social and Historical Context.
          N.Y.: Columbia University Press.

Ranulf, Svend
1938      Moral Indignation and Middle Class Psychology: A Sociological Study.
[1964]    Reprinted at N.Y.: Schocken Books.

Reiff, R.
1979      The Invisible Victim: The Criminal Justice System's Forgotten Responsi-
          bility. N.Y.: Basic Books.

Ritchie, James and Terry O'Connell
2001      Restorative justice and the need for restorative environments in bureau-
          cracies and corporations. In Heather Strang and John Braithwaite (eds.),
          Restorative Justice and Civil Society. Cambridge, U.K.: Cambridge
          University Press.

Rock, Paul
1986      A View From the Shadows: The Ministry of the Solicitor General of
          Canada and the Making of the Justice for Victims of Crime Initiative.
          Oxford, U.K.: The Clarendon Press.

# REINVENTING JUSTICE 35

Sampson, Robert J. and John H. Laub
1993    Crime in the Making: Pathways and Turning Points Through Life.
        Cambridge, Mass.: Harvard University Press.

Scheff, Thomas and Suzanne Retzinger
1991    Emotions and Violence: Shame and Rage in Destructive Conflict.
        Lexington, Mass.: D.C. Heath.

Sherman, Lawrence W.
1993    Defiance, deterrence and irrelevance: A theory of the criminal sanction.
        Journal of Research in Crime and Delinquency 30:445–473.
2000    Reducing incarceration rates: The promise of experimental criminology.
        Crime and Delinquency 46:299–314.

Sherman, Lawrence W. and Douglas Smith
1992    Crime, punishment and stake in conformity: Legal and informal control of
        domestic violence. American Sociological Review 57:680–690.

Sherman, Lawrence W., Heather Strang, and Daniel J. Woods
2000    Recidivism Patterns in the Canberra Reintegrative Shaming Experiments.
        Canberra: Australian National University, Research School of Social
        Sciences, Centre for Restorative Justice. www.aic.gov.au/rjustice/rise/index.
        html

Sherman, Lawrence W., Heather Strang, Nova Inkpen, Dorothy Newbury-Birch, and
Sarah Bennett
2002    Developing and Testing Restorative Justice in English Sentencing,
        Probation and Prisons: Sixth Quarterly Report. Philadelphia: University
        of Pennsylvania.

Sherman, Lawrence W., Heather Strang, Geoffrey Barnes, and Daniel J. Woods
2003    Two-year recidivism effects in the Canberra Reintegrative Shaming
        Experiments. Canberra: Centre for Restorative Justice, Research School
        of Social Science, Australian National University. www.aic.gov.au/rjustice/
        rise/index.html

Shumyatsky, Gleb P., Evgeny Tsvetkov, Gael Malleret, Svetlana Vornskaya, Michael
Hatton, Lori Hampton, James F. Battey, Catherine DuLac, Eric R. Kandel, and
Vadim Y. Bolshakov
2002    Identification of a signaling network in lateral nucleus of amygdala
        important for inhibiting memory specifically related to learned fear. Cell
        111:905–918.

Smith, Jane S.
1990    Patenting the Sun: Polio and the Salk Vaccine. N.Y.: Anchor Books.

Social Exclusion Unit
2002    Reducing Reoffending by Ex-Prisoners. London: Cabinet Office, HMSO.

Strang, Heather
2002    Repair or Revenge: Victims and Restorative Justice. Oxford, U.K.:
        Oxford University Press.

Strang, Heather and John Braithwaite (eds.)
2000    Restorative Justice: Philosophy to Practice. Aldershot, U.K.: Ashgate.
2001    Restorative Justice and Civil Society. Cambridge, U.K.: Cambridge
        University Press.

36                       SHERMAN

2002     Restorative Justice and Family Violence. Cambridge, U.K.: Cambridge
         University Press.

Turow, Scott
2002     Quoted in Jodi Wilgoren, Opposing Executions, In Fiction and Real Life.
         New York Times, East Coast Edition, 30 November, B9.

Tyler, Tom
1990     Why People Obey the Law. New Haven, Conn.: Yale University Press.
1998     Trust and Democratic Governance. In Valerie Braithwaite and Margaret
         Levi (eds.), Trust and Governance. N.Y.: Russell Sage Foundation.

Tyler, Tom and Yuen J. Huo
2002     Trust in the Law: Encouraging Public Cooperation with the Police and
         Courts. N.Y.: Russell Sage Foundation.

Uglow, Jenny
2002     The Lunar Men: Five Friends Whose Curiosity Changed the World. N.Y.:
         Farrar, Straus & Giroux.

Urbach, Peter and John Gibson (eds., trans)
1620     Novum Organum. Chicago, Open Court Press.
[1994]

Van den Haag, Ernest
1975     Punishing Criminals: Concerning an Old and Very Painful Question. N.Y.:
         Basic Books.

Van Stokkom, Bas
2002     Moral emotions in restorative justice conferences: Managing shame,
         designing empathy. Theoretical Criminology 6:339–360.

Walsh, Marie-Theres and Timothy G. Dinan
2001     Selective serotonin reuptake inhibitors and violence: A review of the
         available evidence. Acta Psychiatrica Scandanavia 104:84–91.

Webster's
1985     Ninth New Collegiate Dictionary. Springfield, Mass.: Merriam-Webster.

Weitekamp, Elmar
1989     Restitution: A New Paradigm of Criminal Justice or a New Way to Widen
         the Criminal Justice System? Ph.D. dissertation, University of Penn-
         sylvania.

Wilson, James Q.
1983     Thinking About Crime. Rev. ed. N.Y.: Basic Books.

Wolfgang, Marvin E.
1996     Introduction to Cesare Beccaria, Of Crimes and Punishments (1764),
         N.Y.: Marsilio.

Wolff, Nancy
2002     Courts as therapeutic agents: Thinking past the novelty of mental health
         courts Journal of the American Academy of Psychiatry and Law
         30:431–437.

Wolff, Nancy, Dena Plemmons, Bonita Veysey, and Angela Brandli
2002     Release planning for inmates with mental illness compared with those
         who have other chronic illnesses. Psychiatric Services 53 (11):1469–1471.

# [10]

## New Wine and Old Wineskins: Four Challenges of Restorative Justice

*Daniel W. Van Ness*[**]

> *And nobody puts new wine into old wineskins;*
> *if he does, the wine will burst the skins,*
> *and the wine is lost and the skins too.*
> *No! New wine, fresh skins.*
>
> *Mark 2:22*

At the 1987 London conference on criminal law reform that led to the formation of the Society for the Reform of Criminal Law, Justice John Kelly of Australia delivered a remarkable address on the purpose of law.[1] Speaking to two hundred judges, legal scholars, and law reformers from common law countries, he laid aside his prepared comments and spoke with great feeling about the need for criminal law practitioners to see themselves as healers. A purpose of criminal law, he

[**]    Special Counsel on Criminal Justice, Prison Fellowship, Washington, D.C., U.S.A.; B.A., Wheaton College 1971; J.D., DePaul University 1975; LL.M., Georgetown University 1993. I gratefully acknowledge the assistance of Dr. Karen Strong, David Carlson, Thomas Crawford, and Dr. Daniel Dreisbach.

[1]    For a brief account of this conference, see Conference Report, *Reform of the Criminal Law*, 1 Crim. L.F. 91 (1989).

said, should be to heal the wounds caused by crime. Since "healing" is not a word frequently heard in legal gatherings, it was helpful that he illustrated what he meant.

Justice Kelly told of a case in which he had made a special effort to ensure that a rape victim felt vindicated. He had just sentenced the defendant to prison, but before calling the next case he asked the victim to approach the bench. Justice Kelly had watched the complainant throughout the proceedings, and it was clear that she was very distraught, even after the offender's conviction and sentencing. The justice spoke with her briefly and concluded with these words: "You understand that what I have done here demonstrates conclusively *that what happened was not your fault.*" The young woman began to weep as she left the court-room. When Justice Kelly called the family several days later, he learned that his words had marked the beginning of psychological healing for the victim. Her tears had been tears of healing.

The view that justice should bring about healing is, in fact, an ancient concept, one that a growing number of commentators are developing for contemporary application under the rubric of "restorative justice." Advocates of restorative justice face legal and jurisprudential challenges, among these the challenge to abolish criminal law, the challenge to rank multiple goals, the challenge to determine harm rationally, and the challenge to structure community–government coop-eration. This article will consider these four challenges in turn and suggest ways in which they might be addressed.

## ROOTS

We are used to thinking of criminal law as the means through which government prohibits criminal behavior and punishes criminals.[2] We take for granted the distinction between private and public wrongs, which separates the law of torts from criminal law, a distinction

---

[2]      *See, e.g.,* Kenneth Mann, *Punitive Civil Sanctions,* 101 Yale L.J. 1795, 1807 (1992).

ingrained in our common law tradition.[3] But there is another, older understanding of law that resists this duality, affirming that no matter how we administer the law, one of the primary goals of justice should be to restore the parties injured by crime.[4]

Early legal systems that form the foundation of Western law emphasized the need for offenders and their families to settle with victims and their families. Although crime breached the common welfare, so that the community had an interest in, and a responsibility for, addressing the wrong and punishing the offender, the offense was not considered primarily a crime against the state, as it is today. Instead, a crime was viewed principally as an offense against the victim and the victim's family.[5] This understanding was reflected in ancient legal codes from the Middle East, the Roman empire, and later European polities.[6] Each of these diverse cultures responded to what we now call

---

[3]        See, e.g., Atcheson v. Everitt, 98 Eng. Rep. 1142 (K.B. 1775), in which Lord Mansfield wrote: "Now there is no distinction better known, than the distinction between civil and criminal law; or between criminal prosecutions and civil actions." Id. at 1147.

[4]        In his highly regarded book on what he calls "primitive law," E. Adamson Hoebel wrote:

> The job [of primitive law] is to clean the case up, to suppress or penalize the illegal behavior and to bring the relations of the disputants back into balance, so that life may resume its normal course. This type of law-work has frequently been compared to work of the medical practitioner. It is family doctor stuff, essential to keeping the social body on its feet.

E. Adamson Hoebel, *The Law of Primitive Man* 279 (1968).

[5]        E.g., Marvin E. Wolfgang, *Victim Compensation in Crimes of Personal Violence*, 50 Minn. L. Rev. 223 (1965).

[6]        The Code of Hammurabi (c. 1700 B.C.) prescribed restitution for property offenses, as did the Code of Lipit-Ishtar (c. 1875 B.C.). Other Middle Eastern codes, such as the Sumerian Code of Ur-Nammu (c. 2050 B.C.) and the Code of Eshnunna (c. 1700 B.C.) required restitution even in the case of violent offenses. The Roman Law of the Twelve Tables (449 B.C.) required thieves to pay double restitution unless the property was found in their houses; in that case, treble damages were imposed; for resisting the search of their houses, they paid quadruple restitution. The Lex Salica (c. A.D. 496), the earliest existing collection of Germanic tribal laws, included restitution for

crime by requiring offenders and their families to make amends to victims and their families—not simply to insure that injured persons received restitution but also to restore community peace.[7]

This can be seen as well in the language of the Old Testament, where the word *shalom* is used to describe the ideal state in which the community should function.[8] This term signifies completeness, fulfillment, wholeness—the existence of right relationships between individuals, the community, and God.[9] Crime was understood to break *shalom*, destroying right relationships within the community and creating harmful ones. Ancient Hebrew justice, then, aimed to restore wholeness.[10] Restitution formed an essential part of this process, but restitution was not an end in itself. This is suggested by the Hebrew word for "restitution," *shillum,* which comes from the same root as *shalom* and likewise implies the reestablishment of community peace. Along with restitution came the notion of vindication of the victim and of the law itself. This concept was embodied in another word derived from the same root as both *shalom* and *shillum—shillem. Shillem* can be translated as "retribution" or "recompense," not in the sense of revenge (that word in Hebrew comes from an entirely different root) but in the sense of

---

crimes ranging from theft to homicide. The Laws of Ethelbert (c. A.D. 600), promulgated by the ruler of Kent, contain detailed restitution schedules that distinguished the values, for example, of each finger and fingernail. Daniel W. Van Ness, *Restorative Justice,* in *Criminal Justice, Restitution, and Reconciliation* 7, 7 (Burt Galaway & Joe Hudson eds., 1990).

[7]     Hoebel, *supra* note 4, at 279.

[8]     We must distinguish *shalom* from the irrational belief that the world is safe and just. Psychologist Melvin Lerner has argued that human beings need to believe that people basically get what they deserve and that the world is both safe and just, even when events suggest otherwise. This self-delusion, Lerner argues, is necessary in order for people to function in their daily lives. Melvin J. Lerner, *The Belief in a Just World* 11–15 (1980). But the Hebrew word *shalom* does not imply a delusional belief that all is well. To hold healing and *shalom* as goals for society's response to crime is to recognize that hurt and injustice do exist and that they must be healed and rectified.

[9]     G. Lloyd Carr, *Shalom,* in *Theological Wordbook of the Old Testament* 931 (R.L. Harris et al. eds., 1980).

[10]     Van Ness, *supra* note 6, at 9.

satisfaction or vindication.[11] In short, the purpose of the justice process was, through restitution and vindication, to restore a community that had been sundered by crime.

This view of justice is not confined to the far distant past. Many precolonial African societies aimed not so much at punishing criminal offenders as at resolving the consequences to their victims. Sanctions were compensatory rather than punitive, intended to restore victims to their previous position.[12] Current Japanese experience demonstrates a similar emphasis on compensation to the victim and restoration of community peace.[13] The approach (as we will see later) emphasizes a process that has been referred to as "confession, repentance and absolution."[14]

For all of its tradition, the restorative approach to criminal justice is unfamiliar to most of us today. For common law jurisdictions, the Norman invasion of Britain marked a turning point away from this understanding of crime. William the Conqueror and his successors

---

[11]      How is it that a root word meaning "wholeness and unity, a restored relationship" could produce derivatives with such varied meanings?

> The apparent diversity of meanings . . . can be accounted for in terms of the concept of *peace being restored through payment* (of tribute to a conqueror, Joshua 10:1), *restitution* (to one wronged, Exodus 21:36), *or simple payment and completion* (of a business transaction, II Kings 4:7).
> The payment of a vow (Psalms 50:14) completes an agreement so that both parties are in a state of *shalom.* Closely linked with this concept is the eschatological motif in some uses of the term. *Recompense for sin, either national or personal, must be given. Once that obligation has been met, wholeness is restored* (Isaiah 60:20, Joel 2:25).

Carr, *supra* note 9, at 931 (emphasis added).

[12]      Daniel D.N. Nsereko, Compensating Victims of Crime in Botswana (paper presented at the Society for the Reform of Criminal Law Conference on "Reform of Sentencing, Parole, and Early Release," Ottawa, Ontario, Canada, Aug. 1–4, 1988).

[13]      *See, e.g.,* Daniel H. Foote, *The Benevolent Paternalism of Japanese Criminal Justice,* 80 Cal. L. Rev. 317 (1992).

[14]      John O. Haley, *Confession, Repentance, and Absolution,* in *Mediation and Criminal Justice* 195 (Martin Wright & Burt Galaway eds., 1989).

found the legal process an effective tool for establishing the preeminence of the king over the church in secular matters, and in replacing local systems of dispute resolution.[15] The Leges Henrici, written early in the twelfth century, asserted exclusive royal jurisdiction over offenses such as theft punishable by death, counterfeiting, arson, premeditated assault, robbery, rape, abduction, and "breach of the king's peace given by his hand or writ."[16] Breach of the king's peace gave the royal house an extensive claim to jurisdiction:

> [N]owadays we do not easily conceive how the peace which lawful men ought to keep can be any other than the queen's or the commonwealth's. But the king's justice . . . was at first not ordinary but exceptional, and his power was called to aid only when other means had failed. . . . Gradually the privileges of the king's house were extended to the precinct of his court, to the army, to the regular meetings of the shire and hundred, and to the great roads. Also the king might grant special personal protection to his officers and followers; and these two kinds of privilege spread until they coalesced and covered the whole ground.[17]

Thus, the king became the paramount victim, sustaining legally acknowledged, although symbolic, damages.

Over time, the actual victim was ousted from any meaningful place in the justice process, illustrated by the redirection of reparation from the victim to the king in the form of fines.[18] A new model of

---

[15]     Harold J. Berman, *Law and Revolution* 255–56 (1983).

[16]     *Leges Henrici Primi* 109 (L.J. Downer ed. & trans., 1972).

[17]     Frederick Pollock, *English Law before the Norman Conquest,* 14 Law Q. Rev. 291, 301 (1898).

[18]     In the hands of the royal administrators after the Conquest [the king's peace] proved a dynamic concept, and, as Maitland once expressed it, eventually the King's peace swallowed up the peace of everyone else. . . . Already by the time of Bracton, in the thirteenth century, it had become common form to charge an accused in the following terms: "Whereas the said B was in the peace of

crime was emerging, with the government and the offender as the sole parties.

## RESTORATION INTO SAFE COMMUNITIES OF VICTIMS AND OFFENDERS WHO HAVE RESOLVED THEIR CONFLICTS

Criminal justice policy today is preoccupied with maintaining security—public order—while trying to balance the offender's rights and the government's power. These are, of course, vital concerns, but a restorative perspective on justice suggests that fairness and order should be only part of society's response to crime.

And, in fact, other emphases have emerged. These include restitution,[19] victim's rights,[20] rehabilitation,[21] victim–offender reconciliation,[22] community crime prevention,[23] and volunteer-based services for offenders and victims.[24] Some of these movements incorporate proposals

---

God and of our lord the King, there came the said N, feloniously as a felon," etc.

George W. Keeton, *The Norman Conquest and the Common Law* 175 (1966).

[19]     *See* Charles F. Abel & Frank A. Marsh, *Punishment and Restitution* (1984); *Criminal Justice, Restitution, and Reconciliation, supra* note 6; Stephen Schafer, *Compensation and Restitution to Victims of Crime* (1970).

[20]     *See From Crime Policy to Victim Policy* (Ezzat A. Fattah ed., 1983); President's Task Force on Victims of Crime, *Final Report* (1982); Steven Rathgeb Smith & Susan Freinkel, *Adjusting the Balance: Federal Policy and Victim Services* (1988).

[21]     *See* Francis T. Cullen & Karen E. Gilbert, *Reaffirming Rehabilitation* (1982).

[22]     *See Criminal Justice, Restitution, and Reconciliation, supra* note 6; *Criminology as Peacemaking* (Harold E. Pepinsky & Richard Quinney eds., 1991); *Mediation and Criminal Justice, supra* note 14.

[23]     *See* Judith Feins et al., *Partnerships for Neighborhood Crime Prevention* (1983); Richard Neely, *Take Back Your Neighborhood* (1990); Wesley G. Skogan & Michael G. Maxfield, *Coping with Crime* (1981).

[24]     *See* Marie Buckley, *Breaking into Prison: A Citizen Guide to Volunteer Action* (1974); M.L. Gill & R.I. Mawby, *Volunteers in the Criminal Justice System: A*

for systemic change, but for others the criminal justice system is basically irrelevant other than to provide a framework in which (or around which) the programs can function. In any event, the current system's limitations of vision and of participants have begun to be addressed at least in piecemeal fashion.

Some writers have suggested a more comprehensive approach that combines many of these alternatives and that not only recognizes the wisdom of the ancient model but also seeks to apply that wisdom to the present realities of criminal justice. This effort has been championed by legal scholars and criminologists,[25] victim–offender reconciliation practitioners,[26] and adherents of various philosophical, political, and religious perspectives.[27] Several have called this approach "restorative justice"[28]—the overall purpose of which is the restoration into safe communities of victims and offenders who have resolved their conflicts.[29]

---

*Comparative Study of Probation, Police, and Victim Support* (1990); R.I. Mawby & M.L. Gill, *Crime Victims* (1987).

[25]        *E.g.*, Haley, *supra* note 14, at 195; Martin Wright, *Justice for Victims and Offenders* (1991).

[26]        *E.g.*, *Mediation and Criminal Justice, supra* note 14; Mark Umbreit, *Crime and Reconciliation* (1985); Howard Zehr, *Changing Lenses: A New Focus for Crime and Justice* (1990).

[27]        *E.g.*, Wesley Cragg, *The Practice of Punishment* (1992); Daniel W. Van Ness, *Crime and Its Victims* (1986); M. Kay Harris, *Moving into the New Millennium: Toward a Feminist Vision of Justice,* 67(2) Prison J. 27 (1987); Virginia Mackey, Restorative Justice (discussion paper available from the Presbyterian Criminal Justice Program, Lexington, Kentucky, United States, 1990).

[28]        The term "restorative justice" was probably coined by Albert Eglash, *Beyond Restitution,* in *Restitution in Criminal Justice* 91, 92 (Joe Hudson & Burt Galaway eds., 1977), where he suggested that there are three types of criminal justice: retributive justice based on punishment, distributive justice based on therapeutic treatment of offenders, and restorative justice based on restitution. Both the punishment and the treatment model, he noted, focus on the actions of offenders, deny victim participation in the justice process, and require merely passive participation by the offender. Restorative justice focuses instead on the harmful effects of offenders' actions and actively involves victims and offenders in the process of reparation and rehabilitation.

[29]        They have expressed this in different ways. Zehr, *supra* note 26, at 178–81, analogizes to a camera lens and suggests that there are two alternative lenses: retributive

The restorative model seeks to respond to crime at both the macro and the micro level—addressing the need for building safe communities as well as the need for resolving specific crimes.

How might a system of restorative justice achieve its goals? In what ways would such a system differ from current criminal justice practice? While this article is not intended to explore these questions exhaustively, several general comments can be made. First, restorative justice advocates view crime as more than simply lawbreaking, an offense against governmental authority; crime is understood also to cause multiple injuries to victims, the community, and even the offender.[30] Second, proponents argue that the overarching purpose of the criminal justice *process* should be to repair those injuries.[31] Third, restorative justice advocates protest the civil government's apparent monopoly over society's response to crime. Victims, offenders, and their communities also must be involved at the earliest point and to the fullest extent possible. This suggests a collaborative effort, with civil government responsible for maintaining a basic framework of order, and the other parties responsible for restoring community peace and harmony. The work of civil government must be done in such a way that community

---

justice and restorative justice. With regard to restorative justice, he explains that "[c]rime is a violation of people and relationships. It creates obligations to make things right. Justice involves the victim, the offender, and the community in a search for solutions which promote repair, reconciliation, and reassurance." *Id.* at 181.

　　　Cragg, *supra* note 27, at 203, describes restorative justice as a process of "resolving conflicts in a manner that reduces recourse to the justified use of force."

　　　Wright, *supra* note 25, agrees. The new model is one

> in which the response to crime would be, not to add to the harm caused, by imposing further harm on the offender, but to do as much as possible to restore the situation. The community offers aid to the victim; the offender is held accountable and required to make reparation. Attention would be given not only to the *outcome,* but also to evolving a *process* that respected the feelings and humanity of both the victim and the offender.

*Id.* at 112.

[30]　　　*See, e.g.,* Zehr, *supra* note 26, at 181–86.

[31]　　　*See, e.g.,* Wright, *supra* note 25, at 114–17 (proposing a system with the primary aim of restoring—or even improving—the victim's prior condition).

260                    Criminal Law Forum                    Vol. 4 No. 2

building is enhanced, or at least not hampered.[32]

The focus of restorative justice, then, is intentionally holistic. In a restorative paradigm, criminal justice is not merely a contest between the defendant and the state. Criminal justice must take into account, too, the rights and responsibilities of the victim and the community, as well as the injuries sustained by victim, offender, and community.

## CHALLENGES

Ultimately, whole new institutional structures are likely to emerge from the restorative approach, just as the rehabilitation model gave birth to penitentiaries, probation and parole systems, and juvenile courts,[33] and as the just deserts model of fairness in sentencing gave rise to determinate sentences and sentencing guidelines.[34] One such initiative is victim–offender reconciliation, which permits these two parties to meet with a trained mediator to discuss the crime and its aftermath and to develop a strategy to "make things right."[35]

There is great value in model programs such as victim–offender reconciliation: they explore new horizons in criminal justice theory, and they provide data with which to evaluate and modify not only the programs but the theory behind them as well.[36] But more than models is needed—there is a continuing need for analytical precision in understanding the new vision, articulating purposes and outcomes, developing

---

[32]      *See* section *infra* entitled "The Challenge to Structure Community–Government Cooperation."

[33]      *See* Edgardo Rotman, *Beyond Punishment* 21–57 (1990).

[34]      *See* Dean J. Spader, *Megatrends in Criminal Justice Theory*, 13 Am. J. Crim. L. 157, 180–95 (1986).

[35]      For an excellent description of victim–offender reconciliation programs, see Zehr, *supra* note 26, at 158–74.

[36]      This phenomenon has been aptly described as "theory overtaking practice" in Wright, *supra* note 25, at 41–45.

strategies for accomplishing those purposes, and evaluating results.[37]

Legal scholars and jurists can offer an invaluable service here, since a number of legal and jurisprudential challenges to criminal law and procedure are raised by the suggestion that a fundamental purpose of criminal justice should be to promote restoration of those touched by crime. This article examines four such challenges: (1) the challenge to abolish criminal law, (2) the challenge to rank multiple goals, (3) the challenge to determine harm rationally, and (4) the challenge to structure community–government cooperation.

## The Challenge to Abolish Criminal Law

Currently, both the criminal law and the civil law of torts deal with intentional behavior by one person that violates the rights of another. In criminal cases, the offender is prosecuted by an agent of the government and punished; to convict, the prosecutor must prove the offender guilty beyond a reasonable doubt. In tort cases, the defendant–offender is sued by the plaintiff–victim and is required to pay damages or otherwise make right the harm done; the plaintiff must prove the defendant liable by a preponderance of the evidence.[38] But since the underlying harmful action is basically the same in criminal and tort cases, why are the two treated differently? The answer most often given is that while civil cases are concerned with the violation of individual rights, criminal cases are concerned with broader societal rights; criminal cases should not be initiated by victims, since vindication of public policy should not depend on an individual victim's decision to institute legal proceedings.[39]

---

[37]    It must be remembered that criminal justice history is filled with visionary people whose visions failed to be realized because they neglected to engage in the requisite analytical work. This phenomenon is neatly summarized in the title of Blake McKelvey's *American Prisons: A History of Good Intentions* (1977).

[38]    For an excellent discussion of the distinctions between what he calls the criminal justice and the civil justice "paradigm," see Mann, *supra* note 2, at 1803–13.

[39]    *But see id.* at 1812 n.61, where Mann argues that while this is the conventional argument for the paradigmatic distinction between criminal and civil justice, the practical

But as we have seen, excluding victims' interests from criminal cases is a relatively recent development. How does the emphasis in restorative justice on repairing the damage caused by crime affect our understanding of criminal law? Should a separate criminal law be maintained?

Randy Barnett and John Hagel, early proponents of restitution as a new paradigm of criminal justice, have argued for what would effectively be the end of criminal law, replacing it with the civil law of torts:

> A specific action is defined as criminal within the context of this theory only if it violates the right of one or more identifiable individuals to person and property. These individuals are the victims of the criminal act, and only the victims, by virtue of the past infringement of their rights, acquire the right to demand restitution from the criminal.
>
> This is not to deny that criminal acts frequently have harmful effects upon other individuals besides the actual victims. All that is denied is that a harmful "effect," absent a specific infringement of rights, may vest rights in a third party.[40]

Barnett and Hagel define crime by examining not the offender's behavior but the victim's rights, particularly "the fundamental right of all individuals to be free in their person and property from the initiated use of force by others."[41] They agree that there may be broader social goals but argue that settling the private dispute will "vindicate the rights of the aggrieved party and thereby vindicate the rights of all persons."[42] Barnett and Hagel conclude that, among other things, this means there can be

---

distinction is blurred by RICO statutes, which authorize private prosecution, and by SEC actions, in which the government is authorized to seek compensation for private individuals.

[40]      Randy E. Barnett & John Hagel, *Assessing the Criminal*, in *Assessing the Criminal: Restitution, Retribution, and the Legal Process* 1, 15 (Randy E. Barnett & John Hagel eds., 1977).

[41]      *Id.* at 11.

[42]      *Id.* at 25.

no "victimless crimes."

But vindicating the rights of direct victims does not vindicate the rights of all other persons. Though the injuries are not easy to quantify, *secondary victims* are also injured by crime:

> [C]rime imposes three distinct kinds of costs on its indirect victims. There are, first, the *avoidance costs* that are incurred by anyone who takes steps to minimize his chances of becoming the direct victim of crime. Installing locks and burglar alarms, avoiding unsafe areas, and paying for police protection, whether private or public, all fall into this category. Indirect victims may also have to pay *insurance costs*—costs that increase as the rate of crime in an area increases. And, finally, "as crime gives rise to fear, apprehension, insecurity, and social divisiveness," indirect victims are forced to bear the *attitudinal costs* of crime.[43]

Interestingly, these costs directly affect the right to be free in person and property that Barnett and Hagel espouse. This suggests that the first rationale for maintaining criminal law is that civil law fails adequately to vindicate the rights of secondary victims.

Second, criminal law offers more than vindication of individual rights. It also provides a controlled mechanism for dealing with those accused of crossing the boundaries of socially tolerable behavior. In a thoughtful and disturbing essay entitled "Retributive Hatred," Jeffrie Murphy notes that crime arouses "feelings of anger, resentment, and even hatred . . . toward wrongdoers."[44] He argues that criminal justice should restrain these feelings. "Rational and moral beings . . . want a world, not utterly free of retributive hatred, but one where this passion is both respected and seen as potentially dangerous, as in great need of reflective

---

[43]     Richard Dagger, *Restitution, Punishment, and Debts to Society*, in *Victims, Offenders, and Alternative Sanctions* 3, 4 (Joe Hudson & Burt Galaway eds., 1980) (citations omitted).

[44]     Jeffrie G. Murphy, Retributive Hatred: An Essay on Criminal Liability and the Emotions 2 (paper presented at a conference on "Liability in Law and Morals," Bowling Green State University, Bowling Green, Ohio, United States, Apr. 15–17, 1988).

and institutional restraint."[45] While one may argue with his description of the desires of "rational and moral beings," few would dispute that the retributive impulse must be restrained.

Third, there are procedural advantages to governmentally prosecuted criminal cases. The experience of European countries that permit varying degrees of victim participation in the prosecution of criminal cases bears this out.[46] The victim typically lacks the expertise, financial resources, and time to prosecute. Furthermore, the goals of consistency, fairness, and efficiency can best be pursued by coordinated governmental action, since public prosecutors can weigh decisions in light of stated policies and rely on the help of investigatory agencies. Moreover, prosecutors are presumably less influenced than are victims by personal motivations such as revenge.[47]

In summary, maintaining the criminal law is desirable inasmuch as it provides an effective method of vindicating the rights of secondary victims, it restrains and channels in acceptable ways retributive emotions in society, and it offers procedural efficiencies in enforcing public values.

### The Challenge to Rank Multiple Goals

Given that the overall purpose of restorative justice is to resist crime by building safe and strong communities, this goal can be achieved only when multiple parties (victims, offenders, communities, and governments) pursue multiple goals (recompense, vindication, reconciliation, reintegration, atonement, and so forth). Is it possible for so many parties

---

[45]     *Id.* at 31.

[46]     *See, e.g.,* Matti Joutsen, *Listening to the Victim: The Victim's Role in European Criminal Justice Systems,* 34 Wayne L. Rev. 95 (1987).

[47]     *But see* Abraham S. Goldstein, *Defining the Role of the Victim in Criminal Prosecution,* 52 Miss. L.J. 515, 555 (1982). Governmental prosecution of offenses also has its limitations: the prosecutor administers an agency of government with its own administrative, political, investigative, and adjudicative objectives, any of which can lead prosecutors to focus less on a just resolution of the particular case and more on the effective use of limited resources. In addition, political forces may lead prosecutors to cater to, rather than restrain, retributive impulses in the community.

to pursue so many goals in such a way as to achieve restoration?

The current criminal justice system faces the challenge of balancing multiple goals,[48] usually expressed as deterrence, incapacitation, rehabilitation, and retribution (desert). The first two can be classified as utilitarian, with the focus on crime control. The third can either be similarly classified or be justified as a social value in and of itself. The last limits the nature and extent of the sentence, emphasizing proportionality. Paul Robinson has suggested that the attempt to pursue these four goals raises questions at two levels. First, does any one of them (such as crime control or proportionality) take precedence as an overarching goal of criminal justice? Second, which of the goals have priority when they cannot all be accommodated (when, for example, rehabilitation is prevented by a sentence sufficiently harsh to deter others)?[49]

At first glance, this confusion appears to grow geometrically under the restorative justice model, which adds such goals as recompense and vindication. But, in fact, the more holistic perspective of restorative justice may actually help society successfully manage multiple goals because it identifies restoration as the overarching goal of criminal justice.

How can the goals of deterrence, incapacitation, rehabilitation, and retribution be organized so that they help achieve the overarching purpose of restoration? Robinson, a former member of the U.S. Sentencing Commission, has explored approaches that permit multiple goals to interact with each other in a principled and consistent way. He proposes that a first step is to clarify which goals *determine* the sentence and which simply *limit* the nature or duration of the sentence.[50] A "determining goal" requires that certain features be included in the sentence; it recommends a sentence. A "limiting goal," in contrast, requires that certain features be excluded.[51] So, for example, rehabilitation as a determining goal might produce a recommendation of an indefinite period of treatment, whereas desert as a limiting goal would

---

[48]    Paul H. Robinson, *Hybrid Principles for the Distribution of Criminal Sanctions,* 82 Nw. U. L. Rev. 19 (1987).

[49]    *Id.* at 25–28.

[50]    *Id.* at 29–31.

[51]    *Id.*

266                    Criminal Law Forum                    Vol. 4 No. 2

establish maximum and minimum periods of time.

Although this approach was designed to rank sentencing purposes under the current paradigm, it could be adapted by restorative justice advocates. For example, with regard to specific crimes, the determining goal of the criminal justice process would be resolution of the conflict; community safety would be a limiting goal only. This means that restitution would be presumed and that sentences providing for incarceration, which effectively precludes or substantially delays restitution (since most offenders are impoverished and few prison industry programs exist), should be used solely as a last resort. Any social controls imposed on the offender should not unduly obstruct the determining goal of resolution.

Likewise, with reference to crime as a community phenomenon, the determining goal of the community and the government would be safety, with specific strategies limited by the need appropriately to resolve individual crimes when they occur. Similar analysis is needed in considering the other subsidiary goals: recompense and redress through the formal criminal justice system; rehabilitation and reconciliation through community-based programs. The challenge is to prioritize restorative outcomes over procedural goals. The test of any response to crime must be whether it is helping to restore the injured parties.

### The Challenge to Determine Harm Rationally

The current paradigm of criminal justice gives scant attention to the harm resulting from the offense and focuses instead on the offender's actions and state of mind. The extent of harm to victims and their neighbors is, with some exceptions, ignored. When this form of injury is considered in offenses such as theft, it is only to establish the seriousness of the crime (misdemeanor versus felony), and the inquiry is typically limited to whether the property was worth more or less than a specific statutory amount.[52] Under recent sentencing and parole guidelines, the extent of harm also has been considered to determine the

---

[52]     *See, e.g.,* Ill. Ann. Stat. ch. 720, § 5/16-1(b) (1993) (providing that theft of property under $300 is a misdemeanor, and over that amount a felony).

length or severity of the sentence,[53] but again the categories are broad and general, and typically they are used to determine the amount of punishment as opposed to the amount of reparation.

In a restorative justice model, however, victim reparation is a determining goal. Consequently, calculating the amount of loss sustained by victims assumes great importance; to do such calculations, there must first be clarity about the kinds and extent of harms to be considered. This means that three categories of issue will need to be addressed: the kinds of victim to be reimbursed, how harms should be quantified, and how questions of disparity should be addressed.

## WHAT KINDS OF VICTIMS SHOULD BE REIMBURSED?

Most people would intuitively define the victim as the person directly harmed by the offense—the person whose house was burglarized, for example. That person is certainly the primary victim. But others are also affected adversely by crime. Family members and neighbors may suffer increased fear, as well as direct and indirect financial costs. The criminal justice system (and the community as well) may be called on to expend resources. An employer may lose money because of the absence of a victim who is at court or in the hospital. And so on.

Which victims should be considered for reparation? The answer to this question may vary depending on the offense. For example, immediate family members of a homicide victim might be made eligible to recover the costs of psychiatric counseling, while members of a theft victim's family might not. But at a minimum, two groups of victims should always be eligible for restitution: the direct victim and the community, with the direct victim having priority over all secondary victims, including the community.

Alan Harland and Cathryn Rosen have made an excellent case for differentiating direct victims from their communities and, therefore, for treating restitution differently from community service:

> [U]nlike victim restitution that is based upon (and limited by) a case-by-case determination of victim injuries, the "harms" on

---

[53]     E.g., Albert W. Alschuler, *The Failure of Sentencing Guidelines*, 58 U. Chi. L. Rev. 901, 908–15 (1991).

which the offender's community service liability is predicated are far less specific, and the metric against which the amount of service owed is assessed tends to be no less arbitrary than the amount of a fine, probation, incarceration, or any other penal rather than compensatory sanction . . . . [I]t is perhaps not unreasonable to question whether community service has any claim at all to be part of the presumptive norm of restitution, and to ask why it is useful to continue to treat the two sanctions as merely different examples of a uniform concept.[54]

Harland and Rosen are right on all counts. But while this does not necessarily preclude the use of community service as a form of reparative sanction, it does require that we clarify the nature and extent of the harm done to the community, as well as the most appropriate means for the offender to repair that harm.

### HOW DO WE QUANTIFY THE HARM THAT SHOULD BE REPAIRED?

While society incurs indirect costs as a result of crime, it is impossible to quantify with absolute accuracy the indirect costs related to a particular crime. But it is reasonable and necessary to make an effort at approximating these costs. Here the concept of "rough equivalences" developed by Norval Morris and Michael Tonry might be helpful.[55] They argue that pure equivalence between similar offenders is neither possible nor desirable. Instead, Morris and Tonry propose that the ideal should be to achieve "a rough equivalence of punishment that will allow room for the principled distribution of punishments on utilitarian grounds, unfettered by the miserable aim of making suffering equally painful."[56]

A similar approach could be taken in relating reparative sentences to levels of harm. While Harland and Rosen are right that such a system

---

[54] Alan T. Harland & Cathryn J. Rosen, *Impediments to the Recovery of Restitution by Crime Victims,* 5(2) Violence & Victims 127, 132 (1990).

[55] Norval Morris & Michael H. Tonry, *Between Prison and Probation: Intermediate Punishments in a Rational Sentencing System* (1990).

[56] *Id.* at 31.

is more arbitrary than case-by-case restitution, it is certainly less arbitrary than current, entirely punitive sanctions.   Criteria must be established and applied uniformly throughout the entire sentencing structure within a jurisdiction.   Great Britain did this several years ago by devising guidelines for restitution.   Ironically, they look a great deal like the Anglo-Saxon King Ethelbert's restitution schedules promulgated fourteen hundred years ago:

> Under guidelines sent to the country's 27,710 magistrates, attackers can be forced . . . to compensate their victims by the punch.   Sample penalties:   $84 for a simple graze, $168 for a black eye, $1,428 for a broken nose, $2,940 for a fractured jaw, and as much as $13,440 for a serious facial scar.   Said Home Office Minister John Patten:   "I am anxious that the victims get a better deal."[57]

Two things should be noted about the modern British approach:   it restricts compensable harms to direct victims and it uses rough equivalences for the amount of restitution to be ordered.

  While it is neither feasible nor, perhaps, desirable to attach monetary values to every conceivable type of harm, a serious effort to grapple with the issue is necessary.   Otherwise, types and amounts of reparation may be simply arbitrary and no different in nature from the abstract "fine," except for who receives the money.   If victims are to be paid back, and if offenders are to see their reparation as linked to the specific harm done, then restitution, like community service, should be as closely related to the particular injury as possible.

### How Do We Avoid Unwarranted Disparity?

This leads us directly into the question of disparity—whether particular offenders or victims will receive orders for restitution that are not comparable to those given to other offenders or victims.   Disparity can happen in several ways.

---

[57]      *World Notes:  Socking It to the Bad Guys,* Time, Oct. 3, 1988, at 43; *see* Home Office Circ. No. 85/1988; Magistrates' Ass'n of England and Wales, *Sentencing Guidelines* at iv (1992).

First, if each offender is sentenced according to the type of offense alone, the restitution order may fail to reflect the actual harm caused, because similar offenders committing similar crimes can bring about dramatically different injuries. Consider two burglaries in which a vase is stolen—if one is from a five-and-ten-cent store while the other is an authentic Ming, treating the offenders alike because their actions were similar would have a disparate effect on the two victims.

Second, if each offender is sentenced according only to the actual harm caused, then similar illegal conduct may result in dramatically different sentences. In the preceding example, the offender who stole the Ming vase could take years to repay the victim, while replacing the dime-store vase would be a matter of days or hours. Both victims and offenders would therefore receive significantly different treatment.

Finally, differing circumstances on the part of victims and offenders may lead to a disparate effect even when the offense and the financial loss are the same. Wealthy offenders may be able to complete their sentences simply by writing a check, while impoverished offenders may have to work long and hard to satisfy the judgment. Similarly, wealthy victims may have far less trouble recovering from crime than those who are without adequate financial resources.

Of course, not all disparity is wrong, nor is it possible to avoid it entirely. However, justice requires that victims and offenders be treated consistently, and that as much as possible outcomes not fall more heavily on some than on others for social, economic, or political reasons.

The earlier discussion on balancing multiple goals may offer guidance here. Should the emphasis be on *consistency* in dealing with offenders' actions or on victims' *harms?* This question calls for a prioritization of goals. Since restoration is the determining goal, the issue of fairness becomes a limiting goal.[58] Therefore, in a restorative justice system, guidelines outlining minimum and maximum amounts of restitution might be established for particular offenses. These would be related to typical losses of primary and secondary victims. If an agreement were not reached through negotiation, victims would present evidence of their actual losses to the sentencing judge, who would then

---

[58]     In the United States, it is likely that constitutional provisions requiring equal protection and prohibiting cruel and unusual punishment would yield this result.

set an amount within the pertinent range.[59]  If the actual loss were less than the minimum established, the victim would receive only the actual loss, and the balance would be set aside into a victim compensation fund for those victims whose loss exceeded the range.

A similar approach might help address the issue of economic imbalance between otherwise comparable offenders.  The Swedish "day fine" approach, which bases the sanction on the offender's daily wages, multiplied by a figure that represents the seriousness of the offense, could be adopted here as well.[60]  Once again, the determining goal would be reparation to the victim, and fairness would be a limiting goal.  Under this approach, one offender might actually be ordered to pay less than the indicated amount of restitution, with the balance made up from a compensation fund; another offender might be required to pay more, with the excess going into that fund.

### The Challenge to Structure Community–Government Cooperation

Under restorative justice, it is argued, civil government and the community cooperate both in enabling the victim and the offender to resolve the crime successfully and in building safe communities.  Is this kind of cooperation feasible?  Two concerns have been raised in this connection.

First, can community-based programs be linked with agencies of the criminal system without losing their restorative values?  This concern has been sparked by the experience of some reconciliation and mediation programs in the United States and England, which started with visionary objectives and then found those goals being redirected by a much larger criminal justice system with its own—and different—vision.  For example, a reconciliation program may begin to be measured by the *number* of offenders it diverts from prison, rather than by the peacemak-

---

[59]      "[G]iving offenders opportunities to demonstrate a willingness to accept responsibility for their offences is not incompatible with treating like cases alike and assuring that sentences arrived at reflect in appropriate ways the gravity of the offences committed."  Cragg, *supra* note 27, at 216.

[60]      Martin Wright, *Making Good: Prisons, Punishment, and Beyond* 87–88 (1982).

272                    Criminal Law Forum              Vol. 4 No. 2

ing results of the mediation.[61]

Howard Zehr, a pioneer in reconciliation program development, has suggested three reasons that dependence on the criminal justice system can distort the vision of such programs: the criminal justice system's interests are retributive not restorative; its orientation is with the offender not the victim; and its inclination when challenged is self-preservation.[62] To these could be added the observation that the procedures of traditional criminal justice systems are coercive, which tends to mitigate against reconciliation or mediation.[63]

A second concern is that community–government collaboration will result in expanded state control. This is the well-known problem of net widening, and it happens in subtle ways.[64] Suppose, for example, that to develop credibility a community-based diversion program agrees to accept referrals of minor offenses from the local court. The court may respond by referring cases that are so minor they would have been dismissed otherwise. If offenders who fail to comply with the reconciliation agreement are then brought back before the judge and sentenced to jail or prison, the unintended effect of this arrangement, which was designed to be an *alternative* to incarceration, may actually be that more offenders are locked up.[65]

---

[61]      Zehr, *supra* note 26, at 232–36.

[62]      Dependence on the criminal justice system is one of three forces that Zehr argues can lead to distortion of vision; the other two are nongovernmental. They include the "dynamics of institutionalization"—such as the need for easily quantified and achieved administrative goals and measurements to justify the organization's existence; the tendency for programs to take on the values of their funding sources; differences between the goals of leaders and staff; and the difficulty of building "prophetic" functions into the organization's structure. The second of these is the design and operation of the program. If goal conflicts are not identified and resolved early on, they carry the potential of diverting the organization from a visionary mission. A succession of seemingly small policy decisions may change the long-range direction of the organization. *Id.* at 233–35.

[63]      Cragg, *supra* note 27, at 199.

[64]      *See, e.g.,* Thomas G. Blomberg, *Widening the Net: An Anomaly in the Evaluation of Diversion Programs,* in *Handbook of Criminal Justice Evaluation* 572 (Malcolm W. Klein & Katherine S. Teilmann eds., 1980).

[65]      *See, e.g.,* Christa Pelikan, *Conflict Resolution between Victims and Offenders in Austria and in the Federal Republic of Germany,* in *Crime in Europe* 151, 164–65 (Frances

But government does not exist apart from society; it is part of society, with specific powers and interests. This observation suggests that community–government cooperation must be fluid and dynamic in keeping with the nature of society itself. And it permits us to draw certain conclusions about what can make the cooperation effective. First, such an undertaking requires that both parties share the same overarching goal, and not just *any* goal. It is likely even now that government and community share the common goal of security. If the mutual goal is to be restoration of the victim, as well as of community safety, then a significant political and public education campaign lies ahead. This is true in the community, as well as in the governmental sphere.

Second, influence flows both ways. Thus, community programs themselves have affected the structure and the goals of the criminal justice system. Peter Kratcoski has outlined a pattern of evolving volunteer activity in criminal justice. At the outset, private groups set up new programs. These programs then have to turn to government assistance when services outstrip existing private resources. At some point, however, the government begins to underwrite the program fully, using volunteers to fill in gaps.[66] An example is the probation system, which grew out of a volunteer program initiated by John Augustus in 1842. Eventually the program was absorbed into the criminal justice system, but with a continuing mission to help offenders.[67]

Third, although government and community must seek the same overarching goal, they also play different roles not only in responding to individual offenders and victims but also in establishing community safety. Both of these objectives must be pursued with equal vigor.

---

Heidensohn & Martin Farrell eds., 1991). Pelikan describes a pilot program in which prosecutors were granted discretionary authority to divert juvenile offenders into a mediation program, as well as the steps taken to avoid net widening.

[66]     Peter C. Kratcoski, *Volunteers in Corrections,* 46(2) Fed. Probation 30 (1982).

[67]     A report several years ago from the Missouri Probation and Parole Department stated that it viewed its mission as helping the community determine its goals for offenders under supervision and then helping the community achieve them. On this program, see Steve German, *Knowledge Is Not Enough: Addressing Client Needs in Probation and Parole,* in *Community Corrections* 15, 17 (Amer. Correctional Ass'n 1981).

While the obstacles to accomplishing this collaboration are daunting, we can be encouraged by reports from Japan. According to John Haley, criminal justice in that nation operates on two tracks. One is similar to the formal criminal justice system found in Western nations:

> Paralleling the formal process, however, is a second track to which there is no Western analogue. A pattern of confession, repentance and absolution dominates each stage of law enforcement in Japan. The players in the process include not only the authorities in new roles but also the offender and the victim. From the initial police interrogation to the final judicial hearing on sentencing, the vast majority of those accused of criminal offenses confess, display repentance, negotiate for their victims' pardon and submit to the mercy of the authorities. In return they are treated with extraordinary leniency; they gain at least the prospect of absolution by being dropped from the formal process altogether.[68]

To illustrate this leniency, Haley notes that prosecutors proceed in only about 5 percent of all prosecutable cases. The vast majority of such cases are handled in uncontested summary proceedings in which the maximum penalty is a fine of $1,000–1,350. By the time cases have reached this point, the offender has demonstrated remorse, paid restitution, and secured the victim's pardon. Haley concludes:

> In this respect the West, not Japan, should be considered remarkable. The moral imperative of forgiveness as a response to repentance is surely as much a part of the Judeo-Christian heritage as the East Asian tradition. . . . Whatever the reason, unlike Japan Western societies failed to develop institutional props for implementing such moral commands. Instead the legal institutions and processes of Western law both reflect and reinforce societal demands for retribution and revenge.[69]

---

[68]     Haley, *supra* note 14, at 195 (citation omitted).

[69]     *Id.* at 204. Other observers have written about the distinctive role of apology and settlement in how the Japanese respond to crime. *See, e.g.,* Foote, *supra* note 13;

For a pattern like Japan's to develop in Western justice systems, victims and offenders (as well as the formal criminal justice system) will need to work together. But what if they fail to interact in the cooperative and voluntary way Haley describes? Clearly they cannot be forced to participate in community-based, informal mechanisms for repairing injuries; only the government is authorized to use this kind of force to secure participation in the criminal justice system.

Current criminal justice procedures are highly coercive for both victims and offenders. They are built on the reasonable assumption that not all defendants will willingly take part in the trial process or voluntarily complete their sentences. But they are also predicated on the assumption that not all *victims* will cooperate in the prosecution of their offenders; unwilling victims may have to be subpoenaed to testify at trial.

Restorative justice, with its emphasis on full and early participation of the parties in addressing the injuries caused by crime, places a premium on *voluntary* involvement. For offenders, this demonstrates willingness to assume responsibility for their actions. For victims, it reduces the likelihood that they will be victimized a second time by the formal or informal responses to crime. When such involvement is not forthcoming, however, what should happen? How this question is answered depends to a certain extent on whether the uncooperative party is the victim or the offender.

An uncooperative offender will need to have sufficient coercion applied to ensure participation in the criminal justice system. However, it should be the least amount of coercion necessary, and voluntary assumption of responsibility should be encouraged. Of course, there is no such thing as completely voluntary action in a coercive environment (as when an offender agrees to restitution during a victim–offender reconciliation meeting conducted before sentencing). But assumption of responsibility by the offender should be encouraged.

Victims may also choose to participate or not in the process. If they choose not to, they should be permitted to waive any rights they may have to pursue restitution as a part of the criminal case. The offender should then be required to make compensation payments to the

Hiroshi Wagatsuma & Arthur Rosett, *The Implication of Apology: Law and Culture in Japan and the United States*, 20 Law & Soc'y Rev. 461 (1986).

victim compensation fund. However, there may be situations in which the actual and potential injuries to the community may necessitate the victim's involvement in order to secure a conviction. Under such circumstances, the government should have the authority (as it does today) to subpoena the victim as a witness. Yet even this should be done in a context that will be as protective and supportive as possible, in order that the victim's participation, though coerced, will still contribute to a measure of restoration.

## CONCLUSION

Dissatisfaction with the current paradigm of criminal justice is leading to new programs with different visions. Some, such as restitution, can be incorporated into existing structures. Others, such as victim–offender reconciliation, point to a possible new approach to criminal justice—restorative justice. In some ways, restorative justice is simply a new application of an ancient vision. It is new wine from old vines. But those of us who celebrate the harvest are advised to remember the parable of new wine and old wineskins. Before we begin to pour—before we insert restorative features into familiar responses to crime—we would do well to reflect on what the consequences may be.

This article has considered four likely consequences: the challenge to abolish criminal law, the challenge to rank multiple goals, the challenge to determine harm rationally, and the challenge to structure community–government cooperation. Although each challenge is significant, I have argued that all can be effectively addressed. Indeed, they must be if criminal justice is to become—using Justice John Kelly's image—a means of healing the wounds of crime.

# [11]

## Restoration and Retribution

### Antony Duff

#### I. SEEKING RECONCILIATION

Though philosophers are as fond as other academics of confrontation, they some-times pursue a strategy of reconciliation, which seeks to resolve a controversy by dissolving the problem about which it rages. The reconciler argues that both sides are right in the important aspects of what they claim, but wrong to think that they must disagree if they are to maintain what matters to them: they are wrong, that is, on the very issue on which they agree—that their positions are incompatible.[1]

This paper seeks such a reconciliation in relation to the controversy over 'restorative' and 'retributive' justice. Advocates of 'restorative justice' argue that our responses to crime should seek restoration: we must therefore eschew retri-bution and punishment, since they preclude restoration. On the other side, advo-cates of punishment argue that the primary state response to crime should be to punish offenders in accordance with their deserts: 'restoration' should therefore not be the primary aim, since restoration precludes punishment, and is liable to be inconsistent with the values (justice, proportionality and fairness) which are central to punishment. Thus, it seems, we must choose between 'restorative' and 'retributive' justice,[2] or between the 'punishment paradigm' and the 'restorative paradigm' (Ashworth, 1993).

I will argue that restorative theorists are right to insist that our responses to crime should seek 'restoration', whilst retributive theorists are right to argue that we should seek to bring offenders to suffer the punishments they deserve; but that both sides to the controversy are wrong to suppose that these aims are incom-patible. Restoration is not only compatible with retribution: it *requires* retribu-tion, in that the kind of restoration that crime makes necessary can (given certain deep features of our social lives) be brought about only through retributive pun-ishment (see also Daly, 2000).

---

[1] A good example of this strategy is the compatabilist attempt to reconcile free will with deter-minism: see Watson, 1982.

[2] See eg Christie, 1981: 11; Marshall, 1988: 47–8; Zehr, 1990: 178–81; Walgrave, 1994: 57, and in this volume; Dignan, 1999: 54, 60; Braithwaite, 1999: 60, and in this volume. For further references and apt criticism, see Daly and Immarigeon, 1998: 32–34.

**44**   *Antony Duff*

There are of course genuine contrasts that connect to the supposed contrast between 'restorative' and 'retributive' justice: most obviously, there are sharp contrasts between what goes on in the kinds of programmes that are formally labelled as 'restorative', and what goes on, under the name of punishment, in our criminal justice systems. Advocates of each species of justice also often hold *conceptions* of 'restoration', 'retribution' and 'punishment' given which the pursuit of one does preclude the pursuit of the other. I will argue, however, that those conceptions are inadequate, and that more plausible conceptions will enable us to see how retributive punishment is the appropriate way of achieving the kind of restoration that crime makes necessary.

This argument lays me open to attack from both sides. Advocates of 'restorative justice' might accuse me of a punitive obsession which blinds me to the non-punitive possibilities of restorative processes; and advocates of punishment might accuse me of abandoning the central principles of penal justice. I do not expect to persuade committed advocates of either position that they are wrong: but I hope at least to show that there is an alternative.

## II. 'RESTORATION' AND 'RETRIBUTION'

To understand what 'restorative justice' could be, we must ask what is to be restored, to and by whom, when a crime has been committed. To see how it can require 'retributive justice', we must also ask what 'retribution' can amount to.

Restorative justice is 'a process whereby parties with a stake in a specific offence collectively resolve how to deal with the aftermath of the offence and its implications for the future' (Marshall, 1999: 5). Its purpose 'is the restoration into safe communities of victims and offenders who have resolved their conflicts' (Van Ness, 1993: 258). The vagueness of these definitions is inevitable, given the diversity of the 'restorative justice' movement (see Van Ness, this volume): but we must ask what it is about the 'aftermath' and 'implications' of an offence that the parties must 'deal with'—and what would constitute success or failure in dealing with it; what these 'conflicts' involve, and how they can be 'resolved'.

Crimes typically cause various kinds of 'harm' which we might then seek to 'repair'. The simplest case is that of material harm: someone's property is destroyed or damaged or stolen. Three features of this case should be noted. Firstly, such harm can usually be fully repaired: the property can be returned, or the damage made good, or a functionally equivalent replacement provided. Secondly, the harm can be understood as a harm independently of its causation by a criminal action: the same harm could be caused by an innocent action, or by natural causes (see Feinberg, 1984: 31). Thirdly, the harm could in principle be repaired by anyone—by the victim, by other people, by the state, or by the offender. It is just that the offender should pay for the repair if she has the resources to do so, since she culpably caused the harm[3]: but it could be adequately provided by anyone.

Of course, even in property crimes matters are not typically that simple: the 'harm' done is not limited to material damage to or loss of replaceable property. The property itself might not be reparable or replaceable: if the watch I inherited from my father is lost, a new watch cannot fully replace it. The victim might suffer psychological effects—anger, anxiety, loss of trust—which typically depend on how the harm occurred: the psychological effects of (what is perceived as) a crime typically differ from those of naturally caused harm. Such effects can spread beyond the immediate victim: his intimates might be distressed and angered on his behalf; those who know about the crime might be rendered anxious lest they become victims. We can also begin to talk here (as restorative theorists often talk) of damage to relationships: to the relationship between victim and offender, or between offender and wider community. We will need to look more carefully at the character of such 'damage', however, in particular at the question of whether it can be understood in empirical terms: is it just a matter of how the people concerned are now disposed to feel about and behave towards each other?

These points become even more obvious when we move from property crimes to other kinds of crime—especially those involving attacks on the person; the three features which characterised the case of simple material harm are no longer clearly present.

Firstly, it becomes less clear what, if anything, could count as 'fully repairing' the harm. This is true even when the crime causes a harm which can be identified as such independently of its criminal causation (a physical injury caused by an assault, for instance). Of course, many physical injuries can be repaired without long term physical effects: but some cannot; and even with those that can, it is not clear that their 'repair' can (as the repair or restoration of property can) make it as if they had never occurred. It is even more clearly true when we look at other kinds of harm—for instance the emotional distress caused to victims of criminal attacks. The victims of such harms might still be offered, and accept, financial compensation: but we need to explain the sense in which money could 'repair' these kinds of harm, since it cannot repair them in the straightforward way in which it can repair financial loss or loss of functional property.

Secondly, it becomes harder, if not impossible, to identify the harm independently of the crime that caused it. Such independent identification is doubtful even when it seems possible: it is at least arguable that one whose property is stolen, or who is physically attacked, suffers a *different* harm from that suffered by one who simply loses her property or suffers a natural injury—the harm of being stolen from, or of being wrongfully attacked (see Duff, 2002). But it becomes more clearly impossible in other cases. If we are to understand the harm suffered by a

---

[3] Which is how tort law would decide the matter, see Ripstein, 1999.

46   *Antony Duff*

rape victim, for instance, or by someone who is burgled, we might see it as manifest in their psychological distress: but to understand that we must understand it
as a response to the wrong that they suffered. The same is true of damage to
relationships: even if we focus on the way in which the people concerned are now
disposed to feel about and behave towards each other, we can understand those
changed dispositions only as responses to a perceived wrong. I will return to this
point shortly.

Thirdly, whatever kind of 'repair' is possible, it is not clear that it is something
that anyone other than the offender could provide. Others can of course do much
for the victims of crime: friends and fellow citizens can offer material help and
sympathetic support, of a kind that is sensitive to the fact that the victim suffered
criminal, not merely natural, harm; the state can provide more formalised versions of such help, as well as financial compensation—though this again raises the
question of how money can help to repair such harm.[4] But once we move away
from the straightforward repair or replacement of material property, the meaning
and efficacy of reparative measures come to depend crucially on who offers them;
and there may be kinds of repair that *only* the offender can provide. If, for
instance, apology is an essential reparative measure, the offender must be involved:
for whilst others might pay the financial compensation that I owe to the person
I wronged, they cannot apologise for me.

These comments point towards something which should anyway be obvious
enough: that any talk of 'restoration' in the context of crime must be sensitive to
the fact that the victim of crime has been not just harmed, but *wronged*; he has
suffered a wrongful, as distinct from a natural or merely unlucky, harm. Some
restorative theorists reject the very concepts of crime and wrong: rather than
talking of the 'wrong' the offender did or the 'crime' she committed, we should
talk about the 'conflict' or 'trouble' that needs to be resolved.[5] Others, however,
rightly insist that we must retain the concept of crime (and the criminal law as
providing an authoritative specification of criminal wrongs), and recognise that
crimes typically involve a victim who is wronged.

This does not yet distinguish criminal law from tort law, which enables those
who suffer wrongful loss to gain redress or compensation, by making those who
caused the loss pay for it. I cannot pursue this issue in detail here, but we can
suggest two identifying features of the kinds of wrong that should be criminal
rather than (merely) tortious.

First, in tort law the focus is on the loss or harm that was caused, which can
typically be identified independently of its relation to any wrongful action. Fault
becomes relevant only in deciding who should bear the cost of that loss: if it was
caused by another's negligence, its cost can legitimately be transferred to her (see
Ripstein, 1999: chs 2–4). By contrast, criminal law focuses primarily on the wrong

---

[4] On what the state owes to victims of crime, see especially Ashworth, 1986, 1993: the fact that the
state offers victims of crime compensation that it does not offer victims of natural misfortune reflects
the difference between criminal and natural harms.

[5] See eg Christie, 1977; Hulsman, 1986. In response see Duff, 2001: 60–64.

that was done. This is most obvious in the case of crimes—such as attempts or crimes of endangerment—that might cause no harm of a kind that could ground a tort claim, but that can still constitute serious criminal wrongs (see Ashworth, 1993: 285), but it is also true of crimes that cause such harm. The wrong done to the victim of rape, or wounding, or burglary, is in part constituted by, but also part constitutes, the harm that she suffers: to understand such harm, we must understand it as a *criminal* harm—as a harm that consists in being *wrongfully* injured.

Secondly, it is often said that crimes are 'public' wrongs: but it is hard to explain the sense in which they are 'public' wrongs, without denigrating the victim's standing by implying that they are wrongs against 'the public' *rather than* the victim. We could, however, say that they are 'public' in the sense that, while they are often wrongs against an individual, they properly concern 'the public'—the whole political community—as wrongs in which other members of the community share as fellow citizens of both victim and offender.[6] They infringe the values by which the political community defines itself as a law-governed polity: they are therefore wrongs for which the polity and its members are part-responsible in the sense that it is up to them, and not just up to victim and offender as private individuals, to make provision for an appropriate response.

This brings us back, however, to the question of what an 'appropriate response' would be when such a wrong has been committed, and what the notion of 'restoration' could amount to in this context; and we can now see more clearly why the three features that characterised the simple case of material harm do not carry across to criminal wrongs.

First, it is not clear what could count as 'repair' or 'restoration', or whether there could be a complete repair or restoration. Property can be repaired or replaced; physical injuries can be healed; psychological suffering and distress might be assuaged, traumas eventually healed: but what can 'repair' or 'restore' the wrong that has been done? It is here that talk of apology, of shaming, even of 'confession, repentance and absolution',[7] becomes appropriate: but I will argue that this brings us into the realm of punishment.

Secondly, we cannot separate the harm that needs repair from the wrong that was done: for the wrong partly constitutes the relevant harm. This is true even of crimes that involve some independently identifiable harm: the victim of wounding suffers not just the harm of physical injury, but the distinctive harm of being wrongfully attacked. It is also true when the harm is manifest in the victim's psychological suffering, or when we talk of damage to relationships. The victim's anger or fear expresses his understanding of what he suffered as a wrong, and it can be appraised as a reasonable or unreasonable response to that wrong—an appraisal which has implications for what we think is due to him by way of

---

[6] See Marshall and Duff, 1998; and on the relevant idea of political community, Duff, 2001: chs 2, 5.

[7] JO Hayley, as quoted by Van Ness, 1993: 255. See also Christie, 1977.

reparation. The damage done to the offender's relationships—with the victim, with others—might be described in apparently empirical terms: the victim, or others, no longer trust her, or feel at ease with her as a friend, or colleague, or fellow citizen. But it is crucial to a proper understanding of this kind of harm that these are reasonable responses to a wrong that was done—for instance that they cease to trust her because she showed herself, by committing that wrong, to be *untrustworthy*. There is also a significant kind of damage to the offender's relationships that does not consist in and need not involve (though it might be recognised in) any such actual responses: she has by her crime violated the values that define her *normative* relationships with her victim and with her fellow citizens. If I betray my friend, my action is destructive of the bonds of friendship even if she never finds out, and even if we can maintain what looks like an undamaged friendship: for such an action denies the values, the mutual concern, by which a friendship is defined. So too, when I wrong a fellow citizen, my action damages the normative bonds of citizenship,[8] which raises the question of how those bonds can be repaired.

Thirdly, we must ask who could provide the kind of 'reparation' or 'restoration' that crime, as involving wrongdoing, makes necessary—but also to whom such reparation must be made. Where there is an identifiable victim, she is the obviously appropriate recipient of reparation, since it is she who was harmfully wronged: but the political community as a whole is also owed something, since it shares in the victim's wrong as a violation of its public values. The community can of course do something towards repairing or restoring the victim, by offering help, and sympathetic recognition of what she has suffered: but in so far as the harm consists in a wrong done to the victim, or damage to the normative relationship between offender and victim (and between offender and wider political community), there is a kind of 'repair' that only the offender can provide.

In the next section I will flesh out this idea, which informs many restorative programmes, and will argue that it is a kind of 'repair' that involves the offender's punishment. However, since my claim is that we should seek restoration through retribution, I should say something about retribution, to ward off some likely misunderstandings.

Talk of retribution conjures up in many minds the image of a vindictive attempt to inflict hardship—to 'deliver pain' (see Christie, 1981)—'for its own sake'; and who could argue in favour of *that?* I will argue, however, that the retributivist slogan—that 'the guilty deserve to suffer'—does express an important moral truth; and that in the case of the criminally guilty it is the state's proper task to seek to ensure that they suffer as they deserve.

The retributivist slogan says nothing about *what* the guilty deserve to suffer; the crucial task in making retributivism morally plausible is to explain this. Once we recognise that the offender has done *wrong*, we can identify two kinds of 'suf-

---

[8] Thus even if victim and offender had no actual contact before the crime, they were related normatively as fellow citizens; and it is that relationship that the crime damages.

fering' that he deserves in virtue of that wrong. First, he deserves to suffer remorse: he should come to recognise and repent the wrong that he did—which is necessarily a painful process. Secondly, he deserves to suffer censure from others—which might be a formal censure, or the angry, ferocious censure of the victim or her friends; this too, if taken seriously, must be painful. There is also a third kind of 'suffering', a third kind of 'burden', that might be appropriate, that of making reparation to the victim. Some restorative theorists argue that the hardship involved in making reparation is a side-effect of the restorative process, not its aim, thus seeking to distance themselves from any species of 'punishment' (eg Walgrave, 1994: 66) but I will argue that reparation *must* be burdensome if it is to serve its restorative purpose.

I can best develop my argument that the kind of restoration that crime makes necessary should involve the offender's punishment by contrasting two models of mediation—a 'civil' and a 'criminal' model: this will occupy the next section.

## III. MEDIATION: CIVIL VERSUS CRIMINAL

For restorative theorists, the process is as important as (or more important than) the product (see Dignan, this volume): restoration is achieved as much by the process of discussion and negotiation between victim, offender and others as by whatever reparative measures flow from that process. That process takes a variety of different forms in different programmes.[9] In particular, the range of people involved varies—as between, for instance, victim-offender mediation programmes in which individual victim and individual offender are the only lead players and group conferences that also involve their families, friends or 'supporters'. There is much to be said about who should participate (about who has responsibility, or standing, in the matter) but I will concentrate here on the simple case of victim-offender mediation, and on the contrast between two simple models of mediation.

*Civil* mediation is a matter of negotiation and compromise, aimed at resolving conflict. I am in conflict with my neighbour over her constant early morning Do-it-yourself work; my complaints have proved fruitless. Rather than going to law, we try mediation to resolve our conflict: we must find a way to live together as neighbours; going to law would probably be an expensive way of failing to achieve that. The mediation process consists initially in mutual explanation, and complaint. I complain about her DIY work; she argues that I am exaggerating things, and accuses me of keeping her awake with my late night parties. However, we recognise that we must move beyond trading complaints and harping on past misdeeds. Perhaps we should each admit that we have been variously in the wrong in the past, but now look to the future, to find a mutually acceptable *modus vivendi*. That will

---

[9] See generally Marshall and Merry, 1990; Daly and Immarigeon, 1998; Braithwaite, 1999; Kurki, 2000; also Roberts and Roach, Schiff, in this volume.

50   *Antony Duff*

involve negotiating a compromise between our conflicting habits: we might agree
that she will avoid noisy DIY work before 9.00 am, whilst I will hold no more than
one late party a fortnight. We might also pay compensation for any past damage—
damage to her hedge by my guests, to my walls by her building work; and we
might exchange general apologies for any past wrongs. But the compensation will
be focused purely on any material damage that was done; and the apologies might
be formal (we do not aspire to the sort of friendship in which apologies are worthwhile only if sincere) and unfocused (we do not list every wrong).

Some such civil mediation process is often the appropriate way of dealing with
conflicts, including many which involve criminal conduct. Perhaps my neighbour
has committed what counts in law as criminal damage against me, as my guests
have against her: but it would be stupid to call the police and demand that they
press charges. This is partly because there have been similar, minor, wrongs on
both sides, but also because our relationship is one of rough equality: neither has
been oppressing the other. We have each failed to think carefully enough about
our relationship, but we can remedy that through informal mediation.

Sometimes, however, such a process is inappropriate: if mediation is possible
at all, what is required is *criminal* mediation, under the aegis of the criminal law.

Criminal mediation is focused on a wrong that has been done. A woman has
been beaten by her husband, or her house has been burgled and vandalised; the
parties agree to mediation. It matters, first, that the relevant facts be established,
either before the mediation or as its first stage—that this was a serious criminal
assault, or burglary and criminal damage. (Whereas in the civil case, it is less
important or helpful thus to focus on the past.)

Secondly, the process will include discussion and mutual explanations of those
facts: the victim can explain how the crime affected her; the offender might
explain how he came to commit it. The offender's explanation might include
mitigating factors: but he is not allowed to argue that his conduct was justified—
that husbands have the right to 'chastise' their wives, for instance. For the criminal
law, under whose aegis the process takes place, defines what counts as a crime and
as a justification: whatever else is negotiable, the wrongfulness of the offender's
conduct is not.[10] (Whereas in civil mediation each party might initially seek to
justify their own conduct, before realising that this is futile.)

Part of the aim of the process is precisely this communication between victim
and offender: the victim has a chance to bring the offender to grasp the wrong he
did her, and to understand his action from her perspective; the offender has the
chance to explain himself, and to grasp more clearly what he has done. Censure
is integral to this exercise: to try to bring the offender to grasp the wrong that he
did involves at least implicitly condemning his action as wrongful (not to
condemn it would be implicitly to deny that it was a wrong, or that its wrongfulness mattered); and if he comes to grasp it as a wrong, he will censure himself for
doing it.

---

[10] Compare Dobash and Dobash, 1992: ch 7, on the CHANGE project for violent men.

Thirdly, however, the process also aims to reconcile offender and victim: but what does this involve? Minimally, the aim is to reconcile them as fellow citizens (if they had no closer relationship that could be salvaged): to repair or restore the normative relationship of fellow-citizenship, so that they can treat each other with the acceptance and respect that fellowship in the polity requires. The offender's crime violated the values which define that normative relationship, and was thus injurious to it; that injury must be repaired.

Now in civil mediation, reconciliation is achieved partly by a compromise between the conflicting interests of the parties concerned: but since the wrongfulness of the crime is not negotiable, we cannot seek reconciliation in the criminal case through a similar compromise—for instance one that allows the husband to beat his wife occasionally. Nor can reconciliation be achieved merely by the kind of reparation that civil mediation can involve, for even if the independently identifiable harms suffered by the victim could be repaired, what is required is a response that addresses the *wrong* done to her. That must at least involve an apology, which expresses the wrongdoer's recognition of the wrong she has done, her implicit commitment to avoid such wrongdoing in future, and her concern to seek forgiveness from and reconciliation with the person she wronged. Apologies own the wrong as something that I culpably did, but disown it as something that I now repudiate; they also mark my renewed recognition of the person I wronged as one to whom I owe a respect that I failed to display, and with whom I must reconcile myself by making up for what I did to her.[11]

But a merely verbal apology might not be enough, for relatively serious wrongs. This is partly because verbal apologies can easily be insincere—mere words that lack depth or truth; but also because even a sincere verbal apology might not do enough to address the seriousness of the wrong. We often need to give more than merely verbal expression to things that matter to us. We express gratitude for services done to us by gifts or, in the public realm, by public rewards or honours; we express our grief at a death through the rituals of a funeral. Such more-than-merely-verbal modes of expression have two purposes: they make the expression more forceful, and they help to focus the expresser's attention on what needs to be expressed.

Similarly, an apology is strengthened if it is given a more than merely verbal form—if I make some kind of material reparation to the person I wronged. Thus the mediation process typically aims to end with an agreement on what reparation the offender should make. This might consist in something superficially identical to the reparation to which civil mediation can lead: if I damaged another's property, I might pay for its repair, or even repair it myself. But such direct repair is not always possible: the wrongdoer might need to find some other benefit he can provide for the victim (or for others; the offender might agree to undertake some charitable activity). Furthermore, even if such direct repair is possible, it has

---

[11] Compare Gaita, 1991: chs 1–4, on remorse as involving a recognition of the *reality* of the other person.

52    *Antony Duff*

a different meaning in the criminal case, as a forceful expression of the offender's recognition of his wrongdoing—a forceful apology.

One striking difference between reparation in the civil and in the criminal case concerns its burdensome character. Civil reparation can be burdensome, depending on what is required and on the repairer's resources: but it is not designed to be burdensome, and repairs the harm no less efficaciously if it is entirely unburdensome. Criminal reparation, by contrast, must be burdensome if it is to serve its purpose: only then can it express a serious apology for a wrong done; if it cost the wrongdoer nothing, it would mean no more than empty verbal apology.[12]

I have spoken so far of how sincere apology can be adequately and forcefully expressed; and we could see the paradigm of moral reparation for a wrong as the voluntary undertaking of some designedly burdensome reparative task which will express the wrongdoer's sincerely remorseful apology. But life, especially of the kind that involves criminal mediation, is not always like that: what can I say about cases in which the offender is not sincerely apologetic, or in which the victim is not ready to accept such an apology? I will comment on the latter possibility in section V, but should make two initial points about the former possibility here.

Part of the purpose of criminal mediation is, as I have noted, to bring the offender (if she needs bringing) to recognise her crime as a wrong—and thus to recognise the need for some apologetic reparation. But that might not happen; and the question is whether, on my account, there can then be any appropriate point to requiring her to undertake a reparative task,[13] if it does not express a sincere apology. There is an appropriate point, in two ways.

First, the process of undertaking the reparation can help to induce what it is intended to express—the offender's repentant recognition of the wrong he has done. Just as the rituals of a funeral can serve both to express and to induce an understanding of the significance of the person's death by focusing the mourners' attention on it, so undertaking reparation can focus the wrongdoer's attention on the meaning of his wrongdoing, so inducing him to repent it as a wrong, and to see the reparation as an appropriate way of expressing that repentance.

Secondly, even if this does not happen, requiring the wrongdoer to undertake a reparative task serves a legitimate purpose. It makes it forcefully clear to him that he has done wrong, and that he owes this to his victim by way of apologetic reparation: we require him, in effect, to apologise to her in order to make clear to

---

[12] John Braithwaite asks why restoration must be burdensome: why can it not be achieved by a hug, or a gift from victim to offender (in discussion; see Braithwaite, 1999: 20 fn 6)? We need to know more about the context before we can understand whether a hug or a gift could have a suitably restoring meaning (in his example, the villagers' gift of rice to the thief expressed their shame that 'one from our village should be so poor as to steal', which implies their partial responsibility for the theft): but my concern is with what the offender owes the victim, rather than with what the victim or others can do for the wrongdoer.

[13] It might seem that I am here smuggling a 'requirement' into what was initially presented as, and what should surely be, a *voluntary* process of mediation resulting in an *agreed* mode of reparation: but I will argue that offenders could properly be required to enter mediation and to undertake reparation.

him why he ought to do so. It sends a message to the victim—that we recognise and take seriously the wrong she has suffered. There is also still a sense in which victim and offender are reconciled by the very ritual of reparation, even if it does not express a sincere apology. In more intimate relationships only sincere apologies have value: but in the more distant relationships in which we stand to each other simply as fellow citizens we can often make peace with each other by going through the ritual motions of making and accepting an apology without inquiring into its sincerity.[14]

We can, I suggest, see criminal mediation and reparation as a kind of secular penance: as a burden undertaken by the wrongdoer, which aims to induce and express her repentant and apologetic understanding of the wrong she has done, and thus to secure reconciliation with those she has wronged. Religious penances are addressed to God, against whom the sinner has offended. Secular penances are addressed initially to the direct victim of the wrongdoing (when there is one), as the person to whom apology is most obviously owed; but they are also addressed to the wider community, against one of whose members the wrong was committed and whose values were violated. Crimes as public wrongs require public apology: an apology addressed to the whole community as well as to the individual victim.

We should also, I claim, recognise criminal mediation and reparation as punitive, indeed as a paradigm of retributive punishment.

## IV.  CRIMINAL MEDIATION AND PUNISHMENT

Criminal mediation, as described here, certainly fits the standard definitions of punishment, as something intentionally painful or burdensome imposed on an offender, for her crime, by some person or body with the authority to do so—and, we can add, intended to communicate censure for that crime.[15]

It focuses on the offender and his crime: on what he must do to repair the moral damage wrought by his crime. It is intended to be painful or burdensome, and the pain or burden is to be suffered *for* the crime. The mediation process itself aims to confront the offender with the fact and implications of what he has done, and to bring him to repent it as a wrong: a process which must be painful. The reparation that he is then to undertake must be burdensome if it is to serve its proper purpose. The aim is not to 'make the offender suffer' just for its own sake: but it is to induce an appropriate kind of suffering—the suffering intrinsic to

---

[14] I do not pretend that the notion of apology, and the role I give it here, are unproblematic: some of the problems are highlighted by Bottoms, by Daly and by von Hirsch, Ashworth and Shearing in this volume. For preliminary attempts to deal with some of the problems, see Duff, 2001: ch 3.6 and ch 3.7.4.

[15] This is not the place for a detailed (and ultimately fruitless) exploration of the definitional complexities of the concept of punishment: see Scheid, 1980 on the definitional debate, and (on censure as a defining feature) Feinberg, 1970.

confronting and repenting one's own wrongdoing and to making reparation for it. Criminal mediation takes place under the aegis of the criminal law and the authority of a criminal court: a court must determine that the defendant committed the offence charged, supervise the mediation process, approve its outcome (the reparation the offender is to make), and deal with offenders who refuse to take part or to make the agreed reparation (see further section V below).

It might seem that criminal mediation and reparation still cannot constitute punishment, since punishment is imposed against or regardless of the offender's will, whilst mediation and reparation must be consensual: the offender must agree to enter mediation, and to undertake reparation. However, first, punishment can be *self*-imposed: an offender who willingly enters mediation and undertakes reparation can be said to be punishing herself.[16] Secondly, most of the punishments imposed by our courts are not strictly 'imposed' in the sense that the offender is simply their passive victim or recipient: more usually, they consist in *requirements*—to pay a fine, to undertake the specified community service, to visit the probation officer[17]—which it is up to the offender to carry out for herself; and offenders could likewise be required to take part in the mediation process and to undertake the specified reparation. There are, of course, sanctions against offenders who fail to do what is required of them, which will involve, in the end, something strictly imposed on the offender: but restorative processes must also be backed up by ultimately coercive sanctions against offenders who fail to do what is required of them.[18]

However, my claim that criminal mediation and reparation should be seen as punishment is not simply definitional: this process can serve the appropriate aims of criminal punishment.

First, mediation is a communicative process. The procedure consists in communication between victim and offender about the crime's implications, as a wrong against the victim; the reparation that the offender undertakes communicates to the victim and others an apology for that crime. But it is a process of *punitive* communication: it censures the offender for his crime, and requires some burdensome reparation for that crime. Criminal punishment must, I believe, be justified (if it can be justified at all) as a communicative enterprise between a state or political community and its members; criminal mediation is certainly such an enterprise.

Secondly, criminal mediation is retributive, in that it seeks to impose on (or induce in) the offender the suffering she deserves for her crime, and is justified in those terms. She deserves to suffer censure for what she has done: mediation aims to communicate that censure to her, in such a way that she will come to accept that she deserves it. She deserves to suffer remorse for what she has done:

---

[16] Compare Adler, 1992: ch 2, on the 'conscientious paradigm' of punishment.

[17] And even, in some countries, to present oneself on a specified date or at weekends to serve a prison term: see Walker and Padfield, 1996: 142–4.

[18] See Walgrave, 1994: 70–1, and this volume; Braithwaite, 1999: 56–7, 61–7.

mediation aims to induce remorse in her, by bringing her to recognise the wrong she has done. She ought to make apologetic, burdensome, reparation to her victim: mediation aims to provide for such reparation. By seeing criminal mediation as punishment, we can thus make plausible sense of the retributivist idea that the guilty deserve to suffer, by showing what they deserve to suffer, and why. What they deserve to suffer is not just 'pain' or a 'burden', but the particular kind of painful burden which is integral to the recognition of guilt: they deserve to suffer that because it is an appropriate response to their wrongdoing; and criminal mediation aims precisely to impose or induce that kind of suffering.

Thirdly, the reparation that the offender undertakes is a species of penal hard treatment: it is intentionally burdensome, making demands on his time, money or energies, independently of its communicative meaning. But we can now see how penal hard treatment can be justified as an essential aspect of a communicative penal process: the hard treatment that reparation involves is the means by which the offender makes apologetic reparation to the victim, and a vehicle through which he can strengthen his own repentant understanding of the wrong he has done.[19]

Fourthly, although criminal mediation is retributive, looking back to the past crime, it is also future-directed. It aims to reconcile victim and offender, through apologetic reparation by the offender. It aims to dissuade the offender from future crimes: to bring her to repent the wrong she has done is to bring her to see why she should not commit such wrongs in future. This is not, however, to posit a consequentialist 'general justifying aim' (see Hart, 1968) for criminal mediation or for punishment. On consequentialist accounts, the relationship between punishment and the good it aims to achieve is instrumental and contingent: punishment is, as a matter of fact, an efficient technique for achieving that good. But the relationship between criminal mediation and the goods it aims to achieve is not merely instrumental. For the ends themselves determine the means which are appropriate to them: the reconciliation which is to be achieved must involve a recognition of and apology for the wrong that was done, and must therefore be achieved by a process which includes such recognition and apology; the offender is to be dissuaded from future crime by her recognition of the wrong she has committed.[20]

Although I have argued that we should see criminal mediation of the kind described here as a paradigm of punishment, it might strike you that this process is still very different from the criminal punishments typically imposed under our existing penal systems; and so it is and should be. For although I believe that punishment is in principle a necessary and appropriate response to criminal wrongdoing, I am not seeking to justify our existing penal practices, or anything very like them. However, a criminal mediation process of the kind I have described will by no means always be possible or appropriate: I should therefore say something

---

[19] On 'hard treatment', and the problem of justifying it from a communicative perspective, see Feinberg, 1970; von Hirsch, 1993: 12–13.

[20] For a fuller account of the conception of punishment sketched here, see Duff, 2001.

56   *Antony Duff*

about how criminal mediation should fit into a larger system of criminal justice—
a system that will also impose more familiar kinds of punishment; this will also
involve some comments on the proper role of the criminal courts, and will thus
address some further concerns of critics of the 'restorative paradigm'.[21]

## V.   RESTORATIVE PUNISHMENT AND THE COURTS

I have suggested that criminal mediation should be conducted under the aegis and
authority of a criminal court. The court has an important role even when there
is an identifiable victim, when both victim and offender are willing to engage in
mediation, and when (with the help of a mediator) they agree on a suitable mode
of reparation; but its role is more prominent when these conditions are not
satisfied. In both cases, however, its central role is as guarantor of punitive justice.

The court's initial task is to establish whether the alleged offender did commit
the crime charged, and to convict him if he is proved guilty. One of the protections that a liberal state should provide for its citizens is that they must not be
subjected to the critical public attention that criminal mediation involves unless
they are proved to have committed a public wrong—a task which cannot be safely
left to informal procedures. It is also appropriate for the court to mark the public
character of the wrong by convicting, and thus condemning, the defendant if his
guilt is proved.

If victim and offender agree to mediation, the court has a role both as protec-
tor of each party's rights (protecting each against exploitation or bullying), and
as guardian of the public interest: since the crime is a public wrong, the victim
(and her supporters, if the mediation process includes them) must speak not just
for herself, but for the community as a whole; and the offender must speak not
just to her, but through her to the whole community. This role is best discharged
by a court-appointed mediator, who can speak with the voice and authority of
the law and of the polity whose law it is. Two other aspects of the court's role as
guarantor of punitive justice are worth emphasising.

First, the court and the mediator must ensure that the offender is only required
to discuss, and make reparation for, the crime proved against her. Restorative
theorists sometimes take it to be a merit of 'informal justice' that it allows a wider,
unconstrained discussion of whatever problems exist in the offender's relationships with others, or in her life as a whole: but this is not something in which
offenders should be required to participate. What justifies mediation, and the
demand that the offender take part in it, is her crime. A community that is to
respect the privacy of its citizens must respect certain limits on how far it seeks
to intrude into their lives or thoughts—which, in this context, means that it

---

[21] See also the 'making amends' model suggested by von Hirsch, Ashworth and Shearing in this
volume: this section addresses some of the concerns that they raise.

should inquire only into the crime, her reasons for it, and its implications: that is their business, but other aspects of her life are not.

Secondly, the court must approve the reparation that is agreed between victim and offender to ensure that it is appropriate. What makes it appropriate depends in part on its character: is it, for instance, degrading? But it also depends on its proportionality to the crime: whilst the fact that a certain reparation has been agreed counts strongly in its favour as being just (as the outcome of a just, participatory process), it is not dispositive. The reparation must constitute an adequate apology to the victim, and to the wider community, and so must communicate an adequate conception of the crime to the offender, the victim and others: this must include a conception of its seriousness, which is marked by the onerousness of the reparation. So whilst on this account we should not seek a strict proportionality between crime and reparation, or make proportionality our positive aim, we must respect the demands of a rough and negative proportionality: the reparation must not be *disproportionate* in its severity to the seriousness of the crime.[22]

The court's role becomes more prominent when direct victim/offender mediation is not possible or appropriate. Mediation is clearly not possible if there is no identifiable individual victim; or if the offender or the victim refuses to take part, or cannot take part, in the process. In such cases, the offender will undergo a punishment of a more familiar kind: but I would argue, though I cannot develop the argument here, that the sentencing process should as far as possible be a formal analogue of the victim-offender mediation process (a mediation process, we might say, between the offender and the political community);[23] and that the offender's punishment should resemble, in its meaning and purpose, the reparation to which criminal mediation leads, as a kind of apologetic reparation that the offender is required to make to the wider community—the community which might be the only identifiable victim of the crime.

A trickier question is that of when direct victim-offender mediation followed by punitive reparation would be possible but inappropriate: are there kinds of crime for which mediation, even if it leads to onerous reparation, is not an appropriate response? I am not sure about this. Some might fear that even criminal mediation as I have described it makes crime too much of a private matter between victim and offender—and that for serious crimes we need a stronger public dimension to the response than mediation involves. But criminal mediation, as I have described it, presupposes a public condemnation of the crime

---

[22] The role of proportionality on my account thus has something in common with the role that Morris and Tonry give it, as a negative constraint on sentencing rather than a positive aim (eg Morris and Tonry, 1990: ch 4; Tonry, 1998): but see Duff, 2001: 137–9, 141–3. Note too that, since the focus is on the wrong done to the victim, the seriousness of the crime, and so the onerousness of the reparation, is to be measured by the seriousness of the wrong; the amount or cost of the harm caused will be relevant only insofar as it bears on the seriousness of the wrong. All this provides part of an answer to Ashworth's worries in Ashworth, 1993.

[23] Compare Cavadino and Dignan, 1998; for more detail, see Duff, 2001: chs 3–4.

58   *Antony Duff*

through a criminal conviction; the wider community's voice is heard in the process through the mediator; and the reparation constitutes an apologetic communication to the victim and to the wider community.

Perhaps, however, one reason for insisting in some cases on a more public determination of sentence has to do with the nature and meaning of the sentence. For instance, the meaning of imprisonment is that the offender has, by his crime, made it morally impossible for his fellow citizens to live with him in ordinary community: the appropriate response to his crime is therefore temporary exclusion from such a community. Now such a punishment, with such a meaning, can be appropriate, for the most serious kinds of crime that deny the community's most basic values: but the judgement that it is appropriate should fall to be made not by victim and offender in a mediation process, but by a criminal court that speaks directly for the community from which the offender is to be excluded.

I cannot pursue this issue further here. What I have argued is that criminal mediation should be seen as a secular penance which, precisely as a kind of punishment for the wrong the offender has done, aims to secure repentance and apologetic reparation from the offender, and thus to achieve a reconciliation between the offender and those she has wronged. It aims, that is, to achieve restoration, but to achieve it precisely through an appropriate retribution. That is also, I would argue, the proper aim of criminal punishment more generally: but there is much more to be said about the relationship between criminal mediation and other modes of punishment than I can say here.

## REFERENCES

Adler, J (1992) *The Urgings of Conscience* (Temple University Press, Philadelphia).

Ashworth, AJ (1986) 'Punishment and Compensation: Victims, Offenders and the State' 6 *Oxford Journal of Legal Studies* 86–122.

—— (1993) 'Some Doubts about Restorative Justice' 4 *Criminal Law Forum* 277–99.

Braithwaite, J (1999) 'Restorative Justice: Assessing Optimistic and Pessimistic Accounts' in M Tonry (ed), *Crime and Justice: A Review of Research* (University of Chicago Press, Chicago IL) vol 25, 1–27.

Cavadino, M and Dignan, J (1998) 'Reparation, Retribution and Rights' in A von Hirsch and AJ Ashworth (eds), *Principled Sentencing* 2nd edn (Hart Publishing, Oxford).

Christie, N (1977) 'Conflicts as Property' 17 *British Journal of Criminology* 1–15.

—— (1981) *Limits to Pain* (Martin Robertson, London).

Daly, K (2000) 'Revisiting the Relationship between Restorative and Retributive Justice' in H Strang and J Braithwaite (eds), *Restorative Justice: Philosophy to Practice* (Ashgate, Aldershot).

Daly, K and Immarigeon, R (1998) 'The Past, Present, and Future of Restorative Justice' 1 *Contemporary Justice Review* 21–45.

Dignan, J (1999) 'The Crime and Disorder Act and the Prospects for Restorative Justice' 1 *Criminal Law Review* 48–60.

Duff, RA (2001) *Punishment, Communication, and Community* (Oxford University Press, New York).

—— 'Harms and Wrongs' (2002) 5(1) *Buffalo Criminal Law Review* 13–45.

Feinberg, J (1970) 'The Expressive Function of Punishment' in J Feinberg, *Doing and Deserving* (Princeton University Press, Princeton NJ).

—— (1984) *Harm to Others* (Oxford University Press, New York).

Gaita, R (1991) *Good and Evil: An Absolute Conception* (Macmillan, London).

Hart, HLA (1968) 'Prolegomenon to the Principles of Punishment' in HLA Hart, *Punishment and Responsibility* (Oxford University Press, Oxford).

Hulsman, L (1986) 'Critical Criminology and the Concept of Crime' 10 *Contemporary Crises* 63–80.

Kurki, L (2000) 'Restorative and Community Justice in the United States' in M Tonry (ed), *Crime and Justice: A Review of Research* (University of Chicago Press, Chicago IL) vol 27, 235–304.

Marshall, SE and Duff, RA (1998) 'Criminalization and Sharing Wrongs' 11 *Canadian Journal of Law and Jurisprudence* 7–22.

Marshall, TF (1988) 'Out of Court: More or Less Justice?' in R Matthews (ed), *Informal Justice* (Sage, London).

—— (1999) *Restorative Justice: An Overview* (Home Office, London).

Marshall, TF and Merry, S (1990) *Crime and Accountability: Victim/Offender Mediation in Practice* (HMSO, London).

Morris, N and Tonry, M (1990) *Between Prison and Probation: Intermediate Punishments in a Rational Sentencing System* (Oxford University Press, New York).

Ripstein, A (1999) *Equality, Responsibility and the Law* (Cambridge University Press, Cambridge).

Scheid, DE (1980) 'Note on Defining "Punishment"' 10 *Canadian Journal of Philosophy* 453–62.

Tonry, M (1998) 'Interchangeability, Desert Limits and Equivalence of Function' in A von Hirsch and AJ Ashworth (eds), *Principled Sentencing* 2nd edn (Hart Publishing, Oxford).

Van Ness, DW (1993) 'New Wine and Old Wineskins: Four Challenges of Restorative Justice' 4 *Criminal Law Forum* 251–76.

von Hirsch, A (1993) *Censure and Sanctions* (Oxford University Press, Oxford).

Walgrave, L (1994) 'Beyond Rehabilitation: in Search of a Constructive Alternative in the Judicial Response to Juvenile Crime' 2 *European Journal of Criminal Policy and Research* 57–75.

Walker, N and Padfield, N (1996) *Sentencing Theory, Law and Practice* 2nd edn (Butterworths, London).

Watson, G (ed) (1982) *Free Will* (Oxford University Press, Oxford).

Zehr, H (1990) *Changing Lenses: A New Focus for Crime and Justice* (Herald Press, Scottsdale PA).

# [12]

## PROSECUTING VIOLENCE: A COLLOQUY ON RACE, COMMUNITY, AND JUSTICE

### Goodbye to Hammurabi: Analyzing the Atavistic Appeal of Restorative Justice

Richard Delgado*

*A recent innovation in criminal justice, the restorative justice movement has serious implications for the relationship among crime, race, and communities. Restorative justice, which sprang up in the mid-1970s as a reaction to the perceived excesses of harsh retribution, features an active role for the victims of crime, required community service or some other form of restitution for offenders, and face-to-face mediation in which victims and offenders confront each other in an effort to understand each other's common humanity.*

*This article questions whether restorative justice can deliver on its promises. Drawing on social science evidence, the author shows that the informal setting in which victim-offender mediation takes place is apt to compound existing relations of inequality. It also forfeits procedural rights and shrinks the public dimension of disputing. The article compares restorative justice to the traditional criminal justice system, finding that they both suffer grave deficiencies in their ability to dispense fair, humane treatment. Accordingly, it urges that defense attorneys and policymakers enter into a dialectic process that pits the two systems of justice, formal and informal, against each other in competition for clients and community support. In the meantime, defense attorneys should help defendants find and exploit opportunities for fair, individualized treatment that may be found in each system.*

* Jean Lindsley Professor of Law, University of Colorado-Boulder. J.D., 1974, U.C. Berkeley. I gratefully acknowledge the assistance of Andrea Wang in the preparation of this essay.

## INTRODUCTION

The relationship among race, crime, and community is complex and multiform. Although every crime is a violation of community,[1] community concerns acquire special significance with interracial and interclass crimes where offenses can easily be seen as injuries one of *you* inflicted against one of *us*.[2]  Enforcement of crime may also take on an interclass or intergenerational dimension, such as when police enforce anticruising ordinances against teenage drivers or antigraffiti laws against inner-city youth.[3] *Non*enforcement can also raise class and community concerns as well, such as when the black community charges the police with lax enforcement of street crime because of subconscious racism and devaluation of black life.[4]

The prosecution and defense of crime may take on an implicit or explicit community dimension as well.  Consider, for example, a defense attorney who advances a cultural defense that, if successful, will mitigate his or her client's punishment but only at the cost of stigmatizing the defendant's group as subcultural, violent, or bizarre.[5]  In these cases, the community issue is what one of us (the defendant) is doing to the rest of us (the community).[6] Finally, sexual violence cases demonstrate how the manner of prosecuting a case may affect the community.  When a victim of sexual assault is forced to recount her sexual history on the stand, all women receive a warning not to complain of mistreatment at the hands of men.[7]

This essay addresses a recent dynamic movement that seeks to address the effects of crime on community.  Restorative justice, which began in the mid-1970s as a reaction to perceived excesses of incarceration, as well as

---

1. This is so because the community defines crime and punishes those whose actions violate these standards. On the role community condemnation plays in the criminal law, see Henry M. Hart, Jr., *The Aims of the Criminal Law*, 23 LAW & CONTEMP. PROBS. 401, 402-06 (1958).

2. *See, e.g.*, JODY DAVID ARMOUR, NEGROPHOBIA AND REASONABLE RACISM: THE HIDDEN COSTS OF BEING BLACK IN AMERICA 81-101 (1997); KATHERYN K. RUSSELL, THE COLOR OF CRIME: RACIAL HOAXES, WHITE FEAR, BLACK PROTECTIONISM, POLICE HARASSMENT, AND OTHER MACROAGGRESSIONS 1-13 (1998).

3. *See* John Larrabee, *Cities Wish Artists Would Find Another Canvas*, USA TODAY, June 29, 1999, at 4A; Roesslein, *These Motorists Are Cruising for Trouble*, MILWAUKEE J. SENTINEL, Sept. 8, 1998, at 14.

4. *See* RANDALL KENNEDY, RACE, CRIME, AND THE LAW 76-135 (1997) (arguing that nonenforcement of crime in black neighborhoods erodes quality of life). *But see* Regina Austin, *"The Black Community," Its Lawbreakers, and a Politics of Identification*, 65 S. CAL. L. REV. 1769, 1771-72 (1992) (noting that some black communities rally behind certain offenders).

5. *See, e.g.*, Peter Margulies, *Identity on Trial: Subordination, Social Science Evidence, and Criminal Defense*, 51 RUTGERS L. REV. 45, 53-54 (1998) (pointing out that cultural defenses can stigmatize the defendant's community). *See generally* Leti Volpp, *(Mis)Identifying Culture: Asian Women and the "Cultural Defense,"* 17 HARV. WOMEN'S L.J. 57 (1994).

6. *See* Margulies, *supra* note 5, at 46-47, 53-57.

7. *See, e.g.*, SUSAN ESTRICH, REAL RAPE 51-53 (1987) (giving examples of victim humiliation at trial).

754                    STANFORD LAW REVIEW                    [Vol. 52:751

inattention to the concerns of victims, offers a new paradigm for structuring the relationship among crime, offenders, and communities.[8] Featuring new ways of conceptualizing crime, along with innovative mechanisms for dealing with it, restorative justice constitutes a radically new approach to criminal justice.

Part I reviews the origins and ideology of restorative justice, including what it hopes to accomplish and its purported advantages over the current system. Parts II and III then critique the movement, first offering an internal assessment that evaluates the new approach on its own terms, followed by an external critique that examines it in light of broader values. Part IV reviews some of the deficiencies in our current system, particularly for disadvantaged, minority, and young offenders. Part V offers suggestions for strengthening community bonds while dealing fairly and consistently with those who have breached them.

## I. THE RESTORATIVE JUSTICE MOVEMENT AND VICTIM-OFFENDER MEDIATION

In ancient times, crime was dealt with on an interpersonal level, with restitution or even private resources, rather than official punishment, the main remedy.[9] The state played little part. For example, the Code of Hammurabi provided that individuals who had injured or taken from others must make amends, in service or in kind.[10] Other early systems, such as the Torah and Sumerian Code,[11] required that offenders make their victims whole, as

---

8. For excellent overviews of the new movement, see generally PACT INST. OF JUSTICE & MCC OFFICE OF CRIMINAL JUSTICE, THE VORP BOOK (Howard Zehr ed., 1983); DANIEL VAN NESS & KAREN H. STRONG, RESTORING JUSTICE (1997); MARTIN WRIGHT, JUSTICE FOR VICTIMS AND OFFENDERS: A RESTORATIVE RESPONSE TO CRIME (2d ed. 1996); Mark S. Umbreit, *The Development and Impact of Victim-Offender Mediation in the United States*, 12 MEDIATION Q. 263 (1995); Daniel W. Van Ness, *New Wine and Old Wineskins: Four Challenges of Restorative Justice*, 4 CRIM. L.F. 251 (1993); Henry J. Reske, *Victim-Offender Mediation Catching On*, A.B.A. J., Feb. 1995, at 14, 14; David Van Biema, *Should All Be Forgiven?*, TIME, Apr. 5, 1999, at 55, 55; Howard Zehr, *Restorative Justice: The Concept*, CORRECTIONS TODAY, Dec. 1997, at 68.

For critiques and evaluations of the restorative justice movement or victim-offender mediation, see generally RESTORATIVE JUSTICE ON TRIAL (Heinz Messmer & Mans-Uwe Otto eds., 1992); Andrew Ashworth, *Some Doubts About Restorative Justice*, 4 CRIM. L.F. 277 (1993); Jennifer Gerarda Brown, *The Use of Mediation to Resolve Criminal Cases: A Procedural Critique*, 43 EMORY L.J. 1247 (1994); Terenia Urban Guill, *A Framework for Understanding and Using ADR*, 71 TUL. L. REV. 1313 (1997); Sheila D. Porter & David B. Ells, *Mediation Meets the Criminal Justice System*, 23 COLO. LAW. 2521 (1994).

9. *See, e.g.*, VAN NESS & STRONG, *supra* note 8, at 8; Van Ness, *supra* note 8, at 253-56; Brown, *supra* note 8, at 1254 (discussing blood feuds and private vengeance).

10. *See, e.g.*, VAN NESS & STRONG, *supra* note 8, at 8-9.

11. *See id.; see also* Fred Gay & Thomas J. Quinn, *Restorative Justice and Prosecution in the Twenty-First Century*, THE PROSECUTOR, Sept./Oct. 1996, at 16 (noting that the Sumerian method has roots in the 600 A.D. Laws of Ethelbert). On the Torah's preference for compensation of vic-

did Roman law.[12] Then, in the eleventh century, William the Conqueror expanded the king's authority by declaring certain offenses crimes or "breaches of the king's peace," redressed only by action of the king's courts.[13] Accordingly, private vengeance was forbidden, fines were paid directly to the state, rather than to the victim, and punishment, rather than restitution or making amends, became the main sanction for antisocial behavior.[14] This approach, with the state wielding monopoly power over the prosecution and punishment of crime, has reigned unchallenged until recently.

## A. *Restorative Justice*

Many proponents of restorative justice believe that our current approach to criminal justice should be reexamined and that we should try to recapture many of the values of the earlier, pre-Norman approach. Specifically, restorative justice advocates argue that incarceration offers little in the way of rehabilitative opportunities for offenders. Many emerge from prison more hardened and angry than when they entered, setting up a cycle of recidivism that serves neither them nor society.[15] Moreover, although the victims' rights movement has begun to clamor for restitution as a part of court-ordered sentencing,[16] relatively few victims receive compensation for their injuries, and fewer still receive anything resembling an apology from the perpetrator.[17]

The movement's proponents argue that the traditional criminal justice system does a second disservice to victims, by forcing them to relive their ordeal at trial.[18] Because the American criminal justice system conceptualizes crime as a wrong against the state, it uses the victim for her testimony, while offering little, if anything, in the way of counseling services or sup-

---

tims, see STEVEN SCHAFER, COMPENSATION AND RESTITUTION TO VICTIMS OF CRIME (2d ed. 1970); Brown, *supra* note 8, at 1254 n.20; *Victim Restitution in the Criminal Process: A Procedural Analysis*, 97 HARV. L. REV. 931, 933 n.18 (1984).

12. *See* VAN NESS & STRONG, *supra* note 8, at 8-9. Early Saxon justice had similar provisions. *See* SCHAFER, *supra* note 11, at 3-7; Brown, *supra* note 8, at 1254-55 n.22.

13. *See, e.g.*, VAN NESS & STRONG, *supra* note 8, at 9-11; Van Ness, *supra* note 8, at 255-56.

14. *See* VAN NESS & STRONG, *supra* note 8, at 9-11; WRIGHT, *supra* note 8, at 14 (noting that collecting fines and forfeits proved to be profitable); Van Ness, *supra* note 8, at 256.

15. *See, e.g.*, VAN NESS & STRONG, *supra* note 8, at 43; WRIGHT, *supra* note 8, at 11, 40; Van Ness, *supra* note 8 at 257-60.

16. On the victims' rights movement, which advocates restitution and a more participatory role at trial for victims of crime, see, e.g., NATIONAL VICTIM CTR., CHRONOLOGY OF THE VICTIMS' RIGHTS CONSTITUTIONAL AMENDMENT MOVEMENT (1991). For a critique of this movement, see Lynne N. Henderson, *The Wrongs of Victim's Rights*, 37 STAN. L. REV. 937 (1985).

17. *See* Brown, *supra* note 8, at 1255-57 (describing the nascent victims' rights movement, which is attempting to address these perceived differences).

18. *See* NATIONAL INST. OF CORRECTIONS, DEP'T OF JUSTICE, RESTORATIVE JUSTICE: WHAT WORKS 3 (1996); Umbreit, *supra* note 8, at 263.

port.[19] For the same reason, district attorneys rarely consult with the victim at key times during the course of the trial, so that he experiences a lack of control as key events take place without his input.[20]

In response to these perceived shortcomings, proponents of the Restorative Justice Movement believe that those affected most by crime should play an active role in its resolution. The movement intends to redefine crime as an offense against an individual, providing a forum for the victim to participate in the resolution and restitution of that crime.[21] This is achieved through programs in which the victim, offender, and community play an active role.

## B. *Victim-Offender Mediation: Restorative Justice in Action*

Of the numerous programs bearing restorative justice roots, Victim-Offender Mediation (VOM) is the most well established.[22] Although VOM takes slightly varying forms,[23] all share the same basic structure. Most receive referrals from the traditional justice system, are predicated on an admission of guilt, and, if successful, are conducted in lieu of a conventional trial.[24] The VOM process generally consists of four phases: Intake, Preparation for Mediation, Mediation, and Follow-up.[25] During intake, a pre-

---

19. This limitation is inherent in the prosecutor's role—she prosecutes in the name of the state. Unlike a tort lawyer who sues on behalf of an assigned client and, of course, is under a professional obligation to consult with that client at critical stages, the victim of a crime is not the client of either the prosecutor or defense counsel and has no right, under conventional law or professional codes, to be consulted as to his wishes at critical stages. *See* Henderson, *supra* note 16, at 942-53 (describing recent changes affording victims a measure of participation rights).

20. *See* Brown, *supra* note 8, at 1256-57 (describing the beginnings of a movement to provide victims such input).

21. *See* VAN NESS & STRONG, *supra* note 8, at 43; Mark S. Umbreit & William Bradshaw, *Victim Experience of Meeting Adult vs. Juvenile Offenders: A Cross-National Comparison*, 61 FED. PROBATION, Dec. 1997, at 33, 33. On the general movement to reincorporate the victim in our treatment of crime, see generally DAVID W. VAN NESS, CRIME AND ITS VICTIMS (1986).

22. *See* Gordon Bazemore & Curt Taylor Griffiths, *Conference, Circles, Boards, and Mediations: The "New Wave" of Community Justice Decisionmaking*, FED. PROBATION, June 1997, at 25, 27; Zehr, *supra* note 8, at 268-70.

Other restorative justice programs include community policing, community corrections, and family conferencing circles. *See* Bazemore & Griffiths, *supra*; Russ Immarigeon & Kathleen Daly, *Restorative Justice: Origins, Practices, Contexts, and Challenges*; 8 ICCA J. ON COMMUNITY CORRECTIONS 13, 13-16, 26, 28-30, 35, 37-39 (1997). On various aspects of community corrections, see ROBERTA C. CRONIN, NATIONAL INST. OF JUSTICE, BOOT CAMP FOR ADULT AND JUVENILE OFFENDERS, OVERVIEW AND UPDATE (1994) (describing boot camp punishment, youth leadership camps, and similar programs for offenders); NATIONAL INST. OF CORRECTIONS, STRIVING FOR SAFE, SECURE AND JUST COMMUNITIES (1996) (essays on approaches to community corrections that emphasize community and neighborhood participation and control).

23. *See* Brown, *supra* note 8, at 1264 (describing the different implementations of VOM).

24. *See* Mark S. Umbreit, *Mediation of Victim Offender Conflict*, 1988 J. DISP. RESOL. 85, 88 (1988).

25. *See id.* at 87.

screening occurs. Here, the mediator, who is either a trained community volunteer or a staff person,[26] accepts the victim and offender into the VOM process if both parties express a readiness to negotiate and show no overt hostility toward each other.[27] In the Preparation for Mediation stage, the mediator talks with the victim and the offender individually and schedules the first meeting. If the mediator does not feel she has effectively established trust and rapport with each of the parties, the case is remanded to court.[28] In the Mediation stage itself, the parties are expected to tell their versions of the story, talk things over, come to understand each other's position, and agree upon an appropriate solution, usually a restitution agreement or work order.[29] If they cannot do so, the case is remanded to court. A final Follow-up stage monitors the offender's performance and cooperation with the work or restitution agreement, with the goal of assuring compliance.[30]

### 1. *VOM success: far-reaching and still growing.*

While the majority of VOM programs concentrate on first- and second-time juvenile offenders,[31] some include adult felons, including alleged killers, armed robbers, and rapists.[32] In a recent year, VOM dealt with 16,500 cases in the United States alone, while the number of programs in the United States and Canada approached 125.[33] Endorsed by the ABA,[34] the movement shows no sign of slowing.[35]

### 2. *VOM's departure from today's criminal justice system.*

Like other programs born of the Restorative Justice Movement, VOM seeks to cure perceived problems with the traditional criminal justice process. While an adversarial dynamic may create the appearance of greater justice, it also provides minimal emotional closure for the victim and little direct

---

26. *See* MARK S. UMBREIT & NATIONAL INST. OF CORRECTIONS, DEP'T OF JUSTICE, VICTIM OFFENDER MEDIATION: CONFLICT RESOLUTION AND RESTITUTION 9 (1985).

27. *See id.*

28. *See* Umbreit, *supra* note 24, at 88.

29. *See id.* at 90-91.

30. *See id.* at 92; Brown, *supra* note 8, at 1265-67.

31. *See* Umbreit, *supra* note 8, at 270; Mark S. Umbreit & Jean Greenwood, *National Survey of Victim-Offender Mediation Programs in the United States*, 16 MEDIATION Q. 235, 239 (1999).

32. *See* MARK S. UMBREIT, PACT INST. OF JUSTICE, VICTIM OFFENDER MEDIATION WITH VIOLENT OFFENSES 11-18 (1986); WRIGHT, *supra* note 8, at 90, 159 (noting that VOM is beginning to be considered for cases of domestic violence and sexual assault); Brown, *supra* note 8, at 1262; Barbara Hudson, *Restorative Justice: The Challenge of Sexual and Racial Violence*, 25 J.L. & SOC'Y 237, 245-53 (1998); Umbreit & Greenwood, *supra* note 31.

33. *See* Guill, *supra* note 8, at 1327.

34. *See* Reske, *supra* note 8.

35. *See* Mike Dooley, *The NIC on Restorative Justice*, CORRECTIONS TODAY, Dec. 1997, at 110.

accountability by the offender to the victim.[36]  On the other hand, VOM deals more openly with the direct human consequences of crime.  Through a face-to-face meeting and discussion, the victim is able to receive information about the crime, express to the offender the impact his actions have had on her, and, it is hoped, gain a sense of material and emotional restoration.[37] Similarly, the offender is forced to face the consequences of his actions and accept responsibility for them, while also playing a role in fashioning the remedies.[38]  The offender's restitution should also lead to increased public confidence in the fairness of the system.[39]  A further advantage for the of- fender is that VOM offers an alternative to the ravages of incarceration:  Be- cause successful mediation serves in lieu of a trial, a defendant who cooper- ates and performs the agreed service will escape confinement entirely.

In summary, proponents of VOM maintain that the program will em- power the victim while reducing recidivism among offenders.[40]  It offers the hope that victims and offenders may come to recognize each other's common humanity and that offenders will be able to take their place in the wider community as valued citizens.  Through restitution, the victim will gain back what was lost.  Accordingly, VOM proponents advocate the program as "a challenging new vision of how communities can respond to crime and vic- timization. . . . deeply rooted in . . . the collective western heritage . . . of re- morse, forgiveness, and reconciliation."[41]

## II.  CAN RESTORATIVE JUSTICE DELIVER ON ITS PROMISES? AN INTERNAL CRITIQUE

Critics of the Restorative Justice Movement and VOM voice two con- cerns: (1) they charge that restorative justice does not deliver what we expect from a system of criminal justice, and (2) they contend that the movement

---

36. *See* Umbreit, *supra* note 8, at 266.

37. *See* Van Biema, *supra* note 8, at 55-56; *see also* Hon. Robert Yazzie, *"Hozho Nahas- dlii"—We Are Now in Good Relations: Navajo Restorative Justice*, 9 ST. THOMAS L. REV. 117, 123-24 (1996) (discussing a traditional parallel system of restorative justice among the Navajo).

38. *See* UMBREIT & NATIONAL INST. OF CORRECTIONS, *supra* note 26, at 3; Guill, *supra* note 8, at 1327-28; Yazzie, *supra* note 37, at 123.

39. *See* Gordon Bazemore & Mark Umbreit, *Rethinking the Sanctioning Function in Juvenile Court: Retributive or Restorative Responses to Youth Crime*, 41 CRIME & DELINQ. 296, 297-98, 302-03 (1995).

40. *See* William R. Nugent & Jeffrey B. Paddock, *The Effect of Victim-Offender Mediation on Severity of Reoffense*, 12 MEDIATION Q. 353, 363, 365 (1995).

41. Umbreit, *supra* note 8, at 275.  *But see* Brown, *supra* note 8, at 1295 (arguing that this goal is unrealistic in a culturally diverse society and that VOM advocates hunger for a "simpler, more homogeneous time").

may render a disservice to victims, offenders, or society at large. The following two sections discuss these two sets of criticisms in turn.[42]

### A. Can Restorative Justice Deliver What We Expect from a System of Criminal Justice?

Among the elements that society may reasonably expect from a criminal justice system are consistency, equality of bargaining power, due process, punishment, state control, and widespread applicability.

### 1. Consistency.

Consider first the problem of inconsistent results. The traditional criminal justice system aims at uniformity, employing a system of graded offenses and sentencing guidelines designed to assure that like cases are treated alike.[43] Although far from perfect in realizing this goal, the system at least holds consistency up as an ideal and includes measures designed to bring it about.[44] Moreover, judges, prosecutors, and defense attorneys are repeat players who tend to see cases in categorical terms (e.g., a car accident: pedestrian versus driver) rather than in terms of ascribed qualities of the participants (e.g., black driver, white pedestrian).[45] However, VOM lacks both an obvious "metric" (e.g., what is the appropriate number of hours of community service for a shoplifting offense?[46]) and the repeat-player quality of formal adjudication.[47] The mediator may have seen many cases similar to the one at hand, but the victim and the offender will most likely be in their

---

42. The term "internal critique" describes a critique or assessment that takes as its point of departure goals and values that its new movement professes, or that reasonably may be attributed to it.

43. *See, e.g., A Symposium on Sentencing Reform in the States*, 64 U. COLO. L. REV. 645 (1993).

44. *See, e.g.*, Leonard Orland & Kevin R. Reitz, *Epilogue: A Gathering of State Sentencing Commissions*, 64 U. COLO. L. REV. 837, 844 (1993).

45. The "social contact hypothesis," a leading school of social science thought, holds that interacting with large numbers of people of different races diminishes prejudice, because the individual learns, through experience, that people of different races and ethnicities are similar to those of her own group—some good, some bad. For a summary of this theory and its leading contender, the "confrontation theory," see Richard Delgado, Chris Dunn, Pamela Brown, Helena Lee & David Hubbert, *Fairness and Formality: Minimizing the Risk of Prejudice in Alternative Dispute Resolution*, 1985 WIS. L. REV. 1359, 1385-87 (summarizing social science studies suggesting that a regime of firm rules and sanctions is best calculated to suppress racist impulses, even the unconscious kind).

46. On this lack of a readily available metric for compensatory justice, see Ashworth, *supra* note 8, at 280-85, 290-94 (noting that harms to "the community" are especially hard to quantify).

47. In mediation, the mediator may be somewhat of a repeat player (although not so much as a judge), but the victim and offender are likely to be first-time (or at least infrequent) participants. *See* Delgado et al., *supra* note 45, at 1365.

situation for the first time.[48] Without any prior experience, different victims and offenders may decide similar cases differently, leading to inconsistency in punishment.

### 2. *Inequality of bargaining power.*

VOM gives great power to the victim, and mediators and judges reinforce that power, placing defendants in an almost powerless position. For example, the mediator frequently advises the offender that he will be referred back to the court system for trial if he and the victim cannot reach a restitution agreement.[49] The mediator may also tell the offender that the judge will take his lack of cooperation into account at the time of sentencing. This leaves the victim with the power to price the crime based on her subjective reaction, while at the same time confronting the offender with a harsh choice: cooperate or go to jail.[50]

### 3. *Waiver of constitutional rights.*

Related to the above-mentioned coercive quality of mediation is the issue of waiver of constitutional rights.[51] Enacted during a period when the "king's peace" view of crime and criminal justice prevailed, rather than during the earlier period when private restitution served as chief remedy,[52] our Constitution and Bill of Rights guarantee the criminally accused certain rights, including the right to confront witnesses, to be represented by counsel, and to avoid self-incrimination.[53] Fearing abuse by the powerful state, the Framers incorporated these protections against overzealous prosecution and police practices.[54] However, because VOM pressures offenders to accept informal resolution of the charges against them and to waive representation by a lawyer, trial by jury, and the right to appeal, it would seem to stand on constitutionally questionable ground.[55] Moreover, mediation takes place early in the criminal process, at a time when the offender may be un-

---

48. *See* note 45 *supra* and accompanying text.

49. *See* Brown, *supra* note 8, at 1267, 1269-70.

50. *See* note 46 *supra* and accompanying text; *see also* Brown, *supra* note 8, at 1249.

51. *See* notes 28-31, 48-50 *supra* and accompanying text.

52. *See* notes 9-14 *supra* and accompanying text.

53. *See* U.S. CONST. amend. V, VI; *see also* JEROLD H. ISRAEL, YALE KAMISAR & WAYNE R. LAFAVE, CRIMINAL PROCEDURE AND THE CONSTITUTION 33-54 (1999) (discussing the way in which these rights were extended to all criminal defendants).

54. *See* WAYNE R. LAFAVE & JEROLD H. ISRAEL, CRIMINAL PROCEDURE § 2.1 (2d ed. 1992).

55. *See* notes 28-31, 48-50 *supra* and accompanying text.

aware of the evidence against him, or the range of defenses available.[56] Furthermore, social science evidence compiled by VOM's defenders is one-sided, adulatory, and lacking basic elements of scholarly rigor—such as blind studies, controls for variables, and randomization—that one would wish in connection with a widespread social experiment.[57] In the current state of research, neither offenders nor their advisors can predict what mediation will really be like.[58] Thus, a defendant may be unable to waive his rights "knowingly and intelligently" as required by the Constitution.[59]

### 4. *Punishment.*

Our society has further expectations of any system of criminal adjudication. These include the traditional goals of criminal punishment—deterrence, rehabilitation, increased societal safety, and retribution.[60] Mediation may accomplish some of these objectives in individual cases, but only incidentally and as a byproduct of its principal objectives of compensating the victim and avoiding incarceration for the offender.[61] During mediation, if an offender is willing to apologize and make restitution, he is released immediately into society with little check on whether he is fully rehabilitated.[62] Accordingly, society's need for retribution or vengeance remains unsatisfied. This is not surprising: Most restorative justice theorists consider retribution an illegitimate relic of a more barbaric age.[63]

### 5. *State control.*

Another troubling aspect of VOM is that it may upset social expectations by casting a wider net of state control than we expect. One way this may happen is that minor cases that ordinarily would have been dismissed or treated summarily in the traditional system receive full-blown treatment under VOM.[64] Indeed, one study showed that VOM *increased* incarceration

---

56. *See* Brown, *supra* note 8, at 1263-64.

57. *See, e.g.,* Elmar Weitenkamp, *Can Restitution Serve as a Reasonable Alternative to Imprisonment?, in* RESTORATIVE JUSTICE ON TRIAL, *supra* note 8, at 84, 94.

58. *See id.; see also* Guill, *supra* note 8, at 1327-28 (arguing that the literature is dismissive of problems and objections).

59. *See* Johnson v. Zerbst, 304 U.S. 458, 465 (1938) (holding that waiver of constitutional rights must be knowing and voluntary).

60. On these four classic goals of criminal punishment, see JOSHUA DRESSLER, CASES AND MATERIALS ON CRIMINAL LAW 21-35 (1994).

61. *See* text accompanying notes 9-41 *supra* (discussing the objectives and ambitions of restorative justice).

62. *See* Robert Carl Schehr, From Restoration to Transformation: Victim Offender Mediation as Transformative Justice 19-21 (1999) (unpublished manuscript, on file with author).

63. *See, e.g.,* WRIGHT, *supra* note 8, at 133, 135; Van Ness, *supra* note 8, at 251-52, 258-59, 266.

64. *See* Weitenkamp, *supra* note 57, at 81-84.

because many offenders who would not have received jail time entered into a restitution agreement, but then failed to carry it out. These offenders were then referred back to court, where they were sentenced for failure to complete their restitution bargain.[65]

### 6. *VOM's limited applicability.*

Finally, mediation cannot be applied, without radical modification, to victimless crimes, such as drug offenses or crimes of attempt, or to offenses against the state or a corporation.[66] In these cases, no ordinary victim is available to meet with the perpetrator and discuss restitution, nor has the perpetrator victimized a specific individual or community who could be made whole.

### B. *Disservice Toward Particular Groups*

Defenders of restorative justice and VOM frequently assert that this type of informal justice is beneficial to society, offenders, and victims. What they neglect to mention, however, is that informal justice may also have a number of downsides for both victims and offenders.

### 1. *Victims.*

Mediation may disserve victims by pressuring them to forgive offenders before they are psychologically ready to do so.[67] Mediators, who typically want both parties to put aside their anger and distrust, may intimate that victims are being obstructionist or emotionally immature if they refuse to do so. Such victims may in fact harbor perfectly understandable anger and resentment over the crime.[68] A victim who already blames herself may magnify that self-blame; this risk is most severe if the offender is an acquaintance or intimate partner of the victim.[69] Furthermore, VOM casts the victim in the role of sentencer, holding the power of judgment over the offender. Not only does this lead to a lack of proportionality and consistency,[70] but it may also place an unwelcome burden on the victim who will end up determining the

---

65. *See, e.g., id.*

66. In these cases, either no victim exists, or the harm is so diffuse as to make restitution and compensatory justice impracticable. *See* WRIGHT, *supra* note 8, at 147-48 (noting that where no individual victim exists, restitution might go to the community as a whole, or it may not be required if the victim does not want it); Ashworth, *supra* note 8, at 284.

67. *See,* Brown, *supra* note 8, at 1273-76.

68. *See id.* at 1266, 1273.

69. *See id.* at 1278-81.

70. *See* text accompanying notes 43-48 *supra.*

fate of an often young and malleable offender. Not every victim will welcome this responsibility.[71] In pressuring the victim to "forgive and move on" and handing him the power of sentencer, VOM may end up compounding the injury received from the crime itself.

### 2. *Offenders.*

At the same time, VOM may disserve offenders, who lose procedural guarantees of regularity and fair treatment.[72] Offenders are urged to be forthcoming and admit what they did, yet often what they say is admissible against them in court if the case is returned.[73] Finally, as mentioned earlier, mediation may not meet social expectations for a system of criminal justice: It dismisses retribution, a valid social impulse; abjures incapacitation, even for serious offenses; offers little in the way of deterrence (a forty-five minute session is not unpleasant enough); and reduces recidivism little, if at all, perhaps because offenders' basic attitudes are unchanged, and the compulsory nature of the mediation induces only superficial expressions of shame and regret.[74]

### III. EXTERNAL CRITIQUE: LARGER, SYSTEMIC PROBLEMS WITH RESTORATIVE JUSTICE AND VICTIM-OFFENDER MEDIATION

As we have seen, restorative justice, in some respects, falls short of achieving its professed goals, or, indeed, those that any system of criminal justice, even narrowly understood, should be expected to accomplish. This section examines restorative justice in light of broader political and social values, such as its ability to spark needed social change, moral reflection, or altered relationships between offender and victim communities. As will be seen, restorative justice raises troubling issues when viewed through this lens as well.

### A. *Restoration of the Status Quo Ante*

One difficulty with restorative justice inheres in the concept itself. Restorative justice, like tort law, attempts to restore the parties to the status quo ante—the position they would have been in had the crime not occurred—through restitution and payment.[75] But if that status quo is marked by radical

---

71. *See* Brown, *supra* note 8, at 1266-67.

72. *See* notes 54-55 *supra* and accompanying text; Brown, *supra* note 8, at 1284-86 (noting that VOM may be especially hard on minorities and the tongue-tied).

73. *See* Brown, *supra* note 8, at 1288-90 (noting the risk of self-incrimination).

74. *See* note 85 *infra* and accompanying text; *see also* WRIGHT, *supra* note 8, at 27 (describing punishment as the "deliberate infliction of pain" and rehabilitative sanctions as constructive measures); Ashworth, *supra* note 8, at 283-86 (doubting whether society is prepared to forfeit retributive punishment in favor of a restorative justice approach).

ugh restitution and payment.[75] But if that status quo is marked by radical inequality and abysmal living conditions for the offender, returning the parties to their original positions will do little to spark social change. The mediation agreement ordinarily requires payment from the offender to the victim, when in many cases it will be the offender who needs a better education, increased job training, and an improved living environment. Offenders rarely are assigned work that will benefit them or lead to new job opportunities; rather, they end up performing menial services for the victim, such as cutting his grass, painting his porch, or making simple repairs.[76] When the offender performs services for the community, they typically take the form of unskilled labor, such as clearing brush, picking up trash in city parks, or painting over graffiti.[77]

A key component of VOM consists of shaming the offender—making him feel the full force of the wrongfulness of his action, thus causing him to experience remorse.[78] Yet, this adjustment is all one-way: No advocate of VOM, to my knowledge, suggests that the middle-class mediator, the victim, or society at large should feel shame or remorse over the conditions that led to the offender's predicament. Of course, many offenders will be antisocial individuals who deserve little solicitude, while many victims will have well-developed social consciences and empathize with the plight of the urban poor. But nothing in restorative justice or VOM encourages this kind of analysis or understanding.[79] In most cases, a vengeful victim and a middle-class mediator will gang up on a young, minority offender, exact the expected apology, and negotiate an agreement to pay back what she has taken from the victim by deducting portions of her earnings from her minimum-wage job. Little social transformation is likely to arise from transactions of this sort.

---

75. *Cf.* WRIGHT, *supra* note 8, at 124, 129 (acknowledging that restitution can be regressive, but noting that this is not a frequent concern); Schehr, *supra* note 62 (noting that restitution is arguably inherently conservative, since its goal is to restore parties to the situation that prevailed before their interaction took place).

76. On the range of work assignments, see Bazemore & Griffiths, *supra* note 22, at 28; Schehr, *supra* note 62, at 3-5, 21-22 (on menial work assignments, in general); Reginald A. Wilkinson, *Community Justice in Ohio*, CORRECTIONS TODAY, Dec. 1997, at 100-01.

77. *See* note 76 *supra*.

78. On shame as an ingredient in VOM and restorative justice, see generally VAN NESS & STRONG, *supra* note 8; Brown, *supra* note 8. On shame as a crime control strategy, see generally JOHN BRAITHWAITE, CRIME, SHAME, AND REINTEGRATION (1989). For critiques of the shaming approach, see generally Toni M. Massaro, *Shame, Culture, and American Criminal Law*, 89 MICH. L. REV. 1880 (1991); Robert Weisberg, *Criminal Law, Criminology, and the Small World of Legal Scholarship*, 63 U. COLO. L. REV. 521 (1992).

79. *See generally* Schehr, *supra* note 62.

## B. *Unlikelihood of Sparking Moral Reflection and Development*

By the same token, it seems unlikely that VOM will produce the desired internal, moral changes in the offender.[80] In theory, bringing the offender to the table to confront the victim face-to-face will enable him to realize the cost of his actions in human terms and to resolve to lead a better life.[81] Some offenders may, indeed, have a crisis of conscience upon meeting the person she has victimized. But a forty-five minute meeting is unlikely to have a lasting effect if the offender is released to her neighborhood and teenage peer group immediately afterwards.[82] If the offender-victim encounter is brief and perfunctory, and the ensuing punishment demeaning or menial, young offenders will learn to factor the cost of restitution into their practical calculus the next time they are tempted to commit a crime and to parrot what is expected of them when caught. Most offenders are at an early stage of Kohlberg's moral development, seeing right and wrong in pragmatic terms— the action is right if you can get away with it, wrong if you are caught and punished.[83] A short encounter with a victim is unlikely to advance them to a higher stage. Reports of young offenders show that most have little self-esteem,[84] yet both the mediation and the ensuing work an offender performs for the victim or his community come perilously close to degradation rituals. Rarely, if ever, is the offender ordered to do something that will benefit him. For all these reasons, VOM is apt to do little to make an offender a better person; indeed, in a few studies, recidivism increased, compared to a similar group subject to the ordinary criminal justice system.[85]

## C. *Inequality of Treatment of Offenders and Victims*

Mediation treats the *victim* respectfully, according him the status of an end-in-himself, while the offender is treated as a thing to be managed, shamed, and conditioned.[86] Most surveys of VOM programs ask the victim if he felt better afterwards. By contrast, offenders are merely asked whether

---

80. On the hope that VOM will transform hardened criminals into thoughtful, law-abiding citizens, see Brown, *supra* note 8, at 1259-61.

81. *See id.* at 1259-60.

82. In other words, the reinforcing effect of the neighborhood and peer group is likely to be much more enduring and influential than that of mediation.

83. *See* JAMES Q. WILSON & RICHARD J. HERRNSTEIN, CRIME AND HUMAN NATURE 392-93 (1985); Bruce A. Arrigo & Robert C. Schehr, *Restoring Justice for Juveniles: A Critical Analysis of Victim-Offender Mediation*, 15 JUSTICE Q. 629, 653 (1998).

84. *See, e.g., Turning Society's Losers into Winners, an Interview with Dennis A. Challeen*, 19 JUDGES J. 4, 5 (1980).

85. *See* P. R. SCHNEIDER, RESTITUTION AS AN ALTERNATIVE DISPOSITION FOR SERIOUS JUVENILE OFFENDERS (1982); Weitenkamp, *supra* note 57, at 84. *But see* VAN NESS & STRONG, *supra* note 8, at 10 (finding small, insignificant reductions in recidivism).

86. *See* notes 12-18, 36-40 *supra* and accompanying text.

they completed their work order and whether they recidivated.[87] Offenders sense this and play along with what is desired, while the victim and middle-class mediator participate in a paroxysm of righteousness. In such a setting, the offender is apt to grow even more cynical than before and learn what to say the next time to please the mediator, pacify the victim, and receive the lightest restitution agreement possible.

The offender's cynicism may not just be an intuition; it may be grounded in reality: Informal dispute resolution is even more likely to place him at a disadvantage than formal adjudication. In court, a panoply of procedural devices serve as a brake against state power and overzealous prosecution.[88] Each defendant is assigned a lawyer, who has a prescribed time and place for speaking.[89] The state bears a heavy burden of proof.[90] Moreover, visible features of the American Creed, such as the flag, the robes, and the judge sitting on high, remind all present that principles, such as fairness, equal treatment, and every person receiving his day in court, are to govern, rather than the much less noble values we often act upon during moments of informality.[91] In less formal settings, the same individuals who will behave with fairness during occasions of state will feel much freer to tell an ethnic joke or deny a person of color or a woman a job opportunity.[92] This "fairness and formality" thesis, solidly grounded in social science understandings of the dynamics of prejudice,[93] counsels against using VOM for offenders who are

---

87. *See, e.g.,* MARK S. UMBREIT, VICTIM MEETS OFFENDER: THE IMPACT OF RESTORATIVE JUSTICE AND MEDIATION (1994) (reporting studies of satisfaction in four juvenile courts that employed victim-offender mediation); WRIGHT, *supra* note 8, at 129; William Bradshaw & Mark S. Umbreit, *Crime Victims Meet Juvenile Offenders: Contributing Factors to Victim Satisfaction with Mediated Dialog,* JUV. & FAM. CT. J., Summer 1998, at 17, 19, 21-24; Stella P. Hughes & Anne L. Schneider, *Victim-Offender Mediation: Characteristics and Perceptions of Effectiveness,* 35 CRIME & DELINQ. 217, 229 (1989) (finding victims satisfied and offenders unlikely to recidivate); Schehr, *supra* note 62; Mark S. Umbreit & Jean Greenwood, *National Survey of Victim-Offender Mediation Programs in the United States,* 16 MEDIATION Q. 235, 244-45 (1999) (asking survey victims about their feelings and degree of satisfaction and focusing on whether offenders completed the restitution agreement).

88. *See* notes 54-55 *supra* and accompanying text; Delgado et al., *supra* note 45, at 1367-75, 1402.

89. *See* Delgado et al., *supra* note 45, at 1402.

90. *See e.g.,* DRESSLER, *supra* note 60, at 8-9 (discussing the burden of proof in criminal cases).

91. *See* Delgado et al., *supra* note 45, at 1383-84 (pointing out that at moments of intimacy and informality, individuals are more likely to tell a racist joke, favor friends in job searches, or disparage minorities or women).

92. *See id.* at 1383-85, 1388.

93. *See id.* at 1375-83, 1402-04 (discussing the social science foundation of the fairness-and-formality hypothesis).

young, black, Latino, or otherwise different from the white, middle-class norm many Americans implicitly embrace.[94]

## D. *Racial and Social Inequality*

The prime architects of the VOM movement seem to believe that mediators can balance, or counter, inequalities among the parties.[95] However, their own writing about race is replete with stereotypes.[96] Rather than

---

94. *See id.* at 1387-89, 1402-04 (noting that deformalized adjudication exacerbates preexisting power differentials among the participants and increases the likelihood of a biased outcome).

95. *See* Umbreit, *supra* note 8, at 270 (expressing this faith).

96. For example, a leading proponent of VOM, addressing the problem of mediation when one of the parties is a minority group member, writes of African Americans that "understanding the cultural base from which the client is operating" is key. MARK S. UMBREIT, NATIONAL INST. OF CORRECTIONS INFO. CTR., VICTIM OFFENDER MEDIATION IN URBAN/MULTI-CULTURAL SETTINGS 12 (1986). Citing other authorities, seemingly with approval, this author goes on to assert that this understanding includes that blacks are church-oriented, share "child care, food, money, and emotional support," and affirm "a value system which embraces a sense of 'we-ness.'" *Id.* at 13. Moreover, blacks supposedly exhibit an interpersonal style that is "'animated, interpersonal and confrontational,'" while whites are cool and impersonal. *Id.* Black talk is said to be "'heated, loud, and generates affect.'" *Id.* Whites use argument to express anger; blacks, routinely, use argument when trying to persuade. *See id.* at 13-14. Blacks have no respect for authority—merely because something is published "or in some other way certified by experts in the field is not sufficient for many blacks to establish its authority." *Id.* at 14 (citing authorities). Blacks are said to follow a value system in which it is permissible to interrupt, "rather than waiting for their turn," and in which spontaneity of expression is routine. *Id.* They do not understand rules regarding generalization, so that statements like "'white people are racists'" are "not intended to be all inclusive." *Id.* at 15. "Within black culture, the applicable rule is 'If the shoe fits, wear it.'" *Id.*

Further generalizations about blacks related by the same author deal with eye contact, "hot" versus "cool" interactive style, use of titles and surnames, and boastfulness (tolerated and approved of in the black community). *See id.* at 16-17.

Latinos ("Hispanic people") do not come off much better. Latinos are supposedly deeply respectful of authority. "Whether the locus is nature, fate, age, God, or authority, it tends to be more external than internal," in contrast to Anglos who see themselves in charge of their fates. *Id.* at 6-7. Challenging a person's opinion is evidence of "disrespect," a major sin. *Id.* at 7. Hispanic people live in a "hierarcial [sic] world," in which respect and calling people by their last names are of utmost importance. *Id.* at 7-8. The culture is said to encourage dependency, so that the mediator or social worker must "be sure the individual understands you through use of language that is clear, concise, and simple. Second, be warm and personal . . . (yet not) overly friendly, effusive. . . ." *Id.* at 8.

For further stereotypes about minority communities, see Howard H. Irving, Michael Benjamin & Jose San-Pedro, *Family Mediation and Cultural Diversity: Mediating with Latino Families*, 16 MEDIATION Q. 325, 327-30 (1999), which includes the following wisdom about Latinos for fellow mediators:

- Group-oriented (family over all);
- Obsessed with machismo and honor;
- "Sensitive to insult or criticism;"
- Devoid of any sense of time urgency (time is flexible);
- "Emotions are close to the surface;"
- Prone to escalating conflict rapidly, and unable to let it go; and
- Susceptible, in the case of men, to "shame, which in turn promotes marital . . . desertion . . . and divorce."

breaking down the barriers and preconceptions that parties bring to the table, mediation is apt to compound preexisting power and status differentials even more systematically and seriously than formal, in-court resolution.[97]  VOM sets up a relatively coercive encounter in many cases between an inarticulate, uneducated, socially alienated youth with few social skills and a hurt, vengeful victim.  This encounter is mediated by a middle-class, moralistic mediator who shares little background or sympathy with the offender, but has everything in common with the victim.  To label this encounter a negotiation seems a misnomer, for it is replete with overt social coercion.

### E.  *Prompting Recognition of Common Humanity*

Nothing is wrong with requiring persons who have harmed others without justification to make restitution.  But forcing a needy person who has stolen a loaf of bread to do so is regressive, unless accompanied by measures aimed at easing his poverty.[98]  In VOM, all the onus is placed on the offender to change; the victim is required only to come to the bargaining table, discuss how the crime has affected him, negotiate a restitution agreement, and accept an apology.  Why not require victims to take a bus tour of the offender's neighborhood and learn something about the circumstances in which he lives?  In traditional adjudication, judges, prosecutors, defense attorneys, and jurors will all be privy to this information and be able to consider it when charging and sentencing, but with mediation, the mediator and the victim often will not.  Mediation aims at emotional closure,[99] but without a reciprocal exchange of information, any closure is apt to occur only on the most superficial level.  If the objective of VOM is to have both sides recognize their common humanity, measures of this sort ought to be considered.  Why not even encourage the *victim*, in appropriate cases, to perform service to the offender or his or her community as a condition of receiving restitution (for example, by serving as a mentor or big brother/sister to a youth like the of-

---

Mediators are urged to cultivate patience, respect the existing hierarchy and macho practices, and be ready for a parade of "allusions, proverbs, folk tales, storytelling, humor, metaphor, and reframing." *Id.* at 332-33.  Because of Latinos' concept of extended time, mediators also need to be ready for clients who miss appointments or show up late.  *See id.* at 334; *see also* Cherise D. Hairston, *African Americans in Mediation Literature: A Neglected Population,* 16 MEDIATION Q. 357, 360-61 (1999) ("A review of mediation literature indicates minimal awareness of and sensitivity to historical, political, societal, and cultural influences.").

   97. *See* Delgado et al., *supra* note 45, at 1388-89, 1402-03; text accompanying notes 116-123 *infra.*

   98. Recall the famous line from Anatole France about how the law, in its majesty, forbids rich and poor alike from sleeping under bridges or stealing bread.  *See* DICTIONARY OF QUOTATIONS 363 (Bergen Evans ed., 1968).

   99. *See* Brown, *supra* note 8, at 1263; Reske, *supra* note 8, at 14-15; Mark S. Umbreit, *Restorative Justice through Mediation,* J.L. & SOC. WORK, Spring 1995, at 1, 2.

fender)? Countless studies of mediated crime adopt the feelings of the victim as the principal measure of success or failure—the better the victim feels afterwards, the more successful the mediation.[100] Yet, sometimes in a successful mediation, the victim should feel *worse*, or at least realize that matters are not as simple as she might have thought.

F. *Which Community is to be Restored?*

In a similar vein, VOM will frequently lead to a restitution agreement that includes service to "the community."[101] Indeed, one of the principal advantages of VOM is said to be its ability to repair the breach that the offender's crime has opened between himself and that same community.[102] Yet proponents of restorative justice rarely focus on the precise nature of that community. In a diverse, multicultural society, many collectivities may vie for that status. To which does the offender owe restitution? If, for example, the offender is to rake leaves, should he be required to do it in a park near where the victim lives? In a large municipal park serving the entire city? In one in his own neighborhood? Descriptions of successful mediation abound with stories of offenders made to perform services to victims' churches, for example.[103] Apart from obvious issues of separation of church and state, such privatized, particularized service is troublingly reminiscent of peonage and prison labor gangs.

G. *Erasing the Public Dimension of Criminal Prosecution*

Moreover, such particularized mediation atomizes disputes, so that patterns, such as police abuse or the overcharging of black men, do not stand out readily. It forfeits what Owen Fiss and others call the public dimension of adjudication.[104] Mediation pays scant attention to the public interests in

---

100. *See* Reske, *supra* note 8; Van Biema, *supra* note 8 (using feelings as a measure of success).

101. *See, e.g.,* text accompanying note 77 *supra*; Bazemore & Griffiths, *supra* note 22, at 28. For critiques of the notion that, in a diverse society like ours, anything like a unitary community exists, see Massaro, *supra* note 78, at 1922-23; Sally Engle Merry, *Defining "Success" in the Neighborhood Justice Movement, in* NEIGHBORHOOD JUSTICE 172, 175-77 (Roman Iomasic & Malcolm M. Feeley eds., 1987); Daniel R. Ortiz, *Categorical Community*, 51 STAN. L. REV. 769 (1999).

102. *See* note 77 *supra* and accompanying text; Bazemore & Griffiths, *supra* note 22, at 28.

103. *See* Bazemore & Griffiths, *supra* note 22, at 25 (describing a work assignment under which the offender was sent to work in a food bank sponsored by victim's church); *see also* WRIGHT, *supra* note 8, at 151 (warning that restitution can be corrupted to serve private gain); Burt Galaway, *Victim Participation in the Penal-Corrective Process*, 10 VICTIMOLOGY: AN INT'L J. 617, 624-25 (1985) (addressing the concern that restitution can be corrupted to serve private gain).

104. *See* Owen Fiss, *Against Settlement*, 93 YALE L.J. 1073, 1085 (1984). Mediation, as observed earlier, takes place in private settings, and the results are rarely recorded or reported in a newspaper or anywhere else.

criminal punishment, particularly retribution.[105] It also lacks the symbolic element of a public trial, trying instead to compensate by formalized talking among private participants. The criminal justice system, of course, is a principal means by which society reiterates its deepest values; loss of that opportunity is cause for concern.

The timing of VOM's advent is also curious: It first appeared when the United States' demographic composition was beginning to shift rapidly in the direction of a majority nonwhite population.[106] Juries were beginning to contain, for the first time, substantial numbers of nonwhite members, and at least one scholar of color would soon encourage black jurors to acquit young black men, who are, in their view more useful to the community free than behind bars.[107] Could it be that VOM arose, consciously or not, in response to the threat of jury nullification?

### H. *Treating Conflict as Pathology*

Perhaps the above concerns can be captured in the notion of conflict as pathology.[108] Like many forms of mediation, VOM treats conflict as aberrational, and the absence of it as the desired state.[109] Yet, in a society like ours, tension among groups may be normal, and not a sign of social pathology.[110] With a history of slavery, conquest, and racist immigration laws, the United States today exhibits the largest gap between the wealthy and the poor of any Western industrialized society.[111] Until recently, Southern states segregated school children by race[112] and criminalized marriage between whites and blacks.[113] Surely, in such a society, one would expect the have-nots to attempt to change their social position (by legal or illegal means), and the

---

105. *See* notes 60-63 *supra* and accompanying text; Albert W. Alschuler, *Mediation with a Mugger: The Shortage of Adjudicative Services and the Need for a Two-Tier Trial System in Civil Cases*, 99 HARV. L. REV. 1808, 1809-10 (1986) (questioning whether mediation satisfies the public's demand for accountability); Ashworth, *supra* note 8, at 284 (also questioning whether mediation satisfies the public's demand for accountability).

106. In the late 1970s and early 1980s, when society was first becoming aware of the growth in minority populations.

107. *See generally* Paul Butler, *Racially Based Jury Nullification: Black Power in the Criminal Justice System*, 105 YALE L.J. 677 (1995). For a forerunner of the Butler thesis, see Austin, *supra* note 4, at 1771-72.

108. *See* Richard Delgado, *Conflict as Pathology: An Essay for Trina Grillo*, 81 MINN. L. REV. 1391 (1997) (first coining the term).

109. *See id.* at 1397.

110. *See id.* at 1397, 1400-02.

111. *See* Tom Teepen, *It's True: Rich Just Get Richer; Poor, Poorer*, MILWAUKEE J. SENTINEL, Sept. 7, 1999, at 10.

112. *See* Brown v. Board of Education, 347 U.S. 483 (1954).

113. *See* Loving v. Virginia, 388 U.S. 1 (1967).

haves to resist these attempts. Conflict is a logical and expected result.[114] One also would expect the majority group to use the criminal law, at least in part, as a control device—a means of keeping tabs on any behavior of subordinate groups that threatens or irritates, such as loud music, congregating on sidewalks, writing graffiti on freeway overpasses, and shoplifting.[115] Insofar as restorative justice aims at smoothing over the rough edges of social competition and adjusting subaltern people to their roles, it is profoundly conservative. While restoration and healing are emotionally powerful objectives, it is hard to deny that they can have a repressive dimension as well.

## IV. "BUT CONSIDER THE ALTERNATIVE": THE CRIMINAL JUSTICE SYSTEM

Before rejecting restorative justice and VOM for the reasons mentioned in Parts II and III of this essay, it behooves us, as its advocates urge, to consider the alternative—the conventional criminal justice system. For if informal adjudication of offenders is imperfect, the traditional system may be even worse. And when one does examine the traditional system, one discovers that it is far from the safe haven that formal settings generally provide for the disempowered. Instead, as a result of a slow evolution, our criminal justice system has emerged as perhaps the most inegalitarian and racist structure in society. Our prisons are largely black and brown.[116] Indigent defendants are assigned a lawyer from the underfinanced public defender's office and encouraged to plead guilty to a lesser offense in return for a shorter sentence, even if they are innocent or have valid defenses to the charges against them.[117] Minority defendants receive harsher sentences than middle-class whites charged with the same offense, while black men convicted of murdering whites receive the death penalty ten times more often than do whites who kill blacks.[118] Police focus on minority youth congregating on street corners; they stop black motorists and Latino-looking men at airports so regularly that the black community refers to the traffic stops as "DWBs"

---

114. *See* Delgado, *supra* note 108, at 1397-1402.

115. On the use of the criminal law to demonize and control minority groups of color, see Richard Delgado, *Rodrigo's Eighth Chronicle: Black Crime, White Fears: On the Social Construction of Threat*, 80 VA. L. REV. 503 (1994).

116. *See generally* MARC MAUER, THE SENTENCING PROJECT: YOUNG BLACK MEN AND THE CRIMINAL JUSTICE SYSTEM: A GROWING NATIONAL PROBLEM (1990) (discussing disproportionate number of black men in penal institutions).

117. On the difficult conditions under which most public defenders work, see James M. Doyle, *"It's the Third World Down There!": The Colonialist Vocation and American Criminal Justice*, 27 HARV. C.R.-C.L. L. REV. 71 (1992).

118. On the racial gap in sentencing, see MAUER, *supra* note 116; Andrea Blum, *Jail Time by the Book: Black Youths More Likely to Get Tough Sentences Than Whites, Study Shows*, A.B.A. J., May 1999, at 18. On the death penalty, see DAVID C. BALDUS, GEORGE WOODWORTH & CHARLES A. PULASKI, JR., EQUAL JUSTICE AND THE DEATH PENALTY (1990) (examining the role of racial bias in the application of the death penalty).

("Driving While Black").[119]  Meanwhile, the war on drugs causes police to target minority communities, where drug transactions tend to be conspicuous, rather than in middle-class areas where use is more covert.[120]  Black judges face recusal motions more often than their white counterparts often from white litigants concerned that the judge may rule against them because of their race.[121]  Studies of the behavior of mock jurors show that baby-faced defendants are acquitted more often than less attractive ones against whom the evidence is exactly the same.[122]

The criminal justice system, then, may be the lone institution in American society where formal values and practices are worse—more racist, more inegalitarian—than the informal ones that most citizens share.  As previously mentioned, the situation in this society is generally the opposite:  Our formal values, the ones that constitute the American Creed, are exemplary—every person is equal, everyone deserves full respect as a moral agent, one person one vote—while informality harbors risks for women, blacks, and members of other outgroups.[123]  In our criminal justice system, however, the opposite situation prevails.  There alone, as in South Africa under the old regime, the formal values are implicitly or explicitly racist.  Just as in South Africa, in former times, a black, such as a stranded motorist, might receive kind treatment from the occasional white traveler while the official police would pass him by, members of stigmatized groups today are apt to receive harsher treatment from U.S. police, judges, and juries than they might get, with luck, at a mediation table.  As with Jews in Holland during the Third Reich, private kindness is at least possible; the official kind, unlikely.  Despite the main drawbacks of privatized, decentralized, informal mediation, offenders will often be better off taking their chances within VOM than within the formal system.

---

119. *See generally* City of Chicago v. Morales, 527 U.S. 41 (1999) (striking down anti-gang ordinance that prohibited congregating on the streets as impermissibly vague).  On "driving while black," see AMERICAN CIVIL LIBERTIES UNION, DRIVING WHILE BLACK: RACIAL PROFILING ON OUR NATION'S HIGHWAYS (1999); Michael A. Fletcher, *Driven to Extremes: Black Men Take Steps to Avoid Police Stops*, WASH. POST, Mar. 29, 1996, at A1; Kevin Johnson, *ACLU Campaign Yields Race Bias Suit*, USA TODAY, May 19, 1999, at 4A.  On profiling of Latinos, see Julie Amparano, *Waiting to Celebrate*, A.B.A. J., July 1999, at 68, 69.

120. On the racial impact of the war on drugs, see Andrew N. Sacher, *Inequities of the Drug War: Legislative Discrimination on the Cocaine Battlefield*, 19 CARDOZO L. REV. 1149 (1997).

121. *See* Sherril A. Ifill, *Judging the Judges: Racial Diversity, Impartiality and Representation on State Trial Courts*, 39 B.C. L. REV. 95, 114 (1997) (describing case in which defendants insisted that Judge Leon Higginbotham disqualify himself for this reason).

122. For a study of the role that baby-faced features and physical attractiveness play in determining length of sentence, see Michael G. Efran, *The Effect of Physical Appearance on the Judgment of Guilt, Interpersonal Attraction, and Severity of Recommended Punishment in a Simulated Jury Task*, 8 J. RES. PERSONALITY 45 (1979).

123. *See* Delgado et al., *supra* note 45, at 1367-75, 1383-85, 1402-03.

## V. WHAT, THEN, TO DO? A DIALOGIC APPROACH BASED ON COMPETITION BETWEEN THE TWO SYSTEMS

Assuming they have a choice, blacks, Latinos, and others subject to prejudice should examine both systems carefully before opting for one or the other. In white-dominated regions, as Rodney Hero has recently pointed out, blacks are apt to receive poor formal treatment;[124] they may be better off taking their chances with VOM. Where, by contrast, the jury pool is racially mixed and the judge sympathetic, formal adjudication may be the better choice. While these pragmatic calculations are taking place, conscientious legislators and reform-minded lawyers should work to improve both systems.

### A. *Within the Formal Criminal Justice System*

Within the formal system of courtroom justice, defense lawyers should serve as guides and native informants, helping defendants find and exploit any known niches of sympathy and fair treatment. Examples include regions where the jury pool is racially and economically mixed, where judges are trained to look behind police testimony and a record of prior convictions for possible bias and overcharging.[125] Because the formal values have become corrupted by an overlay of discriminatory practices, participants must constantly remind everyone to follow the American Creed. Legislators and community groups should urge "superformality"—new layers of formality aimed at keeping the police, prosecutors, and other agents of official power honest. Examples include police and prosecutor review boards, laws requiring the police to keep statistics on traffic stops, and instructions aimed at encouraging members of the jury to consider whether race is affecting their judgment.[126] In short, progressive lawyers and community activists should bolster the in-court version of criminal justice by expanding any informal

---

124. *See* RODNEY HERO, FACES OF INEQUALITY: SOCIAL DIVERSITY IN AMERICAN POLITICS 74-79 (1998) (examining the racial makeup of judges and juries in state courts).

125. *See generally* Doris Marie Provine, *Too Many Black Men: The Sentencing Judge's Dilemma*, 23 L. & SOC. INQUIRY 823 (1998) (discussing the problems of avoiding disproportionate conviction and sentencing of African American males); Katheryn K. Russell, *"Driving While Black": Corollary Phenomena and Collateral Consequences*, 80 B.C. L. REV. 717, 728 (1999) (describing Judge Nancy Gerstner's refusal to sentence a black motorist to a long term under a "three-strikes" type statute, because of the way police target black motorists for zealous enforcement). On the need for skepticism over eyewitness identification in cross-racial settings, see John Gibeaut, *"Yes, I'm Sure That's Him,"* A.B.A. J., Oct. 1999, at 26.

126. *See* Matt Ackerman, *Special Jury Instructions Needed if Cross Racial ID Uncorroborated*, N.J. L.J., Apr. 19, 1999, at 1, 1; Gibeaut, *supra* note 125 (noting that social scientists support the need for caution in cross-race situations); Cynthia Lee, *Race and Self-Defense: Toward a Normative Conception of Reasonableness*, 81 MINN. L. REV. 367, 482 (1996) (urging a "race switching" jury instruction aimed at requiring jurors to consider whether their verdict would be the same if the defendant and the victim were of different races).

links to justice, while seeking to impose new levels of formal oversight on the rest of the system.

## B. *Within Alternative, Informal Justice*

Reformers and critics need to call attention to the way mediation's informality can easily conceal race and class bias underneath an overlay of humanitarian concern.[127] Minority communities need to understand how this happens, so they can avoid its seductive appeal. Minorities should also lobby for structural improvements to VOM, such as more mediators of color, participation by defense attorneys, and studies that test some of VOM's overenthusiastic claims. Where VOM seems fairer than the formal justice system, defendants should "take the bait" and opt for it, while keeping alert for possible abuse and unfairness. The defense bar should attempt to counteract the powerfully conservative, status-quo-enforcing thrust of restorative justice by insisting that community and religious groups (its main sponsors) reform it. For example, minority groups could demand that work assignments benefit the offender and her community, rather than merely enhancing the middle-class or suburban communities where most victims live. Just as mediation now provides for a full airing of the victim's story, mediation should allow the offender's history be heard as well. If the offender is inarticulate, someone should be appointed to speak for him, so that those present become better informed of the social conditions that give rise to crime in a substantial sector of the population. Optimistically, this knowledge will inspire further social reform.

## C. *Short and Long-Term Strategies*

In short, persons dissatisfied with both approaches to criminal justice should adopt a short-term and a long-term strategy. The short-term would consist of steering defendants to the system where they are likely to experience the fairest treatment. The long-term strategy would focus on forcing dialog and competition between the two systems, drawing comparisons between them, making criticism overt, and attempting to engraft the best features of each onto the other. This frank merging and borrowing should promote dialog between practitioners of conventional, courtroom justice and informal mediation—something that, except in a few locations, is not taking place now. Both systems should be made to compete with each other for resources, participants, and approval in the eyes of the various constituencies that make up the criminal law's public.

---

127. *See* notes 88-95 *supra* and accompanying text.

This process, if carried out persistently and intelligently, can harness two principal theories for controlling prejudice—confrontation and social contact[128]—by challenging the conventional system and the emerging one, reminding each of its myths and values, and demanding that each equal or exceed the other in pursuit of the common goal of racial and social justice. Ultimately, no form of criminal justice, either of the traditional or the restorative variety, will work if the target community lacks a hand in designing and operating it. Blacks, Latinos, whites, middle-class, and blue-collar people must be permitted, indeed encouraged, to work together to counter exploitative arrangements that oppress them and render our society one of the most fearful and crime-ridden in the Western developed world.

---

128. *See* note 45 *supra* (explaining these two approaches).

# [13]

## CONDITIONS OF SUCCESSFUL REINTEGRATION CEREMONIES

### Dealing with Juvenile Offenders

JOHN BRAITHWAITE and STEPHEN MUGFORD*

*Shifting criminal justice practices away from stigmatization and toward reintegration is no small challenge. The innovation of community conferences in New Zealand and Australia has two structural features that are conducive to reintegrative shaming: (a) selection of the people who respect and care most about the offender as conference participants (conducing to reintegration); and (b) confrontation with victims (conducing to shaming). Observation of some failures and successes of these conferences in reintegrating both offenders and victims is used to hypothesize 14 conditions of successful reintegration ceremonies.*

The spectre of failure haunts modern criminology and penology. Deep down many feel what some say openly—that 'nothing works': that despite decades of study and debate, we are no nearer deterrence than we ever were and/or that more 'humane' forms of treatment are mere masquerades concealing a descent into Kafaesque bureaucracy where offenders suffer a slow and silent suffocation of the soul. Worse still, we fear that even when something does work, it is seen to do so only in the eyes of certain professionals, while 'outside' the system ordinary citizens are left without a role or voice in the criminal justice process.

This paper takes a different view. Rejecting the pessimism that pervades discussions about crime and punishment, it offers an optimistic view of at least one area—the punishment of juvenile offenders. It argues that it is possible to develop practices that 'work'—both in the sense of reducing recidivism and reintegrating offenders into a wider web of community ties and support and, at the same time, in giving victims a 'voice' in a fashion that is both satisfying and also socially productive. Further, it links a theory (reintegrative shaming) and a practice (the reintegration ceremony) which explain how to understand and how to implement this success.

While there are elements that are quite distinctive about both the theory and practice of reintegrative shaming, there is also a great deal in common with the theory and practice of 'making amends' (Wright 1982); restorative justice (Cragg 1992; Galaway and Hudson 1990; Zehr 1990); reconciliation (Dignan 1992; Marshall 1985; Umbreit 1985); peacemaking (Pepinsky and Quinney 1991); redress (de Haan 1990) and feminist abolitionism (Meima 1990). We differ from abolitionists, however, in believing that it is right to shame certain kinds of conduct as criminal in certain contexts.

The rest of the paper has two sections. The second section outlines some fieldwork

* Division of Philosophy and Law, The Research School of Social Sciences, The Australian National University.
We would like to thank John McDonald, Gabrielle Maxwell, David Moore, Jane Mugford, Terry O'Connell, and Clifford Shearing for the stimulation and critique they provided in developing the ideas in this paper.

JOHN BRAITHWAITE AND STEPHEN MUGFORD

which we have undertaken to examine such ceremonies, makes a relatively brief series of arguments which connect the theory of reintegrative shaming to the seminal paper by Garfinkel on degradation ceremonies and outlines how the latter must be transformed to cover reintegration ceremonies. The major point of this section is a specification of the conditions for successful reintegration ceremonies. The third and longer section follows the logic of such ceremonies, illustrating each point with material derived from the fieldwork and offering comments about policy and implementation.

### Background to the Argument: Reintegrative Shaming in Theory and Practice

The theory of reintegrative shaming (Braithwaite 1989, 1993) has been offered as a way of achieving two major aims. First, to recast criminological findings in a more coherent and productive fashion. Secondly, to offer a practical basis for a principled reform of criminal justice practices. Central to the endeavour is an understanding of the relationship between crime and social control which argues for the shaming of criminal *acts* and the subsequent reintegration of deviant *actors* once suitable redress and apology have been made. It is argued that societies that have low rates of common types of crime (such as Japan) rely more upon this type of social control, working hard at reforming the deviant through reconstructing his or her social ties. Conversely, high crime societies (such as the US) rely upon stigmatization, thus doing little to prevent cycles of re-offending.

This theory has clear practical implications and people involved in various reform programmes have drawn on it in various ways—sometimes as an inspiration for reform blueprints (see e.g., Howard and Purches 1992; Mugford and Mugford 1991, 1992; O'Connell and Moore 1992), often as a way to articulate what they are trying to achieve and give it a sharper focus. Some, such as the New Zealand Maoris, have comprehended and applied the principles of the theory for hundreds of years (Hazlehurst 1985). Where we have heard of or been involved in programmes, we have sought to carry out some limited fieldwork which would help us to understand both what is practically possible and how we might refine our ideas.

This paper utilizes such ongoing fieldwork, specifically observations of community conferences for 23 juvenile offenders in Auckland, New Zealand, and Wagga Wagga, Australia. In New Zealand, these conferences are called family group conferences. While there are differences between the approaches adopted in the two cities, both involve diverting young offenders from court and keeping them out of exclusionary juvenile institutions. Both programmes subscribe to the philosophy of reintegrative shaming as outlined above. Shame and shaming is commonly used in both programmes to describe what is going on; reintegration is commonly used in Wagga, while healing is more commonly used in Auckland for this aspect of the process. The approach in both cities involves assembling in a room the offender and supporters of the offender (usually the nuclear family, often aunts, uncles, grandparents, sometimes neighbours, counsellors, even a teacher or football coach) along with the victim of the crime (and supporters of the victim, usually from their nuclear family) under the supervision of a co-ordinator—a police sergeant in Wagga, a youth justice co-ordinator from the Department of Social Welfare in Auckland. Auckland conferences usually only have single offenders, but can have multiple victims in the room. Wagga conferences often bring together multiple offenders who were involved jointly in the same offences with

CONDITIONS OF SUCCESSFUL REINTEGRATION CEREMONIES

multiple victims. In the conferences we observed, the number of people in the room ranged from five to 30. More systematic data from New Zealand puts the average attendance at nine (Maxwell and Morris 1993: 74). At both sites, the offender(s) plays an important role in describing the nature of the offence(s). The psychological, social, and economic consequences of the offence—for victims, offenders, and others—are elicited in discussions guided by the co-ordinator. Disapproval, often emotional disapproval, is usually communicated by victims, and often by victim supporters and family members of the offender. At the same time, the professional who co-ordinates the conference strives to bring out support for and forgiveness towards the offender from participants in the conference.

A striking common feature of both locations is that the formal properties of the cautioning conference have come to take on a ceremonial or ritual character, based partly upon 'common sense', itself expanded and tempered by experiences of what does and does not seem to work well. With varying degrees of accomplishment, co-ordinators have developed procedures designed to ensure that the potential for shaming and reintegration of offenders is realized in practice. In so doing, they have effectively invented the reintegration ceremony, even if that is not what they would always call it. In this ceremony, identities are in a social crucible. The vision that an offender holds of himself as a 'tough guy' or that victims have of him as a 'mindless hooligan' are challenged, altered, and recreated (for example, as a 'good lad who has strayed into bad ways').

Viewing these events as a reintegration ceremony recalls the seminal contribution of Harold Garfinkel (1956) on 'Conditions of Successful Degradation Ceremonies'. Perhaps the same kind of social structures and socio-psychological processes he analyses in that paper are at work here, but in different combination and directed to different ends? Posing the problem that way has been a productive way for us to organize our views of reintegration ceremonies and so we choose to use the Garfinkel approach as a way of outlining this rather different set of events.

By degradation ceremonies, Garfinkel meant communicative work that names an actor as an 'outsider', that transforms an individual's total identity into an identity 'lower in the group's scheme of social types' (1956: 420). Most criminal trials are good examples of status degradation ceremonies and this view of them became a central idea in the sociology of deviance, especially among labelling theorists (see Becker 1963; Schur 1973). For Erikson (1962: 311), for example, this communicative work constitutes 'a sharp rite of transition at once moving him out of his normal position in society and transferring him into a distinctive deviant role'. Moreover, Erikson continues, an '. . . important feature of these ceremonies in our culture is that they are almost irreversible' (1962: 311).

Such a view, however, is simplistic, exaggerated, and overly deterministic (Braithwaite 1989). Most people who go into mental hospitals come out of them; many alcoholics give up drinking; most marijuana users stop being users at some point in their lives, usually permanently; most kids labelled as delinquents never go to jail as adults. Labelling theorists did useful empirical work, but their work was myopic, exclusively focused on 'front-end' processes that certify deviance. Above all, they envisaged individuals as having 'total identities'. We suggest that by employing instead the notion of multiple identities one can recast the interest in transformation ceremonies, asking questions as much about ceremonies to decertify deviance as to certify it.

141

JOHN BRAITHWAITE AND STEPHEN MUGFORD

While degradation ceremonies are about the sequence disapproval–degradation–exclusion, reintegration ceremonies are about the sequence disapproval–non-degradation–inclusion. In a reintegration ceremony, disapproval of a bad act is communicated while sustaining the identity of the actor as good. Shame is transmitted within a continuum of respect for the wrongdoer. Repair work is directed at ensuring that a deviant identity (one of the actor's multiple identities) does not become a master status trait that overwhelms other identities. Communicative work is directed at sustaining identities like daughter, student, promising footballer, in preference to creating 'master' identities like delinquent.

Considerable analytic and policy implications follow this refocusing from degradation to reintegration. Indeed, we suggest that the implication is a redesign of everything about contemporary criminal justice systems and everything about the labelling theory critique of those institutions. To achieve this, however, it is necessary to show where one must transcend earlier accounts. As a first step, we juxtapose in Table 1 Garfinkel's conditions of successful degradation ceremonies with our own conditions of successful ceremonies of reintegration. These latter were condensed from our observations and cast in a form that allows comparison and contrast. Eight of the conditions we specify for reintegration ceremonies involve presenting a deliberate twist on Garfinkel's conditions. The other six are based on observations and discussions and, we feel, address some of the theoretical neglects of the ethnomethodological tradition.

### Reintegration Ceremonies in Practice

In this section, we outline each of the 14 conditions identified in Table 1. For each one, we provide a detailed discussion, drawing on our field work observations.

### (1) The event, but not the perpetrator, is removed from the realm of its everyday character and is defined as irresponsible, wrong, a crime

Courtroom ceremonies tend to degradation rather than reintegration—that is, they remove both event *and* perpetrator from the everyday domain in just the way suggested by Garfinkel. This is because the production-line technocracy and discourse of legalism makes it easy for the offender to sustain psychological barriers against shame for acts that the court defines as wrongful. It is hard for a person who we do not know or respect, who speaks a strange legal language, who forces us into a relationship of feigned respect by making us stand when she walks into the room, to touch our soul. Thus event and perpetrator remain united. One casts out both or neither. So the denunciation of the judge may degrade the offender, but the process is so incomprehensible, such a blur, that all the judge usually accomplishes is some authoritative outcasting.

In contrast to formal courtrooms, community conferences in New Zealand and Wagga are held in less formal spaces. Conference co-ordinators purposively assemble actors with the best chance of persuading the offender of the irresponsibility of a criminal act. Close kin are prime candidates for commanding the respect that enables such persuasion, but with homeless or abused children the challenge is to discover who

## CONDITIONS OF SUCCESSFUL REINTEGRATION CEREMONIES

### TABLE 1

| Conditions of successful degradation ceremonies | Conditions of successful reintegration ceremonies |
| --- | --- |
| 1. Both event and perpetrator must be removed from the realm of their everyday character and be made to stand as 'out of the ordinary'. | 1. The event, *but not the perpetrator*, is removed from the realm of its everyday character and is defined as irresponsible, wrong, a crime. |
| 2. Both event and perpetrator must be placed within a scheme of preferences that shows the following properties:<br>(a) The preferences must not be for event A over event B, but for event of *type* A over event of *type* B. The same typing must be accomplished for the perpetrator. Event and perpetrator must be defined as instances of a uniformity and must be treated as a uniformity throughout the work of the denunciation.<br>(b) The witnesses must appreciate the characteristics of the typed person and event by referring the type to a dialectical counterpart. Ideally, the witnesses should not be able to contemplate the features of the denounced person without reference to the counter-conception, as the profanity of an occurrence or a desire or a character trait, for example, is clarified by the references it bears to its opposite, the sacred. | 2. Event and perpetrator must be uncoupled rather than defined as instances of a profane uniformity. The self of the perpetrator is sustained as sacred rather than profane. This is accomplished by comprehending: (a) how essentially good people have a pluralistic self that accounts for their occasional lapse into profane acts; and (b) that the profane act of a perpetrator occurs in a social context for which many actors may bear some shared responsibility. Collective as well as individual shame must be brought into the open and confronted. |
| 3. The denouncer must so identify himself to the witnesses that during the denunciation they regard him not as a private but as a publicly known person. | 3. Co-ordinators must identify themselves with all private parties—perpetrators, their families, victims, witnesses—as well as being identified with the public interest in upholding the law. |
| 4. The denouncer must make the dignity of the supra-personal values of the tribe salient and accessible to view, and his denunciation must be delivered in their name. | 4. Denunciation must be both by and in the name of victims and in the name of supra-personal values enshrined in the law. |
| 5. The denouncer must arrange to be invested with the right to speak in the name of these ultimate values. The success of the denunciation will be undermined if, for his authority to denounce, the denouncer invokes the personal interests that he may have acquired by virtue of the wrong done to him or someone else. | 5. Non-authoritative actors (victims, offenders, offenders' families) must be empowered with process control. The power of actors normally authorized to issue denunciations on behalf of the public interest (e.g., judges) must be decentred. |
| 6. The denouncer must get himself so defined by the witnesses that they locate him as a supporter of these values. | 6. The perpetrator must be so defined by all the participants (particularly by the perpetrator himself) that he is located as a supporter of both the supra-personal values enshrined in the law and the private interests of victims. |
| 7. Not only must the denouncer fix his distance from the person being denounced, but the witnesses must be made to exprience their distance from him also. | 7. Distance between each participant and the other participants must be closed; empathy among all participants must be enhanced; opportunities must be provided for perpetrators and victims to show (unexpected) generosity toward each other. |
| 8. Finally, the denounced person must be ritually separated from a place in the legitimate order, i.e., he must be defined as standing at a place opposed to it. He must be placed 'outside', he must be made 'strange'. | 8. The separation of the denounced person must be terminated by rituals of inclusion that place him, even physically, inside rather than outside. |
| | 9. The separation of the victim, any fear or shame of victims, must be terminated by rituals of reintegration. |
| | 10. Means must be supplied to intervene against power imbalances that inhibit either shaming or reintegration, or both. |
| | 11. Ceremony design must be flexible and culturally plural, so that participants exercise their process control constrained by only very broad procedural requirements. |
| | 12. Reintegration agreements must be followed through to ensure that they are enacted. |
| | 13. When a single reintegration ceremony fails, ceremony after ceremony must be scheduled, never giving up, until success is achieved. |
| | 14. The ceremony must be justified by a politically resonant discourse. |

143

JOHN BRAITHWAITE AND STEPHEN MUGFORD

the child does respect.[1] Perhaps there is an uncle who he feels sticks up for him, a football coach he admires, a grandmother he adores. The uncle, the football coach, and the grandmother must then be urged to attend. Normally, they are flattered to be told that they have been nominated as one of the few human beings this young person still respects. So they come. They come when the appeal to them is 'to support and help the young person to take responsibility for what they have done'. Thus the setting and the ceremonial character seek to 'hold' the offender while allowing separation from the offence.

Victims play a crucial role in this, for they are in a unique position to communicate the irresponsibility of the *act*. Much delinquency is casual and thoughtless (O'Connor and Sweetapple 1988: 117–18). The offenders who thought all they had done was to take 50 dollars from the house of a faceless person find that person is a vulnerable elderly woman who did without something significant because of the loss of the money. They learn that as a result of the break-in she now feels insecure in her own home, as does her next door neighbour. Both have invested in new security locks and are afraid to go out in the street alone because they have come to view the neighbourhood as a dangerous place. Collateral damage from victimization is normal rather than exceptional and co-ordinators become expert at drawing it out of victims and victim supporters. Techniques of neutralization (Sykes and Matza 1957) that may originally have been employed, such as '. . . I am unemployed and poor while the householder is employed and rich' are seriously challenged when confronted by the elderly victim. Sometimes this shocks the offender. Other times it does not. Many of the worst offenders have developed a capacity to cut themselves off from the shame for exploiting other human beings. They deploy a variety of barriers against feeling responsibility. But what does not affect the offender directly may affect those who have come to support her. The shaft of shame fired by the victim in the direction of the offender might go right over the offender's head, yet it might pierce like a spear through the heart of the offender's mother, sitting behind him. It is very common for offenders' mothers to start to sob when victims describe their suffering or loss. So while display of the victim's suffering may fail to hit its intended mark, the anguish of the offender's mother during the ceremony may succeed in bringing home to the offender the need to confront rather than deny an act of irresponsibility.

Indeed, in our observations mothers often seize the ceremony of the occasion to make eloquent and moving speeches that they have long wanted to make to their child:

I imagine life as a family living in a valley and the children gradually start to venture out from the family house in the valley. Eventually they have to climb up the mountain to get out of the valley. That mountain is adolescence. At the top of the mountain is a job. When they have that they can walk gently down the other side of the mountain into life. But there's another way they can go. They can decide not to climb the path up the mountain but to wander in the easier paths out into the valley. But those paths, while they are easier, lead to greater and greater

[1] A common cynicism when we have spoken to American audiences about these ideas has been that it sounds like a good idea for sweet, sheep-loving New Zealanders, with their intact families, but that it could never work in the face of the family disintegration of American slums. This is an odd perspective, given the empirical reality in New Zealand that Youth Aid Officers saw 'poor family support/background' as the most important factor *in favour of* opting for referral of a case to a family group conference rather than some other disposition (Maxwell and Morris 1993: 60–1). Moreover, in practice, 14 per cent of young people processed in family group conferences do not live with their families, compared to 4 per cent of those processed by informal police diversion (Maxwell and Morris 1993: 64, 66).

## CONDITIONS OF SUCCESSFUL REINTEGRATION CEREMONIES

darkness. I'm concerned that my little boy took one of those paths and I'm losing him into the darkness.

Co-ordinators work at bringing out collateral damage. Parents are asked: 'How did this episode affect the family?' Offenders are asked: 'How did mum and dad feel about it?' Typically, the offender will admit that their kin were 'pretty upset'. In Wagga, the co-ordinator then routinely asks why and in a large proportion of cases, young people will say something to the effect that the parents care about them or love them. This is the main chance the reintegrative co-ordinator is looking for. Once this is uttered, the co-ordinator returns to this again and again as a theme of what is being learnt from the conference. In the wrap-up, he will reaffirm that 'Jim has learned that his mum and dad care a lot, that his Uncle Bob wants to help . . .' This is not to deny that this strategy of reintegration can be mismanaged:

Co-ordinator: 'James, why are your parents upset?'
James: [Silence]
Co-ordinator: 'Do you think it's because they care about you?'

James: 'Don't know.'

Another way this path to reintegration can be derailed is when the parents indulge in outcasting attacks on their child. Co-ordinators sometimes manage this problem by intervening to divert stigmatization before it gets into full swing:

Mother: 'He used to be a good boy until then.'

Co-ordinator interrupts: 'And he still is a good boy. No one here thinks we're dealing with a bad kid. He's a good kid who made a mistake and I hope he knows now that that's what we all think of him.'

Even when serious stigmatic attacks are launched, the communal character of the encounter creates the possibility of reintegrative amelioration. The worst stigmatic attack we observed arose when the mother of a 14-year-old girl arrived at the conference. She told the co-ordinator that she was unhappy to be here. Then when she saw her daughter, who preceded her to the conference, she said: 'I'll kill you, you little bitch.' A few minutes into the conference, the mother jumped up from her seat, shouting: 'This is a load of rubbish.' Then pointing angrily at her shaking daughter, she said: 'She should be punished.' Then she stormed out. These events might have created a degradation sub-ceremony of great magnitude. Instead, the other partici-pants in the room were transformed by it and developed a quite different direction. Victim supporters who had arrived at the conference very angry at the offender were now sorry for her and wanted to help. They learnt she was a street kid and their anger turned against a mother who could abandon her daughter like this. This dramatic example highlights two common processes seen in the conferences—the alteration of perspectives and the generation of social support. We believe these processes occur for two reasons:

1. the more serious the delinquency of the young offender, the more likely it is to come out that she has had to endure some rather terrible life circumstances. Rather than rely on stereotypes they see the offender as a whole person (a point we return to later); *and*

JOHN BRAITHWAITE AND STEPHEN MUGFORD

2. participants at the conference have been invited on the basis of their capacity to be supportive to either the offender or the victim. Being supportive people placed in a social context where supportive behaviour is expected and socially approved, they often react to stigmatic attacks with gestures of reintegration.

Even as they use stigmatic terms, ordinary citizens understand the concept of communicating contempt for the deed simultaneously with respect for the young person. An adult member of the Maori community caused tears to trickle down the cheeks of a huge, tough 15-year-old with the following speech:

Stealing cars. You've got no brains, boy . . . But I've got respect for you. I've got a soft spot for you. I've been to see you play football. I went because I care about you. You're a brilliant footballer, boy. That shows you have the ability to knuckle down and apply yourself to something more sensible than stealing cars . . . We're not giving up on you.


*(2) Event and perpetrator must be uncoupled rather than defined as instances of a profane uniformity. The self of the perpetrator is sustained as sacred rather than profane. This is accomplished by comprehending: (a) how essentially good people have a pluralistic self that accounts for their occasional lapse into profane acts; and (b) that the profane act of a perpetrator occurs in a social context for which many actors may bear some shared responsibility. Collective as well as individual shame must be brought out into the open and confronted*

In speaking of degradation ceremonies, Garfinkel (1956: 422) says: 'Any sense of accident, coincidence, indeterminism, chance or momentary occurrence must not merely be minimised. Ideally, such measures should be inconceivable; at least they should be made false.' There must be no escape, no loophole. Rather, degradation insists upon fitting an identity of total deviant with a single, coherent set of motives into a black and white scheme of things. In contrast, a condition of successful reintegration ceremonies is that they leave open multiple interpretations of responsibility while refusing to allow the offender to deny personal responsibility entirely. In degradation ceremonies, the suppression of a range of motives and the insistence upon one account of responsibility allow the criminal to maintain (at least in her own eyes) an identity for herself as 'criminal as victim', to dwell on the irresponsibility of others or of circumstances. When the crime is constructed as the bad act of a good person, uncoupling event and perpetrator, a well-rounded discussion of the multiple account-abilities for the crime does not threaten the ceremony as an exercise in community disapproval. The strategy is to focus on problem rather than person, and on the group finding solutions to the problem. The family, particularly in the New Zealand model, is held accountable for coming up with a plan of action, which is then ratified by the whole group. The collective shame and collective responsibility of the family need not detract from individual responsibility for the crime nor from community respons-ibilities, such as to provide rewarding employment and schooling for young people. Yet the collective assumption of responsibility moves the ceremony beyond a permanent preoccupation with the responsibility of the individual that might stall at the point of stigmatization and the adoption of a delinquent identity. The practical task of designing a plan of action is a way of putting the shame behind the offender, of moving from a shaming phase to a reintegration phase. Agreement on the action plan can be an

## CONDITIONS OF SUCCESSFUL REINTEGRATION CEREMONIES

even more ceremonial decertification of the deviance of the offender through institutionalizing a signing ceremony where offender, family, and police put their signatures side by side on the agreement. In signing such an agreement, the responsible, reintegrated self of the offender distances itself from the shamed behaviour. The sacredness of the self is sustained through its own attack upon and transcendence of the profane act. Similarly, the collectivity of the family acknowledges its shame and takes collective responsibility for problem solving in a way that transcends its collective shame.

*(3) Co-ordinators must identify themselves with all private parties—perpetrators, their families, victims, witnesses—as well as being identified with the public interest in upholding the law*

Garfinkel's third condition of successful degradation ceremonies is that the denouncer must claim more than a private role but must communicate degradation in the name of an [imaginary, unified, and static] public. This condition is explicitly incorporated into Western criminal law, wherein the police and the judge in a criminal trial are legally defined as fiduciaries of public rather than private interests. In community conferences, this totalizing fiction is put aside. Co-ordinators have responsibilities to, and identify with, a plurality of interests. Reintegration and consensus on an agreement is quite unlikely unless the co-ordinator identifies with and respects all the interests in the room. Outside interests will put the agreement at risk unless the co-ordinator also speaks up on behalf of any public interest beyond the set of private interests assembled for the conference. This sounds demanding, perhaps even impossible. How can so many interests be juggled and a workable outcome reached? Our answer is simple—in practice consensus is reached more than 90 per cent of the time at both research sites and in most of these cases the consensus is implemented (Maxwell and Morris 1993: 121).[2]

*(4) Denunciation must be both by and in the name of victims and in the name of supra-personal values enshrined in the law*

For Garfinkel, degradation ceremonies are enacted in the name of the supra-personal values of the tribe. We have seen that successful reintegration requires confronting the private hurts and losses from the crime as well. A key condition for the success of reintegration ceremonies is to get the victim to turn up. Where victims are institutions (like schools), this means getting victim representatives to turn up (e.g., the principal, elected student representatives). Blagg (1986) has discussed the greater problems of making reparation meaningful with impersonal victims. Victim or victim representative attendance has been nearly universally achieved in Wagga, but in New Zealand the success rate has been under 50 per cent (Maxwell and Morris 1993: 75), though there is reason to suspect that the latter disappointing statistic has been improving in more recent times in New Zealand.[3] Some will be surprised at the near-universal

---

[2] See, however, the discussion of professionally manipulated consensus under point (5) and in the conclusion to this article.

[3] The main reason for non-attendance for victims in New Zealand was simply their not being invited, followed by being invited at a time unsuitable to them (Maxwell and Morris 1993: 79), a result of poor understanding of the philosophy of the reform by conference co-ordinators, heavy workload, and practical difficulties, such as the police failing to pass on the victim's address. Only 6 per cent of victims said they did not want to meet the offender (Morris *et al.*, in press).

success in Wagga and the recent higher success in New Zealand in getting victims along to conferences. But when the co-ordinator issues a combined appeal to private interest, public virtue (playing your part in getting this young person back on track) and citizen empowerment, the appeal is rather persuasive. In the words of Senior Sergeant Terry O'Connell—the key actor in adopting and developing the programme at Wagga—the key is to 'make the victim feel important and they will come'. And important they are: in New Zealand victims can effectively veto any agreement reached at the conference, but only if they actually attend and listen to the arguments. Even in conventional dyadic victim–offender reconciliation programmes in a non-communitarian society such as the United States, victim interest in participation is quite high (Weitekamp 1989: 82; Galaway 1985: 626; Galaway and Hudson 1975: 359; Novack *et al.* 1980; Galaway *et al.* 1980). Some of this may be sheer curiosity to meet the person who 'did it'.

When the victim and victim supporters turn up, of course, there remains the possibility that private hurts and losses will not be fully communicated to the offender. Sometimes the victim says that they suffered no real loss. For example, at one conference we attended, the victim said that the car stolen for a joy ride was found as soon as he noticed it to be missing and he could detect no damage. Here the co-ordinator must reiterate the public interest in being able to assume that one can park a car somewhere without constant worry that it might be stolen. Pointing out that '. . . it was a lucky thing for you and Mr X [the victim] on this occasion' reinforces responsibility in the absence of specific private harm. Furthermore, in stressing the public as well as the private view of a crime, if the absence of private harm means that there is no direct compensation to be paid or worked for, conferences will usually agree to some community service work for the offender. Often there will be both private compensation and community work, signifying both the private and the public harm. The gesture of restoration to both community and victim, even if it is modest in comparison to the enormity of the crime, enables the offender to seize back pride and reassume a law-respecting, other-respecting, and self-respecting identity.

*(5) Non-authoritative actors (victims, offenders, offenders' families) must be empowered with process control. The power of actors normally authorized to issue denunciations on behalf of the public interest (e.g., judges) must be decentred*

Degradation ceremonies for Garfinkel are about privileging authoritative actors with the right to denounce the profane on behalf of the tribe. Judges, for example, silence the denunciations of victims or pleas for mercy from relatives. Their role in the courtroom is simply as evidentiary fodder for the legal digestive system. They must stick to the facts and suppress their opinions. Consequently, they often emerge from the experience deeply dissatisfied with their day in court. For victims and their supporters, this often means they scream ineffectively for more blood. But it makes no difference when the system responds to such people by giving them more and more blood, because the blood-lust is not the source of the problem; it is an unfocused cry from disempowered citizens who have been denied a voice.

Reintegration ceremonies have a [dimly recognized] political value because, when well managed, they deliver victim satisfaction that the courts can never deliver. In

## CONDITIONS OF SUCCESSFUL REINTEGRATION CEREMONIES

Wagga, a standard question to the victims is: 'What do you want out of this meeting here today?' The responses are in sharp contrast to the cries for 'more punishment' heard on the steps of more conventional courts. Offered empowerment in the way we have suggested, victims commonly say that they do not want the offender punished; they do not want vengeance; they want the young offender to learn from his mistake and get his life back in order. Very often they say they want compensation for their loss. Even here, however, it is suprising how often victims waive just claims for compensation out of consideration for the need for an indigent teenager to be unencumbered in making a fresh start.

Clifford Shearing attended two of the Wagga conferences with us. Struck by the readiness of victims not to insist on compensation claims but to press instead for signs of remorse and willingness to reform, Shearing said, '. . . they all wanted to win the battle for his [the offender's] soul[4] rather than his money'.

How can we make sense of outcomes that are so at odds with preconceptions of vengeful victims? In fact, even in traditional stigmatic punishment systems, victims are not as vengeful as popular preconceptions suggest (Weitekamp 1989: 83–4; Heinze and Kerstetter 1981; Shapland, Willmore, and Duff 1985; Kigin and Novack 1980; Youth Justice Coalition 1990: 52–4). Citizens seem extremely punitive and supportive of degradation ceremonies when asked their views in public opinion surveys. Distance, a stereotyped offender, and a simplification of evil conduce to public support for degradation ceremonies. But the closer people get to the complexities of particular cases, the less punitive they get (Ashworth 1986: 118; Doob and Roberts 1983, 1988). As we noted earlier, the reality of the meeting between victim, offender, and others tends to undermine stereotyping. Instead, immediacy, a particular known offender and a complex grasp of all the situational pressures at work conduce to public support for reintegration.

Some reconciliations at family group conferences are quite remarkable. The most extraordinary case we know of involved a young man guilty of aggravated assault with a firearm on a woman who ran a lotto shop. The offender locked the woman at gunpoint in the back of her shop while he robbed her of over $1,000. When the time for the conference came, she was mad, after blood. Yet after considerable discussion, part of the plan of action, fully agreed to by the victim, involved the victim housing the offender while he did some community work for her family! This is not an isolated case, although it involves the most dramatic shift of which we became aware. Occasionally, victims make job offers to unemployed offenders at conferences.

Unresolved fury and victim dissatisfaction is, of course, the stuff of unsuccessful reintegration ceremonies. An important recent New Zealand evaluation shows that failure as a result of such dissatisfaction remains (Maxwell and Morris 1993: 119). In fact over a third of victims who attended conferences said they felt worse after the conference, a result of insufficient attention to victim reintegration (see point (9) below).

It is not only victims who can benefit from the empowerment that arises from having cases dealt with in this non-traditional setting. Offenders and offenders' families are also very much empowered when community conferences work well. Maxwell and Morris (1993: 110) found that New Zealand conferences work better at empowering

---

[4] An allusion to Rose (1990) and his discussion of 'governing the soul'.

JOHN BRAITHWAITE AND STEPHEN MUGFORD

parents than offenders.[5] This is probably true in Wagga as well, though the Wagga approach rejects the Auckland tendency to give the arresting police officer the first opportunity to explain the incident of concern. Instead, the young person, rather than police or parents, are always given the first opportunity to describe in their own words what has brought them to the conference. We see this Wagga practice of temporally privileging the accounts of the young persons as a desirable way of seeking to empower them in the dialogue. For all parties, success is predicated upon a significant degree of agency. On the other hand, when agency is denied the ceremonies fail. Then there is the pretence of empowerment, with families and offenders being manipulated into agreements that are developed by the police or youth justice co-ordinators, an outcome that is not uncommon (Maxwell and Morris 1993: 112). There can be little real experience of shame when apology and remedial measures are forced on the offender and his family rather than initiated by them. Empowerment is crucial to reintegration, while manipulation makes instead for degradation.

*(6) The perpetrator must be so defined by all the participants (particularly by the perpetrator himself) that he is located as a supporter of both the supra-personal values enshrined in the law and the private interests of victims*

This condition of successful reintegration is accomplished by having the offender's responsible self disassociate itself from the irresponsible self. Apology is the standard device for accomplishing this, as Goffman pointed out:

An apology is a gesture through which an individual splits himself into two parts, the part that is guilty of an offence and the part that disassociates itself from the delict and affirms a belief in the offended rule (1971: 113).

At all the conferences we attended, the offenders offered an apology.[6] Often they agreed to follow up with a letter of apology or a visit to apologize again to the victim and other members of the family. Often there was also apology to parents, teachers, even the police. A common feature of successful reintegration ceremonies can be a rallying of the support of loved ones behind the disassociation of self created by a genuine apology. After one moving and tearful statement by a Maori offender in Auckland, for example, elders offered congratulatory speeches on the fine apology he had given to his parents.

The verbal apology can be accompanied by physical acts. The most common physical accompaniment to apology is the handshake. Female victims sometimes hug young offenders, an especially moving gesture when it reaches across a racial divide. In Maori conferences,[7] kissing on the cheek, nose pressing and hugging occur among

---

[5] This is not to downplay the wonderful successes with offender empowerment that can and do occur within the New Zealand process: 'I felt safe because my whanau [extended family] were there with me. I would have felt like stink if I had to face it on my own. My auntie explained it so I understood. It was good that she allowed me to take a role' (young person quoted in Maxwell and Morris 1993: 78).

[6] In this regard, we were somewhat surprised by Maxwell and Morris's (1993: 93) finding that an apology was formally recorded as offered in only 70 per cent of their sample of conferences. We wondered if all of the more informal means of apology (including backstage apology) were counted in this result.

[7] With Samoan conferences, it is common for offenders to apologize on their knees, a degrading form of apology in Western eyes, but perhaps not so when the cultural context is to elevate the offender quickly, embracing his restored identity. That is, for the Samoan, the kneeling may represent part of a reintegrative sequence rather than signifying degradation.

## CONDITIONS OF SUCCESSFUL REINTEGRATION CEREMONIES

various of the participants (even visiting sociologists!). Ritual bodily contact is not the only form of physical act to accompany apology. Other common acts include the handing over of compensation or the offer of a beverage. In a recreation of the theme that commensalism celebrates solidarity, successful ceremonies have ended with victim and offender families arranging to have dinner together after the conference.

Despite the manifestly successful effect of apology, it is not something encouraged by court rooms. Criminal trials tend to leave criminal identities untouched by attacks from responsible, law-abiding, or caring identities. Indeed, degradation tends to harden them. It is not a major challenge in identity management for a tough guy to sustain this identity during a criminal trial. The challenge is more difficult in an open dialogue among the different parties assembled for a community conference. Usually, there are some things that the police know about the offender's conduct that his parents do not know and there are vulnerabilities the parents know that the police do not. The traditional criminal process enables the offender to sustain different kinds of stories and even different identities with parents and police. Conferences can expose these multiple selves to the partitioned audiences for which these selves are differentially displayed. Out of one conference, Wagga parents learned that their teenage son had punched a 14-year-old girl in the face; then the police learned that the boy had beaten his mother before, once with a broom; then everyone learned that he had also hit other girls. There are some lies that the offender can live in the eyes of the police; others in the eyes of his parents; but many of them cannot stand in the face of a dialogue among all three that also enjoins victims.

All this is not to deny that apology, even the sincerest apology, can be secured without challenging a delinquent identity that remains dominant over a law-abiding identity. In one case, a 14-year-old girl acknowledged that the effect of stealing a cheque from the mail-box of an elderly woman had been 'awful' for the victim and she apologized with feeling. But when it came to the action plan, she was intransigently against the idea of returning to school: 'No. I don't like school.' Even a modest proposition from the group for community service work of 20 hours over four weeks was bitterly resisted: 'It's too much time. I want to be a normal street kid and if you're a street kid you need time to be on the street. That would take up too much of my time.' Nothing was going to interrupt her career path as a street kid! This is a familiar theme in literature on identity maintenance from writers associated with labelling and similar perspectives. There comes a point where a change which seems both possible and advantageous in the immediate context is resisted because of the degree of commitment to a path and the consequent 'side bets' (Becker 1960) that an individual has made in following that path.

Interestingly, however, our empirical observations match the general case we made earlier: namely, that while such commitment to deviance is possible, it is also rare. The norm is strongly towards the reversibility rather than irreversibility of the deviant identity and, as in the case just described, in contrast to the labelling claim, irreversibility seems more connected to the individual commitment to an identity (agency) than to structural features that prevent reversion. No doubt, the matter of commitment is not exhausted by these brief comments. We might suppose that as adults get older, deviant identities might become more encrusted and harder to change (and hence shaming and reintegration less relevant). For some people such a process probably occurs. But as data on the relationship between age and deviance shows

JOHN BRAITHWAITE AND STEPHEN MUGFORD

(Hirschi and Gottfredson 1983; Youth Justice Coalition 1990: 22–3) reversion from deviant to mainstream identities is the norm with progressing age. Thus the idea that shaming and reintegration ceremonies are valuable only for the young is not well founded. Indeed, preliminary qualitative evidence indicates that it may be extremely valuable for individuals well into middle age.[8]

*(7) Distance between each participant and the other participants must be closed; empathy among all participants must be enhanced; opportunities must be provided for perpetrators and victims to show (unexpected) generosity toward each other*

At the start of conferences, victims and offenders, victim supporters, and offender supporters tend to work hard at avoiding eye contact. By contrast, at the end of a successful reintegration ceremony, participants are looking each other in the eye. Reintegration ceremonies succeed when one side makes an early gesture of self-blame or self-deprecation. In one case, an offender wrote a long letter of apology to the victim before the conference was convened. At another conference, a mix-up by the police resulted in the victim being advised of the wrong date for the conference. Despite this, she came within 15 minutes of a 'phone call at 6 p.m. in the middle of preparing for dinner guests'. The conference co-ordinator said that she agreed to drop everything to come 'if it would help the boys'. 'What do you think of that?' said the co-ordinator. 'She's a nice lady', said one of the offenders. 'And I bet you were frightened to go out from your own house after this', added the mother of another offender.

In many cases, the offender's family does not wait for their offspring to come under attack from the victim. They pre-emptively launch the attack themselves in terms so strong that the victim can be moved to enjoin that the family '[Not] be too hard on the boy. We all make mistakes.' Self-deprecating gestures from either side can facilitate reintegration, which is powerfully facilitated by exchanges such as:

Victim: 'It was partly my fault. I shouldn't have left it unlocked.'

Offender: 'No that's not your fault. You shouldn't have to lock it. We're the only ones who should be blamed.'

A common strategy of all parties for seeking to elicit empathy from others is to refer to how they may suffer these problems themselves in another phase of their own life cycle. Offender's uncle to offender: 'In a few years you will be a father and have to growl at your boys.' Co-ordinator to victims: 'You were once parents of teenagers yourselves.'

---

[8] In Australia, we have been experimenting with reintegrative conferences with white-collar crime, cases that illustrate the problem of victim shame. A recent case has involved action by the Trade Practices Commission against a number of Australia's largest insurance companies in what have been the biggest consumer protection cases in Australian history. The victims were Aborigines in remote communities who were sold (generally) useless insurance and investment policies as a result of a variety of shocking misrepresentations, even the misrepresentation that the Aborigine would be sent to jail if he did not sign the policy. Victims sometimes escaped through the back door when the government man in the white shirt arrived to interview them, fearing that *they* had done something wrong. Many shook and cried throughout their interviews. They felt shame at losing the little money their families had. The apologies issued by company chief executives at highly publicized press conferences were about communicating the message that it was the company who had to face 'the same job' (as Aborigines put it). Moreover, full compensation with 15 per cent compound interest would acquit the shame victims felt as providers. In addition, insurance company top management were required to attend negotiation conferences at Wujal Wujal, where they faced their victims, apologized to them and lived the life conditions of their victims, sleeping on mattresses on concrete floors, eating tinned food, during several days of negotiation. For more details on this and other cases of corporate shaming praxis, see Fisse and Braithwaite (1993) and Braithwaite (1992).

CONDITIONS OF SUCCESSFUL REINTEGRATION CEREMONIES

One case we attended involved a father and son who had a stormy relationship. A Maori elder counselled the father that he should put his arm around his boy more often, advice the father conceded that he needed to take. The father was a harsh and tough man, once a famous rugby forward with a reputation as an enforcer. The attempt of a Maori police officer to elicit empathy in these difficult circumstances was both innovative and effective, since tears began to stream down the face of the young offender, who up to this point had managed the impression of being a young tough:

Policeman: 'Look what you have done to your father and mother. If your father hit you, you'd stay hit. You wouldn't be getting up. But he hasn't.' [Offender gasps, his chest heaving with unnatural struggling for air]. 'I was always angry and bitter at my father. He was a hard man.'

Uncle interjects: 'Yes, he'd hit you first, then ask questions afterwards.'

Policeman continues: 'Then he died. Then I realised how I loved and missed the old bastard. Don't wait till your father dies, Mark.'

At this point the mother buried her head in her lap with quiet sobbing. Then the father and then the son cried, by which point all in the room had tears in our eyes. How impressive an accomplishment this was—eliciting such empathy for a father about whom it was clearly difficult to say anything laudatory. Taken out of context, it does not seem a very positive thing to say about a father that he has refrained from ironing out his son. But for a son who himself was enmeshed in the culture of rugby and who knew his father's history of ironing out a great number of other human beings, the tribute was deeply moving.

*(8) The separation of denounced persons must be terminated by rituals of inclusion that place them, even physically, inside rather than outside*

Already we have mentioned a number of rituals of inclusion: apology and its acceptance, handshaking, the putting of signatures side by side on an agreement, and so on. In a traditional Samoan context, this is taken further. Following an assault, the Matai, or head of the extended family unit of the offender, will kneel on a mat outside the house of the victim family until he is invited in and forgiven. Sometimes that will take days. There may be something to learn from the Samoans here on the conditions of successful reintegration ceremonies, namely the provision of a spatio-temporal dimension to the imperative for reintegration. For how long should I continue to avoid eye contact with this person who still kneels in front of me? When do I conclude it by embracing him in forgiveness? The sheer physicality of his remorse makes ignoring him indefinitely a rather limited third option. The ceremony is driven by a spatial imperative. Indeed, most successful ceremonies in our own society specify place (e.g., a church, a presentation dais) and a time when it is appropriate and fitting to carry out that ceremony. Moreover, in moving individuals through space and time, those movements are not haphazard—they fit the messages of transformation or reaffirmation that the ceremony seeks to convey.

In Wagga, the spatial arrangement that is employed to convey both the unity of the community and yet the tension between victim and offender, is a horseshoe seating arrangement. At one end of the horseshoe sits the offender(s) with her family(ies) sitting in the row behind. At the other end sits the victim(s) with his family(ies) sitting

JOHN BRAITHWAITE AND STEPHEN MUGFORD

in the row behind him. The horseshoe symbolizes the tension of the meeting, part of one community but at widely separated points on this matter. Moreover, movements within the space can and do occur, such as when people cross the central space to shake hands at certain moments. These are culturally contingent matters; offending boys are commonly made to sit on the floor during Polynesian conferences, a temporary obeisance that seems culturally appropriate to them rather than debasing. Sometimes they are asked to come out and stand at the front for their formal apology, after which they return to their seat in a circle. In each of these, the physical space is used constructively to convey important messages. And, as we shall see later, the separation of the overall space into front and backstage areas also has its uses.

The symbolic meanings signified by space rarely surface in the discursive conscious-ness of the participants (or so we presume) but the successful use of space is not predicated upon that level of reflection. In all probability, more still could be done with the symbolic use of space in such ceremonies—one could take this even further by placing offenders alone in the centre of the horseshoe for the first stage of the conference, though one might worry about this intimidating them into silence. These are matters that require more detailed exploration, but note here merely that there is a fine line between artifice and artificiality.

The temporal dimension of the ceremony is also important. The phases in a successful ceremony are clearly visible in the way that participants comport themselves and a 'winding down' is often discernible. Indeed, the phased structure is not dissimilar to that described by Bales (1950) in his work on interaction process analysis. As Bales argued there, the social group that has formed to handle a particular risk (in this case for the ceremony) comes to develop a bounded process of its own, marking its phases with different styles of comportment and mood. Although breaks in the meeting are rarely used in Wagga,[9] one could conceivably have a coffee break once there had been good progress toward a settlement during which the protagonists could physically mix; after the break, offender families could come back side by side with their children to present their plan of action. Certainly, such activities are used to mark the end of the formal ceremony and handle transitions back to the 'outside world' and at such moments drinking together, whether coffee or—as might be appropriate in other contexts, alcohol—serves to mark that transition (Gusfield 1987; cf. also Bott 1987; Hazan 1987).

It is also important to note here that the physical act of handing over money as compensation or a bunch of flowers (as happened in one case) creates a strong imperative for an apology–forgiveness interaction sequence. Most English-speaking people find it normal to cancel grudges at the moment of a physical act of compensating wrongdoing by uttering the word 'sorry'. Faced with such an utterance, only unusual victims resist the imperative to return a word of forgiveness, to 'let bygones by bygones', or at least to show acceptance, thanks, or understanding.

Regrettably the common legal processes of a gesellschaft society sanitize such physical moments out of transactions. They are, in the Weberian sense, 'disenchanted'. With the loss of that enchantment they lose also powerful opportunities for transforma-tions of self and context. Rational actor models of the world notwithstanding, successful

---

[9] In New Zealand, it is usual to have a break in the proceedings during which the offender's family meets on its own to prepare a plan of action.

## CONDITIONS OF SUCCESSFUL REINTEGRATION CEREMONIES

practice of justice is not merely a technical-rational action. When restitution is reduced to 'the cheque is in the mail' (likely put there by the clerk of the court) matters of deep moral concern have been reduced to mere money, to the ubiquitous question 'how much?' (Simmel 1978). In contrast, successful reintegration ceremonies put reintegrative physicality back into the process. In so doing they transcend the merely rational to speak to vital concerns of human conscience.

*(9) The separation of the victim, any fear or shame experienced by victims, must be terminated by rituals of reintegration*

The objective of reintegrating offenders is advanced by reintegrating victims; the objective of reintegrating victims is advanced by reintegrating offenders.[10] Victims are invisible in Garfinkel's model, but our thesis is that effective reintegration ceremonies are victim-centred, a centrality described under conditions (3), (4), and (5). Victims often suffer from bypassed shame (Scheff and Retzinger 1991) and bypassed fear. The girl who is sexually assaulted by a young man often feels that the incident says something about the respect in which she is held by males. She feels devalued to have been treated with such disrespect (Murphy and Hampton 1989). One way to rehabilitate her self-respect is a ceremonial show of community respect for her. Apology from the man who disrespected her is the most powerful way of resuscitating this self-esteem and community shaming of the disrespecting behaviour is also powerful affirmation of the respect for her as a person.

Victims often continue to be afraid after a crime and at an apparently irrational level. When a break-in causes a victim to feel insecure in her home, it is good for this fear to be openly expressed. For one thing, there is practical advice the police are usually able to give that can leave the victim both safer and feeling more assured of being safe.

In one Wagga conference involving teenage lads who inflicted a terrifying assault on a much younger boy and girl, the boys offered to come around to the home of the victim family to apologize more formally to all members of the family. The young girl looked afraid and said that she did not want them coming near her home. So it was decided they would apologize in writing. But from that point on in the conference, the cautioning sergeant highlighted the fact that there was no particular meaning to the choice of these two children as victims. It was a one-off incident that could have happened to anyone. At the end of the conference, the sergeant ushered the offenders and their supporters out, asking the victim family to stay behind. Then he asked the children if they now felt assured that these boys would not come after them again. He asked them what they thought of the boys and they said that the conference had put it all behind them now. They felt more sorry for the boys than afraid of them. The mother said later that she had come to see them as frightened little boys. This interpretation

---

[10] In practice, the Wagga process has been more oriented from the outset to reintegrating victims than the New Zealand process. Many New Zealand co-ordinators, interpreting literally a clause in the New Zealand Children, Young Persons and Their Families Act, have been reluctant to allow victim supporters to attend the conference. There has been a lot of learning in New Zealand on this question, but in some parts there is still a fear of the vindictiveness of victims and, more particularly, of victim supporters. If victims are to be reintegrated, however, caring supporters are a necessary ingredient. Our strongest criticism of the New Zealand reform effort has been the half-hearted commitment to victim reintegration in many quarters.

155

was confirmed by a minister of religion who met with the family immediately after the conference.

Note here the importance of two smaller backstage conferences after the formal conference—a further instance of the significance of space referred to earlier. Backstage conferences can do some reintegrative work for both offenders and victims that cannot be accomplished front stage. Every conference we have attended broke up into some important little backstage meetings after the main conference. At times, the reintegrative work that happened after the conference was more significant than that transacted within it. A boy who maintained a defiant demeanour throughout the conference shed a tear when his uncle put his arm around him after the conference (his identity as nephew allows him to cry, but not the identity he must maintain in the face of his mates). A mother confesses that she does not believe she can get her daughter to attend the agreed community work and another uncle volunteers to 'make sure she gets there'. Backstage intimacy can allow some masks to be removed that actors feel impelled to sustain during the conference proper. A practical implication is not to rush the exit from the theatre.

### (10) Means must be supplied to intervene against power imbalances that inhibit either shaming or reintegration, or both

Of the various criticisms we have heard raised about the ceremonial process that we are describing in this paper, one of the most common concerns the imbalance of power in society and the way that this must spill over into, and hence structure in negative ways, the reintegration process. How, they ask, can this process disassociate itself from wider matters of class, race, patriarchy, and age stratification? If such disassociation does not occur, how can the ceremony act other than to reproduce that same patterning of ageism, class, race, and patriarchy? The risk is obvious. The ethnomethodologists of the 1960s, among whom Garfinkel is counted, were rightly condemned by the marxists of the 1970s (Taylor, Walton, and Young 1973) for inattentiveness to issues of power. By using Garfinkel's work as a starting point might we not fall into the same trap, blithely praising a ceremony whose deeper realities are much darker than we sense? Are the ceremonies of reintegration we are discussing capable of intervening against power imbalances in any serious way?

Our answer to this falls into several parts, and these parts relate to what we have seen in our observational work.

First, in no sense is intervention to deal with individual offences the most important thing we can do to respond constructively to the crime problem: attacking deeper structures of inequality is more important (Polk 1992; Braithwaite 1991, 1993). But let us not underestimate how important a basis of inequality criminal justice oppression is to (say) Aboriginal Australians. The structure of laws and the daily routines of the police and the courts contribute mightily to that oppression. Thus, to alter the police-court process is an important step, even if it is not a sufficient step. Indeed the very history of the Antipodean conferences we are discussing here begins with Maori frustration with the way the Western state disempowered them through the criminal justice system (Report of the Ministerial Advisory Committee 1986). These reforms 'came from below' and were explicitly understood by Maori protagonists to introduce

156

CONDITIONS OF SUCCESSFUL REINTEGRATION CEREMONIES

communitarian reintegrative features into a system that lacked them and which stigmatized their young people in destructive ways. In this sense, if in no other, we advocate the reintegration ceremonies because they are valuable in the eyes of most of those who are involved in them.[11]

Our second point is more theoretical. At the core of the criticism about power imbalances undermining the ceremony is a failure to think through the precise nature of the ceremony. The current of mainstream sociology that has dealt with ritual and ceremony has principally been conservative and functionally oriented (Cheal 1988). As a result, the tendency has been to emphasize static, system-integrative, and totalizing aspects of rituals over dynamic aspects, multiple identities, and social change. But that shortcoming is a feature of the theory, not the ceremony. If commentators associate conservatism with ceremony for this reason, they do so out of habit rather than evidence. There are dynamic features to these ceremonies which emphasize agency and social freedom (within obvious bounds) not merely totalizing conformity. No doubt, there are meanings which ceremonies permit and others they do not and no doubt some of those privilegings and silencings may be problematic. But we dispute that they can be 'read off' in advance.

Third and last, the criticism implies that anyone who pursues the course we describe here is utopian—class, race, and patriarchy are so ingrained in 'the system', it can be said that the system can never transcend them. Perhaps. But our view is quite different. We see that the existing 'system'—which is not particularly systematic in that it lacks unity, coherence, and direction—is racked with problems arising from differences in power which we can identify as 'class, race, and patriarchy'. But we go on to argue that if so, this identifies the places where we need to work relentlessly for change. Moreover, we suggest that our observations of such ceremonies indicate that while power imbalances remain ineradicably within what we describe, they also provide a greater space in which people can be agents than the existing processes. More voices are heard, saying more things than in conventional courts and that is a positive thing. Concrete examples may help to make the point.

It is an empirical question whether powerful outside voices are likely to be raised in a conference or a court against a father who dominates his daughter. Here we observe that the condition of the successful reintegration ceremony is that the co-ordinator act on this fact of domination by asking the daughter *who she would like* to be there to stick up for her against her father.

The philosophy of the New Zealand reforms (Children, Young Persons and Their Families Act 1989) is that when families are in deep trouble, a social worker from the state is not likely to be the best person to straighten out their problems (Maxwell and Morris 1993). However big a mess the family is in, the best hope for solving the problem of families resides within the families themselves and their immediate communities of intimate support. What the state can do is empower families with resources: offer to pay to bring Auntie Edna from another city for the conference (as they do in New Zealand), offer to pay for a smorgasbord of life skills, job training, remedial education, anger control courses, but with *the power of choice from that*

---

[11] In New Zealand, 53 per cent of the offenders processed through family group conferences are Maori (Maxwell and Morris 1993: 69). On Maori perceptions of the value of the reforms, see n. 13 below.

JOHN BRAITHWAITE AND STEPHEN MUGFORD

*smorgasbord resting entirely with the young offender and her support group.*[12] Processes like this do offer a redress of power imbalances centred upon race, albeit not completely. In New Zealand, where the Maori community contribute half the cases processed by the New Zealand juvenile justice system, conferences offer an important redress in a criminal justice system that is otherwise not a peripheral but a central source of their disempowerment. The same point can be made about racial minorities in all the English-speaking countries. It is a small blow against black oppression when the white father of the victim of a brutal assault offers to go with the family of the Aboriginal offender to argue the reversal of a decision to expel him from school because of the assault. Conferences will never usher in revolutionary changes; they do, however, give little people chances to strike little blows against oppression.

The possibilities for improving the position of women within criminal justice processes also seem to us to be quite promising. This is illustrated by the Wagga case mentioned earlier of the mother who was being beaten by her son. Court-based criminal justice systematically obscures the fact that in Australia we have a massive problem of son–mother violence. Domestic violence is constructed in the literature as spouse abuse because mothers keep the problems with their sons submerged, blaming themselves, refusing to complain against their own children. If the Wagga case discussed earlier had gone to court, it is most unlikely that the assault on the girl would have led on to a discussion of the wider problem of the assault on the mother and other females. The family group conference approach enabled community confrontation of this 15-year-old boy with the problem of his violence at an early enough age for such a confrontation to make a difference. But most mothers and sisters are unlikely to co-operate in a stigmatic or punitive vilification of their young son or brother. Ceremonies must be perceived as reintegrative, directed not only at getting the boy to take responsibility for his actions but also at supporting and helping him, before most mothers and sisters will break the silence.

We could add that the economic prospects of offenders, which are often very dim, are not always neglected in these conferences. While this is not a widespread feature, sometimes the unemployed are helped to find jobs; sometimes the homeless are found homes; often the school dropouts are assisted in getting back to school or into some alternative kind of technical training or educational development. Clearly there are many more important fronts on which to struggle for a more just economic system than through family group conferences, but these conferences are at worst not deepening the problems that the young offenders face.

In short, while the reintegration ceremonies we write of here do not overcome inequalities, they can be and are sensitive to them and do what they can to allow for and/or redress some of those inequalities. In so doing, they create spaces for agency and voice; they return conflicts that are 'stolen' by state professionals to ordinary citizens (Christie 1977). This, we think, is a progressive move. The structural feature of successful conferences that we hypothesize to be most critical here is proactive empowerment of the most vulnerable participants—offenders and victims—with the choice of caring advocates, who may be more powerful than themselves, to exercise countervailing power against whoever they see as their oppressors.

---

[12] With the weak welfare states that exist in both Australia and New Zealand, the range of such choices effectively available to young people, in most localities but particularly in rural localities, is very poor (Maxwell and Morris 1993: 180).

CONDITIONS OF SUCCESSFUL REINTEGRATION CEREMONIES

*(11) Ceremony design must be flexible and culturally plural, so that participants exercise their process control constrained by only very broad procedural requirements*

We should be pluralist enough to see that a good process for Maoris will not necessarily be a good process for Europeans, or even for some Maoris who say they don't believe in 'too much shit about the Maori way' (Maxwell and Morris 1993: 126).[13] At the same time, we should not be so culturally relativist as to reject the possibility of Europeans learning something worthwhile from Maori practice. Family group conferences are essentially a Maori idea, but the idea has been very favourably received by white communities in New Zealand and Australia, Australian Aboriginal communities, and Pacific Islander communities living in New Zealand. The reason is the flexibility built into the approach. Because Samoan participants have genuine process control, they can choose to encourage kneeling in front of the victim. Maori communities can choose to break the tension during proceedings by singing a song, something Westerners would find a rather odd thing to do on such an occasion. Maori conferences often signify the sacredness of the public interests involved (conditions 3 and 4) by opening and closing the conference with a (reintegrative) prayer.

Every conference we have attended has been completely different from every other conference. Indeed, flexibility and participant control of the process are the reasons why this strategy can succeed in a multicultural metropolis like Auckland. This is not a communitarian strategy for the nineteenth century village, but for the twenty-first century city. Flexible process, participant control—these are keys to delivering the legal pluralism necessary for the metropolis. Another key is that this is an individual-centred communitarianism, giving it a practical edge for constructing community in an individualistic society. The authors of this paper choose not to attend Neighbourhood Watch meetings, because the appeal of community obligation is not sufficient to motivate our participation. In contrast, if one of us were asked to attend a family group conference on the basis that either a victim or an offender from our neighbourhood or family had nominated us as a person who could lend support, we would go. We would be flattered to have been nominated by the individual. This is what we mean by the practical appeal of individual-centred communitarianism. Helping an individual is more motivating to citizens than abstractions such as 'contributing to making your neighbourhood safer'.

While the reintegrative strategy is firmly grounded in the theory of legal pluralism, certain basic procedural rules cannot be trumped. The most important of these is that if the offender denies committing the alleged offences, she has the right to terminate the

[13] While it is easy to find Maoris who resist the notion that there is a lot of point in turning back the clock to a pre-European society and others who see family group conferences as a corruption and debasement of Maori traditions by the Western justice system, we suspect the predominant Maori reaction is as expressed by the Maori researchers on the Maxwell and Morris project in the following quote—accepting the need for mutual accommodation between Maori and Western justice systems, especially when victims and offenders come from different cultures:

'We feel that the Act for the most part is an excellent piece of legislation which promises exciting possibilities for the future. When the processes outlined in the Act were observed, Maori families were indeed empowered and able to take an active part in decisions concerning their young people. It is not difficult to see the beneficial influences that the Act may eventually exert on wider Maori, Polynesian and Pakeha society. Maori society could gain immensely from legislation that acknowledges and strengthens the hapu and tribal structures and their place in decisions regarding the wellbeing of young people and [from legislation] that provides them with an opportunity to contribute to any reparation and to support those offended against. The same scenario would apply to Pacific Island peoples. Pakeha society would also benefit from a process which acknowledges the family and gives redress to victims' (Maxwell and Morris 1993: 187).

JOHN BRAITHWAITE AND STEPHEN MUGFORD

conference, demanding that the facts be tried in a court of law. She does not have to plead guilty. The conference can proceed only if she chooses 'not to deny' charges made by the police. Some of the more informal ground rules that co-ordinators enforce, such as 'no name calling' and 'no badgering of the young person' have the effect of tipping the balance against degrading discourse in favour of reintegrative dialogue. What such basic procedural rules do is constitute a generally acceptable framework within which a plurality of dialogic forms can flourish (see Habermas 1986).

Given a commitment to flexibility and participant empowerment, one central concern is the prospect of standardization and routinization. It would be easy for ceremonies to be converted into Foucauldian 'discipline', extending the net of state control. Disturbing signs of this as a future trend can be discerned, for example in the near-automatic tendency of some state officials at New Zealand conferences to suggest a curfew as part of the plan of action. Families can and do argue against their children being put on a rigid curfew, suggesting that a degree of participant control of the process is prevailing against pressures for standardized response, but the routinization of the suggestion without apparent consideration of case details implies a standardizing tendency. Similarly, after a training conference for co-ordinators in Wagga that we attended with Clifford Shearing and Jane Mugford, they expressed concern to us that some of the contributions to the training by local social workers and psychologists undercut the shifts away from stigmatization and toward community empowerment. The tendency there was to speak and reason in abstract categories such as 'problem youth' in a way that, taken seriously, would erode the agency and voice of participants in favour of the imposition of control by 'experts'.

These tendencies notwithstanding, our view is that, at present, the family group conferences do not extend the net of state control (see also Moore 1992), but rather extend the net of community control, partly at the expense of state control, partly at the expense of doing something about problems that were previously ignored (such as mother-bashing by sons).[14] Conferences can be used by communities to co-opt state power (formalism harnessed to empower informalism) (Braithwaite and Daly, in press); or they can be used by state authorities to expand their net of coercion by capturing informal community control (as in the net-widening critique). The contingent potential for both these developments and for the re-emergence of professionalized routinization need to be kept in mind in planning the expansion of such programmes.

*(12) Reintegration agreements must be followed through to ensure that they are enacted*

In the early days of the family group conferences in both New Zealand and Wagga, there was poor follow-up to ensure that agreements reached at the conference were implemented. Now more systematic procedures are in place in New Zealand to ensure, for example, that where monetary compensation is involved, victims do receive it. For a sample of 203 family group conferences held in 1990, Maxwell and Morris (1993: 102) found that in 59 per cent of cases agreements were completely implemented within three to four months and partly completed in a further 28 per cent of cases, leaving only

[14] Maxwell and Morris's (1993: 176) New Zealand data support this interpretation. They find that the result of the New Zealand reforms is fewer children going to court, fewer receiving custodial penalties, but more children whose delinquency was previously ignored altogether or discharged by the court experiencing moderate interventions such as formal apology, compensation, and community service decided through family group conferences or police diversion.

CONDITIONS OF SUCCESSFUL REINTEGRATION CEREMONIES

13 per cent of cases in which the tasks were largely uncompleted in this time frame—a very good result. At Wagga, young offenders and their families are invited to at least one follow-up workshop to close out the process. Families have an opportunity to swap notes at the workshop on the difficulties they have faced in implementing their plan of action. The Wagga police also see a reintegrative rationale for the workshop in helping families to overcome their shame by working with other families in the same situation. It is possible that this interpretation is right, as illustrated by the following passage from our fieldwork notes:

Of the three offenders [in this particular case] George was the one who seemed totally unmoved by what the victim and his family said at the conference. George's mother got together with mothers of George's friends who had also been in trouble, to talk about their problems. One of the mothers said that her boy had been sexually assaulted and that was one thing that upset him. Later George's mother said to George that he has not had it so tough as John, who had been sexually assaulted. George said nothing. Later, he called his mother back, broke down and said he had been sexually assaulted too (by the same person, we assume). George's mother now dates the assault as marking the time since which George had been getting into trouble. Her social construction of George is no longer as a boy who went bad. Now it is of a boy who was good, who went through a bad time as a result of a sexual assault, and who is now coming to terms with what happened to him and is coming out of it—a 'good boy' again.

Implementation of agreements from family group conferences is more effective than with court ordered compensation largely because the compensation is a collective obligation entered into by voluntary collective agreement.[15] Moreover, the co-ordinator will often secure the nomination of a relative who will be responsible for ensuring that the offender complies with the terms of the agreement. Dr Gabrielle Maxwell has made the same point about completion of community work orders: 'The community work projects that work are the ones the family comes up with itself.'

*(13) When a single reintegration ceremony fails, ceremony after ceremony must be scheduled, never giving up, until success is achieved*

Traditional criminal justice processes paint themselves into a corner because of two imperatives: the desire to give kids another chance; notwithstanding this, the desire to signal that 'the system is tough and next time you will not be so lucky'. These two imperatives intersect with the empirical reality that young offenders offend a lot during their years of peak offending. Most will come through this peak period within two or three years if the criminal justice system does not make things worse by degradation ceremonies (such as institutionalization). The two imperatives and the empirical pattern of offending intersect to cause the criminal justice system to do exactly what its

---

[15] As an aside, it is worth noting here the implications for the justice model which provides a critique of family group conferences as inferior to courts. Courts, according to this critique, provide singular, consistent justice, in contrast to the plural, inconsistent justice of conferences. It is an interesting empirical question whether in practice, as opposed to theory, courts do deliver more just sanctioning when compensation, fines, and community service ordered by the court are defied in the majority of cases. It is not inconceivable that even though there is greater inequity in the sanctions ordered by group conferences, in the sanctions actually implemented there is greater equity for the group conference than for the court process.

JOHN BRAITHWAITE AND STEPHEN MUGFORD

practitioners know is the worst thing to do, that is, set up a self-defeating chain of events:

| | |
|---|---|
| Conviction 1: | 'Take this as a warning.' |
| Conviction 2: | 'I'll give you a second chance. But this is your last chance.' |
| Conviction 3: | 'With regret, I must say that you have already been given your last chance.' |

The policy in New Zealand is to avoid this slippery slope. While some cases in the juvenile justice system continue to slide down it, most do not and since 1988 the rate of institutionalization of young offenders has dropped by more than half (Maxwell and Morris 1993: 176), possibly by 75 per cent (McDonald and Ireland 1990: 16). Now, most detected offences are judged not to warrant the cost of convening a family group conference, and informal warnings to juveniles on the spot or at the police station remain the predominant response for very minor offences (Maxwell and Morris 1993: 53). Taking no action beyond a formal letter of warning from the police is also common (Maxwell and Morris 1993: 59). Visits by the police to the offender's home to arrange informally for reparation and apology to the victim occur in a quarter of non-arrest cases (Maxwell and Morris 1993: 53). Only if these steps are insufficient is a full conference arranged.

In addition to these informal pre-conference measures, some New Zealand young offenders have been through six or seven formal conferences for different offences. The New Zealand Police Association, which strongly supports the family group conference strategy for most offenders, has reservations about repeated use of the approach on 'hardened' offenders. They illustrated the problem with examples such as this:

Ngaruawahia reports that a 16 year old youth had a Family Group Conference on 26 June 1990 for three offences, another on 10 July for six offences, another on 20 July 1990 for two offences, Youth Court hearing on 24 July 1990, another Family Group Conference on 14 February 1991 for two offences. The youth committed suicide at Weymouth Boys Home in April 1991 (New Zealand Police Association 1991: 19).

Of course, such a case seems a 'failure'. But what kind of failure is it? We can think of three ways of categorizing it: (a) a failure of the family group conference; (b) the likely failure of any approach with the most difficult cases; or (c) the failure of giving up on the family group conference in favour of the court-institutionalization route. The implication of the passage is that this is a failure of type (a), but we suspect that it is better understood as type (b) and/or (c).

Of course, it would be naïve to expect that a one- or two-hour conference can normally turn around the problems of a lifetime. In any case, the theory of the conference is not really that what is said at the conference will change lives in an instant and irreversible way—a conference is a social activity, not a genie from a bottle. Rather the hope for the conference is that it will be a catalyst for community problem solving. Viewed in this way, when there is re-offending after a conference, it is to some extent the community that has failed. The failure of the conference was in not catalysing the right sort of community support for the offender. If the failure is not inherent to the conference process, but is a failure in the community catalysis of the intervention, then one conference after another, each time seeking to catalyse community support in a different way, or with different invitees, makes sense.

## CONDITIONS OF SUCCESSFUL REINTEGRATION CEREMONIES

To achieve a successful reintegration ceremony, then, it is necessary that co-ordinators must never give up, that they act as if there is always a reason for the failure of the last intervention *other than* the irretrievable badness of the offender. Even if the offender dies before the community succeeds in preventing his offending, by trying again and again with reintegrative approaches, the co-ordinator believes that she has at least refrained from accelerating his criminal career path during the time he lived. The typical criminal career is a useful touchstone, here. Knowing the pattern typical of some offenders, it is *dis*abling to conceive success in terms of stopping offending. At the same time, it is *en*abling to define success as a downward shift in the slope of a criminal career path and failure as allowing an upward shift. Unless the offences are extreme,[16] it is always better to keep plugging away with a strategy that neither succeeds nor fails than to escalate to one that fails. At least the former does no harm.

Is there a practical way of implementing the attitude of never giving up? Below is an example of how the police might react to the first eight detected offences of a career criminal under a reintegrative strategy.

*First offence:* Boy warned by the police on the street for a minor offence. 'If I catch you at this again, I'll be in touch with your parents about it.'

*Second offence:* Same type of minor offence on the street results in a formal letter of warning and a visit to the family home to discuss the warning.

*Third offence:* Family group conference. Still a fairly minor offence, so no elaborate follow-up or detailed plan of action, just the reintegrative shaming of the offender and calling on the offender and the family to take responsibility for the problem in their own way. For the over-whelming majority of such minor offenders, this is the last the juvenile justice system will see of them, so any more detailed intervention is wasteful overkill.

*Fourth offence:* Second family group conference. More rigorous conference. What did the participants do, or fail to do, after the last conference? More detailed plan of action to respond to this analysis of the problem. Designation of offender supporters to monitor and report on implementation. Follow-up by co-ordinator to report back to participants on implementation. Modest quantum of community work.

*Fifth offence:* Third family group conference. Escalation of shaming of offender: 'You gave undertakings to your family at the last conference that you have broken in the most thoughtless way. You breached the trust your parents put in you with that agreement.' Redesign the plan of action. This time, secure a more solemn oath to the parents. Follow through. More community work.

*Sixth offence:* Fourth family group conference. New invitees. The smorgasbord of intervention options that the family group can choose (life skills or work skills courses, remedial education, church-run programmes, anger control courses, regular meetings with the school counsellor,

---

[16] There will be rare cases where the offender is so dangerous that escalation to institutionalization is inevitable and necessary. We have no dispute with such a course of action in those cases.

outward bound, drug rehabilitation programmes, etc.) is put before them in a different way. 'We chose the wrong option before. That was our mistake. But we believe in the caring side of you that your family sees so often, so eventually you will find with them the right option to assist you to consider the hurt you cause to victims like Mrs Smith and to consider your own future.' Keep up the shaming, this time focused on the particular circumstances of Mrs Smith. Work for Mrs Smith.

*Seventh offence:* Fifth family group conference. Try again basic strategy of fourth conference with a different victim, different participants, and a different way of presenting the smorgasbord of intervention options.

*Eighth offence:* Sixth family group conference. Change tack. Eventually come back to the fact that the offender is still responsible for this particular criminal act, but lead off with collective self-blame: 'As a group, your parents, your sister, grandfather and aunt, your teacher, Mrs Brown, who has such a soft spot for you, and me as the co-ordinator of this conference, we all feel responsible that we have let you down. We haven't listened to you well enough to come up with the right ways to help you. We need you to tell us where we have gone wrong.' Various other options can follow, such as one family member after another coming along prepared to give a speech on the mistakes they have made in the course of the saga. A search could be initiated by the family to find some new participants in the conference to add fresh perspectives, even asking another couple to become 'god-parents'. An option on the co-ordinator's side could be to bring in a consultant professional of some sort with new ideas to participate in the conference.

Obviously, it gets very difficult to keep coming up with new angles, to keep projecting faith in the essential goodness of the offender, to persist with the never-give-up ideology. The relentless optimism that successful reintegration enjoins may eventually surrender in the face of a natural human pessimism. We saw one stigmatizing conference for an offender (his fourth) which exemplified this surrender. During this encounter, the exasperated co-ordinator described the offender as a 'Yahoo'. Before inviting the offender to give his side of the story, he turned to the family and asked them what they thought was wrong with the boy. He said: 'The responsibility is the parents, not ours. I don't care. The Department doesn't care. We can just send it on to court.' The Youth Advocate said that she saw the key question as being whether 'his friends were bad or he was the bad one'. She supported the interpretation of the police that escalation to institutionalization was the track the boy was heading down. The police, the co-ordinator and the youth advocate had given up and everything they said gave the impression that they had given up on him. Even when the boy apologized, the co-ordinator evinced utter cynicism when he retorted dismissively, 'That's what you said last time.' This was a fully fledged degradation ceremony rather than an attempt at reintegration.

Pessimism is a natural human reaction to repeated misfortune and eventually the most determined commitment to 'never giving up on the offender' may succumb to it.

### CONDITIONS OF SUCCESSFUL REINTEGRATION CEREMONIES

But a tenacious commitment to the ideology of never giving up will allow co-ordinators to cling to it for the fourth conference after the failure of the third. A slightly more tenacious commitment allows optimism to survive the fifth conference into the sixth. At each stage, more and more offenders drop off never to return, their criminal careers coming to an end without being inflicted with degradation ceremonies. Very few offenders indeed will make it through to a sixth conference. If we can hold out with optimism until then, the criminal justice system will have been transformed to a 99 per cent reintegrative institution. That can hardly be a bad outcome.

True disciples of reintegration, including ourselves, take the injunction to never give up on offenders to the absolute extreme. Even when a criminal career has continued to the point of the offender being the most powerful organized criminal in the country, the best hope for dealing with him is conceived as persuading him to convert his illegitimate capital into a legitimate business, giving his children a better future, a more respectable future, than the shame of his criminal empire. Going further still, as we have illustrated earlier (see n. 8 above), we think even the top management of certain Australian insurance companies are best negotiated with reintegratively! In the extraordinary cases where offenders are such a danger to the community that incarceration is defensible, we should not give up on pushing for reintegration, even though the degradation ceremony of confinement makes this maximally difficult.

*(14) The ceremony must be justified by a politically resonant discourse*

Shaming and reintegration are terms that we think have merit (that we will not defend here) in the discourse of criminological theory. These days, they have surprising currency among the police and community of Wagga. But in New Zealand, the terms that have more currency are, respectively, young offenders and their families 'taking responsibility' and 'healing'. The discourse of responsibility and healing may have more popular political appeal than that of shame and reintegration, as evidenced by the wide political support it has attracted in New Zealand and the growing support throughout Australia (Interim Report of the Select Committee on the Juvenile Justice System 1992; Tate 1992).

Much more crucial to this political and media support has been the marketing of this reintegration strategy as victim-centred and family-centred. It is a progressive reform that calls the hand of conservative politicians. They are forever claiming that victims are the forgotten people of the criminal justice system and bemoaning the declining importance of the family in contemporary society. Here is a reform that empowers victims and at the same time values and empowers families. Such a reform puts conservatives in a vulnerable position when they seek to oppose it.

Moreover, conservatives have also found in Australia and New Zealand that they cannot count on their allegedly 'natural allies' in law and order campaigns, the police. The Australian and New Zealand Police Federation carried a resolution at its 1991 conference supporting the New Zealand juvenile justice reforms. In New Zealand, 91 per cent of the time, police report that they are satisfied with the outcomes of the conferences in which they participate, a higher level than for youth justice co-ordinators (86 per cent), parents (85 per cent), offenders (84 per cent) and victims (48 per cent) (Morris and Maxwell 1992). Perhaps this should not surprise us. The approach appeals to the common sense of police. On balance, it cuts their paperwork

JOHN BRAITHWAITE AND STEPHEN MUGFORD

and economizes on criminal justice system resources; they often feel empowered by the capacity the conference gives them to make practical suggestions to the family on what might be done about the problem (an opportunity they are rarely given by courts); they like to treat victims with the decency that they believe courts deny them (in particular, they like to see victims actually getting compensation); and they find that the programme builds goodwill toward the police in communities that are empowered through the process. Most critically, they find participation in community conferences more interesting, challenging, and satisfying work than typing up charges and sitting around in courthouses for cases that are rushed through in a matter of minutes. This is by no means a universal police reaction. But we can certainly say that the strongest support for these reintegrative programmes in Australia has come from the police. While New Zealand reform was Maori-driven, the Australian reform is being police-driven.

Finally, the political appeal of the process is that it can be advocated in the discourse of fiscal restraint. In New Zealand, one of the most conservative governments in the Western world liked a reform that helped the budget deficit by allowing them to sell most of the institutions for juvenile offenders in the country. We were told that the Department of Social Welfare alone estimated that in 1991, they saved $6 million as a result of the reform. In this area of criminal justice, youth justice co-ordinators not only do the job more effectively than judges in court, they are cheaper than judges. By the same token, youth justice advocates are cheaper than prosecutors and public defenders. At all levels of the criminal justice system there are savings—not always massive savings, but rarely trivial.[17]

At the same time, reintegration ceremonies offer an attractive political package for a reforming politician. Presented properly, it can satisfy the otherwise incompatible imperatives of keeping the police and the finance ministry happy at the same time. It can even put the victims movement and liberally minded criminal justice reformers—who so often seem diametrically opposed—together on the same platform of support.

### Conclusion

A useful way of thinking about ceremonies for dealing with rule breakers is in terms of the ratio of stigmatic to reintegrative meanings during the ceremony. When that ratio is high, we have a degradation ceremony; when low, a reintegration ceremony. There are few, if any, actors who are perfectly faithful to the theory of reintegrative shaming during such ceremonies. Typically, messages are mixed, as with the Maori participant quoted above: 'You've got no brains, boy (stigmatization) . . . But I've got respect for you (reintegration) . . .' There are many actors like this one who communicate shame while also sustaining a high ratio of reintegrative to stigmatizing meanings. The subtleties in the ways shaming and reintegration are mixed by practical human communicators are myriad. We noted one police sergeant who addressed male offenders by their names whenever he was engaging them in responsibility talk, but

---

[17] Against this view, economists might say that we should cost the (considerable) time involved in the attendance of victims and supporters, for example. If we calculated these costs, perhaps there would be no savings. But why should we make a negative entry for victims in the economic calculus when the fact is that the reform increases utility for victims? To enter the costs would make sense only if we could value the benefits. And if we did that, then no doubt the system we describe would again show a better balance sheet.

CONDITIONS OF SUCCESSFUL REINTEGRATION CEREMONIES

who called them 'mate' whenever he switched to reintegrative talk. When we pointed out this observation and asked him whether he was aware of the pattern, the sergeant told us it was a conscious communication strategy.

In Giddens's (1984) terms, many actors have practical but not discursive consciousness of the idea of reintegration; some actors, like this sergeant, have both. A feasible objective is to increase the proportion of actors who are conscious of the virtues of reintegration. This is not best achieved by lectures from theoretical criminology texts, but from telling stories (Shearing and Ericson 1991) and simple homilies such as that of one police constable: 'Just because we sometimes do stupid things; that does not mean we are a stupid person.' It could be that if there is a key principle of successful reintegration ceremonies, it is that there should not be too many principles. Training of co-ordinators should be kept simple, leaving them wide discretion to implement flexibly a few broad principles.

Stigma cannot be rooted out of confrontations between people who are angry and affronted by acts of rule breaking. But the ratio of stigmatization to reintegration can be shifted substantially by story-based training methods that focus on a few core principles—empower the victim, respect and support the offender while condemning his act, engage the offender's supporters. Just by having a process that is more victim-centred, problem-centred, and community-oriented, rather than centred on the offender and his pathologies, we institute a logic that produces less stigmatization and more reintegration. Obversely, the offender-centred logic of the courtroom or the psychiatrist's couch institutionalizes stigmatization.

One of the inevitable problems is that the stigmatizing, disempowering professional knowledges of the court and consultancy rooms penetrate the reintegration ceremony. Most depressingly, this was observed in New Zealand with the role of certain youth advocates, private lawyers contracted by the state to watch out for the rights of young offenders during conferences. Sometimes they 'earn their fee' by taking charge, telling the family what sort of action plan will satisfy the police and the courts. Or worse, we see 'the practice of law as a confidence game' (Blumberg 1967) where advocate, co-ordinator and police conspire to settle a practical deal among the professionals, then sell that deal to the conference participants, a deal that in at least one case seemed to us a sell-out of both the offender and the victim.

We commented earlier about the observations made by Clifford Shearing and Jane Mugford after a Wagga training session. Their point was that the reform process must create a new knowledge, a citizen knowledge, otherwise the old professional knowledges would colonize the spaces in the programme. We agree—hence the importance of the simple principles outlined above and the importance of the central involvement of local police–citizen consultative committees and other community groups in guiding reform. At the same time, however, we think the professional knowledges also include the seeds of their own reform. Reintegrative concepts have a major place in psychological and particularly social work discourse. These can be brought to the fore through reforms such as we are seeing in New Zealand and Wagga. While the youth advocates were criticized by a number of people we spoke to in New Zealand for importing professional control into family group conferences, some of these critics also pointed out how many advocates had changed their legalistic habits to accommodate the communitarian ideology of the conferences. Finally, there can be no doubt that these reforms are part of wider changes in police knowledges in Australia and New Zealand—away

167

*Correctional Ethics*

from 'lock-'em-up' law enforcement and toward community policing. None the less, at the crucial middle management levels, the old punitive knowledges of policing continue to predominate and must be confronted by reasoned cases based on the success of alternative practices. Reformers can't lock professional knowledges out of the process. Hence, reformers must be engaged with police education, counter-colonizing that area with reintegrative ideas.[18]

There are no criminal justice utopias to be found, just better and worse directions to head in.[19] The New Zealand Maori have shown a direction for making reintegration ceremonies work in multicultural metropolises such as Auckland, a city that faces deeper problems of recession, homelessness, and gang violence than many cities in Western Europe. Implementation of these ideas by the white New Zealand authorities has been riddled with imperfection—re-professionalization, patriarchy, ritualistic proceduralism that loses sight of objectives, and inappropriate net-widening. The important thing, however, is that the general direction of change is away from these pathologies; it is deprofessionalizing, empowering of women, oriented to flexible community problem-solving and, for the most part, narrowing nets of state control (Maxwell and Morris 1993: 25, 134, 136, but see 128, 176; on net-narrowing at Wagga see Moore 1992; O'Connell 1992). Most critically, it shows that the conditions of successful reintegration ceremonies that criminologists identify when in high theory mode can be given practical content for implementation by police and citizens.

As both Max Scheler and Garfinkel point out: 'There is no society that does not provide in the very features of its organisation the conditions sufficient for inducing shame.' (Garfinkel 1956: 420). The question is what sort of balance societies will have between degradation ceremonies as a 'secular form of communion' and reintegration ceremonies as a rather different communion. Garfinkel showed that there was a practical programme of communication tactics that will get the work of status degradation done. We hope to have shown that equally there is a practical programme of communication tactics that can accomplish reintegration.

### REFERENCES

ASHWORTH, A. (1986), 'Punishment and Compensation: Victims, Offenders and the State', *Oxford Journal of Legal Studies*, 6: 86–122.

BALES, R. (1950), *Interaction Process Analysis*. Cambridge: Addison Wesley.

BECKER, H. S. (1960), 'Notes on the concept of commitment', *American Journal of Sociology*, 66: 32–40.

—— (1963), *Outsiders: Studies in the Sociology of Deviance*. New York: Free Press.

BLUMBERG, A. S. (1967), 'The Practice of Law as a Confidence Game: Organizational Cooptation of a Profession', *Law and Society Review*, 1: 15–39.

---

[18] Something the senior author has been actively engaged with since 1986 as a member of the NSW Police Education Advisory Council.

[19] There is no persuasive evidence that the reforms we have described actually work in reducing delinquency. That would require random allocation experiments. We can say that official statistics do not support the conclusion that they are failing. Crime rates in Wagga Wagga seem to have fallen since the juvenile justice reforms were introduced. In New Zealand, juvenile crime rates were falling slightly before the Children, Young Persons and Their Families Act 1989 was passed, and continued to fall slightly after its introduction (Maxwell and Morris 1993: 45).

CONDITIONS OF SUCCESSFUL REINTEGRATION CEREMONIES

BLAGG, H. (1985), 'Reparation and Justice for Juveniles: The Corby Experience', *British Journal of Criminology*, 25: 267–79.

BOTT, E. (1987), 'The Kava Ceremonial as a Dream Structure', in M. Douglas, ed., *Constructive Drinking: Perspectives on Drinking from Anthropology*. Cambridge: Cambridge University Press, pp. 182–204.

BRAITHWAITE, J. (1989), *Crime, Shame and Reintegration*. Cambridge: Cambridge University Press.

—— (1991), 'Poverty, Power, White-Collar Crime and the Paradoxes of Criminological Theory', *Australian and New Zealand Journal of Criminology*, 24: 40–58.

—— (1992), 'Corporate Crime and Republican Criminological Praxis', Paper to Queens University Conference on Corporate Ethics, Law and the State, Kingston.

—— (1993), 'Inequality and Republican Criminology', in John Hagan and Ruth Peterson, eds, *Crime and Inequality*. Palo Alto: Stanford University Press.

BRAITHWAITE, J., and DALY, K. (in press), 'Masculinities, Violence and Communitarian Control', in T. Newburn and B. Stanko, eds, *Just Boys Doing Business? Men, Masculinity and Crime*. London: Routledge.

CHEAL, D. (1988), 'The Postmodern Origins of Ritual', *Journal for the Theory of Social Behaviour*, 18: 269–90.

CHRISTIE, N. (1977), 'Conflict as Property', *British Journal of Criminology*, 17: 1–26.

CRAGG, W. (1992), *The Practice of Punishment: Towards a Theory of Restorative Justice*. London: Routledge.

DE HAAN, W. (1990), *The Politics of Redress: Crime, Punishment and Penal Abolition*. London: Unwin Hyman.

DIGNAN, J. (1992), 'Repairing the Damage: Can Reparation Work in the Service of Diversion?', *British Journal of Criminology*, 32: 453–72.

DOOB, A., and ROBERTS, J. (1983), *Sentencing: An Analysis of the Public's View of Sentencing. A Report to the Department of Justice, Canada*. Department of Justice: Canada.

—— (1988), 'Public Attitudes towards Sentencing in Canada', in N. Walker and M. Hough, eds, *Public Attitudes to Sentencing*. Aldershot: Gower.

ERIKSON, K. T. (1962), 'Notes on the Sociology of Deviance', *Social Problems*, 9: 307–14.

FISSE, B., and BRAITHWAITE, J. (1993), *Corporations, Crime and Accountability*. Sydney: Cambridge University Press.

GALAWAY, B. (1985), 'Victim-Participation in the Penal Corrective process', *Victimology*, 10: 617–30.

GALAWAY, B., and HUDSON, J. (1975), 'Issues in the Correctional Implementation of Restitution to Victims of Crime', in J. Hudson and B. Galaway, eds, *Considering the Victim*. Springfield, IL: Charles C. Thomas.

—— (1990), *Criminal Justice, Restitution and Reconciliation*. Monsey, NY: Criminal Justice Press.

GALAWAY, B., HENZEL, M., RAMSEY, G., and WANYAMA, B. (1980), 'Victims and Delinquents in the Tulsa Juvenile Court', *Federal Probation*, 44: 42–8.

GARFINKEL, H. (1956), 'Conditions of Successful Degradation Ceremonies', *American Journal of Sociology*, 61: 420–4.

GIDDENS, A. (1984), *The Constitution of Society*. Berkeley, CA: University of California Press.

GOFFMAN, E. (1971), *Relations in Public*. New York: Basic Books.

GUSFIELD, J. R. (1987), 'Passage to Play: Rituals of Drink in American Society', in M. Douglas, ed., *Constructive Drinking: Perspectives on Drinking from Anthropology*. Cambridge: Cambridge University Press, pp. 73–90.

HABERMAS, J. (1986), 'Law as Medium and Law as Institution', in Gunther Teubner, ed., *Dilemmas of Law in the Welfare State*. Berlin: Walter de Gruyter.

HAZAN, H. (1987), 'Holding Time Still with Cups of Tea', in M. Douglas, ed., *Constructive Drinking: Perspectives on Drinking from Anthropology*. Cambridge: Cambridge University Press, pp. 205–19.

HAZLEHURST, K. (1985), 'Community Care/Community Responsibility: Community Participation in Criminal Justice Administration in New Zealand', in K. Hazlehurst, ed., *Justice Programs for Aboriginal and Other Indigenous Communities*. Canberra: Australian Institute of Criminology.

HEINZ, A., and KERSTETTER, W. (1981), 'Pretrial Settlement Conference: Evaluation of a Reform in Plea Bargaining', in B. Galaway and J. Hudson, eds, *Perspectives on Crime Victims*. St. Louis, MO: Mosby.

HIRSCHI, T., and GOTTFREDSON, M. (1983), 'Age and the Explanation of Crime', *American Journal of Sociology*, 89: 552–84.

HOWARD, B., and PURCHES, L. (1992), 'A Discussion of the Police Family Group Conferences and the Follow-Up Program (Stage 2) in the Wagga Wagga Juvenile Cautioning Process', *Rural Society*, 2: 20–3.

Interim Report of the Select Committee on the Juvenile Justice System (1992). Adelaide: Parliament of South Australia.

KIGIN, R., and NOVACK, S. (1980), 'A Rural Restitution Program for Juvenile Offenders and Victims', in J. Hudson and B. Galaway, eds, *Victims, Offenders and Alternative Sanctions*. Lexington, MA: Lexington Books.

MARSHALL, T. F. (1985), *Alternatives to Criminal Courts*. Aldershot: Gower.

MAXWELL, G. M., and MORRIS, A. (1993), *Family Victims and Culture: Youth Justice in New Zealand*. Wellington: Institute of Criminology, Victoria University of Wellington.

McDONALD, J., and IRELAND, S. (1990), *Can It be Done Another Way?* Sydney: New South Wales Police Service.

MEIMA, M. (1990), 'Sexual Violence, Criminal Law and Abolitionism', in B. Rolston and M. Tomlinson, eds, *Gender, Sexuality and Social Control*. Bristol: European Group for the Study of Deviance and Social Control.

MOORE, D. B. (1992), 'Facing the Consequences. Conferences and Juvenile Justice', *National Conference on Juvenile Justice*. Canberra: Australian Institute of Criminology.

MORRIS, A., and MAXWELL, G. (1992), 'Juvenile Justice in New Zealand: A New Paradigm', *Australian and New Zealand Journal of Criminology*, 26: 72–90.

MORRIS, A., MAXWELL, G., and ROBERTSON, J. P. (in press), 'Giving Victims a Voice: A New Zealand Experiment', *Howard Journal of Criminology*.

MUGFORD, J., and MUGFORD, S. (1991), 'Shame and Reintegration in the Punishment and Deterrence of Spouse Abuse'. Paper presented to the American Society of Criminology Conference, San Francisco, 20 November.

—— (1992), 'Policing Domestic Violence), in P. Moir and H. Eijckman, eds, *Policing Australia: Old Issues, New Perspectives*. Melbourne: MacMillan, pp. 321–83.

MURPHY, J. G., and HAMPTON, J. (1989), *Forgiveness and Mercy*. New York: Cambridge.

New Zealand Police Association (1991), Submission to the Review of the Children, Young Persons and their Families Act 1989. Wellington: New Zealand Police Association.

NOVACK, S., GALAWAY, B., and HUDSON, J. (1980), 'Victim and Offender Perceptions of the Fairness of Restitution and Community-Service Sanctions', in J. Hudson and B. Galaway, eds, *Victims, Offenders and Alternative Sanctions*. Lexington, MA: Lexington Books.

## CONDITIONS OF SUCCESSFUL REINTEGRATION CEREMONIES

O'CONNELL, T. (1992), 'It May Be the Way to Go', *National Conference on Juvenile Justice*. Canberra: Australian Institute of Criminology.

O'CONNELL, T. and MOORE, D. (1992), 'Wagga Juvenile Cautioning Process: The General Applicability of Family Group Conferences for Juvenile Offenders and their Victims', *Rural Society*, 2: 16–19.

O'CONNOR, I., and SWEETAPPLE, P. (1988), *Children in Justice*. Sydney: Longman-Cheshire.

PEPINSKY, H. E., and QUINNEY, R. (eds) (1991) *Criminology as Peacemaking*. Bloomington: Indiana University Press.

POLK, K. (1992), 'Jobs not Jails: A New Agenda for Youth', *National Conference on Juvenile Justice*. Canberra: Australian Institute of Criminology.

Report of the Ministerial Advisory Committee on a Maori Perspective for the Department of Social Welfare (1986), *Puao-Te-Ata-Tu* (day break). Wellington, New Zealand: Department of Social Welfare.

ROSE, N. (1990), *Governing the Soul: Shaping the Private Self*. London: Routledge and Kegan Paul.

SCHEFF, T. J., and RETZINGER, S. M. (1991), *Emotions and Violence: Shame and Rage in Destructive Conflicts*. Lexington, MA: Lexington Books.

SCHUR, E. M. (1973), *Radical Non-Intervention: Rethinking the Delinquency Problem*. Englewood Cliffs, NJ: Prentice-Hall.

SHAPLAND, J., WILLMORE, J., and DUFF, P. (1985), *Victims in the Criminal Justice System*, Cambridge Studies in Criminology. Brookfield, VT: Gower.

SHEARING, C. D., and ERICSON, R. V. (1991), 'Towards a Figurative Conception of Action', *British Journal of Sociology*, 42: 481–506.

SIMMEL, G. (1978), *The Philosophy of Money*. London: Routledge.

SYKES, G., and MATZA, D. (1957), 'Techniques of Neutralization: A Theory of Delinquency', *American Sociological Review*, 22: 664–70.

TATE, SENATOR M. (1992), Opening Address, *National Conference on Juvenile Justice*. Canberra: Australian Institute of Criminology.

TAYLOR, I., WALTON, P., and YOUNG, J. (1973), *The New Criminology: For a Social Theory of Deviance*. London: Routledge and Kegan Paul.

UMBREIT, M. (1985), *Crime and Reconciliation: Creative Options for Victims and Offenders*. Nashville, TN: Abigton Press.

WEITEKAMP, E. (1989), Restitution: A New Paradigm of Criminal Justice or a New Way to Widen the System of Social Control? Unpublished Ph.D dissertation, University of Pennsylvania.

WRIGHT, M. (1982), *Making Good: Prisons, Punishment and Beyond*. London: Hutchinson.

Youth Justice Coalition (1990), *Kids in Justice: A Blueprint for the 90s*. Sydney: Law Foundation of New South Wales.

ZEHR, H. (1990), *Changing Lenses: A New Focus for Criminal Justice*. Scottdale, PA: Herald Press.

# [14]

## SETTING STANDARDS FOR RESTORATIVE JUSTICE

JOHN BRAITHWAITE*

*Three types of restorative justice standards are articulated: limiting, maximizing, and enabling standards. They are developed as multidimensional criteria for evaluating restorative justice programmes. A way of summarizing the long list of standards is that they define ways of securing the republican freedom (dominion) of citizens through repair, transformation, empowerment with others and limiting the exercise of power over others. A defence of the list is also articulated in terms of values that can be found in consensus UN Human Rights agreements and from what we know empirically about what citizens seek from restorative justice. Ultimately, such top-down lists motivated by UN instruments or the ruminations of intellectuals are only important for supplying a provisional, revisable agenda for bottom-up deliberation on restorative justice standards appropriate to distinctively local anxieties about injustice. A method is outlined for moving bottom-up from standards citizens settle for evaluating their local programme to aggregating these into national and international standards.*

### Pluralizing State Power

This essay will explore the tensions between restorative justice as a bottom-up social movement and the fact that its philosophical fundamentals require it to exercise power accountably (Roche 2001). Top-down managerialist accountability of an 'audit society' that takes the techniques of the discipline of business accounting into fields to which they are not well adapted (Power 1997) does not have an encouraging history in criminal justice (Jones 1993). Managerialist restorative justice is also anathema to the bottom-up democratic (civic republican) ethos of the social movement. Yet this essay develops two philosophical positions: (a) that top-down accountability of some form is needed with top-down standards that are contestable bottom-up; (b) that human rights must be protected by restorative justice processes (Braithwaite and Pettit 1990). It will be argued that human rights meta-narratives that come from above can be made concretely meaningful by local standards that have contextual relevance to restorative justice programmes. This concrete experience can then generate democratic impulses that can inform the reframing of top-down human rights discourse (Habermas 1996).

In the article Northern Ireland is selected as a least likely case study (Eckstein 1975) for such an approach in Western societies—a case study selected as one where the approach would prove least likely to be feasible. Northern Ireland is a context where political trust is low, where there is a long history of democratic impulses from below being blocked by blood and domination and which has not had an exemplary rights culture. It is of course not as unlikely a case study as Afghanistan, but in the West we can plausibly advance Northern Ireland as a least likely case. If it can be shown that the approach can be

---

* Professor in the Law Program, Research School of Social Sciences, Australian National University, Canberra.

developed in a feasible way in the least likely case, then the methodological idea is that the approach might have prospects of being robustly relevant in many contexts.

One of the reasons restorative justice gathers modest support in reformist politics is that many can identify with a commitment to combating oppressive state structures of inhumane reliance on prisons. It also involves empowering citizens with responsibility for matters that over the past few centuries came to be viewed as state responsibilities. For most restorative justice advocates, restorative justice is consequentialist philosophically, methodologically, and politically. The restorative method is to discuss consequences of injustices and to acknowledge them appropriately as a starting point toward healing the hurts of injustice and transforming the conditions that allowed injustice to flourish. Politically, if citizens can see that there are consequences for offenders in taking responsibility for dealing with all of this, they may see less need for punishment because 'something needs to be done' and punishment seems the natural thing to do with crime. Notwithstanding this consequentialism, many of the limits that retributivists regard as central are also found to be important standards of restorative justice. The article considers what those standards should be and how they should be refined. But if restorative justice is about shifting power to the people, surely reimposing the state to set standards for restorative justice shifts the power back to the state?

It may. And there is certainly a worry here, especially in contexts like Northern Ireland. In Northern Ireland, as in South Africa, Bougainville (Howley 2002) and other post-conflict situations, all sides have their historical reasons for distrusting moves by the state that might disempower their people. Equally, there are historical reasons for the state to distrust paramilitary elements in civil society who they fear will use control of informal justice to sustain an armed tyranny over local communities. So we need state standards to render the empowerment of restorative justice robust. In popular justice throughout the ages we have seen all manner of disempowerment of minorities by majorities, of those without guns by those with guns (Abel 1981, 1982; Nader 1980). State-sanctioned human rights are vital for regulating the tyrannies of informal justice. They are also vital for regulating the tyrannies of the police, of state-sanctioned torture and violence, which in Northern Ireland have been considerable problems.

State standards can enable the deliberative democracy of the people or it can disable it. It all depends on what the standards are and how they are implemented. So we must get down to detail. But before we do that, it is worth mentioning that part of the genius of restorative justice as a policy idea is that many of its most precious ideals are invulnerable to state power. An example is Kay Pranis's (2000) great insight about how empowerment works with restorative justice. Pranis says we can tell how much power a person has by how many people listen to their stories. When the prime minister speaks from his podium many listen; when the pauper on a street corner mutters his stories we walk past. The deadly simple empowering feature of restorative justice here is that it involves listening to the stories of victims and accused offenders, both groups which the criminological literature shows to be disproportionately poor, powerless and young (Hindelang *et al.* 1978; Braithwaite and Biles 1984). The empirical evidence is that women's voices are actually slightly more likely to be heard in restorative justice conferences than men's voices (Braithwaite 2002: ch. 5), a very different reality from the voices that are heard in the corridors of state power and judicial power. Pranis's point is that by the simple fact of listening to their story we give them power. So long as the core listening principle of restorative justice is retained, this kind of empowerment cannot be threatened by state standards.

## *Dangers in Standards*

While it is good that we are now having debates on standards for restorative justice, it is a dangerous debate. Accreditation for mediators that raises the spectre of a Western accreditation agency telling an Aboriginal elder that a centuries-old restorative practice does not comply with the accreditation standards is a profound worry. We must avert accreditation that crushes indigenous empowerment.

We should also worry about standards that are so prescriptive that they inhibit restorative justice innovation. We are still learning how to do restorative justice well. The healing edge programmes today involve real advances over those of the 1990s and the best programmes of the 1990s made important advances over those of the 1980s. We should even worry about regulatory proposals that are highly prescriptive about how we should define what a standard or a principle of restorative justice is, or which matters should be formulated as rights that are guarantees that should never be breached. I am not sure we have learnt enough yet about what happens in restorative processes to be ready for such prescription.

We must be careful in how we regulate restorative justice now so that in another decade we will be able to say again that the healing edge programmes are more profoundly restorative than those of today. Unthinking enforcement of standards is a new threat to innovating with better ways of doing restorative justice. It is a threat because evaluation research on restorative justice is at such a rudimentary stage that our claims about what is good practice and what is bad practice can rarely be evidence-based.

At the same time, there is such a thing as practice masquerading as restorative justice that is outrageously poor—practice that would generate little controversy among criminologists that it was unconscionable, such as the conference discussed in the next section where a child agreed to wear a t-shirt announcing 'I am a thief'. Such practices are an even greater threat to the future of restorative justice. So we have no option but to do something about them through a prudent standards debate. We can craft open-textured restorative justice standards that allow a lot of space for cultural difference and innovation while giving us a language for denouncing uncontroversially bad practice. This contribution to the standards debate will be a modest one that will not seek to be exhaustive in defining the issues standards must address.

## *The Principle of Non-Domination*

From my civic republican perspective (Braithwaite and Pettit 1990; Pettit 1997), a fundamental standard is that restorative processes must seek to avoid domination. We do see a lot of domination in restorative processes, as we do in all spheres of social interaction. But a programme is not restorative if it fails to be active in preventing domination. What does this mean in practice? It means that if a stakeholder wants to attend a conference or circle and have a say, they must not be prevented from attending. If they have a stake in the outcome, they must be helped to attend and speak. This does not preclude special support circles for just victims or just offenders; but it does mandate institutional design that gives every stakeholder a meaningful opportunity to speak and be heard. Any attempt by a participant at a conference to silence or dominate another participant must be countered. This does not mean the conference convenor has to intervene. On the contrary, it is better if other stakeholders are given the space to speak up against dominating speech. But if domination persists and the stakeholders are afraid to confront it, then the convenor must confront it by specifically asking to hear more from the voice that is being subordinated.

Often it is rather late for confronting domination once the restorative process is under way. Power imbalance is a structural phenomenon. It follows that restorative processes must be structured so as to minimize power imbalance. Young offenders must not be led into a situation where they are upbraided by a 'roomful of adults' (Haines 1998). There must be adults who see themselves as having a responsibility to be advocates for the child, adults who will speak up. If this is not accomplished, a conference or circle can always be adjourned and reconvened with effective supporters of the child in the room. Similarly, we cannot tolerate the scenario of a dominating group of family violence offenders and their patriarchal defenders intimidating women and children who are victims into frightened silence. When risks of power imbalance are most acute our standards should expect of us a lot of preparatory work to restore balance both backstage and frontstage during the process. Organized advocacy groups have a particularly important role when power imbalances are most acute. These include women's and children's advocacy groups when family violence is at issue (Strang and Braithwaite 2002), environmental advocacy groups when crimes against the environment by powerful corporations are at issue (Gunningham and Grabosky 1998).

Of course, holding the threat of a punishment beating, of kneecapping, over the head of a person is an intolerable violation of the principle of non-domination. Common ground among all the restorative justice initiatives in Northern Ireland seems to be to transcend this particular form of domination, though there are competing visions of how to accomplish this. While I am in no position to adjudicate these competing visions, I would like to submit the principle of non-domination and the values that flow from it as a values framework for the debate.

Due process is perhaps the major domain where there have been calls for standards. It seems reasonable that offenders put into restorative justice programmes be advised of their right to seek the advice of a lawyer on whether they should participate in the programme. Perhaps this would be an empty international standard in poorer nations where lawyers are not in practical terms affordable or available for most criminal defendants. But wealthier nations like the United Kingdom can afford higher standards on this issue. Arresting police officers who refer cases to restorative justice processes should be required to provide a telephone number of a free legal advice line on whether agreeing to the restorative justice process is prudent.

In no nation does it seem appropriate for defendants to have a right for their lawyer to represent them during a restorative justice process. Part of the point of restorative justice is to transcend adversarial legalism, to empower stakeholders to speak in their own voice rather than through legal mouthpieces who might have an interest in polarizing a conflict. A standard that says defendants or victims have a right to have legal counsel present during a restorative justice process seems sound. But a standard that gives legal counsel a right to speak at the conference or circle seems an unwarranted threat from the dominant legal discourse to the integrity of an empowering restorative justice process. This does not mean banning lawyers from speaking under any circumstances; if all the participants agree they should hear some expert opinion from a lawyer then that opinion should certainly be invited into the circle. Moreover, I have argued that where lawyers have signed a collaborative law agreement and been trained in collaborative law values and methods, there may be special virtue in hearing from them (Braithwaite 2002: 250–1).

The most important way that the criminal justice system must be constrained against being a source of domination over the lives of citizens is that it must be constrained against ever imposing a punishment beyond the maximum allowed by law for that kind of offence. It is therefore critical that restorative justice never be allowed to undermine this constraint. Restorative justice processes must be prohibited from ever imposing punishments that exceed the maximum punishment the courts would impose for that offence. As someone who believes that restorative justice processes should be about reintegrative shaming and should reject stigmatization, it seems important to prohibit any degrading or humiliating form of treatment. We had a conference in Canberra where all the stakeholders agreed it was a good idea for a young offender to wear a t-shirt stating 'I am a thief'. This sort of outcome should be banned.

Another critical, albeit vague, standard is that restorative justice programmes must be concerned with the needs and with the empowerment not only of offenders, but also of victims and affected communities. Programmes where victims are exploited as props for programmes that are oriented only to the rehabilitation of offenders are morally unacceptable (Braithwaite 2002: ch. 5). Deals that are win-win for victims and offenders but where certain other members of the community are serious losers, worse losers whose perspective is not even heard, are morally unacceptable. The key principle here is equal concern for all stakeholders. The most important way to manifest that concern is through respectful listening, which is also the obverse of banning disrespectful or humiliating, degrading ways of reacting or punishing.

The right to appeal must be safeguarded (Brown 1994; Warner 1994). Whenever the criminal law is a basis for imposing sanctions in a restorative justice process, offenders must have a right of appeal against those sanctions to a court of law. That said, not all of the accountability mechanisms of criminal trials seem appropriate to the philosophy of restorative justice. For example, if we are concerned about averting stigmatization and assuring undominated dialogue, we may not want conferences or circles to be normally open to the public. But if that is our policy, it seems especially important for researchers, critics, journalists, political leaders, judges, colleagues from restorative justice programmes in other places, to be able to sit in on conferences or circles (with the permission of the participants) so there can be informed public debate and exposure of inappropriate practices. Most importantly, it is critical that restorative justice processes can be observed by peer reviewers whose job it is to report on compliance with the kinds of standards I will discuss.

### International Standards

In general, UN Human Rights instruments give quite good guidance on the foundational values and rights restorative justice processes ought to observe. The first clause of the Preamble of the Universal Declaration that most states have ratified is:

Whereas recognition of the inherent dignity and of the equal and inalienable rights of all members of the human family is the foundation of freedom, justice and peace in the world . . .

Obviously freedom, justice and peace have a lot of appeal to someone who values republican freedom to frame the pursuit of justice and peacemaking in restorative justice. In its 30 Articles the Universal Declaration defines a considerable number of slightly more specific values and rights that seem to cover many of the things we look to restore and protect in restorative justice processes. These include a right to protection from having one's property arbitrarily taken (Article 17), a right to life, liberty and security of the person (Article 3), a right to health and medical care (Article 25) and a right to democratic participation (Article 21).

From the restorative justice advocate's point of view, the most interesting Article is 5: 'No one shall be subjected to torture or to cruel, inhuman or degrading treatment or punishment.' Of course, all states have interpreted Article 5 in a most permissive and unsatisfactory way from a restorative justice point of view. The challenge for restorative justice advocates is to take the tiny anti-punitive space this Article creates in global human rights discourse and expand its meaning over time so that it increasingly acquires a more restorative interpretation. This is precisely how successful NGO activists have globalized progressive agendas in many other arenas—starting with a platitudinous initial rights framework and injecting progressively less conservative and more specific meanings into that framework agreement over time (Braithwaite and Drahos 2000: 619–20).

We can already move to slightly more specific and transformative aspirations within human rights discourse by moving from the Universal Declaration of 1948 to the less widely ratified International Covenant on Economic, Social and Cultural Rights of 1976 and the International Covenant on Civil and Political Rights of 1966. The former, for example, involves a deeper commitment to 'self-determination' and allows in a commitment to emotional wellbeing under the limited rubric of a right to mental health. The 1989 Second Optional Protocol of the Covenant on Civil and Political Rights includes a commitment of parties to abolish the death penalty, something most restorative justice advocates would regard as an essential specific commitment. Equally most restorative justice advocates would agree with all the values and rights in the United Nations Declaration on the Elimination of Violence Against Women of 1993, the United Nations Standard Minimum Rules for Non-Custodial Measures of 1990 (the Tokyo Rules) and the Declaration of Basic Principles of Justice for Victims of Crime and Abuse of Power adopted by the General Assembly in 1985. The latter includes some relevant values not so well traversed in other human rights instruments such as 'restoration of the environment' (Article 10), 'compassion' (Article 4), 'restitution' (various Articles), 'redress' (Article 5) and includes specific reference to 'restoration of rights' (Article 8) and 'Informal mechanisms for the resolution of disputes, including mediation, arbitration and customary justice or indigenous practices' which 'should be utilized where appropriate to facilitate conciliation and redress for victims'. (Article 7).

## A Proposal

So a proposal for a starting framework for a debate on the content of restorative justice standards might take the values discussed above, all of which can be found in the UN human rights instruments I have discussed. From a civic republican perspective we can distinguish constraining standards that specify precise rights and limits and maximizing standards which, while they might justify specific constraints, are also good consequences in themselves which we should want to maximize.

*Constraining standards*

- Non-domination
- Empowerment
- Honouring legally specific upper limits on sanctions
- Respectful listening
- Equal concern for all stakeholders
- Accountability, appealability
- Respect for the fundamental human rights specified in the Universal Declaration of Human Rights, the International Covenant on Economic, Social and Cultural Rights, the International Covenant on Civil and Political Rights and its Second Optional Protocol, the United Nations Declaration on the Elimination of Violence Against Women and the Declaration of Basic Principles of Justice for Victims of Crime and Abuse of Power.

*Maximizing standards*

- Restoration of human dignity
- Restoration of property loss
- Restoration of safety/injury/health
- Restoration of damaged human relationships
- Restoration of communities
- Restoration of the environment
- Emotional restoration
- Restoration of freedom
- Restoration of compassion or caring
- Restoration of peace
- Restoration of a sense of duty as a citizen
- Provision of social support to develop human capabilities to the full
- Prevention of future injustice.

Not only are these values that can be justified from the text of UN human rights instruments, as outlined above, they are also consistent with the empirical experience of what victims and offenders say they want out of restorative justice processes (see Strang 2000), at least at our present limited state of knowledge of these matters. The privileging of empowerment on the first list of standards we are constrained to honour means that stakeholders are empowered to tell their own stories in their own way to reveal whatever sense of injustice they wish to see repaired. This can mean at times quite idiosyncratic conceptions of justice that are not reflected in the second starting list of maximizing standards. The idea is that we must honour the standards on the constraining standards list, but that we are not constrained to accomplish always the standards on the maximizing standards list. Constraining standards (list 1) versus maximizing values (list 2) against which we can evaluate the performance of restorative justice in comparison to its alternatives without always being required to honour the standard. With many types of crime, restoration of the environment, for example, will simply not be relevant, as will healing physical injuries not be relevant when a crime is non-violent. With the maximizing standards, the measure is not that they are always secured, but that they are more likely to be increased across a large number of cases that go into a restorative justice programme compared to cases that do not, and more likely to be increased after a restorative justice process than before. So they are certainly the stuff of useful yardsticks for evaluating restorative justice programmes.

Together these values imply parsimony in the use of punishment; together they say there are many positive approaches to regulation that we can consider before we consider our reluctant willingness to resort to punishment. The first 11 standards on the second priority list are different forms of healing that can all be justified in terms of values in the UN human rights instruments above and the empirical experience of what participants often say is the healing they want out of restorative justice processes. Beyond saying that, I will not mount a detailed defence of them. Obviously, there are many dimensions of a value like emotional restoration—some want relief from the emotion of fear, others from hate, others from shame, others vindication of their character.

The twelfth standard—providing social support to develop human capabilities to the full—is essential as a corrective to the concern that restorative justice may be used to restore an unjust status quo. The key design idea here is that regulatory institutions must be designed so as to nurture developmental institutions. Too often regulatory institutions stultify human capabilities, the design of punitive criminal justice systems being a classic example.

For the final standard, preventing future injustice, there are as many modalities of evaluation as forms of injustice. The one being most adequately researched at this time is prevention of future crime, an evaluation criterion that has shown progressively more encouraging results over the past three years (Braithwaite 2002: ch. 3).

*Emergent standards*

- Remorse over injustice
- Apology
- Censure of the act
- Forgiveness of the person
- Mercy.

As a list of specific restorative values, the maximizing standards list is unsatisfactorily incomplete. The above list of what we will call emergent standards is nowhere to be found as values in these UN documents. The list of emergent standards differs from the earlier list of maximizing standards in a conceptually important way. It is not that the emergent values are less important than the maximizing values. When Desmond Tutu (1999) says 'No Future Without Forgiveness', many restorative justice advocates are inclined to agree. Forgiveness differs from say respectful listening as a value of restorative justice in the following sense. We actively seek to persuade participants that they ought to listen respectfully, but we do not urge them to forgive. It is cruel and wrong to expect a victim of

SETTING STANDARDS

crime to forgive.[1] Apology, forgiveness and mercy are gifts; they only have meaning if they well up from a genuine desire in the person who forgives, apologizes or grants mercy. Apart from it being morally wrong to impose such an expectation, we would destroy the moral power of forgiveness, apology or mercy to invite participants in a restorative justice process to consider proffering it during the process. People take time to discover the emotional resources to give up such emotional gifts. It cannot, must not, be expected. Similarly, remorse that is forced out of offenders has no restorative power. This is not to say that we should not write beautiful books like Tutu's on the grace that can be found through forgiveness. Nor does it preclude us evaluating restorative justice processes according to how much remorse, apology, forgiveness and mercy they elicit. Some might be puzzled as to why reintegrative shaming does not rate on my list of restorative values. It is not a value, not a good in itself; it is an explanatory dynamic that seeks to explain the conditions in which remorse, apology, censure of the act, forgiveness, mercy and many of the other values above occur. There is redundancy in listing remorse, apology and censure of the act because my theoretical position is that remorse and apology are the most powerful forms of censure since they are uttered by the person with the strongest reasons for refusing to vindicate the victim by censuring the injustice. However, when remorse and apology are not elicited it is imperative for other participants to vindicate the victim by censuring the act.

Let us clarify finally the distinctions among these three lists of standards of restorative justice. The constraining list are standards that must be honoured and enforced as constraints; the maximizing list are standards restorative justice advocates should actively encourage in restorative processes; the emergent list are values we should not urge participants to manifest—they are emergent properties of a successful restorative justice process. If we try to make them happen, they will be less likely to happen in a meaningful way.

Many will find these values vague, lacking specificity of guidance on how decent restorative practices should be run. Yet standards must be broad if we are to avert legalistic regulation of restorative justice that is at odds with the philosophy of restorative justice. What we need is deliberative regulation where we are clear about the values we expect restorative justice to realize. Whether a restorative justice programme is up to standard is best settled in a series of regulatory conversations (Black 1997, 1998) with peers and stakeholders rather than by rote application of a rulebook. That said, certain highly specific standards are so fundamental to justice that they must always be guaranteed—such as a right to appeal.

Yet some conventional rights, such as the right to a speedy trial as specified in the Beijing Rules for Juvenile Justice, can be questioned from a restorative perspective. One thing we have learnt from the victims' movement in recent years is that when victims have been badly traumatized by a criminal offence, they often need a lot of time before they are ready to countenance healing. They should be given the right to that time so long as it is not used as an excuse for the arbitrary detention of a defendant who has not been proven guilty.

---

[1] As Martha Minow (1998: 17) puts it: 'Forgiveness is a power held by the victimized, not a right to be claimed. The ability to dispense, but also to withhold, forgiveness is an ennobling capacity, part of the dignity to be reclaimed by those who survive the wrongdoing.'

This is an illustration of why at this point in history we need an international frame-work agreement on standards for restorative justice that is mainly a set of values for framing quality assurance processes and accountability in our pursuit of continuous improvement in attaining restorative justice values. There is some hope that the Committee of Experts established in pursuance of the Declaration of Vienna from the 2000 UN Congress on the Prevention of Crime and the Treatment of Offenders will accomplish precisely that.

### Not Waiting for the United Nations

At the local level what we need to think about is how to make the quality assurance processes and accountability work well. We don't have to wait for the United Nations for this. A local restorative justice initiative can take a very broad list of values, such as the ones I have tentatively advanced here, and use them as the starting point for a debate on what standards they want to see accomplished in their programme. A few discussion circles with all the stakeholders in the programme may be enough to reach a sufficient level of shared sensibility to make quality assurance and accountability work. Not every contested value or right has to be settled and written down. The unsettled ones can be earmarked for special observation in the hope that experiential learning will persuade one side of the debate to change their view or all sides to discover a new synthesis of views. I will illustrate with the restorative justice standards debate in Northern Ireland.

Northern Ireland actually has a more mature debate on standards and principles of restorative justice than any society I know. It is certainly a more sophisticated debate than in my home country of Australia. I suspect this is because Northern Ireland has a more politicized contest between state and civil society models of restorative justice than can be found in other places. Such fraught contexts are where there is the greatest risk of justice system catastrophes. But they also turn out to be the contexts with the richest prospects for rising to the political challenges with a transformative vision of restorative justice. During a short visit to Northern Ireland in 2000 I found the restorative justice programmes in both the Loyalist and Republican communities inspiring. Partly this is because of the courage and integrity of the community leaders involved and the reflective professionalism of those in the state who are open to restorative justice. I have been struck by the way so many ex-prisoners from both sides I met, who agree on very little politically, share remarkably similar restorative justice values. We saw them discover these shared values with other community leaders sitting in the same circle in a conference organized in Belfast by Kieran McEvoy and Harry Mika (2001). There is hope in this for Northern Ireland.

The drafting of local charters, as commended in the 'Blue Book' (Auld, Mika and McEvoy 1997) discussed in Harry Mika and Kieran McEvoy's paper (this issue, see also McEvoy and Mika 2001a, 2001b and Mika and McEvoy 2001), is consistent with the approach I commend here. So is the approach Greater Shankill Alternatives has developed through its local 'Principles of Good Practice' (drafted by Debbie Watters and Billy Mitchell). There are a lot of similarities between these principles (from the Loyalist community) and those articulated by the Republican community through statements such as the 'Standards and Values of Restorative Justice Practice' of Community Restorative Justice Ireland (from the Republican side). The latter has some distinctively

SETTING STANDARDS

interesting standards as well, such as 'flexibility of approach' and 'evaluation' (and both 'confidentiality' and 'transparency'). There is also indigenous distinctiveness in the proposal that key elements of the charters 'are slated to appear as large murals at strategic locations, in spaces that have traditionally been reserved for the political iconography that is well known within and outside Northern Ireland' (McEvoy and Mika, 2001b). For all the local distinctiveness, both the Republican and Loyalist charters have values that sit comfortably beside the values I have derived from the UN human rights instruments and beside those that the Northern Ireland Office has derived from European human rights instruments (for example, in *Restorative Justice and a Partnership Against Crime* 1998).

Recent email correspondence with Kay Pranis revealed the important work she has been doing on bottom-up values clarification in Minnesota. Let me quote at length from her email:

During the training we do a values exercise right away that becomes a touchstone throughout the rest of the training. We give participants a family conflict dilemma, suggest that the siblings come together for a day to try to work it out and then ask them to imagine they are driving home after the day with their siblings. We pose the question: what would you hope was true of your behavior that day working through the problem with your siblings, regardless of the outcome? They make a list individually, then group in pairs to come up with a consensus list for the pair, then group in fours to develop a consensus list and then we go to the large group and put together a consensus list—which is a list of values. There is always general acknowledgement that the list represents who we would like to be but we don't often achieve that—especially in our conflicts. I then talk about circles as a space that tries to maximize the possibility of staying close to those values in our behavior—the circle is designed to help us be our best selves.

In the training with the staff from time to time someone would say 'But these kids don't have these values so the circle won't work with them.' I didn't think it was true (because every group we do the exercise with comes up with essentially the same list) but didn't have a basis to refute that claim until I did the training with the kids. I modified the conflict situation to make it more relevant for the kids but kept it close to the original and used exactly the same process I use with adults. The kids produced a wonderful list—like the adults but even more elaborate. It was so exciting. Who they want to be looks just like who the adults want to be—but what became apparent in the training was that they don't think the world is a safe place to be that kind of person.

Anyway, it was a great experience for me. The kinds of kids who were in the training would have been very intimidating to me as an adolescent. I was very shy and had no idea of the kinds of environments that other kids experienced—so I only saw the defiance or bullying. It was very healing for me to experience them in their humanity and vulnerability.

Systematic empirical work on such initiatives could test Pranis's observation that surprising degrees of consensus over restorative justice values emerge bottom-up from the normally disenfranchised and could document what those values are. Over time compilations of such empirical work from around the world could be bottom-up democratic inputs for revising the hoped-for UN standards. Compilations for one nation can inform the restructuring of national law.

Once there has been a preliminary discussion of the principles, standards and rights a local programme should honour, training is needed for all new restorative justice convenors to deepen the furrows of shared sensibility around them. Training carries a risk of professionalization. This risk can be to some extent countered by making the training participatory, by giving trainees the power to reframe the curriculum. It need not be long. Three days of training followed by a period when convenors work with an experienced mentor and a follow-up day of reflection on the initial period of practice can turn out excellent convenors. Most people do not make good restorative justice facilitators. But I believe that in any large group of people, say in any 7th grade schoolroom, there will be someone with the ability to be an empowering facilitator of a restorative justice circle with only limited training.

It follows from this view that quality assurance is more important than training. I have sat through more restorative justice training sessions than any sane human being would aspire to and taught many others. As well trained as I am, a good quality assurance programme would weed me out as someone whose talents were better suited to other roles. My main deficiencies as a restorative justice conference facilitator are that I am sometimes too intellectually curious about things that are not important to the parties, I am sometimes more emotionally engaged than is best and my personality causes me to have too much dominance in a room; even when I have my mouth shut, my body language is too inured to leadership—communicating encouragement or doubt when all I should be communicating is attentive listening.

Many deficiencies of this kind can be cured by colleagues who sit in on our circles and communicate with us frankly about how we can improve. Other failings may require that we be gently steered into making a contribution somewhere other than in this front-line role. Either way, the crucial remedy is peer review complemented by feedback from participants. The feedback I mean involves the peer reviewer talking to participants after a conference or circle to elicit any concerns they have about the way the facilitator played out their role. It is this process of post-conference regulatory conversations about the conduct of the conference itself that helps clarify how we should give life to the principles, standards and rights that restorative justice must honour. The 'regular inspection by the independent criminal justice inspectorate' recommended by the Criminal Justice Review for Northern Ireland could be crafted to fulfil this role.[2]

## Conclusion

The suggestion here is to do something like the following before setting up a new restorative justice programme:

(1) Assemble stakeholders to reflect on a starting set of principles, standards or rights. These starting objectives might be grounded in the values and rights in UN or European human rights instruments.

---

[2] One of the referees pointed out the double standard that this inspectorate was to be 'created exclusively for restorative justice (and not for any independent inspection of conventional justice organizations or practices)'. I do not know enough to have a view on whether this inspectorate as the referee implies is a statist conspiracy to crush community justice. But on the double standard of restorative justice having to face superior accountability mechanisms than state justice, of the courts being a sufficient check on poor prosecutorial practice but not on poor restorative conference practice, of restorative justice being set evaluation research expectations much higher than have ever been set for the efficacy and justice of courts, these double standards are a good thing. This is because the accountability standards of extant criminal justice institutions are intolerably unsatisfactory from the perspective of restorative justice philosophy, certainly from a civic republican one (see Roche 2001).

SETTING STANDARDS

(2) Secure through this local democratic deliberation a set of local commitments to standards that are widely shared. Secure commitment to continuing regulatory conversations around other standards that stakeholders consider important, but where sensibilities are not shared.

(3) Try to resolve the contested standards through reflexive praxis—restorative justice practice that reflects back on its starting assumptions.

(4) Avoid didactic training. Make the training sessions, especially role-plays, part of this locally reflexive praxis that continually rebuilds the ship of restorative justice while it sails the local seas.

(5) Use peer review not only to counsel against practices that threaten the consensually shared standards but also to advance our understanding of the contested standards through regulatory deliberation.

(6) Aggregate these local regulatory conversations into a national regulatory conversation. If the local regulatory conversations converge on the importance of certain rights that should never be infringed, then the state should stand behind those rights, for example by legislating for them or threatening programme funding when they are flouted. But where there is no democratically deliberated consensus, the state should be wary of national standards that threaten local innovation and local cultural difference.

At the end of the day it is better that restorative justice learn from making mistakes than that it make the mistake of refusing to learn. This mistake usually takes the form of believing that standards and rights should be grounded in the rulings of lawyers whose eyes are blinkered to the reflective practice of justice by the people. Recent experience is ground for optimism that if we regulate flexibly, being mindful of all the local ideas for innovation, richer models of restorative justice can blossom. Critics who believe in a univocal justice system as opposed to a legal pluralist one will look askance at the long list of standards I have suggested might emerge from allowing a thousand flowers to bloom bottom-up. But it may be that citizens will find they like a criminal justice system with a lot of bottom-up aspirations for reducing injustice and perhaps a rather smaller number of top-down constraints on what sort of flowers should be allowed to bloom. Designing research that asks citizens with experience of a restorative justice process to evaluate it on 20 or 30 criteria is actually not difficult, just as it is not impossible to collect objective outcome data on multiple criteria of evaluation. If the worry is that justice innovations that seek to accomplish many things will actually do the most important things badly, then this worry can be tested empirically by such research.[3] Of course we already have a criminal law that at some levels aspires to most of the objectives canvassed here. It aspires to enact criminal laws and execute enforcement that *protects the environment*, without manifesting much interest in empirical research on whether its criminalization strategies actually do improve the environment. Defenders of our criminal law claim that it does many of the things it does to *protect the dignity* of citizens without demanding evaluation

---

[3] If they are right, such critics will be able to specify a set of core evaluation criteria. Programmes that perform well on a large number of non-core standards they set out to maximize will produce poor results on the core criteria. Of course, my hypothesis is that this will prove wrong. My reasons are that injustice is variegated and requires creativity to confront in all its forms and that injustice in the periphery (a refugee camp) is a cause of injustice at the core (the World Trade Centre). While it equally sounds plausible that the best way to advance knowledge might be to create knowledge institutions with highly focused objectives, empirically it is non-focused institutions called universities that win most Nobel Prizes, not specialist research institutes or business laboratories.

research on how dignified citizens believe they have been treated by said institutions, and so on. Evidence and innovation from below instead of armchair pontification from above should be what drive the hopes of restorative justice to replace our existing injustice system with one that actually does more to promote justice than to crush it. It would be a less tidy justice system, but tidiness seems decisively not a good candidate for a justice standards framework.

## REFERENCES

ABEL, R. (1981), 'Conservative Conflict and the Reproduction of Capitalism: The Role of Informal Justice', *International Journal of the Sociology of Law*, 9: 245–67.

——(1982), 'The Contradictions of Informal Justice', in R. Abel, ed., *The Politics of Informal Justice, I: The American Experience*, 1–13. New York: Academic Press.

AULD, J., GORMALLY, B., McEVOY, K. and RITCHIE, M. (1997), 'Designing a System of Restorative Community Justice: A Discussion Document', *The Blue Book*. Belfast: The Authors.

COMMUNITY RESTORATIVE JUSTICE IRELAND (n.d.), *Standards and Values of Restorative Justice Practice*. Belfast.

BLACK, J. (1997), *Rules and Regulators*. Oxford: Oxford University Press.

——(1998), 'Talking About Regulation', *Public Law*, Spring: 77–105.

BRAITHWAITE, J. (2002), *Restorative Justice and Responsive Regulation*. New York: Oxford University Press.

BRAITHWAITE, J. and BILES, D. (1984), 'Victims and Offenders: The Australian Experience', in *Victimization and Fear of Crime: World Perspectives*, edited by R. Block. Washington, DC: US Department of Justice.

BRAITHWAITE, J. and PETTIT, P. (1990), *Not Just Deserts: A Republican Theory of Criminal Justice*. Oxford: Oxford University Press.

BROWN, J. G. (1994), 'The Use of Mediation to Resolve Criminal Cases: A Procedural Critique', *Emory Law Journal*, 43: 1247–309.

ECKSTEIN, H. (1975), 'Case Study and Theory in Political Science', in N. Greenstein and N. Polsby, eds., *Handbook of Political Science*, Vol. 7: Strategies of Enquiry. Reading, MA: Addison-Wesley.

GUNNINGHAM, N. and GRABOSKY, P. (1998), *Smart Regulation: Designing Environmental Policy*. Oxford: Clarendon Press.

HABERMAS, J. (1996), *Between Facts and Norms: Contributions to a Discourse Theory of Law and Democracy*. London: Polity Press.

HAINES, K. (1998), 'Some Principled Objections to a Restorative Justice Approach to Working with Juvenile Offenders', in *Restorative Justice for Juveniles: Potentialities, Risks and Problems for Research*, in L. Walgrave, ed., selection of papers presented at the International Conference, Leuven, 12–14 May 1997, pp. 93–113. Leuven: Leuven University Press.

HINDELANG, M. J., GOTTFREDSON, M. R. and GAROFALO, J. (1978), *Victims of Personal Crime: An Empirical Foundation for a Theory of Personal Victimization*. Cambridge, MA: Ballinger.

HOWLEY, P. (2002), Breaking Spears and Mending Hearts, Sydney: Federation Press.

JONES, C. (1993), 'Auditing Criminal Justice', *British Journal of Criminology*, 33: 187–202.

McEVOY, K. and MIKA, H. (2001a), 'Punishment, Politics and Praxis: Restorative Justice and Non-Violent Alternatives to Paramilitary Punishments in Northern Ireland', *Policing and Society*, 11: 359.

——eds. (2001), 'International Perspectives on Restorative Justice', conference report. Belfast: Queen's University.

SETTING STANDARDS

MIKA, H., and McEVOY, K. (2001), 'Restorative Justice in Conflict: Paramilitarism, Community and the Construction of Legitimacy in Northern Ireland'. *Contemporary Justice Review*, 3/4: 291–319.

MINOW, M. (1998), *Between Vengeance and Forgiveness: Facing History after Genocide and Mass Violence*. Boston: Beacon Press.

NADER, L., ed. (1980), *No Access to Law: Alternatives to the American Judicial System*. New York: Academic Press.

PETTIT, P. (1997), *Republicanism*. Oxford: Clarendon Press.

POWER, M. (1997), *The Audit Society: Rituals of Verification*. Oxford: Oxford University Press.

PRANIS, K. (2000), 'Democratizing Social Control: Restorative Justice, Social Justice and the Empowerment of Marginalized Populations', in L. Walgrave and G. Bazemore, eds., *Restoring Juvenile Justice: An Exploration of the Restorative Justice Paradigm for Reforming Juvenile Justice*. Monsey, New York: Criminal Justice Press.

ROCHE, D. (2001), *First By Persuasion: Accountabilities of Restorative Justice*, PhD dissertation. Australian National University, Canberra.

STRANG, H. (2000), *Victim Participation in a Restorative Justice Process: The Canberra Reintegrative Shaming Experiments*, PhD dissertation. Australian National Universityj, Canberra.

STRANG, H. and BRAITHWAITE, J., eds. (2002), *Restorative Justice and Family Violence*. Melbourne: Cambridge University Press.

TUTU, D. (1999), *No Future Without Forgiveness*. London: Rider.

VAN NESS, D. and STRONG, K. H. (1997), *Restoring Justice*. Cinncinnati, OH: Anderson Publishing.

WARNER, K. (1994), 'The Rights of the Offender in Family Conferences', in C. Alder and J. Wundersitz, eds., *Family Conferencing and Juvenile Justice: The Way Forward or Misplaced Optimism?* Canberra: Australian Institute of Criminology.

ZEHR, H. (1990), *Changing Lenses: A New Focus for Criminal Justice*. Scottsdale, PA: Herald Press.

# Part IV
# Correctional Policy

# [15]

## Prison Reform amid the Ruins of Prisoners' Rights

James B. Jacobs

Prisons and jails need continuous "reform" because there are constant financial, political, administrative, psychological, and even biological pressures threatening to undermine conditions, practices, and programs. Penal institutions often seem to be in decline if not in crisis (Christianson 1998). At the beginning of the twenty-first century, it remains a tremendous challenge to keep prisons and jails safe, clean, hygienic, operational, and humane (Stern 1998).

In our 1,400 federal and state prisons and many thousands of county jails and local lockups, conditions and operations are only to a limited extent determined by correctional ideologies and philosophies. Humane values and correctional "philosophies" are important, but they are insufficient to ensure humane conditions. Resources and administrative competence are far more important (see Lin 2000; Bottoms 1999).

Money does not guarantee decent prison conditions and operations, but lack of money assures the opposite. At present, our states and localities are experiencing very serious budget crises that may persist for years. State and local officials are combing through their programs to identify places to make budget cuts. Jails and prisons will certainly be a prime candidate. While imprisonment has been wildly successful in the late twentieth century in garnering support for more beds in more facilities, that is entirely different than garnering support for maintaining and improving intra-prison conditions, operations, and programs.

Unlike practically all other programs, penal institutions have no political constituency, except perhaps for the prison officers' unions in some states (e.g., California). Prisoners are not seen as among the "deserving poor." Allocating scarce resources to improve or maintain humane prison conditions (in contrast with spending money to provide more beds) will not win votes or acclaim. Thus, when it comes to choosing whether to cut funding for prisons and jails, schools, higher education, roads, and health care, prisons and jails will always be the first choice unless public officials are forced (by courts, riots, or something else) to spend the money (see Berk and Rossi 1977).

How budget reductions impact on jail and prison conditions, practices, and programs is an important topic for empirical research. We can expect, at a minimum, that expenditures for maintenance and renovations will suffer. Prisons do not age gracefully. Many penal institutions are more than 50 years old, some of the largest institutions date from the nineteenth century. Maintenance, much of it performed by prisoners themselves, is often shoddy. There is always a crying need for repairs to plumbing, electricity, heating, windows, painting, kitchens, grouting, and so on.

When money is scarce, prison officials will not be successful in their attempts to upgrade out-of-date industrial equipment and workshops. As the machinery wears out or becomes obsolete, intra-prison worksites and vocational training programs are cut back and shut down; certainly, no new ones are opened. "Unemployment" and idleness increase. Even small budget items fall victim to the budget cutters. Athletic equipment and televisions are not replaced. The prison library stops making acquisitions. There are fewer special events and not enough staff on duty to supervise them. In contrast to the decline in living conditions, inmate expectations have risen steadily over the last century as the general societal living standard has steadily improved. Thus, prison conditions that inmates of past generations might have considered endurable, today's prisoners will experience as unendurable. As prison conditions and operations deteriorate, inmate morale decreases and staff morale follows suit.

Maintaining the physical infrastructure is not the only, or even the most important, challenge of prison reform. The crisis in state and local budgets also impacts on salaries and the number and type of positions that can be funded. Sufficient attention, especially academics', has never been paid to the importance of the human infrastructure of prisons and jails and its management. (There are approximately 440,000 persons working in adult corrections; 260,000 are uniformed correctional officers.) It takes many capable and dedicated people to run a penal institution efficiently and safely—for example, wardens, assistant wardens, and other central office administrators, shift commanders, cell block sergeants, vocational teachers, industrial foremen, and treatment personnel. Indeed, it takes intelligence, maturity, and confidence to function effectively as a line correctional officer in a cell house, recreational area, or kitchen/dining room. And even all of the efforts of competent people at the institutional level can go for naught if the correctional department's central office is marked by incompetence.

Jails and prisons are hard on staff as well as inmates (Lombardo 1981). Locked in like the prisoners, employees are exposed on a daily basis to unpleasant, dangerous, and unhealthy conditions (noise, odor, hostility, violence, disease, and high levels of stress). They spend their working lives in close interaction with inmates loaded with anger, self-loathing, violent impulses, manipulative personalities, mental illness, and infectious diseases, including tuberculosis, hepatitis, and HIV. There are complicated and fractious divisions among the inmates based upon race, gang affiliation, personal fealties, feuds, and animosities (see Morris 1995). Given such working conditions, it is hardly surprising that prison staff, especially without competent training, support, and supervision, burn out or worse. Very high staff turnover and daily absenteeism are the reality in many penal facilities, greatly complicating, if not overwhelming, effective management. The risk and reality of staff corruption, capitulation to inmates, and brutality constantly threaten the goal of a humane and smooth functioning organization.

Recruiting, training, nurturing, promoting, and improving prison personnel should be seen as a prerequisite and top priority for prison reform. Unfortunately, little attention is given to identifying the qualities needed for prison staff, recruiting and training such people, identifying potential leaders and developing their expertise, retaining the most capable people, and structuring rewarding careers in corrections. Recruitment is typically haphazard, training cursory and shallow (often half of the recruits are gone within the first six months), work unpleasant, stressful, dangerous, and unhealthy. Promotions are not keyed to competence. Status is low. It is not surprising that most employees do not find prison work satisfying.

Many good people quit; there is a constant flow of the most competent staff to the private sector and to other public sector jobs. Staff turnover undermines administrative systems. Those left behind feel "stuck." Absenteeism proliferates. Management positions go unfilled. Decisions are left hanging. Morale plummets. It becomes harder to recruit new employees into an organization that is "troubled," chaotic, and dangerous.

Even in the best of times, it is a major challenge to maintain decent prison conditions. But the beginning of the twenty-first century is not the best of times for prisons and jails, fiscally or politically. Pay is extremely low, given the magnitude of the responsibility and the difficulty of the work. In January 2001, going into the current fiscal crisis, the average annual starting salary for correctional officers was approximately $24,000; the average maximum salary was $38,000.[1] The average minimum salary for wardens was $54,250, while the average maximum salary was $86,275. If salaries fail to keep pace with inflation, or actually lose ground, the forces of demoralization become even stronger so that recruiting and retaining competent replacement will become even tougher.

Crowding is the relentless opponent of humane prison conditions, over-whelming improvements to physical plant, programming, and staff. At the turn of the twenty-first century, despite massive prison construction in the previous two decades, most American prisons operate at more than 100 percent rated capacity, some at much more than 100 percent.[2] Mass incarceration reigns as the entrenched criminal justice policy of the United States (Garland 2001). While, in the last few years, prison population growth has slowed down, there has certainly been no reversal; there remains plenty of pent-up demand for prison beds—desire for more severe sentences, desire to punish new crimes, desire for more "productive" (in terms of arrests/convictions) police work (see Hallinan 2001).

The prevailing law and order politics, embraced by both political parties, has produced a chronic crowding problem that affects every aspect of institutional life. The greater the crowding, the more and greater the negative impacts; a smaller percentage of inmates has any kind of job or educational placements. Less recreational space/time per prisoner means a much less satisfactory recreational program (e.g., more people competing for a ball or a game opportunity). The waiting list to see doctors and counselors lengthens. More prisoners are crammed into cells where they spend more hours per day (in many cases practically all 24 hours). Less space and less privacy generate more friction and conflict. The same number (or fewer) prison officers for more inmates means less supervision and declining safety. Rising prison population without commensurate increases in staff and improvement to the built environment inevitably and inexorably undermines prison conditions. Moreover, the prevailing ethos is not sympathetic to prisoners (Zimring, Hawkins, and Kamin 2001). To the contrary, there is political pressure to cut back on or cut out "amenities" like weight lifting and college programs and to establish "no frills prisons." Such cuts are all the more likely in the context of serious public sector budget crises. And such cuts, of course, contribute to the spiral of decline.

## Sources of Prison Reform

What are the forces that operate to counteract the pressures that constantly undermine prison conditions, programs, and operations? In the last half century, the most important, by far, has been the willingness of judges, especially federal judges, to enforce prisoners' rights, especially the right to be free from cruel and unusual punishment. Other forces that, in the past, have generated pressure for humane prison conditions, and that may play a role in the future, are prisoners' riots and protests, correctional leaders' lobbying and innovations, advocacy and watchdog groups' campaigns, and privatization.

## Rise and Fall of the Prisoners' Rights Movement

The heyday of the prisoners' rights movement roughly spanned the period from 1960 to 1980. Prisoners challenged every aspect of the prison regime, from censorship to disciplinary confinement, from prohibitions on wearing jewelry to no-contact rules in the visiting room, from denial of access to the Bible and Koran to racial discrimination in cell and work assignments, from lack of access to the courts to arbitrary disciplinary procedures (Jacobs 1980). The lawsuits with the largest impact on the institution of imprisonment were class actions challenging the constitutionality, under the Eighth Amendment's cruel and unusual punishment clause, of the totality of prison conditions, including cell size, quality of lighting, ventilation, sanitation, nutrition, and medical care (Feeley and Rubin 1998; Schlanger 1999).

Unlike other areas of court-initiated social change, the U.S. Supreme Court did not play a powerful role in the prisoners' rights movement. True, there were a few decisions in the early years that guaranteed religious freedom and access to the courts. *Wolff v. McDonald* (418 U.S. 539 [1974]), a case about prison discipline, supplied the most stirring language by announcing that no iron curtain separated prisons from the rest of American society. But there is no single watershed Supreme Court decision to match *Brown v. Board of Education* (for school desegregation) or *Roe v. Wade* (for abortion rights). In the area of prisoners' rights, the most important decisions were rendered at the district court level and were strongly rooted in the facts, the conditions and operations at particular prisons and jails (Jacobs 1995).

The prisoners did not win most of their cases but, in the early years, they won many. The prison officials, used to ruling as autocrats, were arrogant and ineffective witnesses. They could rarely point to written rules and regulations; existing rules were vague and authoritarian (e.g., "insolent eyeballing" and "unruly conduct"). And even when the inmates did not prevail, their litigation reinforced the point that prisons are sociopolitical institutions that must function under the rule of law and that prisoners are citizens behind bars entitled to constitutional protections (see Jacobs 1977, 1980).

The active involvement of courts in prisoners' rights cases meant that prison reform that was not achievable in the political arena was achievable in the judicial forum. Federal judges examined every aspect of prison conditions and operations in a way that had never been done before, and they (even "conservative" judges) found many of these conditions deplorable and unconstitutional. Wide-ranging and thorough reform was imposed upon prisons, which were ordered to provide prisoners decent light, heat, cell space, showers, food, safety, sanitation, nutrition, recreation, medical care, and, to some extent, fair and rational procedures (see Feeley and Rubin 1998).

The potential of judicially driven prison reform is much weaker at the turn of the twenty-first century. Forward momentum has been halted and, arguably, the willingness and ability of courts to set and enforce minimum standards of decency in jails and prisons is waning. How and why this reversal happened is a subject that will take years to understand fully, but understand it we must if we are to understand the potential and limits of prison reform in the twenty-first century.

Perhaps all social movements carry the seeds of their own reversal. In the case of the prisoners' rights movement, a clash between the political branches of government and the judiciary was inevitable. The political branches always preferred to allocate resources to causes and constituencies that produce votes, certainly not to inmates of prisons and jails. On occasions, governors and powerful legislators publicly defied or vilified the courts. More frequently, they ignored or dragged their feet with respect to compliance with court orders, and explicitly or implicitly encouraged prison officials to do the same. This led to some very protracted, sometimes decades-long struggles between, on the one side, plaintiffs' counsel and special masters working for the courts and, on the other side, local and state officials (see, e.g., Martin and Ekland-Olson 1987). (Over the years, however, many front-line prison officials came to see that their working conditions and jobs generally would be easier and more satisfying if the court-mandated changes were implemented. In some cases, they welcomed and even colluded in the prisoners' lawsuits.)

Conservative scholars excoriated federal judges for being duped by plaintiff prisoners and for handing down decisions that undermined the authority of savvy prison officials (DiIulio 1987). The Supreme Court and lower federal courts' support for prisoners' rights lawsuits steadily diminished in the 1980s and 1990s (see Branham 1976). It is not so much that the courts reversed themselves (although the Supreme Court did rein in lower courts on a number of occasions with decisions like *Turner v. Safley*, 482 U.S. 78 [1987]), as that the courts drew a line in the sand: "this far and no further." Most existential rights have been recognized in whole or in part, and the principle that the Eighth Amendment protects prisoners from inhumane conditions (admittedly difficult to define) has become part of our constitutional jurisprudence. Nevertheless, the Supreme Court has made it abundantly clear that federal courts must show substantial deference to prison officials (e.g., *Rhodes v. Chapman*, 452 U.S. 337 [1981]) and that the exigencies of prison organization necessarily mean that constitutional rights in prison cannot be exercised as freely and fully as on the outside (e.g., *Baxter v. Palmigiano*, 425 U.S. 308 [1976]; *Hudson v. Palmer*, 468 U.S. 517 [1984]).[3]

The most profound blow to the prisoners' rights movement was passage of the Prison Litigation Reform Act of 1995 (PLRA) (Pub.L. No. 104–134; 110 Stat. 1321, Sections 801–810), an ideologically motivated federal law that represents the political branches' efforts to prevent the judiciary from recognizing and enforcing prisoners' rights (Kuzinski 1998). The PLRA, a plank in the Republicans' "contract with America," but signed without protest by President Bill Clinton, sought to deter prisoners from filing federal lawsuits, lawyers from representing them, courts from granting them wide-ranging equitable relief, and special masters from enforcing court decrees.[4] What is more, the PLRA allows prison officials to open up and cast off reforms, long ago agreed to in negotiated settlements with plaintiff prisoners.[5]

The PLRA's first strategy is to increase litigation costs to prisoners in order to deter or prevent them from suing their captors. The law requires prisoners to exhaust all administrative (grievance-type) remedies before filing a lawsuit. It also puts financial barriers in their way. Whereas for decades inmates could avoid filing costs by bringing their suits *in forma pauperis*, the PLRA requires even the most impecunious prisoners, as long as they have money in their prison accounts, to pay a filing fee. Moreover, a prisoner who has had three previous lawsuits dismissed must pay the full filing fee in advance. Furthermore, the PLRA instructs the court not to waive certain litigation costs (e.g., transcripts of depositions) that could be levied against a losing prisoner plaintiff.

The PLRA's second strategy is to make it more difficult for prisoners to obtain legal representation in institutional litigation. Until passage of the PLRA, prisoners' rights attorneys, like all other civil rights lawyers, were entitled to "reasonable compensation" from the defendant government in the event they were successful; that provided an incentive for private attorneys to take on prisoners' cases that they thought had a reasonable chance of succeeding. The PLRA caps an attorney's fee at 150 percent of the total monetary judgment awarded the inmate or 150 percent of the hourly rate paid to criminal defense lawyers for representing indigent federal criminal defendants, whichever is the lesser. This makes it financially difficult or impossible to take on cases that, while important in principle, are not likely to produce large monetary judgments for the plaintiff inmates. The law redefines "reasonable compensation" for lawyers representing prisoners to 150 percent of the hourly rate authorized for court-appointed criminal defense lawyers rather than the market-based rate that previously applied.

Third, the PLRA limits the remedies that federal judges can impose in prisoners' rights cases. Courts may neither grant nor approve any relief other than money damages, "unless the court finds that such relief is narrowly drawn, extends no further than necessary to correct the violation of the federal right, and is the least restrictive means necessary to correct the violation of the federal right." In other words, the PLRA seeks to restrict courts to redressing individual grievances (restricted to compensating inmates for physical injury) and not the problems of classes of plaintiffs. Even if plaintiffs can vault the class action hurdle, relief must be limited to correcting the specific constitutional violations giving rise to the suit. In addition, judges cannot impose population caps except in circumstances in which other, less intrusive relief, have failed to remedy the constitutional violation. Only a specially convened three-judge panel can impose a cap.

Federal judges have enforced their remedial decrees in condition of confinement cases by appointing special masters to operate as the judge's eyes and ears on the scene. The special master, often with the assistance of a staff, has devoted full-time or substantial part-time attention to a particular case, has carried out investigations on compliance, hired special consultants to draw up standards and strategies for reform, and reported to the court on the defendant prison officials' progress. On occasion, the special masters have sought to have defendant prison officials held in contempt for dragging their heels. The importance of the role of special master in late twentieth-century prison reform cannot be exaggerated; the expertise, persistence, and negotiating skills of many of these masters is the single most important factor in the success of major institutional reform litigation.[6] The PLRA attempts to neutralize special masters by limiting their remuneration to 150 percent of the hourly rate for counsel appointed to represent indigent defendants in federal criminal cases, a fraction of what masters have been awarded in the past. The hope of the PLRA's sponsors is that the most experienced and competent special masters will be driven from the field.

Finally, defendants are entitled to termination of any prospective relief two years after it is granted, unless the court finds a "current and ongoing violation" of the federal law. The PLRA even opens up old consent decrees, agreements negotiated between prisoners' lawyers and the state. While they are under attack by prison officials, the courts are instructed to treat them as null and void.

The PLRA is an extraordinary politico-legal event, representing a broad-side attack on the whole jurisprudence of prisoners' rights and, what is more, an attempt by the legislature to supplant the courts as the ultimate arbiter of what prison conditions and operations are acceptable. Nevertheless, it would be an exaggeration to say that the PLRA and conservative court decisions have eliminated the prisoners' rights movement as a source of prison reform in the twenty-first century. Some prisoners' cases will be successfully brought in state courts, although those courts historically have been far less receptive to prisoners' complaints than the federal courts. Crafty litigators have found ways around some of the PLRA's restrictions and some federal judges who resent the congressional effort to curtail their jurisdiction seek ways to reach results they think are just. Some prison and jail conditions and operations will be so deplorable and violative of humane standards that prisoners' rights lawyers will have no difficulty overcoming the hurdles that the PLRA places in their path. Parties can contract around the provision allowing for consent decrees to sunset in two years.

A final caveat: the prison reform litigation of the late twentieth century may have contributed to the emergence of a new form of super-maximum-security incarceration that scrupulously respects the letter of the law, while constituting a prison regime remarkable for a new form of inhumanity, marked by massive control and minimal interpersonal human contact. These institutions utilize high-tech security with remote controlled gates, voice recognition equipment, and omni-present surveillance. To find these "state of the art" institutions unconstitutional would take a wholly new understanding of human suffering and "cruel and unusual punishment" as well as breathtaking judicial ingenuity and audacity (see *Madrid v. Gomez*, 889 F. Supp. 1146 [N.D. Cal. 1995]). How could such institutions be reformed when, according to a new model, they are the quintessence of reformed?

## Prison Riots and Protests

Prisoners have little influence over the prison conditions, operations, and programs. Indeed, they are disenfranchised in most states. Ironically, perhaps, inmates' main contribution to prison reform has been due to riots. Major jail/prison riots (e.g., Attica, N.Y. 1971; New Mexico 1980; Strangeway Prison [U.K.] 1989) have focused media attention and thus public attention on these institutions, led to the formation of prestigious committees (New York State Special Commission 1972; Woolf 1991) and to sensible recommendations for reforms aimed at ameliorating the conditions and practices that caused the riots. Although the record on following through on such recommendations is spotty, there is no doubt that riots and fear of riots generates some pressure to address prisoners' and staffs' grievances.

We cannot dismiss the possibility that in the twenty-first century riots will turn out to be an important force for addressing inhumane prison conditions, but there is no reason to predict that this will happen. In the last decade or two, U.S. penal institutions have become much more riot-resistant. Prison officials have more and better anti-riot hardware (including rubber bullets, gas bombs) and SWAT units, better anti-riot training and more sophisticated strategies for dealing with disturbances. The "hardening" of penal facilities over the last generation has made rioting less likely and, if it occurs, more controllable.

Prisoners have also been known on rare occasions to engage in self-mutilation, hunger strikes, and other types of protests to make known their grievances and to bring about improvements in the conditions of their confinement (see Cummins 1994). While a possible source for future prison reform, these kinds of protests are not very likely. American prisoners historically have not been good at or experienced in organizing and protesting. Moreover, it would be extremely difficult, within the context of its conflict-ridden inmate culture, for prisoners to effectively organize and demonstrate for prison reform. Finally, such protests would have to be extremely dramatic to draw public and political attention and achieve results.

### Professionalism as a Force for Reform

There have always been particular prison officials (e.g., Thomas Mott Osborne in New York and Alexander MacConochie in Norfolk Island), themselves reformers, who have pressed for more humane penal conditions (see Morris 2002). While historically the point was not always obvious to them, prison officials have a substantial community of interest with prisoners in safe, humane, and constructive prison conditions, operations, and programs. This point is now widely recognized. What was new in the latter decades of the twentieth century was the emergence of the American Correctional Association, a professional prison officials' organization that linked professionalism to safe, clean, efficient, and richly programmed penal institutions (see American Correctional Association 2002).

Whereas at previous points in U.S. history, prison staffs have seen themselves locked in a zero-sum struggle with prisoners over authority, many of today's prison officials are much more professional and sophisticated than their predecessors. They are graduates of colleges and universities, much more closely tied to mainstream society, more integrated with public administration generally, less politicized, and more likely to define themselves as professional public sector managers whose aim is to secure the most resources they can toward the goal of safe, secure, and humane institutions. When living conditions are safe and relatively pleasant for inmates, working conditions for employees will be safe and relatively pleasant. When inmates feel that rules and procedures are fair and uniformly enforced, there will be fewer challenges to staff authority. When inmates are busy, there will be less violence and conflict; staff will find their work more relaxed and more rewarding.

Professionalism is very important to the self-identity of today's prison wardens and managers. For almost two decades the American Correctional Association (ACA) has promulgated best practices standards for jails and prisons and has encouraged its members voluntarily to seek "accreditation" of their institutions. (The process involves an ACA team carrying out a thorough evaluation of compliance with ACA standards.) Managers of more than 1,200 jails and prisons have invested millions of dollars in training and renovation in order to comply with ACA standards.

Nevertheless, while prison officials may become more important as a force pushing for decent and rational prison reform, there are limits to what they can accomplish. For one thing, it remains unclear how much professionalization can take place around a sense of mission as limited and lackluster as safe and secure warehousing of convicted offenders. For another thing, for today's correctional professional to survive and advance in state politics, it is necessary to be a team player, loyal to the governor. Lobbying is mostly confined to the executive branch where prison officials compete with representatives of other government agencies for position on the governor's list of priorities. In this competition, their great disadvantage is that they do not provide services for a politically significant constituency. They have to compete with government agencies that represent powerful and politically salient groups. Furthermore, the top corrections officials can only lobby so much and so openly. As members of the governor's team, they cannot denounce, embarrass, or threaten the governor and his or her administration. Only the guards' union could play the role of a no-holds-barred pressure group and perhaps they will do so more aggressively in the years to come (see generally, Parenti 1999).

Even without more resources, prison officials could contribute to better prison conditions and operations by being capable and imaginative managers, who are good problem solvers, get the most out of their staffs, promote fairness, and keep morale high. The National Institute of Corrections has made important but limited contributions to professionalizing and training the managerial ranks of prison officials. In the twenty-first century, there is enormous opportunity for improvements in professional educational programs in prison administration. An expanded federal National College of Corrections that offered year-round short and long courses for middle and upper corrections managers could make an enormous contribution to the operation of our prisons.

### Privatization as a Force for Reform

It certainly could be argued that one reason prison conditions have historically been so bad is that penal institutions have, for most of U.S. history, been handed over to a public monopoly that has no or little incentive to innovate, to do things better or more efficiently. Americans, at least at this point in our history, are likely to think of competition as being the great engine of innovation and efficiency. If the operation of prisons is farmed out to a variety of private sector contractors, would we not reap a benefit in terms of better managed prisons? Unlike public prison departments, private prison providers would have a powerful incentive to perform well so that they would be hired to run more institutions in more states. Indeed, a highly publicized failure would be very bad for business (see Harding 1997).

The private prison companies are run by some of the best known and most highly respected former public sector prison managers. If successful, privatization would allow them to earn more money and to leverage their expertise over more institutions. In theory, they could, by use of financial incentives, hire the best people, promote them more flexibly, and adopt all sorts of innovations that would not be possible in the public sector. Moreover, the private prisons could be seen as laboratories for reform where, unfettered by muscle-bound bureaucracies, managers could experiment with new administrative strategies and ideas. Any successes that they achieve could be replicated in other institutions, public and private.

So far the jury is still out on whether private prisons have been a positive force for American corrections. Many studies have failed to confirm that private prisons have produced better prison regimes (Greene 2003a, 2003b; Greene et al. 1999). Indeed, there have been disturbing cases of chaotic and unsuccessful private prisons. Nevertheless, I think there is reason to believe that private prisons, in some form, can and will be a positive force in American corrections in the twenty-first century.

Perhaps the public sector officials who contract for and supervise the contracts of private prisons will have to develop greater expertise in performing their role. The same fiscal pressures that drive down conditions and operations in public prisons lead public officials to focus primarily or solely on cost in contracting for and evaluating private prison providers. If cost is going to be the only criteria on which public contractors are going to evaluate private prisons, it will hardly be surprising that the resulting institutional regimes do not do well on all sorts of measures of good conditions, operations, and programs. You get what you pay for.

*Citizens Prison Reform Groups*

There have always been idealistic private citizens, some of them ex-prisoners, who have dedicated themselves to improving the lot of jail and prison inmates. Groups like the John Howard Association, the Fortune Society, the Osborne Association, and Prison Fellowship Ministries in the United States, the Howard League in the United Kingdom (Schone 2001), and Amnesty International, which investigates prisons all over the world, have played a positive role throughout the twentieth century in bringing deplorable conditions to public attention and in campaigning for better conditions and more resources. Sometimes these groups have achieved formal or quasi-formal status in corrections by being given authority to freely visit prisons and make reports (see, e.g., Morgan 2001).

While these publicly spirited NGOs will undoubtedly continue to be a force for prison reform in the twenty-first century, their role is limited by several realities. First, there are today far more prisons and prisoners than there were a generation ago, but the size of the NGO prison reform groups has not grown commensurately. Thus, there are fewer prison reformers to monitor far more institutions and inmates. Second, in a period of fiscal crisis, these organizations, which depend upon private donations, will have to struggle just to keep running. It will become harder and harder to prevent layoffs and reduction of activities. It will also be harder to wring concessions and initiatives out of public officials when these officials are under pressure from groups and constituencies of all types.

## New Sources for Prison Reform

The best hope for a brand new source of prison reform would come from adoption of some sort of national service program or ethos that would require or encourage young Americans to give one or two years of service to their country (see Moskos 1988). Just as tens of thousands of young people today serve a stint in the armed forces and just as other young people, under the auspices of Americorps, tutor and mentor youth, build affordable housing, teach computer skills, clean parks and streams, run after-school programs, and help communities respond to disasters, thousands could be directed to our correctional facilities where they could work (for a national service stipend) in office jobs, in the visiting room, as counselors, teachers, or staff aids to the administrators, or as line officers.

Consider the benefits that would flow from filling 10 percent of prison staff positions with young people meeting their national service responsibility. At a minimum, they would inject an "outsiders" presence into the closed world of the prison. Because these young people would be available to bear witness to deplorable conditions and staff brutalities and illegalities, they would deter them from occurring and help remedy them when they do occur. In effect, they would undermine the prison's equivalent of the "blue wall of silence." They would bring to the parochial prison society new ideas and perspectives that might make operations more efficient and fair. They would create a much stronger link between the prison and the larger society.

A corps of young National Service volunteers would help the prisons run more smoothly. Extra hands could improve the records office, the commissary, the visiting room, the school, and the infirmary. In addition, the program would provide a pool of potential recruits that would otherwise not be available to corrections.

Perhaps most importantly if, over time, tens or hundreds of thousands of young people had a first-hand experience working in prisons, they might form the basis for an informed and active political constituency for prison reform. At a minimum their participation in the society's core institution of punishment would democratize the institution of punishment and bolster the prison's legitimacy.

Admittedly, there is no reason to predict that Congress will establish a national service system any time soon. Nevertheless, volunteerism remains a powerful theme in U.S. society and recent years have seen the formation of Peace-Corps-type organizations in education and the environment. Some states (e.g., Texas) have experimented with internships in corrections. A program of short-term service in corrections might appeal to an idealistic element among today's youth. We will not know until we have tried.

## Conclusion

The twenty-first century has begun with American prisons and jails under more than usual pressure. The national inmate population is at an all-time high, indeed six times higher than it was in the early 1970s. Hundreds of prisons have been opened in the last two decades. Thousands of correctional personnel have been hired. Experienced officials have been spread thinner and thinner over more and more institutions. Still, a crowding crisis endangers the smooth and humane operation of this American gulag. And a serious fiscal crisis now calls into question the capacity of state and local governments to manage their much-expanded penal facilities and inmate populations consistent with humane and constitutional standards.

Funding and administering decent penal facilities is one of the toughest challenges our society faces and one of the most important. Yet political realities do not assign the task a high priority. For the last several decades the courts took over the role of monitoring the prisons and guaranteeing that conditions be kept to certain standards. Now the courts are in retreat, and there is no other actor available to pick up the slack. In my view, only a national service program aimed at prisons and jails would supply the manpower and energy to really make a significant impact. But I have floated the idea before and regrettably have never seen it seriously discussed.

Of course, we should always be modest in trying to make future forecasts. Forces now unforeseen may come to the rescue of our prisons and jails. Perhaps today's fiscal crisis will prove to be short-lived? Perhaps our two-decade-long experiment with mass incarceration will suddenly and dramatically reverse itself? Perhaps the courts will get a second wind and come roaring back into prison cases? Perhaps one or more horrific riots will persuade the populace and the politicians that prison conditions cannot be ignored? Perhaps a wave of humanitarianism, stimulated by the voices of humanists like Norval Morris, will capture the imagination and spirit of a new generation that will take more seriously its responsibility to ensure that all citizens under state confinement are treated with respect and decency (Morris and Jacobs 1974).

## Notes

1. These figures are taken from the *2001 Corrections Yearbook* (Camp and Camp 2002). Line officers can increase their take home salary by working overtime. But working a lot of overtime may also take its toll on individuals and the organization.

2. According to the *2001 Corrections Yearbook* (Camp and Camp 2002), as of January 1, 2001, states reported that their penal institutions were operating at 107.2 percent of capacity. Rhode Island reported operating at 88.9 percent capacity, while Washington State reported operating at 135.7 percent of capacity.

3. *Baxter* held that Miranda warnings need not be given inmates facing disciplinary hearings. *Hudson* held that, under the Fourth Amendment, prisoners have no reasonable expectation of privacy in their cells and that destruction of their property does not constitute an unconstitutional "seizure" because the exigencies of prison security require that prison officials have authority to seize inmates' property.

4. There is a growing research literature on the extent to which prisoners' lawsuits, before the PLRA, were a burden on the federal judiciary. Professor Margo Schlanger (2003) has carried out the most comprehensive research. She finds that in 1995, inmates filed over 40,000 new federal civil lawsuits, 15 percent of the federal civil docket. Of course, many of these complaints were given very short shrift. In 1997, just two years after passage of the PLRA, the number of inmate filings had declined 30 percent.

5. Before passage of the PLRA, the Supreme Court had opened the door to opening up and modifying old consent decrees in *Rufo v. Inmates of Suffolk County Jail*, 502 U.S. 367 (1992).

6. Professor Norval Morris served as special master in *Williams v. Lane*, 1988–1992, which dealt with the conditions and operations of protective custody at Illinois's Stateville Penitentiary and in *K.L. v. Edgar*, 1993–1996, which dealt with conditions in Illinois's mental hospitals. The jurisdiction of both cases was the Northern District of Illinois.

## References

American Correctional Association. 2002. *Standards for Adult Correctional Institutions*. 4th ed. Washington, D.C.: American Correctional Association.

Berk, Richard A., and Peter H. Rossi. 1977. *Corrections Reform and State Elites*. Boston: Ballinger Press.

Bottoms, Anthony E. 1999. "Interpersonal Violence and Social Order in Prisons." In *Prisons, Crime and Justice: A Review of Research*, vol. 26, ed. Michael Tonry and Joan Petersilia. Chicago: University of Chicago Press.

Branham, Lynn S. 1976. *The Law of Sentencing, Corrections, and Prisoners' Rights*. 5th ed. 2002. West Group.

Camp, Camille G., and George M. Camp. 2002. *2001 Corrections Yearbook*. Middletown, Conn.: Criminal Justice Institute.

Christianson, Scott. 1998. *With Liberty for Some: 500 Years of Imprisonment in America*. Boston: Northeastern University Press.

Cummins, Eric. 1994. *The Rise and Fall of California's Radical Prison Movement*. Stanford, Calif.: Stanford University Press.

DiIulio, John, Jr. 1987. *Governing Prisons: A Comparative Study of Prison Management*. New York: Free Press.

Feeley, Malcolm M., and Edward L. Rubin. 1998. *Judicial Policy Making and the Modern State: How the Courts Reformed America's Prisons*. Cambridge: Cambridge University Press.

Fitzgerald, Mike. 1977. *Prisoners in Revolt*. Harmondsworth: Penguin.

Garland, David. 2001. *The Culture of Control: Crime and Social Order in Contemporary Society*. Oxford: Oxford University Press.

Greene, Judy. 2003a. "Bailing Out Private Jails." In *Prison Nation: The Warehousing of America's Poor*, ed. Tara Herival and Paul Wright. London and New York: Routledge Press.

―――. 2003b. "Lack of Correctional Services: The Adverse Effects on Human Rights." In *Capitalist Punishment: Prison Privatization and Human Rights*, ed. Andrew Coyle, Rodney Neufield, and Allison Campbell. Atlanta: Clarity Press.

Greene, Judy, et al. 1999. "Comparing Private and Public Prison Services and Programs in Minnesota: Findings from Prison Interviews." Minneapolis: University of Minnesota Law School Institute on Criminal Justice. Available: http://www.law.umn.edu/centers/crimjust/sentence.php.

Hallinan, Joseph. 2001. *Going up River: Travels in a Prison Nation*. New York: Random House.

Harding, Richard. 1997. *Private Prisons and Public Accountability*. New Brunswick, N.J.: Transaction Pub.

Howard League. 1975. Boards of Visitors of Penal Institutions: Report of a Committee Set up by Justice, the Howard League for Penal Reform, the National Association for the Care and Resettlement of Offenders.

Jacobs, James B. 1977. *Stateville: The Penitentiary in Mass Society*. Chicago: University of Chicago Press.

―――. 1980. "The Prisoners Rights Movement & Its Impacts." In *Crime and Justice: An Annual Review of Research*, vol. 2, ed. Norval Morris and Michael Tonry. Chicago: University of Chicago Press.

―――. 1995. "Judicial Impact on Prison Reform." In *Punishment and Social Control*, ed. Thomas G. Blomberg and Stanley Cohen. New York: Aldyne de Gruyter.

Johnson, Robert. 1996. *Hard Time: Understanding & Reforming the Prison*. Boston: Wadsworth Publishing Co.

Kuzinski, Eugene J. 1998. "The End of the Prison Law Firm? Frivolous Inmate Litigation, Judicial Oversight, and the Prison Litigation Reform Act of 1995." *Rutgers Law Review* 29:361–399.

Lin, Ann Chih. 2000. *Reform in the Making: Implementation of Social Policy in Prisons*. Princeton: Princeton University Press.

Lombardo, Lucien X., 1981. *Guards Imprisoned: Correctional Officers at Work*. New York: Elsevier.

Martin, Steve J., and Sheldon Ekland-Olson. 1987. *Texas Prisons: The Walls Came Tumbling Down*. Austin: Texas Monthly Press.

Mathiesen, Thomas. 1990. *Prison on Trial: A Critical Assessment*. London: Sage.

Morgan, Rod. 2001. "International Controls on Sentencing and Punishment." In *Sentencing and Sanctions in Western Countries*, ed. Michael Tonry and Richard S. Frase. New York: Oxford University Press.

Morris, Norval. 1995. "The Contemporary Prison: 1965–Present." In *Oxford History of the Prison: The Practice of Punishment in Western Society*, ed. Norval Morris and David J. Rothman. New York: Oxford University Press.

―――. 2002. *Maconochie's Gentlemen: The Story of Norfolk Island and the Roots of Modern Prison Reform*. New York: Oxford University Press.

Morris, Norval, and James B. Jacobs. 1974. "Proposals for Prison Reform." *Public Affairs Pamphlets*, no. 510.

Moskos, Charles. 1988. *A Call to Civic Service: National Service for Country and Community*. New York: Free Press.

New York State Special Commission on Attica. 1972. *The Official Report*. New York: Bantam Books.

Parenti, Christian. 1999. *Lockdown America: Police & Prisons in the Age of Crisis*. London: Verso.

Schlanger, Margo. 1999. "Beyond the Hero Judge: Institutional Reform Litigation as Litigation." *Michigan Law Review* 97: 1994–2036.

———. 2003. "Inmate Litigation." *Harvard Law Review* 116(6): 1555–1706.

Schone, J. M. 2001. "The Short Life and Painful Death of Prisoners' Rights." *Howard Journal* 40:70–82.

Stern, Vivien. 1998. *A Sin against the Future: Imprisonment in the World*. Boston: Northeastern University Press.

Woolf, Lord Justice H. 1991. *Prison Disturbances, April 1990: Report of an Inquiry*. London: H.M. Stationery Office.

Zimring, Franklin, Gordon Hawkins, and Sam Kamin. 2001. *Punishment and Democracy: Three Strikes and You're Out in California*. New York: Oxford University Press.

# [16]

## Cell Out

### Renting Out the Responsibility
### for the Criminally Confined

### Jess Maghan

---

### Accountability in the Privatization
### of Corrections

In a society in which organizations compete either for economic resources or for the loyalty and support of group members, the prison has
a unique position. It is noncompetitive in the sense that no other organization challenges it directly. The prison therefore need not, as ultima
ratio of its existence, maintain competitive standards, adapt itself rapidly to technological progress, or respond to fluctuations of market conditions; nor is it immediately dependent on the good will, benevolence,
or loyalty of a group of sponsors or followers, as are many other nonprofit organizations. (Grosser, 1969)

Grosser's characterization of the prison as a noncompetitive institution
clearly demonstrates the dramatic reappearance of private prisons. Private-
for-profit incarceration companies now maintain an aggressive market enterprise in the United States and globally. This market parallels in scale the
military defense industry of recent times. Concurrently, it is also strongly
influenced by privatization in law enforcement, public safety, security, and
social welfare services, as well as the vast new markets in the cybernetics and
communication technology fields (Bernstein, 1996; Crenshaw, 1995; Hobsbawm, 1994; Lilly and Knepper, 1992; Maghan, 1995; Stolz, 1997). Private-
for-profit incarceration portends much of the emerging character of correctional custody in the twenty-first century.

## Criminal Justice Institutions

50

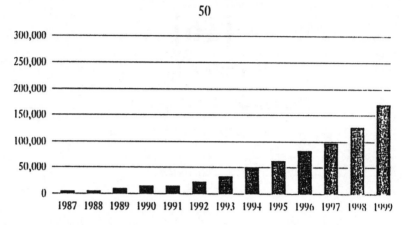

Fig. 4-1. The growth of private prisons. Shown are the number of secure adult prison beds operated by private management companies since 1987 (with estimates for the years 1997–1999). *Source:* Center for Studies in Criminology and Law, University of Florida.

## Feasibility of the Privatization of Correctional Services

The private prison business has become one of the fastest-growing industries in the nation. It is here to stay for the foreseeable future. Private-for-profit incarceration is now past the point where a single scandal will kill the movement. Until it becomes clear that private correctional facilities are neither cheaper nor better than public facilities, the growth of private correctional facilities will continue. The number of inmates in privately managed or owned prisons is expected to exceed 80,000 in 1996, up from 3,122 in 1987, with projected annual growth of 35 percent over the next few years. Figure 4-1 profiles this growth.

## The Standard-Bearers of Correctional Privatization

The Correction Corporation of America and Wackenhut Security are now substantially larger than many public-sector departments of correction and certainly larger than most jail systems. The Corrections Corporation of America (CCA) is now one of the fastest-growing companies traded on the New York Stock Exchange. In 1995, CCA shares soared from eight to thirty-seven dollars a share, an increase of 385 percent. As of October 1997, the value of CCA shares had reached approximately $3.5 billion. Wackenhut Corporation follows as a close contender in these growth stock trends of privatized prison and security systems. These figures clearly reflect an exponential

## Cell Out

### 51

growth of private-for-profit incarceration and demonstrate a viable market. On the industrial-product side, these two giants of private-for-profit incarceration appeal to politicians as an immediate cost-savings alternative to public prisons. The boundaries are yet to be defined.

## Organizational Theory

The political nature of the public sector correctional system, reporting to the executive branch of government at the local, state, and federal level, leaves it vulnerable to a host of external forces, particularly regarding budget and operational philosophy. The public correction system is a residual agency. Positioned downstream from all other components of the criminal justice system, it has always been prey to the ideology of the political majority (Maghan, 1997). This situation is described as a matter of territorial concern, a level of concern that is increasingly manifested in "strategic political issues" relating to community perceptions of crime and crime control policies (Mullen, Chaotar, and Cartow, 1985:74).

In 1992, a survey of perceptions of privatization among public sector prison wardens (Kinkade and Leone, 1992) found that privatization, as established on the fringes of public jails and prisons (such as minimum security alcohol/substance abuse centers and immigration detention centers), represented no threat to public prison wardens. These private correctional facilities were actually perceived as providing additional alternative sentencing options. The current spin of privatization into medium and maximum security prisons, however, is engendering propriety concerns among both public sector prison wardens and prison watchdog groups. Organizations maintain their domains by differentiating themselves from competitors and by maintaining autonomous control over their respective areas (Aldrich, 1979). The external competition from the private sector is raising new concerns of encroachment by the private sector on a domain long held by public sector officials.

## The Past Is a Prologue

The cause and effect issues of contemporary correctional privatization are markedly similar to those of the privatization movement of the 1860s—increasing prisoner populations and a declining economy in the larger society. Likewise, past problems intrinsic to contractual arrangements, such as failure to meet contract stipulations, costs associated with contracts, and quality of contractors' services, are also reappearing (Durham, 1989, 1993; Lewis, 1965; McConville, 1987; McKelvey, 1977).

Smith (1993) cites the convergence of three trends in the mid-1980s as

## Criminal Justice Institutions

### 52

instrumental to the current correctional privatization movement: (a) the ideological imperatives of the free market; (b) the huge increase in the number of
prisoners; and (c) the concomitant increase in imprisonment costs.

---

### Economic Politics

The connection between economics and the intolerance of crime is a major
platform issue in the politics of the 1990s. The Republican majority that captured Congress in the 1994 elections has had a direct impact on state and
local correctional agencies. The demand for tougher criminal laws, longer
prison sentences, mandatory life sentences for repeat offenders, more executions with fewer delays, and harsher forms of incarceration is manifest in the
public mind. Currently, a conservatively bound definition of modern confinement precludes much of the public debate on the purpose of incarceration, its
costs, and the alternatives. "The current conservative penology is a new fantasy of control, as dubious in its assumptions, yet as historically significant as
Bentham's panoptic vision. In blunt terms, it is markedly less concerned with
responsibility, fault, moral sensibility, diagnosis, or intervention and treatment of the individual offender. Rather, it centers on techniques to identify,
classify and manage inmates in groupings sorted by dangerousness. The task
is managerial, not transformative" (Feely and Simon, 1992:452).

Views about private imprisonment services are closely linked to deeper political values, making it difficult to resolve the public policy debate about contracting. Knowing more about the actual experiences and consequences of
contracting will go a long way toward identifying the desirable combinations
of public and private responsibilities and interests.

The Florida Corrections Commission (FCC) has developed a detailed
oversight map for identifying and monitoring costs and quality of services
relating to privatization. This process represents a promulgation of processes
and procedures in evaluating privatization decision making. The chapter appendix outlines these oversight factors.

---

### Accountability in the Privatization
### of Correctional Services

That private prisons have not been declared unconstitutional does not resolve
the question of whether contractual delegation of administrative authority
over imprisonment is proper or desirable. In a legalistic sense, the inmate has
injured the interest of the state and not an individual. Since it is the state that
has been injured, it is the state's duty to punish the transgressor. There have
been no lawsuits to challenge the fundamental idea of contracting out correc-

## Cell Out

### 53

tional services. The existing lawsuits regarding private correctional contractors are essentially the same as those concerning public agencies—claims of poor medical care, excessive use of force—that is, operational issues. A particular jurisdiction may need statutory authorization to contract, but this is not a definitive situation.

The June 23, 1997, ruling by the U.S. Supreme Court (*Richardson v. McKnight*), however, denied entitlement of qualified immunity to private prison staff. This is the first formal legal precept regarding the legal responsibilities of private prisons. It further narrows both the operational liability and cost disparities between private and public correctional facilities. The question remains: Can state or local government delegate its power to punish (Collins, 1987; Dilulio, 1990; Logan, 1990; Maghan, 1991; McDonald, 1990a; Robbins, 1988)?

> The real danger of privatization is not some innate inhumanity on the part of its practitioners but rather the added financial incentives that reward inhumanity. The same economic logic that motivates companies to run prisons more efficiently also encourages them to cut corners at the expense of workers, prisoners, and the public. Private prisons essentially mirror the cost-cutting practices of health maintenance organizations: Companies receive a guaranteed fee for each prisoner, regardless of the actual costs. Every dime they don't spend on food or medical care or training for guards is a dime they can pocket. (Bates, 1997:7)

### The Social Impact of Privatization

The internal logic of privatization consists of mutually reinforcing a set of beliefs that are inherently expansionistic (Gilbert, 1996a). In that view, there is literally no limit to either the amount or type of social control functioning that could be privatized. Presumably, even capital punishment could again be privatized, and, through privatization, as many people as possible could be confined (Gilbert, 1996b). Consequently, the social impact of private-for-profit incarceration presents the potential for an ever-widening capacity for imprisoning more inmates. The possibility that a private prison industry lobby could affect important decisions, such as whether to develop alternatives to imprisonment, seems credible (Maghan, 1991; Morris and Rothman, 1995). The current trend toward privatization of corrections, which is forcing criminal justice into the business world, may escalate the need for increased attention to ethical issues in criminal justice (Silvester, 1990).

In this context, cost should not be the single motivating factor in prisons, but rather the issue of who is to punish those who refuse to abide by the rules

## Criminal Justice Institutions

### 54

of the state. However, the goal of cost efficiency requires a correctional manager to prioritize, for example, where and how incoming funds are to be spent.
Doing this appropriately requires that the manager have not only a solid grasp
of the demands of the marketplace but also an understanding of the ethical
ramifications of decisions that are made. For example, labor costs in a service-
delivery business are usually one of the major expenses, and consequently
they constitute an area in which reduced expenditure can directly affect net
income. Cost-cutting in this area has implications for the quality of service
delivered. Individual states have a tremendous responsibility for the custody
of inmates that cannot be delegated to the private sector without strict surveillance of contractor performance.

Accountability for the private entrepreneur is always the profit margin as
the baseline of cost-effectiveness (Gandy and Hurl, 1987; Harrison and
Gosse, 1985; Walker, 1994). As Silvester (1990) notes: "When settings are
created in which the pragmatic concerns of the business world interact with
the ethical dilemmas produced by the conflicting ideologies intrinsic to the
justice system, individuals unseasoned in the principles of ethical decision-
making are faced with an increasing array of problems. What appear to be
simple decisions of policy, such as which staff to hire and how to train them
or which clients to accept and when to refer, begin to take on new meaning
when money and careers are directly impacted" (68).

The assumption by many privatization advocates that private markets and
self-interest economics are inherently self-regulating cannot be supported.
The invisible hand of free market forces has clearly not prevented market failures or abuses of public interest. As epitomized with the 1980s collapse of
American Savings and Loan, private economic interests have exploited public
interests as opportunity targets in a deregulated marketplace (Denhardt,
1988; Fasenfest, 1986; Luttwak, 1996; Starr, 1987; Wolfe, 1989).

---

### Differing Definitions of Accountability

Spurred by a tax revolt that spread across the United States in the late 1970s
and early 1980s, citizens were voting down bonding proposals, even though
they were at the same time demanding that more criminals be imprisoned in
the hope of making their communities safer. Public officials saw the lease-
purchase arrangements as a convenient way out of this dilemma—a rent payment can be paid out of government operating budgets (McDonald, 1994). A
recurring controversy cited in government and academic studies of privately
run correctional facilities is the practice of lease/purchase financing as a
method of circumventing the debt ceilings and referenda requirements of
general-obligation bonds. Because no voter approval is required, lease/pur-

## Cell Out

### 55

chase agreements undeniably reduce citizen participation in corrections policy (Johnson, 1985).

In the traditional business arena, the knowledge that when service is poor
the paying customers eventually stop coming serves as a safeguard. Privatized
correctional services, however, serve "clients" who have been ordered there by
the courts, who have little political influence, and who, therefore, have minimal immediate impact on or control over the finances of the business.

Private prison corporations answer criticism by insisting that their prisons
run efficiently without scrimping on essentials or impinging on prisoners'
rights. The Corrections Corporation of America notes in its 1994 annual report that the stock options it offers to employees foster a sense of ownership
and makes them more receptive to complaints from prisoners.

### Privatization in Texas:
### A National Model

The reemergence of the private sector's involvement with the Texas prison
system signaled a new era in Texas corrections, an era distinguished by progressive methods for aiding the thousands of Texas inmates. The most important aspect of this privatization experiment pertains to the type of facility
that is operated by the private companies. By using small (five-hundred-man)
facilities that offer prerelease programs, lawmakers are taking major steps toward preparing inmates for life outside prison walls.

The operation and management of small, specialized facilities that house
low-risk inmates has been championed as a possible role for the private sector
in the nation's correctional system (Folz and Scheb, 1989; Johnson and Ross,
1990). Other states might follow the example of Texas. According to Logan
(1990), this already may be a trend: Most of the privately operated state
prison units in the United States house fewer than five hundred low-risk inmates.

A second feature of the Texas privatization experiment is the financing
scheme contrived to pay for the construction and operation of prerelease centers. Lawmakers devised a bonding mechanism that did not need voter approval. By using lease revenue bonds, the state does not technically create a
debt. Although the use of such bonds proved successful in Texas, the issuance
of bonds that do not need voter approval to pay for prison construction has
been criticized because the government can expand prison construction without public input (Leonard, 1990; McDonald, 1989).

A third aspect of the Texas privatization experience pertains to the contract negotiations between the state and private companies. On the basis of
the original contracts, the contract monitors' reports, and the companies' re-

## Criminal Justice Institutions

### 56

sponses to the reports, it appears that some portions of the contracts were ambiguous (for example, educational programs, vocational programs, and pre-release programs). As a result, the companies and the Texas Department of Corrections spent a great amount of time and money in reaching agreements on how to carry out the contracts properly (Ethridge and Marquart, 1993).

---

## The Dilemma of Cost-Benefit Analysis

Krulwich (1981:12) refers to the series of costs related to inappropriate or inadequate regulation as "secondary effects that are rarely considered in the rush and newness of privatization." For example, regulation at times causes delay, which, in turn, imposes its own set of costs. Failing to take into account effects that accumulate over time has been suggested as one cause of some of these problems. More often, costs (and benefits) that economists cannot measure are ignored or merely cited as possibilities the agency also considered without attempting to quantify.

In a profile analysis entitled *Privately Managed Prisons—At What Cost?* the Prison Reform Trust of the United Kingdom provides an analysis of cost factors. This analysis concludes that privately managed prisons are not the benchmark on which to base publicly managed prison budgets. A detailed account of the consternation of attempts at comparative cost analysis and the concomitant political and bureaucratic foray involved in the public use of private prisons continues to raise concerns. For example:

• Comparisons between public and private prisons are complex, as it is difficult to establish true "like with like" conditions. For example, in addition to the stated overall contract price for a private prison, as compared with the annual budget for a publicly run prison (even if they were the same kind of prison, of the same age, with the same design, number, and category of prisoners from the same locality with exactly the same needs and services provided—all of which must be unlikely), there are a myriad of hidden costs to be taken into account. These would include prison service headquarters costs; the resources of outside agencies, such as police, fire department, local authorities, national health services, health and safety agencies, and other central government departments and voluntary groups that provide services to prisons; the public provision of local infrastructure to prisons; and not least, the cost to taxpayers of the entire privatization itself.

• Taxpayers also foot the bill for costs that are exclusive to the private sector and that are included as an element of the contract price, such as the need to make profits, create returns on capital investment and dividends for shareholders or payments to parent companies for technical know-how, expertise,

## Cell Out

### 57

or management/administrative fees. There is also the loss in corporation tax revenue if the company makes a loss.

• Despite the claim that privately managed prisons are cheaper to run, the Prison Service has been unable to publish meaningful cost comparisons. It is arguable that this exercise might not even be possible. (Nor has the issue been resolved in the United States or Australia, both of which have had longer experience of privately managed prisons than has the U.K.)

• The claim that privately managed prisons automatically provide better value for the money is also, at best, unproven, as the performance of three of the existing privately managed prisons in the U.K. testifies. The fourth, Buckley Hall, has not yet been independently evaluated (Penal Lexicon Home Page: United Kingdom, September 15, 1996).

---

### Accountability:
### Private Versus Public Prisons

Privatization advocates discount concerns over the erosion of governmental sovereignty. They argue that sovereignty is retained through the contract and enforced by the government's power to terminate the contract. This view fails to recognize the fact that progressive privatization of correctional production (that is, the creation and delivery of correctional services) gradually transfers public policy making functions to the private sector (Dahl and Glassman, 1991; Gilbert, 1996a; Keating, 1990; Kolderie, 1986; Leonard, 1990; McDonald, 1990b; USGAO, 1991).

A vivid test of the sovereignty of governmental oversight occurred in the June 18, 1995, riot at the 350-bed Immigration and Naturalization Service (INS) Detention Center in Elizabeth City, New Jersey, contracted at $54 million to Esmore Correctional Services, Inc., a private correctional management firm (J. Sullivan, 1995).

The INS, a federal agency with little experience (and few options) for operating a custodial detention center for illegal immigrants, had sought private contractors out of the sheer expediency of creating detention facilities quickly. These minimum security centers, located in unobtrusive locations, provoked little controversy or even notice. The convenience of contracted detention services pre-empted INS concern for contracted detention centers. This matter continues to play out with protracted litigation on behalf of the immigrant detainees. In this tragedy it has become painfully obvious that accountability is not always a clear-cut matter in this mix of private and public prisons.

As Mullen et al. (1985) speculated it would, the correctional privatization movement appears to be shifting from initial declarations of cost savings to

## Criminal Justice Institutions

### 58

more neutral issues of "flexibility and the provision of special services" (7). Essentially, there is little evidence of anything imaginative or exciting coming out of the new private prison facilities. To date, the development, design, operation, and management of private prisons has turned out to be much like those of their traditional counterparts. The administrative ranks of the private prisons continue to grow with managers and supervisors that have been mostly recruited (or are retired) from public sector correctional agencies.

### Privatized Correctional Services
### Have a New Cell Mate

Private welfare management and training companies are lining up for a market that expanded overnight when President Clinton, in September 1996, signed the new law to replace the sixty-year-old guarantee of federal aid to poor children with lump grants to the states. Privatization is now being championed as an enhancement for the new welfare law. For the first time, the law allows states to buy not only welfare services but also gatekeepers to determine eligibility and benefits. The privatization of social-welfare functions has become a dominant theme for twenty-first-century human resource functions, including education, health and medical services (HMOs), and a growing range of social infrastructure maintenance services. Because of a mutuality of the clients served, linkages with these newly privatized human service agencies will engender collaborative services with and among public and private correctional programs.

The tough job ahead for both public and private penal experts is to continue to create constitutionally protected justice environments geared to both economic and social improvements. The past decade of aggressive privatization in correctional services is clarifying fundamental demarcations of privatization claims. Consider what privatization might and might not do: (a) It cannot ease the credit crunch caused by budget deficits; (b) it cannot relieve government of its social responsibilities; (c) it isn't likely to make monopolies more efficient; and (d) it may even temper political demands for inefficient operations. The real hope for innovative change lies in a middle ground.

### Possibility Thinking and the Privatization
### of Correctional Services

The racial demographics of our prison population mirror deeper social problems, problems that prisons are increasingly being asked to solve. The American prison system already functions as a surrogate national public health sys-

## Cell Out

### 59

tem, a national job training and literacy program, and, unfortunately, as a second-rate mental hospital. Tapping into the emerging public-private partnerships evolving out of the past decade of privatization may help solve this crisis.

## Potential Partnerships

It is time to redefine the purpose of the prison, to peel away all of these social engineering tasks the prisons are assuming. Let the prisons truly become a penal system for long-term and dangerous inmates and turn remaining custodial control into a restructured system of correctional programs leading to positive behavior, such as community service and boot camp programs. Such centers (public and private), concentrating on programs of self-esteem and personal development skills for inmates, can put our correctional system back into balance with other criminal justice and social service agencies. This could well be the beginning of a correctional version of the popular and successful community policing programs throughout the United States. In this context, accountability for both public and private prisons can be linked to creativity and community partnership. How can this process be achieved?

While the United States represents a pioneer market in the incarceration-for-profit industry, it can also serve as a laboratory for the development of a new "social contract" with private correctional entrepreneurs. The utility of these partnerships will emerge as government seeks new modes for custodial care of geriatric prisoners, prisoners with alcohol- and drug-related problems, and prisoners with emotional and mental problems (Cullen, 1986; Matthews, 1989). One of the most significant outcomes of the privatization debate is that a fundamental rethinking of every facet of the existing system is widely recognized as not only desirable but very necessary (Matthews, 1989). These partnerships are stimulating new forms of oversight responsibility by both government and private agencies (Crants, 1991; Cullen, 1986; Matthews, 1989, 1990).

The privatization movement has now matured enough to bring some reasoning to the usual reactive stance of both advocates and adversaries. There is an emerging community of interests that recognizes a mutuality of mission in meeting the ever-growing correctional custodial needs of the nation. It can be hoped that this community of interests will lobby for increasing legislation to create privatized minimum security centers for drug addicts, alcoholics, and special-need offenders.

It is not science fiction to speculate that the prisons (private and public) of the twenty-first century will constitute even more gigantic correctional complexes, providing a full range of institutionalized geriatric and public health

## Criminal Justice Institutions

### 60

services. The mix of public and private correctional systems is inevitable. The maintenance of the social accountability and integrity of these new partnerships must be inculcated in the institutions of both sectors. This necessitates a return to the teaching of vocational and economic civics: public and private partnerships.

---

## Subjective Social Costs of Prison Privatization

As a prelude, the current intoxication with the return of private-for-profit incarceration is the most recent indicator of an emergent fourth wave of correctional reform at the cusp of the twenty-first century. The reappearance of prisons-for-profit as a fourth wave reform movement is opening old wounds and creating new dilemmas of social engineering and the possibilities for positive change. The net-widening capabilities of privatized incarceration are ominous. In this context, privatization manifestly represents *less eligibility reborn*. Sparks (1996) offers a resounding cautionary tone: "The prospect that penal services might be provided by a private sector not 'incentivized' toward relentless improvement but instead constrained by a rhetoric of austerity exposes a range of impending troubles for the legitimacy of the private corrections industry which have until now been largely suppressed" (89).

This is a keenly insightful point shadowing the current reprogramming of private-for-profit incarceration. Prison privatization confronts us with subjective social costs that are not so readily quantifiable. There is a concern for the consequences of commercialization in influencing current criminal justice policy. International human rights experts are joining in voicing concerns that privatization of prisons is not in accordance with international human rights law (Beyens and Snacken, 1996). The embodiment of new public and private correctional partnerships may be the end product of this aggressive correctional privatization. The mix of public and private correctional systems is inevitable. Reforms that will define and ensure the social accountability and integrity of these new partnerships will constitute the dominant interplay in the institutions of both sectors. The importance of prisoner rights advocacy in both private and public prisons must now shift to an expanded corporate model. The dilemma continues.

---

## Appendix
### Florida Corrections Commission

PROJECT: Identify Costs and Quality of Service Factors Relating to Privatization of State Prisons

# Cell Out

## 61

1. ISSUE: Identify factors to consider for evaluating costs and quality of services for use in comparing private versus state prisons.

2. BACKGROUND/HISTORY: The increase in privatization of correctional facilities in the late 1980s and first half of the 1990s was part of a philosophical shift toward privatization of many government services. The advantages of privatization are said to be its cost efficiency, similar or better quality services, and its ability to bring facilities on-line quickly. Opponents believe that one of the core functions of government is punishment and that private companies profit motives have no place in the administration of justice, where it may create a conflict of interest between the public safety and private profit.

Private involvement with adult correctional institutions has three major models:

(1) private financing and construction of prisons;
(2) private industry involvement in prisons through vocational, academic, work and support programs; and,
(3) the management and operation of an entire correctional facility by a private contractor.

There is general agreement that privatization is a management tool that, when used, requires government to make a series of decisions. These decisions are policy decisions to determine:

- the level of privatization;
- which services may be considered for privatization;
- cost/benefit decisions to determine whether the public or private sector could produce those services most effectively and efficiently;
- evaluation decisions whether output or outcome evaluation should be utilized to determine if privatization decisions made are meeting intended goals.

Many state corrections agencies believe that privatization in corrections has sufficient merit to justify further study. Some advocates of privatization believe that cost savings can be realized from increased flexibility in competitively shopping for prices. Most private companies involved in corrections do not offer traditional pension plans to its employees, but rather offer vested employees opportunities in profit-sharing plans. Advocates state that one feature of private involvement in corrections is the capacity of the private sector to expand criminal sanctions, through new forms of intermediate level control and new surveillance and control technologies.

Criminal Justice Institutions

62

SECTION 944.105(1)—FLORIDA STATUTES, authorizes the Department of Corrections to enter into contracts with private vendors for the provision of the operation and maintenance of correctional facilities and supervision of inmates. It requires that prior to entering into or renewing a contract for a privatized prison, the DOC must determine that the contract offers substantial savings and that the contract provides for the same quality of services as that offered by the department.

3. CHAPTER 957: The Auditor General is charged with certifying to the Correctional Privatization Commission actual costs associated with the construction and operation of similar facilities or services; and developing and implementing an evaluation of the costs and benefits of each contract entered under this Chapter.

The evaluation must include a comparison of the costs and benefits of constructing and operating prisons by the state versus by private contractors. The Auditor General (again, by agreement, OPPAGA [Office of Program Policy Analysis and Government Accountability] will conduct these reviews) is further charged with evaluating the performance of the private vendor at the end of the term of each management agreement and making recommendations to the Legislature as to continue the contract.

By contract, the private vendor must provide a full-time contract monitor, who is appointed and supervised by the Correctional Privatization Commission.

DESCRIPTION/SCOPE OF WORK: This FCC issue would require the cooperation and support of the Correctional Privatization Commission, the Department of Corrections, and individual private correctional contractors (Wackenhut Corporation, U.S. Corrections Corporation, Esmor Correctional Services, and the Corrections Corporation of America). FCC activities would include, but not necessarily be limited to, contacting other states with multiple privatized prisons to determine:

- The model(s) of privatization utilized;
- The profile of offender populations (adult, pre-release, jail, juvenile) at the contracted facilities;
- The statutory authorization for contracting correctional facilities;
- The statutory authorized entity for contracting correctional facilities;
- The cost and quality of services contractually required for the continued operation and renewal of contract;

## Cell Out

### 63

- The cost and service quality criteria reviewed to determine contractual compliance;
- The entity which reviews and evaluates the cost and service quality criteria of private prisons;
  The availability of evaluations comparing the cost and service quality criteria of private v. public prisons.

Review existing research literature to identify methods and criteria utilized in measuring and evaluating costs and quality of services in private versus public prisons.

Review all Florida contracts for privatized prisons for language pertaining to cost savings and the provision/quality of services—including academic, vocational training, and substance abuse program services.

Identify innovative facility design or program operations of privatization facilities.

Develop cost and service quality factors for statutory authorized entities to consider for evaluating and comparing private versus public prison operations in Florida.

4. BENEFIT OF PROJECT: The primary benefit of FCC conducting an analysis to identify cost and service quality factors would be to policy and decision makers involved in privatization of correctional facilities. Sections 944.105 and 944.710-719, Florida Statutes, and Chapter 957, Oversight via Florida Statutes, each prescribe varying responsibilities for cost savings, audits and monitoring contract compliance. Although cost comparison will be an essential part of the Auditor General's review, that review will not occur until completion of the second year of operation, in preparation for the decision of renewing the contract. (Florida Corrections Commission, 1996)

## References

Aldrich, H. E. (1979). *Organizations and Environments*. Englewood Cliffs, N.J.: Prentice-Hall.

Bates, Eric (1997). "Private Prisons." *Nation* 8 (1):11–38.

Bernstein, Nina (1996). "Giant Companies Entering Race to Run State Welfare Programs." *New York Times*, September 11, 14.

Beyens, Kristel, and Sonja Snacken (1997). "Prison Privatization: An International Perspective." Pp. 240–65 in *Prison 2000: An International Perspective on the Cur-*

## Criminal Justice Institutions

### 64

*rent State and Future of Imprisonment*, Roger Matthews and Peter Francis, eds. New York: St. Martin's.

Collins, William C. (1987). "Privations: Some Legal Considerations from a Neutral Perspective." *American Jails* 1:28–34.

Crants, Doctor R. (1991). "Private Prison Management: A Study in Economic Efficiency." *Journal of Contemporary Criminal Justice* 7 (1):49–59.

Crenshaw, Martha (1995). *Terrorism in Context*. University Park, Penn.: Pennsylvania State University Press.

Cullen, F. (1986). "The Privatization of Treatment: Prison Reform in the 1980s." *Federal Probation* 50:8–16.

Dahl, J. G., and A. M. Glassman (1991). "Public Sector Contracting: The Next Growth Industry for Organizational Development." *Public Administration Quarterly* 14 (winter):483–97.

Denhardt, K. G. (1988). *The Ethics of Public Service*. New York: Associated Faculty Press.

DiIulio, John J. (1990). "The Duty to Govern: A Critical Perspective on the Private Management of Prisons and Jails." Pp. 116–28 in *Private Prisons and the Public Interest*, D. C. McDonald, ed. New Brunswick, N.J.: Rutgers University Press.

Durham, Alexis M., III (1989). "Origins of Interest in the Privatization of Punishment: The Nineteenth and Twentieth Century American Experience." *Criminology* 27:107–39.

—— (1993). "The Future of Correctional Privatization: Lessons from the Past." Pp. 33–49 in *Privatizing Correctional Institutions*, G. W. Bowman, S. Hakim, and P. Seidenstat, eds. New Brunswick, Conn.: Transaction.

Ethridge, Philip A., and James W. Marquart (1993). "Private Prisons in Texas: The New Penology for Profit." *Justice Quarterly* 10 (1):30–48.

Fasenfest, D. (1986). "Using Produce Incentives to Achieve Social Objectives: An Assessment of the Marketplace and Public Policies." *Policy Studies Review* 5 (February):634–42.

Feeley, S., and J. Simon (1992). "The New Penology: Notes on the Emerging Strategy of Corrections and Its Implications." *Criminology* 30 (4):449–74.

Florida Corrections Commission (1996). *Project: Identify Costs and Quality of Service Factors Relating to Privatization of State Prisons*. Tallahassee, Fla.: OPPAGA.

Folz, David H., and John M. Scheb, II (1989). "Prisons, Profits and Politics: The Tennessee Privatization Experiment." *Judicature* 73 (2):98–102.

Gandy, J., and L. Hurl (1987). "Private Sector Involvement in Prison Industries: Options and Issues." *Canadian Journal of Criminology* 29:185–204.

Gilbert, Michael J. (1996a). "Private Confinement and the Role of Government in a Civil Society." Pp. 13–20 in *Privatization and the Provision of Correctional Services: Context and Consequences*, G. Larry Mays and Tara Gray, eds. Cincinnati: Academy of Criminal Justice Sciences (ACJS) and Anderson Publishing.

—— (1996b). "Making Privatization Decisions Without Getting Burned: A Guide for Understanding the Risks." Pp. 61–73 in *Privatization and the Provision of Correctional Services: Context and Consequences*, G. Larry Mays and Tara Gray, eds. Cincinnati: Academy of Criminal Justice Sciences (ACJS) and Anderson Publishing.

Cell Out

65

Grosser, George H. (1969). "External Setting and Internal Relations of the Prison." P. 11 in *Prison within Society*, L. Hazelrigg, ed. Garden City, N.Y.: Anchor Books.

Harrison, E., and M. Gosse (1985). *Privatization: A Restraint Initiative. Policy Report*. Victoria: British Columbia Ministry of Correction.

Hobsbawm, Eric (1994). *The Age of Extremes: A History of the World, 1914–1991*. New York: Pantheon Books.

Johnson, Byron R., and Paul P. Ross (1990). "The Privatization of Correctional Management: A Review." *Journal of Criminal Justice* 18:351–58.

Johnson, Judith (1985). "Should Adult Correctional Facilities Be Privately Managed?" *National Sheriff* 38 (2):18–21.

Keating, J. M. (1990). "Public over Private: Monitoring the Performance of Privately Operated Prisons and Jails." Pp. 87–94 in *Private Prisons and the Public Interest,*. D. C. McDonald, ed. New Brunswick, N.J.: Rutgers University Press.

Kinkade, Patrick T., and Matthew C. Leone (1992). "The Privatization of Prisons: The Wardens' Views." *Federal Probation* 56 (4):58–65.

Koldrie, T. (1986). "The Two Different Concepts of Privatization." *Public Administration Review* 46 (July–August):285–91.

Krulwich, Andrew S. (1981). "Cost-Benefit Evolves under Regulators, Legislators." *Legal Times of Washington*, June 8, pp. 12–13.

Lampkin, Linda M. (1991). "Does Crime Pay? AFSCME Reviews the Record on the Privatization of Prisons." *Journal of Contemporary Criminal Justice* 7 (1):41–48.

Leonard, H. B. (1990). "Private Time: The Political Economy of Private Prison Finance." Pp. 48–60 in *Private Prisons and the Public Interest*, D. C. McDonald, ed. New Brunswick, N.J.: Rutgers University Press.

Lewis, W. D. (1965). *From Newgate to Dannemora*. Ithaca, N.Y.: Columbia University Press.

Lilly, J. Robert, and Paul Knepper (1992). "An International Perspective on the Privatization of Corrections." *Howard Journal* 31 (3):174–91.

Logan, Charles H. (1990). *Private Prisons Cons and Pros*. New York: Oxford University Press, 1990.

Luttwak, Edward (1996). "The Middle Class Backlash: Turbo-Charged Capitalism and Its Consequences." *Harper's Magazine*, May, pp. 48–60.

Maghan, Jess (1991). "Privatization of Corrections: Anticipating the Unanticipated." Pp. 135–49 in *Perspectives on Deviance: Dominance, Degradation and Denigration*, Robert J. Kelly and Donald E. J. MacNamara, eds. Cincinnati: Anderson Publishing.

—— (1995). "Terrorist Mentality." Unpublished keynote presentation, Fifth European Conference of Law and Psychology, Budapest, Hungary, September 2.

—— (1997). "Training Cannot Do What Management Cannot Do: The Evolvement of Centralized Training in Modern Correctional Services." *Corrections Management Quarterly* 1 (1): 40–48.

Matthews, Roger (1989). *Privatizing Criminal Justice*. Thousand Oaks, Calif.: Sage Publishers.

—— (1990). "New Directions in the Privatization Debate?" *Probation Journal* 37 (2):50–59.

McConville, Sean (1987). "Aid from Industry? Private Corrections and Prison

## Criminal Justice Institutions

### 66

Crowding." In *America's Correctional Crisis: Prison Populations and Public Policy*, S. Gottfredson and S. McConville, eds. Westport, Conn.: Greenwood Press.

McDonald, Douglas C. (1989). "The Cost of Corrections: In Search of the Bottom Line." *Research in Corrections* 2:1–6.

—— (1990a). "When Government Fails: Going Private as a Last Resort." Pp. 179–99 in *Private Prisons and the Public Interest*, D. McDonald, ed. New Brunswick, N.J.: Rutgers University Press.

—— (1990b). "The Costs of Operating Public and Private Correctional Facilities." Pp. 28–37 in *Private Prisons and the Public Interest*, D. C. McDonald, ed. New Brunswick, N.J.: Rutgers University Press.

—— (1994). "Public Imprisonment by Private Means: The Reemergence of Private Prisons and Jails in the United States, the United Kingdom, and Australia." *British Journal of Criminology* 34:29–48. (Special issue)

McKelvey, B. (1977). *American Prisons: A History of Good Intentions*. Montclair, N.J.: Patterson Smith.

Morris, Norval, and David J. Rothman, eds. (1995). *The Oxford History of the Prison: The Practice of Punishment in Western Society*. New York: Oxford University Press.

Mullen J., K. Chaotar, and D. Cartow (1985). *The Privatization of Corrections*. Washington, D.C.: National Institute of Justice.

Prison Reform Trust (1996). *The Penal Lexicon Home Page*. United Kingdom, September 15:12–14.

Robbins, Ira (1988). *The Legal Dimensions of Incarceration*. Washington, D.C.: American Bar Association.

Silvester, Deanna Buckley (1990). "Ethics and Privatization in Criminal Justice: Does Education Have a Role to Play?" *Journal of Criminal Justice* 18:65–70.

Smith, Phil (1993). "Private Prisons: Profits of Crime." *Convert Action Quarterly* 18 (2):26–46.

Sparks, Richard (1996). "Penal 'Austerity': The Doctrine of Less Eligibility Reborn?" Pp. 74–93 in *Prison 2000: An International Perspective on the Current State and Future of Imprisonment*, R. Matthews and P. Francis, eds. New York: St. Martin's.

Starr, Paul (1987). "The Limits of Privatization." In *Prospects for Privatization*, vol. 36, no. 3, S. H. Hanks, ed. New York: Proceedings of the Academy of Political Science.

Stolz, Barbara Ann (1997). "Privatizing Corrections: Changing the Corrections Policy-Making Subgovernment." *Prison Journal* 77 (1):92–111.

Sullivan, Harold J. (1989). "Privatization of Corrections and the Constitutional Rights of Prisons." *Federal Probation* 53 (2):36–42.

—— (1993). "Privatization of Corrections: A Threat to Prisoners' Rights." Pp. 139–55 in *Privatizing Correctional Institutions*, G. W. Bowman, S. Hakim, and P. Seidenstat, eds. New Brunswick, N.J.: Transaction Publishers.

Sullivan, John (1995). "Six Guards in New Jersey Charged with Beating Jailed Immigrants." *New York Times*, October 14: A12.

United States General Accounting Office (1991). *Private Prisons: Cost Savings and BOP's Statutory Authority Need to Be Resolved*, GAO/GGD-91-21.

Walker, Donald B. (1994). "Privatization in Corrections." Pp. 570–85 in *Correctional*

## Cell Out

### 67

*Counseling and Treatment*, P. C. Krateoski, ed. Prospect Heights, Ill.: Waveland Press.

Wolfe, A. (1989). *Whose Keeper? Social Science and Moral Obligation.* Los Angeles: University of California Press.

## Case Cited

*Richardson v. McKnight*, No. 96–318, U.S. Supreme Court (1997).

# [17]

# *The Hardness of Hard Treatment*

JOHN KLEINIG*

In February, 1996, Rosemary West was convicted of ten murders of young women, including a daughter and stepdaughter. The British public were shocked by the gruesome details as they gradually unfolded. West (whose co-defendant husband committed suicide in custody) was sentenced to life imprisonment on each count.[1] In a subsequent newspaper article, Stephen, Rosemary's eldest son, reportedly complained about the apparently comfortable life his mother had in prison. His mother was reading the classics, attending seminars, and working 40 hours a week making toys: 'She is happy and quite content and has found a lot of friends. This is disappointing, really. I wonder if you can call it punishment at all?'[2]

In the USA, Stephen West's concern has been expressed and acted upon for some time. Boot camps have grown in popularity; at least two states have re-introduced chain gangs;[3] several others have begun to remove inmate facilities such as gym equipment and television sets; and others have banned cigarettes, or scaled down telephone access, or food choice. Just how hard should the hard treatment of imprisonment be?

There are, of course, various motivations at work in such initiatives. Some are obvious and inherently reasonable, albeit at times improperly exploited[4]—such

---

* I have little doubt that this contribution would have been improved had Andrew von Hirsch been able to review it beforehand. Nevertheless, I am very grateful for comments on earlier versions by Derek Brookes, Tziporah Kasachkoff, Charles Lindner, Margaret Leland Smith, and Larry E. Sullivan.

[1] West subsequently appealed her conviction, but was unsuccessful. See *Rosemary Pauline West* [1996] 2 Cr.App.R. 374.

[2] *The Times*, 19 March 1996, p. 5.

[3] In one one those states—Alabama—the threat of a suit and international criticism has led to their discontinuance. However, the state retained the use of 'hitching posts'—something like a pillory, and only recently has a federal judge ruled against them. See Adam Nossiter, 'Judge Rules Against Alabama's Prison "Hitching Posts" ', *New York Times*, 31 January 1997, p. A14. In a variation, prisoners employed in 'chain' gangs are sometimes being kept under control by means of stun belts, which allow corrections officers to deliver an 8-second burst of 50,000 volts to the kidneys from up to 300 feet away. See Peter L. Kilborn, 'Revival of Chain Gangs Takes a Twist', *New York Times*, 11 March 1997, p. A18; William F. Schulz, 'Cruel and Unusual Punishment', *New York Review of Books*, 24 April 1997, pp. 51–2.

[4] I am mindful of Hugo Bedau's observation that 'along with patriotism, security—national security and prison security—is the last refuge of scoundrels': 'Prisoners' Rights', (1982) I, 1 *Criminal Justice Ethics* (Winter/Spring) 38.

as the need to maintain a secure and untroubled environment. Other reasons are blatantly politico-economic. Budgetary concerns are taxpayer and therefore voter concerns, as is crime, and in the lead-up to an election year American politicians found it useful to talk tough on crime. Although the huge investment in imprisonment is costing the American taxpayer plenty, it is made more palatable for many if prison life cannot be painted in glamorous terms.[5]

Though institutional and politico-economic concerns do much to drive change, they are supported by other, more ideological considerations. Some, such as Stephen West's, are retributive: a sense that proportionality between offence and punishment has been lost where imprisonment seems to lack a suitably reprobative and penitential dimension. Alternatively, it is argued that those who offend forfeit their claims to or become less eligible for the comforts of life, and cannot complain if their conditions are cheerless and hard. Others, however, argue that considerations of deterrence are of central importance: if prisoners find gaol too congenial, their incarcerative experience will fail to inhibit future criminality. And since, for many of the homeless, impoverished, and drug addicted, even the confinement of gaol is likely to provide better conditions than they are used to and can easily expect outside prison, these critics would argue that conditions should be spartan, if not hard.[6]

How hard may hard treatment be? What factors should determine or limit its hardness? In section 1 I review very briefly what I consider to be the major argument for prescribing the hard treatment that constitutes punishment. The standardization of (much of) that hard treatment as imprisonment is briefly recounted in section 2. In section 3 I consider several factors that might be appealed to in limiting the hardness of the hard treatment of imprisonment, claiming in particular that imprisonment must be neither inhumane nor degrading. In section 4 I suggest some positive, restorative directions that should be pursued when imposing hard treatment. Finally, in section 5 I relate the earlier discussion to some incarcerative practices—those concerning space and environment, work and activity, amenities, visitation and access, and opportunities.

I should make it clear at the outset that, because of the scale of the problems involved, I will generally confine myself to custodial sanctions, and to the hardness that may be associated with them—not primarily by virtue of their length, but with reference to the deprivations or additional impositions that may be associated with incarceration. Of course, length of sentence cannot be separated too sharply from the deprivations that are associated with it. In terms of proportion-

---

[5] In 1995, Richard Zimmer, then a New Jersey Representative, introduced what was termed the 'No Frills Act', designed to make a state's eligibility for prison construction money dependent on its commitment to removing weight-lifting equipment, in-cell coffee pots, and inmate access to computers, to ending the showing of R-rated movies, and to ensuring that prison food was no better than that served in the Army. See Mark Curriden, 'Hard Time', 1995, LXXXI *ABA Journal* (July) 73.

[6] In the USA the two are usually distinguished, gaols (jails) being locally run centres of detention/correction for misdemeanants, and prisons being state and federally run structures for felons; but I shall treat them as one here. My concerns apply most critically to prisons, though conditions in many gaols are woefully inadequate. Overcrowding has led to a mixing of the populations.

ality, a short hard sentence may be considered equivalent to a longer sentence without any added hardships. My main concern, however, will be with the conditions under which a prison term is served out rather than with its duration.

## 1. PUNISHMENT AS HARD TREATMENT

Punishment, it is said, is hard treatment.[7] That is, it involves not merely condemnation, rebuke, or censure, but some substantial imposition on a wrong-doer. Why *hard treatment*, as distinct from condemnation or censure, should be justified, has engaged the attention of philosophers from the very beginning. The classical theories of punishment—deontological and consequentialist—are largely attempts to answer such a question.

Here I do little more than rehearse what I believe to be the strongest considerations in favour of the practice of punishment.[8] Punishment is punishment *for* and, unlike mere penalization, which is a deliberate imposition for some rule infraction, punishment has a distinctively expressive character. It involves a stigmatizing condemnation of the punished. It does so, because the person punished has been judged to be guilty *inter alia* of some *moral wrong-doing*, that is, of violating basic conditions of our human engagement.[9] I leave aside the specific character of the wrong-doing and, for the present, the issue of a punisher's authority to punish.[10] It is sufficient at this point to note that what punishment is *for* is a breach of standards that are believed to be of fundamental significance in our human intercourse.[11]

We might, of course, respond to moral wrong-doing in a number of ways. We can criticize, censure, or rebuke the wrong-doer. And generally that would not be out of place. Were that all we did, however, it would be inadequate. Merely to rebuke or censure the wrong-doer would fail to register the seriousness of what was done. Some *proportionate* response is called for, as a simple matter of fairness or justice. Proportionality is not simply an optional add-on to the censure, but is

---

[7] I associate the phrase with Joel Feinberg, 'The Expressive Function of Punishment' (1968), reprinted in *Doing and Deserving* (Princeton: Princeton University Press, 1970), pp. 95–118.

[8] I have provided a fuller discussion in 'Punishment and Moral Seriousness', (1991) XXV, 3–4 *Israel Law Review* 401–21, and even earlier in *Punishment and Desert* (The Hague: Martinus Nijhoff, 1973).

[9] Here of course I make the controversial assumption that crimes are to be distinguished from mere administrative offences in part because an element of moral wrong-doing is involved. I have tried to say something in favour of this claim in *Punishment and Desert*, (1973), n. 8 above, Ch. 2, and in (1986) V, 1 'Criminally Harming Others', *Criminal Justice Ethics* (Winter/Spring) 3–10 (though see Joel Feinberg's response to the latter in the same issue).

[10] Any full theory of punishment—especially of institutionalized punishment—must address this issue. At this point I am concerned with what justifies the punishing of a person and not with what might justify *my* or *someone else's* being the one to punish the person.

[11] It is, I believe, the pre-eminence of moral considerations in human interaction that gives moral breaches the significance that punishment registers. Nevertheless, it is also my view that not every moral breach is appropriately punished by the State. The State has a limited function and some acts that are deserving of punishment are better left to others or, as some would sometimes put it, to God.

276 *John Kleinig*

implicit in it. When we censure others for their wrong-doing, we mark them out as worthy of punishment. Where others have been harmed, endangered, or otherwise set back by the moral derelictions of another, some significant deprivation is signalled as appropriate.[12] Not only does the imposition serve to impress on the wrong-doer the character of what s/he has done, it also acknowledges the personhood of the victim and the seriousness of what was done to him. The complaint often heard, that some offenders are given no more than a slap on the wrist by the criminal justice system, registers the intuition that mere censure or disapprobation, detached from some proportionate response, is not enough.[13] *Ceteris paribus*, unless the disgraced person is also deprived, the offence is not given its due.

In saying that some proportionate response is *called for*, as a matter of fairness or justice, I should not be taken to imply that punishment should (all things considered) be inflicted or that punishment is all that we should pursue in our dealings with offenders. Other concerns may sometimes override those of retributive justice and some form of victim-offender reconciliation might also be sought. Nevertheless, in the absence of other considerations, wrong-doing normally provides sufficient reasons for punishment (albeit not legal punishment, for which other conditions may also be necessary).

## 2. Hard Treatment as Imprisonment

But even if we can grant that the hard treatment that punishment involves can be justified, further questions of hardness must be addressed. Here I want to distinguish two related issues.

There is, first of all, a question about *how much* punishment a wrong-doer should receive. This is what usually engages punishment theorists who have progressed beyond: 'Why punish at all?' As with the prior question, answers to: 'How much?' have retributive/consequentialist disputation as their traditional backdrop. Thus they have focused on issues of proportionality, commensurability, equality, and *lex talionis*, on the one hand, and incapacitation, deterrence, rehabilitation, and the maximization of utility, on the other. As with the prior question, I would answer the latter in retributive terms. The severity of punishment, I would argue, should be proportionate to the wrong-doing that has justified punishment in the first place. Unless it is so answered, at least in part, I believe that the retributive claims made in response to the prior question will be undermined.[14]

---

[12] Punishment is not 'hard-wired' to wrong-doing. The 'ought' of deservedness is 'ought, *ceteris paribus*' not 'ought, all things considered'.

[13] Those who find it difficult to see this connection might compare disapprobation and censure with gratitude. Gratitude may sometimes be shown by expressions such as 'thank you'. But 'thank you' is frequently insufficient as an expression of gratitude. A willingness to do something proportionate for the other is also called for. For the argument in connection with gratitude, see Terrance McConnell, *Gratitude* (Philadelphia: Temple University Press, 1993).

[14] This of course is subject to all sorts of refinements. The notion of proportionality needs to be explicated; the issue of fixing penalty scales has to be addressed; the relevance of prior record must be

## The Hardness of Hard Treatment 277

A further question concerns *the form* that punishment will take. Although this question too can be approached via an engagement with retributive and consequentialist considerations, it does not do so quite as readily or exclusively. Here we might ask whether imprisonment, fines, community-based sanctions, confiscation, whipping and mutilation, demotions, and exclusions are appropriate ways of punishing or, since imprisonment is to be our focus, we might ask what what deprivations and impositions should be associated with it? Should those who are imprisoned also be required to perform hard labour, have their mail censored, be deprived of cigarettes, conjugal visits, access to the entertainment and news media, and so forth? It is with aspects of this latter question that I shall here be concerned.

### (a) The birth of the prison

We need to remember that imprisonment, as a method of punishment as distinct from a method of detention, is relatively modern.[15] That is not to impugn it, though some who have reflected on the inadequacies of the prison system have seen its recency as evidence of its merely pragmatic value and its failure to have deep roots in moral consciousness. Certainly the speed with which imprisonment superseded other traditional forms of legal punishment, and has come to represent a largely unquestioned resource of the criminal justice system,[16] might give us pause and lead us to wonder whether it is not too convenient a device for dealing with the complexities of human failure. In the USA, with its massive problems of urban crime (despite recent declines), imprisonment has reached crisis proportions, and many communities no longer know how to cope with the demand for prison resources.[17]

However, rather than denigrating imprisonment as an overly convenient ('out of sight, out of mind') response to criminality, we can also view it as a more humane alternative to forms of punishment that prevailed until the nineteenth

dealt with. Andrew von Hirsch has grappled with some of these questions in *Past or Future Crimes: Deservedness and Dangerousness in the Sentencing of Criminals* (New Brunswick, NJ Rutgers University Press: 1985); *Censure and Sanctions* (Oxford: Clarendon Press, 1993); and 'Desert and Previous Convictions in Sentencing', (1981) LXV *Minnesota Law Review* 591–634.

[15] For a good overview, see Norval Morris and David J. Rothman (eds.), *The Oxford History of the Prison: The Practice of Punishment in Western Society* (New York: Oxford University Press, 1995).

[16] That is putting it too strongly. In parts of Europe there is a strong anti-incarcerative tradition. See, for example, the articles included in the section on 'Alternatives to Punishment' in (1991) XXV, 3–4 *Israel Law Review* (Summer-Autumn) 681–791.

[17] In 1995, there were nearly 1.6 million people in American federal, state, and local prisons, a figure of 600 for every 100,000 people—up from 455/100,000 in 1991 (see 'Prison and Jail Inmates', *Bulletin*, Bureau of Justice Statistics, NCJ-161132 (August, 1996) ). The latter figure compared with 311 people in South Africa and 177 in Venezuela, the USA's closest rivals. In the USA, the rate for African-American and Hispanic males was 3,370/100,000, compared to 681/100,000 for black males in South Africa. In 1994, an additional 3.6 million people were under some form of correctional supervision (see 'Correctional Populations in the United States, 1994', *Executive Summary*, Bureau of Justice Statistics, NCJ-161559 (July, 1996) ).

century. In his graphic account of 'the birth of the prison', Michel Foucault made much of the way in which the various corporal punishments of the eighteenth century sought to reproduce in the body of the condemned person the heinousness of the crimes s/he had committed. The procession of public torture was a 'penal liturgy' through which the convicted person confessed to, accepted the punishment for, repented of, and represented the crimes for which s/he had been found guilty.[18] The move to imprisonment coincided with and to some extent expressed a humanitarian turn in nineteenth century penology, a belief that reduction of rights rather than infliction of pain represented a more acceptable— 'civilized'—response to wrong-doing. Furthermore, according to Foucault, it represented a dramatic change in the ends of punishment—movement away from a retributive and socially educative focus to one that was consequentialist and individually reformative.[19] The prison, particularly in the view of some of its earlier advocates, was to be disciplinary rather than merely punitive. What had previously been inflicted in public was now to be imposed in private.

Early reformatively-oriented prisons were austere institutions, designed, according to their advocates, to instil in their inmates habits of discipline and virtue. The austerity of prison life freed the prisoner from worldly distractions and enabled him to reflect on his deeds and to respond penitentially to them. But in addition the disciplines of prison life—its routines, religious requirements, and labour—were meant to transform the presumed idleness and social irresponsibility of the prisoner into more constructive social dispositions and behaviour.

Reality, of course, rarely matched theory, and many prisons remained little more than warehouses for the socially unacceptable. In time, there would be more insistent and sometimes effective calls and demands for improved conditions and a questioning of the presumption of the humaneness of prison life.

As Foucault properly recognizes, one of the motivating factors behind the ideology of 'imprisonment as punishment' was its constitution as a humane alternative to the corporal assaults that had until then prevailed. The emerging egalitarianism of the enlightenment tradition acknowledged both the rights and the moral responsibility of the offender, and shifted the locus of punishment from body to soul. The offender was seen as rational, redeemable, and potentially useful, and the State was not to squander its human resources. The deprivation of liberty had penitential and social possibilities that the corporal tradition had too often ignored. Despite some of the capital penal legislation of the late eighteenth and early nineteenth century, only in the more serious of cases did the offender actually forfeit all future claims to human society.

---

[18] Michel Foucault, *Discipline & Punish: The Birth of the Prison* (NY: Vintage, 1977), p. 47.

[19] That change was itself connected with a move towards secularization—a loosening church/State nexus diminished the State's role as executor of God's retributive justice. The State came to have independent ends of its own.

## (b) Prison reform

But what should determine the conditions under which the sentence is to be served? The imprisonment that presaged a more humanitarian approach to punishment did not deliver what it promised. Squalid conditions, solitariness or invasive and predatory behaviour, neglect, and abuse characterized many prisons of the eighteenth and early nineteenth centuries, and it was only through the diligent efforts of reformers such as John Howard in England and Elizabeth Fry in the USA that conditions began to improve. Not only were some of the more unsanitary and demoralizing features of prison life ameliorated, but constructive work and training programmes were introduced, prison personnel were gradually professionalized, and various health and legal services provided. Even so, the seclusion of prison life continued—and has continued—to make it possible for inmates to be housed under conditions that are frequently scandalous.

At the same time—at least in the USA, whose prison population is now over one and a half million, and in which illegal overcrowding of gaols and prisons is almost the norm—there are now insistent calls for the removal of many of the benefits that have been slowly exacted from a reluctant system. Imprisonment is expensive, and a crime-weary and tax-averse public has been responsive to calls to cut back on 'prison perks'.

At this point it is not my intention to deal with the specific exigencies of prison life, but to indicate some general considerations that might mediate decisions about the kinds of conditions under which a term of imprisonment is properly served. When I have outlined these, I will then turn to specific features of the prison experience.

## 3. Limiting the Hardness of Hard Treatment

I begin with two side-constraints of long standing. Both the English Bill of Rights of 1689 and Eighth Amendment (1789) to the US Constitution eschew punishments that are 'cruel and unusual'.[20] Although these constraints have recently occasioned considerable debate in the USA, much of it has been directed to the question whether capital punishment should be considered cruel and unusual.[21]

---

[20] More recent documents, such as the Universal Declaration of Human Rights (1948) and the European Convention for the Protection of Human Rights and Fundamental Freedoms (1953) outlaw 'cruel, inhuman or degrading' and 'inhuman and degrading' punishment, respectively, and it is the latter that provide the focus for A. Ashworth and E. Player in Ch. 10 of this book, above. I shall later come close to this position by suggesting that the categories of 'inhumane' and 'degrading' best capture the constraints to be placed on punishment/imprisonment. But see n. 47 below.

[21] *Furman* v. *Georgia*, 408 US 239 (1972). See Margaret Jane Radin, 'The Jurisprudence of Death: Evolving Standards for the Cruel and Unusual Punishments Clause', (1978) CXXVI, 5 *University of Pennsylvania Law Review* (May) 989–1064; Hugo Adam Bedau, 'Thinking of the Death Penalty as a Cruel and Unusual Punishment', (1985) XVII *University of California, Davis, Law Review* 873–925.

I shall leave aside the issue of capital punishment's constitutional status. Here I ask the more general questions: What would make punishment, and the conditions of imprisonment in particular, cruel and unusual? And what would make for the unacceptability of such punishment? Although cruelty and unusualness have usually been considered together, and were possibly intended by their constitutional draughtsmen to be interpreted as a complex unity, I believe that somewhat different considerations are suggested by each, and so I shall first discuss them separately.[22]

## (a)  Cruelty

As its philological origins in the Latin *cruor* (gore, spilled blood) suggest, cruelty has paradigmatically involved 'the wilful inflicting of physical pain on a weaker being in order to cause anguish and fear'.[23] But the focus has now shifted from physical pain to include suffering in general, and remarks no less than blows may be deemed cruel. There is still the vexed question whether the cruelty of acts is a function (subjectively) of the motives, intentions, or state of mind of the cruel agent or (objectively) of the necessity of the suffering or the point of view or experience of or injury to his/her victims,[24] or, perhaps more likely, either one or the other, depending on the circumstances. Even though the central cases of cruelty concern suffering that has been deliberately inflicted, there is some reason to think that both individuals and institutions can operate cruelly from lack of sensitivity no less than from design.[25]

The wrongness of deliberate cruelty is almost foundational. That is, causing

---

[22] There has been a tendency in Eighth Amendment jurisprudence to see the phrase 'cruel and unusual' as something like the phrase 'null and void', a unitary and intensifying designation rather than as a dual disqualification. Thus, in relation to the contribution made by 'unusual', Justice Brennan remarked: 'The question, in any event, is of minor significance; this Court has never attempted to explicate the meaning of the Clause simply by parsing its words' (*Furman* v. *Georgia*, 408 US 238, at 276 n. 20 (1972) ). See the discussion in Bedau, 'Thinking of the Death Penalty as a Cruel and Unusual Punishment', (1985), n. 21 above, pp. 880–3. However, Justice Scalia assumed a distinction between them when speaking for the Court in *Harmelin* v. *Michigan*, 111 S. Ct. 2680, 2686–87, 2701 (1991). And in the 1776 Maryland Bill of Rights, 1776 Constitution of North Carolina, and 1780 Massachusetts and 1784 New Hampshire Declarations of Rights, 'cruel' and 'unusual' are disjunctively rather than conjunctively related. For a listing of conjunctive and disjunctive references, see Peter Mathis Spett, 'Confounding the Gradations of Iniquity: An Analysis of Eighth Amendment Jurisprudence in *Harmelin* v. *Michigan*', (1992) XXIV, 1 *Columbia Human Rights Law Review* (Winter) 228–9 n. 126. I shall suggest later that different (albeit related) considerations might well be indicated by the two terms.

[23] Judith Shklar, *Ordinary Vices* (Cambridge, MA: Belknap Press of Harvard University Press, 1984), p. 8.

[24] Until recently, American courts expected serious injury to be involved as an objective indicator of cruelty. However, in a fairly recent decision it was held that cruelty could be established in the absence of 'significant' injury, at least as long as the other 'objective' elements were present—i.e. the need for the force, the degree of force in relation to the need, and the perceived threat to the officer at the time. See *Hudson* v. *McMillian*, 112 S.Ct. 995, at 999 (1992). In this case, it was allowed that where the force was applied 'maliciously and sadistically', the charge of cruelty could be sustained.

[25] I will suggest, however, that if we look at the wider category, inhumaneness, of which cruelty is a type, the notion of neglectful suffering is more easily accommodated.

## The Hardness of Hard Treatment                                   281

suffering to another is an evil that stands in need of justifying reasons, and, when suffering is inflicted with a view to the hurt that is involved (whether or not pleasure is taken in inflicting it), justifying reasons are disavowed.[26] Infliction of suffering for the sake of proportionate good may be justified, but that is usually because such suffering is seen as part of an organic whole (as in retribution)[27] or as an unfortunate—though presumably necessary—means to some worthwhile end.

In jurisprudential discussion, objective approaches have led to the characterization of *excessive* or *disproportionate* punishments as cruel. Somewhat different ideas tend to be conveyed by each. Excessiveness looks to some end that is being pursued or sought. Disproportionality looks back to the offence for which the suffering is imposed. An excessive punishment will cause more suffering than is necessary to deter, rehabilitate, or achieve whatever other socially acceptable goals are being sought. A disproportionate penalty will be one that is out of keeping with the seriousness of the offence for which it is imposed.[28] So-called draconian penalties are disproportionate. I am inclined to give moral priority to disproportionateness in deciding whether to characterize a punishment as cruel rather than simply unnecessary. That is, a penalty that is more severe than is necessary to rehabilitate will not be cruel if it is not disproportionate to the offence for which it is inflicted, whereas a penalty that is disproportionate to the offence but not more severe than is necessary to rehabilitate or deter might well be considered cruel.[29]

Cruelty to a sentient being is bad enough. Cruelty to a rational sentient being is worse, because it is dehumanizing. As is also the case with coercion, one of the manifest effects of suffering—at least of certain types and degrees of suffering[30]— is to shift what moves us to act from a consideration of the merits of the case to whatever will relieve our situation. Such suffering tends to undermine that which constitutes our human distinctiveness, our capacity for appraisal.[31] Our

[26] The suffering sanctioned by retributive theory is for wrong-doing and intended to express reprobation rather than the desire to cause suffering. Nevertheless, Hugo Bedau seriously considers the possibility of justified cruelty if the stakes are high enough ('Thinking of the Death Penalty as Cruel and Unusual Punishment', (1985), n. 21 above, pp. 886–9).

[27] The idea of an organic whole goes back to Plato (presuming that the *Greater Hippias* is a Platonic dialogue), but is discussed at length by G. E. Moore in *Principia Ethica* (Cambridge University Press, 1903), pp. 27–36.

[28] In the legal discussion, the disproportionality condition can be violated even if the punishment is not particularly onerous. Thus it would violate the Eighth Amendment were a person to be sentenced to just one day in prison for the 'crime' of having a cold (*Robinson* v. *California*, 370 US 660, at 667 (1962) ). Thus the legal and moral notions of what constitutes 'cruelty' may diverge.

[29] However, teleologically justified suffering *will* be characterizable as cruel if it is wilfully excessive: the dentist who drills without offering an anaesthetic.

[30] The qualification is important. Suffering may also 'bring us to our senses', a function which may have deep roots in the physiological value that pain has as a warning mechanism.

[31] I do not, of course, want to deny that (cruelly inflicted) suffering may provide a vehicle through which we may emerge ennobled. However it is precisely because suffering threatens our humanity that our ability to rise above it is ennobling. The latter possibility can hardly constitute a justification for inflicting it.

282                              *John Kleinig*

autonomy is expressed in our ability to reflect on options and to make choices based on a consideration of those options. Cruelty involves the infliction of a suffering that threatens to overwhelm our capacity to perform these basic operations. It tends to reduce us to the level of what we may characterize as animality—responsiveness primarily to the promptings of pleasure or pain. Actually, it may be worse than that, since both physical and mental cruelty often exacerbate suffering through an exploitation of the imaginative possibilities of our human consciousness.[32]

The potential for cruelty is endemic to prison society. The imbalance of power, and the environment of disgrace in which prisoners must live, create opportunities—even temptations—for the perpetration of cruelties both physical and mental. The potential for deprivations and requirements that cause suffering is enormous, and if deprivations and impositions are forced upon inmates simply or even primarily because of the suffering they will cause, or if they are disproportionate to the occasioning offence, some measure of cruelty will almost certainly be involved. Even more likely, deprivations that are imposed without regard to the suffering they will cause will likely be seen as cruel or at least inhumane. Unless there has been some conscious and conscientious trading off or balancing of suffering against some other essential and significant end (such as security or the demands of communal living) to be achieved at the cost of the deprivation or imposition, the charge of cruelty will be hard to defeat.

Cruelty in prisons may attach to the *kind* of additional deprivations involved, the *amount* of imprisonment, or the *procedures* that surround the ordering of prison experience. Extended periods of solitary confinement, unless they can be justified for security reasons, may well be cruel, since they deprive the individual of a basic human need, social engagement.[33] A legal provision such as the 'three strikes law' could also be considered cruel by virtue of its disproportionateness.[34] And strip search practices that have little regard for the sensitivities of inmates might also be thought cruel.[35]

The evil of cruelty in punishment should be calculated not only by reference to

[32] Physical torture is an almost exclusively human form of cruelty, especially in its more exquisite manifestations. Consider also the cases of a parent being forced to watch the torture of a child or of a prisoner who has a manuscript on which he has been labouring confiscated and burned before his eyes.
[33] In the court cases that have linked prison deprivations with Eighth Amendment interests, the denial of any or adequate medical treatment to prisoners has been seen as cruel, as has indifference to shocking prison conditions. See *Estelle* v. *Gamble*, 429 US 97, at 104 (1976); *Holt* v. *Sarver*, 309 F. Supp. 362, at 372–3 (E. D. Ark. 1970), *affirmed* 442 F.2d 304 (8th Cir. 1971).
[34] See, for example, Mark W. Owens, 'California's Three Strikes Law: Desperate Times Require Desperate Measures—But Will it Work?' (1995) XXVI, 3 *Pacific Law Journal* (April), 881–919. The California initiative was not novel. Similar penalties for recidivism had been previously imposed and upheld—see, for example, the Texas case, *Rummel* v. *Estelle*, 445 US 263 (1980).
[35] See Tracy McMath, 'Do Prison Inmates Retain Any Fourth Amendment Protection from Body Cavity Searches?' (1987) LVI *University of Cincinnati Law Review* 739–55. However, see *Payton* v. *Vaughn*, 798 F.2d 258, at 261–2 (E.D. Pa. 1992), where 'embarrassment' was held not to be sufficient to establish a claim to cruel and unusual treatment. See, further, *Jordan* v. *Gardner*, 986 F.2d 1521, at 1526–7 (9th Cir. 1993), where a cross-gender, clothed body search was held to be both 'unnecessary' for security and 'without penological justification'.

what it is for its victims, but should also have some regard to the effect that cruelty has on those who inflict it. Although some warped personalities will enjoy the infliction of suffering on others, most of those who act cruelly will need to anaesthetize themselves against the suffering they cause. And a society that fails to deal with cruelty will probably also need to develop mechanisms to desensitize itself to suffering. In so doing, it will diminish itself.[36]

## (b) Unusualness

It may seem odd to reject punishment simply because it is 'unusual'. After all, what is unusual may be no more than what falls outside some statistical norm, and there is nothing normatively significant in that.[37] In the case of punishment, however, even statistical abnormality may be inherently problematic. For in cases in which impositions are novel, we are likely to lack assurance that what is done will not also constitute an affront to human dignity: 'frequency of use furnishes evidence of wide acceptability, and . . . the very fact of regular use diminishes the insult'.[38] That is not quite right, though it does gesture towards the US Supreme Court's claim that the constitutional proscription of cruel and unusual punishment 'must draw its meaning from the evolving standards of decency that mark the progress of a maturing society'.[39] As it turns out, what are characterized as unusual punishments tend to be not only statistically but also normatively abnormal. They generally distinguish in a way that humiliates. In the ongoing debate, such punishments have included bodily mutilation, branding, and certain forms of corporal punishment, and their effect has been not only to disgrace wrong-doers but also to bring them into contempt.[40]

---

[36] The jurisprudence of cruelty goes further than I do here. In *Robinson* v. *California*, a punishment was deemed to fail the Eighth Amendment test because it was prescribed for what the court deemed a 'chronic condition' or 'status' rather than some voluntary act (370 US 660, at 665–6 (1962) ). Perhaps a kind of disproportionality is involved, though the failure seems more radical than that. Also, in the death penalty cases, punishment has been deemed cruel if the rationale for selecting those on whom it has been imposed is considered arbitrary and capricious. See *Furman* v. *Georgia*, 408 US 238 (1976).

[37] Thus, in *Trop* v. *Dulles*, Chief Justice Warren, speaking for the Court, stated that 'unusual' added nothing to the Eighth Amendment clause besides signifying 'something different from that which is generally done' (356 US 86, at 100–1 n. 32 (1958) ).

[38] Laurence H. Tribe, *American Constitutional Law* (Mineola, NY: Foundation Press, 1978), p. 917.

[39] *Trop* v. *Dulles*, 356 US 86, at 101 (1958) (Warren CJ). In *Weems*, the unusualness, as well as the cruelty, of the *cadena temporal*, was a factor. It was noted that the punishment was 'unusual in its character',—that 'it has no fellow in American legislation' and 'comes under the condemnation of the bill of rights, both on account of [its] degree and kind' (*Weems* v. *US*, 217 US 349, at 377 (1910) ). However, there is nothing conceptually to prevent the novelty of a punishment from being a peculiarly apt and restorative imposition.

[40] The issue of the 'surgical and chemical castration' of persistent sex offenders has proven more controversial. See William L. Baker, 'Castration of the Male Sex Offender: A Legally Impermissible Alternative', (1984) XXX, 2 *Loyola Law Review* (Spring) 37–399; Pamela K. Hicks, 'Castration of Sexual Offenders: Legal and Ethical Issues', (1993) XIV, 4 *Journal of Legal Medicine* (December) 641–67; Kenneth B. Fromson, 'Beyond an Eye for an Eye: Castration as an Alternative Sentencing

284                                *John Kleinig*

Avishai Margalit has recently argued that a decent society, one to which he believes we should aspire, is characterized by institutions that do not humiliate people.[41] On his account, humiliation has two dimensions—the rejection of a person from the human commonwealth and the loss of basic control. The former provides a sound reason for a person to consider his or her self-respect to be injured, and the latter is the effect of diminished self-respect. It is Margalit's task to show how certain social set-ups that reject the specific forms of life in which people express their humanity may effect such humiliation.

It is clear how a prison system may effect the humiliation of its inmates.[42] Even though prisoners are rightly disgraced by their imprisonment, and are prevented from exercising some of the rights of citizenship, they should still be permitted to retain the respect and dignity that is the due of every human being. Indeed, as Chief Justice Warren noted, 'the basic concept underlying the Eighth Amendment is nothing less than the dignity of man'.[43] A non-humiliating prison system will not reject prisoners from the human commonwealth by treating them as though they have forfeited the right of personhood—and thus may be exposed or presented in ways that would be expected to detract from their self-recognition as responsible and redeemable beings. Nor will it treat prisoners in ways that remove from them those elements of control that are fundamental to their standing as rational and sensitive beings. Such was part of the case against torture; but it could apply equally to punishments that have the effect of transforming a person's capabilities (as in mutilation) or of exposing a person to ongoing contempt (as with branding). We might want to say much the same about the use of chain gangs and certain kinds of prison garb, even though, unlike mutilation and branding, their effects need not be permanent. Chain gangs are often operated in public view, and the chaining together of prisoners, like beasts of burden, is designed to elicit contempt and create a sense of belittlement. Striped prison garb, too, has long associations that 'mark one out' as contemptible and wretched.[44]

Other features of prison life might also be seen as humiliating. In the early case of *Weems* v. *US*, a Philippine statute prescribing the penalty of *cadena temporal* was ruled unconstitutional in the case of an official who had made a false

Measure', (1994) XI, 2 *New York Law School Journal of Human Rights* (Spring) 311–37; Daniel L. Icenogle, 'Sentencing Male Sex Offenders to the Use of Biological Treatments: A Constitutional Analysis', (1994) XV, 2 *Journal of Legal Medicine* (June) 279–304.

[41] Avishai Margalit, *The Decent Society*, trans. Naomi Goldblum (Cambridge, MA: Harvard University Press, 1996). Margalit distinguishes this from a civilized society, in which *individual members* do not humiliate one another, and both from a *just* society.

[42] In the late 1960s, Chief Judge Henley spoke of imprisonment within the Arkansas Penitentiary as amounting to 'banishment from civilized society' (*Holt* v. *Sarver*, 309 F. Supp. 362, at 381 (E.D. Ark. 1970), *affirmed*, 442 F.2d 304 (8th Cir. 1971) ). I am of course prescinding from the question whether imprisonment itself may involve humiliation. Although I sidestep the question, I do not want to dismiss it. See the concluding section 6 below.

[43] *Trop* v. *Dulles*, 356 U.S. 86, at 100 (1958).

[44] It is not the uniformity of garb as such, but the distinctiveness and associations of certain kinds of garb that is the problem here. Compare the yellow stars that Jews were required to wear in National Socialist Germany.

statement in a public record. Not only had he been sentenced to an inordinately long time in prison (15 years), but also under conditions that were seen as humiliating. The penalty required that he be chained from the wrist to the ankles, do 'hard and painful labor', receive no outside assistance, be under surveillance for life, be disqualified forever from public office, and lose various rights—'of parental authority, guardianship of person or property, participation in the family council, marital authority, the administration of property, . . . to dispose of his own property by acts *inter vivos*', to vote, and to receive retirement pay.[45] Stripped not only of liberty, the official was also stripped of the conditions of self-respect.

I have focused on cruel and unusual punishment because it provides a useful starting point for discussion of the limits to hard treatment. But the category—or categories—of cruel and unusual can be seen as specifying more general constraints that might be placed on hard treatment. Punishment that is cruel is more generally and appropriately characterized as *inhumane*.[46] And punishment that is unusual might be seen more generally as *degrading*. This is much closer to the terminology of contemporary statements of the side-constraints on the conditions of confinement.

### (c) Inhumaneness

Generally we treat people inhumanely when we disregard their sensibilities as human beings.[47] More precisely, our inhumaneness is constituted by our failure to have an appropriate concern about the suffering that we cause them. If cruelty most often involves the deliberate infliction of suffering for the sake of the hurt involved, inhumanity toward others may just as often be registered by an indifference to suffering that is being caused. The inhumane may simply lack the empathy that enables them to see how the suffering that they cause to others is experienced by those others.[48]

The inhumane treatment of prisoners may be as much a matter of neglect as of deliberate policy. Overcrowded and vandalized prison facilities, an inadequate low calorie diet, lack of oversight that allows predatory behaviour to flourish,

---

[45] *Weems* v. *US*, 217 US 349, at 364–5 (1910).

[46] A child may be cruel without being inhumane, since its moral sensibilities have not yet been developed. Cruelty may be shown to animals, but inhumaneness is generally shown toward those with human feelings.

[47] It is the focus on sensibilities that distinguishes treatment that is inhumane from that which is inhuman: inhuman treatment is treatment that is not fit for or appropriate to human beings; there is no (explicit) implication about the way in which it affects the sensibilities of those on whom it is imposed. Clearly, though, the two notions are very close.

[48] Michael Davis has attempted to make inhumaneness a function of the *shock* that a particular treatment causes to our sensibilities, rather than the *disregard* for suffering that is shown by those who have caused it. For him no act is intrinsically inhumane, and judgements of inhumaneness will appropriately differ from society to society. This, I believe, confuses the *concept* of inhumaneness with a particular *conception* of inhumaneness. See his 'The Death Penalty, Civilization, and Inhumaneness', (1990) XVI, 2 *Social Theory and Practice* (Summer) 249–51.

unsanitary conditions that go unrectified, and an atmosphere of uncertainty and dread—all contribute to an environment that is properly describable as inhumane.

Humaneness, on the other hand, recognizes individuality and the varied ways in which people may suffer, and seeks to preserve them from suffering that is inappropriate to their situation.[49] Treating people humanely does not mean treating them softly or even subjecting them to conditions that are less than spartan. Hard treatment may be onerous, tiring, difficult, vigorous, austere, and rigorous without being inhumane. The athletics coach and military sergeant may both subject their charges to rigorous activity that aches and fatigues, but it is not thereby inhumane. It might be, of course, if the exercises are not carefully modulated and well suited to the essential ends of such activity—game- or battle-fitness.

The US Supreme Court debate is notable for the reluctance that the justices have shown to involve themselves in prison conditions. Historically, the Court took the view that it was not part of its task to supervise prison conditions. In part this reflected a belief in the separation of powers, the Courts' lack of expertise, and a policy of federalism.[50] But by the 1970s this had changed, and a range of prison conditions had been brought within the ambit of the Eighth and other Amendments.[51] However, it did not take too long for an increasingly conservative Court to rein in its involvement with the conditions of incarceration. A phrase used in *Estelle*—'deliberate indifference'—became the precondition for establishing an Eighth Amendment case where inhumane or otherwise degrading conditions were experienced by prisoners.[52] The inhumaneness of the conditions was not itself sufficient.[53]

---

[49] This might be a reason for concessions—particularly in regard to prison conditions—for those who are sickly or very old. See Nancy Neveloff Dubler, 'Depriving Prisoners of Medical Care: A "Cruel and Unusual" Punishment', (1979) *Hastings Center Report* (October) 7–10; Cristina J. Perierra, 'Do the Crime, Do the Time: Should Elderly Criminals Receive Proportionate Sentences?' (1995) XIX, 2 *Nova Law Review* (Winter) 793–819.

[50] See Note, 'Beyond the Ken of the Courts: A Critique of Judicial Refusal to Review the Complaints of Convicts', (1963) LXXII, 3 *Yale Law Journal* (January) 506–58. The courts took the view that the intention of the Eighth Amendment was to exclude certain kinds of penalties—torture, crucifixion, burial alive, burning at the stake, boiling in oil, live disembowelment, public dissection, and so on. See *Wilkerson v. Utah*, 99 US 130, at 136 (1879); *In re Kemmler*, 136 US 436, at 446–7 (1890). Once the Eighth Amendment was applied to the states during the years of the Warren Court, it was probably only a matter of time before it would be directed to prison conditions.

[51] See Michael S. Feldberg, Comment, 'Confronting the Conditions of Confinement: An Expanded Role for Courts in Prison Reform', (1977) XII, 2 *Harvard Civil Rights—Civil Liberties Law Review* (Spring) 367–404.

[52] *Estelle v. Gamble*, 429 US 97, at 105–6 (1976). An attempt to unpack the phrase 'deliberate indifference' was made in *Farmer v. Brennan*, 114 S. Ct. 1970 (1994), where Justice Souter, writing for the Court, interpreted it in the familiar criminal law terms of subjective recklessness (*ibid*, at 1979–80). The use of this subjective standard is criticized in Melvin Gutterman, 'The Contours of Eighth Amendment Prison Jurisprudence: Conditions of Confinement', (1995) XLVIII *SMU Law Review* 395–9.

[53] In cases in which actions are taken to restore order, a stronger subjective standard has been applied—whether, in causing suffering, prison officials acted 'maliciously and sadistically for the purpose of causing harm' (*Whitely v. Albers*, 475 US 312, at 321 (1986), quoting *Johnson v. Glick*, 481

## (d) Degradingness

To degrade another is to detract from the other's dignity as a human being. Just as pornography is often said to degrade women by characterizing them in ways that detract from their rationality and autonomy, representationally reducing them to the status of sexual playthings,[54] what is sometimes done to prisoners is also said to be degrading insofar as it treats them as and reduces them to less than rational, autonomous beings. When the degradation of prisoners occurs, however, it is not simply representational, but actual. Prisoners who are degraded have been portrayed or forced to act in ways that are demeaning of their status as humans. What Kant demanded of capital punishment might be demanded of punishment generally, namely, that it be 'kept entirely free from any maltreatment that would make an abomination of the humanity residing in the person suffering it'.[55]

Although the notion of a universal human dignity probably has its origins in Stoic and Judaeo-Christian egalitarianism, in post-Enlightenment thought it has come to be ascribed to people in virtue of their capacities as rational beings. The capacity to frame for oneself the choices one makes, the paths one treads, and the goals one pursues is the foundation for human dignity. As well as something that one possesses as a result of one's standing as a human being, dignity may also be given behavioural expression as a kind of manifest bearing. Those who speak of 'dying with dignity' or of 'carrying oneself with dignity' have in mind not simply a standing but a manifest control over the terms of one's life (or death). Margalit speaks of such dignity as 'the external aspect of self-respect'.[56]

On the account of dignity just given, imprisonment may seem to be inherently undignified. For the choices of a prisoner are severely constrained, and prisoners manifestly lack control over the terms of their lives. But though I believe that the conditions of a person's confinement may well be undignifying, I doubt whether imprisonment as such can be seen in that way. The person who has committed a crime has chosen to risk the consequences of law-breaking, and thus the deprivation of some liberty. Moreover, though choices within a prison environment are constrained, they need not be so constrained that the prisoners are deprived of the kinds of choices that manifest their human standing and

---

F.2d 1028, at 1033 (2nd Cir.), *cert. denied*, 414 US 1033 (1973) ). As noted above (n. 24 above), this latter standard has now been extended to other interpersonal encounters between prison officers and inmates. In *Hudson* v. *McMillian*, Justice Sandra Day O'Connor wrote that 'to deny, as the dissent does, the difference between punching a prisoner in the face and serving him unappetizing food is to ignore the "concepts of dignity, civilized standards, humanity, and decency" that animate the Eighth Amendment' (112 S. Ct. 995, at 1000 (1992) ).

[54] I here prescind from a consideration of the accuracy of this claim. For critical discussion, see Alan Soble, 'Pornography: Defamation and the Endorsement of Degradation', (1985) XI, 1 *Social Theory and Practice* (Spring) 61–87.

[55] Kant, *The Metaphysical Elements of Justice* (1797), trans. John Ladd (Indianapolis: Bobbs-Merrill, 1965), p. 102.

[56] *The Decent Society* (1996), n. 41 above, p. 51.

self-respect. We can, indeed, distinguish prison conditions and demands that undermine dignity from those that do not. A prisoner who is expected to get up at a certain hour each morning is not deprived of dignity, whereas a prisoner who is expected to forgo the expression of his political opinions or religious observances in exchange for basic needs (for example, sanitary conditions or association with others) is being expected to sacrifice his dignity.

As part of their dignity, prisoners retain their human rights, albeit in a somewhat circumscribed form. They should be free to worship should they choose, they should be free to express their opinions on various matters, they should be free to have access to the courts, and so on. Their human rights do not evaporate on conviction—they are not 'forfeited'—though to a degree their exercise may be constrained.

A person who acts with dignity is one who possesses self-respect. The servile lack self-respect. Servility is undignified. Even though the servile may possess dignity by virtue of their status, they lack the dignity of manifest control over the way in which they deal with their circumstances. They deny in themselves the status that others should accord them. We acknowledge the dignity of others by according them respect. That is, we acknowledge them as centres of sensibility and rationality, with claims to autonomy that are to be recognized. When we treat others as ends and not merely as means to ends of our own, we show respect for them. When we avoid interfering with their non-invasive choices we show respect for them.

With the degradation of others, there often goes not only disrespect but also, on the part of those degraded, a lack of self-respect. The relation is causal rather than conceptual. To treat others as though they lack claims to our respect, to treat them as tools or playthings, may lead them to have a diminished sense of their own worth, dignity, and rights.

In distinguishing inhumaneness and degradingness as two general constraints on hard treatment, I have not wanted to suggest that they are unrelated. Treatment that is inhumane tends to be degrading, and that which degrades is often inhumane.

## 4. Positive Directions

If hard treatment ought to be bounded on the one side by negative constraints such as inhumaneness and degradingness, it ought also to be shaped on the other side by certain positive ends. Imprisonment is not just proportionate hard treatment, to be imposed without any consideration of what it may and ought to be seeking to accomplish.

We can appreciate the forward-looking dimension of punishment by recognizing that of any proposed punishment it is legitimate to ask: 'Who are *you* to punish?' For even if punishment is deserved and, moreover, ought to be inflicted, it does not follow that just anyone may inflict it. Some standing or authority to punish needs to be established and, as with most authority, the authority to punish is partially justified in terms of ends that it is set up to achieve.[57]

In the case of imprisonment, we are concerned with *legal* punishment, with those punishments that are mandated by the State. And thus we might reasonably ask: What business does the State have in claiming for itself the authority to punish? More particularly, what business does the State have in employing *imprisonment* as a form of punishment? These are large questions, too large to be dealt with at any length here, but they indicate a context within which questions about the positive framing of hard treatment need to be discussed.

Put crudely, if the purposes of State power—and therefore the boundaries of State authority—are essentially negative, if the State's mandate stretches no further than the protection of Lockean rights, then the positive function of punitive hard treatment will be limited to just retaliation against those who have breached those rights. Imprisonment as a particular form of hard treatment might have additional preventive value in its incapacitation and deterrence of those who have so offended. But if, on the other hand, State power is construed in more perfectionist terms, as a means through which a thick conception of the good is realized, then punitive hard treatment will have much more moralistic overtones. The aim of imprisonment will be to educate, reform, and civilize. An acceptable understanding probably lies somewhere between these extremes. A liberal State will seek to sustain a plurality of goods by fostering a communally sensitive autonomy in which individuality may flourish. Imprisonment will be individualized, and will attempt to establish or reinforce in the anti-social an appreciation of the value of constraints in social life and the discipline and knowledge necessary to benefit from and contribute to it.[58]

This is not the place to argue for a particular role for State power. Were I to do so, however, I would wish to defend a conception of State authority that functioned to facilitate personal growth in a context of equal opportunity. In different societies this would manifest itself in different ways. In industrialized, and primarily capitalist societies, it would be the function of the State not only to encourage the development of individual enterprise, but to encourage it in such a way that the gap between the successful and others did not become so great that relations between the two became unconscionably exploitative, manipulative, or oppressive.

It does not require too hard a look at the current prison population to see that a vastly disproportionate number of prisoners come from the disadvantaged

---

[57] In this way, I seek to accommodate the consequentialist dimension of punishment. Although (*pace* von Hirsch, *Censure and Sanctions*, (1993), n. 14 above, p. 12) I believe that retributive considerations are themselves sufficient to justify the hard treatment that is punishment, I claim that justifying the *authority* to impose that punishment may require recourse to consequentialist considerations. See also *Desert and Punishment*, Ch. 4; 'Punishment and Moral Seriousness' (1991), n. 8 above, Sect. VIII.

[58] cf.: 'Having chosen to use imprisonment as a form of punishment, a state must ensure that the conditions of its prisons comport with the "contemporary standards of decency" required by the Eighth Amendment' (*Wilson* v. *Seiter*, 501 US 294, at 311 (1991) (White J concurring) ).

social and economic strata of society. Of course, various explanations for this are possible. Some will focus exclusively on individual deficiencies, others on social handicap. Probably neither is exclusively correct. We are neither independent of our environments nor mere expressions of them. A just social order will be concerned to moderate social disadvantage in ways that diminish the pressure exerted by an unfavourable background. Imprisonment, insofar as it is seen as an appropriate penalty for those who are convicted of crimes, ought to include among its initiatives programmes and services that will assist the incarcerated to live in a more social and personally productive manner. Even inmates who are never to be released might learn, from within the confines of their existence, to make something positively valuable of themselves, even to the extent of making a social contribution.[59]

## 5. PRISON PRACTICE

The foregoing discussion has of necessity been very general, and I will now attempt to indicate how the various factors I have been discussing might bear on some prison conditions.

Whatever else imprisonment involves, it involves a deprivation of 'liberty'. The liberty of which one is deprived is first and foremost freedom of movement. The prisoner is confined to a cell, cell block, or correctional facility for a relatively determinate period of time. But that is not all, for being imprisoned is not like being under house arrest. Prisons are institutions, and total institutions at that. Not only is freedom of movement controlled, but so too are many of the conditions of existence. What is available by way of amenities, what is permitted by way of daily routines, and what access to the larger social world is allowed, is under the control and to some extent subject to the discretion of prison authorities. Each of these dimensions of prison life may be scrutinized by reference to the considerations advanced in sections 3 and 4.[60]

---

[59] Though the incarcerated are denied the ability to move freely within the larger society, they have not thereby been cast out of the human commonwealth; nor need they be denied access to or intercourse with that larger society. There is much to be said for using prison time as an opportunity to create more productive bonds with society, whether this be through artistic and/or literary activity, or through socially useful commercial enterprises. Tragically, support for the latter is often the first thing to go when budgets get tight. It is as though hard time cannot also be productive time.

[60] In the USA, when the courts began intervening in state prisons they sought not only to remove conditions that were deemed cruel and unusual (or in other ways violative of constitutional protections), but also to impose certain minimum positive conditions that would ensure appropriate living conditions and provide particular educational, vocational, and recreational opportunities. For an early but detailed example, see *Pugh* v. *Locke*, 406 F. Supp. 318, at 332–4 (M.D. Ala 1976), *affirmed sub nom. Newman* v. *Alabama*, 559 F.2d 283 (5th Cir. 1977), *certiorari granted in part and reviewed in part sub nom. Alabama* v. *Pugh*, 438 US 781 (1978), *certiorari denied*, 438 US 915 (1978). For an informative review, see Ira P. Robbins and Michael B. Buser, 'Punitive Conditions of Prison Confinement: An Analysis of Pugh v. Locke and Federal Court Supervision of State Penal Administration Under the Eighth Amendment', (1977) XXIX *Stanford Law Review* 893–930 .

## The Hardness of Hard Treatment 291

### (a) Space and environment

Prison life is literally confined. Although—depending on the inmate's offence and demeanour—a prisoner may be allowed to leave his/her cell for a limited period each day, much of his/her life will be spent in a cell equipped with basic necessities—bed, toilet, wash basin, and maybe a few other amenities. But a cell may be too small, too exposed, too hazardous, and too uncomfortable to be humane. Although punishment properly justifies the (temporary) loss of civil rights, one does not thereby forfeit one's humanity, and so there ought to be sufficient space to allow certain basic activities to take place—standing up, walking round, sitting, lying down—and the cell environment should allow for at least a modicum of privacy (compatible with the need for security) and well-being.[61]

In recent times there has been a good deal of controversy over prison smoking policies. As those in the wider society have begun insisting upon smoke-free environments, it has been contended that uncontrolled smoking in prisons should be seen not only as (inescapably) unpleasant for some inmates, but also as unhealthy. It has even been successfully argued that the unwilling exposure to cigarette smoke constitutes cruel and unusual punishment.[62]

Another aggravation of the prison environment, though less seriously taken, is the level of noise that is permitted. The need for security encourages the development of prison space that not only permits the passage of noise from one area to another but, because of the materials used in its construction, ensures that a great deal of noise will be created. Should prisoners be subjected to a noise level that

---

[61] In *Rhodes* v. *Chapman*, the issue of double celling was considered. The Court took the view, expressed by Justice Powell, that there was no constitutional mandate for 'comfortable prisons', and, given other facts about the prison in question, held that double celling *per se* did not contravene the requirements of the Eighth Amendment (452 US 337, at 349 (1981) ). However, Justice Brennan, in a dissenting opinion in which he argued that courts should examine the 'totality of conditions', recognizing their 'cumulative impact', stated that 'The court must examine the effect upon inmates of the condition of the physical plant (lighting, heat, plumbing, ventilation, living space, noise levels, recreation space); sanitation (control of vermin and insects, food preparation, medical facilities, lavatories and showers, clean places for eating, sleeping, and working); safety (protection from violent, deranged, or diseased inmates, fire protection, emergency evacuation); inmate needs and services (clothing, nutrition, bedding, medical, dental, and mental health care, visitation time, exercise and recreation, educational and rehabilitative programming); and staffing (trained and adequate guards and other staff, avoidance of placing inmates in positions of authority over other inmates)' (*ibid*, at 363). And Justice Marshall, also in dissent, noted that most of the prisoners were serving lengthy sentences and that double celling had a debilitating effect on prisoners (*ibid*, at 370). A decade later in *Wilson* v. *Seiter*, Justice Scalia, writing for the majority, argued that claims of a cumulative effect could be sustained only when the conditions 'have a mutually reinforcing effect . . . for example, a low cell temperature at night combined with a failure to issue blankets' (501 US 294, at 304 (1991) ).

[62] In *Helling* v. *McKinney*, 113 S.Ct. 2475 (1993). See Lisa Gizzi, 'Smoking in the Cell Block: Cruel and Unusual Punishment?' (1994) XLIII, 3 *American University Law Review* (Spring) 1091–134; Lana H. Schwartzman, 'Constitutional Law—Eighth Amendment—Involuntary Exposure to Secondhand Smoke in Prison Supports a Valid Cruel and Unusual Punishment Claim if the Risk to One's Health is Unreasonable and Prison Officials are Indifferent to that Risk', (1994) XXV, 1 *Seton Hall Law Review* (Winter) 314–52. There is, however, some evidence of increased violence (from frustration) as prison environments change into non-smoking ones. See Matthew C. Leone, Patrick T. Kinkade, and Mark Covington, 'To Smoke or Not to Smoke: The Experience of a Nevada Jail', (1996) *American Jails* (January/February) 46–52.

most people on the outside would find intolerable? Or is there some reason to consider the noise level of many prisons intolerable, and in need of some moderation? Why should noise that would probably justify a complaint in an apartment house be treated with indifference in a prison setting?

Privacy and security will always be in tension within the prison setting. The value of privacy lies in its recognition of moral space, the need for people to define the terms of their self-presentation. But the recognition of privacy also creates opportunities for activities that will compromise prison security. It is necessary that invasions of inmate privacy be restricted to those for which a security justification can be *convincingly* provided, and that they be implemented in a manner that does not unnecessarily expose inmates to cruel or demeaning treatment. Strip (or even clothed) searches, a staple of prison life, should be conducted with the same constraint, professionalism, and detachment as a gynaecological or medical examination.[63]

One of the most serious problems currently confronting penal institutions in the USA and elsewhere is that of overcrowding. Although there exist (on paper) strict legal requirements regarding space allocations for each prisoner, a lack of coordination between the court and prison system, political intransigence, and reluctance to spend sufficient additional public monies on prison facilities (or alternatives thereto), have led to overcrowding in at least 50 per cent of American prisons. In some cases the overcrowding has reached crisis proportions, and along with this there have come a set of additional problems—severe discontent, an increase in prisoner-on-prisoner abuses, and the drying-up of already inadequate resources for vocational and rehabilitative programmes.

Because prisons are supported by public monies, it is only reasonable that citizens have some say in the way those monies are spent. However, a public that is supportive of increased use of imprisonment and unwilling to pay for the expansion of facilities to carry out its will must face a choice. There is a set of minimum conditions that must be met if prisons are not to be inhumane institutions, and there are facilities that must be provided if positive ends, such as rehabilitation and social reintegration, are to be pursued. Incapacitation and even deterrence are not enough, for the requirement of proportionality will not permit indeterminate or draconian penalties.

If the tax-paying public is not willing to support institutions of punishment that conform to these minima, then it should have to bear the consequences. Offenders should be released and not be cooped up under crowded, inhumane, and degrading conditions. A community makes rules, rules intended to preserve

---

[63] See *Jordan* v. *Gardner*, 986 F.2d 1521 (9th Cir. 1993); also David J. Stollman, 'Female Prisoners' Rights to be Free from Random, Cross-Gender Clothed Body Searches', (1994) LXII, 6 *Fordham Law Review* (April) 1877–1910. Strip and clothed body searches are justified by appeals to security and safety—the safety not only of prison officers but also of other prisoners, who might be assailed with contraband transported via body cavities. It is argued that such intimate searches are necessary, since inmates 'use our cultural sensitivity to touching each other in certain areas as a shield for their misconduct' (*Jordan*, at 1558 (Trott J dissenting) ). The use of cross-gender searches is justified as a way of preserving the element of surprise (*ibid*, at 1554).

a certain quality of public and private life, and it should ensure that the rules are implemented in ways that conform to the moral norms that underlie them. It must therefore ensure that those for whom imprisonment is determined are not cast out of the human community as though they no longer qualify as beneficiaries of those norms.[64]

## (b) Work and activity

Boredom is the psychic equivalent of lack of space. If it is inhumane to deny people adequate opportunities to exercise their bodies, it is degrading to deny them mental stimuli. Humans realize themselves through activity, and though that activity need not be work, productive work activity represents one of the major ways in which we break the bonds of solipsistic subjectivity and are able to influence the world beyond us. The enforced idleness of prison warehousing saps energy and breaks the spirit and does little to assist the reintegration of inmates into the wider community. Although some prisoners might expect to spend the rest of their days behind bars, most will be able to anticipate release, and if their prison experience does little to assist (or even impedes) their return to the wider community, recidivism should come as no surprise.[65]

Although some kinds of work and work conditions can themselves be dehumanizing, there is no reason why prison work should be of this kind. Work that is designed to serve the needs of the prison population itself—the provisions of food, maintenance, cleaning, and agricultural services—is inherently meaningful, and it is reasonable to expect that prisoners should contribute to the conditions of their well-being. Nor should there be any problem about the expectation that prisoners engage in other kinds of productive labour. Even though work assignments may need some individualization and, given the backgrounds of much of the prison population, training may also need to be provided, there is no reason not to require that those prisoners who can should work. Although some kinds of work will be inherently challenging and satisfying, some of the satisfaction of productive work will come from its recognition and valuing by others. Thus prisoners should not be expected to work without remuneration, or be treated as cheap or slave labour. Nevertheless, their remuneration might be discounted to take some account of the costs associated with their 'board and lodging'.[66]

---

[64] As the court in *Wolff* noted, 'there is no iron curtain drawn between the Constitution and the prisons of this country' (*Wolff* v. *McDonnell*, 418 US 539, at 555–6 (1974) ).

[65] Even those who are imprisoned for life without the expectation of parole should be provided with meaningful work. To deny them that just because they will not be released back into the wider society, is to cast them out of the human commonwealth in Margalit's sense.

[66] There is a problem about what to do with the prisoner who refuses to work. Some prisons now expect their inmates to pay not only for 'board and lodging' but also for medical care. If the prisoner works, this may be deducted from their remuneration. If the prisoner refuses to work, then there may be an argument for garnisheeing future earnings. See Wesley P. Shields, 'Prisoner Health Care: Is it Proper to Charge Inmates for Health Services?' (1995) XXXII, 1 *Houston Law Review* (Summer) 271–302; Melody Petersen, 'Charging Inmates for Care Raises Issue of Risk to Their Health', *New York Times*, 23 November 1996, pp. B1, 6.

Although much prison work is likely to take the form of 'factory work', there is nothing inherently demeaning about hard labour. It can be made demeaning, as can all labour, when it is detached from significant social purposes, or when it is organized in the form of a chain gang (intended in part to humiliate). But strenuous labour can also constitute a valuable discipline. The same might also be said—though perhaps with reservations—about boot camps. Run along military lines, the latter subject their participants to intense discipline and physical training. As in the case of military training, they are designed to promote personal and interactive responsibility, increase self-confidence, and improve decision-making skills. As far as the success of such camps in combating recidivism goes, the evidence is mixed, and there is as well the ever-present danger that the power relationships involved will be inappropriately exploited.[67]

Apart from internal work assignments, most prisons do little to provide training and productive work activity. The rapid and huge expansion of the prison population in the USA, coupled with the trimming of prison budgets, has left few programmes in place.[68]

### (c) Amenities

What kinds of creaturely comforts may prisoners expect to have? Should they expect colour TVs, cable access, videoplayers, movies of their choice, coffee-makers, libraries, and so on? Conservative critics of imprisonment often sneeringly refer to prisons as 'country clubs' (albeit ones that they are not in any hurry to join). To the extent that their complaints have had any substance, instances of excess are likely to be isolated (and it is sometimes forgotten that many of the amenities possessed by individual prisoners have been paid for out of their own pockets). Most prisons are poorly provided for, given their large inmate populations, and the weight of the argument should probably be for more amenities rather than fewer.

There are surely some basic amenities to which prisoners should have access—such as disease-free beds, a place to write, sanitary toilet and washing facilities, and access to current information about the world outside. And there is certainly an argument, given that many prisoners will be engaged in legal activity concerning their cases, for giving them reasonable access to essential legal materials.[69]

Among the service amenities to which prisoners should have access are medical and psychiatric care. In some places, attempts have been made to charge

---

[67] See Dale Sechrest, 'Prison "Boot Camps" Do Not Measure Up', (1989) LIII *Federal Probation* 15–20; Doris Layton Mackenzie, 'Boot Camp Prisons: Components, Evaluations, and Empirical Issues', (1990) LIV *Federal Probation* 44–52.

[68] Educational programmes must often be paid for by prisoners, something that they can usually ill afford to do.

[69] The latter has been the subject of a recent U.S. Supreme Court decision, *Lewis v. Casey*, U.S. Lexis 4220; 64 U.S.L.W. 4587 (1996), in which access has been limited.

prisoners for such amenities.[70] The purpose of this has been to reduce what is taken to be an abuse of such provisions: prisoners have sought medical assistance for frivolous reasons—or at least as a strategy for getting temporary relief from the confines of a cell. In principle, this may not be objectionable, though any implementation should take into account the prisoner's resources, as well as other prison conditions (lest prisoners need to use whatever resources they have to relieve other inadequacies in their prison environment).[71]

For some prisoners, the amenities of prison will be better than what they are used to. But this is no argument for not making such amenities available to them. It may mean only that what they are used to is not humanly tolerable.

Although we might reasonably expect prison life to be spartan, it should also provide amenities that enable inmates to develop a richer appreciation of the world in which they are expected to live and to which, in time, most of them will return. Given that there is a significant connection between indigence, social class, and criminal conviction, a prison regime should, despite its hardships, provide incentives and opportunities for people to surmount the obstacles of their situations. If they leave prison reduced in their capacity to value what is available to them in the outside world, their prison experience will have deprived them of goods to which they had a basic claim.

### (d) Visitation and access

Among the most dramatic effects of imprisonment is severance—to a significant degree, at least—from valued social contacts. Inmates are generally permitted controlled and limited weekly visits, visits that may be frustrating and infrequent because of distance or bureaucratic routines. Their mail is often censored, and their ability to have phone access to others is constrained by limited phone availablility.

For some of these restrictions security concerns will be cited. Yet such constraints can be devastating, because inmates' identities are often strongly bound up with those social involvements.[72] What is more, their capacity to stay out of trouble after spending time in prison is likely to be markedly affected by their capacity to sustain and benefit from such relationships.

To this we must add the impact of imprisonment on the other parties in such relationships. If the person who is imprisoned was significantly responsible for family income or family stability, incarceration will place great strains on those who remain outside. Although this may not count decisively against

---

[70] See Wesley P. Shields, Comment 'Prisoner Health Care: Is it Proper to Charge Inmates for Health Services?' (1995) XXXII *Houston Law Review* 271–302.

[71] If, for example, the prison diet is very low in calories, not only may this increase the likelihood of medical problems, but prisoners may seek to use their resources for purchases at the commisary.

[72] It is surely one of the great objections to solitary confinement, except as protection, that it isolates the individual from social contact and thus from one of the central sources of our human flourishing.

imprisonment, it may—especially in view of the need for future social reintegration—provide a reason for providing counselling services and for making access relatively easy and productive.

In responding to these concerns, we might ask whether private conjugal visits should be allowed and other intimate relationships be permitted to develop? One's initial response is affirmative: the sins of one should not (as far as possible) be visited upon innocent others. Every effort should be made to maintain those significant relationships that serve not only to sustain the inmate during his or her prison term, but also to provide a meaningful structure for re-establishing a life after the sentence has been served. Recidivism is not in the public interest.

But although these are strong reasons for trying to accommodate an ongoing conjugality, and also a reason for permitting someone who is incarcerated to marry someone outside the prison environment,[73] there are significant though not overriding security concerns that need to be addressed. What is passed between lovers in such situations may not be limited to bodily fluids.[74] Some balancing of risks and benefits needs to be undertaken. Furthermore, the question of pregnancy needs to be addressed, whether it is the woman who is imprisoned or the man. In the case of long-term imprisonment, does the State condone something which is fundamentally unfair to any child, should conception take place? If the man is imprisoned, does the State have some special responsibility for any child who is conceived in such circumstances?

Along with support for ongoing relationships, there is also an argument for establishing mechanisms that will enable victim-offender reconciliation to take place. Where such reconciliation can be achieved, non-recidivist attitudes and dispositions are also likely to be nurtured.[75]

## (e) Opportunities

Although offenders are to be sentenced in a manner that is proportionate to their offence, most will eventually be released and will be expected to resume a place in the wider society. Imprisonment can increase the difficulties of the latter. Inmates are taken out of the everyday world, and their ability to negotiate its persistent and sometimes considerable demands may well be diminished by their lack of unregimented contact. If a person has been in prison for any significant

---

[73] Donatella Lorch, 'Bride Wore White, Groom Hopes for Parole: Prison Marriages Are on the Increase, Despite Daunting Rates of Failure', *New York Times*, 5 September 1996, B1, 7.

[74] A further problem is posed if the imprisoned party is HIV positive.

[75] Defenders of 'restorative justice' frequently argue that the existing 'punishment paradigm' attends to the violation of social norms, but overlooks the violation suffered by the individual victim of crime. Although the 'restorative paradigm' that is advanced is often seen as an alternative and essentially competing approach to crime management, I am here treating them as complementary. See, e.g., John Braithwaite, *Crime, Shame and Reintegration* (Cambridge University Press, 1989); H. Messmer and H.-U. Otto (eds.), *Restorative Justice on Trial: Pitfalls and Potentials of Victim-Offender Mediation—International Research Perspectives* (Netherlands: Kluwer, 1992).

period of time, s/he is likely to find social expectations difficult to fulfil. Added to this is likely to be the stigma of incarceration.

It is important, therefore, that prisons seek to address these matters, especially if we acknowledge that the State's authority to punish derives in part from the overall value that its punishment will have in maintaining a just and peaceable society. Recidivism is not just a failure of those who lapse again into crime; it also represents some kind of failure for the criminal justice system.

As mentioned earlier, a significant proportion of those who are incarcerated also lack knowledge and skills needed for productive employment; but this extends also to skills necessary for satisfactory social negotiation. And therefore we should expect that prisons will make efforts to provide for both the technical and social skilling of those who are as yet ill-equipped to take a productive place in the wider society. Unfortunately, in economically straitened times, it is just these progammes that are likely to be cut.

## 6. CONCLUSION

In the foregoing discussion I have offered a structure for assessing the appropriate hardness of hard treatment. In so doing, I have sought to extend penal theory beyond the classic debates between retributivism and consequentialism, and have endeavoured to provide a set of considerations that will operate much closer to the interface of theory and practice. In suggesting that imprisonment needs, on the one hand, to avoid practices that are inhumane and degrading and, on the other hand, to foster social goals that fall within the legitimate ambit of the State, I have attempted to provide a test for present practice. My strong impression is that current prison environments, particularly in the USA, commonly fail the test I have provided.

We stand, therefore, at a moral crossroads. We incarcerate those who disregard the norms that should govern our social intercourse, but then treat them in ways that compromise the human regard to which they are entitled. Some would want to argue that this is an inevitable accompaniment of imprisonment,[76] and that alternative ways of dealing with the perpetrators of criminality need to be found. With this I am in partial agreement: some of the problems we currently face are direct products of the huge numbers of those under intensive supervision. The resources being used to build and resource prisons might well be used to sponsor other initiatives that promise lower recidivism, especially on the part of those whose offences might well reflect social conditions and opportunities more than they do a predatory disposition. The Millian encouragement to engage in and foster 'experiments in living' might well be applied to our responses to those who have violated social norms and with whom, therefore, we must now deal.

---

[76] See, for example, Anthony O'Hear, 'Imprisonment', in A. Phillips Griffiths (ed.), *Philosophy and Practice* (1985) (Royal Institute of Philosophy Lecture Series, No. 18), pp. 203–20.

298                              *John Kleinig*

I am, of course, too late—myriad alternatives are being tried, from tent prisons in the desert, to boot camps, to family conferences. Even so, there seems to be increasing pressure on the existing prison system, and as a society we countenance institutional life that violates the basic standards to which we appeal in justifying imprisonment. Perhaps our paralysis reflects the unwillingness and political inability to deal with deeper social problems that find their expression in criminality. For that there is no easy solution.

# [18]

# Penal 'Austerity': The Doctrine of Less Eligibility Reborn?

Richard Sparks[1]

This chapter raises certain arguments and historical analogies which may assist in taking a few preliminary sightings of some distinctive features of the current British penal landscape. I hope to show that some of the present developments, which initially appear rather particular and 'of the moment', interestingly bear comparison with much earlier ideas and events. That comparison may suggest, at least in outline, a way of conceptualizing and responding to the contemporary scene.

I shall begin by sketching some developments in penal policy (and more particularly penal rhetoric) that have occurred during 1993-4, focusing specifically on the claim attributed (via a leaked memorandum) to the British Home Secretary, Michael Howard, that some prison regimes have become insufficiently 'austere', a view which finds ready support in populist media commentary. Secondly, I will suggest that such arguments for more rigorous penal discipline unwittingly but not accidentally reiterate the severe stance that underlay so much of the nineteenth-century penal (and Poor Law) ideology, known as the doctrine of less eligibility. This was, crudely, the view that the level of prison conditions should always compare unfavourably to the material living standards of the labouring poor. Thirdly, I will refer briefly to certain arguments from criminological theory and social histories of crime and punishment which suggest that less eligibility principles are especially characteristic of penal rhetoric during times of economic recession and/or of moments when governments confront crises of popular support and legitimacy. Finally, I will reflect briefly upon how the re-emergence of less eligibility within the penal realm seems likely to impact upon some current debates, especially regarding the privatization of prisons.

## THE PENAL CLIMATE IN 1993-4

It can be suggested that 1993 was a year in which the prevailing 'penal climate' in Britain 'cooled' with some suddenness. The year witnessed a general intensification of long-standing fear and censure over lawless youth and their alleged impunity before impotent courts. Newspapers focused with some delighted outrage on instances of undue judicial leniency (especially over rape sentencing), on the frequency of police cautions, on the imputed reluctance of the Crown Prosecution Service to prosecute, and on the alleged inequities of the new (and short-lived) unit fine system. They reported gleefully on the resignations of some magistrates, while social workers were taken repeatedly to task for permissiveness, coddling and extravagance in their treatment of young offenders. Two pieces of major legislation, the Children Act 1989 and the Criminal Justice Act 1991, were called repeatedly into question (at times by members of the Government which enacted them) for their excessive liberality. Key provisions of the latter were repealed by the Criminal Justice Act 1993, effectively destroying whatever coherence its sentencing framework possessed.

Even before the CJA 1993 took effect sentencing and remanding practices (the latter in part stimulated by a rash of 'bail bandit' stories) appeared to undergo a marked reverse. The reductionist agenda of the CJA 1991 which had produced appreciable falls in the prison population during 1991–2 seemed exhausted. The prison population resumed its underlying upward trend at the startling rate of some 500 per month. This largely cancelled any gains created by the government's extensive and expensive prison building programme. During the year as a whole the prison population increased by some 16 per cent (Ashworth, 1993).

All of this rather quashed the mood of (incautious) optimism which had been detectable among Prison Service insiders and liberal pressure groups in the wake of Lord Justice Woolf's (1991) moderately progressive report. It is notable in this context that the first relevant use of the term 'back to basics' known to this author occurred in a lecture given by the then Director General of the Prison Service in 1992 in which he outlined his interpretation of penal progress in light of the opportunities provided by a falling population (Pilling, 1992; Sparks, 1994). Little more than a year later the term assumed rather different penological implications in the regressive moralizing of the 1993 Conservative Party Conference. Any belief that a rough consensus of informed opinion around the reduction of prison numbers and the enhancement of regimes, backed authoritatively by Woolf, would receive continuity of governmental support dissipated abruptly during 1993.

Certain moments stand out in the destruction of that flicker of optimism. In August 1993 a memorandum from Mr Howard's private office was leaked to the press (*Observer*, 22 August) in which the Home Secretary

76          *Penal 'Austerity': Less Eligibility Reborn?*

reportedly opined that some prisoners 'enjoy a standard of material comfort which taxpayers find difficult to understand'. In September a destructive riot at Wymott prison in Lancashire received extensive press attention. In contrast to Lord Woolf's attempt to find some intelligibility in prison disturbances the popular press voiced an older and more basic construction of prisons as chaotic cauldrons and of prisoners (see Adams, 1992) as a senseless crowd.

It would be unwise to over-interpret such symptomatic readings taken alone. However, in October, Mr Howard's speech to the annual Conservative Party Conference gave this sensed change in the penal climate an explicit political form. To the rapture of his audience and the joy of the Tory press the Home Secretary unveiled a package of '27 points' to crack down on crime. In addition to his specific amendments to penal policy (the youth training order, six new private prisons, more stringent bail conditions) he announced flatly that 'Prison Works', apparently on a freely interpreted mix of retributive, deterrent and incapacitative grounds. Moreover, he declared, if this should mean that more people go to prison then he 'did not flinch' from that.

It matters little in terms of the political effectivity of this declaration that the sentencing principles espoused by Howard are known by their intellectual proponents to 'stand in open and flagrant contradiction' (Bean, 1981). What matters is that they convey a generic feeling of severity. Mr Howard had articulated a particular kind of rhetorical figure composed principally of the revival of deterrence and a strong implication of rigour. This, it is argued, amounts to the reassertion of the doctrine of less eligibility.


## LESS ELIGIBILITY REVISITED

One of the more dispiriting features of the contemporary punitive turn is its apparent ignorance of (or, more accurately, unconcern with) its own historical antecedents. Its populism owes nothing to any developed penological rationale (not even, I will go on to argue, an instrumental control strategy) and everything to an opportunist diagnosis of moral sentiments and popular fears. It is a *discursive* intervention. Its relation to practice, however materially consequential for prisoners, their families and prison staff, is of secondary concern to its author.

Of course, as E. P. Thompson once put it in another context, 'the mind has walked these cliffs before'. The preference for austerity in prison conditions, the elevation of deterrence as a prime aim of punishment, and the association with targeting, discriminating and deserving in welfare provision, are all notions between which a long-standing ideological affinity subsists. This is what the term less eligibility summarizes.

The doctrine of less eligibility received its clearest initial articulation in the late eighteenth century during the period (styled by Foucault as 'the Great Incarceration') when penitentiary imprisonment began to displace more ancient forms of physical punishment, ritual shaming and banishment as a primary penal tactic. The urgent prompting of John Howard and others against the neglect and brutality of the unreformed goals received their sharpest opposition precisely from those who feared that any amelioration in prison conditions would weaken their deterrent effect upon the lower orders. Logically, the more abject the conditions under which the poor survived (or did not) the more extreme the rigours of penal discipline must become.

This is no new discovery of 'revisionist' historiography. In 1939 Hermann Mannheim recorded and anatomized in *The Dilemma of Penal Reform* the hold which less eligibility exerted over all early carceral enterprises. Mannheim explains the inflections which the doctrine underwent. Reactionaries and reformers were divided by their interpretation of it but no one escaped its traces. For the former, whose desire for deterrent control co-existed with a gutsy sense of retributive justice, less eligibility was both practically necessary and morally compelling, since anything else constituted both an invitation and an insult to the honest labourer. For the progressive technocrats of penological engineering such as Jeremy Bentham (for whom considerations of desert were 'nonsense on stilts') the doctrine was moderated into an instrumental requirement of 'non-superiority'.

Such concerns and debates profoundly shaped the forms assumed by early penitentiary regimes. The endlessly careful precautions against comfort and contagion embodied in the silent and separate systems of discipline (Ignatieff, 1978) and the continual debates over the appropriate character of prison labour and diet (Radzinowicz and Hood, 1986) gave the anxiety for less eligibility its material realization. The result was that characteristic ideology of Victorian penality which held that the prison could *perfect* a system of discipline at once unimpeachably humane and unremittingly severe.

These are among the reasons why nineteenth-century penal thought is punctuated by projects for ideal or 'model' systems of imprisonment which are always transfixed between the reforming zeal or philanthropic vocation on the one hand and deterrent criteria on the other. Even transportation (always dogged by allegations of inhuman cruelty) was not immune from allegations of having become self-subvertingly soft when stories of ex-convicts having made good in the new worlds began to filter back to poor relations in the old (Mannheim, 1939; Radzinowicz and Hood, 1986). And the deified icons of Whig interpretations of penal history such as Elizabeth Fry and Mary Carpenter seem never to have disputed that their projects for child saving and the recuperation of fallen women should be consistent with less eligibility principles.

Less eligibility is always sustained by its own sense of justice. Victorian philanthropy was haunted by the knowledge, clearly and repeatedly articulated, of the abject poverty of the mass of the population. Every project of penal improvement was constrained by this knowledge. But such poverty was generally interpreted as a tragic and scarcely alterable fact of nature. Out of a mixture of consideration for the respectable poor and fear of the rough, penal reform could move only within restricted parameters.

The earliest cracks in the dominance of less eligibility, and the counter-assertion of universal criteria in state provision, seem to emerge in the public debate preceding the Royal Commission of 1863.[2] Editorials in *The Quarterly Review* satirize the notion that the rational determination of the prison diet for those in the custody and protection of the state can be pegged to a level believed to exist outside (Radzinowicz and Hood, 1986: 508). But the Royal Commission itself took the standard view, fearing that prisons were 'not sufficiently dreaded'. The meliorist Sir Joshua Jebb died to be replaced by the long ascendancy of the ferocious Sir Edmund du Cane who was absolutely wedded to a principle of uniform deterrence and adamantly resisted any introduction of individuation for prisoners in the guise of rehabilitation (see Garland, 1985, chapter 1).

It is only with the Gladstone Committee of 1895 and the substitution of the rehabilitative 'good and useful life' formula for deterrence as a primary organizing ideology that less eligibility received a serious challenge. The progressivism of early-twentieth-century official penology, registered especially in the institutions of probation and Borstal training, places the doctrine in abeyance as an explicit aim.[3] Among intellectual supporters of rehabilitation, of whom Mannheim is among the most thoroughgoing, less eligibility is identified plainly as an obstacle to be overcome. Mannheim's opposition to less eligibility in *The Dilemma of Penal Reform* is absolute.

Yet Mannheim is only too acutely conscious of the persistence and durability of less eligibility within both lay and jurisprudential penal reasoning. In his view the very contingent and partial status of the victory of rehabilitation during the early and mid-twentieth century penal practice precisely testifies to the doctrine's continued existence as a suppressed but constraining presence. Suffice to say that during periods of penological optimism the dominion of less eligibility is reduced. It is less at home among the development of a universal franchise, welfare entitlement and citizenship than formerly (cf. Jacobs, 1976). Moreover, throughout much of the twentieth century the entrenchment of professional vocationalism (Garland, 1985, 1990) partially insulates penal regimes from the direct impact of less eligibility principles. Thus, even in the wake of the decline of the rehabilitative ideal, the successor languages of 'positive custody' (Home Office, 1979) and 'humane containment' (King and Morgan, 1980) do not betray any marked imprint of less eligibility thinking, even if conservative law-and-order rhetoric, and especially the wilder flights of the *ultras* within Tory ranks (see Pitts, 1989: 41), toy repeatedly with its populist appeal. It is only very recently and for other reasons that less eligibility has resurfaced as an unabashed item of belief and a shaping force in penal politics.

## VICTORIAN VALUES AND FREE MARKET EXPERIMENTS

If, as I contend, less eligibility has lately made something of a comeback in the penal politics of Britain and the United States what reasons can be adduced for its re-emergence? In order for less eligibility principles to apply in any strong sense, certain favourable political and ideological conditions appear necessary: first, that the centrality of punishment to social order be strongly asserted, preferably on quasi-classicist deterrent grounds; second, that this demand for order should be linked to a perception that the integrity of the social fabric is threatened by a rising tide of lawlessness; third, that popular *resentment* be invoked against 'soft' or 'cushy' penal measures using a direct comparison with hardships experienced by law abiding citizens; and fourth that there should therefore be significant numbers of the 'truly disadvantaged' (W. J. Wilson, 1987), some of whom are respectable (and hence potentially seen as hard done by in liberal, 'assistantial' penal measures), while others are decidedly unrespectable (and hence eligible principally for deterrent penalties).

Within academic criminology in the recent past this world outlook has been articulated most clearly by James Q. Wilson (1985) when referring to those rationally parasitic criminals whom he terms 'the calculators'. In politics it is a trope deployed with some enthusiasm and success in the crime control rhetoric of the heydays of the Reagan/Bush and Thatcher eras during the early 1980s (Scraton, 1987; Pitts, 1989; Brake and Hale, 1992; Caringella-Macdonald, 1990). It has also recently become central to the articulation of crime policy under the Major administration in Britain too. Why? What are the conditions most propitious for its successful deployment?

There now exists a substantial body of historical evidence and theoretical reflection which supports the view that variations in the level of punishment and in the intensity of punitive rhetoric have at least an elective affinity with recessionary moments in business cycles (fiscal crisis) and/or with critical moments in the popularity and authority of governments (legitimation crises). The scriptural beginning for such concerns is generally taken to be provided by Rusche and Kirchheimer in *Punishment and Social Structure* (1939).[4] The outlines of Rusche and Kirchheimer's argument are well known and need not be rehearsed at length here (for summaries see Cavadino and Dignan, 1992, chapter 3; Garland, 1990, chapters 4 and 5). In essence, Rusche and Kirchheimer argue that both the level and form of punishment are sensitive to variations in labour market conditions. The latter conditions the value assigned to the offender's life and labour power and underlie the various historical mutations in penal strategy. Roughly speaking, the oversupply of labour in late medieval Europe renders life cheap and gives rise to the notorious savagery of physical punishments in this period. By contrast the demand for labour in the early modern 'mercantilist' period increases the value of life and necessitates that the offender be put to use either domestically (in Houses of Correction) or in the service of colonization and conquest (galley slavery, colonization). Later again, the collapse in labour markets during the early industrial revolution swells the ranks of the unemployed rendering prison labour largely redundant. The resulting sense of fiscal stringency and social alarm ('masterless men', machine breaking) gives rise to a deterioration in both Poor Law provision and prison conditions, with prison labour reserved for purely deterrent, unproductive uses (the treadwheel). Thus the first half of the nineteenth century is the high water mark of less eligibility principles (see Ignatieff, 1978, chapter 7).

Rusche and Kirchheimer's thesis has been widely criticized on both empirical and theoretical grounds (Ignatieff, 1983; Garland, 1990; Zimring and Hawkins, 1991), in particular for its alleged assumption of an hydraulic relationship between economic conditions and punishment. Conversely, however, Rusche and Kirchheimer are widely acknowledged, including by their critics, to have extended the possibilities for the social analysis of penality by severing the formerly presumed relationship between crime and punishment and suggesting the punishment may respond to other conditions and pursue other purposes than simply tracking the crime rate. Later commentators have revised and extended the Ruschean thesis to show the historical susceptibility of punishment to a variable range of ideological and political influences (Ignatieff, 1978; Foucault, 1979; Melossi and Pavarini, 1981; Garland, 1985; Box and Hale, 1986; Box, 1987; Hale, 1989; Barlow, et al., 1993). Perhaps most relevantly for the present argument Box (1987: 197) seeks to rescue the contention that political retrenchments during recessionary periods are registered in increasing prison numbers 'from the quicksand of functionalism and conspiracy theory'. For Box the correlation between increasing unemployment and rising prison populations is mediated by the anxieties of policymakers and sentencers acting logically upon their presumption that unemployment increases crime and disorder.

For later revisionists, therefore, it is the discursive politics of punishment and the resulting vocabularies of penal motive that matter most, rather that its instrumental functions for social control. Punishment as a cultural agent and political tactic may perform a number of roles. It affirms boundaries, draws moral distinctions and imposes identities on its subjects. The capacity to punish effectively, appropriately and judiciously in terms of prevailing rules and norms of procedure is a defining element in the legitimacy of states and governments (Melossi, 1993).

It is therefore also necessary to distinguish clearly between, on the one hand, those transformations in the form and function of penal action which occur, as it were, on a long wave of historical development (Foucault's account of the invention of the penitentiary, Garland's analysis of the birth of the welfare sanction) and, on the other, those manoeuvres and shifts of position within its operation which respond to the press of immediate, conjunctural circumstances and contingencies. We may therefore accept a long-standing tendency towards rule-bound, professionally administered, rationalized penal action (which Garland [1990: 4] summarizes as 'penal modernism'), synthesizing a variety of declaratory, supervisory and corrective objectives, without assuming that this wholly displaces prior and more 'basic' discourses and practices. To the extent that the latter, of which less eligibility is an instance, continue to exist, they may also be drawn upon and invoked for tactical advantage (especially in competitive electoral politics) when the need or opportunity is seen to arise. There is every reason to doubt that all the elements that are in play in any given historical moment form a functionally integrated seamless web.

The results are what Mannheim (1940: 41) termed the 'contemporaneity of the non-contemporaneous' – the simultaneous presence of ostensibly incompatible positions and principles. Thus, as Garland notes (1990: 185) the penal realm may look very different from within (to practitioners, administrators and reformers) and from without (to populist politicians, journalists and the public audiences whom they address). The criteria of legitimacy to which each adhere may conflict sharply. The parameters of the cultural politics of punishment are wide, and the scope for political opportunism within them is great.

Both Garland (1985) and Melossi (1985) suggest that during periods of relative affluence and optimism the centrality of punishment to political debate tends to recede (see also Box, 1987). Penality becomes one element among others in a modernizing political settlement. In the case outlined by Garland of the reforming Liberal governments in Britain in the first years of the twentieth century the tenor of the period is set by the extension of the franchise, the institutionalization of labour disputes and the move towards universalism in welfare provision. Penal relations, increasingly depoliticized and professionalized, bear the imprint of that intellectual and political environment. Something similar would hold for the Progressive era in the United States (conventionally 1900–17, see Degler, 1959), or indeed for the Kennedy–Johnson 'Great Society' period of the 1960s. Such moments are not in the main, as Melossi has it, 'a time for punishment'.

However, Melossi argues, during recessionary periods or more particularly during crises of legitimacy and public order (Melossi, 1993: 266), the field of punishment is apt to be reinvested with political contention. At such times, he suggests, a 'chain of punitive discourse' is established which asserts a connection between the restoration of order and the reassertion of penal power (see also Hall et al., 1978). Somewhat similarly, Habermas's (1976) thesis of 'legitimation crisis' proposes that where states are unable to perform the tasks they have set themselves (which in modern welfare states are more demanding and extensive than formerly) then those functions – previously largely consensually defined – become controversial. The state must either divest itself of its obligations or reassert its competence to fulfil them. Where 'the crisis' combines dimensions of both fiscal stringency and public disorder and anxiety, then the articulation between welfare provision and penalty becomes a problem. Arguments arise for the retrenchment of welfare provision. Commentators assert its economically and socially counter-productive effects (Murray, 1984, 1990). Conservative opinion demands the more vigorous imposition of punishment and an end to its confusion with welfarist aims. Hence the suppressed competition between the possible 'worlds of welfare capitalism' (Esping-Anderson, 1988) becomes more open and intense. Expensive, integrationist penal-welfare strategies are less likely to be politically favoured than other kinds of social regulation – on the one hand the 'liberalization' of labour market 'disciplines' (Aglietta, 1987), on the other a more direct appeal to 'the virtues' (see for example Anderson, 1993) in the control of personal conduct.

It is quite well documented that under such conditions the political party or bloc that successfully represents itself as most responsive to public concerns and anxieties about social disorder is electorally advantaged. In the British case the success of the Conservative party since 1979 is generally acknowledged by both sympathizers (Clark, 1990; Anderson, 1993) and critics (Marquand, 1988; Gamble, 1988; Brake and Hale, 1992) to have owed much to such a form of statecraft. At its height Thatcherism folded together concerns with economic efficiency and fiscal prudence with a sense of urgency in the restoration of propriety and public order to immense political effect. On the one hand it offered an appeal to the private virtues of aspiration, property ownership and consumption *enrichissez-vous, mes enfants!*, on the other the remoralization of the public tasks of welfare and punishment. Such a project is inherently both pragmatic and rhetorical. It has in part to do with the restoration of state legitimacy and the provision of stable conditions for accumulation, in part the invocation of the poetry of political ideas – order, authority, national pride. The punitive turn in Anglo-American penality under Reagan and Thatcher organizes respectable fears of dangerous and undeserving others (the Victorian 'residuum' mutated into the contemporary 'underclass').

Of course we need never assume that such strategies achieve their ostensible aims (least of all the reduction of crime) in order to appreciate their cultural and rhetorical power. In fact the empirical failings of neo-conservative crime control strategies are well known (Matthews and Young, 1986; Currie, 1985; Taylor, 1990; Hudson, 1993), but these have rarely been of central importance to their authors. Rather, the exploitation of ever more well-founded fear may be deployed to buttress the intensification of precisely those same techniques. To the extent that the state grounds its claim to legitimacy in the maintenance of order it must at least symbolically communicate its order-making prowess (Mathiesen's 'action function' of punishment [1990: 138]). In all these respects the politics of punishment necessarily exceed considerations of instrumental social control.

One weakness, therefore, of those commentators who have most closely followed and revised Rusche and Kirchheimer (Box, 1987; Hale, 1989) is their overwhelming preoccupation with punishment *numbers*. The easiest and apparently most conclusive way of demonstrating the turn back towards punishment lies in showing quantitative increases in the allocation of penalties, and especially of prison sentences. Of course this is an important matter and the evidence is indeed startling, especially with respect to the United States where the 'mega-shift' in the prison population since 1980 makes it hard to calibrate on the same scale as those of other advanced societies (Mathiesen, 1990; Christie, 1993; Caringella-Macdonald, 1990). What is frequently forgotten here (though *not* by Rusche and Kirchheimer themselves) is the independent significance of *qualitative* changes in penal style or method, in the conditions under which punishment is undergone, and in vocabularies of motive.[5] But, for Rusche and Kirchheimer it is not just quanta of punishments that matter. Rather, it is less eligibility itself that provides 'the leitmotiv of all prison administration down to the present time' (1939: 94).[6]

Why then should less eligibility – after a quite extended period of comparative abeyance – have recurred with some vigour recently? The reasons, I suggest, are not so very difficult to discern. Much social analysis of the 1980s in Britain (Walker, 1990; Gamble, 1988) and the United States (for example, Currie, 1990) suggests an increasing polarization of shares of national wealth. Such a 'strategy of inequality' is justified by its true believers on the grounds that trickle down effect of affluence for the more successful in Sir Keith Joseph's expression 'lifts all the boats'. Relative inequalities are unimportant by comparison with the optimization of economic performance for the national economy as a whole. Such a view demands the attribution of virtue to the economically successful and insists that any disincentive to free enterprise (redistributive taxation, over-generous transfer payments) is economically irrational. Just as entrepreneurs must be incentivized by the freeing of the market forces, so much concern focuses on the alleged disincentives to the poorest against participation in the labour market presented by the consoling but ultimately disabling embrace of welfare (Murray, 1985; Dennis and Erdos, 1992; Anderson, 1993).

For purists the 'negative freedoms' (Berlin, 1984) of classical liberalism are to be preferred to the positive ambitions of social democracy. The latter inevitably entail an unwelcome and perhaps disastrous over-extension of state action into the private sphere, sapping initiative and personal responsibility. The state should in principle confine itself to the minimally necessary tasks of macro-economic management and the maintenance of law and order. The most appropriate model of social organization is in essence of that social contract theory, in which there may be a sovereign power and an 'invisible hand' but certainly no such thing as 'society'. Individuals are radically accountable for their own character and conduct and must be encouraged to make the best of the benefits and burdens which the moral luck of their market situation affords them. There is thus a necessary symmetry between rewards and deterrents.

One penological sidelight on this world outlook is ingeniously provided by Wilkins (1984) and Pease (1990) in the form of a 'tolerance of inequal-

ity' thesis. For Wilkins and Pease punishment and reward in free market
societies can be thought of most simply as the two ends of a single polar-
ity. Those western societies with the widest ranges of income distribution
(the USA, Great Britain) tend also to have the widest spread of penal
values. That is, the concept of proportionate punishments is translated on
to a more 'stretched out' tariff of penalties than in other comparable
societies. It tends to follow that prison populations will be larger in part
because a higher proportion of very long sentences will be imposed than
in, say, Scandinavia or Japan where income distributions and penal ranges
are both more compressed. Where does this argument lead? The greater
the tolerance of inequality of outcomes the more censoriously a society
regards its deviants? The more rigorously it polarizes punishment and
reward the more centrally it relies upon a system of incentives and deterrents as the calculable levers towards desired conduct? If so, the rational
economic man of classical theory naturally takes as his criminological
counterparts either the successful free rider (Wilson's 'calculators',
Clarke's 'reasoning criminal') or the unsuccessful outsider (the Victorian
pauper or ruffian; the contemporary New Age traveller, the 'social junk' of
the urban underclass).

Pease freely acknowledges that his schema is not much more than a
thought experiment, a statistical *jeu d'esprit*, albeit a provocative one.
What it particularly lacks is any developed awareness of its own potential
links to an actual world of structure and contingency, discourse and action.
That connection seems to me to run somewhat as follows. On the level of
theoretical principle, the economic strategy of inequality speaks a language of reward and penalty based on its assumption of hedonic rationality. Its vocabulary of motives emphasizes a connection between deserving
and rewarding whose mirror image lies in a structure of justly deserved
penalties. But rewards and sanctions are also instruments. Whenever such
a society senses a special difficulty in ensuring desired (or at least com-
pliant) behaviour, or experiences a heightened sense of threat, the discourse of justice is liable to be supplemented or indeed supplanted by that
of deterrence. At such moments the special mixture of censure and
coercion implied by the notion of less eligibility again offers itself as a
favoured option.

This seems to me to describe just the sort of shift of rhetorical gear
which has occurred in British penal politics in recent years. There was a
period in the later 1980s when law and order issues were much less central
to political campaigning than they had been in the early heyday of radical
Thatcherism (indeed they were largely absent from the foreground of the
1987 General Election). Penal policymaking, while still marked by the

86              *Penal 'Austerity': Less Eligibility Reborn?*

liberal individualism of the times took a rather more studied and less ideologically charged form. The principal result was the 1991 Criminal Justice Act with its formalist 'just deserts' framework. 'Law and Order', however has now returned to the political agenda with something of a vengeance. It has done so, moreover, in consequence of a specific conjunction of political circumstances. A successor government presides over an extended and painful recession and stubbornly high unemployment. It stands accused by the ideological ultras within its own ranks (some of whose paternally challenged members are within the Cabinet, indeed the Home Office itself). The government experiences low opinion poll ratings. The governing party is sharply divided on some key issues, especially European policy, in ways which directly bear on its claim to defend the integrity of that key rhetorical entity of Thatcherism, the nation.

Moreover, it is forced to adopt tactics of economic management – first high interest rates, latterly tax increases – which consciously target both private consumption and public expenditure. This tends to induce a sense of relative deprivation (especially compared with the Lawson 'boom' years). This is not just for low income groups. It also squeezes those whose membership of the middle class (especially defined by home ownership) is insecure – people on occupational pensions, the self-employed, older white collar workers who lose their jobs, and so on. And the rage for public spending cuts affects controversial areas – not just welfare provision but, unthinkably to Mrs Thatcher, the police. Key thresholds in social stratification – benefit entitlements, access to housing, access to employment – become politically controversial. They are scarce resources.

The language of discussion that surrounds them comes more and more to include considerations of targeting, discriminating and deserving. It is not simply that any programme of fiscal austerity has implications for the prisons as it does for other public services. Nor is it just that they stand to become overloaded. It is also the case that when governments call upon the general public to accept certain burdens 'in the national interest', they will tend to speak a language of moral injunction which bears down with increasing sharpness on the undeserving and non-contributing, and which underscores more sharply than before the boundary between those who are 'in good standing' and those who are not. A society in such a condition is apt to identify its excluded minorities rather more in terms of their capacity to create trouble than in terms of their needs.

It would appear then that there are moments when a politician's or a party's seizure of a moment of opportunity for self-promotion and the surrounding logic of the situation coincide. The apparent failure of the governing party to deliver on its long-standing undertaking of enhanced community safety and public order itself becomes part of the moment of opportunity, provided that the diagnosis of such failures can be re-interpreted as lying elsewhere – in undue leniency, undiscriminating generosity, middle-class permissiveness. It becomes in itself a reason for reassertion of robustness and hence part of the strategy for coping with a legitimacy deficit. Thus John Major's assertion that we should 'condemn a little more, understand a little less' suppresses and denies what in fact we know of the recent past (the record prison numbers, the drastic public order legislation, the whole uncomprehending and condemnatory discourse of Thatcherism) and insists instead that the remoralization of penalty starts *here*.

## CONCLUSION: LESS ELIGIBILITY, PENAL VALUES AND PRIVATIZATION

It is now, as it has always been, the case that the weight of penal discipline falls disproportionately on the poorest (Hudson, 1993). Recalling the historical tenacity of the discourse of less eligibility reminds us that it is *designed* to do so.

Garland (1985) suggests that the general direction of the twentieth century penal-welfare strategies has been away from less eligibility as a dominant principle and towards reconciling penal action with techniques of inclusion. However 'disciplinary' and invasive the normalizing techniques of the welfare sanction, they were also about the connecting and assimilating properties of social control. Even imprisonment, the most segregative and still stigmatizing penalty, came to be seen in terms of a specific deprivation (of time at liberty) rather than in terms of the deliberate imposition of other hardships; and at least some of its institutions (for example the Borstal) claimed strongly to incorporate a remedial and rehabilitative element, however distantly removed this ideology may have been from practice and real outcomes.

My guess is that the vocational attachments of most penal professionals (whether in the prisons or the 'community') remain to that earlier model of penal action rather than to the present renaissance of a harder edged view. Hanging on to their well-thumbed copies of Lord Woolf's (1991) report and their mission statements, working diligently on their model regimes, prison governors and officers want in the main to be left out of the new vogue for more frequent and more austere punishments. They want to run decent, hygienic, uncrowded, unsmelly prisons. Their professional pride is invested in pre-release schemes, bail information units, visitors' centres, alcohol and drug groups, edible food, suicide prevention initiatives and other signs of penological decency. If they hope that the new renaissance of less eligibility rhetoric will pass them by they may well turn out to be lucky. For its opportunism is palpable. Moreover, it is a language that goes over the heads of those professionals and their practices and speaks directly to 'sound popular feeling' via the medium of the popular press. Maybe then the 'discourse' really is just 'talk'. It does not actually have to be delivered.

Moreover, the vicissitudes of the English prison problem have already had some ironic effects. The nadir of April 1990 and the Strangeways siege generated the somewhat progressive moment of Woolf. Meanwhile, if the politicians give grounds for thinking that they have quit any form of consensus for penal improvement other alliances emerge. Already one can begin to detect a new friendliness between the prison governors, the respectable pressure groups and perhaps the Prison Officers Association (POA) not easily imaginable a few years ago. Those who know better are shrewdly aware that the fragile legitimacy of the prison system, and its avoidance of riot and scandal, depend on defending the gains, not great but real, of the last few years. Taken together these groups form a bloc that even the most studiously reactionary Home Secretary cannot altogether ignore.

But there are also new ingredients in the stew of penal politics. The first is that overcrowding is back, and in no small way. In that respect conditions are again turning in an adverse direction, whatever the best efforts of governors and staff might be. Second, there is privatization. Its position is rendered enormously more complicated by the current harder rhetorical turn. Privatization was mooted and conceived during the eras of just deserts and humane containment. Private imprisonment is thought of by governments principally as a means to certain ends, namely the flexible and cost-effective provision of additional space in which humanely to contain. Private sector agents are not called upon to *want* to punish more people, still less to punish them more. Rather, it is simply that the market only comes into being when governments determine that more prison places should be provided (Sparks, 1994; Shichor, 1993; Lilly and Knepper, 1992a, 1992b).

In the main politicians (Clarke, 1992) and intellectual advocates of privatization (Logan, 1990) argue in conventional terms, but presumably in good faith, that market disciplines and new thinking will produce better and more humane penal environments. However, what has not been thought about in this debate (and certainly not anticipated by the private players) is what happens if better and more humane penal environments are no longer what are desired. The attraction of the privatization case depends on a distinction between the allocation of punishment by the state and the delivery of penal services by its delegated agents. Private sector operators disclaim any interest in making the conditions of imprisonment punitive in themselves (rather than reverse). Many private prison personnel are disillusioned liberals, frustrated at conditions prevailing in the public sector. They posit a close connection between their intervention and penal reform or amelioration. If private sector prisons have preferred penal rationales they lie in the region of neoclassical 'just deserts' thinking and/or selective incapacitation. In either case they are about normalized containment.

But what happens to this argument when the assumed consensus (that prison conditions should be made progressively more tolerable) dissipates? That is, if deterrence is reinstated and less eligibility comes back into the penal equation? For present purposes what is most clearly apparent from these developments is that the more implicit progressivist teleology of Kenneth Clarke's earlier statements during his tenure as Home Secretary (flatly equating privatization with penal improvement) can hardly survive such a deterioration in the surrounding political environment. The idea that the terms on which contracts are offered must inevitably make private prisons preferable from the prisoner's point of view seems more and more open to reasonable doubt. Rather the vaunted responsiveness of the private sector signifies if anything the reverse, namely that prison regimes can be made to react barometrically to the external penal climate (in part by virtue of not being mitigated by the vocational culture – the 'restrictive practices' – of a cadre of administrators and staff steeped in a meliorist public service ethic). The prospect that penal services might be provided by a private sector not 'incentivized' towards relentless improvement but instead constrained by a rhetoric of austerity exposes a range of impending troubles for the legitimacy of the private corrections industry which have until now been largely suppressed. In short, market conditions will have changed because those conditions only exist by grace and favour of the prevailing penal ideology. Either private sector contributors must throw their weight decisively against the deterrence/less eligibility dyad or they must accept the full implications of free market premises, namely that if austerity is what the customer wants, austerity is what they will have.

90            *Penal 'Austerity': Less Eligibility Reborn?*

## Notes

1.  I am most grateful to Pat Carlen, Chris Hale, Nicola Lacey and Joe Sim for their thoughtful comments on an earlier draft of this paper.
2.  The Royal Commission itself and the *Penal Servitude Act 1864* which followed were harshly dominated by less eligibility thinking. This was even more clearly true of Lord Carnarvon's 1863 House of Lords Select Committee into prison discipline which called for more uniformity and deterrent discipline in prisons and for intensified dietary restrictions. This is well summarized by Sim (1990: 33–5).
3.  This does not mean of course that prison conditions uniformly improved or, as Sim (1990) makes clear, that the provision of medical and other facilities to prisoners ceased to be subject to special restrictions. Sim also reminds me (pers. comm.) that in all manner of routine and unacknowledged ways (food, underwear changes, bathing and toilet facilities) prisons remain marked by less eligible features well into the present century.
4.  It is less often remembered (curiously, since Mannheim is generally assigned the role of 'mainstream' commentator to Rusche and Kirchheimer's Marxist outsiders) that the same year also saw the publication of *The Dilemma of Penal Reform*, similarly preoccupied with less eligibility. For all their differences, and Mannheim's sharp criticisms of Rusche and Kirchheimer's economism, both books (but Mannheim's more explicitly) are haunted by the implications of Nazism for the politics of punishment.
5.  In fairness to Box and Hale, of course, one could reasonably argue that under the conditions prevailing in the English prisons during the 1970s and 1980s the problem of less eligibility took care of itself. One did not have to *will* or intend that conditions should become increasingly less eligible; problems of overcrowding and shortage simply made it so willy-nilly (see also McDermott and King, 1989). Moreover, it may well be that, with the notable exception of the 'short, sharp, shock' experiments, that demands of Thatcherite 'law and order' concerns were satisfied by the assurance that more people were in prison, parole conditions made tighter and so on.
6.  This, they go on to say, is the 'inner contradiction' that underlies every reform programme. In this respect they are of course in entire agreement with their contemporary Mannheim. Rusche and Kirchheimer's concern is that each gain in humanitarian reform may be 'surrendered … to the mercy of every crisis in the market'. Conversely, their hope that the spread of affluence may contribute towards a 'more rational and more humane praxis' again suggests more commonality between the 'marxist' and the 'mainstream' commentators than is generally admitted.

## References

Adams, R. (1992) *Prison Riots in Britain and the USA* (London: Macmillan).
Aglietta, M. (1987) *A Theory of Capitalist Regulation* (London: Verso).
Anderson, D. (ed.) (1993) *The Loss of Virtue* (London: Social Affairs Unit).

Ashworth, A. (1993) 'Sentencing by Numbers', *Criminal Justice Matters* (Winter 1993–4).

Barlow, D.; Hickman Barlow, M.; and Chiricos, T. (1993) 'Long Economic Cycles and the Criminal Justice System in the U.S.', *Crime, Law and Social Change*, 19: 143–69.

Bean, P. (1981) *Punishment* (Oxford: Martin Robertson).

Berlin, I. (1984) 'Two Concepts of Liberty', in M. Sandel (ed.), *Liberalism and its Critics* (Oxford: Blackwell).

Box, S. (1987) *Recession, Crime and Punishment*, London: Macmillan.

Box, S. and Hale, C. (1986) 'Unemployment, Crime and Imprisonment and the Enduring Problem of Prison Overcrowding', in R. Matthews and J. Young (eds), *Confronting Crime* (London: Sage).

Brake, M. and Hale, C. (1992) *Public Order and Private Lives* (London: Routledge).

Caringella-Macdonald, S. (1990) 'State Crises and the Crackdown on Crime Under Reagan', *Contemporary Crises*, 14: 91–118.

Cavadino, M. and Dignan, J. (1992) *The Penal System: an Introduction* (London: Sage).

Christie, N. (1993) *Crime Control as Industry* (London: Routledge).

Clark, J. C. D. (ed.) (1990) *Ideas and Politics in Modern Britain* (London: Macmillan).

Clarke, K. (1992) 'Prisoners with Private Means', *The Independent* (22 December): 17.

Currie, E. (1985) *Confronting Crime* (New York: Pantheon).

Currie, E. (1990) 'Heavy with Human Tears', in I. Taylor (ed.), *The Social Effects of Free Market Policies* (Hemel Hempstead: Harvester Wheatsheaf).

Dennis, N. and Erdos, G. (1992) *Families Without Fatherhood* (London: Institute for Economic Affairs).

Degler, C. (1959) *Out of Our Past* (New York: Harper & Row).

Esping-Anderson, G. (1988) *Three Worlds of Welfare Capitalism* (Cambridge: Polity).

Foucault, M. (1979) *Discipline and Punish* (London: Paladin).

Gamble, A. (1988) *The Free Economy and the Strong State* (London: Macmillan).

Garland, D. (1985) *Punishment and Welfare* (Aldershot: Gower).

Garland, D. (1990) *Punishment and Modern Society* (Oxford University Press).

Habermas, J. (1976) *Legitimation Crisis* (London: Heinemann).

Hale, C. (1989) 'Economy, Punishment and Imprisonment', *Contemporary Crises*, 13, 4: 327–49

Hall, S.; Critcher, C.; Jefferson, T.; Clarke, J.; and Roberts, B. (1978) *Policing the Crisis* (London: Macmillan).

Home Office (1979) *Committee of Inquiry into the United Kingdom Prison Services* (May Committee) (London: HMSO).

Hudson, B. (1993) *Penal Policy and Social Justice* (London: Macmillan).

Ignatieff, M. (1978) *A Just Measure of Pain* (Harmondsworth: Penguin).

Ignatieff, M. (1983) 'State, Civil Society and Total Institutions: A Critique of Recent Social Histories of Punishment' in E. Cohen and A. Scill (eds), *Social Control and the State* (Oxford: Blackwell).

Jacobs, J. (1976) *Stateville: the Penitentiary in Mass Society* (Chicago University Press).

King R. and Morgan, R. (1980) *The Future of the Prison System* (Farnborough: Gower).

Lilly J. R. and Knepper, P. (1992a) 'The Corrections-Commercial Complex', *Prison Service Journal*, no. 87.

Lilly, J. R. and Knepper, P. (1992b) 'An International Perspective on the Privatization of Corrrections', *Howard Journal of Criminal Justice*, 31, 3: 174–91.

Logan, C. (1990) *Private Prisons: Cons and Pros* (Oxford University Press).

McDermott, K. and King, R. (1989) 'A Fresh Start: The Enhancement Of Prison Regimes', *Howard Journal of Criminal Justice*, 28: 161–76.

Mannheim, H. (1939) *The Dilemma of Penal Reform* (London: George Allen and Unwin).

Mannheim K. (1940) *Man and Society in the Age of Reconstruction* (London: Routledge and Kegan Paul).

Marquand, D. (1988) *The Unprincipled Society* (London: Fontana).

Mathiesen, T. (1990) *Prison on Trial* (London: Sage).

Matthews, R. and Young, J. (eds) (1986) *Confronting Crime* (London: Sage).

Melossi, D. (1985) 'Punishment and Social Action: Changing Vocabularies of Motive within a Political Business Cycle', *Current Perspectives in Social Theory*, 6: 169–97.

Melossi, D. (1993) 'Gazette of Morality and Social Whip: Punishment, Hegemony and the Case of the USA, 1970–92', *Social and Legal Studies*, 2: 259–79.

Melossi, D. and Pavarini, M. (1981) *The Prison and the Factory* (London: Macmillan).

Murray, C. (1984) *Losing Ground* (New York: Basic Books).

Murray, C., (1990) *The Emerging British Underclass* (with responses by Frank Field, Joan C. Brown, Nicholas Deakin and Alan Walker) (London: Institute for Economic Affairs).

Pease, K. (1990) 'Punishment Demand and Punishment Numbers', in R. V. Clarke and D. M. Gottfredson (eds) *Policy and Theory in Criminal Justice* (Aldershot: Avebury).

Pilling, J. (1992) 'Back to Basics – Relationships in the Prison Service', The Eve Saville Memorial Lecture, Institute for the Study and Treatment of Delinquency. (London: ISTD).

Pitts, J. (1989) *The Politics of Juvenile Crime* (London: Sage).

Radzinowicz, L. and Hood, R. (1986) *The Emergence of Penal Policy* (Oxford University Press).

Rusche, G. and Kirchheimer, O. (1939) *Punishment and Social Structure* (London: George Allen and Unwin).

Scraton, P. (1987) *Law, Order and the Authoritarian State* (Milton Keynes: Open University Press).

Shichor, D. (1993) 'The Corporate Context of Private Prisons', *Crime, Law and Social Change*, 20: 113–38.

Sim, J. (1990) *Medical Power in Prisons* (Milton Keynes: Open University Press).

Sparks, R. (1994) 'Can Prisons Be Legitimate?', *British Journal of Criminology*, 34, 1: 14–28.

Taylor, I. (ed.) (1990) *The Social Effects of Free Market Policies* (Hemel Hempstead: Harvester Wheatsheaf).

Walker, A. (1990) 'The strategy of inequality', in I. Taylor (ed.), *The Social Effects of Free Market Policies* (Hemel Hempstead: Harvester Wheatsheaf).
Wilkins, L. (1984) *Consumerist Criminology* (London: Heinemann).
Wilson, J. Q. (1985) *Thinking About Crime* (New York: Basic Books).
Wilson, W. J. (1987) *The Truly Disadvantaged* (Chicago University Press).

# [19]

# The Virtuous Prison: Toward a Restorative Rehabilitation

Francis T. Cullen,
Jody L. Sundt,
and
John F. Wozniak

The most startling fact in corrections is the seemingly unstoppable rise in the nation's prison population. In 1970, the number of inmates in state and federal prisons on any given day did not reach 200,000; three decades later, this figure was more than six times higher, with the population in excess of 1.2 million (Gilliard, 1998; Langan, Fundis, Greenfeld, and Schneider, 1988). When offenders in jail are added, America's incarcerated population now tops 1.8 million (Gilliard, 1998). Not surprisingly, most criminologists have decried this enormous jump in imprisonment. They often note that, with the exception of Russia, the United States has the highest incarceration rate worldwide—several times higher than most advanced industrial nations (Mauer, 1994). Merely making this observation, it seems, is enough to confirm that something is amiss in our correctional policy.

The most common assertion is that the United States should not place so many of its residents behind bars. Although we largely agree with this contention, we will leave the specific merits of this claim for others to debate (compare, e.g., Bennett, DiIulio, and Walters, 1996 and Reynolds, 1997 with Clear, 1994; Currie, 1998; and Irwin and Austin, 1994). What concerns us here, however, is the concomitant tendency for criminologists to remain silent on precisely *what prisons should be like*. Because criminologists' main concern is that imprisonment should be used sparingly (i.e., only for the incorrigibly violent or for those committing truly heinous crimes), they couple their criticism of the "imprisonment binge" with a call for policy makers to create more viable "alternatives to incarceration."

Although the logic here makes sense—if too many people are locked up, alternatives to prison are essential—this kind of thinking obscures or neglects a related question: Short of releasing them, what should be done with the offenders who remain incarcerated? If at all, criminologists respond with the admonition that prisons should be "more humane." Exactly what this means is only infrequently spelled out (for exceptions, see Johnson, 1996; Toch, 1997).

Why do criminologists generally fail to draft a blueprint for the prison environment? To an extent, their scholarly interests lie outside the substantive area of institutional corrections; instead, their critique of "imprisonment" is part of a broader salvo at the conservatives' "get tough" movement on crime. We suspect, however, that something else is also involved. Since the stunning critique of institutionalization elucidated in Goffman's (1961) *Asylums* and illustrated by the Stanford prison experiment (Haney, Banks, and Zimbardo, 1973), many criminologists have embraced the view that total institutions, and correctional facilities in particular, are *inherently* inhumane. Efforts to improve prisons are thus seen as doomed and, even worse, as serving to *legitimate* the very idea that prisons are *potentially* humane. In this view, a "humane prison" is an oxymoron and a dangerous one at that. The stubborn reality is that even when prison administrators have the best of intentions, institutions will remain coercive and dehumanizing (see, e.g., Rothman, 1980).

This conceptualization of prisons is part of a more general view of *state* social control that has been nearly hegemonic in criminology over the past generation. By the early 1970s, criminologists—by all accounts a progressive group politically—had embraced the view that "nothing works" in corrections and, more generally, that virtually all attempts by the state to control crime were coercive. Scarcely a decade before, they were optimistic—sometimes cautiously, sometimes wildly—that government was an integral part of the solution to crime (President's Crime Commission on Law and Enforcement and Administration of Justice, 1968). The continuing turmoil of the 1960s and revelations of abuse of power by state officials, however, diminished this hope and resulted in a jaundiced view of the willingness and capacity of the government's "agents of social control" to improve offenders' lives (Cullen and Gilbert, 1982; Garland, 1990). Criminologists, especially those of a "critical" perspective, were prone to see virtually any intervention to control crime as a strategy of power concealed beneath a phony rhetoric voiced by naive reformers or disingenuous state officials. In subsequent years, this view became, ironically, uncritically accepted and part of the professional ideology of criminologists.

Binder and Geis (1984) capture this phenomenon in their revealing analysis of how criminologists portray juvenile diversion programs. They note that diversion might legitimately be described as an effort to spare juveniles criminal sanctions in exchange for their participation in programs that provide these youths—many at risk for future illegal conduct—with much-needed social services. These programs are run by youth and nonprofit agencies and provide "family counseling, restitutive arrangements, help with securing work, employment counseling, and intervention with schools" (p. 635). Instead, criminologists commonly portray diversion as "stigmatizing" and as "dramatizing the evil" of "kids." This labeling is carried out by "agents of social control." Positive program results are dismissed as methodologically unsound (see also, Gottfredson, 1979). Most salient, diversion is said to invidiously "widen the net of social control." Such rhetoric, argues Binder and Geis (1984, 630), should be deconstructed to illuminate its ideological purpose:

> The phrase "widening the net" is, of course, employed pejoratively, with the intent to evoke an emotional response. It conjures up visions of a mesh net that is thrown over thrashing victims, incapacitating them, as they flail about, desperately seeking to avoid captivity. The net is maneuvered by "agents of social control," another image-provoking term, this one carrying a Nazi-like connotation. Both terms are employed for purposes of propaganda rather than to enlighten.

Where does this kind of thinking lead us? Binder and Geis (1984, 636) contend that the favored policy recommendation is a preference for "no action"—for nonintervention by the criminal justice system (see also, Travis and Cullen, 1984). When taking "no action" is patently absurd (i.e., when a serious crime has been committed), then the preference is for exercising the least control possible. In this view, the goal should not be to "do good" but to "do the least harm possible" (Fogel, 1988; Gaylin, Glasser, Marcus, and Rothman, 1978). As rising prison populations over the past thirty years reveal, this minimalist approach to crime control has not proven persuasive. It also has led, as we have argued, to an absence among criminologists of systematic thinking about what prisons should be like.

We do not believe that it is responsible for criminologists to refrain from entering the ongoing conversation about what prisons are for and how they should be organized. As noted, the failure to participate in this policy discourse has not stemmed the use of imprisonment in the United States. In this context, the risk of somehow "legitimizing" prisons seems the least of our worries. Worse still, by not articulating a compelling vision for imprisonment—by merely being naysayers for thirty years—criminologists have provided the get-tough crowd with an unprecedented opportunity to redefine the purpose and nature of imprisonment. As Clear (1994) observes, the result has been a "penal harm movement" that has made the infliction of misery on inmates not something to hide but to celebrate. Further, the generic critique of prisons as inherently inhumane, while correct in the sense that all institutions are depriving, ignores the reality that not all prisons are equally depriving (DiIulio, 1987; Wright, 1994). Some facilities expose inmates to violence and inspire fear, some do not; some provide decent amenities, some do not; some provide opportunities to be productive and to change, some do not. To ignore this reality is to forfeit the opportunity to improve the quality of life for America's inmate population.

Given these considerations, we propose that it is time for criminologists—especially progressive criminologists—to speak up and articulate what prisons should be for and like. In the end, we anticipate that a cacophony of voices will be needed to clarify what a progressive approach to institutional corrections should entail. Our purpose here thus must be seen as modest and as advancing but one possible option. This caveat stated, we offer as a model for corrections *the virtuous prison.*

At its core, this approach suggests that the fundamental goal of the prison experience should be to foster "virtue" in inmates, which is usually defined as "moral goodness" or "moral excellence" (*Webster's New Universal Unabridged Dictionary*, 1979, 2042). Prisons should be considered moral institutions and corrections a moral enterprise. Inmates should be seen as having the obligation to become virtuous people and to manifest moral goodness. This statement announces that there are standards of right and wrong and that offenders must conform to them inside and outside of prisons. The notion of a virtuous prison, however, also suggests that the correctional regime should be organized to fulfill the reciprocal obligation of providing offenders with the means to become virtuous. Much like the founders of the penitentiary did when they designed detailed daily routines for inmates to follow (Rothman, 1971), careful attention should be paid to how each prison would be arranged to enhance the goal of moral regeneration. Such efforts should include using existing criminological knowledge on "what works" to change offenders.

The virtuous prison is being advanced as a *progressive* reform—as a way of humanizing imprisonment and of contributing to the commonwealth of communities. We recognize the dangers inherent in preaching morality, but we also suggest that there are dangers—already realized—in rejecting morality. A *progressive* approach is, by its very nature, value-laden, not value-free. We should not be afraid of *rediscovering the morality* that informed earlier, progressive-oriented prison reforms. We also assert that the idea of a virtuous prison has decided advantages over two other models for imprisonment: "the legal prison" and "the painful prison." These issues are explored in the pages ahead.

## REDISCOVERING MORALITY

Progressive criminologists are not without the capacity for moral outrage. They (and we) are indignant about the social and economic injustices that contribute to the uneven distribution of crime in the United States. They show little sympathy for white-collar offenders and castigate corporations who wantonly exploit the environment and commit violence against workers and consumers. Even so, it is politically incorrect or, in the least, unfashionable, to speak of traditional "street" offenders and their misdeeds as "immoral." Take, for example, James Q. Wilson's (1975, 235) now-famous claim that "wicked people exist.

Nothing avails except to set them apart from innocent people." Why should this assertion—arguably correct to a degree—bother progressive criminologists (and us) so much? Why does such moral judgmentalism evoke a visceral feeling of discomfort and make us flush with anger?

In part, we suspect, the rejection of moralism as applied to individual offenders is not so much what it says but what it may unwittingly—or not so unwittingly—obfuscate. By focusing on an individual offender's moral failing, it is easy to ignore the role of the social structure and material inequity—the so-called "root causes"—in the individual's wayward life course. It also is easy to claim that we must "set apart" this individual lawbreaker without pricking our consciences about how we, as a society, may have played a role in the offender becoming "wicked."

Another consideration, however, is the evolving belief among progressives that the trumpeting of morality is not done in good faith but is merely another strategy of power. Moral claims thus are not true but are merely exercises in rhetoric that mask darker political and class-based interests. "Moral crusades" and the speeches of "moral entrepreneurs" are not to be taken at face value but are to be viewed skeptically and deconstructed. What are they really after? What's the hidden agenda?

This view of morality has had salient effects within corrections, most notably with the attack on rehabilitation in the 1970s and beyond. Because advocates often borrowed the language and logic of the medical model, offender treatment has at times been portrayed strictly as a scientific, technical task: finding and using the most scientifically appropriate treatments to change lawbreakers into law abiders. But rehabilitation is, at its core, a moral enterprise. It depends on the existence of social consensus about shared values—about what is right and what is wrong (see Allen, 1981). It is morally judgmental; it accepts a standard for moral and legal behavior and defines those not meeting this standard as in need of adjustment (see Garland, 1995).

Beginning in the late 1960s and early 1970s, progressive criminologists became uneasy about rehabilitation for these very reasons; the treatment ideal's moral claims were seen as illegitimate. Thus, once upon a time, the founders of the penitentiary and of the juvenile court were viewed as humanitarian reformers; now they were unmasked as seeking to "discipline" poor offenders so that they could be productive workers for the capitalists and as becoming "child savers" to reaffirm existing class arrangements and to provide gender-appropriate occupational opportunities (Foucault, 1977; Platt, 1969). Moral crusades thus were redefined as immoral crusades. Similarly, social workers, counselors, and all others tied to the correctional "establishment" were transformed from members of the "helping professions" into "agents of social control" who abused their power so as to control, not improve, offenders (Rothman, 1980). Benevolence thus was supposedly unmasked for what it "really" was: coercion. And offenders, as Binder and Geis (1984, 644) note, became the "underdog, who tends to be seen as a romantic force engaged in a liberating struggle with retrogressive establishment institutions." In its more extreme form, "crime" and "criminals" were reduced to social constructions—words always to be bracketed by quotes to show that there is no objective standard of morality or legality. In its milder form, criminologists simply denied that offenders were different and in need of any change—a position that subsequent research has shown to be foolish (Andrews and Bonta, 1998; Raine, 1993). Moral condemnation of offenders and their harmful behavior was not in vogue. Regardless, if there was nothing really wrong with offenders, then rehabilitation had no legitimate function: there was nothing in them to fix.

Let us hasten to say that these criticisms of rehabilitation had important kernels of truth to them, although not nearly the amount of truth that their advocates confidently imagined (Cullen and Gilbert, 1982; see also, Garland, 1990). This way of thinking, however, also had the distinct disadvantage of directing how a whole generation of criminologists understood corrections. In particular, it became "taken for granted" that prisons were inhumane and immoral places; that "nothing worked" in prisons for the betterment of offenders; and that claims by correctional workers to help offenders were a camouflage for their desire to continue to exercise unfettered discretion over powerless inmates. In this context, there was a tendency to see inmates as twice victimized—once by the social injustices that prompted them to break the law, and a second time by the correctional system that subjected them to inhumane conditions certain to drive them further into crime. The idea that offenders might have engaged in morally reprehensible conduct and that prisons should serve to morally reform them was—and, to a large extent, still is—out of sync with this line of reasoning (Newman, 1983). Discussions of a virtuous prison would have been dismissed out of hand, and those proposing such a foolish venture would have been characterized as criminologically illiterate. This may remain the case.

The difficulty for many criminologists, however, is that they were, and are, largely bereft of any positive agenda for the prison—short, again, of abolishing it or minimizing its use. As they turned away from rehabilitation, most criminologists followed the crowd and embraced the "justice model." They liked this approach because it argued that offenders, including the incarcerated, should be accorded an array of legal rights that would protect them against the power of the state to sanction them unfairly or too harshly. After all, who could be against justice? But this approach was strangely disconnected from the very criminology they practiced. The justice model is based on the legal fiction of the atomized individual offender who freely chooses to break the law and earn the right to be punished. Most criminologists, however, spent their professional lives documenting that, at most, the choice of crime is socially bounded and, in too many cases, that the odds of lawbreaking among people exposed to at-risk environments—the victims of social injustice—are astronomical. We return to the limits of a legal model shortly.

In the end, then, we propose that criminologists, especially progressive scholars, recognize the importance of talking about virtue or morality *in formulating correctional policy in prisons*. This call is not, we believe, a departure from progressive principles but a rediscovery of them. The great reforms in American corrections—for example, the penitentiary and the rehabilitative ideal that led to offender classification and treatment programs—drew their power in large part from the willingness of their advocates to speak about right and wrong and about what prisons should be about. As Zebulon Brockway (1870, 42) eloquently observed more than a century ago in Cincinnati at the National Congress on Penitentiary and Reformatory Discipline:

> It will be noticed that there is a wide difference in these two views of crime; a difference so wide that every prison system must be founded upon one or the other of them, and not by any possibility upon both; for a system, so founded, would be divided against itself, and could not stand. Just here, thorough discussion is needed, for irrevocable choice must be made. If punishment, suffering, degradation are deemed deterrent, if they are the best means to reform the criminal and prevent crime, then let prison reform go backward to the pillory, the whipping-post, the gallows, the stake; to corporal violence and extermination! But if the dawn of Christianity has reached us, if we have learned the lesson that *evil is to be overcome with good*, then let prisons and prison systems be lighted by this law of love. Let us leave, for the present, the thought of inflicting punishment upon prisoners to satisfy so-called justice, and turn toward the two grand divisions of our subject, the real objects of the system, vis.: *the protection of society by the prevention of crime and reformation of criminals.* (Emphasis in the original.)

We recognize that our views risk being discounted as naïve—as ignoring that many progressive reforms have had untoward consequences and that these reforms rarely were constructed to ruffle the feathers of the rich and powerful by calling for the redistribution of valued resources. We cannot fully debate this issue here, but we will make three brief responses. First, critics of past progressive reforms somehow assume that "things would have been better" in the absence of these reforms. Our experiences over the past thirty years, however, provide a sobering rebuttal to the view that the opposite of the traditional progressive model of individualized treatment is the dawn of a new era of humanity in corrections. Second, with appropriate reflection and caution, the mistakes of the past are not inevitably repeated. The alternative view—that all correctional reforms are doomed to corruption and failure—is a recipe for continued inaction. Third, conservatives have rushed into the correctional arena equipped with their moral interpretation of offenders and of what should be done *to*—not *for*—them. Without a competing moral vision, the odds of achieving a more humane approach to corrections are diminished.

Finally, we should take notice that our urging to rediscover morality and to create virtuous prisons are not completely "pie-in-the-sky" ideas. Later, for example, we will discuss a closely allied development: the emergence of faith-based prisons. But we can also draw attention to the growing restorative justice movement (Levrant, Cullen, Fulton, and Wozniak, 1998). This approach, which many progressives are now embracing because it is community-based and not prison-based, is at its core a moral enterprise. It is unabashed in defining the misdeeds of offenders as blameworthy and inexcusable; but it is equally unabashed in holding out the possibility that through the offender's hard work to compensate victims and to change for the better, the gift of forgiveness from victims, and the support of the community, the restoration of offenders—as well as victims and the community—is possible. Whatever its faults and potential problems (Levrant et al., 1998), restorative justice shows that correctional responses are not limited to the infliction of pain but can attempt to achieve nobler goals and real-life outcomes. This is a lesson, we trust, that might be fruitfully generalized to our understanding of prisons—a possibility we will revisit later.


## THE LEGAL PRISON

The attack on rehabilitation in the 1970s fractured the consensus that corrections should be about correcting people. As the hegemony of the treatment ideal shattered, conservatives rushed in to propose an alternative approach: using prisons to inflict pain on offenders for lengthy periods of time. As noted, those on the left, including progressive-oriented criminologists, trumpeted the alternative "justice model of corrections" (see, e.g., Fogel, 1979; Fogel and Hudson, 1981; Morris, 1974).

Within prisons, the prime target of the leftists was the discretion exercised by correctional staff and by parole boards. They bristled at the idea that offenders should be "coerced" into treatment under the threat that their early release from prison depended on program participation and their being "cured." In an inhumane prison environment, staff could not be trusted to exercise their discretion fairly and with expertise. Parole boards were depicted as either political hacks or as well-meaning folks who unwittingly placed inmates in the position of have to "con" board members so as to earn their release from prison. Justice model advocates thus argued that all indeterminacy in sentencing, parole boards, and enforced therapy should be eliminated. But this approach wanted something more: the allocation to inmates of an array of legal rights that would ensure their protection against the abuses visited upon them by correctional staff and by life in an inhumane environment.

In short, whereas advocates of rehabilitation hoped to fashion therapeutic communities, those favoring the justice model wished to construct a "legal prison"—an institutional community built on the principles of restraining state power and of according inmates virtually every legal right available to them in the free society. At times, this approach was characterized as a "citizenship model of corrections." In Conrad's (1981, 17–19) words, the prison "should become a school for citizenship" in which inmates were granted the rights to personal safety, to care, to personal dignity, to work, to self-improvement, to vote, and to a future. Although based on pure speculation, Conrad and other reformers believed that once inmates were offered the opportunity to enjoy and exercise the rights of citizens, the prison would become orderly and more humane. Once citizenship was learned inside prisons, its effects might generalize and make offenders more responsible as they returned to the free society. As Conrad (1981, 19) observed:

> Justice depends on reciprocity between the state and its citizens and among citizens themselves. A man whose rights are not protected by the state has no rights. A man who has no rights cannot be expected to observe the rights of others. If justice is really therapy, as I believe, it can only be administered to a citizen, not to a civilly dead convict.

Although naïve sounding, the justice model is hardly foolish and might even have proved a boon to prison life in a different political context. In the 1970s, those on the political left had reason to believe that the law was an instrument of change and of good. Until this time, inmates had been virtual "slaves of the state" as courts practiced a "hands off" doctrine inside prisons. Prison litigation did much to improve basic standards of living within correctional facilities and to accord offenders religious and legal rights (DiIulio, 1990; Jacobs, 1983). What the justice model advocates did not anticipate, however, was that the expansion of constitutional protections to prisons would, when confronted by more conservative courts, stop far short of ensuring that inmates had a right to citizenship or a humane environment. Instead, the courts have taken a minimalist approach, protecting offenders from "cruel and unusual" prison conditions but not from much more than this (Palmer and Palmer, 1999).

One fundamental problem with the justice model, then, is that it is out of step with the times. In the early 1970s—in the midst of the Civil Rights Movement and in the shocking aftermath of the Attica riot and slaughter—it seemed reasonable to suggest that inmates were victims in need of rights. Today, however, policymakers and the public are likely to concur that inmates "have too many rights." Talk of "democratizing corrections" and turning "inmates into citizens" would prompt skepticism, if not the acerbic query of "who's running the joint now"? The justice model may have done some good, but it has now exhausted itself. It is incapable of fueling a new age of correctional reform in the twenty-first century.

The justice model and its legal prison also failed to provide a compelling answer to the "utilitarian" question of what role prisons would play in reducing crime. Advocates wished to suggest that through "voluntary rehabilitation" and the learning of "citizenship" offenders *might* lower their subsequent criminal participation. But having criticized rehabilitation as coercive and ineffective—the "noble lie" as Morris (1974, 20–22) put it—they were reluctant to say that offenders should change and that corrections *should* ultimately be about facilitating this outcome. As a result, they were wishy-washy on crime, failing to articulate how prisons could be employed to protect innocent citizens—whether through rehabilitation or through tougher means, such as long-term incapacitation. Caught up with rectifying the injustices done to inmates, they largely forfeited the opportunity to show how their progressive-oriented reforms would make society safer. This mistake was not only intellectual but also political; for conservative commentators rushed into this void to tell policymakers and the public how to put an end to the lawlessness in the nation's streets.

## THE PAINFUL PRISON

Clear (1994) characterizes American corrections over the past three decades as being in the throes of a "penal harm movement"—of a concerted effort to inflict increasing amounts of pain on offenders. The most visible sign of this campaign is the successful policy agenda to cram more and more lawbreakers behind bars for longer and longer periods of time. Although given less consideration, a collateral sign of the penal harm movement is the attempt to make inmates' stays in prison not only lengthier but also increasingly physically uncomfortable—what Sparks (1996) calls the policy of "penal austerity."

Given their progressive bent and their attraction to preaching that even the worst among us deserve humane treatment, criminologists have generally been disconcerted by these developments. Even so, while not brutish in their views, some criminologists have warmed to the idea that prisons should be painful rather than, say, therapeutic or contexts in which to practice citizenship.

Take, for example, Newman's (1983) "punishment manifesto" conveyed in his controversial *Just and Painful*. Embracing a retributivist position, Newman argues that imprisonment as a form of punishment should be used sparingly; instead, he favors corporal punishment, delivered most often through electric shocks and calibrated to the seriousness of the crime committed. When prison sentences are given, however, he contends that they should be reserved for those who have engaged in serious and/or repeated crimes. In these cases, the minimum penalty should be fifteen years of incarceration. Most noteworthy for our purposes, he envisions "prisons as purgatory" (p. 61); they should be harsh places so that inmates will suffer. Such punishments are justified, says Newman, because they are deserved and because they offer offenders the opportunity to truly atone for their evil acts and, in a sense, to save their souls.

Newman's proposals are provocative and tempting: would we be willing to take the current massive overuse of imprisonment and exchange it for the application of electric shocks to a great many offenders and lengthy sentences of extreme suffering by few offenders? But this deal will remain hypothetical because of Americans' cultural ambivalence about punishing the body of offenders and their embrace of imprisonment as a preferred sanction. The risk of Newman's proposal, then, is that it will be used in a piecemeal fashion. While it will not reduce the use of imprisonment, it potentially could add legitimacy to claims that prisons should be places in which *all* offenders, not a select few, suffer.

A milder version of the painful prison is set forth by Logan and Gaes (1993). These authors do not favor making prisons a purgatory or exposing inmates to gratuitous pain. They believe that prisons should meet constitutional standards of safety, decency, and amenities and should be governed firmly and fairly, not harshly and arbitrarily. Their "confinement model," however, embraces retribution or just desserts as its guiding principle and sees prison as a means of punishing. Unlike the more liberal advocates of just deserts, who looked to the justice model as a way of protecting inmates from the inherent coerciveness of imprisonment—and more like Newman (1983)—Logan and Gaes favor "punitive confinement" as a way of dramatizing the immorality of the offender's crime and of affirming the offender's "autonomy, responsibility, and dignity" (p. 255).

Logan and Gaes state clearly that they wish offenders to be sent to prison *as* punishment and not *for* punishment. Unless we misread between the lines of their essay, however, this caveat is meant to go only so far. They may not want prisons to be warehouses, but they seemingly do want them to be punitive and to involve no-frills living—to send, as they would say, a "cultural message" to the citizenry that crime is evil and will be judged harshly. Their view of rehabilitation is revealing. Treatment programs, they speculate, are paternalistic and convey the wrong message about crime and criminals to society; they deny offender responsibility and presumably increase the sales of Dershowitz's (1994) *The Abuse Excuse*. Rehabilitation is not to be fully excluded by their confinement model, but it is to be permitted only when it is "voluntary, is separated from punishment, and is not a privilege unavailable to those who are not in prison" (p. 257). Thus, participation in treatment is not to be tied to privileges of any sort; programs are to be delivered after imprisonment or inside prison by outside community social service agencies—and then only to foster institutional order, not to change offenders; and services given to offenders are to be governed by the principle of less eligibility.

Logan and Gaes's model of punitive confinement is principled, but it is not based on principles we wish to embrace. First, as with other retributivists, they must accept the legal fiction that crime is a free and autonomous choice. Even the economists—a discipline based on the assumption of rationality—understand that choice is bounded and is influenced by socially induced "tastes" or "preferences" (see also Boudon, 1998). Although we concur with their desire to hold offenders morally responsible, we believe that this is only half the moral equation: society, too, should be held accountable for its role in the criminal choices offenders make, and the correctional process should reflect this reality. Second, we are equally troubled by their rejection of the utility—the crime savings—that can be achieved through effective correctional intervention, especially with high-risk offenders (Andrews and Bonta, 1998). The easy sacrifice of this goal is tantamount to saying that prisons should play no role in *protecting future victims* from crime. Such a state interest is not only constitutionally permissible but, we believe, moral to pursue. Third, while this may be a case of "what's in the eye of the beholder," we reject their view that prison treatment programs send the cultural message that "crime's not the offender's fault." Rehabilitation can send other messages: that offenders have an obligation to change; that offenders are not a form of refuse but have the human dignity to be renewed; that offenders are worth investing in because they can change and contribute to society; and that we, as a society, are not only about "hating the sin" but, at least under some circumstances, about "loving the sinner."

Perhaps more important, we are troubled that like Newman, Logan and Gaes are seemingly untroubled by the prospect that their call for "punitive confinement" will not go as planned. We worry, however, that once the punitive genie is out of the bottle, it will not prove to be principled but more akin to Jafar—the evil Disney character in the *Aladdin* films who attempted to use his newfound, genie-like powers for self-interest and to harm others. We wonder, in particular, where the restraint will come from if we accept that prisons are an instrument for punishment—pure and simple. What will occur when even responsible scholars such as Logan and Gaes do not challenge the principle of less eligibility? What cultural message will politicians hear, and what can they be trusted to do?

The events from the penal harm movement give us considerable reason for concern. As Lacayo (1995, 31) observes, the "hottest development in criminal justice is a fast-spreading impulse to eliminate anything that might make it easier to endure a sentence behind bars." The roster of these austerity policies is now familiar: sending inmates out on chain gangs; eliminating Pell Grants and opportunities to participate in college programs; banning computers and televisions in cells; forbidding weightlifting; housing inmates in tents; eliminating steak from inmate diets; and so on. These policies are hardly part of a principled confinement model; rather they are intended to ensure that inmates are in prison *for punishment* and are undertaken with the utilitarian and criminologically ill-conceived notion that exposing offenders to rotten living conditions will deter their future wrongdoing. Worse still, these policies are trumpeted by politicians whose newfound campaign to immiserate inmates' lives seems rooted less in morality and more in a calculated desire to capture headlines and electoral capital. Such a vision for corrections should not go unchallenged—a task to which we now turn.

## THE VIRTUOUS PRISON

Because nearly all correctional reforms historically have been misshapen when put into place and have failed to realize their ideals (Cullen and Gilbert, 1982; Rothman, 1990), we approach the task of outlining an alternative vision for the prison with much trepidation. It also is daunting to realize that a crafty critic could soon hone in on our proposal's vulnerabilities (e.g., the potential arrogance in claiming to be virtuous; its embrace of utility as a central correctional goal). Still, as argued previously, we are persuaded that progressives inadvertently have allowed agendas such as the "painful prison" to gain influence by paying insufficient attention to correctional policy as it pertains to life inside institutions. In a very real sense, there is a "culture war" under way over the fate of the nation's prisons. Without fresh ideas—others if not ours—progressives will remain on the defensive and do little to shape prison policies in the time ahead.

## Restorative Rehabilitation

The mission of the virtuous prison is to use offenders' time of incarceration to cultivate moral awareness and the capacity to act virtuously. Although recognizing the deprivations inherent in total institutional life, the approach rejects the progressive view, held by many criminologists, that nothing productive can be accomplished in prison. This approach also rejects the notion of the painful or austere prison as having no utility—other than inflicting suffering—and as inhibiting the inculcation of virtue in offenders. The virtuous-prison approach rejects incapacitation because it is a utilitarian theory that, by not endorsing the goal of offender change, needlessly limits the crime savings—and thus the utility—that prisons can achieve. And this approach rejects retributivist ideas for their disinterest in crime control and for their belief, as Newman (1983, 142) writes, that "the most basic of all freedoms in a society" is "the freedom to break the law" and to be punished for it. The virtuous prison has a different vision—the idea that people, including inmates, have an *obligation* to obey the law, not to harm others, and that societal institutions, including the prison, should be organized to facilitate this goal.

Two principles form the foundation of the virtuous prison: *restorative justice* and the *rehabilitative ideal* (see Wilkinson, 1998). As alluded to earlier, restorative justice hinges on the premise that the harm from crime is morally wrong and that its effects need to be remedied. Offenders thus are called on to announce and publicly accept the blame for their wrongdoing. They are then expected to act virtuously by restoring victims they have harmed. Such restoration for victims might be emotional, such as when offenders apologize for their misdeeds, or might be material, such as when offenders provide restitution. Offenders also must recognize that breaches of the law damage the common welfare; therefore restoring the community through service activities is often mandated. The precise nature of this restorative justice remedy is reached at a conference where the offender, victim, family members, and concerned others meet to express their disappointment and hurt and to work out a way in which the offender can restore the harm he or she has caused. Ideally, and over time, the victim forgives and reconciles with the offender. The community is expected to do its part, too, by reintegrating, not rejecting, the repentant offender. In this whole process, the state is present but involved mainly as an arbiter, helping the parties to reach agreement.

Restorative justice is morally clear and it is unambiguous about requiring offenders to make amends. But this approach is sympathetic as well to the view that people, including lawbreakers, are capable of change. It also proposes that criminal sanctions should be used to rectify harm and to do good—not to heap more suffering on offenders in an aimless way or for purposes of mere retribution. It is backward-looking, shaming the conduct that has occurred; it is present- looking, applying a criminal sanction that does good; and it is future looking, trying to create victims who are restored and offenders capable of moral conduct (see, e.g., Braithwaite, 1998; Hahn, 1998; Van Ness and Strong, 1997).

Can restorative justice, however, be imported into the prison? To date, it has largely been conceptualized as a *community-based* approach; indeed, progressives have rushed to embrace it precisely because it is presented as an alternative to prison (for exceptions, see Hahn, 1998; Van Ness and Strong, 1997; see also, Lund, 1997; Wilkinson, 1998). In an otherwise thoughtful analysis of restorative justice, for example, Braithwaite (1998, 336) will "concede" only that "for a tiny fraction of people in our prisons, it may actually be necessary to protect the community from them by incarceration." This view not only is empirically problematic in its optimistic view of inmates (Logan and DiIulio, 1992), but also errs, we believe, in not seeing the role of restorative justice *within* prisons—a place, again, in which over 1.8 million people now reside in the United States. Regardless, prisons present two challenges to restorative justice: the removal of offenders from the community and a population of more serious, hardened offenders.

Although various scenarios could be devised to reconcile victims with prison-bound or prison-based offenders, the removal of the offender from the local community will make victim-offender conferences less likely to occur. Yet, even if specific agreements with specific victims are not reached, a virtuous prison could be organized around the principle that inmates should be engaged in activities that are restorative (e.g., contributing to a victim compensation fund; community service). In this way, what inmates do would be imbued with a clear moral and practical purpose: to restore harm to society that they and their fellow offenders have caused. In this approach, prisons thus would be an instrument for doing good for society. Although limited, it is noteworthy that prison programs based on restorative justice are beginning to emerge (see, e.g., Lund, 1997; Wilkinson, 1998).

Perhaps the more daunting challenge, however, is the depth of the criminality of the offenders who enter prison. A weakness of restorative justice is that the approach's understanding of offender behavioral change is speculative and based, at most, on only a slice of the criminological research about offenders (see Levrant, et al., 1998). The idea that the kind of high-risk offenders that frequently populate prisons will, with any regularity, be morally regenerated by a two-hour victim-offender reconciliation meeting or merely by furnishing restitution strains credulity. Such an understanding denies the pathology within many offenders that has been developing over a lifetime. It will take tough work and appropriate therapeutic techniques to change offenders—to prepare them to act morally outside the prison walls (see Wilkinson, 1998).

It is at this juncture, therefore, that the rehabilitative ideal should be merged with restorative justice—for two reasons. First, even more strongly than restorative justice, rehabilitation identifies the reform of the offender as a legitimate and important correctional goal—a goal whose attainment simultaneously benefits inmates and, by preventing crime, society. Second, there is now a growing body of empirically based knowledge specifying the correctional interventions that "work" to reduce recidivism, including among high-risk serious offenders (see, e.g., Andrews and Bonta, 1998; Andrews, Zinger, Hoge, Bonta, Gendreau, and Cullen, 1990; Gendreau, 1996; Gibbons 1999; Henggeler, 1997; Lipsey and Wilson, 1998; MacKenzie, 1998). This research suggests that certain "principles of effective intervention" should be followed in seeking to rehabilitate offenders. To a large extent, these principles are consistent with restorative justice because primary targets for change in this correctional approach are offenders' antisocial values and thinking (Gendreau, 1996). In any case, a restorative corrections approach will likely fail to impact recidivism if it is not informed by the extant research on rehabilitation. If one prefers, the principles of effective intervention can be seen as supplying the needed technology for offender restoration.

## Prison Particulars

The goal of prison organization would be to create a "virtuous milieu." The task would be how to surround inmates with positive moral influences. Although our thoughts are still preliminary, we would propose seven general considerations.

*First, inmate idleness would be eliminated.* "Idle hands" may or may not be "the devil's workshop," but they are no friend to virtuous living. Wright (1994) contends that a "productive environment" reduces prisoner violence and disruption and also fosters hope—a sense of purpose—among inmates.

*Second, the activities in which inmates engage would have a restorative purpose.* Prison employment, for example, should not merely be to pass the time or to equip offenders with occupational skills but rather should have a larger purpose beyond the inmate's self-interest. Thus, inmate wages might be used to compensate victims, with offenders writing and sending the checks to victims. Or inmates might be engaged in jobs that produce products for the needy—toys for poor children or prefabricated houses for Habitat for Humanity. Similarly, community service would be encouraged—first inside the prison (e.g., writing to elderly shut-ins, training dogs for the seeing impaired, holding bake sales for "good causes") and then during the day outside the prison (e.g., fixing up a playground, making a house livable for a family) (Lund, 1997). When possible, moreover, inmates would be prompted to help restore one another, such as by tutoring someone who is less educated or leading self-help sessions. Which activities ultimately are implemented is less important than the fact that inmates are engaged in activities that have a *moral purpose*—that provide opportunities to be virtuous (see Van Ness and Strong, 1997, 108–109).

*Third, contact with virtuous people would be encouraged.* Although not unmindful of security risks, the virtuous prison would encourage as many upstanding community people as possible, including those religiously-inspired, to lead and/or participate in prison programs, to mentor inmates, and to visit and socialize with inmates. These volunteers should be seen not as a potential disruption but as a source of valuable human capital who will share their knowledge and values with inmates. Further, by coming into the prison—by devoting their time and effort to a worthy cause—such volunteers are modeling the very kind of pro-social, virtuous behavior that we wish inmates to learn.

*Fourth, inmates would participate in rehabilitation programs that are based on criminological research and the principles of effective correctional intervention* (again, see Andrews and Bonta,1998; Gendreau, 1996). An important principle of the virtuous prison would be that offenders have the *obligation* to seek restoration so as not to misbehave inside the institution or to recidivate in the community. The reciprocal obligation of the state is to provide quality treatment programs that have the greatest chance of facilitating this restoration. In this spirit, criminological knowledge would be welcomed and not dismissed. Programs shown not to work—such as boot camps—would be relegated to the therapeutic dustbin. Alternatively, programs shown to work—cognitive-behavioral interventions—would be implemented and evaluated. In the end, programs would be intended to give offenders the values, understanding of the world, and skills to live a productive life. This approach is much different, we should note, from punitive strategies that threaten offenders with punishment but provide no positive instruction on how to lead a life outside crime.

*Fifth, the standard of inmate living would be as high as possible.* A low standard of living—inflicting pain on offenders—serves no defensible moral or utilitarian purpose. It also is inconsistent with the very purpose of a virtuous prison, which takes seriously the maxim that "virtue begets virtue." Politically, the restorative orientation of the virtuous prison might make it less vulnerable to attempts to immiserate its population. Often, inmates are seen as part of the undeserving poor who no longer should receive social welfare "entitlements." In the virtuous prison, however, inmates will be engaged in activities in which they "give back to victims and the community"; in short, they may become more "deserving" in the eyes of policymakers and thus less attractive as targets for meanness.

*Sixth, prison guards would be encouraged to function as "correctional" officers.* In the virtuous prison, guards would be seen as professionals who deliver various types of human services (Johnson, 1996). Their tasks obviously would involve maintaining order, ensuring custody, and enforcing rules. But they also would be integral to the central institutional mission of fostering virtue in inmates. One cannot bifurcate staff into two neat divisions—"custodial" and "treatment"—because correctional officers are potentially too involved in inmates' daily lives and routines not to affect programmatic outcomes and the quality of the institution. Thus, while guards have their distinctive duties, they should, through participatory management, be brought into the planning of how best to achieve the virtuous prison's central mission. In particular, they should be relied on to advance, not stymie, the restoration or correction of the offenders in their charge. Research suggests that many correctional officers would welcome this enrichment of their occupational role (Cullen, Lutze, Link, and Wolfe, 1989; Johnson, 1996; Toch and Klofas, 1982).

*Seventh, the virtuous prison would not be for all inmates.* We would like to see the model of the virtuous prison spread far and wide, and we are confident that with enough experimentation and organizational development, this model could eventually be effective with a large proportion of the inmate population. Still, we are realistic enough to know that not every inmate could function effectively in this environment (e.g., the intractably recalcitrant, violent, or mentally disturbed inmate). At the very least, however, the virtuous prison would be appropriate for at least *some* inmates, with precisely how many remaining an empirical question to be discovered. If so, then there is reason to undertake an experiment with the prison we have proposed. The salient point is that success with even one model virtuous prison would be valuable because it would show that prisons can serve lofty goals and can be administered, within the limits of good sense, humanely. Some support for these views can be drawn from the current experimentation with "faith-based" prisons.

## Faith-Based Prisons

In April of 1997, Prison Fellowship Ministries—the religiously based prison reform group begun by Charles Colson (of Watergate fame)—initiated the "Inner-Change Freedom Initiative" in a minimum-security prison (Jester II) located outside Houston and under the auspices of the Texas Department of Correction. Based on a model used to reform and administer prisons in Brazil (Leal, 1998), this initiative sought to develop a faith-based prison community. The inmate participants had diverse criminal histories and were required to be within twenty-one to twenty-four months of parole or release from prison. To ensure separation of church and state, Prison Fellowship Ministries funded the program's staff and operation (but not the correctional officers or inmate living costs) and accepted only inmates who volunteered. Other programs are being planned for prisons in Iowa and Kansas (Prison Fellowship Ministries 1999; Mattox, 1999; Niebuhr, 1998; see also, the Internet site of www.ifiprison.org).

The prison initiative is based on the belief that behavior is a reflection of values and worldview. For inmates, it is proposed that rehabilitation depends on a fundamental "inner change" that reconciles the person with Christ. This sacred relationship then allows the offender to reconcile human relationships and to embark on genuine, long-term behavioral change. The special focus on a religious transformation is a distinctive feature of the InnerChange Freedom Initiative. It also is what limits its widespread use, since the separation of church and state sets burdensome legal restrictions on the programmatic services a department of corrections can fund.

From our perspective, however, the InnerChange Freedom Initiative is instructive because the features incorporated into its prison community *besides religion* make it quite similar to the virtuous prison we have proposed. Thus, the Texas initiative largely embraces the dual principles of moral restoration and rehabilitation. It is extensively programmed and relies heavily on church-based volunteers to serve as chaplains, lead small groups, mentor inmates, provide educational and artistic tutoring, facilitate family support groups, and coordinate the community service project. It also has inmates participate in productive work so as to teach them to be "stewards of their time." The initiative is unabashed in expressing its desire not to inflict pain on inmates but to create a community of strong social bonds and love. Further, it is committed to using an aftercare program to reintegrate offenders, upon their release, into a supportive religious community.

To be sure, the appeal of the InnerChange Freedom Initiative stems in an important way from its faith-based orientation and because it was proposed by an influential religious ministry, Prison Fellowship. Still, the kind of prison community being created—a focus on moral restoration, concerted efforts to rehabilitate offenders, substantial support given to offenders during and after incarceration, a lack of mean-spirited rhetoric—did not render this project politically unfeasible. Indeed, by requiring inmates to strive in concrete ways toward change—to show that they were deserving of support—this program was the kind of "compassionate conservatism" that Texas Governor George W. Bush could embrace and use to bump up his ratings in the polls. This initiative thus shows that space exists to experiment with different models of imprisonment. It is relevant as well that, while the American public is punitive toward crime, repeated surveys reveal that there also is substantial support among citizens for the principles of restorative justice and of prison-based rehabilitation (see, e.g., Applegate, Cullen, and Fisher, 1997; Cullen, Fisher, and Applegate, forthcoming). In this context, the prospect of creating a virtuous prison does not seem farfetched.

## CONCLUSION: DOING GOOD

As Binder and Geis (1984) show, criminologists have a tendency to feel happy when they can show that nothing the government does has any effect on crime. At times, there seems to be a special glee—a gotcha!—when scholars can reveal how people who hope to "do good" and express benevolent intentions end up putting reforms into place that have untoward unanticipated consequences. There is, of course, a need to puncture false claims and to save offenders from foolish, if not repressive, efforts to supposedly save them. Pushed too far, however, this professionally supported desire to delegitimate "state control" is smug and counterproductive. Nothing constructive—nothing that can work—is ever proposed.

Prisons, we believe, have suffered from criminologists' unwillingness to entertain the possibility that correctional institutions could be administered more humanely and more effectively. This risk of action is failure and, at times, messing things up. But the past three decades of penal harm should have taught us two lessons about corrections: First, doing good sometimes means that good is actually achieved. And second, doing good is almost always preferable to the alternative—neglect or, even worse, the conscious attempt to inflict pain. The challenge now is to devise those strategies that can, in fact, realize our benevolent sentiments in the difficult area of corrections. The virtuous prison is but one suggestion on how to "do good" in prison. Hopefully, it will soon be followed by many others.

## REFERENCES

Allen, Francis A. 1981. *The Decline of the Rehabilitative Ideal: Penal Policy and Social Purpose.* New Haven: Yale University Press.

Andrews, D. A., and James Bonta. 1998. *The Psychology of Criminal Conduct,* 2nd ed. Cincinnati: Anderson.

Andrews, D. A., Ivan Zinger, R. D. Hoge, James Bonta, Paul Gendreau, and Francis T. Cullen. 1990. "Does Correctional Treatment Work? A Clinically-Relevant and Psychologically-Informed Meta-Analysis." *Criminology* 28:369–404.

Applegate, Brandon K., Francis T. Cullen, and Bonnie S. Fisher. 1997. "Public Support for Correctional Treatment: The Continuing Appeal of the Rehabilitative Ideal." *The Prison Journal* 77:237–58.

Bennett, William J., John J. DiIulio, Jr., and James P. Walters. 1996. *Body Count: Moral Poverty . . .and How to Win America's War Against Crime and Drugs.* New York: Simon & Shuster.

Binder, Arnold and Gilbert Geis. 1984. "*Ad Populum* Argumentation in Criminology: Juvenile Diversion as Rhetoric." *Crime and Delinquency* 30:624–47.

Boudon, Raymond. 1998. "Limitations of Rational Choice Theory." *American Journal of Sociology* 3:817–28.

Braithwaite, John. 1998. "Restorative Justice." Pp. 323–44 in *The Handbook of Crime and Punishment,* ed. M. Tonry. New York: Oxford University Press.

Brockway, Zebulon R. 1871. "The Ideal of a True Prison System for a State." Pp. 38–65 in *Transactions of the National Congress on Penitentiary and Reformatory Discipline,* ed. E. C. Wines. Albany, NY: Weed, Parsons.

Clear, Todd R. 1994. Harm in American Penology: Offenders, Victims, and Their Communities. Albany: State University of New York Press.

Conrad, John P. 1981. "Where There's Hope There's Life." Pp. 3–21 in *Justice as Fairness: Perspectives on the Justice Model,* ed. D. Fogel and J. Hudson. Cincinnati: Anderson.

Cullen, Francis T., Bonnie S. Fisher, and Brandon K. Applegate. Forthcoming. "Public Opinion About Punishment and Corrections." In *Crime and Justice: A Review of Research*, ed. M. Tonry. Chicago: University of Chicago Press.

Cullen, Francis T., and Karen E. Gilbert. 1982. *Reaffirming Rehabilitation*. Cincinnati: Anderson.

Cullen, Francis T., Faith E. Lutze, Bruce G. Link, and Nancy T. Wolfe. 1989. "The Correctional Orientation of Prison Guards: Do Officers Support Rehabilitation?" *Federal Probation* 53 (March):33–42.

Currie, Elliott 1998. *Crime and Punishment in America*. New York: Metropolitan Books.

Dershowitz, Alan M. 1994. *The Abuse Excuse—And Other Cop-Outs, Sob Stories, and Evasions of Responsibility*. Boston: Little, Brown.

DiIulio, Jr., John J. 1987. *Governing Prisons: A Comparative Study of Correctional Treatment*. New York: The Free Press.

———, ed. 1990. *Courts, Corrections, and the Constitution: The Impact of Judicial Intervention on Prisons and Jails*. New York: Oxford University Press.

Fogel, David. 1979. "*. . .We Are the Living Proof. . .:*" *The Justice Model for Corrections*. 2nd ed. Cincinnati: Anderson.

———. 1988. *On Doing Less Harm: Western European Alternatives to Incarceration*. Chicago: Office of the International Criminal Justice, University of Illinois at Chicago.

Fogel, David and Joe Hudson, eds. 1981. *Justice as Fairness: Perspectives on the Justice Model*. Cincinnati: Anderson.

Foucault, Michel. 1977. *Discipline and Punish: The Birth of the Prison*. New York: Pantheon.

Garland, David. 1990. *Punishment and Modern Society: A Study in Social Theory*. Chicago: University of Chicago Press.

———. 1995. "Penal Modernism and Postmodernism." Pp. 181–209 in *Punishment and Social Control*, ed. T. G. Blomberg and S. Cohen. New York: Aldine de Gruyter.

Gaylin, Willard, Ira Glasser, Steven Marcus, and David J. Rothman. 1978. *Doing Good: The Limits of Benevolence*. New York: Pantheon.

Gendreau, Paul. 1996. "The Principles of Effective Intervention with Offenders." Pp. 117–30 in *Choosing Correctional Options That Work: Defining the Demand and Evaluating the Supply*, ed. A. T. Harland. Thousand Oaks, CA: Sage.

Gibbons, Don C. 1999. "Review Essay: Changing Lawbreakers—What Have We Learned Since the 1950s?" *Crime and Delinquency* 45:272–93.

Gilliard, Darrell K. 1998. *Prison and Jail Inmates at Midyear 1998*. Washington, DC: U.S. Department of Justice, Bureau of Justice Statistics.

Goffman, Erving. 1961. *Asylums: Essays on the Social Situation of Mental Patients and Other Inmates*. Garden City, NY: Anchor.

Gottfredson, Michael R. 1979. "Treatment Destruction Techniques." *Journal of Research in Crime and Delinquency* 16:39—54.

Hahn, P. H. 1998. *Emerging Criminal Justice: Three Pillars of a Proactive Justice System*. Thousand Oaks, CA: Sage.

Haney, Craig, W. Curtis Banks, and Philip G. Zimbardo. 1973. "Interpersonal Dynamics in a Simulated Prison." *International Journal of Criminology and Penology* 1:69–97.

Henggeler, Scott W. 1997. *Treating Serious Anti-Social Behavior in Youth: The MST Approach*. Washington, DC: OJJDP, U.S. Department of Justice.

Irwin, John and James Austin. 1994. *It's About Time: America's Imprisonment Binge.* Belmont, CA: Wadsworth.

Jacobs, James B., ed. 1983. *New Perspectives on Prisons and Imprisonment.* Ithaca, NY: Cornell University Press.

Johnson, Robert. 1996. *Hard Time: Understanding and Reforming the Prison.* 2nd ed. Belmont, CA: Wadsworth.

Lacayo, Richard. 1995. "The Real Hard Cell: Lawmakers Are Stripping Inmates of Their Perks." *Time*, September 4, pp. 31–32.

Langan, Patrick A., John V. Fundis, Lawrence A. Greenfeld, and Victoria W. Schneider. 1988. *Historical Statistics on Prisoners in State and Federal Institutions, Yearend 1925-86.* Washington, DC: U.S. Department of Justice, Bureau of Justice Statistics.

Leal, Cesar Barros. 1998. "The Association for the Protection and Assistance to the Convict: A Brazilian Experience." Paper presented at the annual meeting of the American Society of Criminology, November, Washington, DC.

Levrant, Sharon, Francis T. Cullen, Betsy Fulton, and John F. Wozniak. 1999. "Reconsidering Restorative Justice: The Corruption of Benevolence Revisited? *Crime and Delinquency* 45:3–27.

Lipsey, Mark W. and David B. Wilson. 1998. "Effective Intervention for Serious Juvenile Offenders: A Synthesis of Research." Pp. 313–45 in *Serious and Violent Juvenile Offenders: A Synthesis of Research*, ed. R. Loeber and D. P. Farrington. Thousand Oaks, CA: Sage.

Logan, Charles H. and John J. DiIulio, Jr. 1992. "Ten Deadly Myths About Crime and Punishment in the U.S." *Wisconsin Interest* 1 (No. 1):21–35.

Logan, Charles H. and Gerald G. Gaes. 1993. "Meta-Analysis and the Rehabilitation of Punishment." *Justice Quarterly* 10:245–63.

Lund, Laurie. 1997. "Restorative Justice from Prison." *ICCA Journal on Community Corrections* 8 (August):50–51, 55.

MacKenzie, Doris L. 1998. "Criminal Justice and Crime Prevention." Chapter 9 in *What Works, What Doesn't, What's Promising: A Report for the National Institute of Justice*, ed. L. W. Sherman, D. Gottfredson, D. Mackenzie, J. Eck, P. Reuter, and S. Bushway. Washington, DC: U.S. Department of Justice, National Institute of Justice.

Mattox, Jr., William R. 1999. "Prison Program Uses Faith to Transform Lives." *USA Today*, March 15, p. 17A.

Mauer, Marc. 1994. *Americans Behind Bars: The International Use of Incarceration, 1992–1993.* Washington, DC: The Sentencing Project.

Morris, Norval. 1974. *The Future of Imprisonment.* Chicago: University of Chicago Press.

Newman, Graeme. 1983. *Just and Painful: A Case for the Corporal Punishment of Criminals.* New York: Macmillan.

Niebuhr, Gustav. 1998. "Using Religion to Reform Criminals." *New York Times*, January 18, Section 1, p. 16.

Palmer John W. and Stephen E. Palmer. 1999. *Constitutional Rights of Prisoners*, 6th ed. Cincinnati, OH: Anderson.

Platt, Anthony M. 1969. *The Child Savers: The Invention of Delinquency.* Chicago: University of Chicago Press.

President's Commission on Law Enforcement and Administration of Justice. 1968. *The Challenge of Crime in a Free Society.* New York: Avon.

Prison Fellowship Ministries. 1999. *The InnerChange Freedom Initiative: Background, Fact Sheet, History, FAQs, and Legal Basis*. Washington, DC: Prison Fellowship Ministries.

Raine, Adrian. 1993. *The Psychopathology of Crime: Criminal Behavior as a Clinical Disorder*. San Diego: Academic Press.

Reynolds, Morgan O. 1997. *Crime and Punishment in America: 1997 Update*. Dallas, TX: National Center for Policy Analysis.

Rothman, David J. 1971. *The Discovery of the Asylum: Social Order and Disorder in the New Republic*. Boston: Little, Brown.

———. 1980. *Conscience and Convenience: The Asylum and Its Alternatives in Progressive America*. Boston: Little, Brown.

Sparks, Richard.1996. "Penal 'Austerity': The Doctrine of Less Eligibility Reborn?" Pp. 74–93 in *Prisons 2000: An International Perspective on the Current State and Future of Imprisonment*, ed. R. Matthews and P. Francis. Hampshire, UK: MacMillan.

Toch, Hans.1997. *Corrections: A Humanistic Approach*. Guilderland, NY: Harrow and Heston.

Toch, Hans and John Klofas. 1982. "Alienation and Desire for Job Enrichment Among Correction Officers." *Federal Probation* 46 (March):35–44.

Travis III, Lawrence F. and Francis T. Cullen. 1984. "Radical Non-Intervention: The Myth of Doing No Harm." *Federal Probation* 48 (March):29–32.

Van Ness, Daniel W. and Karen H. Strong. 1997. *Restoring Justice*. Cincinnati: Anderson.

*Webster's New Universal Unabridged Dictionary*. 1979. 2nd ed. New York: Simon & Schuster.

Wilkinson, Reginald A. 1998. "The Impact of Community Service Work on Adult State Prisoners Using a Restorative Justice Framework." Ed.D. dissertation, Department of Educational Foundations, University of Cincinnati.

Wilson, James Q. 1975. *Thinking About Crime*. New York: Vintage.

Wright, Kevin N. 1994. *Effective Prison Leadership*. Binghamton, NY: William Neil.

# [20]

# The Correction Officer Subculture and Organizational Change

DAVID DUFFEE

Assistant Professor of Criminal Justice, Division of Community Development,
Pennsylvania State University

Ph.D. (Criminal Justice) 1974, State University of New York (Albany)

*Training and manpower development in correction has become an increasingly important issue. Most such training on the correctional officer level is based upon an academic model of education. This kind of training approach is likely to be ineffective because of a hypothesized officer subculture, the values of which are antagonistic to the policy and values implicit in the training. Three scales, measuring correctional policy, supervisory behavior, and social climate of institutions, were administered in the correction department of a northeastern state in order to test the hypothesis. It was found that officers differed considerably from managers on both policy and social climate. A major explanatory factor appeared to be the way in which the officers perceived themselves to be managed. Suggestions are made for changing the officer subculture values based upon small group dynamics techniques that affect the way in which officers perceive themselves to be managed and alter the perceived rewards for behaving in ways compatible with managerial policy.*

IT IS NOT A RADICAL SUGGESTION that correctional officers might have their own subculture. The police, who face many similar problems, have been called the "blue minority," and research has found police to be a very cohesive group, both on and off duty.[1] Other analogies might be made with foremen in industry,[2] noncommissioned officers in the military, and orderlies and nurses in hospitals.[3] The

correctional officer, like these others, is a man caught in the middle. He is responsible for the control of those below him in accordance with the rules of the organization, but he is usually (1) not given the necessary tools to do that job and (2) caught in the dilemma that full employment of the tools at his disposal usually cause disorder rather than order. He is stuck eight hours a day among a much larger body of men whom he may not like and with whom he is not supposed to fraternize, but with whose objections to his own bosses he can very well identify. Like the inmate, one of his favorite pastimes is identifying dishonesty and hypocrisy in those above him, and like the inmate he feels alienated from middle-class society,

---

1. See Jerome Skolnick, *Justice Without Trial,* New York: Wiley, 1966, pp. 42-70.

2. See Bensman and Gerver, "Crime and Punishment in the Factory: A Functional Analysis," Rosenberg, Gerver, and Houton, eds., *Mass Society in Crisis,* New York: Macmillan, 1964, pp. 141-152.

3. On the similarities in a variety of "total institutions," see Erving Goffman, *Asylums,* Garden City: Doubleday, 1961, pp. 1-25.

which has asked him to do its dirty work and then ignores him completely or condemns him as brutal and inhuman. Like inmates, he feels relegated to the same position in the organization for his entire life stay and explains the selection for the infrequent promotions as owing to "pull" and "politics." Again, like inmates, he feels the rewards of his job are inconsequential and the punishments unavoidable. So why work? Much like inmates, officers have very little idea of the continuity of correction. What becomes of inmates in the end has only a passing connection with their job. Parole is seen in terms of the inmates who return from it, and "the street" is relevant because it is so far away.

Correctional officers, of course, are not inmates. They have a great deal of power over a large number of human beings and they can leave the prison every day. The fact that they spent a lot of time with inmates and have a similar perspective on many aspects of prison life is not in itself sufficient to generate a subculture. A subculture becomes likely when the officers' situation as described becomes problematic.

Because the formation of a subculture is generally a group response to commonly felt conflict, the officer subculture, if it exists, is probably rather recent. While guards may have had a tense, low-paying job fifty years ago, they also had a rather clear-cut role. Officers were in power and inmates were out. Officers told inmates what to do and the inmates obeyed or were punished. In a confrontation, the administration assumed a guard's story was true and an inmate's was a fabrication.

As the image of the inmate has changed considerably in the last fifty years, and he is treated in a considerably different manner by prison administrators, so, too, has the image and treatment of the correctional officer changed. While fifty years ago he guarded subhumans and misbehavior against them was excusable, whenever it was even recognized, today a correctional officer is responsible for the management of human beings, whose word clinically and legally may stand up against his own. More importantly, most correctional officers openly agree that the change in policy is for the better. There may be some regrets about losing the clear-cut rules of yesterday, and there are certainly many complaints about the lack of power and respect today, but most correctional officers do not and would not care to deny that inmates are fellow human beings who should be "getting a better shake." It is only after this fundamental shift in the generally perceived humanity of inmates that the officer subculture has come about. The correctional officer subculture, more than anything else, is born of the frustrating belief that inmates on the whole deserve better treatment than officers (or others) are capable of giving under present circumstances. Just what correctional officers expect of themselves or correctional organizations is not always clear, but in keeping with the new view of inmates, *they expect something more and different from mere order.* As one officer expressed it: "I'm not sure what I'm here for; I know it is not security. Let's face it—the joint's secure. No, I must be good for something different."[4]

4. The quotation is taken from interviews conducted in a minimum security prison, which will be described momentarily. The sentiment expressed was representative of the feeling of roughly half of the officers in the institution.

In part, much of the officer value complex may be built on this flight from ambiguity: that officers have discarded the goal of punishment and find in its place only the competing claims of professors, researchers, politicians, managers, counselors, and inmates, none of which they are willing to accept. They are in the anomic position of working for a goal which is negatively defined as the absence of punishment and is manifested by no acceptably measured results and is mediated by no reliably correlated means.[5]

### EMPIRICAL INVESTIGATIONS OF THE OFFICER SUBCULTURE

While there has been an increasing amount of research into correctional processes and correctional organization, we still know rather little about the men who make up the largest bulk of correctional staff.[6] Much more of the research effort has been expended on the study of the offender. If the behavior of the offender is perceived, reported, and responded to by staff, this research emphasis is fatally inadequate. If the treated are interacting with the treaters, we must also keep systematic information on the treaters.[7] This lack of information also makes difficult any inferences about one segment of that group. It will be difficult to say officers belong to a subculture unless we can see the divergence between the way they feel and the way their superiors feel. Hence, we must also have data about the values of correctional managers.

Several kinds of information about correctional personnel can be gathered. For example, we can seek to know age, educational level, father's social status, number of previous jobs, number of cars owned, kinds of magazines read. Differences between managers and correctional officers on these kinds of variables might point to differences in value, but they would not give us any direct information about the way staff at any level perform in the correctional institution. This kind of background data, of course, might help us to explain some of the differences between values, if we found some. However, the program of action reported here was based on the assumption that organizational variables would have more effect on organizational performance than other kinds of variables. We assumed, for example, that an inference about a warden's treatment of offenders is more safely built on a knowledge of his correctional goals than on a knowledge of the university attended. Likewise, to know how an officer behaves, it is more important to know his values and beliefs about correction than his father's social status or the level of his income. Also, in terms of alternatives of planned change, it seems more likely that interventions can be made to help clarify and influence his views of correction more easily than can interventions be aimed at changing his father's social status or income level.

The investigation of an officer subculture was designed to employ three major variables: correctional policy, managerial behavior, and social climate. By comparing the scores of

5. See Donald Cressey, "Nature and Effectiveness of Correctional Techniques," *Law and Contemporary Problems*, 23 (Autumn 1958), pp. 754-771.

6. John J. Calvin and Loren Daracki, *Manpower and Training in Correctional Institutions*, Joint Commission on Correctional Manpower and Training, Staff Report, December 1969, p. 11.

7. Leslie Wilkins, *Social Deviance*, Englewood Cliffs, N. J.: Prentice-Hall, 1966, pp. 230-231.

various hierarchical levels on these variables on three different questionnaire scales, we can decide whether there is sufficient distance between groups to label the officer scores the manifestation of a subculture.

## THE RESEARCH SITE

The research was conducted in the Department of Correction of a northeastern state. Research entrée was gained during a management training seminar. The top managers of the Central Office and of each of the major institutions in the department responded to questionnaires measuring their correctional policy and their managerial behavior before attending the seminar. During the course of the seminar, it was decided jointly by the managers and the consultants that additional data were desirable about the consequence of managerial strategies. Questionnaires measuring social climate and supervisory behavior were then administered to a random sample of 20 per cent of all staff and inmates in the department.

Additionally, one superintendent volunteered his institution for more in-depth study on the correctional officer and inmate levels. A battery of interviews was conducted at this minimum security prison in order to validate the questionnaire findings and to fill the gaps in our knowledge of the process of policy formulation and implementation. Unless otherwise noted, the data presented in this paper were gathered in the departmental survey of six institutions. Observational and interview data were collected at the minimum security prison.

A major field experiment and organizational change program, the first phases of which are reported at the end of this paper, are now under way at the minimum security prison.

## CORRECTIONAL POLICY

The correctional goals or correctional policy of the various groups in the insitution was measured through the administration of the *Correctional Policy Inventory*.[8] This questionnaire attempts to measure official's relative preferences for four correction models. These models are founded on Kelman's research on qualitative differences in change strategies.[9] Basically, Kelman states that there are three strategies of changing people:

(1) *Compliance,* in which the change agent manipulates the punishment-reward system to guide the changee's responses. Change lasts no longer than surveillance.

(2) *Identification,* in which the changee values the relationship with the change agent. New behavior lasts as long as relationship is salient.

(3) *Internalization,* in which the change agent provides the changee with new information and opportunities. Change tends to be lasting because new behaviors are adopted and internalized as congruent with the changee's value system.

Kelman's typology was "correctionalized" by distributing his change strategies over a two dimensional grid of specifically correctional concerns: concerns for the individual inmate and concern for the community.[10] By

---

8. See Vincent O'Leary and David Duffee, "Correctional Policy: A Classification of Goals Designed for Change," *Crime and Delinquency,* Vol. 7 (October 1971), pp. 373-386. The inventory itself is also available: Vincent O'Leary, *The Correctional Policy Inventory,* Hackensack, N.J.: NCCD, 1970.

9. Herbert Kelman, "Compliance, Identification and Internalization: Three Processes of Attitude Change," *Journal of Convict Resolution,* Vol. 2 (1958), pp. 51-60.

10. See, for example, Daniel Glaser, *Effectiveness of a Prison and Parole System,* Indianapolis: Bobbs-Merrill, 1969, chapter on the parole officers' role (protection and service); Robert P. Schenrell, "Variation and

Diagram 1
Models of Correctional Policy

|  | | LOW | HIGH |
|---|---|---|---|
| CONCERN FOR INDIVIDUAL | HIGH | Rehabilitation<br><br>Identification focus | Reintegration<br><br>Internalization focus |
|  | LOW | Restraint<br><br>Organizational focus (no change) | Reform<br><br>Compliance focus |

CONCERN FOR COMMUNITY

assuming a high and low on both of these concerns, four correctional models emerge.[11] (See Diagram 1.) The inventory using these models was given to top and middle management in the northeastern state before their seminar training, and simpler, adapted forms were administered to officers and inmates at the one minimum security prison. The resulting scores represent the presence of considerable conflict among prison and department personnel. While managers report their policy preference as Reintegration or Rehabilitation (either of which implies high concern for inmates), officers report that they guard inmates in a Reform fashion (high concern for community) and inmates report that they perceive only Restraint in operation (that the prison is run only with administrative ease in mind). (See Table 1.)

These policy configurations are interesting in several respects. First, the policy most desired by administration is not reaching the officer and inmate levels. Second, the same kind of conflict was apparent in interviews conducted at other state institutions, and was apparently not a function of variables limited to one institution. Third, reports from various correctional settings suggests that this trend may be standard nationally.[12]

It appears that, at the demonstration prison, the major policy trans-

Decision Making in Correctional Social Work," *Issues in Criminology,* Vol. 4, No. 2, Fall 1969, p. 101; and Don Gottfredson, *Measuring Attitudes toward Juvenile Delinquency,* New York: National Council on Crime and Delinquency, 1968.

11. Glaser and Schrag use several of the following terms in their description of correctional eras. Daniel Glaser, "The Prospect for Corrections," paper prepared for the *Arden House Conference on Manpower Needs in Corrections,* mimeographed, 1964; Clarence Shrag, "Contemporary Corrections: An Analytical Model," paper prepared for the President's Commission on Law Enforcement and Administration of Justice, mimeographed, 1966.

12. David Street, Robert Vinter, and Charles Perrow, *Organization for Treatment,* New York: Free Press, 1966; Kim Nelson and Catherine Lovell, *Developing Correctional Administrators,* research report to the Joint Commission on Correctional Manpower and Training, December 1969; Mayer Zald, "Power Balance and Staff Conflict in Correctional Institutions," *Administrative Science Quarterly,* Vol 6 (June 1962), pp. 22-49.

TABLE 1
AVERAGE POLICY SCORE BY ORGANIZATIONAL LEVEL*

| Level | Reintegration | Rehabilitation | Reform | Restraint |
|---|---|---|---|---|
| Top Administration (N=30) | 80.0 | 76.8 | 57.7 | 48.2 |
| Middle Managers (N=25) | 69.8 | 80.3 | 66.0 | 56.2 |
| Officers (N=42) | 55.2 | 68.4 | 77.7 | 61.5 |
| Inmates (N-88) | 59.7 | 57.0 | 80.0 | 90.0 |

* Explanation of Table 1. First choice of Level is underscored. All possible t-test differences significant at .01. The correctional policy questionnaire is based on a 1-10 scale for 40 questions. Each policy total has a range from 10-100. Significance of second and third choices may be analyzed in terms of how close they are to first choices. Top administration would rather quickly revert to Rehabilitation (a difference of 3.2 from Reintegration), while officer first choice is much higher than their second choice.

formation occurs at the officer level. Top and middle managers merely reverse first and second choices, while officers have a completely different set of values, preferring change through compliance to any other strategy and opting for the Restraint Model, which offers no change at all, to the Reintegration Model. Since the officers have more contact with inmates than any other organizational members, a significant step in modernizing correctional practice, or implementing policies that have more change potential, is changing correctional officers' values.[13]

---

13. While the work of O'Leary and Duffee is the only material to date that treats "Reintegration" in a measurable and systematic way, many other studies have suggested that Reintegrative Policy is the most promising method of effectuating successful inmate return to the community. Other than studies already mentioned, the work of Harold Bradley seems most convincing. See "Community-based Treatment for Young Adult Offenders," *Journal of Crime and Delinquency,* Vol. 15, No. 3 (July 1969), pp. 359-370, and Bradley *et al., Design for Change: A Program for Correctional Management,* final report, Model Treatment Program, Sacramento, Calif.: Institute for the Study of Crime and Delinquency, July 1968.

THE SOCIAL CLIMATE SCALE

While there may be many different specific reasons for the formation of values, a generalized behavioristic interpretation would be that values help to solve an individual's problems. In this case, we should seek a measure of the way in which the organization affects the individual officer. One way in which the organization affects him is the way in which the social patterns of behavior impress upon the individual and support his acting in certain ways. One measure of the "environmental press" upon individuals was devised by Rudolph Moos. Dr. Moos began his investigations on the effects of mental hospital atmosphere on mental patients. He then altered his instrument for application in correctional institutions. The pretest was administered in juvenile institutions in California.[14] It has since then been

---

14. Rudolph Moos, "The Assessment of the Social Climates of Correctional Institutions," *Journal of Research in Crime and Delinquency,* Vol. 5 (July 1968), pp. 74-88; Ernst Wenk and Rudolph Moos, "Social Climate in Prisons: An Attempt to Conceptualize and Measure Environmental Factors in Total Institutions," *Journal of Research*

utilized in several adult correctional institutions.[16]

Moos broke his social environment into twelve fairly independent dimensions: Spontaneity, Support, Practicality, Affiliation, Order, Insight, Involvement, Aggression, Variety, Clarity, Submission, and Autonomy. These dimensions are relevant to the world of staff as well as the world of inmates. Of interest for the hypothesized existence of an officer subculture are the dimensions as scored by different staff levels, by managerial type, and as correlated with policy scores.

A random sample of correctional staff and inmates was chosen by selecting every fifth name from inmate and staff files. The total population was divided into five hierarchical levels: (1) warden through lieutenants, (2) counselors and teachers, (3) clerical, (4) officers, and (5) inmates. Since the data are used here to analyze the possibility of an officer subculture, the scores of groups 1, 4, and 5 have been chosen as most relevant. The two other groups are tangential to the chain-of-command and to the major set of interactions that we wish to consider here. The social climate dimension means for the three groups are given in Table 2.

Evident in the data of Table 2 is a steady downward decline from warden to officer to inmate on the positive dimensions of the social climate scale

### TABLE 2
### SOCIAL CLIMATE DIMENSION MEANS
### FOR THREE HIERARCHICAL LEVELS

| DIMENSION | MANAGERS N= 32 | OFFICERS 182 | INMATES 430 |
|---|---|---|---|
| SPONTANEITY | 4.03 | 4.13 | 2.45 |
| SUPPORT | 5.84 | 5.41 | 2.79 |
| PRACTICALITY | 6.44 | 5.88 | 4.38 |
| AFFILIATION | 6.69 | 6.39 | 3.39 |
| ORDER | 6.94 | 6.51 | 3.33 |
| INSIGHT | 5.09 | 4.65 | 3.36 |
| INVOLVEMENT | 4.62 | 3.84 | 3.44 |
| AGGRESSION | 6.13 | 6.62 | 7.24 |
| VARIETY | 5.97 | 5.59 | 4.13 |
| CLARITY | 5.41 | 5.02 | 2.16 |
| SUBMISSION | 7.16 | 6.66 | 7.23 |
| AUTONOMY | 3.56 | 3.52 | 2.13 |

and a steady increase from warden to inmate on the negative dimensions. The significance of the difference in the variation from level to level was tested through an analysis of variance. In all cases but on the dimensions of aggression and submission, there was an among-level variation in the dimension scores significant at the .01 level. In other words, these three different levels of the organization felt considerably different environmental presses or the three groups felt considerably different social forces that might influence their behavior.

### MANAGERIAL BEHAVIOR

So far we have seen a considerable variation in the perception of the correctional policy operating in the institution, and a considerable difference in the social climate perceived at three different levels of the organization. A question arises about the process that intervenes between policy formation and daily action. What variable or variables might connect these three levels in such a way that variations in

in *Crime and Delinquency*, Vol. 9, No. 2 (July 1972), pp. 134-148; and "Prison Environments—The Social Ecology of Correctional Institutions," *Crime and Delinquency Literature*, Vol. 4, No. 4 (December 1972), pp. 591-621.

15. In addition to the present study and the Wenk and Moos articles (supra note 14), see Colin Frank and Randy Michel, "Inmate Performance Pay Demonstration Project: Final Report," Federal Bureau of Prisons, Jan. 1, 1972 (mimeo.).

| | |
|---|---|
| 1. The records which are kept in the organization fail to reflect the real work that is being done.  : _ : _ : _ : _ : _ : | The records which are kept in the organization really measure how well the job is getting done. |

policy and social climate might be explained?

O'Leary and Duffee have argued that the managerial style of a supervisor is the most important intervening variable between the statement of a correctional policy and its implementation.[16] Several different methods of measuring managerial behavior have been used. Two of the best known are the two-dimensional approach of Blake and Mouton[17] and the autocratic-democratic continuum of Likert.[18] In order to test the relationships of managerial behavior, policy, and social climate, an "organizational profile" questionnaire was devised and administered to staff along with the social climate scale. The questionnaire was originally designed as a "reversed managerial grid," by which subordinates would rate their supervisors on the two dimensions of concern for employees and concern for production. However, the fifteen questions for each dimension did not prove independent. Therefore, the Blake-Mouton grid-format was discarded and a simple continuum was substituted. While the questionnaire does not measure concern for personnel and concern for organizational needs separately, it does measure the per-

ception by personnel of general managerial "openness" or democratic orientation, and "closure" or autocratic orientation.

The original questionnaire consisted of thirty items. When it was seen that two-dimensionality was not achievable, the decision was made to choose the ten items with the highest correlation to the total score. Each item consists of two statements about a specific organizational activity, separated by a five-space scale. The respondents were asked to check the space that they felt represented the behavior of their organization on that activity (see sample above). The items were scored from zero at the item extreme that represented the perception of insensitivity, inaccuracy, or closure in the organization to four at the item extreme that represented the perception of sensitivity, accuracy, and openness in the organization. The scores on the ten-item questionnaire ranged from 0 (or completely closed) to 40 (or completely open).

Table 3 shows that the organization is perceived as most open by the role incumbents on the managerial level, and the organization is perceived as most closed by the role incumbents on the officer level. The scores for the counselor and clerical groups have been retained in this analysis in order to demonstrate the relationship of officers to all employed staff, and because an inmate comparison is not possible here. Needless to say, comparison of managers and officers alone also yields a significant difference. Table 4

16. Vincent O'Leary and David Duffee, "Managerial Behavior and Correctional Policy," *Public Administration Review* (November/December 1971), pp. 603-616.

17. Robert Blake and Jane Mouton, *The Managerial Grid*, Houston: Gulf, 1964.

18. Rensis Likert, *New Patterns of Management*, New York: McGraw-Hill, 1961; *The Human Organization*, New York: Wiley, 1967.

TABLE 3

ORGANIZATIONAL PROFILE MEANS FOR
FOUR PRISON HIERARCHICAL LEVELS

| | LEVEL | N | MEAN |
|---|---|---|---|
| 1. | MANAGERS | 31 | 22.29 |
| 2. | COUNSELORS, ETC. | 45 | 20.07 |
| 3. | CLERICAL | 14 | 20.71 |
| 4. | OFFICERS | 181 | 16.91 |

shows that the differences in the organizaional profile scores among hierarchical groups are significant at considerably better than .05. There is, then, some evidence of correlation between a relatively healthy environmental press upon the individual and his perception of the organization as open or democratic, and, *vice versa*, there is a relationship between an unhealthy environmental press and the perception of the organization as closed or autocratic.

TABLE 4

ORGANIZATIONAL PROFILE AS REPORTED
BY STAFF, CLASSIFIED BY
HIERARCHICAL LEVEL

| | d.f. | M.S. |
|---|---|---|
| VARIANCE AMONG STAFF LEVELS | 3 | 354.60 |
| RESIDUAL | 267 | 105.43 |
| VARIANCE RATIO | 3.36 | (p>.05) |

SOCIAL CLIMATE DIMENSIONS BY
ORGANIZATIONAL PROFILE

In order to test the hypothesis that the organizational profile may be used to delineate distinct social climates, employee groups were devised that were within or without two standard deviations from the organizational

profile mean. Three employee groups were thereby distinguished: (1) a group perceiving the organization as very open (scores of 28.5+); (2) a middle group perceiving the organization as average (scores from 7.5-28); and (3) a group perceiving the organization as very closed (scores of less than 7.5).[19] The analysis of variance performed on the social climate dimensions for these profile groups yielded significant differences on all dimensions but aggression and submission. (See Table 5.)

In all cases where there is a difference of significance, the comparison of social climate means demonstrates the impact of the perception of an open or democratic organization. (See Table 6.) For example, personnel who feel that they are managed in an open manner have a mean Support score of 7.15, while the average group has a mean of 5.95 and the group that feels managed in a closed manner has a mean of 3.92. The open group has a Practicality mean of 7.60, as opposed to 4.18 for the closed group. In other words, persons who feel that they are managed openly also feel that the prison social climate includes a consideration for the accomplishment of specific practical goals. Personnel who feel that they are managed in a closed fashion feel that the prison has little practical value. In the same way, the group managed openly feels it is much easier to make friends on the job (Affiliation mean of 7.77) than the group managed in a closed fashion (Affiliation mean of 4.94). Likewise, the open group feels more Spontaneity, Order,

19. These three groups may be considered analogous to Likert's System III, II, and I management patterns, respectively, *The Human Organization, op. cit. supra* note 18, pp. 3-12.

Insight, Involvement, Variety, Clarity, and Autonomy in the prison climate.

It seems clear that the way in which men perceive themselves to be managed has considerable influence on the kind of social situation they find themselves in. In general terms, the open-managed group lives in a healthy atmosphere; the closed group, in an unhealthy and strained one. The effects, then, that management can have on the ability of personnel to interact in open and considerate ways with inmates would seem to be great. It would seem much more likely for example, for officers who feel great amounts of Spontaneity, Support, and Practicality about their work situation to extend the much greater effort that is needed in order to make inmates perceive and react to Reintegrative and Rehabilitative behavioral patterns rather than Reform and Restraint patterns.

TABLE 5

SOCIAL CLIMATE DIMENSIONS AS REPORTED BY STAFF, CLASSIFIED BY RESPONSE, ON ORGANIZATIONAL PROFILE QUESTIONNAIRE

| DIMENSION | VARIATION AMONG PROFILE SCORE LEVELS (open, avg. closed) | | RESIDUAL | | VARIANCE RATIO | p. |
|---|---|---|---|---|---|---|
| | degrees of freedom | mean square | degrees of freedom | mean square | | |
| SPONTANEITY | 2 | 15.18 | 268 | 3.52 | 4.31 | p<.05 |
| SUPPORT | 2 | 136.90 | 268 | 4.00 | 34.20 | p<.01 |
| PRACTICALITY | 2 | 157.49 | 268 | 5.25 | 28.54 | p<.01 |
| AFFILIATION | 2 | 107.70 | 268 | 4.13 | 26.06 | p<.01 |
| ORDER | 2 | 53.77 | 268 | 6.45 | 8.34 | p<.01 |
| INSIGHT | 2 | 12.91 | 268 | 3.90 | 3.30 | p<.05 |
| INVOLVEMENT | 2 | 123.31 | 268 | 6.18 | 19.97 | p<.01 |
| AGGRESSION | 2 | 27.31 | 268 | 30.14 | .91 | p>.10 |
| VARIETY | 2 | 31.47 | 268 | 10.15 | 3.10 | p<.05 |
| CLARITY | 2 | 190.00 | 268 | 7.30 | 26.02 | p<.01 |
| SUBMISSION | 2 | 4.10 | 268 | 3.36 | 1.22 | p>.10 |
| AUTONOMY | 2 | 41.32 | 268 | 3.87 | 10.68 | p<.01 |
| POSITIVE HALO | 2 | 19.42 | 268 | 1.44 | 13.52 | p<.01 |
| NEGATIVE HALO | 2 | 11.32 | 268 | 4.84 | 2.32 | p<.10 |

## TABLE 6
### SOCIAL CLIMATE MEANS FOR THREE ORGANIZATIONAL PROFILE LEVELS FOR STAFF IN SIX PRISONS OF A NORTHEASTERN STATE

| Social Climate Dimension | LOW (Closed) N=51 | MEDIUM N=168 | HIGH (Open) N=52 |
|---|---|---|---|
| SPONTANEITY | 3.65 | 4.36 | 4.69 |
| SUPPORT | 3.92 | 5.95 | 7.15 |
| PRACTICALITY | 4.18 | 6.37 | 7.60 |
| AFFILIATION | 4.94 | 6.80 | 7.75 |
| ORDER | 5.73 | 6.76 | 7.77 |
| INSIGHT | 4.27 | 4.91 | 5.25 |
| INVOLVEMENT | 2.75 | 4.48 | 5.83 |
| AGGRESSION | 6.90 | 5.94 | 6.83 |
| VARIETY | 4.75 | 5.57 | 6.31 |
| CLARITY | 3.45 | 5.27 | 7.29 |
| SUBMISSION | 6.63 | 6.58 | 6.15 |
| AUTONOMY | 2.84 | 3.74 | 4.63 |

### CORRELATION OF ORGANIZATIONAL PROFILE AND SOCIAL CLIMATE

In Table 7, the direct relationship between social climate dimensions of Support, Practicality, Affiliation, Order, Involvement, Clarity, and Au-

## TABLE 7
### PRODUCT-MOMENT CORRELATIONS OF SOCIAL CLIMATE DIMENSION SCORES AND ORGANIZATIONAL PROFILE SCORE FOR STAFF OF SIX PRISONS IN A NORTHEASTERN STATE

| | |
|---|---|
| SPONTANEITY | .1942 |
| SUPPORT | .5319* |
| PRACTICALITY | .4441* |
| AFFILIATION | .4293* |
| ORDER | .2859* |
| INSIGHT | .1587 |
| INVOLVEMENT | .4523* |
| AGGRESSION | -.0534 |
| VARIETY | .1202 |
| CLARITY | .4280* |
| SUBMISSION | -.0662 |
| AUTONOMY | .2817* |

N = 271 Correctional Personnel

*P = .01 when r = .254

tonomy and the organizational profile score is visible. The higher, or more open, the employee reports the organization to be in its treatment of him, the higher the social climate dimensions.

### SOCIAL CLIMATE DIMENSIONS AND CORRECTIONAL POLICY

O'Leary and Duffee have demonstrated that there is a strong correlation between particular styles of management and certain correctional policy choices.[20] Although they used the self-reported *Inventory of Managerial Styles*[21] as a measure of managerial behavior rather than the subordinate-reported autocratic-democratic continuum used here, we might expect similar results. Officers who report that management is more open also report a more livable social climate. Since we know that managers who are the most open most frequently espouse Reintegration or Rehabilitation as correctional policy, we might expect the officers with the most healthy climate to behave most frequently in ways supportive of Reintegration or Rehabilitation. Although the data on this point are admittedly slim, this is decidedly not the case. The social climate dimensions that correlated most strongly with open management also correlate, on the officer level, with Reform and Restraint oriented behavior. These relationships are visible in Table 8. Reform oriented officer behavior correlates with Support (.32), Practicality (.40), Affiliation (.36), Order (.34), and Clarity (.56). In other words, the common-sense conclusion that a democratic and open

20. O'Leary and Duffee, note 34 *supra*, p. 611.

21. Jay Hall, Herry Harvey, and Martha Williams, Austin: Teliometrics, 1964.

TABLE 8

PRODUCT-MOMENT CORRELATIONS OF CORRECTIONAL POLICY TOTALS
AND SOCIAL CLIMATE DIMENSION TOTALS FOR CORRECTIONAL OFFICERS

| Climate Dimensions | POLICY | | | |
|---|---|---|---|---|
| | REINTEGRATION | REHABILITATION | REFORM | RESTRAINT |
| SPONTANEITY | .14 | .38 | -.14 | -.38 |
| SUPPORT | -.11 | -.02 | .32 | -.10 |
| PRACTICALITY | .08 | -.06 | .40 | .42 |
| AFFILIATION | .24 | .10 | .36 | -.09 |
| ORDER | .11 | -.27 | .34 | .50 |
| INSIGHT | .46 | .26 | -.07 | -.09 |
| INVOLVEMENT | .08 | -.03 | .03 | .06 |
| AGGRESSION | -.15 | .21 | -.07 | -.57 |
| VARIETY | .19 | -.35 | .12 | .17 |
| CLARITY | .11 | -.18 | .56 | .42 |
| SUBMISSION | .21 | -.18 | -.17 | .45 |
| AUTONOMY | -.16 | .26 | -.01 | -.39 |

N=18 and the resultant matrix should be used only as an indicator of possible relationships. Research into the officer level was not possible under the training grant, except where Managerial Style was an issue. These 18 men filled out additional questionnaires on their own time. They were randomly selected from the officer group, but N is quite small.

management would produce an officer group who were open with inmates is not upheld. The correlation between organizational profile and social climate would suggest that officers *like* democratic superiors, but the correlation between climate and policy suggests that officers feel very uncomfortable if they behave, or are asked to behave, in a democratic manner with their own subordinates, the inmates.

It is evident that changing officer values about correctional policy involves change in a whole set of organizational variables that at the present time reinforce the Reform preference of Officers. Regardless of what administrators desire or research can show to be more effective with (and more desired by) inmates, officers received no reward for changing their own behavior if Reintegration and Rehabilitation strategies make them

less satisfied with the job, or less comfortable in the institutional environment.

Part of the policy formulation-implementation gap must be seen in terms of daily operations of an ongoing prison with considerable history behind it. While most administrators favor policies that involved high concern for inmates,[22] these newer

22. They may do so for many reasons. In the training conferences conducted during this research, Reintegration was most popular with top administrators. They work in a time when the culture demands of professional personnel a new, compassionate view of inmates. The Reintegration Policy "sounds" better when reported to outside community groups. It is also intellectually more satisfying to discover a policy strategy in which concern for inmates and concern for community are seen as compatible, mutually satisfying concerns. Furthermore, this group of managers is highly educated and relatively talented—as well as elevated and isolated

policies have not been implemented from the ground up. Officers who for years have guarded maximum security inmates in the traditional manner of Reform or Restraint have been asked to switch affiliations rather suddenly, but many of their rewards and most of their ideas of what makes a good guard are still based on the traditional system of the paramilitary virtues of aloofness to their subordinates, strict adherence to rules, and unquestioning loyalty to the warden.[23] Hence, the new policies have remained intangible goals on lower organizational levels, and the tangible goals used in the evaluation of daily activity are a poor translation of long-range departmental desires. In such situations, officers are unlikely to perform "above and beyond the call of duty."[24]

SUMMARY OF RESEARCH FINDINGS

The research in this project involved three questionnaires measuring staff and inmate scores on the three scales of Correctional Policy, Organizational Profile, and Social Climate. The data of Table 1 demonstrated a significant divergence between top- and middle-management report of the policy they preferred and the officer and inmate report of the policy being implemented in the institution. Table

2 demonstrates that the social climate or environmental press impinging upon managers, officers, and inmates was also different. Managers perceived a relatively healthy social climate; officers, a considerably more strained or unhealthy atmosphere; and inmates, the most unhealthy social climate.

It was hypothesized that, at least on the staff level, divergencies in policy and climate might be explained by the way in which staff perceive themselves to be managed. The organizational profile questionnaire was devised to test these differences along an autocratic-democratic continuum. Table 3 demonstrated that managers perceived the organization to be most democratic and officers perceived the organization to be most autocratic. Table 4 showed these differences to be statistically significant.

Since there was a differential perception of organization by hierarchical level, and also a differential social climate by hierarchical level, the relationship between organizational profile and social climate was tested by analyzing the social climate by level of democracy-autocracy perceived by the respondents. Table 5 demonstrates that this analysis significantly distinguishes different social climates on all but two subscales. In Table 6 the social climate dimension means for the three organizational profile groups demonstrated that staff perceiving the most democratic supervision also perceive the healthiest social climate, and the staff perceiving the most autocratic supervision also perceive the least healthy social climate. Table 7 underscores the relationship of organizational profile and social climate in a different way, by presenting correlations of the two scores. There is a direct relationship between a healthy

---

from the kind of pressure felt by officers. Indeed, all organizational pressures at the top level press for Reintegration, which, as a systemic policy, is most easily comprehended from the top, where interrelation of the entire department is recognized.

23. See Donald Cressey, "Contradictory Directives in Complex Organizations: The Case of the Prison," *Administrative Science Quarterly*, 4 (June 1959), pp. 1-19.

24. See W. Keith Warner and A. Eugene Havens, "Goal Displacement and the Intangibility of Organizational Goals," *Administrative Science Quarterly*, 12, 9 (March 1968), pp. 539-555.

social climate and more democratic organizational profile scores.

Finally, Table 8 presents correlations that were available between correctional policy scores and social climate for officers. The assumptions that underlie this data presentation are most important to our conclusions. First, we have seen that the goals of the correctional institution chosen by managers are not implemented. Second, we have seen that different managerial behavior patterns are clearly related to the degree of comfort or health that staff feel in their social climate. Third, we have seen that officers, like everyone else, feel more comfortable under democratic supervision. The essential question, then, is what kind of social climate, which might be interpreted as the kind of social reward, do officers feel to be associated with the four correctional goals. Although the number of officers tested is small, the present data suggest that officers are fairly uncomfortable with the social climates associated with Reintegration and Rehabilitation. They find much stronger social reward with Reform and Restraint policies.

This finding contrasts strongly with previous research that O'Leary and Duffee conducted with correctional managers. On the managerial level it was found that the most democratic managers also preferred Reintegration and Rehabilitation policies. The present data suggest that while democratic supervision does provide a healthy social climate for officers, officers do not perceive a healthy climate to be associated with the goals of that supervision: namely, Reintegration and Rehabilitation policy.

*In toto*, the data seem to support the hypothesis of an officer occupational subculture, the values of which

are antagonistic to the successful implementation of managerially desired correctional policy. While officers will find rewarding the social consequences of democratic management, they do not find rewarding the social consequences of the correctional policy desired by their superiors. It becomes crucial, then, to devise ways of changing the correctional officers' perception of the social rewards that they perceive to be associated with modern correctional policy.

## IMPLICATIONS FOR TRAINING

While we now seem aware that changing an inmate is a much more complex, time consuming, and interesting activity than a high-flown lecture on morality and civil duty, most training for correctional officers (where any is offered) amounts to little more than that. In the course of an orientation class or within the rubric of a training academy, correctional officers may be given several hours of lecture on such things as "Role of the Counselor," "Human Behavior," and "Leadership and Employee Attitudes."[25] While the goal of such training is admirable and its implementation is long overdue, the process used to convey the content is not always compatible with the kind of behavior desired in correctional officers as a result of the training. The most common format of these sessions is straight, stand-up lecture by selected governmental personnel who have some functional relation to the topic to be covered. Lectures may be broken by films and on-site visits, and there is generally some time for question-an-

---

25. Lecture topics have been taken from the Basic Training School course catalogue from one Eastern State. Other training academies provide similar offerings.

swer-discussion sessions[26] after the formal talk. In other words, the "courses" in the training academies often tend to be taught in the style of a several-period lecture on the freshman level in a university.

It is likely that an hour or two of lecture on a particular subject has a miniscule effect on even the best students listening to the best professor in a good university. Such lectures are only effective as they counterpoint carefully selected readings and occur within the peculiar university atmosphere where foreign ideas, even in the least interested students, enjoy some prestige. Such is not the case in a correctional training academy where many officers hold little respect for "book learning,"[27] or for the men whose learning is from books rather than the real life of the cell block.

In spite of such problems, the usual educational techniques may be of some value—*so long as the goal of the educator is to impart information.*

26. Trainees at two academies that the author is acquainted with personally usually select the discussion periods as the most rewarding.

27. The lack of respect, of course, may be caused by a number of other factors such as envy and anger at those who are educated, threat to self-image for not being educated, anger at and resentment of economic demands that precluded education, or disenchantment with college or academy programs that do not reflect the realities of custodial supervision. Also, the suggestion was made elsewhere that traditional university education is only effective in the context of the campus culture. When training or retraining is to provide trainees with information and the ability to use it in non-university settings, considerably more attention must be paid to the process (as opposed to the content) of training. See Roger Harrison and Richard Hopkins, "The Design of Cross-cultural Training: An Alternative to the University Model," *Journal of Applied Behavioral Science*, Vol. III, No. 4 (1967), pp. 431-460.

While it is true that our schools and colleges do change the behavior of the students who attend, it seems likely that changes in behavior can be attributed to the forceful socialization processes that occur in the institutions of education, not to the content of lectures. A quantum of information itself *may* change a person's behavior but it is likely to change his tactics *within* a pre-set perspective and pattern of behavior.[28] The information itself is likely to be received and interpreted within that mental and emotional framework. Within somebody else's circumstances, that piece of information may bring quite a different response. In correctional training where courses have been devised in order to change correctional officer behavior, it is quite possible that the wrong design is being used. If the major goal is to change behavior (i.e., to increase cooperation between custodial and treatment staff), a more effective design would be one that could cut through the ideological differences between the people involved. An analogous problem occurs when a counselor tries to break through the values of the inmate caste in order to reach the individual inmate.

We would no longer plan to change an inmate subculture by lecturing to inmates on the advantages of "doing your own time," or the virtues of obeying the rules. On the contrary, we are aware that such a subculture breaks down when it ceases to have pay-off, as when new careerists take on paraprofessional roles and learn new ways of gaining status, prestige, and

28. Within the "ideology," as that term is used by John Griffiths, "Ideology in Criminal Procedure or a Third Model of the Criminal Process," 79 *Yale Law Journal* (1970) at 359, footnote 1.

money.[29] Similarly, the typical training program conducted for correctional officers ignores the problem that information received by officers in the course of training will be interpreted in terms of the values that they hold important. If the goal of officer training is to change officer behavior (i.e., to make it compatible with a certain policy), then methods of training should be employed that can change the weight that officers place on certain kinds of information.

### Changing the Officer Subculture

There is no reason why the method most recently employed and most successful in breaking down the inmate culture might not also be used in undermining the officer value-set. This strategy involves "use of products of a social problem in coping with the social problem."[30] The basic notion in this mode of change is that people will accept as trainees information and behavior that they would not accept as changees. Toch has had success both with violent inmates and violent policemen when they were enlisted in a project to study and change violent behavior in others.[31]

The problem to be confronted by this kind of technique used with correctional officers is not to reduce violence, but to reduce the pressures on the officer that lead him to be more comfortable with Reform and Restraint behavior patterns. The published literature at this point is so devoid of any reliable reports of what officers think about, want to do, or want to see changed in correction that it is difficult at this time even to guess what these pressures might be. The suggestions advanced here are a summary of conclusions from a project that followed the research reported in this paper.[32]

The project began as a weekly discussion session involving six correctional officers and the author. The charge to the group was rather vague, because it was thought that locking the officers into particular issues should be avoided. The relevant goal of the group, as far as this discussion of an occupational subculture is concerned, was simply to examine the

29. See, for example, *Ex-offenders as a Correctional Manpower Resource*, proceedings of a seminar of the Joint Commission on Correctional Manpower and Training, Washington, D.C.: American Correctional Association, 1966.

30. U.S. Department of H.E.W., *Experimental in Culture Expansion*, Report of Proceedings of a Conference on "The Use of Products of a Social Problem in Coping with the Problem," held at the California Rehabilitation Center, Norco, Calif., July 10, 11, and 12, 1963; and see Donald Cressey, "Social Psychological Foundations for Using Criminals in the Rehabilitation of Criminals," *Journal of Research in Crime and Delinquency*, Vol. 2 (1965), pp. 44-55.

31. Hans Toch, *Violent Men*, Chicago: Aldine, 1970; and Hans Toch, J. D. Grant,

and R. Galvin, *Agents of Change: Study in Police Reform*, Cambridge: Schenkeman, 1974. This type of change strategy is generally traced to Kurt Lewin's war work in changing buying habits of civilians. See Lewin, *Resolving Social Conyicts*, New York: Harper and Row, 1948; and "Group Decision and Social Change," in T. Newcomb and E. Hartley (eds.), *Readings in Social Psychology*, New York: Holt, Rinehart, and Winston, 1947.

32. A full report of the activities conducted by the officer discussion groups are available in David Duffee, *Using Correctional Officers in Planned Change*, final research report, National Institute of Law Enforcement and the Administration of Justice, NI-71-115 PG, October 1972. The fact that the National Institute of Law Enforcement and Criminal Justice furnished financial support to the activity described in this publication does not indicate the concurrence of the Institute in the statements or conclusions contained therein.

goals and operations of the institution in order to determine what problems the officers perceived as most relevant to their own echelon. The assumptions upon which the project started were that, if officers were given the role of helping to analyze organizational conflict and contributing to the resolution of conflict, part of that resolution would include changes in their own attitudes and behaviors toward inmates and toward managers. The results of fifty-two weeks of discussion were fairly rewarding. Not only did the officers identify several short-range but crucial problems, but they took organized steps to solve them.

Perhaps the project of greatest risk that they undertook involved changing a departmental policy that required urinalysis of inmates returning from furlough. The departmental policy stated that inmates should be selected at random for this test, the assumption being that the furloughed inmates' knowledge of the impending random selection would reduce drug abuse on furloughs. The officers took the position, however, that it was highly unfair for a man returning from furlough to be subjected at random to 48-hour lockup, if the test results were negative. The fact that six officers with an average length of service of thirteen years should take this position was surprising in and of itself. More telling, perhaps, is that the officers at the beginning of the discussion group project would definitely not have taken the inmates' point of view. It seemed to be the process of the group dynamics approach that changed their reference point.

They became so interested in doing a proficient job of seeking out and solving organizational problems that they began to adopt a researcher's point of view about the value of valid information. Thus, the furlough problem was identified and the officers' strategy to solve it was based upon discussions with disgruntled inmates. It became so important to this group to find out the other side of the story that both an ex-offender and an inmate were invited to become permanent discussion group members.

Through the discussion of the furlough problem and several other tasks that were undertaken, it became evident that the trainee or cohort role was an effective one for changing an officer's perception about the "best way to run a prison." As the project began, the officers were preoccupied with how inmates or superiors impinged upon them, placing them in double-bind situations that could not be resolved. As the discussions progressed, however, their perspective shifted to how all the groups in the prison were, or could be, organized in order to achieve more satisfactory results for everybody.

The major stumbling block that the group encountered turned out to be not their relationships with inmates, but their relationships with superiors. They much more readily accepted the inmates' point of view as valid than they did the point of view of the superintendent. Regardless of the fact that the superintendent had approved the project and had sanctioned their investigation of problems that were traditionally handled by middle-managers, the officers viewed the superintendent's hypothetical veto power as the greatest potential threat to their work and to their new point of view. This attitude on their part underlines the importance of carefully designing such projects from an organizational standpoint. If such a group changes while the organizational environment does not, the potential for damage is great.[33]

The major point for this research, however, is not the development of specific change strategies but the evidence that value-changing techniques were rather effective in changing the behavior of six correctional officers. Based upon these principles, many parallel groups with different tasks have sprung up in the same prison. It seems likely to this researcher that traditional manpower development

techniques, such as those discussed at the beginning of this section, would have considerably less utility. The transfer of information about correctional policy and "modern correctional practices," in and of itself, is not sufficient to change the behavior of correctional officers. Attention must also be given to the process by which information is gathered and disseminated. Officers in the discussion group had a commitment to gathering and using information about new correctional policy and opposing points of view in the institution. A retroflexive consequence of that activity was change in their own behavior, because they began to perceive social rewards for that behavior that they had previously doubted.

---

33. For an example of administrative cooptation of a project that had not gained administrative policy approval, see Elliot Studt, Sheldon L. Messinger, and Thomas P. Wilson, *C-Unit: Search for Community in Prison*, New York: Russell Sage, 1968.

# Part V
# Correctional Ethics as Professional Ethics

# [21]

# Appreciative inquiry and relationships in prison

ALISON LIEBLING, DAVID PRICE AND CHARLES ELLIOTT
*University of Cambridge, UK*

## Abstract

Staff–prisoner relationships are at the heart of the prison system and a stable prison life depends to a large extent on getting these relationships right, particularly in long-term maximum security establishments in the UK. Despite their significance, few studies have explored empirically how these relationships develop and operate. Understanding staff–prisoner interactions requires a detailed and firmly grounded appreciation of the broader tasks prison officers carry out and the nature of prison officer work. Staff–prisoner relationships are invested with an unusual amount of power. This power is, however, 'held in reserve' most of the time, as Sykes argued in 1958. Previous studies have generally regarded prison staff superficially and critically. The study reported in this article employs an innovative 'appreciative' methodology, seeking to allow staff to focus on the best aspects of their work and role, and the conditions in which they function especially well. Two important features of their work – the peacekeeping aspects and the use of discretion – must be considered in any attempt to describe how staff–prisoner relationships are accomplished.

## Key Words

appreciative inquiry · methodology · peacekeeping · prison officers · relationships

'A little example if you want . . . A couple of weeks ago there were some people across from the American service, from Texas. I had a long chat; one was a warden, their equivalent of our Governor. And I toured him around the wing, and he was asking about the regime, how many staff we've got, what type of prisoner we've got on here. He just shook his head in amazement. He said this would never work in America – how do you do it? Well, we talk to prisoners. How can you do that? He just didn't believe what we did. He said that, over there, if you get more than 20 prisoners in a room, they go in there mob-handed with shotguns. And we just go in on our own and talk to them. He couldn't believe it. But we do it; I don't know how we do it, but we do. It's a good example of how professional we are, or how professional we can be, and the goodwill of the prisoners. It works.' (Senior Officer)

'What sort of relationship are you aiming at? . . . It has to be based on honesty, openness, clarity of purpose, boundaries, the ability to exercise humanity, discretion, flexibility where circumstances clearly require it. It's about stepping back from the immediacy of the relationship between criminal and captor; and it's about occasionally remembering that these are husbands, fathers, sons, Buddhists, Christians, artists, well people, sick people. It's about being able to remember that.' (Governor grade)

Despite the centrality of staff–prisoner relationships to prison life, there exists no satisfactory analysis of the nature of this relationship. The word relationship means 'alliance', 'association', 'connection', or 'dependence'. There is a flow of interaction and dependence in two directions (e.g. see Shapira and Navon, 1985), although, in the coercive environment of a prison, the relationship is invested with an unusual amount of power (the ability of one party to influence or determine the behaviour of another party). This power is 'held in reserve' most of the time, so the relationship takes place without explicit reference to it, but both staff and prisoners are aware of who has how much power, and prisoners may try to challenge it, overturn it, or keep it to a minimum. By 'relationship' in the prison context, we mean (something like) sustained periods of interaction, including interaction of a non-rule-enforcing – or rule-resisting – nature. The relationship is made up of some rule-enforcing and many non-rule-enforcing encounters.

It is this special dimension of relationships in prison – the unusually significant place of power – which led us to consider the role of discretion (that is, the use of power) as a primary site for analysis. Prison officer work is 'low visibility' work. The exercise of discretion, which has been recognized as a highly significant field of interest in the policing literature, has not been directly studied in relation to prison life, although it has been raised as an issue of some interest (see, for example, Sparks et al., 1996; also Sykes, 1958; Mathiesen, 1965; Jacobs, 1977; McDermott and King, 1988) and there have been some interesting US studies on the use of authority (Hepburn, 1985; Herbert, 1998; Gilbert, 1997). A few studies exist on aspects of what prison officers *think* (e.g. Colvin, 1977; Lombardo, 1981; Willet, 1983; Marsh et al., 1985; Kauffman, 1988), but little is known about what prison officers in English prisons *do*, particularly in this area of decision-making and the use of power. Decisions prison officers make occur as part of a network of relationships (Hawkins, 1992). The dynamics of prison life exist within this context of complex and embedded relationships, particularly in a dispersal (maximum security) prison,[1] where the sentences served are very long, and staff get to know prisoners well. Power flows through them. What 'goes on' in prison goes on primarily through relationships. They transmit, or contain, degrees of power and authority, *and* degrees of trust and respect. Relationships matter because they influence action. They frame, inform, constrain and facilitate staff and prisoner behaviour.

Research which has considered prison staff has tended to regard the over-use of power as its key – or major – concern. Prison staff are often either neglected or negatively stereotyped in the existing literature (e.g. Morris and Morris, 1963; Cohen and Taylor, 1972; however, see also Thomas, 1972; Jacobs, 1977; Sparks et al., 1996). Their arguably primary *peacekeeping* role, achieved through talk, has been largely overlooked (contrast Bittner, 1967; Sykes and Brent, 1983; McKenzie and Gallagher, 1989; Chan, 1997 for a discussion of this aspect of policing). Prison officers may *under-use* their power more often (and to better effect) than they over-use it. These issues – albeit critical to our understanding of prison life – have rarely been addressed.

In this article, we begin a process of discovery: what is the nature of the staff–prisoner relationship; how do prison officers see their main role in this area of their work; and can this low visibility dimension of prison officer activity be usefully analysed? How is staff power deployed? If, as we believe, there is much to learn from such a study, what is the appropriate methodological approach to take?

## INVESTIGATING STAFF–PRISONER RELATIONSHIPS

The project on which this article is based forms part of a major research programme into staff–prisoner relationships at the Cambridge Institute of Criminology. The research is aimed at developing a better understanding of the nature of such relationships in long-term prisons, and of the ways in which these relationships function and can differ. There are four main components to the overall research strategy:

(i)     A literature review, tendered by the Prison Service and awarded to the Institute of Criminology, researching what is known about prison officers and staff–prisoner relationships, and identifying gaps in that knowledge. The results of this review are being published elsewhere (Price and Liebling, 1998).

(ii)    A detailed ethnographic study of life at a maximum security prison in East Anglia, providing a thorough exploration of 'the prison officer at work' and of staff–prisoner relationships within the prison. This study, now complete, has been published by the Prison Service (Liebling and Price, 1999).

(iii)   A 'relational audit'[2] of the prison providing mainly quantitative data about the state of relationships at the prison. This part of the research is being conducted by the Relationships Foundation, which has pioneered such audits, under the supervision of the project team.

(iv)    The development of an appropriate methodological approach to this area of prisons research, leading towards a longer-term empirical project examining staff–prisoner relationships across the Prison Service but with particular concentration on establishments for long-term prisoners.

The particular project reported on here seeks to provide a detailed scrutiny of staff–prisoner relationships at a maximum security prison in East Anglia, aiming to provide both immediate practical benefits and long-term theoretical reflection to staff and senior management at the prison. This article therefore relates to parts (ii) and (iv) of this wider programme.

### Background

The centrality of staff–prisoner relationships to the operation of any prison has long been recognized in official accounts of the prison (Home Office, 1984; Dunbar, 1985; Pilling, 1992; Sparks et al., 1996), albeit, as we argue here, at a superficial or uncritical level of analysis. The large proportion of long-term and Category A prisoners in the dispersal system – where the need for safe custody and the maintenance of order and control are vital – makes these relationships especially important and complex. Yet very little is known about how these relationships develop and function. They can be (and have been) 'too close', 'too distant', 'too flexible' and 'too oppressive' (see, for example, Jacobs, 1977; Home Office, 1991, 1994, 1995; Scraton et al., 1991; Bottomley et al., 1994). Recent changes to prison life – a tightening up of security and control – have arguably substantially altered the basis and dynamics of relationships between staff and prisoners, as styles of authority and the distributions of power in prison alter.[3] The way in which prisons are 'policed' can vary from 'liberal-permissive' to near 'zero-tolerance' – between wings, between establishments and over time. There is no satisfactory account of what a good or right relationship is.

In 1997, the Cambridge Institute of Criminology was successful in a national tender invited by the Prison Service to conduct a literature review examining staff–prisoner relationships (see Price and Liebling, 1998). The review aimed to provide a synthesis of existing empirical knowledge about prison officers and their work, and place this in a theoretical context that examines prison officer decision-making, the use of authority and discretion, and the effects of organizational change upon the work of prison staff. The findings highlighted the difference between 'good' and 'right' relationships. 'Right' relationships may be 'good' (close, fair, open, etc.) but they are also 'vigilant'. Much more research on rule-enforcement, the use of discretion and 'law in action' has been achieved in policing (see Smith, 1986; Dixon, 1997), but the lessons from this research have not been applied to the study of prison officers, despite certain similarities – but also some important distinctions – between 'policing the community' and the maintenance of order in a prison.[4] The need for a ground-breaking research strategy in this area was established.

**The study**

As part of the work carried out for the literature review, visits were made to a dispersal prison and several other establishments. The discussions held, and the relationships developed during these visits, led to an empirical pilot project, to be carried out at the dispersal prison.[5] This project has now been published in full (Liebling and Price, 1999). The project was primarily *descriptive*, seeking positively to articulate the nature of prison officers' work with prisoners (see later in this article). The research concentrated on everyday routines and relationships. It also examined critical incidents such as assaults and adjudications, and the subsequent influence and consequences of these incidents. The research programme included an extended period of observation of daily life at the establishment; the shadowing of particular prison officers through shifts; the researchers' attendance at more formal aspects of prison life, such as adjudications, wing boards,[6] senior management meetings; the collection of institutional data giving basic information as to the structure and organization of the prison (for instance, prisoner data, number of staff, age, gender, length of time at the prison, sick and transfer rates, etc.); attendance at a weekly prisoner dialogue group;[7] a series of semi-structured and unstructured recorded interviews with officers, prisoners and senior managers; the identification of 'role model' prison staff (those whom others felt performed especially well in the job), 'high adjudicating' and 'low adjudicating' staff (those resorting to formal disciplinary procedures either especially frequently or rarely), for observation, shadowing and interview; and occasional focus group discussions convened by the research team with (i) prisoners; (ii) prison officers; and (iii) selected members of the senior management team.

The purpose of the project was to build a detailed and informed picture of the nature of staff–prisoner relationships, to explore important features of these relationships, including the question of boundaries, to discover what drives such relationships in long-term prisons, and to look for 'best practice' as regards the work and skills of prison officers. We intended from the outset to attempt to articulate this picture *appreciatively.*[8] We decided that one method that might repay exploratory usage at this early stage in our research was 'appreciative inquiry' (Elliott, 1999).

In the remainder of this article, we shall outline the method of appreciative inquiry, showing how it differs from (or is larger than) Matza's concept of appreciation (Matza, 1969), and how it can be used as one important tool in the search for 'the truth' about social reality. We also explore its limitations and discuss how far this method – applied to the prison world – takes us towards explanation.

## CORRECTION, APPRECIATION AND APPRECIATIVE INQUIRY

Matza argued that the traditional social-scientific correctional, pathological or critical stance towards deviancy could be contrasted with an appreciative stance which accepted, and sought to understand, the complexity, diversity and subjectivity of human action (Matza, 1969). To be 'intrigued', he argued (Matza, 1969: 17), commits the researcher to seek to comprehend social reality as it appears to those who inhabit it. Appreciative inquiry adopts this position, as we shall outline later, but, as a method of inquiry, it seeks to extend its scope beyond what Matza referred to as naturalistic appreciation by encouraging social actors to reflect explicitly upon their most positive experiences. This inquisitive approach has been conceived as a tool for stimulating organizational growth and change (see Cooperrider, 1990). Here, we are exploring its potential not primarily as a tool for change but, within Matza's original framework, as part of our search for understanding and explanation. We explore these ideas further below.[9]

### Appreciative inquiry in prison

The recent literature on the 'appreciative inquiry' method, then, seeks to supplement 'problem-oriented' research methodology with a search for 'affirming' knowledge and positive imagery (which might ask questions like, 'under what circumstances do you feel that you function at your best as a prison officer?', etc.). This method has been used in developing countries and recently in the National Health Service and in other public organizations as a method of achieving constructive change in complex social systems. It is 'an attempt to generate a collective image of a new and better future by exploring the best of what is and has been' (Bushe, 1995). The basic process of appreciative inquiry is to begin with a grounded observation of the 'best of what is', then through vision and logic collaboratively articulate 'what might be' (Bushe, 1995). We felt that this empathetic approach might have a particular value in a sensitive and beleaguered organization in which staff often felt at the receiving end of sometimes savage criticism. It would supplement 'problem-oriented' knowledge with alternative readings of the nature of prison officers' work, in an attempt to look in new ways for 'the truth' about what they do.

This research approach is distinct in that it begins by reflecting on what is best. It is in this sense (as we argue later) deliberately *partial* (and therefore, on its own, incomplete). We were led by this approach, for example, to appreciate a point made in the policing literature that the key role of law enforcement agencies is often *peacekeeping* and the *avoidance of conflict*, rather than the use of force. Prison staff, by talking about their best experiences of their work, talked to us at length about their highly prized skill of repeatedly moving the atmosphere on a wing from tension to order. More on this below. The aim of this approach is not to deny 'the darker side' of social reality or the realities of the flow and abuse of power in prison, but to deliberately seek to include other realities, to tap into the positive resources, experiences and imaginations of staff and prisoners, and to transcend typical research (and practitioner) preoccupation with 'what doesn't work' and what staff 'get wrong'. Both extremes of social reality 'delude us', but, brought together, can 'inform us in unique ways'. This research enterprise seeks to shift staff from an exclusive focus on 'deficits and deficiencies' to 'accomplishments and achievements' (Elliott, 1999). The deficits do not have to have 'the last existential word' (Elliott, 1999), but they ask important and rare questions. What gives staff life and energy? What are their highest expectations of the job? Under what circumstances does their work give them the greatest satisfaction? What are the establishment's best memories? When have they got things really right? Used in this exploratory way, this is not 'action research' per se, but represents an attempt to incorporate into our research design some effort to stimulate articulation of valuable perspectives which lie beyond the imaginative horizons reached by standard evaluation research, or by typically critical prison studies. An appreciative stance – in the sense that we are using it here – fosters self-confidence, energy, faith. This can be a more creative and future-oriented process than the type of critical evaluation often carried out in prison. The process permits emotional space (cf. Goffman, 1963; Fromm, 1994), but deliberately encourages hope as well as grief, or positive as well as negative projections, to fill that space in a healthy process of self-reflection. As Elliott argues:

> [P]eople may well be feeling persecuted, misunderstood, undervalued, patronised, not taken seriously – and therefore, often, torn apart ... But, by being challenged to reread their own script and that of the organisation and, in the process, by being empathetically listened to within an appreciative environment – that is, one that takes them seriously as people in their own subjectivity – the people concerned are able to acknowledge those feelings as real but not determinative ... [T]hey are given the emotional space and ability to move into the future. (Elliott, 1999)

We chose to pursue this part of our research mainly through lightly structured talk: through the interview. Every social researcher is aware of the ambiguities that surround collecting data through interviews. Every method, every setting, every subconscious or unconscious transaction between interviewer and interviewee influences the outcome and therefore raises questions about the 'truthfulness' of the material that is subsequently analysed. In the context of the critical (and especially administrative) social sciences, we have tended to collect interview data with an essentially Newtonian conception of reality in the background. That is to say, we have tended to look for 'the problem' by a process of dis-aggregation and de-composition in the belief that this will enable us to produce an analytical reconstitution of reality out of which 'a solution' will emerge. Whether intentionally or not, this has inevitably led to a research style which is problem- or deficiency-focused. The object of the research has been to locate the problem; analyse it; and suggest a solution.

It is not our position here to reject that style of research entirely, or to deny the influence of Matza's notion of appreciation, or 'the Sykesian tradition' on our own research approach. It is, however, our intention to reflect on the structural biases that a problem-oriented procedure introduces to the very process of the research and especially into the interviewing phase of that research. To put it simply, if one seeks problems, problems will be found. If the interview is set up in problem mode, however skilfully disguised, the direction of the interview is already determined, and so is the psychic dynamic that flows between the interviewer and the interviewee.

It is easy to illustrate this point. If the object of the research is to assess, let us say, the adequacy of the training of the prison staff, the assumption of most critical social science will be that the training is somehow inadequate and that those areas where training is deficient will be revealed via deficiencies in the performance of the trained staff on the wings. Convention in the interviewing process will be designed to uncover those deficiencies, no doubt with great sensitivity. However, interviewees will quickly understand that the object of the inquiry is to uncover their failings. Inevitably, they feel defensive. The researcher is left with the difficult and invidious task of analysing the data knowing that there is a bias in the material designed to defend the objects of the research from presumed criticism. We thus have a situation that verges on the tragicomic. The interviewee will consciously as well as unconsciously distort 'the truth' to serve a particular end and the interviewer will have to double-guess the data in order to construct a version of 'the truth' which may be very different from that of the interviewee.

It is not part of our argument that there is one single 'truth' or that social reality exists ideally, independent of reconstructions that we all put upon it (Gergen, 1982; Wheatley, 1992). Indeed, we start from a social constructionist epistemology but we are very conscious of the choices that we make, at least initially, in that construction. By using *appreciative* inquiry, in the precise way in which we use the term here, we are seeking to establish a dynamic between interviewer and interviewee which enables the interviewee to speak out of their best experience, rather than out of a presumed need to defend or justify their worst or near worst experience (Barrett and Cooperrider, 1990).

It is worth exploring further precisely what we mean by appreciative in this context. It is not synonymous with positive, either in the popular American or social-scientific sense. It is rather the appreciation of which Matza wrote when describing two alternative ways of 'constructing' hobos in New York (Matza, 1969, describing a study by Anderson, 1923). As he pointed out, they can be constructed as social deviants who are a menace to polite society; or as people who have chosen a particular way of adapting to difficult circumstances. In either case, the data gathered by the researcher will be similar but the appreciative researcher starts from a construction of empathy and supportive interest, rather than from judgementalism or condemnation (Vickers, 1968). The charge is sometimes made that appreciation in this sense leads to a Pollyannaish refusal to face negativity. The data reported later in this article will refute that allegation.

Indeed, a moment's reflection will suggest that, by *starting* from an explicitly appreciative position, one will often be led into a wider and deeper understanding of the negativities that are subsequently reported. We shall return to this below but for the moment emphasize only that appreciation or appreciative inquiry starts from accepting the construction of reality by the interviewee on its own terms and supporting that construction by a moderate degree of empathy so that the interviewee does not feel judged or criticized nor constantly brought up against the 'difficulties' or 'problems' of a situation *by the interviewer* (Isen and Shalker, 1982; Long and Newton, 1995).

Usually, appreciative inquiry is part of a larger process, e.g. the development of a strategic plan or a large-scale evaluative exercise. In this larger process, the dynamic of appreciative questioning leads on to the formation of action priorities. Central here is what the originator of appreciative inquiry, David Cooperrider, has called the heliotropic principle (Cooperrider, 1990). This is the observation that, if an organization is enabled to appreciate what gives its members energy, satisfaction, fulfilment and meaning, the organization will *automatically* move in that direction. The contrast with problem-focused, critical social science is thus marked: the latter tends to generate defensiveness and a reluctance to move organizationally: it is the ambitious claim of appreciative inquiry that it makes such movement almost irresistible by bringing to consciousness in individuals and in work groups not only knowledge of best practice in the conventional sense, but also the knowledge of most fulfilling practice which gives meaning and self-worth to work in the organization.

In the project reported in this article, we were not concerned, at least at this early stage, to initiate organizational development in this sense. Rather, we were gathering data for a process of wider reflection on the nature of the staff–prisoner relationship. It is worth reporting – as will become clear later in the article – that in some instances there was clear evidence of a change of consciousness by the interviewee that, had it been put in a wider organizational context and supported by a developmental process, would certainly have brought about change in practice. In that sense, we were sometimes aware of a potential dynamic within the inquiry process that had to go, at least for the moment, unrealized.

The sceptic may be surprised that lifers, very long-term prisoners convicted of the most serious crimes, and apparently highly conservative prison staff with a strong 'control' orientation in a maximum security jail would have much to 'appreciate' (Sloterdijk, 1988). Indeed, when we first considered using this technique in a prison, we were anxious about the kind of responses that appreciative questions might elicit. We were afraid of cynicism and negativity. One of us has used appreciative inquiry in social situations which were almost as difficult – for example, amongst nomads in the Sahara who have had their herds wiped out by drought and are in the process of making the immensely stressful transition from a nomadic life to a settled agricultural life in one of the most hostile environments on earth; and among street children in Accra who, like Anderson's New York hobos, are usually constructed as petty thieves, prostitutes, drug dealers and gangsters, and whose access to the basic constituents of a reasonable standard of living is minimal at best (reported in Elliott, 1999). In both of these applications, the researchers had the same initial anxieties, so steeped are we in problem-focused social science, yet in both cases – one an exercise in developmental planning; the other in organizational evaluation – the inquiries revealed not only a remarkable richness of data but also a change of dynamic, from dependency to self-reliance, as the interviewees began to see themselves not as victims but as responsible actors.

Armed with this experience, then, and conscious of the more limited objectives of our intervention, we thought it well worth while as an experiment in criminological method to set about gathering data, not only on best practice and best experience, but also on the affective mode that has accompanied these practices and experiences. Thus, we were not only interested in what *works* best, essentially a functionalist approach, but also in what methodology *feels* best to both staff and prisoners.

The first step in the inquiry was to produce an appreciative protocol which is simply a list of generative questions which form the starting point of a larger, wider appreciative conversation. It is worth emphasizing the point because misunderstandings arise when the protocol is interpreted as an interview schedule and administered with the routinization of a structured questionnaire. The protocol is not a schedule in this sense; it is rather a list of opening gambits designed to move and hold the interviewee in appreciative mode while a particular topic is explored. The questions were not necessarily asked in strict order, nor were they all necessarily asked.

A reading of the appreciative protocol shown in Table 1 will reveal a degree of repetition and overlap which a conventional researcher would do their best to remove.

---

● **TABLE 1. Appreciative protocol for use with staff and prisoners at a maximum security prison**

---

1  Tell me a story about what it is like when life is at its best here.
2  Can you describe for me, in as much detail as you like, the day you remember as the best day of your life as a prison officer [as a prisoner]?
3  [If you were a prison officer/prisoner] What sort of relationship would you think it most beneficial to cultivate with prisoners/prison officers?
4  Reflecting on other prisons you know, where/when do you think relations between staff and prisoners have been at their best?
5  What is your ideal for staff–prisoner relationships?
6  Tell me about a time that you have experienced when staff–prisoner relations were neither too oppressive nor too relaxed. What do you recall as being special about that time?
7  What do you see as the downside of relationships that are too relaxed? . . . too repressive? How do you think that downside can be avoided?
8  If you had one wish for staff–inmate relationships here, what would it be?
9  If you were in charge of training prison staff, what would you most emphasize about how they should relate to inmates? . . . about where they should draw the boundaries?
10 Some prisons draw the line too harshly; some too leniently. Neither produces contented prisoners, a safe environment or a reasonable quality of life for prisoners and staff. Where would you rate this prison? How could it best move to the ideal position?
11 Tell me a story about life in a prison when everyone has 'got it right' between staff and prisoners.
12 Here is a map of what relationships between staff and prisoners might be like. Where do you think this prison is on this map? Where should it be if it is to be the best prison in the country?[a]

---

*Note:*[a] *The map had two dimensions: close-distant; and consistent-flexible. It was borrowed from Hay and Sparks, 1990.*

We sometimes found ourselves inwardly impatient or anxious about asking a question that seemed to us to cover ground already visited. In nearly every case, such fears were misplaced. This supported our experience gained elsewhere that, because one is seeking to get the interviewee in touch with deeply meaningful experiences of their own life and/or some of their most treasured hopes for their working environment, there is no sense of the well running dry. Many data-gathering methods function on a one-to-one correspondence. In other words, there is a question and one appropriate answer. On this view, it is the interviewer's task to elicit the appropriate answer. In appreciative inquiry, there is no such one-to-one correspondence. There is an invitation to explore at the cognitive and affective levels a territory that is as vast as it is usually under-visited. It was thus no surprise to us that interviews were sometimes still in full flow after two-and-a-half hours.

A feature of the appreciative approach is that, because it draws on memory and imagination, it is often best conducted in narrative form. Story-telling is at a premium. (This has implications for the construction of social reality and should need no further emphasis.) We wondered how well inmates and staff would respond to the invitation to 'tell us a story about . . .'. As, with the wisdom of hindsight, one might expect, there was great variability amongst both staff and inmates. Some clearly found story-telling a more natural mode of communication than did others. It is one of our cultural handicaps that we tend to be distrustful of our own stories and feel more secure, perhaps both intellectually and personally, in abstract generalization, *however poorly based that generalization is* (Boje, 1991; Brison, 1992). We thus found ourselves frequently repeating the invitation to move back into narrative mode and abandon the search for generalization. We recognize that this leaves us with a heuristic difficulty: we have a mixture of generalizations we can't test and stories about whose representativeness we are inevitably ignorant. There is therefore necessarily and unashamedly a subjective element in the interpretation of the data that we have collected. We have had to take views about both of those issues. Is this a one-off story? What does this generalization represent? In the end, we have had to construct our own reality about the way relationships between staff and prisoners work – in exactly the same way as is true of any form of social research (Scott and Christensen, 1995).

We said in the last paragraph that appreciative inquiry draws on the imagination and seeks to elicit interviewees' best vision of the future. From that, it might be inferred that it trades in utopian wish-lists that have no relationship to 'reality'. That has not been our experience in other applications of appreciative inquiry and it certainly wasn't the case in this prison. Even the most disenchanted prisoners and the most disillusioned officers know and (at least in one sense) accept the constraints within which a prison is run. When asked what might look like utopian questions, *within the context of their own experience*, they answered with a surprising sensitivity to the constraints of budget, manpower, confused aims and the need to maintain an orderly regime. It seemed to be the case that, having drawn them into an appreciative reflection of their own situation and their own best experiences, their visions and ideals were conditioned by those best experiences, rather than by some fanciful dreaming. The best imaginable, to put it shortly, was the generalization of the rare best experience.

As might be expected, some interviewees found it difficult to get into appreciative mode at all and others slipped very easily from the appreciative to the analytical. It was our job to help them back into the appreciative mode by re-framing their analytical comments. For example, many prisoners complained about the inconsistency with which rules are applied by the staff on the wing (so did some staff). Reflections on this inconsistency could easily become a long recital of perceived maladministration and petty injustice. Without ignoring the truthfulness of the affect associated with this recital, once we had heard them, and responded to them, we tried to re-frame these complaints in a way that allowed the interviewee to re-enter the appreciative mode. For example, we found ourselves responding to the recital by summarizing it and saying: 'What I hear you saying is that it is really important to you that the rules are clear; that they don't change often; and that they are enforced consistently. Is that right? What do you notice about life on the wing when that happens?' Usually, such re-framing, perhaps repeated two or three times, enabled the interviewee to shift from a critical, deficiency-focused account back into identifying the conditions that need to be met for life to be as good as it can be.[10]

## What we learned

We carried out 32 interviews (17 staff and 15 prisoners) at this stage in our research. The interviews lasted around an hour each, although some took much longer.[11] Most of the interviews were tape-recorded (some were not and notes were taken). They were transcribed, our own notes were added and they were analysed using NUD*IST.[12] The appreciative interviews formed part of a larger study involving hours of observation, a longer programme of interviews, informal discussion and the shadowing of officers in their work. These observations and other sources of information have inevitably informed our analysis, and form the 'whole' through which we seek to move towards a fuller understanding of the nature of prison officer work and of their relationships with prisoners. The account we present here relates primarily to the appreciative interviews held with staff.

'Life at its best' for staff was quiet, 'a day going by with no trouble', when there is a feeling of team work ('when we all pull together'), and of support, mainly from immediate colleagues but also from wider management. The lack of tension and confrontation made a good day. This did not mean a day without work, but a day without major incidents. The challenges could be enjoyable, as staff enjoyed solving problems and making decisions. Taking part, being fully involved and being expected to 'deliver' made the job agreeable ('if you do something right, you feel good when you've done it right, and I enjoy being able to do that'), but staff all began with the absence of trouble. The senior management team had on their walls their most desired media headline: 'Well Run Prison Has Quiet Day'. This 'vision of the best kind of day' was very strongly shared by officers. At first, we wondered whether staff were describing their successful days negatively – as *simply* the 'absence of trouble' or as a mundane concern for routine administration – but we realized that this is precisely the conceptual problem outlined above. Resolving and avoiding conflict, avoiding the use of force and under-enforcing some of the rules were not *omissions*, but were acts requiring skill, foresight, diplomacy and humour:

> You couldn't really say what an ideal day is, because an ideal day is no trouble. So any day with no trouble is an ideal day. I mean, you'll get the inmates come up to the gate ranting and raving, but if it's dealt with without any violence then that's an ideal day, simple as that really.

> The best day … um, I suppose it would be the day [describes an incident] – it went very smoothly, there were no injuries, no unnecessary force or anything like that, it was very professional.

This was often *despite* difficulties with routine administration – staff smoothed over bumps, tied loose ends together through informal means and solved endless problems. Senior managers recognized the demands of this type of work for officers and the difficulties of fully accepting the authority of their role, not retreating from it:

> I:   Can you talk about what life's like when it's at its best here?
> R:   When it's at its best here, all over the jail [prison] there are people *holding their little bits of anxiety*, whatever it is and dealing with it. And the worst day is when all that anxiety gets crumpled up into a big ball and ends up on my desk. It's when people are doing their job at their various levels. They're acting within their authority, within their legal power, they're dealing with the big problems and the small problems that come up, they're referring their problems when it's appropriate to refer them, but they're dealing with problems that are within their power. That's when it's a good day. When the whole thing ticks over nicely. There's enough to do when everything's going well. (Senior Manager)

Officers described what we have called 'peacekeeping' (they did not use this term themselves, but we recognized it in the policing literature) as a key part of the best of their work. Their positive efforts to negotiate peace – to *achieve* 'quiet' – tend to be overlooked and undervalued:

> A successful day is one where you open up in the morning with 120 inmates, and at the end of the day you've got the same 120 inmates and the routines have run well, there's been no need for confrontation and staff and inmates are quite happy. Inmates aren't happy being in prison, but if, at the end of the day, they can say 'they've treated us fair, they haven't stitched us up, we've had our meals, had our exercise, had our association, done our work but there's been nothing that I've wanted to have a go about to someone' – then that's got to have been a successful day – and it hasn't sent staff stress levels peaking. And I can go home and not have to think that I need half an hour to sit down and get the jail out of my system before I can sit and talk to my wife and children. (Prison Officer)

There is an important gap here – in the literature, in research and in prison officers' self-conscious grasp of what it is that makes their job highly skilled. The movement from tension to 'peace' is not described:

> I remember one in particular, one Monday on here that stands out, I'll never forget it as long as I live. It was just so frustrating, I was nearly in tears I was that angry. Things were going wrong and I was losing control of them, and it was my job to make sure that these things did not go wrong and eventually things came together but I had to work very hard to do it. (Senior Officer)

The 'very hard work' involved in re-establishing order, in retaining or restoring relationships and in keeping communication flowing is absent from all verbal and written accounts of prison officer work. This general lack of consideration of the nature of prison officer work was identified by Hay and Sparks in a 1991 article in the *Prison Service Journal*:

> Like a footballer who can score a wonderful goal but not really describe how he did it, prison officers sometimes exercise social skills of great refinement and complexity without dwelling upon or articulating what they are doing. (Hay and Sparks, 1991: 3)

It is significant that staff (and others) take for granted (regard as 'common sense') their negotiation or 'peacemaking' skills. Solving situations, and defusing tension, were definite skills which were deployed often. Successful interventions in potentially conflictual situations signalled competence and professionalism:

> I:  Can you give me an example of a time when you felt that you really got it right between you and a prisoner(s)?
> R:  I feel that I am quite good if a con has been gobbing [*shouting*] to talk him down and get rid of it. Which I have done a few times. (Prison Officer)

This kind of activity involved judgement, experience and sensitivity to the specific context of the wing:

> When you first come on to a new area, as a new officer, you basically say 'what happens here?' and they say 'it's done like this'. So you do it like that, but the regular staff do it their own way, which is the relaxed way and you say 'no it's like that' – then you get abuse. A few times I got that. I remember a con had a go at me once here, shouting, and the whole wing watched. I didn't shout back, I didn't lose my temper, and nobody got hurt. (Prison Officer)

As an officer, what you could do was limited not only by 'the rules' but by confidence, credibility and *relationships*:

> You can't walk straight in as a new officer, because the prisoners will spot you a mile away, and start calling the shots and throwing their weight around. You can legally! – but the cons don't accept that. You have to earn the respect of the prisoners. There have been quite a lot of new officers who have turned up in the past few months, and they try to copy the old officers straight away – and this doesn't really work. You must develop your own style. You can be influenced by people in a certain extent – you've got to be as you do that in any job – but you must establish your own personality within the job. (Prison Officer)

So, being a good prison officer involved being good at *not* using force, but still getting things done; it meant being capable of using legitimate authority, and being in control without resorting to the full extent of their powers. It meant establishing relationships and investing those relationships with real aspects of one's personality. This routine part of prison officers' work was highly valued among officers themselves – but was not often seen (or perceived as seen) by those who manage and reward them.

Their best moments in the job ('the best day you remember as a prison officer') often involved promotion, recognition and reward – some specific acknowledgement that they are 'good at the job'. But 'good days' were defined by the atmosphere of the prison: 'when things turn out right', all the bits work ('if we're asking for movements [to other parts of the prison] we're getting it, or if we're not, we're getting a reason why not'); when communication is good. There were, in fact, two types of 'good' days:

*Correctional Ethics*

I: When do you most enjoy coming to work here . . . a day when you went home and thought, 'Woah, really good day today'?

R: That's difficult, because you can have good days, which *are* good, and you can also have bad days which are good.

I: Is there any difference in what's good about them?

R: Yeah. A *good* good day, if you wish, could be a day where you come on in the morning and everything seems to go right from half-past-seven, everyone turns up for work, prisoners are happy, they all go to work, all the feeding goes properly, nothing goes wrong – everything runs smoothly, and you feel at the end of the day, great, everything's gone well. I've had no prisoners shouting at me, threatening me, all the staff have been good, they've done their jobs, all the prisoners have done their jobs, everyone's got what they want, and you feel good about it. I can go home of a night, or you go for a pint afterwards with a few lads and you think, yeah, no problems. And then you can have a bad day which can also turn out good. If you have an incident, albeit a fairly major one, and the reason it turns out good is because you know what you've done and you know what your staff have done, they've done professionally and to the best of their abilities. For example, a cell fire that we had four or five weeks ago – all the staff knew what they had to do, I knew what decisions I had to make, the orders I gave to the staff they carried out without question, the orders I gave to the prisoners they carried out without question, there was no arguing, no what ifs?, buts, can I have this?, nothing, everybody did everything correctly and it all fitted together like a jigsaw should. It worked perfectly. Although it was a real horrible day, and people went home smelling of smoke and there was water everywhere and prisoners were upset and staff were totally shattered, it was a good day. Because, although it didn't go 'right', because when things did go pear-shaped, everybody did things as they should have done, when they should have done, and how they should have done, and it turned out great. (Senior Officer)

Most of the staff mentioned 'working with people' – their relationships – as the most enjoyable aspect of the job:

I: You seem to enjoy being a prison officer.

R: Love it. Dealing with people. I've always liked it. (Prison Officer)

What makes life here good? I think teamwork. We're a good team, good relationships. When I say the team I don't mean just officers, I mean everybody. We all seem to be striving for the same ends – to get on with the job; to do it professionally. Yes, we do have a laugh in-between but that's the way it gets done, and I think that helps to keep the tempo on the wing . . . I think for where we are, working in a dispersal with the type of prisoners we're looking after, it's a pat on the back for everybody. (Prison Officer)

The sorts of relationships staff tried to cultivate with prisoners were – at their best – fair, honest and good humoured. Good relationships were 'right' relationships:

Yeah. I think, staff–prisoner relationships are essential; a good healthy working relationship where there's a degree of mutual respect. I wear a uniform and I've got pips on my shoulder. I expect my rank to be respected, but I can't expect me as an individual to be respected, I have to earn that respect from inmates and the only way I'm going to do that is by being fair with them. (Senior Officer)

Good relationships did not require 'being a yes man' (giving in to prisoners), which was not appropriate and had dangerous consequences. One of the officers most admired by other staff was a relatively strict adherent to the rules:

> I do say 'no' to inmates but I think there's an art to saying no – we shouldn't just say no and push them away. If you say no and explain why, they might not agree with the decision but they accept it a lot more. [. . .] I've always been able to talk to inmates. I spend quite a lot of time, even as an SO, out on the landings. I get the feel of the wing, inmates know I'm supporting staff but they also know they can speak to me [. . .]. (Senior Officer)

Consistency was important:

> To survive you have to be the same with all of them. If you want to be a bad lad, a fair but firm officer, you've got to be that all of the time. Not just with the little ones. You've got to be quite consistent – that is what the cons relate to: consistency. (Prison Officer)

But so was flexibility. There were disagreements amongst staff as to where the appropriate boundaries lay; what kinds of people prisoners were and what sort of relationship was appropriate. Should officers play pool with prisoners, offer them biscuits, accept a cooked meal, disclose any personal information – and so on? Are these the significant issues around which decisions about consistency revolve? Or are problems of consistency restricted to the use of power and authority? This question was crystallized in relation to Sex Offender Treatment Programme (SOTP) work, where officers were involved in therapeutic activities with prisoners, and in the Special Security (exceptional risk) Unit, where relationships between staff and the very small group of prisoners it contained were strictly controlled. The question of what sort of relationships staff and prisoners should develop came up over and over again:

> I:  What sort of relationship do you think you should be cultivating with inmates?
> R:  Professional, really. I had a conversation with an inmate yesterday who's appealing [against conviction], and he hasn't done the SOTP. Refused to even speak about doing offence-related work, which I have a lot of interest in. And he said, well, as soon as you walk out the gate, you don't care any more. I said, well, I do go home but the work I do group-workwise I'm doing it all my way, I'm doing all the planning and the preparation [at home]. If I wasn't interested in people I wouldn't be doing it. So I said, we'll have a chat. And that's encouraging, really. Especially at the other end, the hard-men didn't want to do it – and it was brilliant to see the effect. People look at you differently, too. You're still in uniform but they see – because you're sharing experiences you wouldn't normally do, they look at you differently, and it's quite an advantage in relationships with them. And it comes as a complete surprise to them that you do work at home, and so on.
> I:  Does it change the way you do the job, this involvement – that they see another side of you, that you see another side of them?
> R:  Yeah: I think I'm more forgiving, if I can use that word. A lot of people, it's 'he's a con, that's it'. But I can see both sides, the weaknesses as well.
> I:  Does that bring on any response from staff who don't share your perspective?
> R:  Well, since groupwork started, it's not an MSL task.[13] So it's had varying degrees of support from management – it's the 'care-bear' against the [others] . . . And if you get a one-to-one with a member of staff you can explain it. And I've got some staff involved who have

85

been quite anti to begin with. It's difficult to get something going because the natural reaction to anything here is to piss-take, constantly – it's a defensive thing. You don't tend to get conversations of any kind of depth unless you see people outside the job. And that's only about three or four people, for me. (Prison Officer)

Staff found it difficult to articulate precisely 'where the boundary lay'. Each individual had a slightly different sense of 'where the line is'. Everyone knew that relationships needed to be policed:

Certainly not too deep a relationship. I think the best word to describe a relationship with any prisoner is a relationship of compromise. You have to be seen to be firm but fair. Treat everybody equally, irrespective of race, colour or creed. I'm not saying that we, any prison officer, doesn't like one prisoner more than he likes another, because we all do, that's human nature, but, by the same token, if you put two of them on the same line, you've got to treat them both equally. It comes down to the regime on the wing or in the prison, or a decision to do with disciplinary rules, or any decision that might affect their sentence or whatever, it can be something as silly as something they want from the canteen or the library or the gymnasium, you've still got to treat them equally, irrespective of whether you like them or don't like them. So, yeah, firm but fair, and equal. But I think you've got to reach a compromise all the time. There are two points to an argument, and sometimes prisoners do have good points to an argument to put up. (Prison Officer)

There were different types of relationships in different parts of the prison – in each area, the style was different; the amount of power used or required was different. There were times when staff felt the balance was just right. There were places and times where staff knew that relationships were not appropriate:

I:  Of the jobs you've done, on the seg, X Wing, the DST[14] and here [another wing], which of those would you say had the best model for staff–prisoner relationships?

R: Got to be the wing. Got to be. Because you deal with them every day. You deal with them on a one-to-one basis every day. That's where the best relationship is built up. The seg's a punishment area, the DST's a punishment group, they come and take things off you. I was on visits, and they're okay as long as you're not interfering with their visits. But the wings are definitely where you build the rapport with the inmates.

I:  Is there any difference between the relationship you had on X Wing to the relationship you have here?

R: Yeah. On here, it's – well, for me, I grew up on the streets and that, so I've seen all they've seen, and there's a bit of mutual respect there because, at the end of the day, there but for the grace of God go I. You know, at a very early age, you think 'hang on a minute' or you carry on. So I was lucky there. On X Wing [a Vulnerable Prisoner Unit], it was totally different because they had that little bit of fear of us, you could get them to do anything. And I'm not saying you used to threaten them or anything like that, there was nothing involved like that, but from day one, when it first opened, the majority of staff were very strong characters, so they got a regime up and running so that, when the inmates came and said 'oh we're not doing that', it was 'oh you are doing that', and they were told from day one. There's never been any major trouble on X Wing, never. And when I came on there from the seg unit, because I'd been in there as well, they see an aura for a seg officer, so they had that little bit of fear there, and when you work in a seg you do have an attitude because you're talking to people who are aggressive all day long, so you're aggressive back, so when I first went on there I suppose I was a little bit aggressive and they stood back a bit, you know. It is totally different. (Prison Officer)

The balance had to be right between being in control, being civil, being human and being firm. Staff wanted involvement, but they also wanted safety and respect:

> You can relate to inmates, you can be friendly, you can be talkative, you've got to know which subjects you can talk about, and . . . you've got to be professional. You've got to be respectful – if you want them to respect you, then you've got to respect them. Being polite and courteous costs nothing, because that's how you'd expect to be treated. In every respect, I'd say treat people how you want to be treated yourself. But having said that . . . you don't have to be best friends. Because at the end of the day you're there for a security purpose as well as everything else. You've got to be open because there's not just security; you've got to be approachable. Because you're also their link to wherever, even if it's because someone decides to become suicidal or has another problem. You've got to be approachable because you don't want that problem to fester, you want to feel as though he can come and speak to you and that you will then take that on board and deal with it, you'll sort it out yourself or give it to the necessary agencies. I think, if you're firm but fair, they'll appreciate that and that will then gain respect. I'll use the word again – consistent. But you cannot be over-friendly, particularly in dispersals. (Prison Officer)

Staff understood that 'grey areas' required limits. They checked each other's limits sometimes and had views about the boundaries other staff kept:

> I:  What do you see as the downside of relationships that are too relaxed?
> R:  We get taken for a run. We can be manipulated. There is a very great danger that they'll run circles around us. So we must be able to recognize when we're being used, when they're gleaning information for which they have no use.
> I:  What's the downside of relationships that are too firm?
> R:  I think, if you came into a disturbance or an unsettling situation, if you get on well with the inmate, he will shout and rave but he'll still support you. If you've been a bully or been oppressive, then look out. If he doesn't like you, then he's going to make sure that you're a target.
> I:  How can those two extremes be avoided?
> R:  I think you rely on your colleagues, possibly, to observe and comment – being open. In the SSU, before and after each session, there was a debriefing and staff used to tear each other apart if they thought there was a problem. So possibly staff briefing and de-briefing each other, supporting each other – if you see something getting too near. (Prison Officer)

On the wings, and even in the Special Security Unit, there was little consensus about detail:

> I:  Is there generally a consensus among staff about appropriate relationships?
> R:  Unfortunately not, no. (Prison Officer)

Shifts had 'styles' and, within shifts, individuals had styles. On the wings, officers who had not worked in the Special Security Unit often felt that different styles of relationship were beneficial, or even vital to the smooth running of the wing. Different approaches were taken with different prisoners. But staff articulated an overall sense of 'where they stood' in the establishment (the framework or tone of which was to a large extent set by senior management) and what type of relationships existed.

Staff were, on the whole, satisfied that their relationships with prisoners at this establishment were good. They were certainly better than they had been in the past ('we don't come across as being scared of them any more'), and they were considerably better than at a lot of other prisons. There was agreement that staff felt 'in control' and that prisoners 'know where they stand', but that there was good humour and a certain amount of respect on both sides. This was not a vision shared by all staff, or by all prisoners by any means, although prisoners, too, generally argued that most staff at the prison were reasonably fair. There were serious complaints from prisoners about 'tightening up', the removal of privileges, about 'winding up' and about some staff attitudes. There were also particular incidents and some individual officers who were considered unfair. There were limits to relationships, because of being in a prison environment and because there was always room for improvement:

> [This prison] stands out because we relate a bit better, the overall atmosphere in the place is settled. Occasionally, the relationships are strained a bit because there are lock-downs and so on; at the end of the day there always will be 'them' and 'us', but most of the time that's forgotten about just to get on with life – this is a community we're all in, and when we have a lock-down or a serious incident you revert back to the 'them and us' bit, and you see that mostly if there is hands on; if staff have been assaulted or if there's a need to restrain a prisoner then that is usually, it can be very frightening, very surprising how the 'them and us' bit comes back in. (Prison Officer)

What we felt, however, was that a positive or appreciative vision of staff–prisoner relationships and of prison officer work was achievable.[15] Inevitably, this is a complex task. At the end of the day, prisons coerce; and prisoners resist. What for staff can sometimes be described as a game, because they have most of the power and freedom, is deadly serious to prisoners. Most of the time, in a dispersal environment, staff recognize this and they understand the risks to their own safety if inappropriate liberties are taken. They have a vested interest in treading carefully and in seeking a sustainable form of legitimate authority, with minimal resort to the powers they do have. This is for reasons of practice and principle. Most of the staff we observed and interviewed recognized the weight and the depth of a long sentence of imprisonment (cf. Downes, 1988; King and McDermott, 1995). Those who didn't were considered dangerous to work with. Honesty, fairness, respect, openness, communication and trust were all important aspirations. Safe and appropriate boundaries could be consistent with good and right relationships. Self-confidence, optimism and energy were helpful assets in the job. Officers' vision of better staff–prisoner relationships involved more consistency, more management support, less political interference in prison and more 'professionalism'. Some went further:

> I:  If you had one wish for staff–inmate relationships here, what would it be?
> R:  I think it would be that, when a man goes on a visit with his family, as his personal officer I'd go down there and say, 'Hello, I work with John', and say something about him. You could see his community a bit, see him as a family man, as a dad, as a husband. A few words of praise, just a few minutes, and then off. I've done it, it does work and the families love to

hear a few good comments about what's happening to their son in here. I've done it a number of times, and it ends up with the mum or dad saying, 'Oh, remember us to officer so-and-so'. They like to think that their son is doing well, is doing [his] best, that someone cares about him. (Prison Officer)

So, what did we learn? We learned how enthusiastically staff respond to unconditional positive regard; we learned how quick they are to trust uncritical observers of their work; how ready they are to communicate, to explain and to be generous; how little is needed to stimulate their co-operation and interest. Staff describe their ideal working environment as rather like the conditions of an appreciative inquiry: they are seen, heard, respected, rewarded; they feel safe, supported and nurtured. An initial lack of confidence that their own perspective may be of value to others is quickly overcome and they 'grow' in self-esteem as the interview progresses. Some initial defensiveness gives way to an open, honest and deeply felt sense of the complexity and significance of their work. Their humility regarding 'intellectual' and 'abstract' reasoning is displaced, and they demonstrate rare abilities in the art of human communications and management. The first lesson of the exercise was that staff do have a clear and positive vision of their working environment and of their own role in prison life. This vision is relatively easily tapped and articulated – despite expectations held to some extent by ourselves and certainly by others that staff are (as a group, if not individually) fixed in a position of cynicism and negativity.

They articulate a sense of uncertainty about the 'modern' way of being a prison officer, although they are clear about the need for balance between care and control. They understand at a 'deep' level the concepts of respect, boundaries and honesty, and they see these things as crucial to the successful performance of their work. Yet, exactly how 'respect' and 'boundaries' were practised by officers differed. They are committed to a view of their job which requires all problems to be resolved verbally (through relationships and communication) where at all possible. They also believe that their own position has to be moulded around their own personalities – that their personality characteristics should shape the job of being a prison officer. This can work extremely well and constitutes a kind of integrity which is fundamental to successful prison officer work. Staff are aware of the tensions between consistency and personality; they are constantly picking their way through this minefield. Prisoners and staff have highly refined 'bullshit-detector' skills. They know how difficult and dangerous human behaviour can be. Inevitably, individual differences result in variety among staff: this variety is seen by most as highly valuable (within a fairly broad range). Staff also recognize that different approaches may be required towards different individual prisoners. Complex assessments and adjustments develop over time, so staff assess what works with different individuals. Prisoners do the same. Staff need continuity for this very valuable 'relationship negotiating' dimension of their work and they derive satisfaction from 'getting it right' with a wide range of prisoners (especially difficult ones).

The second lesson was that staff are highly motivated to, and derive considerable satisfaction from, 'getting relationships right'. They are proud when they manage to 'create a pleasant atmosphere on the spur'. Relationship building behaviour establishes credit, which officers expect to (and often can successfully) draw on at difficult or testing times.

## CONCLUSIONS

This article outlines an experiment in methodology and a new way of looking at the work of prison officers. We have drawn three conclusions about staff–prisoner relationships and three broad conclusions about the appreciative inquiry method from our research so far.

### Staff–prisoner relationships

First, relationships matter in complex ways in prison. 'What goes on' is mediated through relationships. The use of power is limited as well as transmitted by them. The realm of practices and relations in prison is under-explored, despite its emergence in penology as a crucial site for analysis (see Garland, 1990, 1997).

Second, staff–prisoner relationships are highly complex at an empirical level. Prisoners and prison officers seem to be trapped in a paradox. Prisoners value consistency, over time and between individuals, sometimes (it appears) even above fairness. Staff recognize this, but they also recognize that the type of degree of consistency that prisoners want is impossible to deliver, because of real differences between individuals, between situations and over time. Absolute consistency may be (a) impossible, and (b) a qualified good. Having a mix of staff with slightly different positions may be valuable. Getting relationships right involves a lot more than 'being consistent'. In fact, there exists a huge degree of inconsistency among staff in relation to even apparently 'trivial' practices, such as the use of first names, the acceptability of swearing, the playing of games with prisoners and so on. If there is to be consistency, these are probably the easiest things to be consistent about. Does this type of inconsistency matter? Some dialogue should take place on these questions of prison life. A conversation about apparent detail would raise awareness about the broader issues. What is trivial and what is significant? Why? Should inconsistencies be minimized and structured according to principle? Which inconsistencies and why? What is legitimate? Are there tensions between what is 'right' and 'what works'? Staff do not generally discuss questions of practice or principle in this way – even at regular staff meetings designed to encourage communication and consistency. There may be more room for flexibility in some areas than in others. It may be useful to distinguish between formal and informal aspects of officers' work. For examples, see Table 2.

Third, prison officers spend a great deal of their time and energy negotiating 'peaceful co-existence' with and between prisoners. They avoid conflict, resolve tensions; they humour and challenge. Lines are constantly drawn and redrawn by conversation, both between staff themselves and between staff and prisoners. Talk frames formal events such as adjudications, steering their impact and their meaning. Most of the time, prisons

● **TABLE 2. Examples of formal and informal aspects of officers' work**

|                       | FORMAL            | INFORMAL (SUBSTANTIVE)  |
| --------------------- | ----------------- | ----------------------- |
| Relationships         | No discretion     | Significant discretion  |
| Rules and procedures  | Little discretion | Little discretion       |
| Privileges            | No discretion     | Little discretion       |

are relatively ordered and peaceful. This peacemaking – line-drawing – rule-enforcing aspect of prison officers' work with prisoners is under-valued, under-theorized and under-estimated. We do not know enough about what prison officers do. This is especially true of prison officer decision-making, the use of discretion and the 'peacekeeping' aspects of their work. Some of the lessons of the existing policing literature could be usefully applied to this neglected aspect of prison life. Prison officers are agents of social control. Serious academic discussion of what constitutes the central prison officer task and what is the nature of their authority has been neglected.

## Appreciative inquiry

We reflected, at the end of the process, on our experiences of the research approach we had taken. We were particularly interested to explore whether there was anything distinct about carrying out appreciative inquiry (AI) in a (maximum security) prison. We drew three broad conclusions relating to appreciative inquiry as a research method carried out in this setting.

First, it was notable that, despite the very real feeling that we had 'broken new ground', and had succeeded in transforming typical research-led conversations and in achieving a 'vision' of the best staff have to offer, the scope of our reflection was in the end relatively narrow (compared to other experiences of the AI method). Officers' experiences of their 'best day' stopped at the end of the shift, or at the absence of conflict. The imaginative horizons were confined; the language used was restricted. What was it about the prison experience that so constrained the reflections or aspirations of our participants?[16] Through control, routine, indifference to the human spirit, or the damage done, prison constrains language and imagination.

In addition, and related to our first point, the language used in prison seemed restricted disproportionately towards negativity. There is a language for 'bad behaviour' but not for 'good behaviour'; a language for 'failure' but not for 'success'; a language for 'punishment' but not for 'reward'; and so on. This is as true for staff and staff behaviour as it is for prisoners. The (relative) lack of creativity discovered is coupled with a culture of 'despairing cynicism'. It is not surprising that prison constrains hope. If language reflects thought and expectation, then we found institutionalized expertise in negativity and very little expertise in responsivity to success. Was this connected to the paradox of successful prison officer work meaning that, at the end of the day, 'nothing happened'? Given the 'success' of our research endeavour in reframing perspectives, could the enduring negative culture of the prison officer world be challenged at an institutional level?

This is linked to our third point, about approaches to prisons research. The appreciative inquiry method is, in its pure form, action research (Elliott, 1999). It seeks to transform organizations, to encourage a spirit of hope and growth, and to lead towards constructive change. Its integrity as a method is linked to its search to engage with 'possible bests'. Once fully engaged in by participants, those 'possible bests' should surely be sought? Our exploratory use of the appreciative inquiry method fell far short of this 'ideal'. How far this 'reforming' stance is an acceptable position for prisons research to take is a vexed question on which we as a research team might take up quite different positions. Is the aim of the method to bring about transformation, thus making prisons less brutal, more humane institutions; or can a research method stop at 'appreciative

PUNISHMENT AND SOCIETY 1(1)

understanding´; at descriptive empiricism; at exposure, or at theory? How far does appreciative inquiry take us as part of a search for 'the truth' about social reality? We close our article with these incomplete reflections about the ethics of prisons research as an activity, about the contribution AI can make, and hope that we have at least revitalized the dialogue about prisons and prisons research. We found the method opened doors to data and interpretations that may have remained firmly shut in other research environments, and it clearly made a significant difference to the way at least some prison officers conceived of their role. The discipline of having to focus on 'the best' in themselves and their colleagues gave them a sense of being valued. Whether or not our experiences with our research participants exceeded the familiar Hawthorne effect (and we suspect that it did), our impression, for at least a significant minority was that, even after only one long interview, consciousness was beginning to shift in a deep and significant way. As an *instrument for change*, the possibilities are endless. As a *research method*, AI takes us in new directions also. There are complex questions about its focus, and perhaps about the risks of 'romanticism' which Matza discussed in his account of the 'appreciative stance' in 1969. As a research tool, it offers some significant pathways in the (we argue here) broader search for 'verstehen' understanding.

## Final thoughts

So, finally, a small amount of appreciation has quite dramatic effects on prison officers. They told us (and demonstrated) that they were enlivened by our conversations and by other examples they gave of 'being appreciated':

I:  Can you describe your best day in the Service?
R:  My best day . . . Funnily enough it was at X prison. I was having a truly appalling day. Absolutely nothing had gone right. I was sat at my desk. There was a Gov 5 in the Lifer Unit and a Principal Officer, and the Principal Officer had been off long-term sick, so I was by myself. There were lots and lots of things to do and it was all going wrong. And it was about four in the afternoon and the phone went – and it was Mr [Bloggs] who was then in Lifer Management Unit. And he said, 'I think you're doing a good job there. And I'm going to nominate you for the Butler Trust.'[17] I didn't know what the Butler Trust was, but it really mattered to me that the phone had gone when I was in my depths of despair and someone had said to me, 'I think you're doing a good job'! I was really lucky, I went on to do the Butler Trust Overseas Scholarship. So that was the best day – the worst day and the best day. Someone gave me a stroke when I'd had lots of kicks.

There is, of course, a real complexity to this world we are seeking to describe. The views that prison officers believe prisoners to hold about them – as generally fair, honest and attempting to do their best – may not be views actually held by prisoners. The perception of prisoners granting 'goodwill' to officers, granting 'order and legitimacy' because of the fairness of officers (see Sparks, 1994; Sparks and Bottoms, 1995; Sparks et al., 1996), may be a construct produced through the way officers frame their world. Terms like 'firm but fair' may have sinister implications which prisoners understand only too well. Conversations with prisoners suggest that they are inevitably far more aware of the power and potential for force underlying the authority of the prison officer's role than most of those who inhabit the role, or try to manage it.

We can conclude that the method of appreciative inquiry has a distinct power and

LIEBLING, PRICE AND ELLIOTT   Appreciative inquiry and relationships in prison

relevance in the prison setting. There is something distinctly energizing about the exploration of the best expectations of people and organizations. The narratives we took away with us were open and curiously life-giving. Appreciative inquiry seems to us to constitute an important new way of looking for 'the truth' about what prison officers – and organizations – do.

## Acknowledgements

We would like to thank Professor Anthony Bottoms for his assistance with the research strategy on staff–prisoner relationships, and for clarifying our thoughts as we wrote this article. We would also like to thank Professor Keith Bottomley for his helpful comments and the Governor, staff and prisoners at our research establishment for their trust. Finally, our thanks are due to three anonymous reviewers who offered us helpful comments and suggestions for final revisions.

## Notes

1 Dispersal prisons hold an increasing proportion of Category A prisoners within a population of dispersal-allocated Category B prisoners. Category A prisoners are maximum security and tend to be serving very long sentences. There are five dispersal prisons in England and Wales. Dispersal prisons traditionally have quite liberal regimes (thought to be appropriate to long-term confinement) and close staff–prisoner relationships, in the interests of order and control (see Home Office, 1984).

2 A 'relational audit' is designed to measure the structure and quality of staff–prisoner relationships in individual prison establishments (see Schluter and Lee, 1993; and for a review of this method, Price and Liebling, 1998).

3 Some of the 'tightening up' policies to have been introduced since 1995 include restrictions on temporary release, a system of earned privileges, greater restrictions on telephone use and property, and significant increases in both perimeter and internal security (searching, the use of CCTV cameras, intelligence gathering, etc.). See Liebling et al., 1997 for an account.

4 As one of our referees pointed out, the early sociologies of imprisonment and the classic ethnographies of policing had some common intellectual origins, but the questions of discretion and peacekeeping have gone on to receive greater development in the policing literature. Some of the areas of overlap in prison and policing studies which are ripe for contemporary analysis include the 'crisis of legitimacy', 'permissive policing' versus 'zero-tolerance', 'the maintenance of order and social control', 'devolution, empowerment and accountability', etc.

5 The Governor was particularly receptive to the relationships work, as he saw the issue of staff–prisoner relationships as especially pertinent to life in his establishment at the time of our review. The precise shape of the research project was negotiated with the Governor, as an 'extended pilot' exercise, intended to pursue the question of how best to approach the staff–prisoner relationships issue methodologically, but also as a self-contained research project which may be of benefit to the establishment.

6 For example, sentence planning boards, at which decisions would be made about prisoners' progress based on reviews of behaviour and work performance.

7 This was a weekly discussion group meeting between prisoners, facilitated by an outside group-worker and attended by others. Its purpose was to enable prisoners and others to talk together in an exploratory way about subjects which held deep meaning for the participants, without violence or dispute; 'to enquire together through conversation' (see Garrett, 1997). Staff sometimes attended the discussion group too.

8 This does not mean that we wished to avoid or overlook negative features of staff–prisoner relationships. On the contrary, as we shall explain further below, our experience has been that this appreciative route can lead to a richer understanding of those negative features which appear. There are of course dangers that our empathetic approach simply introduces a different (albeit less common) bias into research on prison staff. We are aware of the dangers of this position (e.g. recently expressed by Carlen, 1994: that prisons are 'romanticized' by campaigners and reformers; and that prisons should be studied as sites of punishment). The former is not our intention, as we hope to show. See Matza on this point and the avoidance of 'romanticism' (Matza, 1969: 16–17). The latter, that is, the study of the prison as a site of punishment and the relations between penal practices and other institutions, is the broader project towards which our work aims to contribute.

9 We became aware that thus shifting the focus of inquiry, from a strategy of change to a strategy of understanding, distorted the dynamic of appreciative inquiry in important ways. First, it laid the foundations for change which may or may not ultimately happen but which will certainly be detached from this process. Second, it omitted the stage of a normal appreciative inquiry where different accounts of or perspectives on 'best experiences' are systematically compared and digested by the social actors themselves. Third, it omitted the discipline of using the 'best experiences' as a springboard for inventing new social processes that would make more common the substance of the best experiences. In this sense, by thus detaching understanding from strategizing-for-change, we did not complement the empathetic hearing with the planning-for-action which is at the heart of appreciative inquiry as originally developed by Cooperrider. Nonetheless, as we shall show later in this article, we were impressed with the appreciative approach's capacity for unearthing data that structured questions would have left in the ground.

10 We acknowledge that this is, in one sense, quite a directive process. But the direction is to mode, not to content.

11 None of the individuals we approached declined our invitation to be interviewed. A small number of staff and prisoners asked to be included. Those we interviewed at this stage comprised an 'opportunity sample' and we make no claims about representativeness. We did deliberately include a wide range of staff and prisoners with different approaches and reputations.

12 NUD*IST is a software program that enables the computer-aided analysis of qualitative data.

13 Minimum staffing level. Certain tasks that prison officers do are included in the MSL. For example, there must be at least one officer per landing on each of the wings when prisoners are unlocked. Group work was not included in this 'profile', which means that, if there are insufficient officers to cover the work, it may be cancelled.

14 Dedicated search team. Officers selected to carry out security searches throughout the prison.

15 It is interesting to observe that the term 'critical' (or 'critique') has several meanings, including rigorous academic credibility. It can also imply censoriousness, derogation and faultfinding. There is no argument between 'critique' and 'appreciation', as Matza's work illustrates. We are simply arguing here that some styles of inquiry are more critical than others.

16 We were reminded of the research by Hutchinson and Buffry on 'The Meaning of Imprisonment'. The authors demonstrated that the range of language used in a maximum security prison is severely restricted, compared to the number and range of words used in conversation in an open prison (Hutchinson and Buffry, 1992).

17 The Butler Trust is a charitable organization founded by R.A. Butler (a former Home Secretary) which aims to recognize unusual initiatives or normal work exceptionally well done.

## References

Ahmad, S. (1996) 'Fairness in prisons', PhD thesis, University of Cambridge.

Anderson, N. (1923) *The hobo*. Chicago: Chicago University Press.

Barrett, F. and Cooperrider, D. (1990) 'Generative metaphor intervention: a new approach for working systems divided by conflict and caught in differences of perception', *The Journal of Applied Behavioural Science* 26: 2.

Bittner, E. (1967) 'The police on Skid Row: a study of peacekeeping', *American Sociological Review* 32(5): 699–715.

Boje, D.N. (1991) 'Story-telling organisation: the study of story performance in an office supply firm', *Administrative Science Quarterly* 36: 106–26.

Bottomley, A.K., Liebling, A. and Sparks, R. (1994) *Barlinnie Special Unit and Shotts Unit: an assessment*. Edinburgh: Scottish Prison Service.

Brison, K. (1992) *Just talk: gossip, meetings and power in a Papua-New Guinea village*. Berkeley, CA: California University Press.

Bushe, G.R. (1995) 'Appreciative inquiry as an organisational development intervention', *Organizational Development Journal* Fall: 44–58.

Carlen, P. (1994) 'Why study women's imprisonment? Or anyone else's?: an indefinite article', *British Journal of Criminology* 34 (Special Issue on 'Prison in Context'): 131–40.

Chan, J. (1997) *Changing police culture: policing in a multicultural society*. Cambridge: Cambridge University Press.

Cohen, S. and Taylor, I. (1972) *Psychological survival: the experience of long-term imprisonment*. Harmondsworth: Penguin.

Colvin, E. (1977) 'The English prison officer: a sociological study', unpublished PhD thesis, University of Cambridge.

Cooperrider, D.L. (1990) 'Positive image, positive action: the affirmative basis of organising', in S. Suresh, D. Cooperrider and Associates *Appreciative management of leadership: a power of positive thought and action in organisations*. San Francisco: Jossey-Bass.

Dixon, D. (1997) *Law in policing: legal regulations and policing practices*. Oxford: Clarendon Press.

Downes, D. (1988) *Contrasts in tolerance: post-war penal policy in the Netherlands and England and Wales*. Oxford: Oxford University Press.

Dunbar, I. (1985) *A sense of direction*. London: Home Office.

Elliott, C.M. (1999) *Locating the energy for change: an introduction to appreciative inquiry*. Winnipeg: IISD.

Fromm, E. (1994) *The art of listening*. London: Constable.

Garland, D. (1990) *Punishment and modern society*. Oxford: Clarendon Press.

Garland, D. (1997) ' "Governmentality" and the problem of crime: Foucault, criminology, sociology', *Theoretical Criminology* 1: 173–214.

Garrett, P. (1997) 'Dialogue and the transformation of memory', in *From learning organisations to learning communities*, proceedings of a conference on 'Systems thinking in action', Orlando. Waltham: Pegasus Communications Inc.

Gergen, K. (1982) *Toward transformation in social knowledge*. New York: Springer-Verlag.

Gilbert, M. (1997) 'The illusion of structure: a critique of the classical model of organisation and the discretionary power of correctional officers', *Criminal Justice Review* 22(1): 49–64.

Goffman, E. (1961) *Asylums: essays on the social situation of mental patients and other inmates*. Harmondsworth: Penguin.

Goffman, E. (1963) *Stigma: notes on the management of spoiled identity*. Harmondsworth: Penguin.

Hawkins, K. (1992) *The uses of discretion*. Oxford: Clarendon Press.

Hay, W. and Sparks, R. (1990) 'Control problems in long-term prisons', unpublished report submitted to Home Office, London.

Hay, W. and Sparks, R. (1991) 'What is a prison officer?', *Prison Service Journal* Spring: 2–7.

Hepburn, J.R. (1985) 'The exercise of power in coercive organizations: a study of prison guards' *Crimonology* 36(2): 343–69.

Herbert, S. (1998) 'Police subculture reconsidered', *Criminology* 36(2): 343–69.

Home Office (1984) *Managing the long-term prison system: the report of the Control Review Committee*. London: Home Office.

Home Office (1991) *Prison disturbances 1990 (The Woolf Report)*. London: HMSO.

Home Office (1994) *Report of the enquiry into the escape from the Special Security Unit at Whitemoor Prison, Cambridgeshire, on Friday 9th September 1994 (The Woodcock Report)*, Cm. 2471. London: HMSO.

Home Office (1995) *Review of Prison Service security in England and Wales and the escape from Parkhurst Prison on Tuesday 3rd January 1995 (The Learmont Report)*, Cm. 3020. London: HMSO.

Hutchinson, W. and Buffry, A. (1992) 'The meaning of imprisonment', prizewinning essay submitted to Prison Reform Trust, London.

Isen, A. and Shalker, T. (1982) 'The influence of feeling state on evaluation of positive, neutral and negative stimuli', *Social Psychology Quarterly* 45(1): 58–63.

Jacobs, J. (1977) *Stateville: the penitentiary in modern society*. Chicago: Chicago University Press.

Kauffman, K. (1988) *Prison officers and their world*. Cambridge, MA: Harvard University Press.

King, R. and McDermott, K. (1995) *The state of our prisons*. Oxford: Clarendon Press.

Liebling, A., Muir, G., Rose, G. and Bottoms, A. (1997) *An evaluation of incentives and earned privileges in prison*. Unpublished report to Home Office, London.

Liebling, A. and Price, D. (1999) *An exploration of staff-prisoner relationships at HMP Whitemoor*. Prison Service Research Report No. 6. Available as Research Findings No. 87. London: Home Office.

Lombardo, L. (1981) *Guards imprisoned: correctional officers at work*. New York: Elsevier.

Long, S. and Newton, J. (1995) 'Educating the gut: an application of psycho-analytic understanding to learning in organisations', paper presented to the Annual Symposium of the International Society for the Psycho-analytic Study Organisations, London.

Marsh, A., Dobbs, J. and Monk, J. (1985) *Staff attitudes in the Prison Service*. London: Office of Population Censuses and Surveys.

Mathiesen, T. (1965) *The defences of the weak*. London: Tavistock.

Matza, D. (1969) *Becoming deviant*. New Jersey: Prentice Hall.

McDermott, K. and King, R. (1988) 'Mind games: where the action is in prisons', *British Journal of Criminology* 28(3): 357–77.

McKenzie, I.K. and Gallagher, G.P. (1989) *Behind the uniform: policing in Britain and America*. St Martin's Press: New York.

Morris, T. and Morris, P. (1963) *Pentonville*. London: Routledge and Kegan Paul.

Pilling, J. (1992) 'Back to basics: relationships in the Prison Service', Eve Saville Memorial Lecture, ISTD.

Price, D. and Liebling, A. (1998) 'Staff-prisoner relationships: a review of the literature', unpublished report submitted to the Prison Service.

Schluter, M. and Lee, D. (1993) *The R Factor*. London: Hodder and Stoughton.

Scott, W. and Christensen, S., eds (1995) *Institutional construction of organisations*. London: Sage.

Scraton, P., Sim, J. and Skidmore, P. (1991) *Prisons under protest*. Milton Keynes: Open University Press.

Shapira, R. and Navon, D. (1985) 'Staff–inmate co-operation in Israeli prisons: towards a non-functionalist theory of total institutions', *International Review of Modern Sociology* 15: 131–46.

Sloterdijk, P. (1988) *Critique of cynical reason*. Minneapolis: University of Minnesota Press.

Smith, D. (1986) 'The framework of law and policing practice', in J. Benyon and C. Bourne (eds) *The police*. Oxford: Pergamon.

Sparks, R. (1994) 'Can prisons be legitimate? Penal politics, privatisation, and the timeliness of an old idea', *British Journal of Criminology* 34 (Special Issue on 'Prison in context'): 14–28.

Sparks, R. and Bottoms, A.E. (1995) 'Legitimacy and order in prisons', *British Journal of Sociology* 46(1): 45–62.

Sparks, R., Bottoms, A.E. and Hay, W. (1996) *Prisons and the problem of order*. Oxford: Clarendon Press.

Sykes, G. (1958) *The society of captives*. Princeton, NJ: Princeton University Press.

Sykes, G. and Brent, E. (1983) *Policing: a social behaviourist perspective*. New Jersey: Rutgers University Press.

Thomas, J.E. (1972) *The English prison officer since 1850*. London: Routledge and Kegan Paul.

Vickers, G. (1968) *Value systems and social process*. London: Tavistock.

Wheatley, M. (1992) *Leadership in the new science: learning about organisation from an orderly universe*. San Francisco: Berrett Koehler.

Willet, T. (1983) 'Prison guards in private', *Canadian Journal of Criminology* 25: 1–18.

ALISON LIEBLING is a Senior Research Associate at the Institute of Criminology, Cambridge. DAVID PRICE is a Research Assistant at the Institute of Criminology, Cambridge. CHARLES ELLIOTT is a Lecturer in Economics at the University of Cambridge and the Dean of Trinity Hall.

# [22]

# Health Care in the Corrections Setting: An Ethical Analysis

## Kenneth Kipnis

Ethics may have the most to learn at societal interfaces. Where differing cultural values and social practices brush up against each other in ways that force accommodation, the collision of normative systems can sometimes provide the ethical theorist with fascinating data even as it affords the ethicist-practitioner with an opportunity to participate creatively in a process of principled reconciliation. Such an interface can be found at the boundaries of medicine and corrections. For health care professionals who work in prison settings—nurses and psychologists as well as doctors—and for the corrections officers who sometimes work alongside them, there can be a sense of working at the margin. It will be the purpose of this chapter to characterize the types of normative conflict that arise for correctional health care professionals (CHCPs) and to set out some strategies for engaging them. I will, in the process, make some observations about how to understand the generic nature of these insufficiently studied ethical issues.

## The Incarcerative Backdrop

Much of the appeal of *M.A.S.H.*, both the film and the television series, was in its surrealistic foregrounding of a close-knit team of devoted healers against the grim backdrop of a vast military organization, optimized to inflict death and serious injury upon an enemy. The drama, with its regular doses of black humor, drew heavily on the value conflicts inherent in that context. It was easy to appreciate why most of these well-meaning doctors and nurses were cynically alienated from military life, and why they drank.

In some ways, the social responsibilities of prison health care professionals are comparable to those of the military in wartime. Like the army, prisons do not serve to promote health care. The constituting task of penal institutions is readily grasped when we recollect that those convicted of sufficiently grave offenses are, as we say, remanded to the warden's custody. In doing so, the judicial system solemnly entrusts prison administrators to carry out the penal sentences imposed by the courts. Aside from the restrictions placed on probationers, retributive loss of liberty is the predominant form that judicial punishment takes: there are about two million persons in American jails and prisons.

Although more philosophical work needs to be done on the nature and justification of imprisonment as a form of punishment, we should not be surprised, in our society, to see retribution take the form of loss of liberty. For it is common for those reared in liberal democracies to celebrate personal freedom as the preeminent political good. Liberal democratic societies are, perhaps by definition, informed by the value that rational persons are presumed to place on liberty. So the first of John Rawls's two principles of justice reads: "each person is to have an equal right to the most basic liberty compatible with a similar liberty for others."[1] And Joel Feinberg has devoted much of his career elaborating the Millian view that, unless there are good reasons to the contrary, individuals should be at liberty to do as they choose.[2] Accordingly, if liberty is embraced as a preeminent political good, then official punishment, as a societally imposed form of hard treatment, might well take the form of imprisonment: that is, an officially imposed, systematic suspension of liberty. Not only could loss of liberty be reasonably supposed to be, broadly, undesirable enough to deter rational malefactors, but additionally, its imposition upon those convicted of serious offenses could persuade law-abiding citizens that, so retributed, crime does not pay.

Accordingly we do not take issue here with the premises that wrongdoers should be punished; that the forfeiture of liberty is, here and now, a societally appropriate punishment in many cases; and that the prison— more or less as we understand it—is an appropriate means of implementing such a punishment. So conceived, prisons are institutions in which the presumption in favor of liberty is in large measure reversed: that is, unless there are good reasons to the contrary, inmates should not be at liberty to do as they choose. So conceived, prisons exist as societally constituted institutions for the purpose of systematically and generally denying opportunities to those convicted of serious offenses.

Jurisprudentially, the prison's implementation of this inverted liberal principle has historically taken the form of judicial deference to experienced prison administrators. Adopting a hands-off policy, courts have generally given wardens broad latitude to implement institutional policies that further proper penal purposes. But these purposes—a motley agglomeration of goals, some perhaps central to the prison's mission and others more or less peripheral to it—are often controversial. Along with prison's role in implementing a retributive forfeiture of liberty, commentators have spoken of the value of rehabilitation, encouraging repentance, incapacitating convicted wrongdoers, deterring extramural crime, making available a population of tightly controlled research subjects, generating revenues through the use of a monitored labor force, promoting institutional efficiency, earning profits, reducing an excess labor force, administering suffering, and so on. Hence the need, noted earlier, for further philosophical inquiry.

But notwithstanding this variety, there is one salient fact that sharply narrows a warden's focus: prisons are, by their very nature, coercive institutions. The inmates have been arrested, their sentences have been imposed on them, and, from the moment a prisoner first hears the heavy steel doors slam shut, the elements of everyday life are palpably shut off. Accordingly, those who are remanded to the warden's custody are presumed to be (1) intent on taking their leave should the opportunity arise and (2) unenthusiastic at best about deferring to the prison's de jure authority. Thus, the rights that inmates will surely forfeit are those that must give way to the warden's responsibilities for prison security: the twin duties to prevent escape and riot. In this regard we point to the authoritarian model of management, the thick walls, the razor wire, the locked doors, the armed guards, the regimentation, and the secondary penal systems that are set up within the penal system. Philosophically, administratively, and physically, these familiar elements of the prison betoken an absence of trust.

## The Mandate of the Correctional Health Care Professional

Although it is relatively easy to discern the warden's ethical situation in the context of prison life, the role responsibilities of the correctional health care professional are somewhat hazier. Notwithstanding the systematic suspension of liberty, it is useful to distinguish between two types of right that inmates can claim.[3] There are, first, what we might call residual rights that properly survive the sentence to prison. The general right to legal counsel, for example, cannot be abridged by wardens, though it is commonly contoured to comport with penal regimes. And second, there are other rights that flow from the status of being in custody: rights, for example, to food and to other living conditions that measure up to our "evolving standards of decency."

Although prison medicine has had a long but not entirely illustrious history in the United States, courts have only occasionally scrutinized the sources and scope of the duty to treat. In 1926, for example, a North Carolina court opined in *Spicer v. Williamson*: "it is but just that the public be required to care for the prisoner, who cannot, by reason of the deprivation of his liberty, care for himself."[4] However it was not until 1973 that the Supreme Court saw fit to set what one might take to be a minimum requirement. Appealing to the constitutional prohibition of cruel and unusual punishment, the Court ruled, in *Estelle v. Gamble*, that

> deliberate indifference to serious medical needs of prisoners consti-
> tutes the "unnecessary and wanton infliction of pain" ... proscribed
> by the Eighth Amendment. This is true whether the indifference is
> manifested by prison doctors in their reponse to the prisoner's needs
> or by prison guards in intentionally denying or delaying access to
> medical care or intentionally interfering with the treatment once pre-
> scribed. Regardless of how evidenced, deliberate indifference to a
> prisoner's serious illness or injury states a cause of action under Sec.
> 1983.[5]

Thus, surprisingly and thanks to *Estelle*, convicted felons are the only population in the United States with a constitutional right to health care.

It is perhaps useful to tease apart these two quite distinct arguments for the prisoner's right to indicated medical treatment. *Estelle*—the more recent Supreme Court case—bases it on the constitutional prohibition against cruel and unusual punishment. Since "deliberate indifference" to the inmate's medical needs adds an extra and illicit measure of suffering to that which is already incident to the licit penalty of imprisonment (that is, loss of liberty), the warden (and therefore all those accountable to that office) have derivative duties to respond to evident medical requirements. It is unconstitutional cruelty to withhold needed health care. No longer merely an element of good penological practice, responsiveness to the inmate's medical requirements has evolved into a constitutionally mandated entitlement.

On the other hand, *Spicer*, the North Carolina case, derives the right from custodial obligations derived from the prisoner's societally imposed deprivation of liberty. In this context, inmates resemble children, at least jurisprudentially. Although there are differences, it is revealing to observe how the legally narrowed liberty rights of children are comparably paired with a reciprocal prohibition against parental neglect. It is, in part, because children—like inmates—are systematically denied the legal powers needed to provide for themselves, that parents and guardians—like wardens—are properly charged with a legal duty to make needed medical services available to those in their custody. In Hohfeldian terms, the constriction of the standard range of liberty-rights is tolerable, in part, because of the presence of special claim-rights. Upon emancipation or completion of a sentence, both the legal adult and the parolee enjoy an immediately enhanced liberty just when they lose their claims to bed, board, and various other necessities of life.

On either of these two jurisprudential analyses, what brings health care professionals into prison are, first, the legal requirement that prison administrators attend to the serious health needs of inmates and, second, the legal prohibition on the unlicensed practice of medicine and nursing. Legally, wardens are under a duty to provide needed health care. But—equally legally—they are generally not licensed to provide it themselves. When we add the duty to make appropriate medical and nursing services available (following *Spicer* and *Estelle*) to the fact of health care licensure, what precipitates is the warden's special obligation to retain health care professionals in the corrections setting.

## Health Care in the Corrections Setting

Now, by their very nature, health care professionals are committed to putting the patient's interests first: striving above all never to harm them, treating decisionally capacitated patients only with informed consent, and scrupulously preserving patient confidences. At the root of this attentive deference, so antithetical to the prison's punitive ambience, is the understandable vulnerability that the ill generally experience when compelled to rely on health care professionals. Infirmity can force us to tell uncomfortable truths to doctors, requiring that we open ourselves in ways that, in other settings, would be embarrassing, shameful, and imprudent. This trust in the integrity of health care professionals is an indispensable element of the therapeutic alliance. It is largely because of these distinctive professional commitments (coupled with the profession's distinctive knowledge and skills) that, first, we as a society have delegated to duly licensed health care professionals the exclusive responsibility to deliver their distinctive services (unauthorized practice being a criminal offense) and, second, that the infirm are as willing as they are to seek out, to trust, and to utilize these specialists.

But although these health care providers serve the needs of the inmate population, they are nonetheless working, directly or indirectly, for prison administration. We have noted how the elements of prison administration betoken both the coercion of and the absence of trust in the inmate. Against this background, the CHCP's foundational duty to nurture the trust and confidence of the inmate/patient runs directly counter to the prevailing ethic in the institution.[6]

In systematically representing a profession's normative commitments, it is often useful to organize them according to the discrete social roles encountered in generic professional practice. Preschool teachers, for example, characteristically have professional dealings with children, parents, colleagues (including supra- and subordinates), specialists in other fields (psychologists and social workers, for example), and, occasionally, with the public. One way of conceiving of a profession's ethics is to try to specify and array the various obligations that practitioners have toward those who occupy each of these generic roles so that, in the end, the obligations are consistent with each other.

In the present context, it is a useful oversimplification to regard the responsibilities of the generic correctional health care professional as vectored toward three discrete parties. As noted earlier and as with all health care professionals, there are the familiar clinical obligations toward the inmate/ patient: centrally, a duty of beneficence toward the patient within the parameters of the patient's consent. Because privacy is largely and commonly forfeited upon conviction, the CHCP's obligation of confidentiality is best seen here as derived from the duty of beneficence. A clinician who is known to reveal medical information to the detriment of patients will soon find that the resulting distrust makes it more difficult if not impossible to respond promptly and appropriately to the medical needs of inmates. A second set of obligations involves duties as an employee of the warden/employer and, derivatively, toward other correctional officers also accountable to the warden. And, finally, there is a third set of public health obligations for the well-being of the inmate population taken as a whole. Quite unlike the clinician's focus upon an autonomous patient, public health concerns may require that a doctor impose treatment for the benefit of a larger group of persons. This third perspective manifests itself in a variety of strategies devised to prevent or slow the spread of illness through a population, strategies that can sometimes pit collective interests against the interests of individuals. In the most dramatic cases—for example, an outbreak of multiple drug resistant tuberculosis in an institutionalized population—infected persons, if they refuse to cooperate, can be properly quarantined against their will.

Many of the ethical dilemmas of correctional health are understandable as conflicts arising out of these three potentially competing sets of obligations: clinical, employee, and public health. Here are four representative examples.

Case 1 illustrates a characteristic clash between clinical and employee obligations.

> 1: You are director of health services for a large correctional facility. The warden has received reliable information from an informant that a certain inmate is sequestering a gun in his rectum. The warden insists that he has probable cause to perform a search and directs you to have it carried out. The inmate will not consent to examination. Except for members of your staff, no correctional personnel are qualified to do X rays or perform body cavity searches.

Cases 2 and 3 illustrate the tension between clinical and public health obligations.

> 2: Following an outbreak of five cases of hepatitis B in one of your units, your investigation points to a prisoner tattooist as the possible source. Though it violated prison regulations, all the infected inmates had recently been tattooed. The tattooist is unwilling to cooperate, refusing to be tested for hepatitis B. Do you test him against his will? If he is a carrier, what do you do then?

> 3: Inmate Richard Wong is a diabetic who has been placed on a special diet by order of the medical staff. He has been hospitalized three times with life-threatening diabetic ketoacidosis following ingestion of candy bars obtained from the inmate canteen. The expenses generated by these unnecessary hospitalizations are forcing you to trim expenditures on other parts of your program, with detrimental results to other inmates/patients. You can initiate disciplinary procedures that will result in his loss of canteen privileges.

Case 4 illustrates a tension between public health obligations and employee responsibilities.

> 4: The encouragement and facilitation of condom usage is a standard and effective public health intervention for managing a sexually active population with HIV seroprevalence. Though condoms do not prevent disease in every instance, their usage significantly reduces the spread of the AIDS virus. Despite evidence that the transmission of HIV (and other STDs) occurs in prison, common administrative policies barring inmates from having sexual relations have been invoked to justify derivative prohibitions on the distribution of condoms to inmates. These restrictions on inexpensive public health efforts contribute to the spread of a deadly and expensive-to-treat disease as they draw heavily on the financial and staff resources of fixed-budget correctional health services. Should health care professionals distribute condoms anyway?

It is useful to distinguish between problems involving conflicts of obligation and those involving conflicts of interest. One has a conflict of obligation when, for example, one owes it to A that one do R but also owes it to B that one not do R. A surgeon, for example, who happens to be a Jehovah's Witness might be the only doctor on duty when an injured non-Witness enters the emergency room in need of an immediate blood transfusion. As a doctor, the surgeon has a clear duty to transfuse, but as a Witness, the surgeon has an equally clear obligation not to. In retrospect, the mistake was to be alone and on duty. The best advice would be scrupulously to avoid placing oneself in situations in which such a conflict could arise. Accordingly, in dealing with potential conflicts of obligation, professionals need to be, first, alert to the possibility of ethical conflict and, second, empowered to configure their responsibilities in advance so that conflicts cannot arise. All four cases can be construed as involving conflicts of obligation.

In contrast, a conflict of interest occurs when, first, the practitioner's role essentially involves some type of fidelity and, second, when some fact reasonably calls that fidelity into question. There is nothing wrong with refereeing a soccer game and nothing wrong with being a parent. But there is something wrong with refereeing a game in which one's own child is a player. While each role is legitimate, one cannot discharge both at once. For we expect parents to be partial to their own children, and that simple fact calls into question the impartiality we want to see in a referee. Given a close call, the parent/referee can be suspected of bias if he favors his child and can be suspected of bending over backward to avoid the appearance of favoritism if he does not. In medicine, fidelity to the patient involves an acknowledgment of the inmate's humanity. Doctors are not supposed to betray, coerce, or harm their patients. A responsible physician honors the duty of fidelity to the patient; this relationship is remarkable in the correctional context, and yet it is the only way to engender a therapeutic alliance, the only way to be a doctor.

Taking these cases as illustrative, what then do health care professionals owe to the inmate/patient, what do they owe to the prison population conceived as a whole, and what do they owe to their prison-administrator employers? While I do not claim to be able to pronounce the final word on this issue, let me propose the following principles as, perhaps, a place to start.

1. *Health care professionals must have the necessary resources and latitude that they need in order to perform their job.*

Correctional health care professionals have the responsibility to provide health services to inmate/patients. Since wardens are not licensed health care professionals, they cannot discharge that responsibility themselves and so they must delegate it to doctors and nurses. Additionally—and crucially important in this context—they must provide these professionals with what they need to do their job. The point that needs making here is not that prison administrators are required to provide health care professionals with everything that they need. From the perspective of professional ethics, it is rather that it is improper for professionals to accept responsibility for the health care of inmates unless they are provided with a level of resources that is adequate to discharge that responsibility. There is a difference between honestly doing one's job and maintaining an illusion of concerned attention.

In the final analysis, the judgment about what professionals need in order to do their work is a professional judgment. Nonprofessionals are typically not competent, for example, to decide what drugs should be in a clinic's formulary. Likewise, because health care professionals need the trust of their patients if they are to discharge their responsibilities to them, prison administrators may not require health care professionals to act in ways that appear to betray that trust. What doctors do to inmate/patients must be done within the framework of the doctor/patient relationship. This line of reasoning supports the second principle.

2. *Health care professionals should scrupulously avoid enlisting in or being conscripted into activities that are not required as part of health care. They must especially avoid complicity in activities that would take advantage of their professional skills to promote prison security or other penal purposes.*

A doctor or nurse is not acting as a health care professional if he or she carries out a body cavity search, conducted against the will of the inmate, for reasons that have nothing to do with the health care of that inmate. The concern here is to keep the two spheres of responsibility—security and health care—separate. Only in this way can doctors and nurses continue to be seen as independent health care professionals rather than as agents of the prison administration. Prison administrators may want to enlist health care providers into the incarcerative mission of the institution, to recruit them, so to speak, into secondary roles as security personnel. But they need to remember that success in this endeavor is likely to undermine the credibility of correctional health care professionals and, as a consequence, damage the prison's ability to discharge its responsibility for inmate health care.

It may be difficult to discern the line that separates the normal practice of medicine from illicit complicity in the punitive mission of the institution. Consider, for example, the use of physicians to pronounce death following executions. At one level, this is merely reliance upon doctors to do what they commonly do every day outside of the penal setting. But notice that when, during the course of a hospital examination and pronouncement, a physician discovers that a patient thought to be dead is, on the contrary, really alive, energetic efforts are characteristically and immediately made to save that patient's life. Contrast that health care response with what happens when a physician discovers, following a penal electrocution, that the condemned has somehow survived the electric chair. The response there is to re-electrocute until death can finally be pronounced. Because the execution is not over until the doctor says it is over, the health care professional in that context is serving as an integral part of a punitive process. Accordingly, even though it may resemble what physicians do elsewhere, wardens should not be able to rely on correctional health care professionals to carry out that task.

But just as wardens must respect the working space that health care professionals require, so too must health care professionals bear in mind the incarcerative mission of the prison. Reciprocally, doctors and nurses must

122                               *Kenneth Kipnis*

remember that their work is to be carried out within procedures that ensure prison security. This leads to our third principle.

3. *While health care professionals should strive to be independent of the incarcerative function of the prison, they must defer to rules and procedures intended to further institutional security.*

    Assuming that such rules and practices do not make it impossible to discharge their health care responsibilities, health care professionals need to appreciate the overriding responsibility that wardens have for prison security. Both health care professionals and prison administrators need to work together to reach a modus vivendi, coordinating the health care and incarcerative responsibilities of prisons. While health care in the corrections setting should not be compromised because of the prison administration's concern for security, the health care staff should nonetheless scrupulously respect reasonable security requirements.

    Applied to case 1, these principles would suggest that prison administrators find alternate ways of dealing with the suspected firearm. Perhaps prison security could be adequately provided for if the inmate were placed in restraints and under guard in a dry room for several days. Were the inmate eventually to request medical attention, health care professionals would then be at liberty to provide it, with the procedure being protected by physician-patient confidentiality. (I assume that the procedure will be carried out in such a way as to ensure protection of the health care staff. Restraints might be used if general anaesthesia is not required.) However once the sequestered firearm comes into the possession of the health care professional, he or she would clearly be ethically prohibited, under principle 3 above, from returning it to the inmate. The health care professional could conceivably convey the gun to the warden. But because of principle 2 above, and apart from conveying the firearm to the inmate, the physician should not be asked to testify against the inmate.

    At bottom, this approach depends upon the abilities of wardens and health care professionals to draw a line between, on the one hand, health care activities that respect reasonable rules that ensure prison security and, on the other hand, activities that constitute complicity by health care staff in the incarcerative mission of the prison. While the former behavior can properly be required of health care professionals, doctors and nurses should uniformly refuse, as a matter of professional ethics, to participate in the latter. Faced with these conscientious refusals, prison administrators should accede to them out of a concern for the effectiveness and professional integrity of their health care staff.

    From a public health perspective, condom availability is a standard intervention in dealing with a sexually active population with some HIV seroprevalence. It seems very likely that there will be significant morbidity and mortality, not only in prisons but outside of them as well, as a consequence of our current prison policies. What all people need is education in the use of prophylactic measures. It could be argued that health care professionals commit professional neglect if they withhold the means for inmate self-protection where condoms are not available from other sources and where high-risk sexual activity occurs and is expected, often, to be less than fully consensual. It could be argued that, in failing to assist in the inexpensive prevention of HIV infection where the ensuing disease can result in costly drains on scarce medical resources, CHCPs are allocating scarce resources unwisely and therefore failing to honor their obligations to respect the claims of other non-HIV-positive inmates with health problems of their own. It could be argued that it is manifestly improper to assume responsibility for the health care of a population when one's employer explicitly prohibits interventions that are known to be effective in preventing the spread of deadly diseases within that population.

In the early decades of this century, university professors, under the aegis of the American Association of University Professors, carried on debate and political struggle over the proper dimensions of professional autonomy in higher education. There was broad agreement that it was manifestly improper for a university administration to hire a capable scholar to pursue responsible judgment in some academic arena and then to specify the conclusions that that scholar could and could not defend. It was plain that if one is going to have scholarship, then one has to allow scholars to pursue arguments wherever they lead, even if they support conclusions that run counter to received doctrine. The academic freedom that is so essential to responsible scholarship is a secured limitation on the employer's right to determine the conditions of employment. Trustees and presidents cannot fire academicians merely because they disapprove of the substance of the work they publish.

If the analysis above is correct, then correctional health services professionals are at a point today that compares to the one that professors occupied prior to 1919. There is some emerging awareness that if health care professionals accept the responsibility to provide care to a population, then they must be free from administrative restrictions that seriously impair their abilities to do that job. Alas, there are also many CHCPs whose professional commitments are evaporating as they align themselves with the incarcerative imperatives that prevail in prison. It is always a political-ethical struggle to retain integrity within institutions that see it as a threat. But lest we think of this problem as one that merely discomfits a criminal element that does not invite our sympathy, we would do well to consider the meteoric ascendancy of managed care. As medicine moves away from its independent fee-for-service transactions toward large-scale, for-profit enterprises in which physicians increasingly think of themselves as employees, the very health of health care will depend on the profession's competence in managing similar

124                                    *Kenneth Kipnis*

pressures. But all of us will be affected then. The lessons of prison medicine (and, for that matter, military medicine) are eminently worthy of philosophical attention.

# Notes

1. *A Theory of Justice* (Cambridge, Mass.: Harvard University Press, 1971), 60.
2. See, for example, his *Social Philosophy* (Englewood Cliffs, N.J.: Prentice-Hall, 1973).
3. Hugo Bedau, "Prisoners' Rights," *Criminal Justice Ethics* 1 (Winter/Spring 1982): 38.
4. 191 N.C. 487, 490 (1926).
5. 429 U.S. 97 (1976).
6. Nancy Dubler and B. Jaye Anno, "Ethical Considerations and the Interface with Custody," in *Prison Health Care: Guidelines for the Management of an Adequate Delivery System*, ed. B. Jaye Anno (Washington, D.C.: United States Department of Justice, National Institute of Corrections, 1991), 55.

# [23]

## Brokering Correctional Health Care

### John Kleinig

It is a rare person for whom the jail or prison experience could be deemed a pleasant one. Indeed, it is almost a principle of punitive incarceration that the custodial experience be less desirable than noncustodial experience. The rationale need not be one of deterrence. If punishment—as retributively deserved—is to be punishment, it must be intended (and normally experienced) as an imposition, as hard treatment. Not only is the experience not pleasant but, as Kipnis notes, the public overseers of jails and prisons do not have the psychological and physical well-being of their clientele among their most significant priorities. Even though the incarcerative institution must have a restorative or reintegrative function if it is to be publicly justifiable,[1] those in control of prisons generally see their role as custodial and incapacitative rather than as educative and reintegrative.

It is understandable therefore that those who are incarcerated will be tempted to seek ways of making their lives a little more comfortable, a little less unpleasant. Exploitation of prison medical facilities may present one such opportunity. Boredom may be relieved, company may be briefly changed, attention may be given. Awareness of such exploitative possibilities might be the most generous explanation for the reluctance of custodial personnel to be responsive to the health care requests of inmates.

That said, it is also likely to be the case that those who are incarcerated will suffer greater infirmities—both psychological and physical—than the general population, even if not always greater than the populations from which they are drawn. If their incarceration is drug related, there is a reasonable chance that they have compromised immune systems or that nutritional deficits have had other health-related sequelae. If their crimes have been violent, there is also a reasonable chance that they have suffered from residual damage themselves. And the conditions of incarceration may generate or exacerbate health hazards of various kinds—the spread of infection, psychological stress, inmate violence, and so on.[2]

## Professionalism Undermined

The body of Kipnis's chapter focuses on the tension that may exist between the professional needs of the health worker and the liberty-limiting and security demands of the jail or prison. And I agree that this tension generates an important cluster of ethical problems for the provision of health care in correctional settings.[3] I am sympathetic to much of what Kipnis says in this connection, adding only that besides the problematic involvement of health personnel in death penalty situations, in which the purpose is not to further the security interests of the prison, but instead to advance its punitive or retributive purposes,[4] he might have also considered their problematic involvement in the management of hunger strikers,[5] in assessments of the suitability of a prisoner for parole,[6] and in judgments about malingering.

Moreover, I think the professional tension that he points out may be more complicated than he indicates—sometimes because of decisions made externally to the correctional institution. The problems that emerged in New York as a result of the contract between St. Bamabas Hospital, Rikers Island jail, and the Manhattan Detention Complex suggest that, by virtue of their interest in profitability, private hospitals may contribute to the ethical problems confronting correctional health care.[7] If health care services are put out for tender, the result may be profit-driven agreements that jeopardize inmate welfare independently of the security needs of the correctional institution.

In yet other cases, ethical problems in correctional health care may have had their primary origin in the health care providers themselves. The provision of correctional health care has little prestige attached to it, and in order to satisfy the demand for health services, correctional institutions have sometimes employed health care personnel who have been found guilty of criminal and/or unprofessional conduct.[8] Even if the health care providers have not previously come to attention for unprofessional conduct, they may still provide medical care that is manifestly substandard, either because, though qualified, they are poor practitioners or because they are poorly qualified.[9] Another source of problems, probably greater in the past than now, is that health care personnel may have research interests that conflict with their care provider interests.[10]

## The Brokers of Correctional Health Care

But there is a further dimension to the issue of health care in a correctional setting. It is referred to—but Kipnis leaves it uncommented on—in the quotation he takes from *Estelle*. Speaking of the "deliberate indifference" that violates the provisions of the Eighth Amendment, the Court there noted that the indifference in question is not limited to that "manifested by prison doctors in their response to the prisoner's needs," but extends to "prison guards in intentionally denying or delaying access to medical care or intentionally interfering with the treatment once prescribed."[11]

I suspect that the ethical problems surrounding health care in a correctional setting may be even more critical in these latter cases. Inmates do not have automatic or immediate access to health care facilities, but are dependent on the discretion—or, if not discretion, the power[12]—of corrections officers. Officers who presume that prisoners are—or that a particular prisoner is—likely to seek access to health facilities for essentially nonmedical reasons or believe that the medical reasons are not serious enough, or see the use of discretion as an opportunity for showing who is in control, will be minded to refuse requests for medical attention or at least to delay compliance until the need for such attention is more manifestly displayed. By then, of course, it may be too late or, if not too late, the problems may have worsened and treatment will need to be prolonged or will be less successful.

Furthermore, prison officers almost certainly see their role as executors of societal retribution with a special responsibility for institutional security needs. If security is given a near-overriding significance, the importance of health care needs is likely to be underplayed. Their responsibility is seen solely as one of containment and warehousing, and not as including preparation for the inmate's eventual return to and productive involvement in the wider society.

Even if officers see their responsibility in broader terms, as ensuring that a social debt is paid, they may consider it important that prisoners "pull their weight" or work and thus place physical and other demands on inmates even when these are medically or psychologically contraindicated.[13]

But why should correctional officers be as responsive to the medical requests or needs of inmates as health professionals? They are not health care professionals, nor are they employed to be health care professionals. How should they, as gatekeepers to the health care professional, as brokers of health care, act in an ethically responsible way? What should an inmate's health care rights be?

## Principles of Brokerage

We can, I think, start with a principle that has been enunciated by the courts but which also makes good moral sense. It is that because an incarcerated

144                                *John Kleinig*

individual "becomes both vulnerable and dependent upon the state to provide certain simple and basic human needs,"[14] it is therefore incumbent on the state's agents to ensure that those basic needs are adequately met. The needs in question include not only food, shelter, and sanitation, but also medical care. Whatever onus may ordinarily lie on the individual to look after his or her own medical needs, it is shifted to the state when the person is incarcerated: "restrained by the authority of the state, the individual cannot himself seek medical aid or provide the other necessities for sustaining life and health."[15]

That principle of course rests on a much more fundamental principle about the inherent dignity of the human individual, a dignity that is not lost or forfeited by wrongdoing even if considerations of desert, justice, and public danger make it appropriate that a person suffers a diminution of the benefits of social life.[16] An incarcerated person has a legitimate expectation that he or she will be provided with the basic human needs compatible with his or her maintenance of dignity and self-respect.

Given this principle, I would suggest that until an individual pattern of behavior shows it to be otherwise,[17] there should be an initial presumption of good faith on the requesting inmate's part, and prison staff should take appropriate steps to provide timely access to professional health care services,[18] or be otherwise responsive to an inmate's health care needs.[19] Morally, this requires more than an absence of deliberate indifference. In a prison situation, with its dependency and vulnerability, it demands an active concern with inmates' health needs, even if they are not always obvious.

Correctional officers are not generally in a position to judge the legitimacy of a request for medical services. Those judgments should normally be left to trained health care personnel who will then exercise their professional judgment. It should be the responsibility of correctional officers and officials to ensure that—compatible with the security needs of the custodial institution—inmates requesting medical assistance are provided with the access they need.

Although the provision of such services might sometimes result in a slight diminution of security, it should generally be possible to provide access to medical services without there being significant compromise, and the inmate's medical interests should normally prevail over any relatively small diminution in security.[20]

Other factors might also be taken into account. If, for example, an inmate requests medical assistance in the middle of the night, when regular health care personnel are not available, some judgment may need to be made as to whether acting on the request can wait till morning. In some cases delay might be appropriate; if, however, the distress appears genuine and serious, prison personnel ought to be under an obligation to respond to it. Doubt should be interpreted in the inmate's favor.[21]

Account should also be taken of the special medical needs of inmates who are under medical supervision. In her chapter, Bomse refers to several cases in which inmates whose medical needs had already been recognized by health care personnel were subjected to conditions that compromised their treatment.[22]

Should the health care personnel—after an appropriate diagnostic investigation—consider the request to be groundless and should a pattern of apparently groundless requests develop, then greater circumspection might be justified and some delay initiated. I say "delay" because, as in the story of the boy who cried "Wolf," it is not unreasonable to assume that medical problems will at some time manifest themselves in a prison or jail setting and that even those who seek to exploit the system will be vulnerable to illness.

Perhaps the most difficult—but also most common—situations in which health care may need to be brokered will concern the mental health needs of inmates. If inmates do not have significant mental health problems before they are incarcerated (and many of them do, often as a factor in the criminality that has led to their incarceration), the custodial environment will itself foster and aggravate such problems.[23] There is a tendency among correctional officers to ignore signs of mental disintegration as long as it does not become a management problem. Barring specific inmate requests, such pathologies are not viewed as treatable so much as manageable. There is some evidence that health care personnel may look at it in the same way, thus reinforcing the status quo and the dehumanized relationship that too often exists between correctional personnel and inmates.[24]

Although, as Kipnis notes, inmates are the only citizens to have a constitutional right to health care, there is an ironic and often tragic gap between this privileged status and reality.[25]

# Notes

1. Even if punishment is retributively deserved, its embodiment in a public institution must have some teleological justification. The reintegrative aspect of custodial care is usually assigned to program/civilian staff rather than to correctional officers. Indeed, there are often deterrents to the latter taking an educative interest in inmates.

2. Consider the spread of HIV—through prison sex/rape—hepatitis, and tuberculosis. In this context, there are important ethical questions concerning screening and segregation. See Leo Carroll, "AIDS and Human Rights in the Prisons: A Comment on the Ethics of Screening and Segregation," in *Correctional Theory and Practice*, ed. Clayton A. Hartjen and Edward E. Rhine (Chicago: Nelson-Hall, 1992), 162–77. Consider also claims about the hazardousness of the enclosed prison environment as a result of environmental tobacco smoke. Here the concern is as much with future as with current health. Though initially one of administrative discretion, the smoking issue has now been settled externally by a Supreme Court deci-

146 *John Kleinig*

sion, *Helling v. McKinney*, 509 U.S. 25, 113 S. Ct. 2475 (1993). See Lisa Gizzi, "Smoking in the Cell Block—Cruel and Unusual Punishment?" *American University Law Review* 43 (Spring 1994): 1091–134. Note, however, the possible link between non-smoking regulations and increased prison violence, discussed in Matthew C. Leone, Patrick T. Kincade, and Mark Covington, "To Smoke or Not to Smoke: The Experience of a Nevada Jail," *American Jails* (January/February, 1996): 46–52.

3. For a valuable overview, see Michael Puisis et al. (eds.), *Clinical Practice in Correctional Medicine* (St. Louis: Mosby, 1998). The book is insightfully reviewed by David Kent in the *New England Journal of Medicine* 340, no. 12 (March 25, 1999): 972.

4. See C. Michalos, "Medical Ethics and the Executing Process in the United States of America," *Medicine and Law* 16 (1997): 125–67; Physicians for Human Rights, American College of Physicians, National Coalition to Abolish the Death Penalty, and Human Rights Watch, *Breach of Trust: Physician Participation in Executions in the United States* (Boston: Physicians for Human Rights, March 1994). The problems here may extend to psychiatric determinations that a prisoner is sufficiently "competent" to be executed. See Richard Bonnie, "Dilemmas in Administering the Death Penalty: Conscientious Abstention, Professional Ethics, and the Needs of the Legal System," *Law and Human Behavior* 14, no. 1 (1990): 67–90.

5. See Lubor Neoral, "Ethical and Medico-Legal Problems Concerning So-Called Hunger Strikers," *Forensic Science International* 69, no. 3 (1994): 327–28; D. Silove, J. Curtis, C. Mason, and R. Becker, "Ethical Considerations in the Management of Asylum Seekers on Hunger Strike," *JAMA* 276, no. 5 (1996): 410–15.

6. See Michael Decaire, "Ethical Concerns within the Practice of Correctional Psychology," <www.uplink.com.au/lawlibrary/Documents/Docs/Doc93.html> (July 25, 2000); cf. also Linda E. Weinberger and Shoba Sreenivasan, "Ethical and Professional Conflicts in Correctional Psychology," *Professional Psychology: Research and Practice* 25, no. 2 (1994): 161–67.

7. Jim Dwyer, "Inmates Suffer for Profits?" *New York Daily News*, October 6, 1998, 8. In this case the contract (essentially a managed-care one) was awarded by the city's Health and Hospital Corporation. But economic factors may also come to play a role in another way. Some prison systems—as part of an attempt to curb what is seen as excessive inmate use of medical facilities—have begun to charge for prison medical services by deducting amounts from what inmates have earned while engaged in prison work. See Wesley P. Shields, "Prisoner Health Care: Is It Proper to Charge Inmates for Health Services?" *Houston Law Review* 32, no. 1 (Summer 1995): 271–302. Consider also the early case of *Tolbert v. Eyman*, in which a prison doctor, skeptical of a prisoner's claim that he suffered from diabetic retinopathy (which was being treated successfully prior to his incarceration), told him he could have the treatment only if he paid for it. 434 F. 2d 625 (1970). In the particular case, however, not even this sufficed to convince the prison authorities to permit him access to it.

8. Andrew A. Skolnick, "Prison Deaths Spotlight How Boards Handle Impaired, Disciplined Physicians," *JAMA* 280 (October 28, 1998): 1387–90, and "Critics Denounce Staffing Jails and Prisons with Physicians Convicted of Misconduct," *JAMA* 280 (October 28, 1998): 1391–92.

9. Although the courts have been rightly reluctant to second-guess medical judgments—at least as constitutional rather than tortious issues—they have not closed that door entirely. See *Tolbert v. Eyman*, 434 F. 2d 625 (1970); *Martinez v.*

*Mancusi et al.,* 443 F. 2d 921 (1970) (a case in which a prison doctor conformed his judgment to institutional convenience—in disregard of the surgeon's instructions); and *Williams v. Vincent,* 508 F. 2d 541 (1974) (in which a doctor chose the "easier and less efficacious treatment" of discarding the inmate's ear and stitching the stump).

10. Edna Erez, "Randomized Experiments in a Correctional Context: Legal, Ethical, and Practical Concerns," *Journal of Criminal Justice* 14 (1986): 389–400. During the heyday of psychosurgical experimentation, prison inmates were frequently induced to "consent" to operations. See Samuel Chavkin, *The Mind Stealers: Psychosurgery and Mind Control* (Boston: Houghton Mifflin, 1978), chapter 5.

11. *Estelle v. Gamble,* 429 U.S. 97, at 104–05 (1976)(notes omitted).

12. Discretion, as I understand it, is a prerogative, an authority to exercise judgment, rather than merely a power to decide.

13. Consider, for example, *Campbell v. Beto,* in which the inmate, Campbell, who suffered documented heart problems, was sent to work in the fields, and whose heart medicine was withheld from him while he was at work. Subsequent to a heart attack, when Campbell initiated a suit against the prison authorities, he was placed in solitary on a restricted diet without mandated medical attention. 460 F. 2d 765 (1972). This case shows the potential for punitive responses should an inmate protest decisions that are made concerning health care. See also *Wilbron v. Hutto,* in which the inmate complained that he was denied medically indicated surgery on an injured hand and was forced to work in the fields, thus aggravating the injury. 509 F. 2d 621 (1975).

14. *Fitzke v. Shappell,* 468 F. 2d 1072, at 1076 (1972)—harking back to *Spicer v. Williamson*: "it is but just that the public be required to care for the prisoner, who cannot by reason of the deprivation of his liberty, care for himself." 191 N.C. 487, at 490, 132 S.E. 291, at 293 (1926). This is not quite the paternalistic principle that I think Kipnis construes it to be: the emphasis is on provision rather than imposition.

15. *Fitzke v. Shappell,* 468 F. 2d 1072, at 1076 (1972). In sufficiently serious cases of denial, the denial may constitute a constitutional violation—either as cruel and unusual punishment (Eighth Amendment) or as a denial of due process (Fourteenth Amendment). Since *Estelle,* the former has predominated.

16. Here I prescind from debates about the compatibility of capital punishment with human dignity. Suffice it to say that opponents generally consider them incompatible and proponents believe them to be compatible.

17. There is a tendency among correctional officers to see inmates as chronic malingerers and to use this profile as a reason for being less than appropriately responsive to individual inmate requests. Although—as I mentioned at the beginning—there are factors in the prison environment that encourage malingering, using a profile to make decisions in an individual case cannot be justified.

18. The courts do not, as far as I can tell, wish to go this far, though I believe it to be ethically required. In *Fitzke v. Shappell,* the court states that constitutional due process does not require that "every request for medical attention must be heeded" but "only where the circumstances are clearly sufficient to indicate the need of medical attention for injury or illness." 468 F. 2d 1072, at 1076 (1972).

19. In *Westlake v. Lucas,* the inmate, Westlake, indicated on admission to the Wayne County jail that he suffered from an ulcer and required a special diet and medication. But jail personnel denied his request until they were ordered to grant it by a doctor, even though they knew that Westlake had received a special diet and

148                              *John Kleinig*

medication at another institution. 537 F. 2d 857 (1976). Had the admitting personnel not known about the special treatment Westlake had received at the other institution, they might have had some reason to demur, though even then an expedited medical examination should have been expected. Westlake had to wait eight days before he received appropriate medical attention.

20. Exceptions can be contemplated. Suppose inmate A has been wounded by inmate B, who is still armed and dangerous. Inmate A's cries for medical assistance may go unheeded while inmate B remains a threat to any who would approach A. But this is an extreme case. Even if an inmate wounds himself as part of an elaborate escape attempt, this would be reason for increased security rather than the denial of health care. See Ted Conover, *Newjack: Guarding Sing Sing* (New York: Random House, 2000), 161.

21. See, in particular, *Fitzke v. Shappell*, where the court noted that "the case before us illustrates the fallacy of the oft-made assumption that one who is dazed or exhibits the symptoms of drunkenness and who may have alcohol on his breath, or who may in fact be intoxicated, requires the 'drunk tank' and not medical attention." 468 F. 2d 1072, at 1079 (1972).

22. Audrey Bomse, "Prison Abuse: Prisoner-Staff Relations," in this volume, 79–104.

23. See, for example, Heather Barr, "First, Do No Harm," in this volume, 125–39.

24. Conover notes the tendency in Sing Sing to refer to mentally disturbed inmates uniformly as "bugs." *Newjack*, 116, 138–51.

25. There is more appearance than reality in this formal privilege. The constitutional right is simply a negative protection against deliberate indifference to a medical condition, gained via a Supreme Court interpretation of cruel and unusual punishment. Those outside prison settings generally have legally secured access to treatment in public hospitals in cases of emergency. This might well serve them better than the constitutional protection possessed by prisoners. My thanks to Margaret Smith.

# [24]

# Management-Staff Relations:
# Issues in Leadership, Ethics, and Values

## Kevin N. Wright

During the late 1970s, Kelsey Kauffman studied the experiences of state corrections officers in Massachusetts. She describes the perception that officers at Walpole maximum-security prison had of their supervisors: "Overriding all else, officers saw administrators 'from the top echelons on down' as uncaring about officers and willing to betray them if necessary to purchase a transient peace. As an officer described their feelings, 'We're alone. We have only each other. The administration does not give a shit for us.'"[1]

Whether this characterization was generally true of Massachusetts's officers at the time and whether it is generalizable to prisons across the United States may be subject to debate. Nevertheless, the sentiment expressed by the Walpole employees raises an extremely important issue: what ethical consideration can prison employees expect from their supervisors? In accepting employment in a prison, does an individual give up the right to a reasonably safe work environment? Must prison employees subjugate their own judgments to those of a capricious supervisor? Does a staff member working in a prison have any right to fair and equal treatment in regard to promotion or termination of employment? What about privacy? In the name of security, can correctional administrators pry into the personal lives of prison employees?

Interestingly, the literature on prison management provides little guidance on these questions. One finds some discussion of what constitutes the ethical treatment of prisoners but virtually nothing about the ethical treatment of prison employees. Kauffman and Jacobs[2] provide some implicit consideration of ethical prison management practices. But if an administrator or scholar wished to find an explicit discussion of ethical treatment of prison employees, he or she would be disappointed.

The few books that examine good prison management are relatively silent about the ethical treatment of staff by supervisors. Neither Phillips and McConnell in *The Effective Corrections Manager*[3] nor Archambeault and Archambeault in *Correctional Supervisory Management*[4] discuss the ethical treatment of employees. John DiIulio, a recognized authority on prison administration, fails to address ethical management in either *Governing Prisons* or *No Escape*.[5] In 1993, McShane and Williams conducted a national survey of prison wardens and published their results in a volume titled, *The Management of Correctional Institutions*.[6] They addressed many aspects of supervision but did not query prison executives about their ethical obligations to employees. In 1994, I made a modest attempt to address the topic in *Effective Prison Leadership*.[7] In a section on integrity, I argued that, to be successful leaders, prison officials must be honest, consistent, and set a good example. Still, my discussion was far from comprehensive.

In 1975, the American Correctional Association adopted its Code of Ethics. It lists seventeen principles that constitute ethical practice toward prisoners, staff, and the community. Four principles apply directly to staff supervision:

- Relationships with colleagues will be of such character to promote mutual respect within the profession and improvement of its quality of service.
- Statements critical of colleagues or their service agencies will be made only as these are verifiable and constructive in purpose.
- Members will not discriminate against any client, employee or prospective employee on the basis of race, sex, creed or national origin.
- Any member who is responsible for agency personnel actions will make all appointments, promotions or dismissals only on the basis of merit and not in furtherance of partisan political interests.[8]

These are fine standards but they are limited in scope.

One might speculate about the paucity of literature concerning the ethical treatment of prison employees. Is it because prisons are closed institutions? Or is it, perhaps, that the traditional paramilitary organization of prisons precludes concern for or attention to questions of ethical practice? I happen to believe that the reason that little has been written about the ethical treatment of prison employees is that relatively little has been written about prison management generally. My purpose here is to suggest a framework for discussion of the ethical supervision of prison staff. I begin with the general question of why organizations have ethical obligations toward their employees. I introduce a set of ethical standards for employees and examine the application of these to employees working within prison settings. I conclude with a discussion of how to ensure that these principles are recognized within the prison work setting.

## The Moral Status of Employees

The United States was founded on a strong belief in and commitment to individual rights and freedoms. Because these rights are recognized in the Constitution and its Bill of Rights, these freedoms have not only moral acclaim but also the force of law. Interestingly, the framers of the American Constitution were principally concerned with the harm that governments could impose on individuals through the denial of liberty, due process, and fundamental human rights. Because the criminal justice system is in the business of denying the liberty of those individuals who have harmed others or pose a threat to public safety, prisoners are afforded legal recourse for the review of the process and conditions by which their rights and freedoms are removed by government.

Prison employees, by contrast, occupy a different legal position from prisoners. As voluntary members of prison organizations who are compensated for their labor, the constitutional protections provided against government interference in one's life do not apply as directly to employees as to prisoners. Instead, a much grayer area of employment ethics must be considered. Here, the force of law generally does not apply.

A belief held by many Americans, and one that has its roots in common law, is that workers are employed at will. That is, employees have the right to choose and change their jobs at will, and employers have the right hire, direct, and fire employees at will. Defenders of this principle claim that it is necessary, for it preserves both the organizations' and the employees' freedom of choice.

Critics claim that the at-will employment principle necessarily places the employee at a disadvantage. If, as a condition of employment, the employee is expected to act responsibly, loyally, and with respect, then the principle of reciprocity demands that the organization must likewise treat the employee responsibly, loyally, and with respect.[9] Just because individuals freely join an organization, they do not relinquish their rights to such fundamental provisions as safety, equal treatment, privacy, free expression, and due process. If organizations have a moral status that affords them some degree of freedom and autonomy, then they also have concomitant moral obligations. These obligations extend to customers or clients, employees, and society.[10]

Proponents of the idea that employees have moral rights identify seven ethical principles that seem applicable to prison employees: safety, fair treatment, due process, freedom of expression, privacy, participation in decision making, and information.[11]

## Safety

It is generally agreed that the most basic human right is the right to life. Without it, all other rights are superfluous and meaningless. To have life, one must have some assurance of safety and security; otherwise, life becomes perilous.

When governments threaten human life through acts of genocide, executions of political prisoners, and torture, those acts can become objects of international attention and, to stop the violence, may result in political, economic, and/or military intervention. Within the international political arena, there appears to be general agreement among people and nations that the sanctity of life overrides national sovereignty. Interestingly, the safety and health of workers in the United States has not always received the same level of concern and protection. Here, we often find an attitude that supports the inviolability of organizational freedom and autonomy even at the expense of individuals' right to safety. This position has kept courts and regulatory agencies from protecting the safety of workers. Only recently has the practice been reversed.

Clearly, jobs vary in the risks they pose to individual safety. Being a librarian is not as risky as being a laborer constructing a skyscraper or a lumberjack harvesting timber in the Northwest. However, workers have the right to understand the risks involved in a particular job and to be protected to the greatest extent possible.

Prison work is clearly more dangerous than many other forms of employment. Risks vary with the security level of the institution and job type within the facility, but the very practice of incarcerating people against their will, particularly a group of people that includes individuals who have demonstrated poor social skills and a propensity to solve interpersonal problems through violence, renders prison work risky. Staff can be assaulted by prisoners and taken hostage during a disturbance. Within such an environment, what rights to safety do prison employees have? What ethical obligations do prison officials have to assure the safety of their employees?

Just as workers employed in other hazardous settings have a right to work conditions that provide maximal safety within the parameters of what is humanly possible and economically feasible, so, too, do prison workers. This means that those responsible for administration have a positive duty to insure that the institution is as safe as possible for its security level.

The physical plant must be sound. Does this require that all facilities be brought up to the most contemporary standards of design and security technology? Probably not. Given the costs of renovation and new construction and the rapidity of technological innovation, such a requirement would be economically unfeasible. There must be balance. States and their prison systems are morally obligated to maintain the physical plant at acceptable levels. Prison structures cannot be allowed to fall into conditions of deterioration and antiquation that make them unsafe.

Beyond the physical plant, there is also a moral obligation to attend to safety practices. Policy governing security practices must be set and reviewed regularly. High expectations are the key to maintaining safe conditions and practices. Key and tool control, attention to inmate movement, and procedures for controlling high-risk prisoners must be reviewed regularly, and corrective action taken when needed. Logs must be maintained. Inmates and staff must be held accountable to standardized procedures. Provisions for emergency response must be in place. Training and retraining are essential to this process.

Prison managers have ethical obligations to inspect operations regularly to ensure compliance with security policy. When noncompliance is detected, corrective action must be taken. Important to the assurance of this right of all staff is responsiveness on the part of the institution as a whole and administrators specifically. To do otherwise is an abdication of moral responsibility.

Throughout this section, I have used the word "right" to safety and have listed a variety of actions that administrators should take if they are to act ethically toward their employees. In reality, the ability of prison managers to perform their duties ethically is constrained by organizational circumstances, budgetary limitations, and competing ethical considerations. For example, sound correctional practice suggests that administrators should do nothing that will significantly alienate the prisoner population. But when prisoners begin to view the conditions of their confinement as unreasonable and unduly harsh, they are much more likely to act out, create a disturbance, or attempt to take control of the facility. This would place staff at greater risk, thus suggesting that the administrator had been acting unethically. However, the institution's budget may be so constrained that there are insufficient funds to employ the staff needed to allow prisoners out of their cells every day. An administrator may have no choice but to lock down the institution on weekends. Such action will alienate the population and increase risk of prisoner reprisal. Administrators must constantly balance decisions that have ethical implications for staff against organizational and budgetary constraints.

Furthermore, prison administrators must struggle with competing ethical obligations. To assure the highest level of staff safety, an administrator may recognize that the facility requires a $50 million renovation. If the ad-

208                                     *Kevin N. Wright*

ministrator aggressively lobbies within the state correctional system and state government for this capital improvement, knowing that if he or she is successful in securing those funds, they will be taken from public monies that would have otherwise gone to public education, is he or she acting ethically?

## Fair Treatment

A second ethical principle that workers share is the right to fair treatment in the workplace. If ethical practices apply to everyone, then individuals must possess those rights equally. Individuals or groups must not possess advantages over others in the provision of and access to moral rights.

The universality of moral rights within the workplace gets expressed in terms of fair treatment. It has a number of elements. First, every person should have equal access to a job and equal consideration on the job. Organizations cannot and should not discriminate against people on the basis of their sex, race or ethnicity, economic background, or religion. Furthermore, employees should receive equal pay for equal work.

Fair treatment also requires that employees not be dismissed without cause. In other words, employees have a right to their jobs. They should be fired only for the following conditions: unsatisfactory performance of duties, criminal activity, drinking or using drugs on the job, disruption of organizational operations without a valid cause, physical or mental incapacitation, and verifiable economic reasons.

Prison staff share the right to fair treatment with other employees. In fact, as public employees, this right is guaranteed legally by the Civil Rights Acts. However, there is a positive moral duty on the part of the organization and its managers to assure that this right is secured. The moral obligation goes beyond a legal one. As with the duty to maintain security, active attention is necessary. Policy that directs hiring, firing, and promotion practices must be firmly established and reviewed.

Within prisons, the right to fair treatment also carries with it an added moral obligation. As law enforcement officers, prison personnel must be prohibited from illegal activities, inappropriate behavior, corruption, and abuses of power. If all employees are to be treated fairly, the organization must be vigilant in detecting staff who engage in prohibited behaviors, and their behavior must be penalized. Not to do so is to treat law-abiding and ethical staff unfairly.

Here, too, ethical decision making and practice are bound by organizational constraints. Fair treatment is frequently influenced by civil service laws and regulations and by union contracts. Fair treatment of employees would dictate that an individual who is particularly derelict or inept in the performance of his or her duties should be removed from service. It is not fair to other conscientious employees that this individual be permitted to shirk responsibility. Such failure could pose a security threat and place other employees at risk of harm. In some systems, the protections of employees provided within the civil service system or through the union contract make it virtually impossible for supervisors to fire employees. Prison managers may be constrained under these circumstances from performing their supervisory functions ethically.

## Due Process

For fair treatment to be sustained in the workplace, checks and balances are required on the capricious exercise of power by supervisors. Otherwise, employees may have a moral right to fair treatment but no guarantee to it since bosses can hire and fire at will. Due process is the method by which rights are protected, either from governmental or organizational intrusion. Before an employee can be fired, demoted, or punished, he or she has the right to peer review and a hearing.

The provision of this right within the justice system takes on added meaning. At the core of the criminal justice system is the right to due process. For government to take away an individual's right to freedom, there must be due process. To provide criminal offenders due process but to deny staff the same right makes a mockery of the very foundation of the system of justice, to say nothing about the impact on employee morale. Surely, staff members have the same moral rights as prisoners. Therefore, for a prison employee to be demoted, sanctioned, or fired, the right to a fair hearing is essential.

As with the two previous ethical principles discussed here, the provision of due process appears to be incontrovertible, but may be limited by the structure and climate of prison. An employee caught bringing drugs into the facility must be suspended immediately. The need to maintain security and to uphold legal behavior outweigh the provision of due process in the moment. A hearing to establish guilt must wait.

In an ideal world, politics would not influence the provision of fair treatment and due process. In reality, however, who gets disciplined is influenced by the politics of various constituencies within an institution. Strong unions can protect some employees. In this circumstance, no matter how correct an administrator believes an action may be, his or her ability to carry it out may be constrained.

## Freedom of Expression

Like due process, freedom of expression serves to balance the distribution of power within organizations and to protect other ethical principles bearing on the treatment of individuals. Employees must have the right to protest, without reprisal, acts of the organization that may be illegal or immoral. The expression of this freedom can take the form of speech, conscientious objection, or whistle-blowing.

The provision and operationalization of this ethical principle for employees working in prisons is troublesome and controversial. Control and predictability are essential in prisons. The prevention of escapes and violence requires a degree of authoritarianism within both the organization and its administration. Traditionally, prisons have been structured as paramilitary hierarchies with clearly differentiated lines of authority and limited discretion for line staff. Recent research has shown that fragmentation within the organizational structure is associated with greater likelihood of riots.[12]

Permitting freedom of expression for staff would appear to be antithetical to the need to maintain control and predictability. Dissension among the staff could threaten the stability of the institution. Again, balance is necessary. Prison staff cannot have unbridled freedom to criticize the administration. Nevertheless, like all employees, prison workers must have the right to protest, without reprisal, against acts of the organization that may be illegal or immoral.

If it is widely recognized that some staff administer their own disciplinary action against aggressive inmates in the form of beatings that take place outside the range of surveillance cameras and, moreover, that prison officials do not take corrective action, then a staff member should be able to report such actions without fear of reprisal. It would be unethical for an administrator to take action against the reporting individual. But what about a prison employee who decides that physical restraints, shackles used while transporting prisoners, are barbaric? Does that individual have the right to go to the press with this belief and to publicly criticize the institution for its use of such devices? Who gets to define "immoral"?

## Privacy

Humans have a moral right to be left alone, to have personal lives, and to be self-directed. For this to happen, they need privacy. Individuals must be able to control what information about themselves is known and disseminated. Werhane explains the necessity of this provision as follows: "Unless their privacy is respected persons lose a sense of self-identity, because what separates one from another, what identifies her to herself, becomes indistinguishable from what others know about her. Without privacy one's personal freedom is, at best, restricted, since the source of free choice, one's autonomy, is not safeguarded."[13]

Within the workplace, privacy involves the separation of personal and work lives. Clearly, employers must have access to certain kinds of personal information, but that access should be limited to work-related information, such as educational background. The personal lives of employees after work hours, provided they are legal, are generally not subjects about which employers have a right to know.

This, too, proves to be a testy issue in prison administration, and one that calls for balance. Two aspects of prison employment impact on the parameters of this right. As law enforcement agencies, prisons are obliged to uphold the highest standards of law-abiding behavior. Prison employees must adhere to this standard, and their institutions have an obligation to assure that this requirement is met. The need to prevent corruption requires some scrutiny into the personal lives of employees.

Illegal behavior among employees can jeopardize security. And prison staff who use drugs or abuse alcohol outside of the workplace may not exercise sound judgment on the job. In this regard, therefore, prison administrators have the right and obligation to maintain surveillance of employees' outside behavior. This may include drug testing.

If, furthermore, prisoners learn of illegal or inappropriate behavior on the part of staff, they may be able to use such information to extort special treatment from staff. Here, too, the organizational need to maintain security and standards of law-abiding behavior demand some restriction and surveillance of employee behavior outside the workplace.

In the examples presented so far, the need of the organization to pry into the personal lives of employees regarding illegal behavior is sufficiently compelling to justify such action. Other instances requiring a balance between personal freedom and organizational needs are not so clear cut. Prison employees who abuse sick leave force their institutions to require other employees to work increased overtime, an expedient that adds to security risks. Does the organization have a right to determine whether the employee is truly sick? Establishing a balance that does not pose undue or overzealous scrutiny and respects the individual autonomy of employees at the same time as protecting organizational needs for security and stability creates a significant challenge for management.

## Participation in Decision Making

Few people would take issue with the notion that individuals have a moral right to freedom of choice and self-determination. These are fundamental elements of individual freedom. Individuals must have autonomy, independence, and the opportunity for self-development.

In accepting employment, do individuals give up the right to freedom of choice and self-determination? Does the organization's autonomy and that of its managers outweigh the autonomy of individual employees? Or are workers left only with the right to leave their employment if they are dissatisfied with the conditions of their jobs or if they find their work experience

212                                    *Kevin N. Wright*

unfulfilling? It would appear that participation in workplace decision making fulfills the promise of purposeful and meaningful work and contributes to employees' self-development. Establishing a balance between the rights of the organization and its managers and the rights of the employees assures freedom of choice and self-control for all members of the organization, not just those in positions of authority and power.

The counterargument to this provision is that such an arrangement infringes unduly upon the right of managers to control the organization. As Werhane points out, participation does not imply the restriction of managers' control but limits their right to control everything.[14] Well-orchestrated participation has been demonstrated to enhance both morale and performance within the organization, thus enhancing the well-being of all with the organization.[15]

As with the preceding ethical issues, providing prison employees with the right to participate in decision making is a challenge for correctional supervisors. The need for control and predictability requires that prison operations be highly structured and that individual discretion be limited and specified. During times of crisis, decision making must be autocratic. However, in the course of day-to-day operations, prison staff should have a right to participate in decision making and to exercise autonomy in job performance within the parameters of policy specification. Not only does this provision allow employees to engage in their own personal development, but it also provides for enhanced correctional outcomes. In previously published empirical research, my collaborators and I demonstrated that participation in decision making resulted in improved employee performance and greater commitment to the organization.[16]

Still, allowing prison staff to participate in decision making and to have job autonomy must necessarily be constrained. What if the employee is a member of the Aryan Nation and expresses racist sentiments or advocates for differential treatment of white and black prisoners? Clearly, such dialogue is inappropriate and the employee's right to participate in decision making is limited. But what if the employee is a member of Amnesty International, an organization that frequently takes the position that practices found in many American prisons are inhumane? Can supervisors restrict this employee's criticisms and his or her promotion of alternative incarceration practices? Who gets to decide the limitations that managers can impose on the provision of this and other ethical principles while remaining ethical in their treatment of employees?

## Information

The final ethical principle to be considered is the right to be informed. All other employee rights hinge upon this right. Since managers control information, employees can exercise other rights only if they know and understand what is going on within the organization and how it impacts on them. For example, employees can know about the risks they face in their jobs only if they are informed about those risks. If their right to safety is to be secured, they need information about the hazards associated with their jobs. Do the materials they work with pose environmental health risks? If employees are knowingly kept in the dark about risks, they do not know that they are in danger and cannot exercise their right to health and safety.

A similar situation exists regarding the right to fair treatment. If information about criteria and decision making associated with hiring and promotions is hidden, then employees have no basis for exercising their right to fair treatment.

The right to be informed can be problematic within the prison organization. With information comes power. Prisoners can use information to gain tactical advantage over staff. Information about such things as prison routines and operation of the control system can be used in planning escapes and prison takeovers. Knowledge about snitches and prisoners' crimes can lead to assaults. Information about movement of prisoners can lead to resistance and disturbances. For these reasons, secrecy and control of information is vital to prison security.

Still, within the parameters of the other six rights, prison employees have a right to know. They should be informed about the safety risks they face. When tension is mounting within the facility, staff have a right to be informed about what is occurring and what precautions are being taken. Staff have a right to know about decisions regarding promotions and other personnel decisions. They have a right to know about policy and changes in policy. Prison administrators have a positive duty to keep staff informed. Acknowledgment is not enough—active communication is required.

## Practices to Assure Ethical Compliance

I have argued that prison employees have seven major ethical rights. However, in considering the application of these rights to prison settings, it became clear that the ability of prison managers to see that these ethical considerations are recognized and respected is constrained by organizational circumstances, budgetary limitations, and competing ethical considerations. It is one thing to claim that employees have the right to as safe a work place as possible and yet another to operationalize that belief in practice. How then should a prison manager proceed to supervise staff in a way that respects the claims of staff?

Larry May, an existentialist philosopher who studies professionalism, proposes the following model of moral responsibility for harm:

> A person is morally responsible for a given harm or character defect
> if:
> (a) the person's conduct played a significant causal role in that
>     harm or defect; and
> (b) the person's conduct was blameworthy or it was morally
>     faulty in some other way.[17]

Compliance with the first of these is generally straightforward. If prison organizations and their administrators act in ways that clearly deny an employee's rights, they have committed a moral harm. If, for example, an employer discriminated against an employee in a promotion decision because of that employee's race, that individual is harmed. It is a morally reprehensible act of commission.

Condition (b) adds a further dimension to moral responsibility for prison organizations and their administrators. If the organization and those who administer it act in a manner that is morally faulty, this, too, can cause blameworthy harm. Prison administrators have a moral responsibility not only to recognize employee rights but to assure them. Acts of omission, the failure to attend to and assure employee rights, is also egregious. Those who administer prisons must create an institutional environment that recognizes, supports, and respects the rules and principles associated with employee rights; otherwise, they will be lost within the bureaucracy and day-to-day operations of the facility.

This second condition shows us how to proceed ethically when decisions are constrained by organizational circumstances, budgetary limitations, and competing ethical considerations. This is important, for May argues that the very nature of bureaucracies works against the recognition and protection of individual rights:

> [I]nstitutional socialization in bureaucracies transforms individuals
> into cogs; that is, these individuals come to think of themselves as
> anonymous. As anonymous cogs, they lack the face-to-face confron-
> tation with one another, and with the consequences of their actions,
> that is necessary for a developed sense of responsibility. Lacking this
> personal dimension in their institutional lives, they are likely to lose
> their sense of responsibility in institutional settings as well.[18]

The loss of identity and sense of responsibility afflicts all members of an organization, worker and manager alike. Nevertheless, the culture of an organization is not fixed. Support and socialization enhance recognition of any organizational value, whether it be quality control, integrity, or ethical behavior. Managers have the authority and responsibility to shape the organizational culture.

To take an example: by its nature, incarceration creates an environment that encourages the abuse of prisoners. Some of those who end up in prisons have demonstrated a proclivity for using violence and disrespecting the rights of others. Incarceration enhances this tendency, and many prisoners therefore resist their keepers. Some lie and manipulate, verbally and physically attack staff, disobey the rules, insult, and even throw feces at staff. In response to the strain posed by such behavior, staff can easily drift into the abuse of their power and disrespect of prisoners. To counter this, those who administer the prison must actively promote a culture that treats prisoners humanely, respectfully, and without brutality.

The prison and its administrators can also promote a culture that recognizes the rights of staff and counteracts organizational pressures to act otherwise. If this is to come about, several factors must be in place. There must be a statement of ethical principles for the treatment of staff. Ideally, it will be part of the organizational mission statement. But to be effective, such principles must not be buried in an institutional document that is seldom visited but be part of a living document that becomes a guiding instrument for institutional culture and operations.

New employees and new managers must be socialized to believe in, adhere to, and attend to these principles. They must be discussed, reinforced, and supported within the day-to-day managerial routine. Both training and regular retraining are essential.

The Federal Bureau of Prisons makes a valuable contribution to the discussion. As part of its mission statement, the Bureau outlines a set of cultural anchors or core values, five of which relate to the treatment of employees:

> 1. *Bureau Family* The Bureau of Prisons recognizes that staff are the most valuable resource in accomplishing its mission, and is committed to the personal welfare and professional development of each employee. A concept of "family" is encouraged through healthy, supportive relationships among staff, and organization responsiveness to staff needs. The active participation of staff at all levels is essential to the development and accomplishment of organizational objectives.

> 2. *Correctional Workers First* All Bureau of Prisons staff share a common role as correctional workers, which requires a mutual responsibility for maintaining safe and secure institutions and for modeling society's mainstream values and norms.

> 3. *Promotion of Integrity* The Bureau of Prisons firmly adheres to a set of values that promotes honesty and integrity in the professional efforts of its staff to ensure public confidence in the Bureau's prudent use of its allocated resources.

> 4. *Career Service Orientation* The Bureau of Prisons is a career-oriented service, which has enjoyed a consistent management philoso-

phy and a continuity of leadership, enabling it to evolve as a stable, professional leader in the field of corrections.

*5. High Standards*   The Bureau of Prisons requires high standards of safety, security, sanitation, and discipline, which promote a physically and emotionally sound environment for both staff and inmates.[19]

These values are frequently published in Bureau documents. They are used in the training of new staff and new managers. They serve as guiding principles in the day-to-day management of institutions and are part of the socialization of personnel into the Bureau culture.

It is important that there is an organizational culture that supports the analysis of ethical considerations. The ways in which ethical principles get bounded and limited, and who gets to determine these restrictions, must be an arena for active discourse. There is a positive duty to attempt to act ethically, and this requires active consideration, discussion, and analysis of ethical challenges.

## Integrity

A discussion of employee rights and their realization within the organization would be incomplete without some mention of integrity. Several studies have been conducted to determine the characteristics that employees most admire in their leaders. Consistently, employees have desired honest leaders. They want the people who direct, guide, and make important decisions regarding their work lives to be trustworthy, ethical, and principled.[20]

Officials who fail to follow through with agreements or make false promises to, deceive, and undermine staff will lose the allegiance, loyalty, and trust of their people. If the organization states that employee rights are important, it must support and protect those values. Hypocrisy is the quickest way to lose trust. Leaders must model the way; they must set the standard for moral and ethical practice.

Integrity rests on consistency. When staff know what their leaders stand for, they do not have to wrestle with uncertainty and try to negotiate some hidden agenda or political game. Knowing the values of the leader avoids confusion, indecision, and conflict. When rules are uniformly applied and no one is able to act with impunity, integrity avoids inequity. Integrity instills within the organization an elemental commitment to inviolable human values.

If the institution makes claim to recognizing and supporting the employees' right to safety, then officials must attend to the business of creating a safe environment. If the institution indicates that employees will be treated fairly, then that provision must be uniformly and consistently applied. Because the need for control and predictability to maintain security impinges on the prison employees' freedom of expression, privacy, and participation in decision making, balance must be sought. The substance of that balance ought to be clearly and openly defined. Employees must know what the rules of the game are and expect that they will be consistently applied.

For prison employees to have basic rights, it all boils down to prison officials acting as moral agents in the task of realizing and assuring them. To act with integrity, prison officials must attend to ethical practice. It has to be part of their vocabulary and managerial practice.

# Notes

1. Kelsey Kauffman, *Prison Officers and Their World* (Cambridge, Mass.: Harvard University Press, 1988), 35.

2. James B. Jacobs, *Stateville: The Penitentiary in Mass Society* (Chicago: University of Chicago Press, 1977).

3. Richard L. Phillips and Charles R. McConnell, *The Effective Corrections Manager: Maximizing Staff Performance in Demanding Times* (Gaithersburg, Md.: Aspen Publications, 1996).

4. William G. Archambeault and Betty J. Archambeault, *Correctional Supervisory Management: Principles of Organization, Policy, and Law* (Englewood Cliffs, N.J.: Prentice-Hall, 1982).

5. John J. DiIulio, Jr., *Governing Prisons: A Comparative Study of Correctional Management* (New York: Free Press, 1987), and *No Escape: The Future of American Corrections* (New York: Basic Books, 1991).

6. Marilyn D. McShane and Frank P. Williams III, *The Management of Correctional Institutions* (New York: Garland Publishing, 1993).

7. Kevin N. Wright, *Effective Prison Leadership* (Binghamton, N.Y.: William Neil Publishing, 1994).

8. Listed in Archambeault and Archambeault, *Correctional Supervisory Management*, 253.

9. Patricia H. Werhane, *Persons, Rights, and Corporations* (Englewood Cliffs, N.J.: Prentice-Hall, 1985), 81–93.

10. Roger Folger, "Fairness as a Moral Virtue," in *Managerial Ethics: Morally Managing People and Processes*, ed. Marshall Schminke (Mahwah, N.J.: Lawrence Erlbaum, 1998), 13–34, 26.

11. These seven principles, along with several others that are not discussed here, are introduced in Werhane, *Persons, Rights, and Corporations*, 81–93.

12. Bert Useem and Peter Kimball, *States of Siege: U.S. Prison Riots, 1971–1986* (New York: Oxford University Press, 1989).

13. Werhane, *Persons, Rights, and Corporations*, 119.

14. Werhane, *Persons, Rights, and Corporations*, 138.

15. For a review of research on the benefits of worker participation in decision making, see Kevin N. Wright, Scott Camp, Evan Gilman, and William G. Saylor, "Job Control and Occupational Outcomes among Prison Workers," *Justice Quar-*

218                                    *Kevin N. Wright*

*terly* 14 (1997): 601–25.

16. Wright, Camp, Gilman, and Saylor, "Job Control and Occupational Outcomes among Prison Workers."

17. Larry May, *Sharing Responsibility* (Chicago: University of Chicago Press, 1992), 15.

18. Larry May, *The Socially Responsive Self: Social Theory and Professional Ethics* (Chicago: University of Chicago Press, 1996), 71.

19. Federal Bureau of Prisons, "Cultural Anchors/Core Values," *Federal Prisons Journal* 3 (Spring 1992): inside front cover.

20. See James M. Kouzes and Barry Posner, *The Leadership Challenge: How to Get Extraordinary Things Done in Organizations* (San Francisco: Jossey-Bass, 1998), 16–19.

# [25]

# The Ethical Dilemmas of Corrections Managers: Confronting Practical and Political Complexity

## Michael Jacobson

In calling for the ethical treatment of correctional staff by correctional administrators, criminologist Kevin Wright acknowledges a difficult and seldom discussed subject.[1] In a total institution that is managed through the threat and use of force, how is the ethical treatment of staff possible? Wright focuses on the ethical obligations of prison administrators to their workers as he attempts to answer, or partly answer, this question. In detailing the ethical obligations of correction administrators toward their staff, he rightly lists among these obligations the provision of safety, fair treatment, due process, freedom of expression, privacy, participation in decision making, and information regarding work-related matters. Yet though these workers rights are eminently fair and reasonable, they raise a host of other thorny issues that are barely addressed in Wright's chapter.

Indeed, precisely because prisons exemplify what Erving Goffman has referred to as "total institutions,"[2] they involve interactions among multiple parties who include, but are not limited to, corrections officers. Discussing ethical issues about corrections as though they exist in a vacuum omits some of the more complex problems and obligations that correctional administrators face. These more complex problems, which include the correctional administrator's ethical obligations to prisoners and their families, to the public, and to furthering rationally conceived correctional policy, all greatly complicate the relationship between administrators and their staffs. Once the correctional administrator's obligations to all these groups, interests, and principles are taken into account, the assessment of what constitutes ethical behavior becomes far more intricate.

Using Wright's discussion as a point of departure, my purpose is to argue for the importance of taking these multiple considerations into account in order to accommodate, rather than oversimplify, the complexity of correctional ethics. First, I address two of Wright's specific policy suggestions; specifically, I suggest that policies beneficial to corrections officers are sometimes at odds with other essential services that government must also provide. Second, I consider ethical obligations that correctional administrators may have not only toward correction officers but also to the larger society of which the prison system is part. And finally, I discuss the way in which the growing privatization of corrections and the influence of private capital have complicated and obscured the effectuation of ethical behavior by corrections administrators. Only the first section responds directly to Wright's own observations. It is because of Wright's tendency to envision correctional ethics rather narrowly that the second and third sections leave his comments behind and place the current problems of corrections managers within a broader social and historical framework.

## What Constitutes the Ethical Treatment of Corrections Officers?

It is hardly controversial to contend, as Wright does, that corrections officers ought to be treated ethically by their supervisors. For corrections officers have one of the most difficult jobs in the criminal justice system. They work inside institutions that are dangerous, and often they must use force to maintain order. On a daily basis, they encounter a wide range of humanity that may include violent prisoners as well as people who are drug addicted and mentally or physically ill. More often than not, these officers are outnumbered by the prisoners they supervise; it is not uncommon for housing officers to supervise as many as 50 to 150 inmates at any time. But even with this intensive workload they are expected to maintain control and order among this captive and frequently hostile population without having to resort to force. Like police, corrections officers must frequently work rotating shifts, but unlike police officers, many work in prisons far from their homes and families. Not surprisingly, the divorce and alcoholism rates among corrections officers are high. The occupation is difficult and stressful for both mind and body.

The people who perform these jobs are certainly entitled to fair and ethical treatment by correctional administrators. But matters are complicated by the fact that prisoners are also constitutionally entitled to fair and humane treatment. This tension—between treating both prisoners and staff fairly—can result in situations in which the assessment of what constitutes ethical treatment of correction officers can become extremely challenging.

Wright says that a crucial ethical obligation of prison officials is to provide due process in cases in which it becomes necessary to discipline correction officers.³ Who would object to the proposition that any progressive correctional system should provide due process and an appeal mechanism for correction officers who must undergo disciplinary proceedings? But, given the extraordinary power that corrections officers possess to control every aspect of prisoners' lives, some traditional notions of due process have a limited relevance. Let me develop what I mean by this seemingly controversial contention.

Abuses of power wielded by correctional administrators and staff are well-documented facts. In the last several years alone, high-profile stories have highlighted the systematic beating of prisoners at a New Jersey detention center for illegal immigrants; the participation of the Georgia prison commissioner in the beating of prisoners; and the fatal beating of an inmate in a Long Island jail after he complained about not receiving his methadone.⁴ Because of such ever-present potential for abuse, the most important characteristic of a humane and well-run correctional facility is that it quickly and severely punishes the unjustifiable use of force by correction officers. By this criterion—also an ethical one—the best run prisons are characterized by the least use of force.

But this means that there may be occasions on which making rapid symbolic points about the unacceptability of abuse in a correctional facility comes into conflict with the expectation of lengthy due process proceedings. Consider the following example. In 1997, during my tenure as New York City correction commissioner, several corrections officers and captains were indicted for participating in the beating of inmates and then covering it up. They were immediately suspended without pay. This accorded with standard practices followed by other law enforcement agencies when officers are indicted for a felony offense. However, in New York City, both city and state law mandate that the New York City Police Department (NYPD) pay its officers after thirty days if the criminal case against them has not been resolved (and most are not). Since the officers must be paid, the police department has the further option of bringing them back to work. Sometimes this has meant that even New York City police officers indicted for the most serious violent felonies are back at work—though not at patrol functions—after thirty days of suspension.

In contrast, city and state law allows New York City's correction commissioner to keep officers on unpaid suspension until their criminal case is disposed. If found guilty of a felony, the officers are immediately terminated; if found not guilty, they are entitled to return to work with their back pay reinstated. My decision in the 1997 case was to keep these indicted corrections officers and captains on unpaid suspension for the duration of their trial, though the criminal proceedings against them, from indictment to trial, lasted nearly two years.

Needless to say, my position was a controversial one. The corrections unions argued strenuously that I was punishing these staff prior to any finding of guilt and that it was un-American to do so. Additionally, the unions pointed out that whereas the police officers who fired forty-one shots in the extraordinarily publicized killing of Amadou Diallo were brought back to work and paid after a thirty-day suspension, these corrections officers, indicted for a far less serious charge (in which the victims were jail inmates), were kept on unpaid suspension indefinitely. The unions questioned how one city government could treat its different uniformed forces so unequally. Clearly, they had a point. It was bizarre that, in one case, police officers had to be paid after thirty days even after allegedly murdering an unarmed man while, in another, correction officers went unpaid for far longer for allegedly committing a less serious crime. However, I felt strongly that the crime with which these correction officers had been charged was exceptionally serious and so potentially harmful to the overriding mission and purpose of the corrections institution that I kept them on unpaid suspension. Moreover, as I knew well in this particular case, the evidence against the officers was overwhelmingly strong.

Could an argument be made that my actions toward these officers violated some due process or moral obligation on the part of administrators to correction officers? Yes. Everyone in this country is presumed innocent in a criminal proceeding prior to its disposition. Additionally, had the officers in this case been police officers accused of beating up suspects, they would have been brought back to work and paid after thirty days. Consequently, these officers were penalized simply because they were corrections officers and by a strange fluke in New York State and City law, which gave me the right to keep them suspended. But, on the other hand, where do the rights of prisoners and their families come in—let alone the right of the public to expect that correctional institutions take every possible measure to ensure a humane and violence-free environment? For practical as well as symbolic reasons, the charge of corrections officers systematically beating prisoners and then covering up this crime from law enforcement authorities should be dealt with in the strictest possible terms.

Here, then, was a situation in which several ethical considerations clashed: fair treatment of correction officers and of prisoners as well as accountability to a broader public. They were not mutually exclusive obligations; nevertheless, not all parties were likely to be pleased with any decision made by the corrections administrator. And so, in cases like the one just delineated, assessing ethical behavior can be complicated. The complications are not sufficiently incorporated into blueprints for the fair treatment of correction officers like the one proposed by Wright.

Wright also suggests other seemingly straightforward moral guidelines. On the subject of working conditions, he writes: "States and their prison systems are morally obligated to maintain the physical plant at acceptable levels. Prison structures cannot be allowed to fall into conditions of deterioration and antiquation that make them unsafe."[5] As before, this seems a patently unobjectionable point: correctional administrators have a basic obligation to provide their staff with a safe working environment. It is a particularly salient responsibility because many corrections officers work in facilities that are quite old. Later in the same section, however, Wright raises a point that introduces a further complexity:

> Furthermore, prison administrators must struggle with competing ethical obligations. To assure the highest level of staff safety, an administrator may recognize that the facility requires a $50 million renovation. If the administrator aggressively lobbies within the state correctional system and government for this capital improvement, knowing that if he or she is successful in securing these funds, they will be taken from public monies that would have otherwise gone to public education, is he or she acting ethically?[6]

This is an insightful and thoughtful question. Unfortunately, Wright does not then proceed to explore its ramifications.

Despite the relatively recent fiscal health[7] of most states' economies, most state budgeting is premised on a zero-sum game. That is, since most governors and state legislatures are likely to cut rather than increase taxes (as occurred in the 1980s and 1990s), budget officials are restricted by finding that there are no more tax levy funds available from the tax proceeds of new years' budgets. Consequently, government agencies must compete for scarce and relatively fixed funds. If, for instance, a state decides to increase the size of its transportation department, this is likely to be achieved at the expense of some other governmental function. In this zero-sum situation, substantial new funding for one governmental function usually creates problems for other governmental agencies. And, of course, the dilemma applies to states' experiences with the relationship between corrections and education budgets. According to the National Association of State Budget Officers (NASBO), the only two governmental functions to increase as a percentage of total state spending from 1987 to 1999 have been Medicaid and corrections. Every other area of state government declined as a percentage of state spending, including primary and secondary education, public assistance, transportation, and environmental protection.[8] Thus, it is no accident that as expenditures on corrections have increased over the last decade, other governmental expenditures—and services—have declined proportionately.

Given this historical trend and current budget practice, the action of a correctional administrator who lobbies aggressively for massive new funding is likely to bring real world consequences for the delivery of other social services. To take a hypothetical though by no means unusual example, a correctional manager who succeeds in obtaining an additional $50 million for needed prison renovation may have also succeeded at preventing the construction of a needed school building in a poor neighborhood. This problem is likely to be especially acute in municipalities in which total budgets are much smaller than those of a huge city such as New York.

Under such circumstances, what is the ethical obligation of the correctional administrator? Is it to let someone else worry about these tradeoffs? After all, it is the correctional administrator's job to be concerned about corrections. One could argue further, moreover, that it is the job of governors and state legislatures to base their resource allocation decisions on the articulated needs of government agency heads. Let the corrections commissioner make her case, the education superintendent make his case, and elected officials can afterward sort it all out. The correctional administrator may adopt this rationale to justify the aggressive pursuit of capital improvements that would benefit both corrections staff and prisoners. In the world of Realpolitik, however, the sophisticated corrections manager knows well that lawmakers will pay much more attention to budget requests from law enforcement agencies that are strongly supported by powerful unions, as is frequently the case with corrections. It is the height of naïveté to believe that these kinds of resource decisions are made by coldly rational policy makers simply on their case-by-case merits.

Thus, the corrections manager cannot so easily get off the hook by projecting such difficult decisions onto other governmental managers. And, consequently, the question remains unanswered as to what ought be done in situations in which, though a newly renovated correctional facility would benefit staff and workers, a new school might provide even greater societal benefit to tens of thousands of school children and teachers. One possibility is that, after weighing the moral costs and benefits involved, the corrections administrator decides not to pursue funding for a correctional facility. Or the administrator might decide not to have her or his actions determined by politically charged budget constraints and call publicly for increased taxes to meet all the legitimate demands for governmental services. Should this last tack be taken, though, the administrator would almost surely lose her or his job. The other possibility is that the corrections administrator decides just "to do my job and let others in government grapple with larger concerns." This is the most pragmatic response and understandably the one most frequently adopted by corrections administrators. Yet even though this is arguably the least ethical of all the responses to securing governmental funds for correctional agencies, it may also be the one that most closely conforms to Wright's criteria for corrections administrators fulfilling moral obligations to their staffs.

Am I saying, then, that all corrections and police administrators should act on the basis of the impact that they believe their actions will have on other parts of government as well as their own? Perhaps not. But I am saying that the dilemma posed by current zero-sum politics is not one that can be blithely ignored. Moreover, it is particularly salient at present when corrections administrators are part of a two-decades-long trend that has witnessed the number of people incarcerated in the United States rising from five hundred thousand to two million and total correctional expenditures now over $41 billion.[9] In this context, corrections administrators do have an ethical obligation to consider how their actions will affect other functions of government. And in some cases this may lead to the conclusion that moral obligations to staff are sometimes outweighed by other, more significant, moral obligations to society.

In practice, no doubt, this is a difficult challenge to operationalize. It would require that correctional administrators be well-informed about the relative health of their local or state budgets as well as about pressing needs elsewhere in government. It would require that these same administrators use this knowledge in the budget process to help guide the size and timing of at least some of their budget requests. Other budget requests would still automatically be made; for example, new staff or space based on increased population should always be funded to ensure the safety of staff and prisoners. Yet there is a subset of all budget requests—new programs, replacement or renovated space, or enhancements to current programs—that probably should be subject to additional examination and critique by correctional administrators in terms of other pressing social needs.

## Are There Greater Moral Obligations for Correctional Administrations to Act Upon?

Thus far, using Wright as a point of departure, I have addressed specific obligations that correctional administrators may have toward prisoners as well as officers and toward society as well as their own agencies. But Wright does not go further to reflect on the overall social and political environment in which corrections managers have had to operate in the 1980s and 1990s. At this point, then, I leave Wright behind and turn to the contemporary character of punishment.

For there are even larger and more fundamental ethical issues that correctional administrators face in the context of increased use of incarceration, eliminated education and rehabilitation programs, harsher sentencing of juveniles as adults, and striking racial disparities in prison populations.[10]

Over the last thirty years, policy making in the field of corrections has witnessed a diminished role for the criminal justice or corrections expert and the increased prominence of state legislatures and governors in making correctional policy. It is elected officials who now largely determine what prisons look like in terms of educational, recreational, and work programs. They are the ones who are usually responsible for increasing lengths of stay driven by the diminished role of parole and mandatory sentencing and for the increasing numbers of ever younger offenders entering adult institutions. In New York, for instance, one of Governor Pataki's first acts upon taking office was to eliminate all college-level education courses in prisons. This was not a particularly surprising decision because other states have also eliminated a variety of education programs in recent years. In 1994, Congress eliminated all Pell grants for prisoners; these grants had helped to pay for higher education classes in prison. Additionally, in the last several years fourteen states have completely eliminated parole,[11] and many other states have reduced historical parole release rates.

Although there are certainly some correction administrators who believe that these recent trends in corrections were long overdue, others—and probably more—feel that they fly in the face of good correctional practice. In fact, even the American Correctional Association (ACA) proclaims that in its legislative priorities for the year 2000 it:

- supports (re)habilitation and prevention programs and services;
- supports management practices that reduce crowding and the deterioration of conditions of confinement in adult or juvenile systems and that provide effective management of community supervision caseloads; and
- supports correctional industry programs.[12]

That the largest professional correctional association in the country supports rehabilitation and industry programs, as well as resources for community supervision, suggests that a large group of corrections professionals disagree with current retributive policies. What, then, is the moral responsibility of corrections administrators when their state governors and/or legislatures make policy that they feel to be antithetical to solid correctional practice? Would the reasoning outlined above again apply—that is, we should do nothing since others (namely, lawmakers) have the constitutional right to enact criminal justice policies restricting prison programs and the use of community corrections and parole? After all, state directors of corrections work for governors. Is it not their job simply to carry out the policy directions set by elected officials? Moreover, being a state corrections director is a prestigious and high-paying government job. As a corrections director, one is in charge of a huge staff, large numbers of prisoners, and significant budgets. It is also a job that entails a good deal of stress as well as a variety of managerial and organizational challenges. These positions are difficult to obtain.

Once one becomes a corrections director, the specter of riots, escapes, or other high-profile events constantly reminds the director that his job security may well be fleeting. In addition to the difficulty of becoming a corrections director and the simultaneous rewards and stresses inherent in the job, do these directors also have a moral obligation to take a public stance against policy and legislation they believe to be harmful to prisoners, staff, and good corrections practice?

The easy answer to this question is yes. After all, if corrections administrators do not protest bad correctional policy, it will be left to advocacy groups and public defenders, and they are easily marginalized and ignored. On the other hand, the political weight on prison system administrators publicly speaking out about the abolition of parole (for instance) would be substantial. There are many corrections administrators who believe that eliminating discretionary parole release and significantly increasing prison length of stays is terrible public policy. The potential harm to staff who manage prisoners who are not rewarded for good behavior, let alone the damage done to prisoners themselves, is very real; the hope of attaining early release has been important in managing correctional facilities. Therefore, were a number of prison administrators, law enforcement officials who are hardly viewed as soft on crime, to criticize this policy publicly, it might change the tenor of public debate.

Why does this not happen? One reason—mentioned above—concerns the problem that corrections administrators would face were they to deplore the zero-sum game of corrections-or-social-service funding: analogously, were corrections directors to speak out against eliminated parole in a state in which the governor supported this policy, they would probably be fired. One of the rules of the game in running a government agency is that you work for the governor, and thus you are expected to support the governor's positions in the public arena. You might express your opposition internally and discreetly, but once a policy decision has been made you must be publicly supportive of it. This is a truism of almost all levels of government. If a disagreement is too strong, the agency head has the option to resign. Thus, the corrections director is faced with some very unpleasant options. He must publicly support, and in some cases must aggressively lobby for, policies that he feels are wrong and unethical. Or he can resign. But resignation means not only the loss of a prestigious and challenging position and of the income and (relative) security that come with it but also being labeled as a troublemaker, a characterization that will greatly limit future employment possibilities with other governors. Neither one of these Hobsonian choices is particularly attractive.

Not all law enforcement officials face such stark choices. District attorneys in cities and counties are usually elected officials. Although they are overwhelmingly conservative on law and order issues (because this is what the voting public generally expects of prosecutors), many prosecutors publicly take surprisingly liberal positions on criminal justice issues. This is possible both because they can make their own decisions on what policies to support or criticize and because they politically calculate that taking some traditionally liberal positions will not hurt them with voters. To take an example, Charles Hynes, the elected district attorney in Kings County, is known nationally for developing alternatives to incarceration programs for drug dealers who would otherwise be sent to prison for long sentences. Ronnie Earle in Austin (Texas) and Michael McCann in Milwaukee County (Wisconsin) have also been known to take public positions on issues such as alternatives to incarceration and the death penalty that are very unusual for prosecutors. The fact that some prosecutors publicly support nontraditional forms of punishment sends a powerful message simply because of who they are. But the structural and political position of prosecutors is quite different from that of correctional directors; it is the latter who, ultimately, have their overall policy set by other elected officials. Although a group of correctional directors taking public positions against the current retributive tide in American corrections would be as influential as these prosecutors taking unpopular positions on law enforcement issues, it is far less likely—and more difficult—for them to do so.

In circumstances such as these, most corrections directors choose some version of the first option. That is, they argue on the inside against policies—such as three-strikes laws, eliminating recreation/weightlifting programs, eliminating or greatly restricting the use of parole—that are considered to be poor correctional practice. Once the internal battle has been lost, a public stance of passive or low-profile support can allow the corrections director to save face and not completely support policies he may find offensive. The rationale for this course of action is fairly clear. Most progressive corrections directors believe it preferable that they be in charge of the prisons system (even if they must tacitly support regressive public policy) than that they be in the hands of the true believers in retributive policies who would be likely to replace them should they be fired on principle. By means of this rationale, corrections administrators can not only keep their jobs but also exert some influence on correctional policy in an otherwise unfriendly, retributive environment.

I return then to this section's basic question: What ethical obligation do corrections administrators who operate in "hostile" environments have to speak out or not speak out? Should they resign over principle or work inside the system for changes that may mitigate perceived harm through managerial control of day-to-day prison operations? Ultimately, I have no simple solution to this complex ethical and personal dilemma. Fighting within the system for change is an admirable pursuit, but it may not result in the public being presented with alternative correctional policies to those that are presently dominant. Speaking out against policies promulgated by one's employer may be politically effective; this may raise issues, at least temporarily, that would otherwise not be aired. Taking positions through professional associations such as the ACA or the Association of State Correctional Administrators (ASCA) may also be useful though probably too low profile to change current public policy and discourse about punishment and corrections. Corrections administrators must make their own decisions or find their own voices in terms of how best to deal with policies with which they disagree. However, it is important for officials to struggle with these issues so that they do not get entirely lost in the day-to-day details and bureaucracy inherent in running large complex organizations. There is meaning simply in wrestling with these larger ethical concerns and in thinking about which kinds of policies exceed one's ability to provide even passive support. Finally, being prepared to speak out when or if the situation arises is important in how correctional administrators live their professional lives as well as for the evolution of corrections.

## What Are the Implications of Privatization for Correctional Ethics?

Private correctional facilities have grown at an astounding rate over the last two decades. From 1989 to 1997 the number of private beds in adult correctional facilities has grown from 15,000 to 64,086.[13] In addition to the growth of privatization in the United States, private correctional firms have been awarded substantial new contracts in Great Britain, Australia, and South Africa. Although the substantial growth of the private prison industry is well documented, the debate about whether private prisons are cheaper or more effective than similar public prisons is still unsettled. There are vocal proponents of increased correctional privatization[14] as well as of its phasing out.[15] Arguments for and against privatization usually tend to make the case that one or the other is more effective and cheaper to operate. However, according to the authors of the latest and most reliable research on the topic: "Our conclusion regarding costs and savings is that the few existing studies and other available data do not provide strong evidence of any general pattern."[16] With regard to effectiveness, this study also found that "given the shortcomings and the paucity of systematic comparisons, one cannot conclude whether the performance of privately managed prisons is different from or similar to that of publicly operated ones."[17]

With a paucity of reliable empirical data to support or oppose private prisons on efficiency grounds, the arguments on both sides of the issue tend to be more ideological. A key pro argument is that the private sector is the epicenter for innovation and creativity, especially in relation to government. It is also claimed that private companies are not encumbered by the same nightmarish bureaucracy, civil service and union rules, and procurement policies as government. Private prisons are therefore a priori likely to be more efficient and effective. The competition between public and private sectors will, moreover, improve the performance of all prisons. On the con side, it is typically argued that corrections constitutes a core governmental function and that only government has the moral right to punish and use force against other citizens. Since private prisons are motivated solely by profits, they will inevitably skimp on training, services, and security, thus resulting in poorly run facilities.

Caught in this debate are correctional administrators who must deal with the practical and ethical aspects of a new phenomenon that is, for the most part, out of their control. Practically speaking, correctional privatization has both advantages and disadvantages for public sector corrections administrators. Private prisons can provide fast relief from overcrowded public prisons and thus help to alleviate one of their most pressing problems. On the other hand, private prisons can fail miserably and thus be the cause of huge political problems for correctional directors who contract with a private prison; this is what recently happened in Louisiana.[18]

However, corrections managers may also experience personal and professional benefits in the growth of private prisons. That is, private prisons have greatly extended the career path and longevity of public prison administrators. Despite the rhetoric that the private sector is the place where innovation and creativity blossoms, an overwhelming number of private prison wardens have come from the public sector. It is not uncommon for a warden of a state or federal prison to retire and then become a warden at a private facility. Not surprisingly, wardens who have had successful careers at managing prisons are very attractive prospects for private firms seeking qualified corrections administrators to run their facilities. This allows the public prison warden not only to collect her or his government pension but also to earn a substantial salary as a private correction administrator. For senior corrections administrators, it is financially a very attractive career.

Thus, corrections directors may find themselves on each side of this issue. But whichever side they are on, complex moral dilemmas are sure to arise. Most correctional administrators are likely to have strong opinions on privatization. To air them publicly may have the same effect as opining on other aspects of correctional policy set by lawmakers in their state: unemployment. Thus, coming out against privatization in a state that, because its legislature and governor both support it, has committed itself to operating private prisons, will certainly put one's career in jeopardy. It will, moreover, likely end the potentially lucrative prospect of becoming an executive in a private correctional firm.

For those correctional administrators who work in private prisons, there is an additional layer of complexity that obscures the determination of ethical behavior. Beyond the multiple parties whose needs must be accommodated in public prisons—guards and their unions, other staff, prisoners, and families of prisoners—there is a further powerful group, namely, investors. The addition of investors into the total institution of prisons compounds the notion of assessing ethical behavior by administrators. Do the interests of staff supersede the financial interests of investors? What may be good for staff (more training) may also be good for prisoners but bad for investors (training costs money). Given this complication, how heavily does the private corrections administrator weigh ethical considerations toward staff? Throwing the interests of private capital into the mix makes it extremely difficult for private correctional administrators to think and act ethically.

## Conclusion

It is not to be doubted that correctional administrators have moral and ethical obligations to their staffs. Nevertheless, prisons are highly complex institutions in which the interests of various parties may conflict. Consequently, assessing what, in particular situations, constitutes ethical behavior becomes an extraordinarily complicated task. The calculus of correctional ethics must take into account not only parties inside but also those outside prisons. A decision that is ethical for one group (for example, bettering the working conditions of correctional staff) may well have a detrimental impact on another (for example, inner-city school children awaiting new school buildings).

Adding further layers of complexity are questions related to whether correctional administrators have an obligation to speak out when correctional practice and policy made by legislators conflict with their own moral and political judgment. Most recent among these areas of disagreement is the issue of private prisons, which, because of the introduction of private capital and its interests, vastly complicates the ethical situation. For public correctional administrators, criticizing privatization may lead not only to their firing from public service, but also to eliminating a career path in the private prison sector. Presumably, a public corrections administrator speaking critically about the entire concept of privatization would not want to become a private correctional administrator. However, an administrator who is critical not of privatization itself but of how privatization is used strategically by the state, or who is critical of specific private prison managements, may also find that his potential for future private prison employment is greatly limited. Corporate CEOs are no more accepting of criticism, no matter how muted, than are governors. For private correctional administrators, on the other hand, weighing the interests of staff and prisoners may put their decisions at odds with the concerns of investors and corporations who are paying their salaries.

There is, therefore, no easy ethical typology by which correction administrators may live. What is clear is that correction administrators have ethical obligations to a variety of groups and interests both inside and outside the prison. For these administrators, it is both a personally and intellectually difficult task to determine what comprises ethical behavior in their institutional role. However, to acknowledge and struggle with this complexity, rather than to pretend that it does not exist, may itself constitute ethical thought and practice. And the struggle has the potential to improve the lives both of those who work and live in prisons and of the communities that surround them.

# Notes

1. Kevin N. Wright, "Management-Staff Relations: Issues in Leadership, Ethics, and Values, " in this volume, 203–18.

2. Erving Goffman, *Asylums: Essays on the Social Situation of Mental Patients and Other Inmates* (Garden City, N.Y.: Anchor Doubleday, 1961).

3. Wright, "Management-Staff Relations," 205.

4. Somini Sengupta, "Immigrants Settle Lawsuit over Jail Beatings for $1.5 Million," *New York Times*, September 21, 1998, B2; Rick Bragg, "Prison Chief Encouraged Brutality, Witnesses Report," *New York Times*, July 1, 1997, A12; David Halbfinger, "Abused Behind Bars: A Special Report," *New York Times*, February 1, 1999, A1.

5. Wright, "Management-Staff Relations," 207.

6. Wright, "Management-Staff Relations," 207–08.

7. In the past several years, state budgets have benefited from the strong national economy. This has allowed some states to spend additional funds without having to commensurably reduce other expenditures as states collect greater amounts of personal income and sales tax from their residents. Despite this recent burst of fiscal health, state budget offices usually try to keep year-to-year expenditures the same (but for inflation and workload increases) with new funds going only toward governors' or legislatures' highest political priorities.

8. National Association of State Budget Officers, *State Expenditure Report* (Washington, D.C., 1999), 9.

9. Bureau of Justice Statistics, *Justice Employment and Statistics Abstracts, 1982–1996* (Washington, D.C., 1999), Table 1.

10. In 1997, the number of whites sentenced to prison per 100,000 was 386 with the corresponding number for African Americans being 3,209. See Ann L. Pastore and Kathleen Maguire (eds.), *Sourcebook of Criminal Justice Statistics*, Table 6.31, <http://www.albany.edu/sourcebook> (November 2000).

11. Paula Ditton and Doris Wilson, *Truth in Sentencing in State Prisons* (Washington, D.C.: U.S. Department of Justice, Bureau of Justice Statistics, 1999).

12. "ACA Legislative Priorities for the Year 2000" at <www.corrections.com/aca/legisl/priorities.html> (11/02/00).

13. Douglas McDonald, Elizabeth Fournier, Malcolm Russell-Einhorn, and Stephan Crawford, *Private Prisons in the United States: An Assessment of Current Practice* (Cambridge, Mass.: Abt Associates, 1998).

14. Charles H. Logan, "Objections and Refutations," in *Privatizing Correctional Services*, ed. Stephen T. Easton (Vancouver, B.C.: The Fraser Institute), 127–38; Charles W. Thomas, "Testimony Regarding Correctional Privatization," testimony before the Subcommittee on Crime of the House Committee on the Judiciary, Washington, D.C., June 8, 1995.

15. Judith Greene, "Prison Privatization: Recent Developments in the United States," paper presented at the International Conference On Penal Abolition, Toronto, Canada, May 2000).

16. McDonald, Fournier, Russell-Einhorn, and Crawford, *Private Prisons in the United States*, v.

17. McDonald, Fournier, Russell-Einhorn, and Crawford, *Private Prisons in the United States*, v.

18. A federal judge in Louisiana found that Wackenhut Corporation ran a juvenile justice facility that routinely brutalized the children in its care. The company agreed to vacate the facility and the state's correction commissioner called the private prison (for whose oversight he was responsible) a failure. See Fox Butterfield, "Settling Suit, Louisiana Abandons Private Youth Prisons," *New York Times*, September 8, 2000, A14.

# Name Index